Lecture Notes in Computer Science　11296

Commenced Publication in 1973
Founding and Former Series Editors:
Gerhard Goos, Juris Hartmanis, and Jan van Leeuwen

More information about this series at http://www.springer.com/series/7409

Ioannis Kompatsiaris · Benoit Huet
Vasileios Mezaris · Cathal Gurrin
Wen-Huang Cheng · Stefanos Vrochidis (Eds.)

MultiMedia Modeling

25th International Conference, MMM 2019
Thessaloniki, Greece, January 8–11, 2019
Proceedings, Part II

Editors
Ioannis Kompatsiaris (iD)
Information Technologies Institute
Centre for Research and Technology Hellas
Thessaloniki, Greece

Benoit Huet (iD)
EURECOM
Sophia Antipolis, France

Vasileios Mezaris
Information Technologies Institute
Centre for Research and Technology Hellas
Thessaloniki, Greece

Cathal Gurrin
Dublin City University
Dublin, Ireland

Wen-Huang Cheng
National Chiao Tung University
Hsinchu, Taiwan

Stefanos Vrochidis
Information Technologies Institute
Centre for Research and Technology Hellas
Thessaloniki, Greece

ISSN 0302-9743   ISSN 1611-3349   (electronic)
Lecture Notes in Computer Science
ISBN 978-3-030-05715-2   ISBN 978-3-030-05716-9   (eBook)
https://doi.org/10.1007/978-3-030-05716-9

Library of Congress Control Number: 2018963821

LNCS Sublibrary: SL3 – Information Systems and Applications, incl. Internet/Web, and HCI

This Springer imprint is published by the registered company Springer Nature Switzerland AG
The registered company address is: Gewerbestrasse 11, 6330 Cham, Switzerland

Preface

These two-volume proceedings contain the papers presented at MMM 2019, the 25th International Conference on MultiMedia Modeling, held in Thessaloniki, Greece, during January 8–11, 2019. MMM is a leading international conference for researchers and industry practitioners for sharing new ideas, original research results, and practical development experiences from all MMM-related areas, broadly falling into three categories: multimedia content analysis; multimedia signal processing and communications; and multimedia applications and services.

MMM 2019 received a total of 204 valid submissions across five categories; 172 full-paper regular and special session submissions, eight demonstration submissions, eight industry session submissions, six submissions to the Video Browser Showdown (VBS 2019), and ten workshop paper submissions. All submissions were reviewed by at least two and, in most cases, three members of the Program Committee, and were carefully meta-reviewed by the TPC chairs or the organizers of each special event before making the final accept/reject decisions. Of the 172 full papers submitted, 49 were selected for oral presentation and 47 for poster presentation. In addition, six demonstrations were accepted from eight submissions, five industry papers from eight submissions, six workshop papers from ten submissions, and all six submissions to VBS 2019. Overall, the program of MMM 2019 included 119 contributions presented in oral, poster, or demo form.

MMM conferences traditionally include special sessions that focus on addressing new challenges for the multimedia community; five special sessions were held in the 2019 edition of the conference. In addition, this year's MMM hosted a workshop as part of its program. Together with the conference's three invited keynote talks and two tutorials, one industry session, and the Video Browser Showdown, these events resulted in a rich program extending over four conference days.

The five special sessions of MMM 2019 were:

- SS1: Personal Data Analytics and Lifelogging
- SS2: Multimedia Analytics: Perspectives, Tools, and Applications
- SS3: Multimedia Datasets for Repeatable Experimentation
- SS4: Large-Scale Big Data Analytics for Online Counter-Terrorism Applications
- SS5: Time-Sequenced Multimedia Computing and Applications

The workshop hosted as part of the MMM 2019 program was:

- Third International Workshop on coMics ANalysis, Processing and Understanding (MANPU)

We wish to thank the authors of all submissions for sending their work to MMM 2019; and, we owe a debt of gratitude to all the members of the Program Committee and all the special events organizers (Special Sessions, Industry Session, Workshop,

VBS) for contributing their valuable time to reviewing these submissions and otherwise managing the organization of all the different sessions.

We would also like to thank our invited keynote speakers, Daniel Gatica-Perez from the IDIAP Research Institute and Ecole Polytechnique Federale de Lausanne (EPFL), Switzerland, Martha Larson from Radboud University Nijmegen and Delft University of Technology, The Netherlands, and Andreas Symeonidis from the Aristotle University of Thessaloniki, Greece, for their stimulating contributions. Similarly, we thank our tutorial speakers, Lucio Tommaso De Paolis from the University of Salento, Italy, and Xavier Giro-i-Nieto from the Universitat Politecnica de Catalunya, for their in-depth coverage of specific multimedia topics.

Finally, special thanks go to the MMM 2019 Organizing Committee members, our proceedings publisher (Springer), and the Multimedia Knowledge and Social Media Analytics Laboratory of CERTH-ITI – both our local organization and support team, and the conference volunteers – for their hard work and support in taking care of all tasks necessary for ensuring a smooth and pleasant conference experience at MMM 2019.

We hope that the MMM 2019 participants found the conference program and its insights interesting and thought-provoking, and that the conference provided everyone with a good opportunity to share ideas on MMM-related topics with other researchers and practitioners from institutions around the world!

November 2018

Ioannis Kompatsiaris
Benoit Huet
Vasileios Mezaris
Cathal Gurrin
Wen-Huang Cheng
Stefanos Vrochidis

Organization

Organizing Committee

General Chairs

Ioannis Kompatsiaris	CERTH-ITI, Greece
Benoit Huet	EURECOM, France

Program Chairs

Vasileios Mezaris	CERTH-ITI, Greece
Cathal Gurrin	Dublin City University, Ireland
Wen-Huang Cheng	National Chiao Tung University, Taiwan

Panel Chair

Chong-Wah Ngo	City University of Hong Kong, SAR China

Tutorial Chair

Shin'ichi Satoh	NII, Japan

Demo Chairs

Michele Merler	IBM T.J. Watson Research Center, USA
Tao Mei	JD.com, China

Video Browser Showdown Chairs

Werner Bailer	Joanneum Research, Austria
Klaus Schoeffmann	University of Klagenfurt, Austria
Jakub Lokoc	Charles University in Prague, Czech Republic

Publicity Chairs

Lexing Xie	Australian National University, Australia
Ioannis Patras	QMUL, UK

Publication Chair

Stefanos Vrochidis	CERTH-ITI, Greece

Local Organization and Webmasters

Maria Papadopoulou	CERTH-ITI, Greece
Chrysa Collyda	CERTH-ITI, Greece

Steering Committee

Phoebe Chen	La Trobe University, Australia
Tat-Seng Chua	National University of Singapore, Singapore
Kiyoharu Aizawa	University of Tokyo, Japan
Cathal Gurrin	Dublin City University, Ireland
Benoit Huet	EURECOM, France
Klaus Schoeffmann	University of Klagenfurt, Austria
Meng Wang	Hefei University of Technology, China
Björn Thór Jónsson	IT University of Copenhagen, Denmark
Guo-Jun Qi	University of Central Florida, USA
Wen-Huang Cheng	National Chiao Tung University, Taiwan
Peng Cui	Tsinghua University, China

Special Sessions, Industry Session, and Workshop Organizers

SS1: Personal Data Analytics and Lifelogging

Xavier Giro-i-Nieto	Universitat Politecnica de Catalunya, Spain
Petia Radeva	University of Barcelona, Spain
David J. Crandall	Indiana University, USA
Giovanni Farinella	University of Catania, Italy
Duc Tien Dang Nguyen	Dublin City University, Ireland
Mariella Dimiccoli	Computer Vision Centre, Universitat de Barcelona, Spain
Cathal Gurrin	Dublin City University, Ireland

SS2: Multimedia Analytics: Perspectives, Tools, and Applications

Björn Þór Jónsson	IT University of Copenhagen, Denmark
Laurent Amsaleg	CNRS-IRISA, France
Cathal Gurrin	Dublin City University, Ireland
Stevan Rudinac	University of Amsterdam, The Netherlands

SS3: Multimedia Datasets for Repeatable Experimentation

Cathal Gurrin	Dublin City University, Ireland
Duc-Tien Dang-Nguyen	Dublin City University, Ireland
Klaus Schoeffmann	University of Klagenfurt, Austria
Björn Þór Jónsson	IT University of Copenhagen, Denmark
Michael Riegler	Center for Digitalisation and Engineering and University of Oslo, Norway
Luca Piras	University of Cagliari, Italy

SS4: Large-Scale Big Data Analytics for Online Counter-Terrorism Applications

Georgios Th. Papadopoulos	Centre for Research and Technology Hellas, Greece
Ernesto La Mattina	Engineering Ingegneria Informatica SpA, Italy
Apostolos Axenopoulos	Centre for Research and Technology Hellas, Greece

SS5: Time-Sequenced Multimedia Computing and Applications

Bing-Kun Bao	Nanjing University of Posts and Telecommunications, China
Shao Xi	Nanjing University of Posts and Telecommunications, China
Changsheng Xu	Institute of Automation, Chinese Academy of Sciences, China

Industry Session Organizers

Panagiotis Sidiropoulos	Cortexica Vision Systems Ltd./UCL, UK
Khalid Bashir	I. University of Madinah, KSA
Gustavo Fernandez	Austrian Institute of Technology, Austria
Jose Garcia	Universidad de Alicante, Spain
Carlo Regazzoni	University of Genoa, Italy
Eduard Vazquez	Cortexica Vision Systems Ltd., UK
Sergio A Velastin	Universidad Carlos III, Madrid, Spain
M. Haroon Yousaf	UET Taxila, Pakistan
Qiao Wang	SouthEast University, China

MANPU Workshop Organizers

General Co-chairs

Jean-Christophe Burie	University of La Rochelle, France
Motoi Iwata	Osaka Prefecture University, Japan
Yusuke Matsui	National Institute of Informatics, Japan

Program Co-chairs

Alexander Dunst	Paderborn University, Germany
Miki Ueno	Toyohashi University of Technology, Japan
Tien-Tsin Wong	The Chinese University of Hong Kong, SAR China

MMM 2019 Program Committees and Reviewers

Regular and Special Sessions Program Committee

Esra Acar	Middle East Technical University, Turkey
Laurent Amsaleg	CNRS-IRISA, France
Martin Aumüller	IT University of Copenhagen, Denmark
Werner Bailer	Joanneum Research, Austria

Bing-Kun Bao | Nanjing University of Posts and Telecommunications, China
Ilaria Bartolini | University of Bologna, Italy
Olfa Ben-Ahmed | EURECOM, France
Jenny Benois-Pineau | LaBRI, CNRS, University of Bordeaux, France
Giulia Boato | University of Trento, Italy
Laszlo Boeszoermenyi | University of Klagenfurt, Austria
Marc Bolaños | Universitat de Barcelona, Spain
Francois Bremond | Inria, France
Benjamin Bustos | University of Chile, Chile
K. Selcuk Candan | Arizona State University, USA
Savvas Chatzichristofis | Neapolis University Pafos, Cyprus
Edgar Chavez | CICESE, Mexico
Zhineng Chen | Institute of Automation, Chinese Academy of Sciences, China
Zhiyong Cheng | National University of Singapore, Singapore
Wei-Ta Chu | National Chung Cheng University, Chiayi, Taiwan
Kathy Clawson | University of Sunderland, UK
Rossana Damiano | Università di Torino, Italy
Mariana Damova | Mozaika, Bulgaria
Duc Tien Dang Nguyen | University of Bergen, Norway
Minh-Son Dao | Universiti Teknologi Brunei, Brunei
Petros Daras | CERTH-ITI, Greece
Cem Direkoglu | Middle East Technical University, Turkey
Monica Dominguez | Universitat Pompeu Fabra, Spain
Weiming Dong | Institute of Automation, Chinese Academy of Sciences, China
Lingyu Duan | Peking University, China
Aaron Duane | Insight Centre for Data Analytics, Ireland
Jianping Fan | UNC Charlotte, USA
Mylene Farias | University of Brasilia, Brazil
Giovanni Maria Farinella | University of Catania, Italy
Fuli Feng | National University of Singapore, Singapore
Gerald Friedland | University of California, Berkeley, USA
Antonino Furnari | Università degli Studi di Catania, Italy
Ana Garcia | I2R, Singapore
Xavier Giro-I-Nieto | Universitat Politècnica de Catalunya, Spain
Guillaume Gravier | CNRS, IRISA, France
Ziyu Guan | Northwest University of China, China
Gylfi Gudmundsson | Reykjavik University, Iceland
Silvio Guimaraes | Pontifícia Universidade Católica de Minas Gerais, Brazil
Pål Halvorsen | Simula and University of Oslo, Norway
Shijie Hao | Hefei University of Technology, China
Frank Hopfgartner | The University of Sheffield, UK
Michael Houle | National Institute of Informatics, Japan

Zhenzhen Hu	Nanyang Technological University, Singapore
Min-Chun Hu	National Cheng Kung University, Taiwan
Lei Huang	Ocean University of China, China
Jen-Wei Huang	National Cheng Kung University, Taiwan
Marco Hudelist	University of Klagenfurt, Austria
Ichiro Ide	Nagoya University, Japan
Bogdan Ionescu	University Politehnica of Bucharest, Romania
Adam Jatowt	Kyoto University, Japan
Debesh Jha	Simula Research Laboratory, Norway
Peiguang Jing	Tianjin University, China
Havard Johansen	University of Tromsø, Norway
Hideo Joho	University of Tsukuba, Japan
Björn Þór Jónsson	IT University of Copenhagen, Denmark
Mohan Kankanhalli	National University of Singapore, Singapore
Anastasios Karakostas	Aristotle University of Thessaloniki, Greece
Sabrina Kletz	University of Klagenfurt, Austria
Eugenia Koblents	UTRC, Ireland
Markus Koskela	CSC - IT Center for Science Ltd., Finland
Ernesto La Mattina	Engineering Ingegneria Informatica S.p.A., Italy
Lori Lamel	LIMSI, France
Hyowon Lee	Singapore University of Technology and Design, Singapore
Andreas Leibetseder	University of Klagenfurt, Austria
Michael Lew	Leiden University, The Netherlands
Wei Li	Fudan University, China
Xirong Li	Renmin University of China, China
Na Li	Dublin City University, Ireland
Yingbo Li	Institut EURECOM, France
Bo Liu	Rutgers, The State University of New Jersey, USA
Xueliang Liu	Hefei University of Technology, China
Jakub Lokoc	Charles University in Prague, Czech Republic
Mathias Lux	University of Klagenfurt, Austria
Jean Martinet	Lille 1 University, France
Jose M. Martinez	Universidad Autonoma de Madrid, Spain
Valentina Mazzonello	Engineering Ingegneria Informatica s.p.a., Italy
Kevin McGuinness	Dublin City University, Ireland
Georgios Meditskos	Aristotle University of Thessaloniki, Greece
Robert Mertens	HSW University of Applied Sciences, Germany
Jochen Meyer	OFFIS Institute for Information Technology, Germany
Weiqing Min	ICT, China
Wolfgang Minker	University of Ulm, Germany
Bernd Muenzer	University of Klagenfurt, Austria
Adrian Muscat	University of Malta, Malta
Phivos Mylonas	National Technical University of Athens, Greece
Henning Müller	HES-SO, Switzerland
Chong-Wah Ngo	City University of Hong Kong, SAR China

Liqiang Nie	Shandong University, China
Naoko Nitta	Osaka University, Japan
Noel O'Connor	Dublin City University, Ireland
Neil O'Hare	Yahoo Research, USA
Vincent Oria	NJIT, USA
Tse-Yu Pan	National Cheng Kung University, Taiwan
Georgios Th. Papadopoulos	Information Technologies Institute, CERTH, Greece
Cecilia Pasquini	Universität Innsbruck, Austria
Stefan Petscharnig	AIT Austrian Institute of Technology, Austria
Konstantin Pogorelov	Simula, Norway
Manfred Jürgen Primus	University of Klagenfurt, Austria
Yannick Prié	LINA - University of Nantes, France
Athanasios Psaltis	CERTH, Greece
Jianjun Qian	Nanjing University of Science and Technology, China
Georges Quénot	Laboratoire d'Informatique de Grenoble, CNRS, France
Miloš Radovanović	University of Novi Sad, Serbia
Amon Rapp	University of Turin, Italy
Stevan Rudinac	University of Amsterdam, The Netherlands
Mukesh Saini	Indian Institute of Technology Ropar, India
Borja Sanz	University of Deusto, Spain
Shin'Ichi Satoh	National Institute of Informatics, Japan
Klaus Schöffmann	University of Klagenfurt, Austria
Wen-Ze Shao	Nanjing University of Posts and Telecommunications, China
Xi Shao	Nanjing University of Posts and Telecommunications, China
Jie Shao	University of Science and Technology of China, China
Xiangjun Shen	Jiangsu University, China
Xiaobo Shen	Nanjing University of Science and Technology, China
Koichi Shinoda	Tokyo Institute of Technology, Japan
Mei-Ling Shyu	University of Miami, USA
Alan Smeaton	Dublin City University, Ireland
Li Su	UCAS, China
Lifeng Sun	Tsinghua University, China
C. Sun	Central China Normal University, China
Yongqing Sun	NTT Media Intelligence Labs, Japan
Pascale Sébillot	IRISA, France
Estefania Talavera	University of Groningen, The Netherlands
Sheng Tang	Institute of Computing Technology, Chinese Academy of Sciences, China
Georg Thallinger	Joanneum Research, Austria
Vajira Thambawita	Simula Research Laboratory, Norway
Christian Timmerer	University of Klagenfurt, Austria
Daniele Toti	Roma Tre University, Italy
Sriram Varadarajan	Ulster University, UK

Stefanos Vrochidis	CERTH-ITI, Greece
Xiang Wang	National University of Singapore, Singapore
Lai Kuan Wong	Multimedia University, Malaysia
Marcel Worring	University of Amsterdam, The Netherlands
Hong Wu	UESTC, China
Xiao Wu	Southwest Jiaotong University, China
Hongtao Xie	University of Science and Technology of China, China
Changsheng Xu	Institute of Automation, Chinese Academy of Sciences, China
Toshihiko Yamasaki	The University of Tokyo, Japan
Keiji Yanai	The University of Electro-Communications, Japan
You Yang	Huazhong University of Science and Technology, China
Yang Yang	University of Science and Technology of China, China
Zhaoquan Yuan	University of Science and Technology of China, China
Matthias Zeppelzauer	University of Applied Sciences St. Pölten, Austria
Hanwang Zhang	Nanyang Technological University, Singapore
Tianzhu Zhang	CASIA, China
Jiang Zhou	Dublin City University, Ireland
Mengrao Zhu	Shanghai University, China
Xiaofeng Zhu	Guangxi Normal University, China
Roger Zimmermann	National University of Singapore, Singapore

Demonstration and VBS Program Committee

Werner Bailer	JRS, Austria
Premysl Cech	MFF, UK
Qi Dai	Microsoft, China
Xiangnan He	National University of Singapore, Singapore
Dhiraj Joshi	IBM Corporation, USA
Sabrina Kletz	University of Klagenfurt, Austria
Andreas Leibetseder	University of Klagenfurt, Austria
Jakub Lokoč	Charles University Prague, Czech Republic
Michele Merler	IBM, USA
Bernd Münzer	University of Klagenfurt, Austria
Ladislav Peska	Charles University Prague, Czech Republic
Jürgen Primus	University of Klagenfurt, Austria

MANPU Workshop Program Committee

John Bateman	University of Bremen, Germany
Ying Cao	City University of Hong Kong, SAR China
Wei-Ta Chu	National Chung Cheng University, Chiayi, Taiwan
Mathieu Delalandre	Laboratoire d'Informatique, France
Seiji Hotta	Tokyo University of Agricultural and Technology, Japan
Rynson Lau	City University of Hong Kong, SAR China

Jochen Laubrock	University of Potsdam, Germany
Tong-Yee Lee	National Cheng Kung University, Taiwan
Xueting Liu	The Chinese University of Hong Kong, SAR China
Muhammad Muzzamil Luqman	University of La Rochelle, France
Mitsunori Matsushita	Kansai University, Japan
Tetsuya Mihara	University of Tsukuba, Japan
Naoki Mori	Osaka Prefecture University, Japan
Mitsuharu Nagamori	University of Tsukuba, Japan
Satoshi Nakamura	Meiji University, Japan
Nhu Van Nguyen	University of La Rochelle, France
Christophe Rigaud	University of La Rochelle, France
Yasuyuki Sumi	Future University Hakodate, Japan
John Walsh	Indiana University Bloomington, USA
Ying-Qing Xu	Tsinghua University, China

Additional Reviewers

Elissavet Batziou	Tor-Arne Nordmo
Lei Chen	Georgios Orfanidis
Long Chen	John See
Luis Lebron Casas	Pranav Shenoy
Gabriel Constantin	Liviu Stefan
Mihai Dogariu	Gjorgji Strezoski
Jianfeng Dong	Xiang Wang
Xiaoyu Du	Zheng Wang
Neeraj Goel	Stefanie Wechtitsch
Xian-Hua Han	Qijie Wei
Shintami Chusnul Hidayati	Wolfgang Weiss
Tianchi Huang	Pengfei Xu
Wolfgang Hürst	Xin Yao
Benjamin Kille	Haoran Zhang
Marios Krestenitis	Wanqing Zhao
Yuwen Li	Yuanen Zhou
Emmanouil Michail	

Contents – Part II

Regular and Special Session Papers

Industry Papers

Demonstrations

MANPU 2019 Workshop Papers

Contents – Part I

Regular and Special Session Papers

Photo-Realistic Facial Emotion Synthesis Using Multi-level Critic Networks with Multi-level Generative Model

Minho Park, Hak Gu Kim, and Yong Man Ro[✉]

Image and Video Systems Laboratory, School of Electrical Engineering, KAIST,
Daejeon, South Korea
{roger618, hgkim0331, ymro}@kaist.ac.kr

Abstract. In this paper, we propose photo-realistic facial emotion synthesis by using a novel multi-level critic network with multi-level generative model. We devise a new facial emotion generator containing the proposed multi-level decoder to synthesize facial image with a desired variation. A proposed multi-level decoder and multi-level critic network help the generator to produce a photo-realistic and variation-realistic facial image in generative adversarial learning. The multi-level critic network consists of two discriminators, photo-realistic discriminator and variation-realistic discriminator. The photo-realistic discriminator in the multi-level critic network determines whether the multi-resolution facial image generated from the latent feature of the multi-level decoding module is photo-realistic or not. The variation-realistic discriminator determines whether the multi-resolution facial image has natural variation or not. Experimental results show that the proposed facial emotion synthesis method outperforms existing methods in terms of both qualitative performance and quantitative performance of expression recognition.

Keywords: Facial variation image synthesis · Adversarial learning
Feature refinement

1 Introduction

In a recent year, deep learning-based studies have shown successful performance in the image processing and computer vision fields. The remarkable success of deep learning is closely related to a large-scale database, which is used for training the deep network with a large number of parameters. Due to the drastically increasing time and cost, it is difficult to not only collect very large-scale datasets and but also annotate them for ground-truth of each data. In particular, in face related applications such as facial expression recognition and face recognition, the rigid requirement to the training and testing sets is one of the most challenges in collecting a large-scale datasets. The rigid requirement on the datasets for face-related applications indicates that it requires the paired sample dataset, e.g., various facial expression images of the same person or face images at different angles of the same person [1–3].

To deal with the issue, nonlinear data augmentation methods [4–6] could be one of the solutions to generative variations of facial images. For example, in facial expression

© Springer Nature Switzerland AG 2019
I. Kompatsiaris et al. (Eds.): MMM 2019, LNCS 11296, pp. 3–15, 2019.
https://doi.org/10.1007/978-3-030-05716-9_1

recognition fields, various facial expression images can be generated from a neutral facial image of the same person. As a result, a large number of facial expression datasets could be built by generating the desired variations. However, it is difficult to generate photo-realistic images while giving the desired variations (e.g., facial expressions) due to the large variations (e.g., from a happy facial expression to sad facial expression).

Recently, various methods based on a generative adversarial network (GAN) [7] were proposed to generate photo-realistic facial expressions. [4] proposed an approximation network for face age progression and regression. In [4], age-progression and regression images were generated by auto-encoder structure. However, the identity of each subject was not maintained since they did not consider the identity information of each subject's face image. [5] proposed a synthesizing expression network using differential discriminator and expression label maker for facial expression image data augmentation. In the differential discriminator [5], by considering the difference image among seven basic facial expression images of the same person, [5] could generate more variation-realistic facial images (i.e., expression-realistic). However, it could lead to artifacts on the generated image because they only focused on generating the variation-realistic image. [6] proposed a multi-domain image-to-image translation method using the generator for mappings among multiple domains in an unsupervised manner. However, it could not generate variation-realistic facial images because it is hard for the generator to learn enough facial variations in an unsupervised manner.

In this paper, we propose photo-realistic facial emotion synthesis by using a novel multi-level critic network and multi-level decoder with generative adversarial learning. The proposed deep learning framework consists of generator, discriminator and multi-level critic networks. The generator consists of encoder and the proposed multi-level decoder. The encoder learns the identity of the input images and the desired facial expression in the semantic features. The proposed multi-level decoder consists of N multi-level decoding modules. The multi-level decoding modules generate various facial images with multi resolutions (see details in Sect. 2). The N-th level decoding module is composed of residual blocks [8] to finally generate desired facial images.

In particular, we introduce novel multi-level critic networks. They are attached to $(N - 1)$ multi-level decoding modules in order to learn multi resolution latent feature maps that make photo-realistic and variation-realistic target images. The proposed one level critic network consists of two discriminators, which are photo-realistic discriminator and variation-realistic discriminator. The photo-realistic discriminator tries to evaluate how realistic the generated images of each level decoding module is compared to the ground-truth multi-resolution target image. It forces the generated images to be closer to the natural image. The variation-realistic discriminator tries to evaluate how the difference between input image and generated target image is realistic compared to the variation difference between the input image and ground-truth target image. It forces the generated facial images to have smooth facial expressions without artifacts. Therefore, they induce generator to synthesize more photo-realistic and variation-realistic images even in large facial variations.

In the training stage with generative adversarial learning, the generator and the discriminator are end-to-end trained with the multi-level critic networks. Due to the influence of the generator and the discriminator, the generator can generate facial variation image maintaining the identity of each facial image. In addition, by multi-level critic networks, the generator can make photo-realistic and variation-realistic image. In the test stage, with only the trained generator, the desired facial expression images can be generated.

To evaluate the performance of the proposed method, we compare the facial expression synthesis performance with the state-of-the-arts methods. The experimental results show that the generator could provide photo-realistic facial expression images minimizing various artifacts.

The remainder of this paper is organized as follows. In Sect. 2, we describe the proposed multi-level critic network in detail. Section 3 shows experimental results for qualitative and quantitative evaluation. Finally, conclusions are drawn in Sect. 4.

2 Proposed Method

2.1 Overview of the Proposed Framework

Figure 1 shows the overall proposed network framework for facial expression synthesizing in training and testing. Let $\mathbf{I}_i$, $\mathbf{I}_t$ and $\mathbf{I}_g$ denote the input, target and generated images, respectively. In Fig. 1(a), the proposed network consists of generator G, discriminator D and multi-level critic networks in training stage. The generator G consists of the encoder for the latent feature encoding and the proposed multi-level decoder for generating facial images with target expression from the encoded features. The discriminator D determines whether the generated image is a photo-realistic or not. The multi-level critic networks are attached to $(N - 1)$ multi-level decoding modules. The critic networks refine multi-resolution latent feature maps of the proposed multi-level decoder to force the generator make photo-realistic and variation-realistic images. The multi-level critic networks determine whether the multi-resolution facial images are photo-realistic or not and variation-realistic or not. By adversarial learning [7] among the generator, discriminator and multi-level critic networks, the proposed network generates photo-realistic and variation-realistic facial expression images. In testing stage, as shown in Fig. 1(b), the facial image with desired expression is generated by the trained generator without target image, discriminator, and multi-critic networks. Details are described in following subsections.

2.2 Generator and Discriminator for Photo-Realistic Image Generation

The overall proposed network consists of three main parts, which are the generator, discriminator and multi-level critic networks. In this section, we describe the proposed generator and discriminator. The role of the generator is to create the facial image with a desired expression while preserving the identity of the image. The role of the discriminator is to distinguish between the generated image and target image. The generator approximates the face manifold by adversarial learning with the discriminator.

The generator G consists of encoder and multi-level decoder. The encoder receives two kinds of inputs, which are the input image, $\mathbf{I}_i \in \mathbb{R}^{128 \times 128 \times 3}$ and label code, $\mathbf{c} \in \mathbb{R}^L$, where L is the number of expressions. The label code $\mathbf{c} \in \mathbb{R}^L$ is passed through

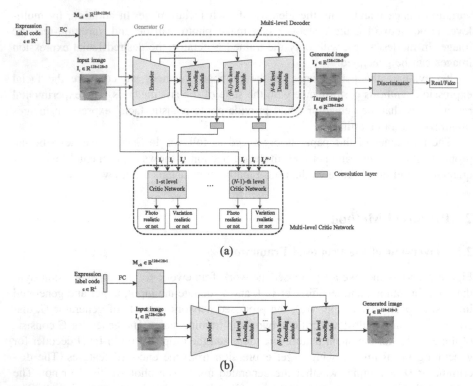

Fig. 1. The overall proposed framework (a) in training and (b) in testing. In training, the proposed network consists of generator, discriminator, and N multi-level critic networks. Expression label code is encoded to label channel map $\mathbf{M}_{ch}$ through fully-connected layers. Concatenating the label channel map to input image, the image with target expression information is fed to the generator. The generator consists of encoder and the proposed multi-level decoder. Through the generator, a facial image with target expression is generated and the discriminator forces the generated image to be photo-realistic. The multi-level critic network refines latent features of the multi-level decoder for generating photo-realistic and variation-realistic images. In testing, the facial image with desired expression is generated by trained generator without target image, discriminator, and multi-level critic networks.

fully connected layers and then its output is reshaped to the label encoded map $\mathbf{M}_{ch} \in \mathbb{R}^{128 \times 128 \times 1}$. By encoding the label code to label map, more abundant condition information of facial expressions can be provided to the generator. Finally, $[\mathbf{I}_i; \mathbf{M}_{ch}]$ is the input of the encoder. By skip-connection [9], the low-level layers in encoder and high-level layers in decoder are connected.

After encoding the facial image and desired expression information, the proposed multi-level decoder generates a facial image, $\mathbf{I}_g \in \mathbb{R}^{128 \times 128 \times 3}$ with the intended expression from the encoded features. The multi-level decoder consists of 1-st to N-th level decoding modules. The decoding modules consist of deconvolution layers and convolution blocks. We proceeded with ($N = 3$) for actual training. Figure 2, Tables 1 and 2 show details of the structures of the encoder and the multi-level ($N = 3$) decoder.

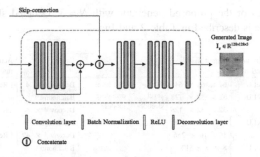

Fig. 2. Architectures of the proposed N-th level decoding module. The first block is residual block that goes through the process of summation of first features and last features of the block. Low-level features of encoder passed through skip-connection is concatenated to the output of residual block. After deconvolution layer and convolution layers, a facial image is generated. Detailed kernel size, activation function and output size of each layer is described in Table 2.

After generating a facial image by the generator, the discriminator D determines whether the generated image, $\mathbf{I}_g \in \mathbb{R}^{128 \times 128 \times 3}$ is photo-realistic or not. The structure of the discriminator is the same as the encoder (see Table 1) of the generator except stride of each convolution layer and the number of convolution layers. The discriminator has 5 convolution layers (except for last convolution layer of the encoder in Table 1). The stride of first two convolution layers is 2 and the stride of the others is 1.

2.3 Multi-level Critic Network for Photo-Realistic and Variation-Realistic Image Generation

Figure 3 shows the proposed n-th multi-level critic network. The network consists of two discriminators, photo-realistic discriminator, D_{pr}^n, and variation-realistic discriminator, D_{vr}^n. The critic networks are used multiple times in the entire network, and each structure is identical. Because the resolution of target and input image is different from generated image $\mathbf{I}_g^n$, target and input image are downsized to $\mathbf{I}_i^n$ and $\mathbf{I}_t^n$ with the same resolution as $\mathbf{I}_g^n$, respectively.

The photo-realistic discriminator, D_{pr}^n tries to distinguish between the generated image, $\mathbf{I}_g^n$ and the target image, $\mathbf{I}_t^n$. D_{pr}^n forces the generator G to synthesize the photo-realistic facial image that is undistinguishable from real image. The structure of the discriminator, D_{pr}^n is same as the discriminator, D.

The variation-realistic discriminator, D_{vr}^n tries to distinguish the difference of facial expression between input and target images and the difference of expression between input and generated images. The effect of difference information is to remove the common spatial features between two images such as identity information. Therefore, D_{vr}^n can focus on the expression variations. The structure of the discriminator is the same as the last three convolution layers of D. The structure of the feature encoder is the same as the first two convolution layers of D except activation function of second convolution layer. The activation function of the second convolution layer is sigmoid function instead of LReLU.

Table 1. Architectures of the proposed generator with $N = 3$. Detailed structure of the N-th level decoding module is described in Table 2 and Fig. 2.

Generator								
Type	Layer	Activation function	Output size	Type		Layer	Activation function	Output size
Encoder	Conv 4 × 4	LReLU	64 × 64 × 64	Multi-level decoder	1-st level decoding module	Deconv 4 × 4	LReLU	4 × 4 × 512
	Conv 4 × 4	LReLU	32 × 32 × 128			Batchnorm	–	4 × 4 × 512
	Batchnorm	–	32 × 32 × 128			Deconv 4 × 4	LReLU	8 × 8 × 512
	Conv 4 × 4	LReLU	16 × 16 × 256			Batchnorm	–	8 × 8 × 512
	Batchnorm	–	16 × 16 × 256			Deconv 4 × 4	LReLU	16 × 16 × 256
	Conv 4 × 4	LReLU	8 × 8 × 512			Batchnorm	–	16 × 16 × 256
	Batchnorm	–	8 × 8 × 512			Deconv 4 × 4	LReLU	32 × 32 × 128
	Conv 4 × 4	LReLU	4 × 4 × 512			Batchnorm	–	32 × 32 × 128
	Batchnorm	–	4 × 4 × 512		2-nd level decoding module	Deconv 4 × 4	LReLU	64 × 64 × 64
	Conv 4 × 4	LReLU	2 × 2 × 512			Batchnorm	–	64 × 64 × 64
	Batchnorm	–	2 × 2 × 512		N-th level decoding module	Conv block (See Table 2 in detail)		128 × 28 × 3

2.4   Objective Functions for Network Training

Discriminator Loss. In order to make the photo-realistic facial image, the discriminator loss can be written as

$$L_D = -\mathbb{E}_{\mathbf{I}_t}[\log(D(\mathbf{I}_t))] - \mathbb{E}_{\mathbf{I}_i,c}[\log(1 - D(G(\mathbf{I}_i, c)))]. \tag{1}$$

The discriminator D tries to minimize L_D to distinguish between generated fake image $\mathbf{I}_g$ and target real image $\mathbf{I}_t$. D forces to the generator mimic the distribution of real image.

Multi-level Critic Network Loss. In n-th multi-level critic network, there are two discriminators D_{pr}^n and D_{vr}^n. First, the loss function of D_{pr}^n can be defined as

$$L_{D_{pr}^n} = -\mathbb{E}_{\mathbf{I}_t}\left[\log\left(D_{pr}^n\left(\mathbf{I}_t^n\right)\right)\right] - \mathbb{E}_{\mathbf{I}_i,c}\left[\log\left(1 - D_{pr}^n(G^n(\mathbf{I}_i, c))\right)\right], \tag{2}$$

where the G^n indicates the part of the generator that includes the encoder and 1-st to n-th level decoding modules. D_{pr}^n tries to minimize $L_{D_{pr}^n}$ to distinguish between the generated low resolution image $G^n(\mathbf{I}_i, c)$ and the down-sampled target image $\mathbf{I}_t^n$. Therefore, D_{pr}^n helps G to generate photo-realistic image by refining the latent features. Second, the loss function of D_{vr}^n can be written as

$$\begin{aligned} L_{D_{vr}^n} = &-\mathbb{E}_{\mathbf{I}_i, \mathbf{I}_t}\left[\log\left(D_{vr}^n\left(f_e^n\left(\mathbf{I}_t^n\right) - f_e^n\left(\mathbf{I}_i^n\right)\right)\right)\right] \\ &- \mathbb{E}_{\mathbf{I}_i,c}\left[\log\left(1 - D_{vr}^n\left(f_e^n(G^n(\mathbf{I}_i, c)) - f_e^n\left(\mathbf{I}_i^n\right)\right)\right)\right], \end{aligned} \tag{3}$$

where f_e^n indicates the feature encoder of n-th level critic network. D_{vr}^n forces the G to generate variations of images that are well formed.

Table 2. Detailed structure of N-th level decoding module.

N-th level decoding module		
Layer	Activation function	Output Size ($w \times h \times c$)
Conv 3×3	ReLU	$64 \times 64 \times 128$
Batchnorm	–	$64 \times 64 \times 128$
Conv 3×3	–	$64 \times 64 \times 128$
Batchnorm	–	$64 \times 64 \times 128$
Deconv 4×4	ReLU	$128 \times 128 \times 256$
Batchnorm	–	$128 \times 128 \times 256$
Conv 3×3	ReLU	$128 \times 128 \times 256$
Conv 3×3	ReLU	$128 \times 128 \times 256$
Conv 3×3	Tanh	$128 \times 128 \times 3$

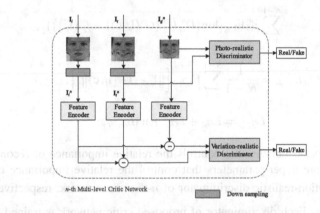

Fig. 3. The structure of n-th multi-level critic network. The proposed network consists of Feature Encoder, Photo-realistic Discriminator, and Variation-realistic Discriminator. To match input image $\mathbf{I}_i$ and target image $\mathbf{I}_t$ to the size of generated image using latent features of decoder $\mathbf{I}_g^n$, $\mathbf{I}_i$ and $\mathbf{I}_t$ are resized. Photo-realistic discriminator determines whether the $\mathbf{I}_g^n$ is photo-realistic or not. On the other hand, Feature Encoder encodes $\mathbf{I}_i^n$, $\mathbf{I}_t^n$, and $\mathbf{I}_g^n$ to input image features, target image features, and generated image features, respectively. After subtracting input image features from target image features and generated image features, Variation-realistic discriminator determines whether the output, facial expression difference features, is variation-realistic or not.

Generator Loss. The generator tries to maximize the discriminator loss, L_D. We adopt L1 distance as reconstruction loss. The objective functions can be written as

$$L_{G_{hr}} = -\mathrm{E}_{\mathbf{I}_i,\mathrm{c}}[\log(D(G(\mathbf{I}_i,\mathrm{c})))], \qquad (4)$$

$$L_{rec,hr} = \mathrm{E}_{\mathbf{I}_t,\mathbf{I}_i,\mathrm{c}}\left[\|\mathbf{I}_t - G(\mathbf{I}_i,\mathrm{c})\|_1\right], \qquad (5)$$

$$L_G = w_1 L_{G_{hr}} + w_2 L_{rec,hr}, \tag{6}$$

where w_1 and w_2 are hyper-parameters that control the relative importance of adversarial loss and reconstruction loss. The overall generator is learned to minimize L_G.

Generator Loss Without N-th Level Decoding Module. After training the overall generator G with L_G, the generator without N-th level decoding module, called $G_{w/o}$, is trained once more. The $G_{w/o}$ tries to maximize the loss of (D_{pr}^1 to D_{pr}^{N-1}) and (D_{vr}^1 to D_{vr}^{N-1}). We also adopt L1 distance as reconstruction of low resolution images. The overall loss functions can be defined as

$$L_{G_{pr}} = -\sum_{n=1}^{N-1} \lambda_{pr}^n \mathrm{E}_{\mathrm{I}_i,\mathrm{c}} \left[\log \left(D_{pr}^n (G^n(\mathrm{I}_i, \mathrm{c})) \right) \right], \tag{7}$$

$$L_{G_{vr}} = -\sum_{n=1}^{N-1} \lambda_{vr}^n \mathrm{E}_{\mathrm{I}_i,\mathrm{c}} \left[\log \left(D_{vr}^n \left(f_e^n (G^n(\mathrm{I}_i, \mathrm{c})) - f_e^n (\mathrm{I}_i^n) \right) \right) \right], \tag{8}$$

$$L_{rec,lr} = \frac{1}{N-1} \sum_{n=1}^{N-1} \mathrm{E}_{\mathrm{I}_t,\mathrm{I}_i,\mathrm{c}} \left[\left\| \mathrm{I}_t^n - G^n(\mathrm{I}_i, \mathrm{c}) \right\|_1 \right], \tag{9}$$

$$L_{G_{w/o}} = L_{G_{pr}} + L_{G_{vr}} + w_3 L_{rec,lr}, \tag{10}$$

where w_3 is a hyper-parameter that controls the relative importance of reconstruction loss. λ_{pr}^n and λ_{vr}^n are hyper-parameters that control the relative importance of photo-realistic and variation-realistic discriminator of n-th critic network, respectively.

Training Scheme. Each discriminator of proposed critic network is trained independently. At each iteration of training process, the discriminator D, $(N-1)$ photo-realistic discriminators and $(N-1)$ variation-realistic discriminators are updated by minimizing L_D, $(L_{D_{pr}^1}, \ldots, L_{D_{pr}^{N-1}})$, $(L_{D_{vr}^1}, \ldots, L_{D_{vr}^{N-1}})$, respectively. Then the overall generator is updated to minimize L_G. Finally, the generator without N-th level decoding module, $G_{w/o}$ is updated to minimize $L_{G_{w/o}}$.

3 Experiments

3.1 Datasets

In experiments, we used one public dataset for training and two public datasets for verifying the effectiveness of our model. PNAS dataset [10] was used only for training and MMI [11] and RaFD [12] datasets were used only for validating performance of our model. Because the images of each dataset we used had different resolutions, we cropped all images in the datasets where the faces were centered and then resized to 128×128. The datasets are as follows:

PNAS Dataset. This dataset consists of 21 distinct expression categories and images of its facial expression are collected from 230 human subjects. For experiment, we used only seven basic expressions (e.g. neutral, anger, disgusted, fearful, happy, sad, and surprised). The number of selected subset was 1,610 and we flipped images in the subset horizontally for data augmentation. The images were used as training set for our model.

MMI Dataset. This dataset consists of 6 basic expressions and 30 subjects. For experiment, we used only neutral expression in the dataset and used this subset as validation set. The number of images in the selected subset was 30. We validated performance of facial expression synthesis of our model with the selected subset.

RaFD Dataset. This dataset consists of 67 subjects with 8 expressions and each subject has three different gaze directions. For experiment, we used only neutral expression in the dataset and used this subset as validation set, like MMI dataset. The number of images in the subset was 201.

3.2 Training Details

Adam optimizer with $\beta_1 = 0.5$ and $\beta_2 = 0.999$ was used to train all models and learning rate was fixed at 0.0002 throughout training process. The batch size for all experiments was set to 16. In order to verify the ability of proposed method as an application of data augmentation through facial image generation, we trained using only PNAS dataset and verified our model with other datasets. We trained our models with Tensorflow on TITAN XP GPU.

3.3 Facial Expression Synthesis

Comparison with Existing Model. In this section, we compared our model with other existing models, Pix2pix [13] and StarGAN [6]. The model of Pix2pix was designed for one-directional image-to-image translation (e.g., from edge to photo). In order to adapt the model to our experiment, we modified it slightly by adding label channel map, M_{ch} to the input of the generator, similar to our model. The model of StarGAN consists of one generator and discriminator based on CycleGAN [14].

Figure 4 shows that Pix2pix model could not preserve the identity of image and made a lot of artifacts. StarGAN model did not produce variation realistic images and the facial expression of generated image was not intensive. On the other hand, our model provided photo-realistic facial images with variation-realistic expression.

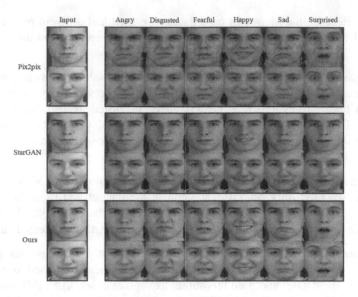

Fig. 4. Facial expression synthesis results on the MMI dataset. From top to bottom row: first row is results by Pix2pix model and second is results by StarGAN model. Final row is results by the proposed model.

Effects of Refining Multi-level Features. Our proposed critic network was used on multi-level features of generator. In this section, we verified that training generator with multi-level critic network achieved better performance than training with single-level critic network. Single-level critic network means that the number of feature level refined by critic network is only one ($N = 2$). In experiments, we used the single-level critic network at low-level feature (32×32) and high-level feature (64×64) and compared the result with outcome of multi-level critic network. The multi-level critic network is used in both low-level feature (32×32) and high-level feature (64×64) ($N = 3$).

Figure 5 shows that the top row is the original input images with neutral expression. In Fig. 5(a), (b), and (c), the expression results for happiness of the generated images were shown. The difference between the expression results is easy to confirm as the happy has large facial variation in the expression category. Figure 5(a) shows the generated facial images with happiness expression using single-level critic network at low-level feature (32×32). The images had artifacts around mouth and skin texture of the images. It did not look like photo-realistic. Figure 5(b) shows the generated facial happiness images using single-level critic network at high-level feature (64×64). The images lose the identity information of original input image. Figure 5(c) shows the generated facial happiness images using multi-level critic network. The images had no artifacts and provided variation-realistic expression while maintaining the identity.

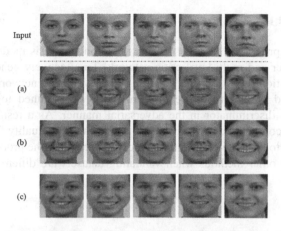

Fig. 5. Generated facial images training with single-level and multi-level critic network. Images in top row are input images with neutral expression of RaFD dataset. (a) is generated facial image with happiness expression using the generator which is trained with single-level critic network ($N = 2$) on low-level feature (32×32). (b) is generated images using the generator which is trained with single-level critic network ($N = 2$) on high-level feature (64×64). (c) is generated images using the generator which is trained with multi-level critic network ($N = 3$).

Facial Expression Recognition. In this experiment, we computed the classification error of a facial expression on generated facial images for a quantitative evaluation. We trained a facial expression classifier on RaFD dataset. We used 90% of the dataset for training and 10% for validating. The AlexNet [15] architecture was used for the classifier and classification error of validation set was 2.86%. After synthesizing the facial images with 7 expressions (including neutral expression) on RaFD dataset using Pix2pix, StarGAN, and our model, the generated images of each model was tested using the above-mentioned classifier. Table 3 shows the classification error of each model. As seen in Table 3, our model achieved the lowest classification error (6.11%). This result indicates that our model produced photo-realistic facial images with distinct expression comparable to real images. On the other hand, the generated images using Pix2pix and StarGAN had poor performance on facial expression classification task.

Table 3. Classification error [%] of synthesized images of each model. The generated images are synthesized using RaFD dataset.

Method	Classification error
Pix2pix	10.73
StarGAN	26.37
Ours	6.11
Real images (RaFD validation set)	2.86

4 Conclusion

In this paper, we proposed the novel facial expression synthesis model by using new multi-level decoder and multi-level critic network. To effectively generate the photo-realistic and variation-realistic facial images, multi-level critic networks consisting of photo-realistic and variation-realistic discriminators were trained together with the generator and the discriminator in the adversarial manner. As a result, the proposed method achieved competitive performance of generating high quality facial expression images compared to the state-of-the-art methods. In particular, the proposed method far has outperformed other methods when validating datasets are different from training dataset.

References

1. Xu, Y., Li, X., Yang, J., Zhang, D.: Integrate the original face image and its mirror image for face recognition. Neurocomputing **131**, 191–199 (2014)
2. Kim, Y., Yoo, B., Kwak, Y., Choi, C., Kim, J.: Deep generative-contrastive networks for facial expression recognition. arXiv preprint arXiv:1703.07140 (2017)
3. Kim, D.H., Baddar, W., Jang, J., Ro, Y.M.: Multi-objective based spatio-temporal feature representation learning robust to expression intensity variations for facial expression recognition. In: IEEE Transactions on Affective Computing (2017)
4. Zhang, Z., Song, Y., Qi, H.: Age progression/regression by conditional adversarial autoencoder. arXiv preprint arXiv:1702.08423 (2017)
5. Gu, G.M., Kim, S.T., Kim, K.H., Baddar, W., Ro, Y.M.: Differential generative adversarial networks: synthesizing non-linear facial variations with limited number of training data. arXiv preprint arXiv:1711.10267 (2017)
6. Choi, Y., Choi, M., Kim, M., Ha, J.W., Kim, S., Choo, J.: Stargan: unified generative adversarial networks for multi-domain image-to-image translation. arXiv preprint arXiv: 1711.09020 (2017)
7. Goodfellow, I., et al.: Generative adversarial nets. In: Advances in Neural Information Processing Systems, pp. 2672–2680 (2014)
8. He, K., Zhang, X., Ren, S., Sun, J.: Deep residual learning for image recognition. In: CVPR (2016)
9. Ronneberger, O., Fischer, P., Brox, T.: U-net: convolutional networks for biomedical image segmentation. In: Navab, N., Hornegger, J., Wells, W.M., Frangi, AlF (eds.) MICCAI 2015. LNCS, vol. 9351, pp. 234–241. Springer, Cham (2015). https://doi.org/10.1007/978-3-319-24574-4_28
10. Du, S., Tao, Y., Martinez, A.M.: Compound facial expressions of emotion. Proc. Natl. Acad. Sci. **111**(15), E1454–E1462 (2014)
11. Valstar, M., Pantic, M.: Induced disgust, happiness and surprise: an addition to the MMI facial expression database. In: Proceedings of 3rd International Workshop on EMOTION (Satellite of LREC): Corpora for Research on Emotion and Affect, p. 65 (2010)
12. Langner, O., Dotsch, R., Bijlstra, G., Wigboldus, D.H., Hawk, S.T., Van Knippenberg, A.: Presentation and validation of the radboud faces database. Cogn. Emot. **24**(8), 1377–1388 (2010)

13. Isola, P., Zhu, J.-Y., Zhou, T., Efros, A.A.: Image-to-image translation with conditional adversarial networks. arXiv preprint arXiv:1611.07004 (2016)
14. Zhu, J.-Y., Park, T., Isola, P., Efros, A.A.: Unpaired image-to-image translation using cycle-consistent adversarial networks. In: Proceedings of the IEEE International Conference on Computer Vision (ICCV) (2017)
15. Krizhevsky, A., Sutskever, I., Hinton, G.E.: Imagenet classification with deep convolutional neural networks. In: Advances in Neural Information Processing Systems, pp. 1097–1105 (2012)

Adaptive Alignment Network for Person Re-identification

Xierong Zhu, Jiawei Liu, Hongtao Xie, and Zheng-Jun Zha(✉)

University of Science and Technology of China, Hefei, China
{zxr8192,ljw368}@mail.ustc.edu.cn,
{htxie,zhazj}@ustc.edu.cn

Abstract. Person re-identification aims at identifying a target pedestrian across non-overlapping camera views. Pedestrian misalignment, which mainly arises from inaccurate person detection and pose variations, is a critical challenge for person re-identification. To address this, this paper proposes a new Adaptive Alignment Network (AAN), towards robust and accurate person re-identification. AAN automatically aligns pedestrian images from coarse to fine by learning both patch-wise and pixel-wise alignments, leading to effective pedestrian representation invariant to the variance of human pose and location across images. In particular, AAN consists of a patch alignment module, a pixel alignment module and a base network. The patch alignment module estimates the alignment offset for each image patch and performs patch-wise alignment with the offsets. The pixel alignment module is for fine-grained pixel-wise alignment. It learns the subtle local offset for each pixel and produces finely aligned feature map. Extensive experiments on three benchmarks, i.e., Market1501, DukeMTMC-reID and MSMT17 datasets, have demonstrated the effectiveness of the proposed approach.

Keywords: Person re-identification · Adaptive alignment
Robust representation

1 Introduction

Person re-identification aims at identifying the same pedestrian across non-overlapping camera views. It has attracted increasing attention due to the wide range of practical applications, such as automated surveillance, activity analysis and person search [10,12,13]. Recent years have witnessed remarkable progress on person re-identification. However, it remains a challenging task due to excessive background, occlusion, as well as dramatic variations in illumination, human pose and viewpoint *etc.* [14].

One critical challenge for person re-identification is the misalignment of pedestrian images, which mainly caused by inaccurate detection of pedestrians and/or dramatic human pose variations across images. For example, Deformable

---

X. Zhu and J. Liu—Equal contribution.

© Springer Nature Switzerland AG 2019
I. Kompatsiaris et al. (Eds.): MMM 2019, LNCS 11296, pp. 16–27, 2019.
https://doi.org/10.1007/978-3-030-05716-9_2

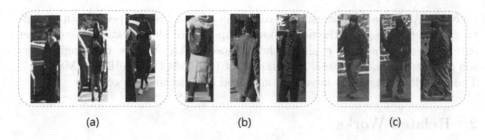

(a)   (b)   (c)

Fig. 1. Illustration of the misalignment challenge for person re-identification: (a) inclusion of excessive background, (b) incomplete coverage of the body, (c) human pose variance.

Part Model [5] and Faster RCNN [15] have been used to automatically detect the bounding boxes of pedestrians in Market1501 [27] and MSMT17 [22] datasets, respectively. The use of automatic detectors can avoid labor-intensive manual labeling. However, detection errors result in undesirable challenges, such as the inclusion of excessive background in pedestrian bounding boxes and incomplete coverage of the body as shown in Fig. 1(a) and (b), respectively. On the other hand, the dramatic variations in human pose also cause the misalignment, as shown in Fig. 1(c).

Recently, a certain number of approaches have been proposed to address the misalignment problem. Existing approaches could be roughly divided into two categories. The first is to use the feature maps from high-level convolutional layers to learn an affine transformation, which is applied on lower-level feature maps to reduce the influence of scale and location variances caused by inaccurate detection [29]. However, affine transformation is not able to handle non-rigid misalignment, such as pose variations. The second is to utilize or design a pose estimation module to localize the body parts for boosting identity matching [20,25]. However, it usually suffers from the pose estimation error and high computational costs.

In this work, we propose a new Adaptive Alignment Network (AAN) to tackle the misalignment problem towards accurate and robust person re-identification. AAN automatically aligns pedestrian features from coarse to fine by learning both patch-wise and pixel-wise alignments, leading to effective pedestrian representation invariant to the variance of human pose and location across images. As illustrated in Fig. 2, AAN consists of a base network, a patch alignment module and a pixel alignment module. The base network is built on ResNet-50 [6] for producing preliminary pedestrian representation. The patch alignment module consists of two convolution layers followed by two fully connected layers. It partitions the feature map from the base network into multiple patches and estimates the alignment offset of each patch. It then conducts patch-wise alignment based on the learned offsets. The pixel alignment module is for fine-grained pixel-wise alignment. It also contains two convolution layers followed by two fully connected layers. It learns the subtle local offset for each pixel within a patch and produces finely aligned feature map. By aligning pedestrian images precisely, AAN is able to learn more discriminative and robust pedestrian presentation and thus improve the performance of person re-identification. We conduct extensive experiments to evaluate the proposed AAN on three challenging person re-identification datasets, i.e., Market1501, DukeMTMC-reID and MSMT17. The experimental results have demonstrated the effectiveness of AAN.

2   Related Works

Recent years have witnessed a certain amount of research efforts addressing the misalignment challenge for person re-identification. This section briefly reviews existing works.

Conventional approaches mainly design hand-crafted descriptors of pedestrian appearance against the misalignment. For example, Farenzena et al. [4] proposed the Symmetry Driven Accumulation of Local Features (SDALF), which exploits the symmetry property of human body to alleviate the influence of human pose variance. Chen et al. [3] proposed the Custom Pictorial Structure (CPS), which localizes the body parts and calculates color histograms from the corresponding body parts. Hirzer et al. [7] combined the horizontally divided Haar features and covariance features for pedestrian matching. It prohibits features that are placed close to the image borders to alleviate the influence of excessive background.

Recently, deep learning techniques have been widely employed for person re-identification. For examples, Su et al. [20] proposed the Pose-driven Deep Convolutional (PDC) network, which explicitly utilizes the human part cues towards alleviating pose variations. A pose driven feature weighting sub-network is designed to adaptively fuse the features of global human body and local body parts. Zhao et al. [25] proposed the Spindle Net, which captures semantic features from different body regions with a region proposal network, and learns aligned features to address pose variations. Zheng et al. [29] proposed the pedestrian alignment network (PAN), which learns an affine transformation to re-localize the pedestrian image and utilizes the re-localized image for better pedestrian matching. Zhao et al. [26] proposed a part-aligned representation. It decomposes human body into parts and aggregates the similarities between the corresponding parts of a pair of probe and gallery images.

3   Adaptive Alignment Network

3.1   Overall Architecture

Figure 2 illustrates the architecture of the proposed AAN, consisting of a base network, a patch alignment module and a pixel alignment module. The base network is built on ResNet-50 [6] due to its effectiveness in learning visual representation. The patch alignment module consists of two convolution layers followed by two fully connected layers. It partitions the feature map from base network into multiple patches uniformly and estimates the alignment offset for each patch.

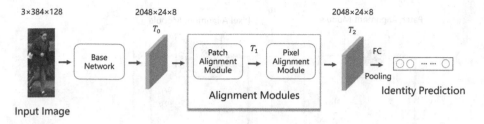

Fig. 2. The overall architecture of the Adaptive Alignment Network (AAN), consisting of a base network, a patch alignment module and a pixel alignment module.

It then conducts patch-wise alignment based on the learned offsets. The pixel alignment module is for fine-grained pixel-wise alignment. It also contains two convolution layers followed by two fully connected layers. It learns the subtle local offset for each pixel within a patch and produces finely aligned feature map. Finally, two fully connected layers are designed to predict the pedestrian identity.

3.2 Base Network

Multiple CNN models have been applied to learn visual representation for person re-identification, such as AlexNet [9], VGGNet [19], ResNet [6] *etc.* In this work, we adopt ResNet-50 model. Compared to other CNNs, ResNet achieves superior performance in learning visual representation by adding a simple skip connection parallel to the layers of convolutional neural networks. The base network contains an initial convolution layer, an initial pooling layer, and four residual blocks. The kernel size of the initial convolution layer is 7×7, which extracts a primitive feature map. The following 3×3 max pooling layer reduces the size of the feature map. Each of the four residual blocks contains several bottleneck building blocks, which consists of three convolution layers. The kernel sizes of the three convolution layers are 1×1, 3×3 and 1×1 respectively. Moreover, the Max-Pooling operation is performed with the first three residual blocks, reducing the size of the feature map.

3.3 Alignment Modules

The proposed AAN performs alignment from coarse to fine. The patch and pixel alignment modules learn patch-wise and pixel-wise offsets and perform feature alignment based on the learned offsets, towards robust representation invariant to variations in human pose and body part location.

As shown in Fig. 3, the patch alignment module contains two convolution layers and two fully connected layers. It takes the feature map T_0 ($2048 \times 24 \times 8$) as input and produces patch aligned feature map T_1 ($2048 \times 24 \times 8$). The patch

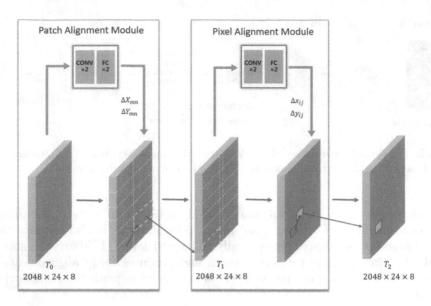

Fig. 3. Illustration of the patch and pixel alignment modules of AAN.

alignment module uniformly partitions the feature maps into 12 patches (the size of each patch is 4×4), and learns the offset of each patch. Afterwards, it replaces a patch P_0 in T_0 by the patch located in the position computed by the corresponding offsets, leading to a roughly aligned feature map T_1.

The configuration of the convolution and fully connected layers in the patch alignment module is as follows. The kernel sizes of the convolution layers are $1 \times 1 \times 16$ and $3 \times 3 \times 4$, respectively. The channels of the fully connected layers are 32 and 24, respectively. In addition, the ReLU operation is performed with the first three layers. The output of the last fully connected layer is a 24-dimension vector, which represents the vertical and horizontal offsets of the 12 patches, $(\Delta X_{mn}, \Delta Y_{mn})$. The patch-wise alignment is conducted following to Eq. (1).

$$P_1(m, n) = P_0(m + \Delta X_{mn}, n + \Delta Y_{mn}) \tag{1}$$

$P_0(m, n)$ and $P_1(m, n)$ represent the patches in T_0 and T_1 at the position (m, n), respectively.

When ΔX_{mn} or ΔY_{mn} is not integer, the pixel $p_0(i + \Delta X_{mn}, j + \Delta Y_{mn})$ in the patch $P_0(m + \Delta X_{mn}, n + \Delta Y_{mn})$ is calculated via the interpolation formulation as follows:

$$
\begin{aligned}
&p_0(i + \Delta X_{mn}, j + \Delta Y_{mn}) \\
&= \sum_{a=1}^{24} \sum_{b=1}^{8} p_0(a, b) \cdot g(i + \Delta X_{mn}, a) \cdot g(j + \Delta Y_{mn}, b)
\end{aligned}
\tag{2}
$$

where $g(x, y) = max(0, 1 - |x - y|)$. Equation (2) is fast to compute since $g(x, y)$ is non-zero only for a few cases.

The pixel alignment module also contains two convolution layers and two fully connected layers. It takes the feature map T_1 as input and produces a finely aligned feature map T_2 ($2048 \times 24 \times 8$) based on the subtle local offset of each pixel in T_1. The kernel sizes of the convolution layers are $3 \times 3 \times 16$ and $3 \times 3 \times 4$, respectively. The channels of the fully connected layers are 512 and 384, respectively. In addition, the ReLU operation is performed with the first three layers. The output of the last fully connected layer is a 384-dimension vector, which represents the subtle local offset $(\Delta x_{ij}, \Delta y_{ij})$ for each pixel. The formulation for pixel-wise alignment is as follows:

$$
\begin{aligned}
p_2(i,j) &= p_1(i + \Delta x_{ij}, j + \Delta y_{ij}) \\
&= \sum_{a=1}^{24} \sum_{b=1}^{8} p_1(a,b) \cdot g(i + \Delta x_{ij}, a) \cdot g(j + \Delta y_{ij}, b)
\end{aligned}
\tag{3}
$$

where $g(x,y) = max(0, 1 - |x - y|)$, $p_1(i,j)$ and $p_2(i,j)$ represent the pixels in T_1 and T_2 at the position (i,j), respectively.

3.4   Loss Function

Cross-Entropy loss is usually leveraged for classification task because of its simplicity and effectiveness. Hence, we adopt the Cross-Entropy loss to optimize the network. Suppose there are K identities for training, we use the classifier to predict K probabilities z_i according to the aligned feature. The loss function is formulated as follows:

$$
L = -log \frac{exp(z_t)}{\sum_{i=1}^{K} exp(z_i)}
\tag{4}
$$

where t is the index of the corresponding identity of an image.

4   Experiments

4.1   Experimental Settings

Datasets. There are several benchmark datasets established for person re-identification. In this work, we conduct extensive experiments on three widely used datasets: Market1501 [27], DukeMTMC-reID [28] and MSMT17 [22].

The Market1501 dataset is one of the largest and most realistic person re-identification benchmark, containing 32,643 images of 1,501 identities captured by 6 cameras. All images are automatically detected by the Deformable Part Model (DPM) detector [5]. Following the protocol used in [27], the dataset is fixedly divided into two parts. One part contains 12,936 images of 750 identities as training set and the other contains 19,732 images of 751 identities as testing set. The proposed method is compared to the state-of-the-art methods under single query evaluation setting.

The DukeMTMC-reID is a subset of the DukeMTMC dataset [16] and is one of the most challenging person re-identification datasets due to similar clothes of different pedestrians and occlusion by trees and cars. It contains 36,411 hand-drawn bounding boxes of 1,812 identities from 8 high-resolution cameras. Following the evaluation protocol specified in [28], it is fixedly divided into two parts respectively, including a training set of 16,522 images of 702 identities and a testing set of 17,661 gallery images of 702 identities. In addition, there are 2,228 query images.

The MSMT17 dataset is collected by a 15-camera network deployed in campus, consisting of 12 outdoor cameras and 3 indoor ones. Faster RCNN [15] is utilized for pedestrian bounding box detection. It contains 126,441 bounding boxes of 4,101 identities. The training set contains 32,621 bounding boxes of 1,041 identities, and the testing set contains 93,820 bounding boxes of 3,060 identities. From the testing set, 11,659 bounding boxes are randomly selected as query images and the other 82,161 bounding boxes are used as gallery images.

Evaluation Metrics. Cumulative Matching Characteristic (CMC) is extensively adopted for quantitative evaluation of person re-identification. The rank-k recognition rate in the CMC curve indicates the probability that a query identity appears in the top-k position. The other evaluation metric is the mean average precision (mAP), considering person re-identification as a retrieval task.

Implementation Details. The implementation of the proposed method is based on the Pytorch framework with one GTX1080Ti. We adopt the pre-trained model on ImageNet to initialize parameters of the base network. The stochastic gradient descent (SGD) algorithm is started with the base learning rate lr of 0.05 (0.005 for the pre-trained layers), the weight decay of $5e^{-4}$ and the Nesterov momentum of 0.9. All the images are resized to the size of $3 \times 384 \times 128$ and normalised with 1.0/256. Meanwhile, the training set is enlarged by data augmentation strategies including random horizontal flipping and random erasing probability of 0.3 during training phase. We set the number of mini-batches to 16 and train the model for 50 epochs in total. The learning rates of all the layers decay to 0.1× of the base after 30 epochs.

4.2   Comparison to the State-of-the-Art

We compare our proposed method to the state-of-the-art methods on the three datasets.

MSMT17. Table 1 shows the performance comparison of the proposed AAN against three state-of-the-art methods in terms of rank-1 recognition rate and mAP. The compared methods include GoogleNet [21], PDC [20] and GLAD [23]. The proposed AAN achieves 70.5% rank-1 recognition rate and 40.9% mAP score. It surpasses other methods by a large margin, improving the 2nd best compared method GLAD by 9.1% rank-1 recognition rate and 6.9% mAP score.

Table 1. Performance comparison to the state-of-the-art methods on the MSMT17 dataset.

Methods	Rank-1	Rank-5	Rank-10	mAP
GoogleNet [21]	47.6	65.0	71.8	23.0
PDC [20]	58.0	73.6	79.4	29.7
GLAD [23]	61.4	76.8	81.6	34.0
AAN	**70.5**	**82.8**	**86.9**	**40.9**

Table 2. Performance comparison to the state-of-the-art methods on the Market1501 and DukeMTMC-reID datasets.

Methods	Market1501		DukeMTMC-reID	
	Rank-1	mAP	Rank-1	mAP
BoW+kissme [27]	44.4	20.8	25.1	12.2
LOMO+XQDA [11]	-	-	30.8	17.0
DNS [24]	55.4	29.9	-	-
Part-Aligned [26]	81.0	63.4	-	-
PAN [29]	82.8	63.4	71.6	51.5
PSE [17]	87.7	69.0	79.8	62.0
DPFL [2]	88.9	73.1	79.2	60.6
MLFN [1]	90.0	74.3	81.2	62.8
DuATM [18]	91.4	76.6	81.8	64.6
SPreID [8]	93.7	83.4	85.9	73.3
AAN	92.0	78.2	84.1	66.4
AAN(RK)	93.6	90.9	88.6	83.8

Market1501. Table 2 shows the performance comparison of the proposed AAN against nine state-of-the-art methods in terms of rank-1 recognition rate and mAP score. The compared methods belong to two categories, i.e., traditional methods based on hand-crafted feature and/or distance metric learning including BoW+kissme [27] and DNS [24], deep learning based methods including Part-Aligned [26], PAN [29], PSE [17], DPFL [2], MLFN [1], DuATM [18] and SPreID [8]. The proposed AAN achieves 92.0% rank-1 recognition rate and 78.2% mAP score. Moreover, AAN achieves significant performance improvement compared to the existing methods for addressing misalignment, i.e., Part-Aligned, PAN and PSE, by 11.0%, 9.2% and 4.3% at rank-1 recognition rate, respectively. AAN(RK) refers to the proposed AAN with re-ranking as used in [8], which is an effective strategy for boosting the performance. With the help of re-ranking, the rank-1 recognition rate and mAP score of AAN are further improved to 93.6% and 90.9%, respectively.

DukeMTMC-reID. We compare the proposed AAN against eight state-of-the-art methods. As shown in Table 2, the proposed AAN achieves the second best result compared to the existing methods, obtaining 84.1% rank-1 recognition rate and 66.4% mAP score. Moreover, AAN achieves significant performance improvement compared to PAN and PSE, by 12.5% and 4.3% at rank-1 recognition rate. With the help of re-ranking, the rank-1 recognition rate and mAP score of AAN are further improved to 88.6% and 83.8%, respectively.

The above experimental results have demonstrated the effectiveness of AAN in dealing with the pedestrian misalignment challenge. By learning both patch-wise and pixel-wise alignments from coarse to fine, AAN is able to produce discriminative and robust features and thus improve the performance of person re-identification.

4.3   Ablation Study

To demonstrate the effectiveness of each component of the proposed AAN, we conduct a series of ablation experiments on MSMT17 dataset. Table 3 shows the ablation study results. "Baseline" refers to the AAN only uses the base network to extract pedestrian feature. "Baseline+Patch" represents the AAN only uses the base network followed by patch alignment module to learn the patch aligned feature. "Baseline+Pixel" represents the AAN only uses the base network followed by pixel alignment module to learn the pixel aligned feature. From Table 3, we can obtain the following observations: (a) Compared to the Baseline, Baseline+Patch achieves significant performance improvement by 6.2% at rank-1 recognition rate. This indicates that the patch alignment module performing patch-wise alignment is able to alleviate the influence of misalignment; (b) Baseline+Pixel boosts Baseline by 6.3% at rank-1 recognition rate, which shows the effectiveness of the pixel alignment module for fine-grained pixel-wise alignment; (c) AAN yields the best performance of 70.5% rank-1 recognition rate. This indicates that AAN can learn effective and robust representation for better pedestrian matching by the patch-wise and pixel-wise alignments.

Table 3. Evaluation of the effectiveness of the proposed AAN on MSMT17 dataset.

Methods	Rank-1	Rank-5	Rank-10	mAP
Baseline	62.0	76.3	81.4	34.1
Baseline+Patch	68.2	81.3	85.5	39.0
Baseline+Pixel	68.3	81.6	85.8	39.7
AAN	**70.5**	**82.8**	**86.9**	**40.9**

Moreover, we conduct experiments to analyze the influence of the size of patches in the patch alignment module on MSMT17 dataset. The experiment results are reported in Table 4. The patches of 2×2, 4×4 and 8×8 obtain the

Table 4. The performance of different sizes of patches in the patch alignment module on MSMT17 dataset.

Size	Rank-1	Rank-5	Rank-10	mAP
2×2	70.1	82.3	86.2	40.2
4×4	**70.5**	**82.8**	**86.9**	**40.9**
8×8	69.6	82.2	86.3	39.6

70.1%, 70.5% and 69.6% rank-1 recognition rate, respectively. The patches of 4×4 yields the best performance, boosting the patches of 2×2 and the patches of 8×8 by 0.4% and 0.9% rank-1 recognition rate, respectively. Thus, in our experiments, we partition the feature map T_0 into 12 patches of 4×4 in the patch alignment module.

5 Conclusion

This paper presented a new Adaptive Alignment Network (AAN) to address the misalignment challenge for person re-identification. AAN learns both patch-wise and pixel-wise alignments from coarse to fine. The patch alignment module partitions the feature map into multiple patches and estimates the offset of each patch. Patch-wise alignment is then conducted based on the learned offsets. The subsequent pixel alignment module learns the subtle local offset of each pixel and produces fine-grained pixel-wise aligned feature map. AAN is able to learn effective and robust pedestrian representation invariant to the variance of human pose and location across images for better pedestrian matching. We conducted extensive experiments on three challenging benchmarks, i.e., Market1501, DukeMTMC-reID and MSMT17. The experimental results have shown that the proposed AAN achieves performance improvements compared to multiple state-of-the-art methods.

Acknowledgement. This work was supported by the National Natural Science Foundation of China (NSFC) under Grants 61622211, 61472392, and 61620106009 as well as the Fundamental Research Funds for the Central Universities under Grant WK2100100030.

References

1. Chang, X., Hospedales, T.M., Xiang, T.: Multi-level factorisation net for person re-identification. In: Proceedings of the IEEE Conference on Computer Vision and Pattern Recognition, vol. 1, p. 2 (2018)
2. Chen, Y., Zhu, X., Gong, S.: Person re-identification by deep learning multi-scale representations. In: Proceedings of the IEEE International Conference on Computer Vision, pp. 2590–2600 (2017)

3. Cheng, D.S., Cristani, M., Stoppa, M., Bazzani, L., Murino, V.: Custom pictorial structures for re-identification. In: Proceedings of the British Machine Vision Conference, vol. 1, p. 6. Citeseer (2011)

4. Farenzena, M., Bazzani, L., Perina, A., Murino, V., Cristani, M.: Person re-identification by symmetry-driven accumulation of local features. In: Proceedings of the IEEE Conference on Computer Vision and Pattern Recognition, pp. 2360–2367. IEEE (2010)

5. Felzenszwalb, P., McAllester, D., Ramanan, D.: A discriminatively trained, multiscale, deformable part model. In: Proceedings of the IEEE Conference on Computer Vision and Pattern Recognition, pp. 1–8. IEEE (2008)

6. He, K., Zhang, X., Ren, S., Sun, J.: Deep residual learning for image recognition. In: Proceedings of the IEEE Conference on Computer Vision and Pattern Recognition, pp. 770–778 (2016)

7. Hirzer, M., Beleznai, C., Roth, P.M., Bischof, H.: Person re-identification by descriptive and discriminative classification. In: Heyden, A., Kahl, F. (eds.) SCIA 2011. LNCS, vol. 6688, pp. 91–102. Springer, Heidelberg (2011). https://doi.org/10.1007/978-3-642-21227-7_9

8. Kalayeh, M.M., Basaran, E., Gökmen, M., Kamasak, M.E., Shah, M.: Human semantic parsing for person re-identification. In: Proceedings of the IEEE Conference on Computer Vision and Pattern Recognition, pp. 1062–1071 (2018)

9. Krizhevsky, A., Sutskever, I., Hinton, G.E.: ImageNet classification with deep convolutional neural networks. In: Conference and Workshop on Neural Information Processing Systems, pp. 1097–1105 (2012)

10. Li, Z., Zhang, J., Zhang, K., Li, Z.: Visual tracking with weighted adaptive local sparse appearance model via spatio-temporal context learning. IEEE Trans. Image Process. (2018)

11. Liao, S., Hu, Y., Zhu, X., Li, S.Z.: Person re-identification by local maximal occurrence representation and metric learning. In: Proceedings of the IEEE Conference on Computer Vision and Pattern Recognition, pp. 2197–2206 (2015)

12. Liu, J., Zha, Z.J., Chen, X., Wang, Z., Zhang, Y.: Dense 3d-convolutional neural network for person re-identification in videos. ACM Trans. Multimedia Comput. Commun. Appl. **14**(4), 9:1–9:18 (2018)

13. Liu, J., et al.: Multi-scale triplet CNN for person re-identification. In: Proceedings of the 2016 ACM on Multimedia Conference, pp. 192–196. ACM (2016)

14. Liu, J., Zha, Z.J., Xie, H., Xiong, Z., Zhang, Y.: CA3Net: contextual-attentional attribute-appearance network for person re-identification. In: Proceedings of the 2018 ACM on Multimedia Conference, pp. 737–745. ACM (2018)

15. Ren, S., He, K., Girshick, R., Sun, J.: Faster R-CNN: towards real-time object detection with region proposal networks. In: Conference and Workshop on Neural Information Processing Systems, pp. 91–99 (2015)

16. Ristani, E., Solera, F., Zou, R., Cucchiara, R., Tomasi, C.: Performance measures and a data set for multi-target, multi-camera tracking. In: Hua, G., Jégou, H. (eds.) ECCV 2016. LNCS, vol. 9914, pp. 17–35. Springer, Cham (2016). https://doi.org/10.1007/978-3-319-48881-3_2

17. Sarfraz, M.S., Schumann, A., Eberle, A., Stiefelhagen, R.: A pose-sensitive embedding for person re-identification with expanded cross neighborhood re-ranking. In: Proceedings of the IEEE Conference on Computer Vision and Pattern Recognition, vol. 7, p. 8 (2018)

18. Si, J., et al.: Dual attention matching network for context-aware feature sequence based person re-identification. arXiv preprint arXiv:1803.09937 (2018)

19. Simonyan, K., Zisserman, A.: Very deep convolutional networks for large-scale image recognition. arXiv preprint arXiv:1409.1556 (2014)
20. Su, C., Li, J., Zhang, S., Xing, J., Gao, W., Tian, Q.: Pose-driven deep convolutional model for person re-identification. In: Proceedings of the IEEE International Conference on Computer Vision, pp. 3980–3989. IEEE (2017)
21. Szegedy, C., et al.: Going deeper with convolutions. In: Proceedings of the IEEE Conference on Computer Vision and Pattern Recognition, pp. 1–9 (2015)
22. Wei, L., Zhang, S., Gao, W., Tian, Q.: Person transfer GAN to bridge domain gap for person re-identification. In: Proceedings of the IEEE Conference on Computer Vision and Pattern Recognition, pp. 79–88 (2018)
23. Wei, L., Zhang, S., Yao, H., Gao, W., Tian, Q.: Glad: global-local-alignment descriptor for pedestrian retrieval. In: Proceedings of the 2017 ACM on Multimedia Conference, pp. 420–428. ACM (2017)
24. Zhang, L., Xiang, T., Gong, S.: Learning a discriminative null space for person re-identification. In: Proceedings of the IEEE Conference on Computer Vision and Pattern Recognition, pp. 1239–1248 (2016)
25. Zhao, H., et al.: Spindle net: person re-identification with human body region guided feature decomposition and fusion. In: Proceedings of the IEEE Conference on Computer Vision and Pattern Recognition, pp. 1077–1085 (2017)
26. Zhao, L., Li, X., Zhuang, Y., Wang, J.: Deeply-learned part-aligned representations for person re-identification. In: Proceedings of the IEEE International Conference on Computer Vision, pp. 3239–3248 (2017)
27. Zheng, L., Shen, L., Tian, L., Wang, S., Wang, J., Tian, Q.: Scalable person re-identification: a benchmark. In: Proceedings of the IEEE International Conference on Computer Vision, pp. 1116–1124 (2015)
28. Zheng, Z., Zheng, L., Yang, Y.: Unlabeled samples generated by GAN improve the person re-identification baseline in vitro. In: Proceedings of the IEEE International Conference on Computer Vision, pp. 3754–3762 (2017)
29. Zheng, Z., Zheng, L., Yang, Y.: Pedestrian alignment network for large-scale person re-identification. IEEE Trans. Circ. Syst. Video Technol. (2018)

Visual Urban Perception with Deep Semantic-Aware Network

Yongchao Xu[1], Qizheng Yang[2], Chaoran Cui[3(✉)], Cheng Shi[1], Guangle Song[3],
Xiaohui Han[4], and Yilong Yin[2(✉)]

[1] School of Computer Science and Technology, Shandong University, Jinan, China
xuyongchao94@gmail.com, shichengcn@gmail.com
[2] School of Software, Shandong University, Jinan, China
yqz.sdu@gmail.com, ylyin@sdu.edu.cn
[3] School of Computer Science and Technology,
Shandong University of Finance and Economics, Jinan, China
crcui@sdufe.edu.cn, glsong921@163.com
[4] Shandong Computer Science Center (National Supercomputer Center in Jinan),
Shandong Provincial Key Laboratory of Computer Networks,
Qilu University of Technology (Shandong Academy of Sciences), Jinan, China
hanxh@sdas.org

Abstract. Visual urban perception has received a lot attention for its importance in many fields. In this paper we transform it into a ranking task by pairwise comparison of images, and use deep neural networks to predict the specific perceptual score of each image. Distinguished from existing researches, we highlight the important role of object semantic information in visual urban perception through the attribute activation maps of images. Base on this concept, we combine the object semantic information with the generic features of images in our method. In addition, we use the visualization techniques to obtain the correlations between objects and visual perception attributes from the well trained neural network, which further proves the correctness of our conjecture. The experimental results on large-scale dataset validate the effectiveness of our method.

Keywords: Visual urban perception · Object semantic information Deep neural network

1 Introduction

Visual urban perception [7,15,22] aims to quantify the associations between the physical appearance of urban environment and the perceived feelings of its inhabitants (e.g., safety, wealth, and beauty). The well-known *Broken Windows Theory* [26] indicates that visual signs of environmental disorder, such as broken windows, litter, vagrancy, and graffiti, can induce negative social outcomes and increase crime levels. Social scientists have also found evidence for the impact of the visual qualities of urban spaces on education [16], health [3], physical activity

© Springer Nature Switzerland AG 2019
I. Kompatsiaris et al. (Eds.): MMM 2019, LNCS 11296, pp. 28–40, 2019.
https://doi.org/10.1007/978-3-030-05716-9_3

[21], etc. For policymakers and urban planners, it is important to understand people's perceptions and evaluate urban spaces, so that they can make cities better places to live for urban residents.

Traditionally, visual urban perception is performed through a filed study by interviewing city residents and manually reviewing photographs, which is undoubtedly a tedious process involving considerable collective efforts [19]. Today, geo-tagged images publicly accessible from social media platforms and street view panoramas have emerged as an invaluable resource to study visual urban perception [7,29]. Besides, the popularity of modern crowdsourcing platforms (e.g., Amazon MTurk) has also made it possible to collect millions of users' opinions about urban places. Both factors jointly facilitate the development of computational methods to automatically infer high-level perceptual attributes of urban environment from the corresponding geo-tagged images.

With the rapid development of computer vision technologies, visual urban perception is initially cast as a regression problem [17,24], where each image of a place is assigned a score indicating the degree to which it relates to certain perceptual attributes. However, it is rather difficult even for human observers to decide the absolute degree, while relative comparison (e.g., *"does this image look safer than the other one?"*) is a more natural way to perceive and evaluate environments in real life. From this perspective, recent studies [15,22] focus on directly predicting the relative ranking of scene images for different perceptual attributes. Meanwhile, research advances also stem from elaborately designing handcrafted features, such as SIFT and HOG, and evolve into automatically learning deep representations for visual urban perception [18]. Currently, Convolutional Neural Network (CNN) has been widely applied to learn effective features, and obtained state-of-the-art performance.

Intuitively, visual urban perception is coupled with the identification of semantic content of images [12]. Humans first make sense of what they are seeing before they perceive an image of urban space as safe, wealthy, or beautiful. To further illustrate this point, we developed a standard CNN with global average pooling [14], and generated an activation map to localize the discriminative image regions for visual urban perception [28]. The process will be thoroughly discussed in Subsect. 3.2. Figure 1 displays the activation maps of some exemplar images for different perceptual attributes. As can be seen, the discriminative regions are usually the parts of images containing some semantic objects. For example, the regions of the object fence is important to identify the attribute *"Safety"*, and the appearance of dirty houses can plays a crucial role in our perception of the *"Depressing"* of the scene. The observations underpin our belief that visual urban perception needs to be accompanied by semantic understanding of urban spaces.

Motivated by the above discussions, in this paper, we propose a double-column CNN architecture to predict visual urban perception by pairwise comparison and get the activation map to show the relationships between objects and perceptual attributes first. We then add the semantic information of the image to each column in the original neural network to get our final network model. Finally, we use the visualization of network to obtain the correlations

Fig. 1. The activation maps for images on six perceptual attributes.

between objects and visual perceptual attributes from the well trained neural network, which further proves the correctness of our conjecture.

The main contributions of our work can be summarized as follows:

- We use a deep neural network predicting the specific perceptual score of each image, and transform the visual perception task into a ranking task by pairwise comparison of image scores.
- We prove the important role of object semantic information in visual urban perception through the attribute activation maps of images, and we combine the objects semantic information with the generic features of images in our network.
- We obtain the correlations between objects and visual perceptual attributes from the pre-trained neural network, using the visualization of network.

The remainder of the paper is structured as follows. Section 2 reviews the related work. Section 3 details the proposed framework of urban perception-semantic fusion network. Experimental results and analysis are reported in Sect. 4, followed by the conclusion and future work in Sect. 5.

2   Related Work

Visual urban perception has received more and more attention because it can play an important role in many fields. The literature on predicting the perceptual responses to images is growing very rapidly, such as aesthetics [11], memorability [10], interestingness [5] and virality [4]. However, these early efforts are mostly based on traditional machine learning methods and extract visual features based on human intuitions. Naik et al. [17] develop an algorithm named Streetscore for predicting the perceived safety of street-level images using generic image features and support vector regression. Orden and Berg [20] use Fisher vectors and DeCAF features to predict the perceive safety and wealthy, and achieve similar conclusions using training data from the Place Pulse 1.0 dataset [24].

With the rise of deep learning in recent years, CNN has been widely used to automatically learn visual perceptual features, and achieve better performance. Dubey et al. [7] develop a double-column CNN with tied weights to capture image features, and predict the image's score on perceptual attributes using a pairwise comparison method. Porzi et al. [22] report a better result to the perception of safety by identifying the mid-level visual elements [6] using CNN. Liu et al. [15] introduce a deep convolutional neural network and an EM algorithm to learn to quantify perceptual attributes of physical urban environments using crowd-sourced street-view images without human annotations. In addition, Law et al. [13] develop a work to estimate house prices through the perceptual features extracted by CNN. All the above methods focus on only the image features extracted by CNN. In contrast, our work proposes a double-column CNN architecture, each column is used to obtain perceptual score of an image, and the accuracy of the pairwise comparison is predicted by comparing the scores of the two images.

Many studies have noted that the object information on the images has an impact on perception. For example, He et al. [9] propose that buildings with dominant shapes and bright colors, historical sites, and intruding signs attract more attention form the people. And Can et al. [1] prove that different objects in the images may indicate different ambiances. However, they have not conducted more in-depth research. In our work, we add the object semantic information to the neural network, which indeed improves the accuracy of the visual perception task. To the best of our knowledge, we are the first to apply semantic information to visual urban perception.

3   Framework

In this section, we formulate the problem of predicting urban perception first. Then, we introduce the activation map technique to highlight image regions that are important to quantify urban perception. Additionally, we propose a fusion network which resorts to semantic recognition to assist urban perception prediction. Finally, we report the object semantic representation.

3.1   Problem Formulation

Given an image, it is hard for people to identify whether it looks safe (classification task) or quantify the degree of its safety (regression task). However, it is more natural for people to pick the safer one from an image pair. Therefore, in this paper, we concentrate on the relative order relationships between different images and cast the urban perception prediction problem as a ranking task.

In this paper, we conduct experiments on Place Pulse 2.0 dataset [7] which gives the pairwise comparisons among images. Formally, we denote each pairwise comparison by a triple $(\mathbf{x}_i, \mathbf{x}_j, y)$, where $\mathbf{x}_i, \mathbf{x}_j \in X$ are images and $y \in \{+1, -1\}$ is a label. Taking *"Safety"* attribute as an example, $y = +1$ denotes that image $\mathbf{x}_i$ is safer than image $\mathbf{x}_j$, and $y = -1$ means the reverse. We denote the dataset consisted of n pairwise comparisons as $D = \left\{ (\mathbf{x}_i^k, \mathbf{x}_j^k, y^k) \right\}_{k=1}^n$. The goal of our task is to learn a mapping function $\boldsymbol{F}_z : X \rightarrow \mathbb{R}$ that predicts a value $\boldsymbol{F}_z(\mathbf{x}_i)$ for each image $\mathbf{x}_i$ perceived by people for one perceptual attribute z. For example, $\boldsymbol{F}_{Safety}(\mathbf{x}_i)$ represents the safety degree of $\mathbf{x}_i$ perceived by people. The desired mapping function $\boldsymbol{F}_z$ is obtained by minimizing the hinge loss function as follows:

$$L = \sum_{(\mathbf{x}_i, \mathbf{x}_j, y) \in D} \max(0, y(\boldsymbol{F}_z(\mathbf{x}_j) - \boldsymbol{F}_z(\mathbf{x}_i)) + 1) \tag{1}$$

3.2   Perception Activation Map

To solve the problem defined in Sect. 3.1, we propose a double-column network taking image pair as input and minimize the loss function Eq. 1 by mini-batch stochastic gradient descent (SGD) algorithm. Figure 2 shows the architecture of our perception rank network (PRN). Two columns are identical and both are ResNet-50 [8] that replaces the last layer containing 1000 neurons with 1 neuron. Each column takes one input image and outputs one real value which reflects the degree of its perceptual attribute.

In order to investigate which regions of an image influence the urban perception mostly, we apply the activation mapping technique based on the global average pooling in CNN to highlight indicative image regions for a specific attribute. In this section, we apply a column of our well trained PRN to generate activation maps. The selected network mainly consists of several convolution layers, a global average pooling layer, and a fully connected layer successively. Given an input image, after a block of convolution layers, the network can generate feature maps, where K is the number of filters in the last convolution layer. On the top of these convolution layers, global average pooling layer takes the average of each feature map and generates a K-dimension vector. Then, the resulting vector connects to the fully connected layer. In our network, the fully connected layer has just one neuron corresponding to the degree of one perceptual attribute. In fact, an activation map for a specific attribute is the weighted sum of K feature

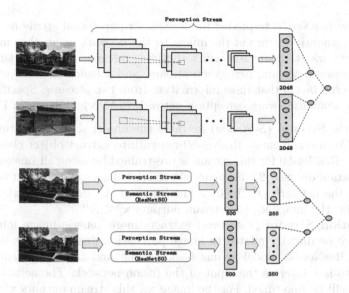

Fig. 2. Two network architectures: PRN (above) and SAPN (below)

maps outputted by the last convolution layer, while the weight of each feature map indicates its importance for that attribute.

Formally, given an image $\mathbf{x}_i$, $f_k^{\mathbf{x}}$ denotes the k-th feature map for image $\mathbf{x}_i$. And the activation map $M_z(\mathbf{x}_i)$ of the image $\mathbf{x}_i$ is computed by

$$M_z(\mathbf{x}_i) = \sum_{k=1}^{K} w_k f_k \qquad (2)$$

Where w_k equals the value from the k-th unit of the vector generated by global average pooling layer to the only neuron in the fully connected layer (here we ignore the bias term).

Figure 1 shows several examples of activation maps for images of six attributes. As we can see from the figure, the highlighted regions for "*Safety*" image include fence and the regions for "*Lively*" image include a store. These regions are relevant to the perceptual attributes, which accords with common sense. From this observation, we believe that semantic information in the images can help us complete the urban perception prediction task.

3.3   Semantic-Aware Perception Network

Inspired by the discovery in Sect. 3.2, we propose doing semantic recognition task simultaneously to assist urban perception prediction task. We believe that it can improve the performance of urban perception prediction task.

In order to verify our conjecture, we reconstruct the original neural network architecture. For each image, we no longer rely solely on the generic features extracted by ResNet-50 to predict its degrees for perceptual attributes. We add the object semantic feature of the image to the network as another input [27]. The sub-network structure to predict the image degree consists of three components: semantic stream, perception stream, and a fusion network with three fully connected layers that fuses information from two streams. Specifically, we develop the semantic-aware perception network (SAPN) as shown in Fig. 2.

- **Semantic Stream** (*S-Stream*) extracts the object semantic features of an image. We use the entire ResNet-50 network to extract object classification features. ResNet-50 for this stream is pre-trained by using all ImageNet 2012 classification dataset [23] that consists of 1000 classes. The output of the last layer of the network ($FC1000$) is the input of the fusion network; in other words, for the image $\mathbf{x}_i$, this stream outputs $\mathbf{x}_i^S \in \mathbb{R}^{1000}$.
- **Perception Stream** (*P-Stream*) extracts more generic image information that may be directly related to image perception prediction. We use a pre-trained ResNet-50 model as our basic model, and take the output of the second-to-last layer as the input of the fusion network. The network in this stream will be fine-tuned. For the image $\mathbf{x}_i$, this stream outputs $\mathbf{x}_i^P \in \mathbb{R}^{2048}$.
- **Fusion Network** is used to fuse features extracted by S-stream and P-Stream and predict the perceptual score of an image according to a three-layer fully connected neural network.

For an image $\mathbf{x}_i$, we obtain the semantic features $\mathbf{x}_i^S$ and perceptual features $\mathbf{x}_i^P$ extracted by S-Stream and P-Stream respectively and adopt them as the inputs of the first hidden layer of the fusion network. There are 500 neurons in the first hidden layer (250 neurons for each stream). The second hidden layer (250 neurons) fuses the outputs of the two streams in the first hidden layer. Then a fully connected layer with just one neuron is added as the output of the fusion network for urban perception prediction. And the output $f_z(\mathbf{x}_i^S, \mathbf{x}_i^P)$ of the fusion network for image $\mathbf{x}_i$ represents the degree of $\mathbf{x}_i$ perceived by people to corresponding perceptual attribute z. Thus, the hinge loss function (see Eq. (1)) can be rewritten as:

$$
\begin{aligned}
L &= \sum_{(\mathbf{x}_i, \mathbf{x}_j, y) \in D} \max(0, y(\boldsymbol{F}_z(\mathbf{x}_j) - \boldsymbol{F}_z(\mathbf{x}_i)) + 1) \\
&= \sum_{(\mathbf{x}_i, \mathbf{x}_j, y) \in D} \max(0, y(f_z(\mathbf{x}_j^S, \mathbf{x}_j^P) - f_z(\mathbf{x}_i^S, \mathbf{x}_i^P)) + 1)
\end{aligned}
\tag{3}
$$

3.4 Semantic Correlation Analysis

Once we trained the SAPN, we can mine the correlations between objects and perceptual attributes using the "visualization" of the network [25]. The goal is to find a pseudo image representation from the semantic stream that maximizes the output score for each of the perceptual attributes. Such object representation identifies the most discriminative objects for the specified urban perception.

As stated in Sect. 3.3, $f_z(\mathbf{x}_i^S, \mathbf{x}_i^P)$ represents the degree of image $\mathbf{x}_i$ perceived by people for corresponding perceptual attribute z. We combine $\mathbf{x}_i^S$ and $\mathbf{x}_i^P$ as

$\overline{\mathbf{x}}_i$ and $f_z(\overline{\mathbf{x}}_i) = f_z(\mathbf{x}_i^S, \mathbf{x}_i^P)$ is the score that represents the degree for perceptual attribute z for image $\mathbf{x}_i$. We try to get an L_2-regularized feature representation, such that the score $f(\overline{\mathbf{x}}_i)$ is maximized with respect to the object:

$$\hat{\mathbf{x}}_z^S = \arg\max_{\mathbf{x}_i^S} f_z(\overline{\mathbf{x}}_i) - \lambda \|\mathbf{x}_i^S\|_2 \tag{4}$$

where λ is the regularization parameter, and the semantic representation $\mathbf{x}_i^S$ can be found by back-propagation with randomly initialized $\overline{\mathbf{x}}_i$. We set the weights of the network fixed and try to obtain the representative objects associated with those perceptual attributes by gradient ascent. Finally, we find an object-perception semantic correlation matrix (SCM):

$$\Pi = \left[\hat{\mathbf{x}}_z^{S^T} \right]_z \tag{5}$$

4   Experiments

In this section, we present the experimental results of the proposed method and several baselines. Experimental results show the benefits of semantic information and the effectiveness of our proposed method.

4.1   Experimental Setup

Datasets. In this paper, we conduct experiments on Place Pulse 2.0 (PP 2.0) dataset [7] which gives the pairwise comparisons among images.

The Place Pulse 2.0 dataset is one of the most challenging and large-scale datasets for street-level image perception. PP 2.0 consists of 110,988 street view images from 56 major cities from 28 countries, and there are 1,169,078 pairwise comparisons in 6 perceptual attributes. The collection of PP 2.0 was designed as an online game. It shows participants two street view images and asks them to choose one in response to questions such as: *"Which place looks safer?"* or *"Which place looks more beautiful?"*. There are six evaluative questions in the datasets. In this paper, we use all the 104,529 images with 1,049,415 pairwise comparisons after cleaning data from PP 2.0 to evaluate the accuracy for six perceptual attributes.

Implementation Details. We train our networks with the mini-batch SGD algorithm under the framework of Keras [2]. Note that there are 1000 neurons in the last fully connected layer in ResNet-50, we change it to one neuron in our PRN model. Both PRN and the perception stream of SAPN use the ResNet-50 with pre-trained weights over ImageNet at the beginning, and we fine-tuned the block-4 and block-5 of the models with the batch size of 32. The learning rate and momentum coefficient are initialized as 10^{-3} and 0.9, respectively. We decrease the learning rate by a factor of 0.1 when the loss on validation set stop declining for 10 epochs. All biases are initialized with zero.

4.2   Visual Urban Perception

In this section, we focus on the effectiveness of the proposed networks. We propose two network structures: PRN and SAPN and we compare the SAPN model against several state-of-the-art methods for visual urban perception prediction [7]. Among them, using ResNet-50 with pre-trained weights and the fine-tuned ResNet-50 are two variants of our models.

- **PRN (ResNet)** takes an image pair as input and consists of two ResNet-50 networks with tied weights which are pre-trained. We change the last layer with 1000 neurons to a fully connected layer with one neuron and all the weights in convolution layers are fixed. It tries to find a mapping function to predict a score for each image and combines two scores with hinge loss;
- **PRN (fine-tuned)** has the same structure as PRN (ResNet). Differently, we fine-tuned the block-4 and block-5 of the ResNet-50;
- **SAPN (ResNet)** combines generic features and semantic information for an image to predict a score for one perceptual attribute. And the weights of the network in perception stream are fixed as the pre-trained weights;
- **SS-CNN** takes an image pair as input, it consists of two disjoint identical sets of layers with tied weights for feature extraction, and a fusion sub-network with softmax loss used to train the network followed the extractor layers;
- **RSS-CNN** is the improvement of SS-CNN. It modifies the SS-CNN by adding a ranking sub-network, consisting of fully-connected weight-tied layers, and it combines softmax loss and ranking loss to train the network.

Table 1 shows the accuracy results of different methods on PP 2.0. For all the experiments, we split the set of triplets for every attribute in the ratio 65-5-30 for training, validation and testing. It can be clearly seen that SAPN (fine-tuned) achieves the best performances for all attributes.

Besides, we note that, SAPN consistently achieves better performance than PRN, which proves the effectiveness of adding semantic information to urban perception prediction task.

Table 1. Results of visual urban perception prediction.

Attribute	PRN		SAPN		SS-CNN	RSS-CNN
	ResNet	Fine-tune	ResNet	Fine-tune		
Safety	59.76	60.63	62.95	**64.87**	60.14	62.12
Lively	58.76	59.90	59.42	**61.09**	60.05	59.95
Beautiful	67.83	68.79	68.30	**69.20**	68.67	69.12
Wealthy	65.44	65.82	64.30	**65.91**	65.53	65.35
Boring	56.32	56.47	56.40	**57.47**	56.34	56.04
Depressing	60.15	61.26	60.80	**62.10**	60.89	61.29

Table 2. Prediction Performance across Attributes

Train / Test	Safety	Lively	Beautiful	Wealthy	Boring	Depressing
Safety	**64.87**	57.78	57.09	58.94	47.42	42.92
Lively	59.05	**61.09**	56.36	59.17	43.24	41.22
Beautiful	64.06	58.28	**69.20**	63.97	48.08	34.83
Wealthy	63.67	62.66	61.78	**65.91**	41.75	36.38
Boring	45.24	42.11	47.60	44.52	**57.47**	54.52
Depressing	39.65	40.01	39.65	39.15	56.41	**62.10**

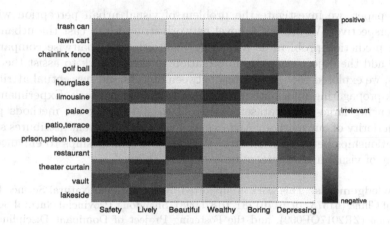

Fig. 3. The relationship between objects and perceptual attributes. Blue stands for positive correlation and red stands for negative correlation. (Color figure online)

4.3   Semantic Correlation Analysis

In the process of gradient ascent, we fixed the weights of the network and set the $\lambda = 1e-3$ and learning rate to 0.8. Finally we get the semantic correlation matrix $\prod$ shown in Fig. 3 after 500 iterations from the trained SAPN for six perceptual attributes.

As we can see from the figure, objects make different contributions to different perceptual attributes. For example, the *"prison"* in the image makes a positive contribution to perceptual attribute *"Despressing"* but has a negative impact on *"Safety"*. The result proves once again that semantic information indeed assists in the visual urban perception task.

4.4   Different Perceptual Attributes Prediction

There are six perceptual attributes in the PP 2.0. To explore the relationships between six perceptual attributes, we train the SAPNs for all attributes and measure the performances for every perceptual attribute on six trained models.

For every perceptual attribute, the test samples are fixed when predicting in six different models. The results are shown in Table 2.

We can see in the result that, the networks trained by "*Safety*", "*Lively*", "*Beautiful*" and "*Wealthy*" show good performance in the prediction of other three perceptual attributes and get poor results in predicting the accuracy in "*Boring*" and "*Depressing*". In the end, we get the conclusion that there are high correlations between different perceptual attributes.

5   Conclusions and Future Work

In this paper, we investigate the problem of visual urban perception with a fresh perspective. We present a novel network structure to cast the urban perception prediction problem as a ranking task, using the pairwise comparison, and we add the object semantic information to the network to assist the task. Besides, we explored the correlations between objects and perceptual attributes by back-propagating information through the trained network. Experiments on a challenging large-scale dataset compared to state-of-the-art methods prove the superiority of our method. And experiment across different attributes shows the relationships between attributes. We shall the relationships to enhance the accuracy of visual urban perception.

Acknowledgements. This work is supported by the National Natural Science Foundation of China (61573219, 61701281, 61876098), Shandong Provincial Natural Science Foundation (ZR2017QF009), and the Fostering Project of Dominant Discipline and Talent Team of Shandong Province Higher Education Institutions.

References

1. Can, G., Benkhedda, Y., Gatica-Perez, D.: Ambiance in social media venues: visual cue interpretation by machines and crowds. In: Proceedings of the IEEE Conference on Computer Vision and Pattern Recognition Workshops, pp. 2363–2372 (2018)
2. Chollet, F., et al.: Keras (2015)
3. Cohen, D.A., Mason, K., Bedimo, A., Scribner, R., Basolo, V., Farley, T.A.: Neighborhood physical conditions and health. Am. J. Public Health **93**(3), 467–471 (2003)
4. Deza, A., Parikh, D.: Understanding image virality. In: Proceedings of the IEEE Conference on Computer Vision and Pattern Recognition, pp. 1818–1826 (2015)
5. Dhar, S., Ordonez, V., Berg, T.L.: High level describable attributes for predicting aesthetics and interestingness. In: 2011 IEEE Conference on Computer Vision and Pattern Recognition (CVPR), pp. 1657–1664. IEEE (2011)
6. Doersch, C., Singh, S., Gupta, A., Sivic, J., Efros, A.: What makes Paris look like Paris? ACM Trans. Graph. **31**(4), 101:1–101:9 (2012)
7. Dubey, A., Naik, N., Parikh, D., Raskar, R., Hidalgo, C.A.: Deep learning the city: quantifying urban perception at a global scale. In: Leibe, B., Matas, J., Sebe, N., Welling, M. (eds.) ECCV 2016. LNCS, vol. 9905, pp. 196–212. Springer, Cham (2016). https://doi.org/10.1007/978-3-319-46448-0_12

8. He, K., Zhang, X., Ren, S., Sun, J.: Deep residual learning for image recognition. In: Proceedings of the IEEE Conference on Computer Vision and Pattern Recognition, pp. 770–778 (2016)
9. He, S., Yoshimura, Y., Helfer, J., Hack, G., Ratti, C., Nagakura, T.: Quantifying memories: mapping urban perception. arXiv preprint arXiv:1806.04054 (2018)
10. Isola, P., Xiao, J., Torralba, A., Oliva, A.: What makes an image memorable? (2011)
11. Joshi, D., et al.: Aesthetics and emotions in images. IEEE Signal Process. Mag. 28(5), 94–115 (2011)
12. Kao, Y., He, R., Huang, K.: Deep aesthetic quality assessment with semantic information. IEEE Trans. Image Process. 26(3), 1482–1495 (2017)
13. Law, S., Paige, B., Russell, C.: Take a look around: using street view and satellite images to estimate house prices. arXiv preprint arXiv:1807.07155 (2018)
14. Lin, M., Chen, Q., Yan, S.: Network in network. arXiv preprint arXiv:1312.4400 (2013)
15. Liu, X., Chen, Q., Zhu, L., Xu, Y., Lin, L.: Place-centric visual urban perception with deep multi-instance regression. In: Proceedings of the 2017 ACM on Multimedia Conference, pp. 19–27. ACM (2017)
16. Milam, A., Furr-Holden, C., Leaf, P.: Perceived school and neighborhood safety, neighborhood violence and academic achievement in urban school children. Urban Rev. 42(5), 458–467 (2010)
17. Naik, N., Philipoom, J., Raskar, R., Hidalgo, C.: Street score-predicting the perceived safety of one million streetscapes. In: Proceedings of the IEEE Conference on Computer Vision and Pattern Recognition Workshops, pp. 779–785 (2014)
18. Naik, N., Raskar, R., Hidalgo, C.A.: Cities are physical too: using computer vision to measure the quality and impact of urban appearance. Am. Econ. Rev. 106(5), 128–132 (2016)
19. Nasar, J.L.: The evaluative image of the city. J. Am. Plan. Assoc. 56(1), 41–53 (1990)
20. Ordonez, V., Berg, T.L.: Learning high-level judgments of urban perception. In: Fleet, D., Pajdla, T., Schiele, B., Tuytelaars, T. (eds.) ECCV 2014. LNCS, vol. 8694, pp. 494–510. Springer, Cham (2014). https://doi.org/10.1007/978-3-319-10599-4_32
21. Piro, F.N., Nœss, Ø., Claussen, B.: Physical activity among elderly people in a city population: the influence of neighbourhood level violence and self perceived safety. J. Epidemiol. Community Health 60(7), 626–632 (2006)
22. Porzi, L., Rota Bulò, S., Lepri, B., Ricci, E.: Predicting and understanding urban perception with convolutional neural networks. In: Proceedings of the 23rd ACM International Conference on Multimedia, pp. 139–148. ACM (2015)
23. Russakovsky, O., et al.: Imagenet large scale visual recognition challenge. Int. J. Comput. Vis. 115(3), 211–252 (2015)
24. Salesses, P., Schechtner, K., Hidalgo, C.A.: The collaborative image of the city: mapping the inequality of urban perception. PloS one 8(7), e68400 (2013)
25. Simonyan, K., Vedaldi, A., Zisserman, A.: Deep inside convolutional networks: visualising image classification models and saliency maps. arXiv preprint arXiv:1312.6034 (2013)
26. Wilson, J.Q.: Broken windows: the police and neighborhood safety James Q. Wilson and George L. Kelling. Criminological perspectives: essential readings 400 (2003)

27. Wu, Z., Fu, Y., Jiang, Y.G., Sigal, L.: Harnessing object and scene semantics for large-scale video understanding. In: Proceedings of the IEEE Conference on Computer Vision and Pattern Recognition, pp. 3112–3121 (2016)
28. Zhou, B., Khosla, A., Lapedriza, A., Oliva, A., Torralba, A.: Learning deep features for discriminative localization. In: Proceedings of the IEEE Conference on Computer Vision and Pattern Recognition, pp. 2921–2929 (2016)
29. Zhou, B., Liu, L., Oliva, A., Torralba, A.: Recognizing city identity via attribute analysis of geo-tagged images. In: Fleet, D., Pajdla, T., Schiele, B., Tuytelaars, T. (eds.) ECCV 2014. LNCS, vol. 8691, pp. 519–534. Springer, Cham (2014). https://doi.org/10.1007/978-3-319-10578-9_34

Deep Reinforcement Learning
for Automatic Thumbnail Generation

Zhuopeng Li and Xiaoyan Zhang[✉]

College of Computer Science and Software Engineering, Shenzhen University,
Shenzhen 518000, China
xyzhang15@szu.edu.cn

Abstract. An automatic thumbnail generation method based on deep
reinforcement learning (called RL-AT) is proposed in this paper. Differing from previous saliency-based and deep learning-based methods which
predict the location and size of a rectangle region, our method models the
thumbnail generation as predicting a rectangle region by cutting along
four edges of the rectangle. We project the thumbnail cutting operations
as a four step Markov decision-making process in the framework of deep
Reinforcement learning. The best crop location in each cutting step is
learned by using a deep Q-network. The deep Q-network gets observations from the recent image and selects an action from the action space.
Then the deep Q-network receives feedback based on current selected
action as reward. The action space and reward function are specifically
designed for the thumbnail generation problem. A data set with
more than 70,000 thumbnail annotations is used to train our RL-AT model.
Our RL-AT model can efficiently generate thumbnails with low computational complexity, and 0.09 s is needed to generate a thumbnail image.
Experiments have shown that our RL-AT model outperforms related
methods in the thumbnail generation.

Keywords: Thumbnail generation · Reinforcement learning
Q-network

1 Introduction

The goal of thumbnail generation is summarizing image contents for effective
searching and browsing while preserving important content as much as possible
in reducing the image size. Manually producing thumbnails for large image collections can be both time-consuming and tedious. Therefore, significant research
has been devoted on developing computational methods for automatic thumbnail
generation.

The intuitive thumbnail generation method is to scale the original image uniformly. However, this strategy causes shrinkage on the image content and fails
to provide a meaningful information at a glance. To solve this problem, content-
aware methods are proposed for image thumbnail generation. The standard operations for thumbnail generation are to crop and scale the original image. Most

© Springer Nature Switzerland AG 2019
I. Kompatsiaris et al. (Eds.): MMM 2019, LNCS 11296, pp. 41–53, 2019.
https://doi.org/10.1007/978-3-030-05716-9_4

methods has mainly focused on extracting the most visually significant part of the image by calculating the saliency region, and then finding an optimum cropping window. These saliency based cropping methods [1,9,15] have a weakness in handling an image with no meaningful objects, such as landscape images. Additionally, they only consider the visually salient parts of the image, and giving less consideration to the background. This may results in incompletion of the image content. Content-aware retargeting methods [16,18] change the aspect ratio or downsize the image while preserving the important image features for adaptive display. Although these methods are effective in composition correction, cropping is still one of the most favored methods comparing to others as it does not cause image distortion. To effectively generate thumbnails, machine learning methods were proposed. An end-to-end deep learning framework is used in [6] to predict the best crop window. The deep learning method shown good performance on thumbnail generation. However, there is still a large room for improving the performance.

This paper proposes a new framework for thumbnail generation. Inspired by the paper cut process, we model the thumbnail generation as predicting a rectangle region by cutting along four edges of the rectangle. The cutting location needs to be decided in each edge cutting step. We project the thumbnail cutting operations as a four step Markov decision-making process in the framework of deep Reinforcement learning. The best crop location in each cutting step is learned by using a deep Q-network. Thumbnails are then generated by predicting the best cropping rectangle region followed by scaling the region to the thumbnail size in special aspect ratio, such as 4:3, 1:1 etc.

The main contributions are listed as follows.

1. The problem of thumbnail generation is modeled as a four step Markov decision-making process in the framework of deep reinforcement learning. Thumbnails can be generated automatically and fast (only 0.09 s is needed for each thumbnail gencration).
2. A simple action strategy is defined based on observing the thumbnail generation problem, which not only reduces the computational complexity, but also facilitates the learning of the optimal strategy for the agent.
3. The center offset distance between the cropping window and the ground truth window is considered as one part of the reward function. It allows us to automatically generate thumbnails in different aspect ratios by re-cropping centered at the original predicted cropping window.

2   Related Work

2.1   Thumbnail Generation

The main steps of thumbnail generation are cropping and scaling. Cropping is to search for a window that covers the most informative content. The most informative content is often calculated by saliency detection. Five saliency maps were calculated based on the interest point distribution in [1]. Then the salience map was binarized by setting a threshold and using values above the threshold to crop the photo. These methods are effective for preserving the foreground content, but consider the background less. This makes the thumbnail information not rich enough. To improve the thumbnail generation effectiveness, learning-based methods were proposed. Handcrafted features were extracted and then a classification method was used to score candidate crops in [9]. Fast-AT method [6] proposed an end-to-end learning framework based on deep learning. Based on the object detection framework, it learns different filters during training and selects the appropriate filter based on the size of the target thumbnail. The deep learning method has achieved the best performance on thumbnail generation.

Scaling involves the scaling scales and the aspect ratio. In [4,5,8,11], the cropping result was directly adjusted to match target size and aspect ratio, which may cause the image to be distorted and objects dificult to identify in the image. Huang et al. [9] fixed the aspect ratio to 4:3 uniformly in generating the thumbnails. In the Fast-AT method [6], different filters were learned for different aspect ratios during training. The appropriate filter was automatically selected in the thumbnail generation. This model results in increasing the difficulty of the training. In our work, the center position offset feedback is considered in the reward function, so that the center offset of the generated thumbnail is greatly reduced. While facing different application scenarios, a new crop window centered at the original cropping window is generated to have the target aspect ratio.

2.2 Reinforcement Learning

Strategies based on reinforcement learning have been successfully applied to many areas of computer vision, including object detection [2,3,10], image description [13], and visual relationship detection [12]. The Tree-RL enhanced tree approach [10] used reinforcement learning to obtain regional proposals. Li et al. proposed to conduct the aesthetics-aware image cropping using deep reinforcement learning (called A2-RL [11]). It modeled the cropping operations as selecting actions from an action space, which including 14 actions involving move, scale, and termination. The cropped image quality gave feedback to the engine by using reward. The A2-RL method has 14 action spaces. It needs more iterations to achieve the best crop which is very time-consuming. In our work, we have built an effective end-to-end deep reinforcement learning model that solves thumbnail generation problem. It only takes 0.09 s to generate a thumbnail.

3 Deep Reinforcement Learning-Based Thumbnail Generation

Just like the paper cut game we play, when we cut the paper, we cut along the edge of the key area, such as cutting an apple, a bird, an airplane and so on. Inspired by the paper cut game, we could crop the region by cutting along four edges of the rectangle. We only need four steps to complete the process. Each step is to cut along one edge. The cut operation needs to decide the cutting location in each step. We propose to model the thumbnail cutting operation as a four step Markov decision-making process in the framework of deep reinforcement learning. The deep reinforcement learning is used to learn the best crop location in each cutting step. Thumbnails are then generated by predicting the best cropping rectangle region followed by scaling the region to the thumbnail size in special aspect ratio. The framework of the proposed method (called RL-AT method) is shown in Fig. 1.

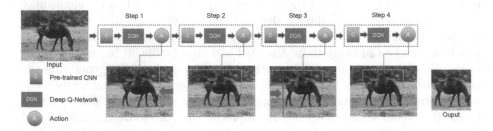

Fig. 1. Each cutting step is summarized as "C-DQN-A". C is the pre-trained CNN model to extract the image features. DQN is a Deep Q-Network, which is using deep neural network to represent the Q-function. Here Q represents the action utility function in Q-learning, which is a classic reinforcement learning algorithm used to solve Markov decision problems. The action (A) represents the cutting location.

In reinforcement learning, the DQN agent receives observation form the current crop window. Then an action is selected from the action space based on the observation and latest history actions. After each action, the agent receives a feedback as reward according to the cropping quality. The goal of the agent is to find the best cropping strategy by maximizing the total cumulative discount reward.

In this section, we will first introduce the state, the action space and the reward function. The architecture of the RL-AT model and the training process is then detailed. Finally, the strategy for generating thumbnails in specific aspect ratio is introduced.

3.1   State and Action Space

The state is a concatenation of the feature vector of the current observation and the vector of history experience. The feature vector of the recent crop region provides the current observation. The history experience captures the history of taken actions. The feature of the region in the recent crop window is extracted from the pre-trained CNN model i.e. VGGNet [14]. The feature is in dimension of 25088. It is utilized as the current observation o_t. The history experience is composed by the predicted values by DQN for actions in the last four steps. As there are 10 actions in each step DQN prediction, therefore the history experience is a 40-dimension vector. We collect the history experience and store them in a replay memory, and a batch randomly sampled from the replay memory is used as the training samples.

For the task of thumbnail generation, we have designed a simple action space. Models with complex action space may make it difficult for the agent to learn the target rule well. Instead of directly predicting the size and location of the cutting bounding box, our method predicts the cutting location of the four edges of the bounding box. It does not cause repeated selection actions. Therefore, our method is fixed to have 4 steps to predict the crop region bounding box. Each step has an action space with 10 actions.

The 10 actions are defined as cutting locations in the cutting direction of the current step. We divide the current observation region into 20 equal blocks along the current cutting direction. The 10 actions are corresponding to the cutting locations at $[0, 1, 2, ..., 9]/20$ length of the current observation region. For example, when action $= 0$ gets the highest value by DQN, the size of the region in the cutting direction is not changed. When action $= 1$ gets the highest value by DQN, one block of the image will be cut out, which is cutting at the $1/20$ location from the boundary. The action space we designed is ingenious and simple. Each step only requires 0.03s in the thumbnail generation.

The choice of action principle is as follow:

$$a^* = \arg\max Q(s_t, a_t) \tag{1}$$

a_t is the output of action values by DQN, and the action a^* is selected as the one corresponding to the maximum value in the current state s_t.

3.2   Reward Function

In designing the reward function, the objective is to design learnable reward functions to motivate the agent to get the desired action. In our work, we explore two different reward definitions. One is feedback based on the cropping quality, the other is feedback on the offset which is the distance between the center of the predicted bounding box and ground truth bounding box. The data set provided by [6] is used to train our model. This dataset includes the coordinates of original image and cropped thumbnail. It is created on Amazon Mechanical Turk. Intersection Over Union (IoU) is used as a criterion for judging the quality of crop images. While the IoU is higher than previous crop result, the machine gets positive feedback, otherwise, the machine gets negative feedback.

Just like the recent research in the deep mind team on the StarCraft game [17], under the guidance of dense reward mechanisms, agents can eventually collect resources and build castles. Inspired by the agent playing games, a rich reward will benefit the agent to learn the optimal strategy. Therefore, rewards in our model are also defined as a set of discrete graded numbers, which are in range of $[-9, 9]$. The reward is formulated as follow:

$$R_{\text{basic}}(s_t, a_t) = floor(10[\text{IoU}(s_t) - \text{IoU}(s_{t-1})]) \tag{2}$$

Where $R_{\text{basic}}(s_t, a_t)$ is the reward for choosing the action a_t when the state s_{t-1} transitions to the state s_t. IoU(b) is the Intersection Over Union ratio of the predict and ground truth bounding box, IoU(b) = $area(b \cap g)/area(b \cup g)$. b is the predicted bounding box, and g is the ground truth bounding box. In order to facilitate the calculation of action values, the IoU difference is multiplied by a factor of 10 to generate graded rewards in a larger range. Since $[(IoU)(s_t) - (IoU)(s_{t-1})] \in (-1, 1)$, so $R_{\text{basic}}(s_t, a_t) \in \{-9, -8, ..., 0, ..., 8, 9\}$.

In order to reduce the center offset of the predicted bounding box from ground truth bounding box, we design the offset as part of the reward function, which is defined as:

$$R(s_t, a_t) = R_{\text{basic}} - \beta \times Dis(C_g - C_b) \tag{3}$$

Where C_b and C_g represent the center coordinates of the predicted bounding box and ground truth bounding box, respectively. $Dis(C_g - C_b)$ is the offset which is calculated as the absolute distance between C_b and C_g. β is the weight for the offset, which is set as 0.005 based on the experiment. $R(s_t, a_t)$ is the final reward combing R_{basic} and offset. Our reward function provides a reasonable hierarchical feedback on the behavior of the agent, allowing the agent to obtain greater positive feedback, thereby maximizing the cumulative reward.

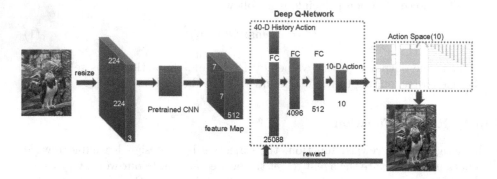

Fig. 2. Deep reinforcement learning model for automatic thumbnail generation.

3.3   The Model and Training

The detailed deep reinforcement learning model for the automatic thumbnail generation is shown in Fig. 2. We resize the input image to 224×224 pixels, and then extract the feature of the current region using pre-trained CNN model. The image feature and historical action are the input of the DQN. The DQN is designed with two fully connected layers and a prediction layer. The DQN predicts the value of the 10 actions, and crops the image based on the action that gets the highest value. Then the DQN gets reward and updates the action values. The action value is updated by

$$Q'(s, a) = Q(s, a) + \alpha[R + \gamma max Q(s', a') - Q(s, a)] \tag{4}$$

Where a' is the action the DQN can select at state s'. State s' is the next state after state s. R is reward, γ represents the discount factor and α represents the learning rate. $Q(s, a)$ is the action value predicted by the DQN and $Q'(s, a)$ is the updated action value. After the DQN getting observation from recent crop region o_{t+1}, history of taken actions h_{t+1} and reward R, the state is updated as $s_{t+1} = (o_{t+1}, h_{t+1})$, and then the action value is updated based on function (4).

In the training, the loss function of the DQN is defined as the squared error between target action values and prediction action values, which is

$$L = (\underbrace{R + \gamma \max Q(s', a')}_{\text{target}} - \underbrace{Q(s, a)}_{\text{prediction}})^2 \tag{5}$$

$R + \gamma maxQ(s', a')$ is the target action value, $maxQ(s', a')$ calculates the action with the highest value in the state s'.

We initialize the Deep Q Network parameters randomly. In each training epoch, VGGNet is used to extract the feature. We use an greedy ε strategy to select action, and the probability of $1 - \varepsilon$ selects the action with the highest action value, $\varepsilon = \varepsilon - 0.1$ until $\varepsilon <= 0.1$. In order to consider more of the future reward, we set discount rate γ as 0.9 and learning rate $\alpha = 10^{-5}$. The back-propagation algorithm is used to update the parameters of the DQN, Adam optimizer is used for training.

3.4   Resolution of Scaling

The thumbnail generation algorithm should have the ability to generate thumbnails in different aspect ratios. In our RL-AT model, offset of the cropped bounding box from the ground truth bounding box is considered in the definition of the reward function, therefore the offset of the predicted bounding box is greatly reduced. This allows us to re-crop the image to have specific aspect ratio by centering at the original cropping region.

Given the aspect ratio of the target thumbnail as G_t, and the aspect ratio, width, and height of the thumbnails generated by our method respectively as P_t, P_w, P_h, where $P_t = P_w/P_h$, we propose to update the height or width of the crop bounding box to fit the target aspect ratio. While $P_t > G_t$, let $P_w = P_h \times G_t$, otherwise, let $P_h = P_w / G_t$. Finally, the image is re-cropped based on updated P_w and P_h while centering at the center of the original crop window.

4   Experiments and Results

4.1   Training Data

Our model is trained by using the dataset provided by [6]. The total dataset consists of 70,048 thumbnail annotations in 28,064 images. Divided into training sets and test sets, the training set has 24,154 images, including 63,043 thumbnail annotations. The test set has 3,910 images containing 7,005 thumbnail annotations. The data between training set and test set is not shared.

Fig. 3. Thumbnails generated by our RL-AT model. Blue bounding box is the cropping bounding box generated by our RL-AT model and red bounding box is the ground truth bounding box. (Color figure online)

4.2 Performance Evaluation

Our RL-AT method can efficiently generate thumbnails. Some thumbnails generated by our RL-AT model are shown in Fig. 3. The predicted thumbnail bounding box is closing to that of the ground truth. In order to quantitatively evaluate the advantage of our RL-AT model, three metrics are assessed, which namely offset, rescaling factor and IoU. Offset measures the absolute distance between the center positions of the ground truth bounding box and predicted thumbnail bounding box. It is calculated in the size space of the original image. Rescaling factor is defined as $\max(S_g/S_b, S_b/S_g)$, where S_g and S_b are the scales for scaling the ground truth and the predicted thumbnail bounding boxes to the size of the target thumbnail size, respectively.

Effect of Action Space and Reward Function. Here we will discuss the advantage of our action space and reward function on thumbnail generation. Our method is fixed to have 4 steps to predict the thumbnail bounding box. Each step has an action space with 10 actions which are cutting locations in the cutting direction of the current step. In order to prove the advantages of our action space definition, our RL-AT method is compared to the A2-RL method [11]. The A2-RL method designed an action space with 14 actions in the deep reinforcement learning framework to conduct image cropping. The action space included actions of adjusting the size, position, and shape of the cropping window. For the analysis of the effect of our reward function, the RL-AT model with our reward function is compared to the RL-AT model using a reward function without offset related feedback (called RL-AT w/o offset). The performance of the three methods is summarized in Table 1.

From Table 1, we could see that our RL-AT method can generate thumbnails with lowest offset and rescaling and highest IoU among the three methods. Compared with the A2-RL method, our RL-AT method reduces the offset by 14.7%, reduces the rescaling factor by 3%, and IoU is increased by 13.3%. The large action space of the A2-RL model can cause the agent to fail to learn the optimal strategy of cropping, and it is possible to select a repeated action. In extreme cases, a thumbnail generation requires hundreds of steps.

Comparing the performance of the RL-AT w/o offset method and our method in Table 1, the offset has a sufficient reduce by considering offset in the reward function, while these two methods have similar IoU. By optimizing the reward function to reduce the offset, we can easily generate thumbnails with different aspect ratios.

Table 1. Comparison with related methods.A2-RL, L-Fang, VFN, Fast-AT, and RL-AT w/o offset, RL-AT with no scaling, RL-AT (4:3) sets the aspect ratio to 4:3, RL-AT (3:4) sets the aspect ratio to 3:4, and RL-AT (1:1) sets the aspect ratio to 1:1.

Model	Offset	Rescaling	IoU
A2-RL [11]	53.6	1.175	0.60
L-Fang [7]	77.2	1.207	0.56
VFN [4]	92.1	1.229	0.62
Fast-AT [6]	55.4	1.154	0.68
RL-AT w/o offset(ours)	50.3	1.159	0.68
RL-AT (ours)	**45.7**	**1.125**	**0.68**
RL-AT (4:3,ours)	45.7	1.116	0.66
RL-AT (3:4,ours)	45.7	1.113	0.65
RL-AT (1:1,ours)	45.7	1.104	0.67

Comparison with Related Methods. Our method is compared to three methods which are also using learning-based methods to predict the cropping region. The three related methods are L-Fang [7], VFN [4], and Fast-AT [6] methods. L-Fang method consider spatial distribution of salient regions and trains a support vector machine classifier to score cropping candidates. The VFN method generates a candidate window by sliding the window to crop the best aesthetic image. Fast-AT proposes a fully convolved deep neural network to achieve multi-scale target thumbnail generation by learning filters of different sizes and aspect ratio thumbnails. To ensure the credibility of the experiment, all the four methods were tested using the same data set with the Fast-AT method. The performance values of Fast-AT method were provided by [6], and the L-Fang and VFN methods were tested in the same environment as our RL-AT method. In our model, we propose to re-crop the image to have a specific aspect ratio based on the original cropping window. The effect of the re-crop on the accuracy in thumbnail generation is also evaluated. We tested on three aspect ratios which are 4:3, 3:4 and 1:1. The performance is summarized in Table 1.

Among the four methods, the L-Fang and VFN methods have the worst performance. The offset of the L-Fang and VFN methods are 77.2 and 92.1 respectively. The reason is that the L-Fang and the VFN methods consider the overall aesthetic in the cropping and it does not take into account the offset. The

Fast-AT method has a good performance in IoU, but it does not consider the deviation of the center position between the predict bounding box and ground truth bounding box during the training. Therefore, the performance of the offset and rescaling factor is poor, where the average offset is 55.4 and the average rescaling is 1.154. They are higher than our RL-AT method. Our RL-AT method has the lowest offset and rescaling factor and almost highest IoU among the four methods. This presents the efficiency of our RL-AT method for thumbnail generation.

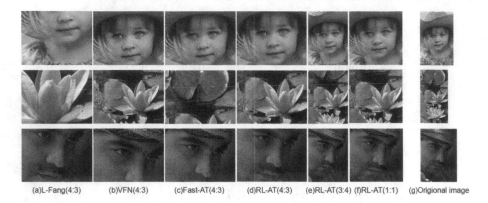

(a)L-Fang(4:3)   (b)VFN(4:3)   (c)Fast-AT(4:3)   (d)RL-AT(4:3)   (e)RL-AT(3:4) (f)RL-AT(1:1)   (g)Original image

Fig. 4. Thumbnail generation examples of L-Fang, VFN, Fast-AT and RL-AT with different aspect ratios.

From Table 1, we also observed that after re-cropping the result by our RL-AT method to a specific aspect ratio, the rescaling factor is much closer to 1, which tell us that the re-cropping result is much closer to the size of the target thumbnail. Though the IoU has a decreasing trend after re-cropping, the IoU is only slightly reduced and also comparable to that of the Fast-AT method. This concludes that using our scaling strategy to match thumbnail size and aspect ratio does not reduce the thumbnail quality.

Several example thumbnails generated by the four methods are shown in Fig. 4. The cropped regions predicted by the L-Fang and the VFN methods are re-cropped to the thumbnail size in aspect ratio of 4:3. They are scaled in the same way as our method. They may lose important information after re-cropping the image to have a specific aspect ratio (e.g 4:3) by centering at the original cropping region. The reason is that they did not consider placing important objects in a central position during training. Comparing our thumbnails in 4:3 (Fig. 4(d)) to those by Fast-AT (Fig. 4(c)), the important contents are preserved better in our thumbnails and without distortions. For example, the flower in the second example and the mouth in the third example are all cropped out in the thumbnails by Fast-AT, however, they are preserved in our thumbnails. When recropping the thumbnails to another aspect ratio using our method, the important contents are also preserved as shown in Fig. 4(e) and (f). This again confirms the effectiveness of our method for thumbnail generation.

4.3 Computational Complexity

In this section, we evaluated the time efficiency of the five models (L-Fang, VFN, A2-RL, Fast-AT, and our RL-AT models). We tested the models of L-Fang, VFN, A2-RL, and our RL-AT in the same environment and compare with the Fast-AT which provide by [6]. The test results are shown as Table 2.

Table 2. Computational complexity comparison among L-Fang, VFN, A2-RL, Fast-AT and RL-AT methods. AvgSteps and AvgTime are the average steps and average time required for each thumbnail generation, respectively. AvgIoU is the average of IoU values.

Method	AvgIoU	AvgSteps	AvgTime(s)
L-Fang [7]	0.56	-	0.87
VFN [4]	0.62	141	1.16
A2-RL [11]	0.60	97	2.29
Fast-AT [6]	0.68	-	0.11
RL-AT (ours)	0.68	4	0.09

As Fast-AT [6] does not provide the test code. We only get the average time for each thumbnail generation without the number of steps required. Therefore, the AvgSteps of Fast-AT is not discussed here. The experimental results show that our RL-AT model requires the shortest time for each thumbnail generation, and the Fast-AT time is equivalent to ours. The L-Fang methods requires handcrafted features for assessing each candidate cropping window. It is time consuming for feature extraction. In the VFN method, a candidate window is generated through a sliding window. Since the number of candidate windows is large, more steps are required. This increases the cropping time. Due to the repeated use of the same action in the A2-RL method, the average number of steps is large and takes a long time. Fast-AT produces thumbnails using a feed-forward network, so it can be faster and has similar computational complexity with our method. In our work, we set the number of thumbnail generation steps to 4, and the agent changes the size of each boundary of the cropping bounding box at each step, which improves the time efficiency.

5 Conclusions

This paper has presented a deep reinforcement learning solution for automatic thumbnail generation problem. We designed the action space and reward function, and built a deep Q-network model to generate thumbnails. Thumbnails can be generated automatically and fast. Only 0.09 s are needed for each thumbnail generation. Experiments have shown that our RL-AT model outperforms related methods in the thumbnail generation process. We also have some failed cases generated by our RL-AT model. When multiple objects appear in the image, the key information may not be at the center of the crop region, and information may be lost after re-cropping. In the future, we will consider adding new constrains in the definition of the reward function to solve the scaling problem mentioned in the limitation.

References

1. Ardizzone, E., Bruno, A., Mazzola, G.: Saliency based image cropping. In: Petrosino, A. (ed.) ICIAP 2013. LNCS, vol. 8156, pp. 773–782. Springer, Heidelberg (2013). https://doi.org/10.1007/978-3-642-41181-6_78
2. Bellver, M., Giró-i Nieto, X., Marqués, F., Torres, J.: Hierarchical object detection with deep reinforcement learning. arXiv preprint arXiv:1611.03718 (2016)
3. Caicedo, J.C., Lazebnik, S.: Active object localization with deep reinforcement learning. In: Proceedings of the IEEE International Conference on Computer Vision, pp. 2488–2496 (2015)
4. Chen, Y.L., Klopp, J., Sun, M., Chien, S.Y., Ma, K.L.: Learning to compose with professional photographs on the web. In: Proceedings of the 2017 ACM on Multimedia Conference, pp. 37–45. ACM (2017)
5. Ciocca, G., Cusano, C., Gasparini, F., Schettini, R.: Self-adaptive image cropping for small displays. IEEE Trans. Consum. Electron. 53(4), 1622–1627 (2007)
6. Esmaeili, S.A., Singh, B., Davis, L.S.: Fast-at: fast automatic thumbnail generation using deep neural networks. In: Proceedings of the IEEE Conference on Computer Vision and Pattern Recognition, pp. 4178–4186 (2017)
7. Fang, C., Lin, Z., Mech, R., Shen, X.: Automatic image croppingusing visual composition, boundary simplicity and content preservation models. In: Proceedings of the 22nd ACM International Conference on Multimedia, pp. 1105–1108. ACM (2014)
8. Goferman, S., Zelnik-Manor, L., Tal, A.: Context-aware saliency detection. IEEE Trans. Pattern Anal. Mach. Intell. 34(10), 1915–1926 (2012)
9. Huang, J., Chen, H., Wang, B., Lin, S.: Automatic thumbnail generation based on visual representativeness and foreground recognizability. In: Proceedings of the IEEE International Conference on Computer Vision, pp. 253–261 (2015)
10. Jie, Z., Liang, X., Feng, J., Jin, X., Lu, W., Yan, S.: Tree-structured reinforcement learning for sequential object localization. In: Advances in Neural Information Processing Systems, pp. 127–135 (2016)
11. Li, D., Wu, H., Zhang, J., Huang, K.: A2-RL: aesthetics aware reinforcement learning for image cropping. In: Proceedings of the IEEE Conference on Computer Vision and Pattern Recognition, pp. 8193–8201 (2018)
12. Liang, X., Lee, L., Xing, E.P.: Deep variation-structured reinforcement learning for visual relationship and attribute detection. In: Proceedings of the IEEE Conference on Computer Vision and Pattern Recognition, pp. 4408–4417 (2017)
13. Ren, Z., Wang, X., Zhang, N., Lv, X., Li, L.J.: Deep reinforcement learning-based image captioning with embedding reward. arXiv preprint arXiv:1704.03899 (2017)
14. Simonyan, K., Zisserman, A.: Very deep convolutional networks for large-scale image recognition. arXiv preprint arXiv:1409.1556 (2014)

15. Sun, J., Ling, H.: Scale and object aware image thumbnailing. Int. J. Comput. Vis. **104**(2), 135–153 (2013)
16. Tan, W., Yan, B., Li, K., Tian, Q.: Image retargeting for preserving robust local feature: application to mobile visual search. IEEE Trans. Multimedia **18**(1), 128–137 (2016)
17. Vinyals, O., et al.: StarCraft II: a new challenge for reinforcement learning. arXiv preprint arXiv:1708.04782 (2017)
18. Zhang, L., Wang, M., Nie, L., Hong, L., Rui, Y., Tian, Q.: Retargeting semantically-rich photos. IEEE Trans. Multimedia **17**(9), 1538–1549 (2015)

3D Object Completion via Class-Conditional Generative Adversarial Network

Yu-Chieh Chen[1], Daniel Stanley Tan[1], Wen-Huang Cheng[2], and Kai-Lung Hua[1(✉)]

[1] Department of CSIE, National Taiwan University of Science and Technology, Taipei, Taiwan
{m10515039,d10515805,hua}@mail.ntust.edu.tw
[2] Department of EE, National Chiao Tung University, Hsinchu, Taiwan
whcheng@gmail.com

Abstract. Many robotic tasks require accurate shape models in order to properly grasp or interact with objects. However, it is often the case that sensors produce incomplete 3D models due to several factors such as occlusion or sensor noise. To address this problem, we propose a semi-supervised method that can recover the complete the shape of a broken or incomplete 3D object model. We formulated a hybrid of 3D variational autoencoder (VAE) and generative adversarial network (GAN) to recover the complete voxelized 3D object. Furthermore, we incorporated a separate classifier in the GAN framework, making it a three player game instead of two which helps stabilize the training of the GAN as well as guides the shape completion process to follow the object class labels. Our experiments show that our model produces 3D object reconstructions with high-similarity to the ground truth and outperforms several baselines in both quantitative and qualitative evaluations.

Keywords: Object reconstruction · Shape completion Generative adversarial network · Object classification

1 Introduction

In a real world setting, data collected from 3D sensors (e.g. Microsoft Kinect, Intel RealSense, LiDAR) are often faced with many problems such as occlusions, sensor noise [8], restricted scanner depth range, limited video frames [9,14], and poor lighting conditions. This results in 3D object models that are noisy and incomplete. For instance, a room scan obstructed by a chair brings about a hole or gap in the 3D desk model. This adds to the difficulty of performing many robotic tasks that requires interaction with objects, such as grasping and navigation, where capturing and understanding the shape of an object is crucial. Humans can easily imagine what these objects might look like given an incomplete image. However, this is a very challenging tasks for robots since there can be many different shape variations of a given object.

© Springer Nature Switzerland AG 2019
I. Kompatsiaris et al. (Eds.): MMM 2019, LNCS 11296, pp. 54–66, 2019.
https://doi.org/10.1007/978-3-030-05716-9_5

We propose a semi-supervised method that can reconstruct and complete the shape of the 3D model given a broken or incomplete 3D object model, as shown in Fig. 1. We combined the benefits of a 3D variational autoencoder (VAE) [11], which can encode meaningful latent representations, and a generative adversarial network (GAN) [7], which can generate realistic samples from a latent representation using a two-player minimax game. Inspired by [4], we introduced a separate classifier that predicts the labels of the generated images and transformed the GAN framework to a three player game instead of two. This stabilizes the training of GANs by constraining the modes of the generated data as well as provide more supervision to the generator through the class labels. Since labels are not always available, we include two additional components that predict pseudo-labels, allowing our model to be trained in a semi-supervised setting. We evaluated our method and compared against several baselines to verify the effectiveness of our method.

Input: Broken 3D object   Output: Complete 3D object   Ground Truth 3D object

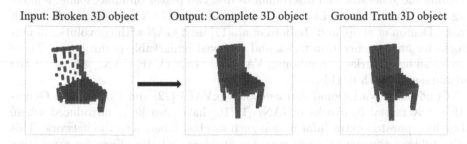

Fig. 1. Our model takes in a broken 3D object as input and produces a reconstruction of how the completed 3D object would look like.

2   Related Work

3D Shape Completion. With the introduction of large scale 3D databases [2, 26], researchers began applying deep learning techniques on 3D computer vision problems. One of the problems that have been gaining traction is 3D shape completion. This is because fixing broken 3D models is usually a necessary preprocessing step. Many research [5,20,23] leveraged on structures and regularities in 3D shapes, such as symmetries in meshes or point clouds, and utilizing them to complete shapes. Although these approaches have shown outstanding results, using hand-crafted design of pre-defined regularities limits the shape space. Sung et al. [23] combines the idea with symmetry-based and data based priors to fill in missing data. However, it assumes that the data contains the same or very similar shapes. This limits the shapes that it can potentially generate. Sharma et al. [20] presented a denoising method with fully convolutional autoencoder to estimate voxel occupancy grids, but they only focus on random noise patterns. In contrast, our method can also accommodate partial range scans that often occur in a real world scenario. Dai et al. [5] built a 3D-Encoder-Predictor Network in a fully-supervised learning-based approach to predict and repair 3D scan.

Generative Models. There have been rapid developments of deep generative models in the past few years. This is largely due to the introduction of two main ideas: Variational Auto-encoder (VAE) [11,18] and Generative Adversarial Network (GAN) [7,17,19]. VAE [11,18] consists of an encoder network that projects the image to a low dimensional latent representation and a decoder that reconstructs the original image from the lower dimensional representation. Different from a standard autoencoder, the latent space of a VAE is designed to be continuous and easy to sample from. A disadvantage of VAE, though, is that the generated samples are usually blurry. GAN [7,19], on the other hand, introduces a discriminator that learns how to differentiate real from fake images. This guides the generator in producing more realistic looking samples by simultaneously training the generator and discriminator in a two player minimax game. Following these advancements, Li and Wand [13] adopted GAN for texture generation tasks. Denton et al. [6] and Radford et al. [17] used GAN with convolutional networks for image generation tasks, and achieved remarkable performance. There have also been works in combining VAE and GAN (VAE-GAN) [12] to get the advantages of both worlds.

Conditional Variational Autoencoders (cVAE) [22] and Conditional Generative Adversarial Networks (cGAN) [15,16] have also been introduced where they incorporated extra information such as class labels into the network. This helps address the one-to-many mapping problem and also allows for generating samples based on a user-specified class. Bao et al. [1] used a conditional VAE-GAN (cVAE-GAN) to produce a new sample of a specified species. Chongxuang et al. [4] proposed a thee-player game that can perform semi-supervised learning (SSL) to address limited labels in the dataset. Few works have explored extending these methods to the 3D setting. 3D Generative Adversarial Network (3DGAN) [24] and 3D Improved Wasserstein Generative Adversarial Network (3D-IWGAN) [21] has shown promising results in generating 3D shapes. However, they requires an independent model for every object category. To deal with the problem, we develop a model that can accommodate multiple object classes in a single model.

3   The Proposed Method

3.1   Background Concepts

Variational Autoencoder (VAE). A variational autoencoder (VAE) [11] consists of an encoder E that encodes a data sample x to a latent vector representation $z \sim E(x) = q(z|x)$, and a decoder or generator G that projects the latent vector back to data space $\hat{x} \sim G(z) = p(x|z)$, as shown in Fig. 2(a). The objective function of VAEs can be separated into two parts, as shown in Eq. 1. The first term is the expected reconstruction error which encourages the network to produce outputs that are similar to the input. It is normally implemented as L_1 or L_2 distance between the input x and the output $\hat{x}$.

$$L_{\text{VAE}} = L_{\text{rec}} + L_{\text{prior}} = -\mathbb{E}_{q(z|x)}[\log(p(x|z))] + D_{KL}\left(q(z|x)||p(z)\right) \quad (1)$$

The second term is a regularizer that encourages the latent vectors to follow some prior distribution $p(z)$. A unit Gaussian prior $p(z) \sim \mathcal{N}(0,1)$ is usually imposed on the encoded latent vectors in order to have a latent space that is continuous and allows for easy random sampling and interpolation. To achieve this, the encoder E is designed to output a mean vector μ and log standard deviation vector $\log(\sigma)$, which are the parameters of a Gaussian distribution. We then use the reparameterization trick to sample a latent vector z, as shown in Eq. 2, where $\odot$ refers to the Hadamard product or element-wise multiplication.

$$z = \mu + \sigma \odot \epsilon, \quad \epsilon \sim \mathcal{N}(0,1) \quad (2)$$

Generative Adversarial Network (GAN). Similar to VAEs, a generative adversarial network (GAN) [7] also consists of two networks, a generator G and a discriminator D, as shown in Fig. 2(b). The generator G is equivalent to the decoder of VAEs wherein it learns to generate an image from a latent vector z that is usually sampled from a uniform distribution or a unit Gaussian distribution. The role of the discriminator D is to learn how to distinguish real images from generated (fake) images. The goal of the generator G is to generate images that are as realistic looking as possible in order to trick the discriminator D into classifying the generated image $G(z)$ as real. This is represented as a minimax optimization in the form shown in Eq. 3, where $p(x)$ and $p(z)$ represent the distribution of the input images x and the distribution of the latent vector z respectively.

$$\min_G \max_D \mathcal{L}_{\text{GAN}} = \mathbb{E}_{x \sim p(x)}[\log D(x)] \\ + \mathbb{E}_{z \sim p(z)}[\log\left(1 - D(G(z))\right)] \quad (3)$$

VAE-GAN. VAEs are trained to optimize pixel-wise reconstruction error using L_2 distance. However, this produces blurry images as the solution would tend towards the mean. The pixel-wise reconstruction error also does not take into account how the human visual perception system would compare images. Since, it is very difficult to mathematically define a distance metric would capture these properties, GANs try to learn this from the data instead. As the GAN discriminator learn to differentiate real from fake images, it also implicitly learns a rich similarity metric for images. By incorporating the GAN discriminator into the VAE framework (shown in Fig. 2(c)), we can combine the advantages of VAEs and GANs to form a hybrid VAE-GAN that can encode an image to a latent vector z and at the same time generate sharper and higher quality images.

Incorporating Conditional Labels. We can further extend these models by conditioning the networks on some auxiliary information y. Instead of learning $p(x)$, the model now learns a conditional probability distribution $p(x|y)$. This makes the learning process easier as it constrains the modes of the distribution and it also allows us to control the data generation process. The conditioning is done by simply concatenating the extra information y, such as class labels, to the inputs of the network, as shown in Fig. 2(d).

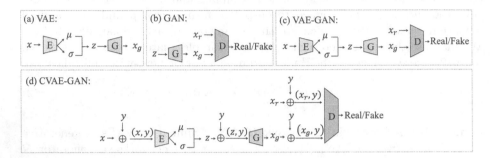

Fig. 2. Comparison of the frameworks of various generative models. $\oplus$ denotes concatenation.

3.2   Problem Formulation

Let x be a voxelized 3D object, belonging to an object class y, which may be broken or incomplete due to various factors such as sensor noise and occlusions causing it to have regions that are missing. Our goal is to generate a reconstruction of how a completed 3D shape of the object may look like. Our approach uses a class-conditional generative adversarial network to learn how these objects would generally look like from the data and hallucinate the missing parts of the incomplete 3D object. Inspired by Chongxuan et al. [4], we formulate our model to have four major components, an Encoder E, a Generator G, a Discriminator D, and a Classifier C. An overview of our framework is shown in Fig. 3.

3.3   Encoder and Generator

Our encoder E and generator G works similarly to a conditional variational auto-encoder (cVAE). The encoder takes in a 3D image x together with class labels y as an input, and outputs a mean vector $\mu \in \mathbb{R}^d$ and standard deviation $\sigma \in \mathbb{R}^d$, where d is a hyper-parameter that controls the dimensions of the latent vector z. We sample z using the reparameterization trick shown in Eq. 2. The generator then generates a reconstruction $x_g = G(z, y)$ of the 3D input image from the latent vector z combined with the class labels y. The encoder is trained to optimize the loss function defined in Eq. 4. The reconstruction objective is

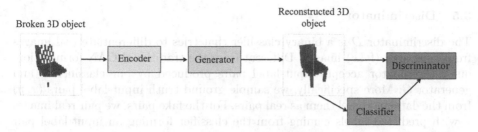

Fig. 3. This figure shows an overview of our proposed framework. The input broken 3D object is fed to the encoder and generator that produces a reconstruction of the complete 3D object. The classifier and discriminator then tries to predict the class of the generated object as well as whether it looks real or fake. The output from the classifier and discriminator are then used as feedback to the generator in order to improve its image generation.

defined using the L_2 distance between the input x and the reconstruction x_r. We apply unit Gaussian prior to regularize the latent space, which is computed as defined in Eq. 6. The generator also optimizes for the reconstruction objective and also tries to generate reconstructions that can trick the discriminator into classifying it as real, as defined in Eq. 7, where δ is a hyper-parameter that controls the relative importance of the reconstruction objective, and C is a separate classifier which we discuss in the next section.

$$L_{\text{Encoder}} = L_{\text{rec}} + L_{\text{prior}} \tag{4}$$

$$L_{\text{rec}} = \mathbb{E}_{x \sim p_{data}}\left[\|x - x_g\|_2^2\right] \tag{5}$$

$$L_{\text{prior}} = -\frac{1}{2}\sum_{j=1}^{d}\left(1 + \exp\left(\sigma_j^2\right) - \sigma_j^2 - \mu_j^2\right) \tag{6}$$

$$L_{Generator} = -\mathbb{E}_{z \sim q(z|x), y \sim p_{data}}\left[\log D\Big(G(z, y), C(G(z, y))\Big)\right] + \delta L_{\text{rec}} \tag{7}$$

3.4 Classifier

The classifier C is a categorical classifier that tries to predict the class labels of the 3D input image. The predicted labels are then used as a conditional information for the discriminator. The classifier C encourages the generator to produce images that can be distinguished as belonging to a particular object class. Having a separate classifier also transforms the GAN objective into a three player game, which makes it more stable [4]. The classifier C is trained to optimize Eq. 8, where $p_c(y|x)$ is the probability distribution over the labels y that the classifier C predicts given and input x.

$$L_{Classifier} = -\mathbb{E}_{x \sim p_{data}}\left[\log D\Big(x, C(x)\Big)\right] - \mathbb{E}_{(x,y) \sim p_{data}}\left[\log\Big(p_c(y|x)\Big)\right] \tag{8}$$

3.5 Discriminator

The discriminator D is a binary classifier that tries to differentiate real images from generated (fake) images. Different from the traditional GAN formulation, our discriminator accepts input-label pairs produced by our classifier C and generator G. More specifically, we sample ground truth input-label pairs (x, y) from the data and label them as real pairs. For the fake pairs, we pair real images x with predicted labels coming from the classifier forming an input-label pair $(x, C(x))$. Similarly, we pair the reconstructed image produced by our generator with its ground truth labels y forming an input-label pair $(G(z, y), y)$. The loss function of the discriminator is defined in Eq. 9, where $\alpha \in (0, 1)$ is a hyper-parameter which controls the relative importance between the generation and classification.

$$
\begin{aligned}
L_{Discriminator} = & - \mathbb{E}_{(x,y) \sim p_{data}} \Big[\log D(x, y) \Big] \\
& - \alpha \mathbb{E}_{x \sim p_{data}} \Big[\log \Big(1 - D\big(x, C(x)\big) \Big) \Big] \\
& - (1 - \alpha) \mathbb{E}_{z \sim q(z|x), y \sim p_{data}} \Big[\log \Big(1 - D\big(G(z, y), C(G(z, y))\big) \Big) \Big]
\end{aligned}
\tag{9}
$$

3.6 Dealing with Missing Labels

Currently, our model requires object class labels in order to generate its reconstruction. However, in many real world applications, we do not always have access to object labels. To address this, we train two additional networks, namely broken and unbroken prediction networks, to predict pseudo-labels to aid in the reconstruction process. Figure 4 shows where these two networks are inserted in our framework. The broken voxel class-predictor network (BPN) accepts broken or incomplete 3D images x_b and tries to predict a label y_b while the unbroken voxel class-predictor network (UPN) accepts unbroken or complete 3D images x_u and predicts its label y_u.

3.7 Network Architecture

Figure 5 shows an overview of our model's network architecture. Our encoder E consists of four 3D convolutional layers with stride length 2 and a kernel size of $4 \times 4 \times 4$ followed by a fully connected layer that projects the image representations to a 2048-dimensional vector. This is then followed by two separate fully connected layers that outputs the 200-dimensional mean and variance vector. We apply batch normalization and ReLU activation at every layer except the output layer.

Our generator G accepts a 200-dimensional latent vector z as input and applies a fully connected layer that projects it to a 2048-dimensional vector. We then reshaped this vector to $2 \times 2 \times 2 \times 256$. This is then followed by four 3D

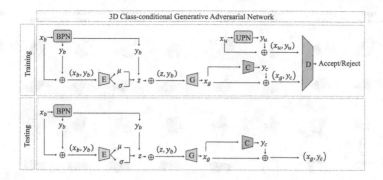

Fig. 4. This figure shows where the broken voxel prediction network (BPN) and unbroken voxel prediction network (UPN) are inserted into our framework.

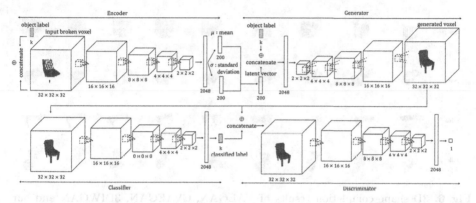

Fig. 5. Network architecture of our encoder, generator, classifier and discriminator, where k denotes the number of object classes.

transposed convolution layers with stride length 2 and a kernel size of $4 \times 4 \times 4$ that up-samples the image representation to $32 \times 32 \times 32$. We apply batch normalization and ReLU activation at every layer except the output layer where we apply a sigmoid activation function.

Similar to the encoder, our classifier C also consists of four 3D convolutional layers with stride length 2 and a kernel size of $4 \times 4 \times 4$ followed by a fully connected layer that projects the image representations to a 2048-dimensional vector. The output layer is a fully connected layer that outputs an k-dimensional vector, where k is the number of classes, followed by a softmax layer that produces a probability distribution across the object classes.

Our discriminator D also shares the same architecture as the encoder and classifier. The only difference is that we apply LeakyReLU activation instead of ReLU. The output layer is a fully connected layer followed by a sigmoid activation function that produces a scalar value corresponding to the probability of being real.

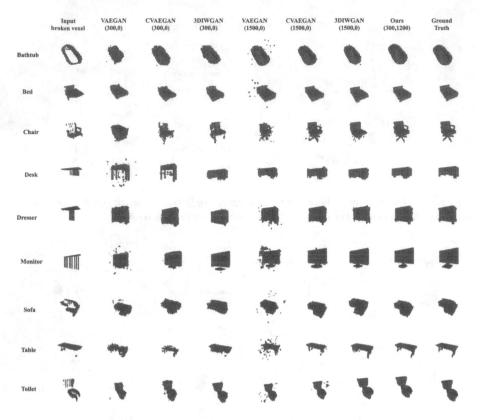

Fig. 6. 3D shape completion results of VAEGAN, CVAEGAN, 3DIWGAN and our method.

4   Experiments

4.1   Datasets

For our experiments, we used the dataset provided by Smith and Meger [21]. They constructed a dataset of broken 3D images with their corresponding ground truth complete images from the ModelNet10 [25] dataset. They also included voxelized representations of the Kindect depth maps sampled from the Large Dataset of Object Scans [3]. Our training set consists of 9 common object categories with each having 1,500 samples per category. This amounts to a total of 13,500 3D image samples with a resolution of $32 \times 32 \times 32$. Our test set, on the other hand, contains 150 samples for each category. To emulate the scenario of not having ground truth labels, we set aside 300 samples with labels per category for training and used the remaining 1,200 samples per category as missing labels.

Table 1. Comparison of different methods evaluated using average Intersection-Over-Union. Note that higher IOU is better. The highest values are highlighted in bold.

Method	Bathtub	Bed	Chair	Desk	Dresser	Monitor	Sofa	Table	Toilet	Mean
VAEGAN [12] (0,300)	0.238	0.492	0.254	0.33	0.634	0.526	0.603	0.227	0.54	0.427
CVAEGAN [1] (300,0)	0.461	0.587	0.331	0.300	0.676	0.600	0.701	0.22	0.593	0.497
IWGAN [21] (0,300)	0.526	0.584	0.28	0.563	0.691	0.613	0.723	0.349	0.617	0.55
VAEGAN [12] (0,1500)	0.484	0.626	0.462	0.581	0.802	0.646	0.784	0.444	0.696	0.614
CVAEGAN [1] (1500,0)	0.614	0.621	0.541	0.64	0.805	0.659	0.823	0.484	0.783	0.663
IWGAN [21] (0,1500)	0.582	0.577	0.435	0.568	0.793	0.683	0.812	0.506	0.717	0.63
OURS (300,1200)	**0.691**	**0.663**	**0.584**	**0.687**	**0.828**	**0.693**	**0.858**	**0.582**	**0.830**	**0.713**

4.2 Implementation Details

We implement our network using the Tensorflow deep learning library and Tensorlayer. The training process takes about four days on a desktop with an Intel Core-i7 CPU and a GeForce GTX1080Ti GPU. We trained for a total of 1500 epochs with a batch size of 30 and a learning rate of 0.0001. We used Adam [10] optimizer with $\beta_1 = 0.5$ and $\beta_2 = 0.9$.

4.3 Results

We compare our model across several baselines in terms of both qualitative and quantitative evaluations. Figure 6 shows the results of the visual comparison across different methods. We trained our model on only 300 labeled examples with 1200 unlabeled examples. The other models, on the other hand, were trained on 1500 labeled examples. We also included the results of the baseline models trained on only 300 labeled examples. The other methods usually have a hard time reconstructing the thin parts of the object. This is most evident in the legs of the chair and table. We can observe that our model is able to reconstruct these well.

Table 2. Comparison of different methods evaluated using the Hausdorff distance (HD). Note that lower HD is better. The lowest values are highlighted in bold.

Method	Bathtub	Bed	Chair	Desk	Dresser	Monitor	Sofa	Table	Toilet	Mean
VAEGAN [12] (0,300)	10.553	7.577	11.575	11.751	10.495	9.842	6.913	8.606	11.548	9.873
CVAEGAN [1] (300,0)	6.995	5.961	8.703	10.844	9.647	8.542	5.734	7.575	10.098	8.233
IWGAN [21] (0,300)	6.893	6.463	8.927	8.420	9.238	8.323	5.607	6.741	10.103	7.857
VAEGAN [12] (0,1500)	6.612	5.779	7.634	7.977	7.505	8.062	4.946	6.452	8.381	7.039
CVAEGAN [1] (1500,0)	5.783	5.712	6.984	7.346	7.712	7.847	4.473	5.932	7.336	6.57
IWGAN [21] (0,1500)	6.615	6.486	8.104	8.262	8.141	7.952	4.939	5.946	8.504	7.217
OURS (300,1200)	**5.491**	**5.611**	**6.931**	**7.175**	**7.155**	**7.611**	**3.995**	**5.719**	**6.616**	**6.256**

We quantitatively evaluated our model using the average Intersection-Over-Union (IOU) and the Hausdorff Distance (HD) between the generated and ground truth images for each category. The results are shown in Tables 1 and 2. We can observe that our method achieves the highest IOU and the lowest Hausdorff Distance, outperforming all the baseline methods.

$$HD\left(A, B\right) = \max\left\{ \max_{a \in A} \min_{b \in B}\left(\|a - b\|\right), \max_{b \in B}\min_{a \in A}\left(\|b - a\|\right)\right\} \qquad (10)$$

5   Conclusions

In this paper, we have proposed a model that can recover the complete 3D object from a broken or incomplete 3D input. Our approach uses a class-conditional hybrid of a 3D variational autoencoder and a three player generative adversarial network that allows it to be trained in a semi-supervised setting. Our experimental results verify the effectiveness of our approach.

References

1. Bao, J., Chen, D., Wen, F., Li, H., Hua, G.: CVAE-GAN: fine-grained image generation through asymmetric training. CoRR, abs/1703.10155 5 (2017)
2. Chang, A.X., et al.: ShapeNet: an information-rich 3d model repository. arXiv preprint arXiv:1512.03012 (2015)

3. Choi, S., Zhou, Q.Y., Miller, S., Koltun, V.: A large dataset of object scans. arXiv preprint arXiv:1602.02481 (2016)
4. Chongxuan, L., Xu, T., Zhu, J., Zhang, B.: Triple generative adversarial nets. In: Advances in Neural Information Processing Systems, pp. 4091–4101 (2017)
5. Dai, A., Qi, C.R., Nießner, M.: Shape completion using 3D-Encoder-Predictor CNNs and shape synthesis. In: Proceedings of IEEE Conference on Computer Vision and Pattern Recognition (CVPR), vol. 3 (2017)
6. Denton, E.L., Chintala, S., Fergus, R., et al.: Deep generative image models using a Laplacian pyramid of adversarial networks. In: Advances in Neural Information Processing Systems, pp. 1486–1494 (2015)
7. Goodfellow, I., et al.: Generative adversarial nets. In: Advances in Neural Information Processing Systems, pp. 2672–2680 (2014)
8. He, F.L., Wang, Y.C.F., Hua, K.L.: Self-learning approach to color demosaicking via support vector regression. In: International Conference on Image Processing (ICIP). IEEE (2012)
9. Hua, K.L., Zhang, R., Comer, M., Pollak, I.: Inter frame video compression with large dictionaries of tilings: algorithms for tiling selection and entropy coding. IEEE Trans. Circ. Syst. Video Technol. 22(8), 1136–1149 (2012)
10. Kinga, D., Adam, J.B.: A method for stochastic optimization. In: International Conference on Learning Representations (ICLR), vol. 5 (2015)
11. Kingma, D.P., Welling, M.: Auto-encoding variational Bayes. In: International Conference on Learning Representations (ICLR) (2014)
12. Larsen, A.B.L., Sønderby, S.K., Larochelle, H., Winther, O.: Autoencoding beyond pixels using a learned similarity metric. arXiv preprint arXiv:1512.09300 (2015)
13. Li, C., Wand, M.: Precomputed real-time texture synthesis with Markovian generative adversarial networks. In: Leibe, B., Matas, J., Sebe, N., Welling, M. (eds.) ECCV 2016. LNCS, vol. 9907, pp. 702–716. Springer, Cham (2016). https://doi.org/10.1007/978-3-319-46487-9_43
14. Li, H.C., et al.: Dependency-aware quality-differentiated wireless video multicast. In: 2013 IEEE Wireless Communications and Networking Conference (WCNC), pp. 2226–2231. IEEE (2013)
15. Mirza, M., Osindero, S.: Conditional generative adversarial nets. arXiv preprint arXiv:1411.1784 (2014)
16. Odena, A., Olah, C., Shlens, J.: Conditional image synthesis with auxiliary classifier GANs. arXiv preprint arXiv:1610.09585 (2016)
17. Radford, A., Metz, L., Chintala, S.: Unsupervised representation learning with deep convolutional generative adversarial networks. arXiv:1511.06434 (2015)
18. Rezende, D.J., Mohamed, S., Wierstra, D.: Stochastic back propagation and approximate inference in deep generative models. arXiv:1401.4082 (2014)
19. Salimans, T., Goodfellow, I., Zaremba, W., Cheung, V., Radford, A., Chen, X.: Improved techniques for training GANs. In: Advances in Neural Information Processing Systems, pp. 2234–2242 (2016)
20. Sharma, A., Grau, O., Fritz, M.: VConv-DAE: deep volumetric shape learning without object labels. In: Hua, G., Jégou, H. (eds.) ECCV 2016. LNCS, vol. 9915, pp. 236–250. Springer, Cham (2016). https://doi.org/10.1007/978-3-319-49409-8_20
21. Smith, E.J., Meger, D.: Improved adversarial systems for 3d object generation and reconstruction. In: Proceedings of the Annual Conference on Robot Learning (2017)
22. Sohn, K., Lee, H., Yan, X.: Learning structured output representation using deep conditional generative models. In: Advances in Neural Information Processing Systems, pp. 3483–3491 (2015)

23. Sung, M., Kim, V.G., Angst, R., Guibas, L.: Data-driven structural priors for shape completion. ACM Trans. Graph. (TOG) **34**(6), 175 (2015)
24. Wu, J., Zhang, C., Xue, T., Freeman, B., Tenenbaum, J.: Learning a probabilistic latent space of object shapes via 3d generative-adversarial modeling. In: Advances in Neural Information Processing Systems, pp. 82–90 (2016)
25. Wu, Z., Song, S., Khosla, A., Tang, X., Xiao, J.: 3d ShapeNets for 2.5 d object recognition and next-best-view prediction. ArXiv e-prints 2 (2014)
26. Wu, Z., et al.: 3d ShapeNets: a deep representation for volumetric shapes. In: Proceedings of the IEEE Conference on Computer Vision and Pattern Recognition (2015)

Video Summarization with LSTM
and Deep Attention Models

Luis Lebron Casas(✉)📵 and Eugenia Koblents(✉)

United Technology Research Center Ireland, Cork, Republic of Ireland
{LebronL,KoblenE}@utrc.utc.com

Abstract. In this paper we propose two video summarization models based on the recently proposed vsLSTM and dppLSTM deep networks, which allow to model frame relevance and similarity. The proposed deep learning architectures additionally incorporate an attention mechanism to model user interest. In this paper the proposed models are compared to the original ones in terms of prediction accuracy and computational complexity. The proposed vsLSTM+Att method with an attention model outperforms the original methods when evaluated on common public datasets. Additionally, results obtained on a real video dataset containing terrorist-related content are provided to highlight the challenges faced in real-life applications. The proposed method yields outstanding results in this complex scenario, when compared to the original methods.

Keywords: Video summarization · LSTM · Attention model
Digital forensics

1 Introduction

In recent years, video summarization has become a very active research field due to the big amount of video content that needs to be monitored in multiple applications [1,2]. For instance, in video surveillance applications, it is often critical to review huge amounts of video content from which only limited fragments are indeed relevant. In the context of the European project DANTE, the goal of the video summarization module is to automatically identify the most relevant video segments in a large collection of video data posted online, in order to assist Law Enforcement Agencies (LEAs) in the identification of potentially terrorist-related activities.

The video summarization task aims to extract a set of key-frames or key-shots that capture the most relevant information in a video. The first works in unsupervised video summarization [3] split the input video into segments and extract key-frames or key-shots based on various heuristic criteria (thresholding color histograms, etc.). The use of additional low-level visual (SIFT [4]) and motion (optical flow [2]) features can help improve their performance in some cases. Other approaches only consider videos that can be classified into specified

© Springer Nature Switzerland AG 2019
I. Kompatsiaris et al. (Eds.): MMM 2019, LNCS 11296, pp. 67–79, 2019.
https://doi.org/10.1007/978-3-030-05716-9_6

categories (such as sports [2] or cooking tutorials [5]), which significantly limits their applicability.

Various criteria could be used to define the importance of a frame or shot in a video, including frame relevance and similarity or the user's interest in the frame content. In [6] the authors employ user-edited videos or photographs from the web with the goal of replicating the user's behavior when summarizing similar videos. In [7] a combination of these criteria is used to define a mixture of cost and benefits. In [8] the use of a textual input query is explored to filter out video shots irrelevant to the user.

In [1] two long short-term memory (LSTM) supervised deep neural networks are proposed, that allow to model both the frame relevance and similarity, with the goal of generating representative and diverse summaries. During the model training phase, the parameters of the network are optimized based on a set of annotated videos, in which one or more users have manually selected the most relevant video segments. Annotations can come in the form of either binary or continuous frame-level importance scores.

In this paper we additionally incorporate a deep attention model into the LSTM architecture in order to represent user's interest without having specific labels for this purpose. Attention models have been used in many deep learning problems to simulate the human behavior and memory mechanism [9], including text summarization [10] and caption generation [11]. In this paper we incorporate an attention model into the vsLSTM and dppLSTM architectures and compare the resulting models with their corresponding baselines in terms of prediction accuracy and computational cost. Quantitative and qualitative comparison results are provided for both public and DANTE video data.

The structure of this document is the following. In Sect. 2 the vsLSTM and dppLSTM models are introduced. In Sect. 3 the attention mechanism is described and the proposed networks are presented. Section 4 summarizes the experimental results obtained in the evaluation of the proposed models, both on public and DANTE datasets. Section 5 is devoted to the conclusions.

2   Video Summarization with LSTM

In this section the vsLSTM and dppLSTM methods proposed in [1] for video summarization are introduced, which allow to generate a representative summary of an input video by extracting the most relevant segments. vsLSTM models frame relevance while dppLSTM additionally accounts for frame diversity in order to avoid redundancy in the generated summary. Both vsLSTM and dppLSTM implement a recurrent neural network (RNN) architecture consisting of forward and backward LSTM chains to model temporal variability in the video.

In the following, let $\mathcal{X} = \{\mathbf{x}_t\}_{t=1}^{T}$ denote a sequence of T frames represented by non-negative visual features $\mathbf{x}_t \in \mathbb{R}^N$. The output of a summarization model is a subset $\mathcal{S} \subset \mathcal{X}$ of the form $\mathcal{S} = \{\mathbf{x}_{t_k}\}_{k=1}^{K}$, where $K < T$ is the desired summary length parameter provided by the user.

2.1 Long Short-Term Memory

LSTM networks are a special kind of RNN that excel at modeling long-range dependencies [12] and have been successfully applied to multiple multimedia processing tasks [10,11]. LSTM cells encode, at each time step, the knowledge of the inputs that have been observed up to that step. Nonlinear sigmoid gates control when the cell retains, updates or forgets its internal state. In the context of video summarization, LSTMs cells are used to learn when to forget or incorporate events occurring in a video sequence [1]. For each input vector $\mathbf{x}_t$, LSTM units compute an output vector $\mathbf{h}_t \in \mathbb{R}^M$, based on the previous output $\mathbf{h}_{t-1}$. The whole sequence of output vectors is denoted as $\mathcal{H} = \{\mathbf{h}_t\}_{t=1}^T$.

2.2 vsLSTM Model for Video Summarization

The vsLSTM model [1], depicted in Fig. 1, employs bidirectional chains of LSTM units, denoted $LSTM^F$ and $LSTM^B$, to model long-term dependencies among video frames in the forward and backward directions, respectively.

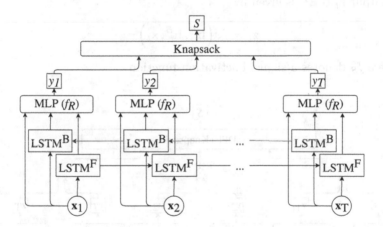

Fig. 1. vsLSTM model [1] composed of forward and backward LSTM layers.

In vsLSTM, the outputs of the two LSTM chains, denoted $\mathbf{h}_t^F$ and $\mathbf{h}_t^B$, are combined with the visual features $\mathbf{x}_t$ using a multi-layer perceptron (MLP) layer. The relevance score $y_t \in [0, 1]$ of each video frame $t = 1, \ldots, T$ is given by

$$y_t = f_R \left(\mathbf{h}_t^F, \mathbf{h}_t^B, \mathbf{x}_t \right), \tag{1}$$

where f_R denotes a sigmoid activation function. Hard binary scores can be computed from the soft frame-level importance scores y_t.

In [1] the authors use Kernel Temporal Segmentation (KTS) [4] to split the input video into R non-overlapping segments $\mathcal{A}_r \subset \mathcal{X}$ of variable length l_r, $r = 1, \ldots, R$. Then, aggregated scores $s_r = \frac{1}{l_r} \sum_t y_t | \mathbf{x}_t \in \mathcal{A}_r$ are computed for each segment. As proposed in [13], the Knapsack algorithm is used to select the optimal subset of segments to be included in the summary, given a score s_r and a length l_r for each segment, and a maximum summary length K.

The vsLSTM model generates the summary based on the predicted relevance of video frames. However, this model does not take into account the similarity among frames and can thus yield redundant summaries. The dppLSTM model [1] additionally accounts for frame diversity and is introduced below.

2.3   dppLSTM Model for Video Summarization

The dppLSTM model [1], illustrated in Fig. 2, combines the vsLSTM network with a determinantal point process (DPP) to additionally model pairwise repulsiveness among video frames. Similarly to the vsLSTM model, in dppLSTM, two bidirectional LSTM chains model forward and backward frame dependencies based on visual features $\mathbf{x}_t$. On one hand, the LSTM outputs $\mathbf{h}_t^F$ and $\mathbf{h}_t^B$ are combined with the input features $\mathbf{x}_t$ as in Eq. (1) to yield relevance scores y_t. On the other hand, the same vectors are combined in an additional MLP branch whose output $\mathbf{z}_t \in \mathbb{R}^P$ is given by

$$\mathbf{z}_t = f_S \left(\mathbf{h}_t^F, \mathbf{h}_t^B, \mathbf{x}_t \right) \tag{2}$$

and where f_S denotes a sigmoid activation function.

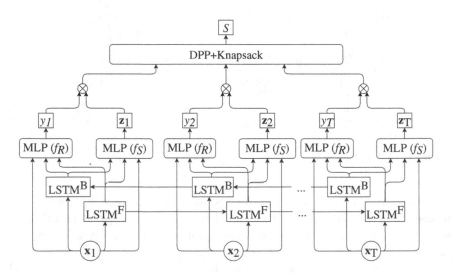

Fig. 2. dppLSTM network [1] that incorporates an additional MLP branch and a DPP layer to represent the pairwise repulsiveness among frames.

In [1] the authors use a DPP probabilistic model of repulsion to model frame diversity. The similarity between frames $\mathbf{x}_t$ and $\mathbf{x}_{t'}$ is modeled by the similarity matrix $\mathbf{L}$, whose components are computed as $L_{tt'} = y_t y_{t'} \mathbf{z}_t^\top \mathbf{z}_{t'}$, for $t, t' = 1, \ldots, T$. Given a set $\mathcal{X}$ of T items (e.g., frames in a video), and a matrix $\mathbf{L}$, the DPP model yields the probability of any subset $\mathcal{S} \subset \mathcal{X}$. This probability is proportional to the determinant of the corresponding sub-matrix $\mathbf{L}_\mathcal{S}$, i.e.,

$$P(\mathcal{S} \subset \mathcal{X}; \mathbf{L}) = \frac{\det(\mathbf{L}_\mathcal{S})}{\det(\mathbf{L} + \mathbf{I}_T)}, \tag{3}$$

where $\mathbf{I}_T$ denotes the identity matrix of size T. The DPP model yields low probability values for subsets including similar frames, thus favoring the generation of diverse summaries. The output of the DPP model is the sequence of K' frames that maximizes the probability in Eq. (3). In [1] the authors claim that K' is usually lower than the desired summary length K. In this case, the Knapsack algorithm is used to increase the summary length up to K frames following the same procedure as described in Sect. 2.2.

3 Video Summarization with LSTM and Attention Models

In this section, extensions of the vsLSTM and dppLSTM models are proposed that incorporate an attention model to learn how the user's interest evolves along the video. We introduce an additional $LSTM^{att}$ layer with input $\mathbf{g}_t \in \mathbb{R}^L$ to model human interest along the video frames in the forward direction. Let $h_t^{att,i}$, $i = 1, \ldots, M$, denote the i-th $LSTM^{att}$ output component at time t and $\mathbf{h}^{att,i} = [h_1^{att,i}, h_2^{att,i}, \ldots, h_T^{att,i}]^\top \in \mathbb{R}^T$. In [10] the authors propose to compute score coefficients α_t^i that represent how much attention should be put on each output component $h_t^{att,i}$. Score coefficients α_t^i are computed as

$$\alpha_t^i = \mathbf{v}^\top \tanh\left(\mathbf{W}_1 \mathbf{h}^{att,i} + \mathbf{W}_2 \mathbf{g}_t\right) \tag{4}$$

where $\mathbf{v} \in \mathbb{R}^V$, $\mathbf{W}_1 \in \mathbb{R}^{V \times T}$ and $\mathbf{W}_2 \in \mathbb{R}^{V \times L}$ are learnable parameters of the model and tanh function operates element-wise. Attention mask coefficients β_t^i are computed as a softmax function of α_t^i, namely,

$$\beta_t^i = \frac{\exp(\alpha_t^i)}{\sum_{j=1}^M \exp(\alpha_t^j)}, \qquad \sum_{i=1}^M \beta_t^i = 1. \tag{5}$$

The attention vector $\mathbf{o}_t \in \mathbb{R}^M$ is computed as a weighted sum of the $LSTM^{att}$ output vectors $\mathbf{h}_t^{att} = [h_t^{att,1}, h_t^{att,2}, \ldots, h_t^{att,M}]^\top \in \mathbb{R}^M$, that is,

$$\mathbf{o}_t = f_{att}\left(\mathcal{H}^{att}, \mathbf{g}_t\right) = \sum_{i=1}^M \beta_t^i \mathbf{h}_t^{att}, \tag{6}$$

where $\mathcal{H}^{att} = \{\mathbf{h}_t^{att}\}_{t=1}^T$. The architecture of the attention model is depicted in Fig. 3, where the output $\mathbf{o}_t$ depends on the input $\mathbf{g}_t$ at time t and the output of the $LSTM^{att}$ cells at all time instants.

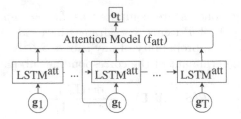

Fig. 3. Attention mechanism to model the temporal evolution of user interest.

3.1 vsLSTM and dppLSTM with an Attention Model

In this section we describe the proposed video summarization models based on the vsLSTM and dppLSTM networks that incorporate an attention mechanism to learn how the user's interest evolves along the video. Figure 4 shows the t-th branch of the proposed vsLSTM+Att (*left*) and dppLSTM+Att (*right*) models for video summarization. The new models incorporate an additional layer for modeling user's attention, which is highlighted in the figure. The dependence of the attention filter on the whole set of $LSTM^{att}$ output vectors is omitted in this diagram for simplicity of representation.

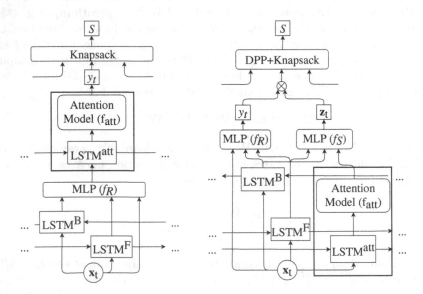

Fig. 4. Branch corresponding to time t of the proposed vsLSTM+Att (*left*) and dppLSTM+Att (*right*) models that incorporate an attention mechanism.

In the vsLSTM+Att network, the attention model is incorporated after the MLP layer (f_R) and provides input to the Knapsack optimization layer. The y_t relevance scores are given by

$$y_t = f_{att}\left(\mathcal{H}^{att}, \mathbf{g}_t\right), \quad \text{where} \quad \mathbf{g}_t = f_R\left(\mathbf{h}_t^F, \mathbf{h}_t^B, \mathbf{x}_t\right). \tag{7}$$

In the ddpLSTM+Att network we include the attention model in the similarity branch instead of the relevance branch as this architecture has shown to yield better accuracy than alternative configurations. The attention mechanism is applied over the input $\mathbf{x}_t$, which is not used as input to the MLP layers but only for the computation of the attention vector. In this case the relevance scores y_t are again computed as in Eq. (1) and $\mathbf{z}_t$ is given by

$$\mathbf{z}_t = f_S\left(\mathbf{h}_t^F, \mathbf{h}_t^B, f_{att}\left(\mathcal{H}^{att}, \mathbf{g}_t\right)\right), \quad \text{where} \quad \mathbf{g}_t = \mathbf{x}_t. \tag{8}$$

In the proposed methods, the final segment selection is performed using the same approach as in the original methods, based on Knapsack and DPP.

4 Experimental Results

In this section we provide comparison results of the original vsLSTM and dppLSTM models and the proposed extensions on two well-known public datasets, namely SumMe [14] and TVSum [13]. SumMe contains 25 high-quality videos, from both static and moving cameras, with highly variable content, including holidays, sports and generic events. On the contrary, TVSum contains 50 Youtube videos grouped into ten highly specific categories such as parkour, flash mob gathering or bee keeping. As suggested in [1], the VSUMM [15] and OVP [16] datasets have also been used to generate an augmented dataset for training purposes. These datasets contain pieces of news, television shows, movies and user generated videos. The vsLSTM methods have also been evaluated on a real and very challenging dataset collected in the context of the DANTE project, containing real videos related to terrorist activities.

Table 1 summarizes some of the main characteristics of the datasets used in the simulations. The total number of videos in public datasets is 175, with a duration between 1 and 10 min each and annotated by several users. Annotations come in the form of discrete frame-level importance scores. On the contrary, the DANTE dataset contains 1084 videos annotated by a single user each. DANTE videos are in general very long and the length of the user summaries ranges between a few seconds and the whole video duration.

4.1 Simulation Setup

Keras 2.0.2 with Theano v.0.9 backend has been used in the experiments, as well as multiple low-level Theano functionalities not included in Keras. As suggested in [1], in the simulations with public datasets, the input video is subsampled to a

Table 1. Main features of the datasets used for video summarization.

	Videos	Duration (min)	Summary	Users per video	Scores
SumMe [14]	25	1–5	5%–15%	15–18	$\{0, 1\}$
TVSum [13]	50	2–10		20	$\{1, \ldots, 5\}$
OVP [16]	50	1–4		5	$\{0, 1\}$
VSUMM [15]	50	1–10		5	$\{0, 1\}$
DANTE	1084	1–120	1%–99%	1	$\{0, 1\}$

2 fps rate to reduce the video redundancy and the computational complexity of the model. InceptionV1 (GoogLeNet) [1] visual descriptors have been extracted from each video frame and used as input vectors $\mathbf{x}_t \in \mathbb{R}^N$, where $N = 1024$.

The dimension of the LSTM output is $M = 256$ for $\mathbf{h}_t^F$ and $\mathbf{h}_t^B$ and $M = 1024$ for $\mathbf{h}_t^{att}$. The output of the MLP sigmoid activation function has dimension 1 for f_R, $P = 256$ for f_S and $M = 256$ for f_{att}, respectively. The summary duration length parameter has been set to $K \leq 0.15 \times T$ in all the simulations.

As suggested in [7], all the mentioned public datasets have been used for training but only SumMe and TVSum have been used for evaluation. The annotation procedure in OVP and VSUMM is inconsistent with the rest of databases and they are barely used for evaluation purposes.

The dataset has been randomly split into three subsets: 60% of the videos for training, 20% for validation and 20% for test. A total of 30 experiments has been run for each video summarization model using different configurations of the network hyper-parameters (number of epochs, batch size, optimization type, learning rate, etc.). The best network configuration has been selected based on the validation set using the F_1-measure between the automatic ($\mathcal{S}$) and the user generated ($\mathcal{U}$) summaries, defined as $F_1 = 100 \times 2PR/(P + R)$. P and R denote precision and recall, respectively, and are computed as $P = \frac{\text{Duration of } (\mathcal{S} \cap \mathcal{U})}{\text{Duration of } \mathcal{S}}$, $R = \frac{\text{Duration of } (\mathcal{S} \cap \mathcal{U})}{\text{Duration of } \mathcal{U}}$. In case $J > 1$ user's annotations are available for a given video, the maximum F_1 score is considered, i.e., $F_1^{max} = \max_{j \in [1, J]} F_1(\mathcal{S}, \mathcal{U}_j)$. Training stops when F_1^{max} decreases for 5 to 10 consecutive epochs on the validation dataset. Finally, the test dataset has been used to compute the final F_1^{max} scores for each model (mean and std over the whole set of videos are reported).

All summarization models have been trained using adaptive moment estimation (Adam) [17] as the optimization strategy. Mean square error (MSE) has been used as the loss function for the vsLSTM-based models and the DPP loss function proposed in [1] for the DPP-based models.

4.2 Simulation Results on Public Datasets

Table 2 summarizes the obtained results for the original and proposed LSTM-based models, in terms of computation time and F_1-measure. The first column reports the training time per epoch in seconds. The total training time can be highly variable among different simulation runs as it depends on the initialization and random network parameters. The second column reports the total testing time for SumMe (obtained on a set of 5 videos with a total duration of 15 min) and TVSum (for 10 videos with a total duration of 35 min). As expected, DPP-based models are computationally more expensive than their vsLSTM counterparts. The proposed models are also more computationally demanding than the baseline methods.

Table 2. Comparison results of the vsLSTM and dppLSTM-based models in terms of train and test time and F_1 (mean and std). F_1 results reported in [1] are also shown.

SumMe	Train (s)	Test (s)	F1	F1 in [1]
vsLSTM [1]	23.8	8.3	42.2 (2.0)	41.6 (0.5)
vsLSTM+Att	71.4	10.8	**43.2 (2.8)**	-
dppLSTM [1]	46.9	14.9	43.2 (2.2)	42.9 (0.5)
dppLSTM+Att	80.1	21.7	43.8 (2.2)	-
TVSum				
vsLSTM [1]	5.3	19.7	57.8 (4.8)	57.6 (0.5)
vsLSTM+Att	8.9	21.4	**63.1(2.1)**	
dppLSTM [1]	8.9	41.7	52.5 (4.9)	59.6 (0.4)
dppLSTM+Att	16.7	55.0	53.9 (5.1)	-

The third column reports the mean and std of the F_1 obtained in our simulations of the baseline and proposed methods, while the last column shows the values reported in [1]. It can be observed that similar average results have been attained, but the obtained std is significantly higher than the one reported in [1], in particular for TVSum. The highest F_1 score has been reached by the proposed vsLSTM+Att model on TVSum, achieving an increment of a 9% with respect to the baseline.

Figure 5 shows a qualitative comparison of the vsLSTM and vsLSTM+Att models on a video example from the SumMe dataset. The sequence of frames corresponds to uniform sampling, vsLSTM and vsLSTM+Att key-frames, respectively. It can be observed that both summaries are rather similar and only differ in a few video segments. vsLSTM+Att selects shots that are spread over the whole video duration while vsLSTM selects several consecutive shots at the beginning of the video.

4.3 Simulation Results on the DANTE Dataset

Finally, in this section, the comparison results of the vsLSTM and vsLSTM+Att models on the DANTE dataset are presented. DPP-based models have been discarded from this analysis since this family of models is very computationally demanding on long videos. The DANTE dataset poses multiple challenges for the

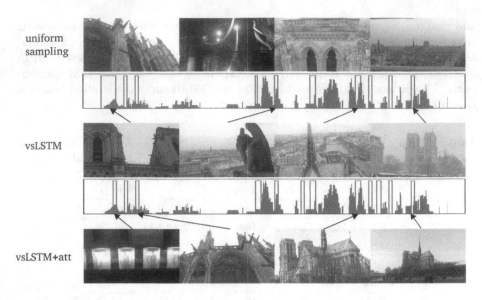

Fig. 5. Comparison of the vsLSTM and vsLSTM+Att models on a SumMe video. The average user score is shown in blue, and the segments selected by the model in red.

video summarization task. On one hand, it contains both long and monotonous videos and short videos with multiple actions. On the other hand, the DANTE videos contain a great variety of content and present very variable image quality, motion and light conditions. Finally, the user's annotation was performed at a much lower level of detail than in public databases and one single annotation per video is available. For this reason, the user generated summaries significantly differ in length and are strongly biased by the user's personal criteria.

Given the length of the DANTE videos, a slightly different approach for the generation of the input features x_t has been followed in this case. In particular, the input video has been segmented using the KTS algorithm [4], based on visual (InceptionV1) and audio features (Mel-frequency spectrum [18]), and keyframes have been selected from each segment. In this case, the input to the summarization models, $x_t \in \mathbb{R}^N$, where $N = 1024$, corresponds to the visual feature vector of each key-frame. The number of input frames is thus significantly reduced with respect to the sub-sampling procedure proposed in [1]. For the performance comparison on the DANTE dataset, both vsLSTM-based models are pre-trained on public databases as described in Sect. 4.2 and then re-trained using the DANTE annotated dataset.

Table 3 shows the comparison results of the vsLSTM and vsLSTM+Att models on the DANTE dataset. The test time corresponds to 125 videos with a total duration of 10 hours. The relatively high testing time is due to the fact that the evaluation procedure during testing considers the whole sequence of video frames, while only key-frames are used during training. It can be observed that the proposed vsLSTM+Att model outperforms the baseline F_1 by a notable 25%

in this challenging scenario. Figure 6 shows an example of the summary generated for a DANTE video by the two compared methods. It can be observed that the annotation is very coarse in this dataset, and only one long segment has been selected as relevant by the user in this example. As a result, the generated summaries are also often composed of longer segments.

Table 3. Comparison of the vsLSTM-based models on the DANTE dataset in terms of train and test time and F_1-measure (mean and std).

DANTE	Train (s)	Test (s)	F1
vsLSTM	846.5	2604.4	41.7 (1.1)
vsLSTM+Att	943.4	3671.7	**52.3 (0.5)**

Fig. 6. vsLSTM versus vsLSTM+Att on a DANTE video. The user annotation and automatically generated summary are shown in blue and red, respectively.

5   Conclusion

In this paper, extensions of the vsLSTM and dppLSTM models have been proposed that incorporate an attention model to learn the user's interest. The proposed methods have been compared to the original models on public databases as well as a real database collected in the context of the European project DANTE, which contains terrorist-related content. The proposed vsLSTM+Att network outperforms the baseline architectures both on public and DANTE data. In particular, the proposed method yields a 25% improvement with respect to vsLSTM on the challenging DANTE dataset. The DPP-based models have shown to be too computationally demanding in this scenario.

Acknowledgements. The work presented in this paper was supported by the European Commission under contract H2020-700367 DANTE.

References

1. Zhang, K., Chao, W.-L., Sha, F., Grauman, K.: Video summarization with long short-term memory. In: Leibe, B., Matas, J., Sebe, N., Welling, M. (eds.) ECCV 2016. LNCS, vol. 9911, pp. 766–782. Springer, Cham (2016). https://doi.org/10.1007/978-3-319-46478-7_47

2. Mendi, E., Clemente, H.B., Bayrak, C.: Sports video summarization based on motion analysis. Comput. Electr. Eng. **39**(3), 790–796 (2013)

3. Wolf, W.: Key frame selection by motion analysis. In: Acoustics, Speech, and Signal Processing, vol. 2, pp. 1228–1231. IEEE (1996)

4. Potapov, D., Douze, M., Harchaoui, Z., Schmid, C.: Category-specific video summarization. In: Fleet, D., Pajdla, T., Schiele, B., Tuytelaars, T. (eds.) ECCV 2014. LNCS, vol. 8694, pp. 540–555. Springer, Cham (2014). https://doi.org/10.1007/978-3-319-10599-4_35

5. Khosla, A., Hamid, R., Lin, C.-J., Sundaresan, N.: Large-scale video summarization using web-image priors. In: Proceedings of the IEEE Conference on Computer Vision and Pattern Recognition, pp. 2698–2705 (2013)

6. Sun, M., Farhadi, A., Seitz, S.: Ranking domain-specific highlights by analyzing edited videos. In: Fleet, D., Pajdla, T., Schiele, B., Tuytelaars, T. (eds.) ECCV 2014. LNCS, vol. 8689, pp. 787–802. Springer, Cham (2014). https://doi.org/10.1007/978-3-319-10590-1_51

7. Gygli, M., Grabner, H., Van Gool, L.: Video summarization by learning submodular mixtures of objectives. In: Proceedings of the IEEE Conference on Computer Vision and Pattern Recognition, pp. 3090–3098 (2015)

8. Sharghi, A., Gong, B., Shah, M.: Query-focused extractive video summarization. In: Leibe, B., Matas, J., Sebe, N., Welling, M. (eds.) ECCV 2016. LNCS, vol. 9912, pp. 3–19. Springer, Cham (2016). https://doi.org/10.1007/978-3-319-46484-8_1

9. Denil, M., Bazzani, L., Larochelle, H., de Freitas, N.: Learning where to attend with deep architectures for image tracking, CoRR, vol. abs/1109.3737 (2011). http://arxiv.org/abs/1109.3737

10. Vinyals, O., Kaiser, L., Koo, T., Petrov, S., Sutskever, I., Hinton, G.: Grammar as a foreign language. In: Advances in Neural Information Processing Systems, vol. 28, pp. 2773–2781. Curran Associates Inc. (2015)

11. Xu, K., et al.: Show, attend and tell: neural image caption generation with visual attention. In: International Conference on Machine Learning, pp. 2048–2057 (2015)

12. Hochreiter, S., Schmidhuber, J.: Long short-term memory. Neural Comput. **9**(8), 1735–1780 (1997)

13. Song, Y., Vallmitjana, J., Stent, A., Jaimes, A.: Tvsum: summarizing web videos using titles. In: Proceedings of the IEEE Conference on Computer Vision and Pattern Recognition, pp. 5179–5187 (2015)

14. Gygli, M., Grabner, H., Riemenschneider, H., Van Gool, L.: Creating summaries from user videos. In: Fleet, D., Pajdla, T., Schiele, B., Tuytelaars, T. (eds.) ECCV 2014. LNCS, vol. 8695, pp. 505–520. Springer, Cham (2014). https://doi.org/10.1007/978-3-319-10584-0_33
15. De Avila, S.E.F., da Luz, A.P.B., de Albuquerque Araújo, A.: VSUMM: a mechanism designed to produce static video summaries and a novel evaluation method. Pattern Recognit. Lett. **32**(1), 56–68 (2011)
16. The open video project. https://open-video.org
17. Kingma, D., Ba, J.: Adam: a method for stochastic optimization, arXiv preprint arXiv:1412.6980 (2014)
18. Stevens, S.S., Volkmann, J., Newman, E.B.: A scale for the measurement of the psychological magnitude pitch. J. Acoust. Soc. Am. **8**(3), 185–190 (1937)

Challenges in Audio Processing of Terrorist-Related Data

Jodie Gauvain[1(✉)], Lori Lamel[2], Viet Bac Le[1], Julien Despres[1],
Jean-Luc Gauvain[2], Abdel Messaoudi[1], Bianca Vieru[1], and Waad Ben Kheder[2]

[1] Vocapia Research, Orsay, France
{jodie,levb,despres,abdel,vieru}@vocapia.com
[2] CNRS-LIMSI, TLP, Orsay, France
{lamel,gauvain,benkheder}@limsi.fr
http://www.vocapia.com
http://www.limsi.fr/tlp

Abstract. Much information in multimedia data related to terrorist activity can be extracted from the audio content. Our work in ongoing projects aims to provide a complete description of the audio portion of multimedia documents. The information that can be extracted can be derived from diarization, classification of acoustic events, language and speaker segmentation and clustering, as well as automatic transcription of the speech portions. An important consideration is ensuring that the audio processing technologies are well suited to the types of data of interest to the law enforcement agencies. While language identification and speech recognition may be considered as 'mature technologies', our experience is that even state-of-the-art systems require customisation and enhancements to address the challenges of terrorist-related audio documents.

Keywords: Automatic speech recognition · Acoustic event detection Language identification · Code switching

1 Introduction

This paper reports on recent research aiming to develop audio analysis technologies to facilitate access to information, helping investigators analysing terrorist-related activities to classify and search through audio or video documents. This research was conducted in the context of a European project focusing on multilingual multimedia data collected from the Web, potentially of interest in law enforcement investigations.

Analysis of this type of data poses a number of challenges rarely found in traditional broadcast data targeted by speech recognition systems. The challenges include: a wide range of recording environments with a variety of background

This work was partially financed by the Horizon 2020 project DANTE - Detecting and analysing terrorist-related online contents and financing activities and the French National Agency for Research as part of the SALSA project (Speech and Language technologies for Security Applications) under grant ANR-14-CE28-0021.

ⓒ Springer Nature Switzerland AG 2019
I. Kompatsiaris et al. (Eds.): MMM 2019, LNCS 11296, pp. 80–92, 2019.
https://doi.org/10.1007/978-3-030-05716-9_7

noises (heavy artillery, strong wind, rain, music, singing, crowd shouting, and other human or mechanically produced noises); the presence of many different native and non-native accents in multiple languages, language switching; and various speaking styles (preaching, chanting, shouting, whispering, ...).

So far, little work has looked into analysing such data, with investigations focusing more on telephone speech recordings for example. But today with the exponential amounts of audiovisual content posted daily on the Web, the growing threat of terrorism and the increasing use of Web platforms by terrorist organisations, it is essential to develnop solutions to efficiently process such content.

In addition to the well-known national and international terrorist investigation units, a growing number of international projects have started addressing the monitoring of such activities in multimedia data. LASIE (www.lasie-project.eu), RAMSES (www.ramses2020.eu), DANTE (www.h2020-dante.eu), PERICLES (www.project-pericles.eu), PROTON (www.projectproton. eu), TAKEDOWN (www.takedownproject.eu), TENSOR (www.tensor-project.eu), RED-ALERT (www.redalertproject.eu) and VICTORIA (www.victoria-project.eu) all aim at retrieving and processing multimedia contents linked to criminal activities for law enforcement purposes, but research is still in its early stages.

2   Audio Analysis Tasks

The proposed audio analysis solutions include identifying the language(s) of an audio document, transcribing speech into text and recognising specific acoustic events. Figure 1 gives a high level use of these technologies in the context of a tool to help humans analyse huge quantities of audiovisual data.

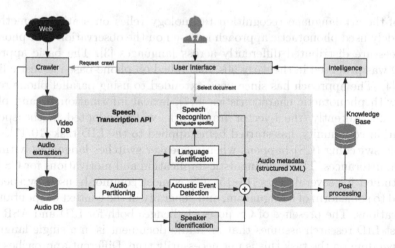

Fig. 1. Elements of the audio analysis process in a high-level context.

Automatic spoken language identification (LID) systems perform automatic detection of the spoken language(s), using the characteristics of the speech signal. LID can be used as a standalone technology, for instance for categorisation purposes, or in association with other technologies, such as automatic speech recognition (ASR). ASR is used to automatically produce a transcript of what is said from the speech signal. Since ASR systems are generally language-specific, it is often useful to combine LID with speech recognisers to provide multilingual transcription functionality [1]. Finally, acoustic event detection (AED) is the task of automatically recognising different types of sounds (whether impulsive, continuous or intermittent) that can be of interest in an audio signal. AED can be used on its own, or in association with other technologies, bringing complementary information to automatic video analysis, for example. Speaker identification from audio is also shown in the figure but is not discussed in this paper.

The three tasks mentioned above all rely on an element called the audio partitioner. It is used to divide the acoustic signal into homogeneous segments, which are further combined into clusters. The partitioner uses a segmentation and labelling procedure based on an audio stream mixture model [2]. After detecting and eliminating non-speech segments, an iterative segmentation and clustering procedure is applied to the speech segments. Each resulting cluster represents roughly a speaker at a given acoustic condition (channel, background noise, etc.) and is assigned a unique label containing gender and channel information.

The data used in the testing phases for each of the audio analysis tasks is a corpus of unannotated terrorist propaganda videos retrieved from the Web. It contains roughly 500 h of audio and 400 h of speech, as detected by the audio partitioner. The tasks and technologies are described in the following sections, along with results and analyses.

3　Language Identification and Code-Switching Detection

State-of-the-art language recognition technology relies on statistical methods. The widely used phonotactic approach is based on the observation that phoneme sequences are distributed differently across languages [3]. The basic approach for LID was proposed in the early 90s, and relied on phone-based acoustic likelihoods [4]. The approach has since been extended to using parallel phone recognisers with phonotactic characteristics [6,7], lexical information [8] and phone lattices [9]. Recently, the i-vector framework, widely adopted in the speaker recognition community, has started being applied to the LID task [10,11].

Code switching (CS) happens when a speaker switches languages within or between utterances. The sociolinguistic implication and motivations for CS have been studied for several years [13–15]. CS is most commonly used by speakers exposed to some form of bilingualism, and generally in the context of spontaneous conversations. The presence of CS poses challenges both for LID and ASR.

Most LID research assumes that an audio document is in a single language, but depending on the task this is not necessarily true. Different approaches were explored to allow the LID system to analyse potential multilingual documents. One option is to determine the predominant language only and another is to output a list of most likely languages with associated scores. An alternative is to partition the audio into speech segments and detect the language of each segment. This approach is suitable for detecting relatively long language segments.

Indeed, LID is highly dependent on the segment duration, and performance can be significantly higher on long segments, for instance longer than 10 s. To ensure a minimal speech duration, LID can be applied to clusters of segments.

3.1 Experimental Conditions

Since LID is a classification problem based upon statistical models of speech, the models have to be trained on data that match the targeted data in order to achieve suitable accuracy levels. In this project, the targeted data consist of video documents containing propaganda or terrorist training instructions. As no task-specific training data were available, broadcast data (principally TV and radio news, talk shows, debates and interviews) were used. This type of data is easily available and was assumed to be the best match among the available corpora. The training data used in this work consists of 1295 h of broadcast news and broadcast conversation shows in 32 languages, collected during several R&D projects. The corpus contains speech from many speakers, several dialects and accents per language, and high variability in acoustic conditions. The amount of training data ranges from 11 to 142 h of speech/language. The test set is composed of the same types of data as used for training, with a total of 96 h of speech in 23 of the 32 languages, with at least 3 h/language.

The baseline LID system's phone decoders make use of HMM-GMM (Gaussian mixture models) acoustic models, whereas the improved system relies on phone decoders with output observation densities produced by (Deep) Neural Networks (DNN) [12]. These models were used to decode the language specific training data in order to estimate phonotactic constraints for each target language. For testing, each data sample is then processed by one or several phone recognisers. In addition, language-specific i-vectors were trained, and during test an i-vector is extracted for each segment and scored against each language-specific vector.

3.2 Experimental Results

The left side of Fig. 2 shows the language error rate (LER) of the baseline and improved LID systems as a function of the minimal cluster duration on a broadcast speech test set. As expected, the performance is seen to depend on the segment cluster duration, being higher for longer segments, and lower for shorter ones. The improved phonotactic system outperforms the baseline by up to 50% relative for the longer segments. The phonotactic and i-vector methods were compared using a single phone decoder. The i-vector system obtains better results on short speech segments (25.2% relative), whereas the phonotactic approach performs better on longer ones (14.3% relative).

Figure 2 (right) shows the LID output on the terrorist propaganda dataset using the segment-cluster mode for processing. Segments shorter than 10 s were removed in order to avoid sections falsely recognised as speech or mislabelled by the LID system. To ensure even higher accuracy, the language confidence scores provided by the system served to narrow down the segments retained. Of the

Duration (sec)	# clusters	System Baseline	System Improved	Relative Reduction
≥ 2.4	3798	6.0	4.3	29.2
≥ 4.0	3744	5.3	3.5	33.3
≥ 8.0	3638	4.4	2.7	38.9
≥ 12.0	3526	3.9	2.1	48.6
≥ 24.0	3060	2.2	1.1	50.7

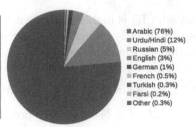

■ Arabic (76%)
■ Urdu/Hindi (12%)
■ Russian (5%)
■ English (3%)
■ German (1%)
■ French (0.5%)
■ Turkish (0.3%)
■ Farsi (0.2%)
■ Other (0.3%)

Fig. 2. Left: LER on a 23-language test set for the baseline and improved phonotactic LID systems as a function of cluster duration on an the internal broadcast data test set. Right: Proportion of speech detected per language in the terrorist propaganda videos.

files where speech was found, 16% were detected as containing more than one language, highlighting the presence of CS in this data.

4   Multilingual Speech Recognition

The last decade has witnessed major advances in speech and language technologies, which are becoming key components for analysing human communication in audio documents. The principles on which ASR systems are based on have been known for many years now, and include the application of information theory to speech recognition [16], the use of a spectral representation of the speech signal, of dynamic programming for decoding, and the use of context-dependent acoustic models [17]. Even though many of these techniques were proposed well over a decade ago, much of the recent progress is due to the availability of large speech and text corpora, and improved processing power which have allowed more complex models and algorithms to be implemented.

Transcription performance varies substantially across data types. While for well-trained ASR systems word error rates (WER) can be in the range of 5–10% on carefully prepared speech, the error rate is easily doubled or tripled for spontaneous speech or in degraded acoustic conditions (WER above 50%). It is widely acknowledged that the performance of a speech recogniser is strongly dependent upon the task, which in turn is linked to the type of user, speaking style, environmental conditions, etc. The emergence of new online-terrorist communities being so recent, very little work has been done on processing the audio contents that they generate. The main challenges lie in the intrinsic variety of such recordings, which can range over any type of quality and real-life situation, not to mention diversity of speakers, emotions, accents, languages, and in particular the use of multiple languages (Code-Switching). All these conditions require specific research in order to go beyond the state-of-the-art.

4.1   ASR System Overview

Most ASR systems have five main components: an audio partitioner, an acoustic model, a statistical language model (LM), a pronunciation dictionary, and a word recognizer [2]. As for LID, no terrorist-related data was available for system development, so broadcast data was used for training and testing as it was assumed to be the best match. The audio partitioner, designed for broadcast speech, generates a sequence of non-overlapping segments and groups them into clusters. Acoustic and language models were trained using statistical methods on large quantities of data. The language model training data includes manual transcriptions of recordings, written dialogues, news and other types of sources that can be gathered from the Web. The acoustic models are triphone-based Hidden Markov Models, with output observation probabilities given by DNNs [12]. For each language, the acoustic models were built using state-of-the-art discriminative training methods and trained on several hundred hours of annotated data (audio recordings and their associated transcriptions). The phone sets cover the language-specific phones and special units to model silence, breath and filler words. The pronunciation dictionaries are built with grapheme-to-phoneme rules derived from linguistic knowledge, complemented with exception rules as needed.

4.2 Experimental Conditions and Results

Six languages are targeted for ASR: Arabic, English, French, Italian, Portuguese and Spanish. Table 1 displays the WER for the baseline and enhanced systems on internal broadcast datasets. Developments for the improved systems involved, in particular, new acoustic modeling based methods on time-delay neural networks (TDNNs) [18] and acoustic data augmentation, including speed and volume perturbation, addition of background noise and reverberation. Both methods have been proven effective to make models more robust to noisy environments and help cope with mismatches between training and testing data [19,20].

Table 1. Word error rate (WER (%)) on an internal broadcast speech development data set with at least 3 h of data from a minimum of 20 speakers per language.

Language	Arabic	English	French	Italian	Portuguese	Spanish
Baseline	9.6	13.3	13.7	9.9	14.2	11.2
Improved	8.9	10.5	11.3	8.1	13.8	10.2

Figure 3 shows an audio excerpt with segments in 3 different languages (English, Arabic and French), with their corresponding automatic transcripts. LID and ASR were jointly applied to produce multilingual speech-to-text.

A subset (7 h) of the terrorist propaganda dataset was manually selected and annotated for testing. This was performed in Arabic, because of its overall predominance in the data, and in English, for demonstration. The ASR system was used to produce a transcript of the audio, and the output was scored against the reference transcripts. Initial results show a considerable decrease in accuracy when compared to those reported in Table 1. The baseline Arabic system obtains a WER close to 30% on this data (compared to 9.6 on the broadcast speech

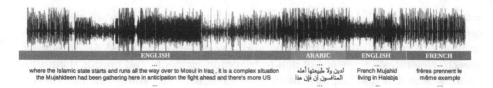

Fig. 3. ASR an audio excerpt containing segments in 3 different languages.

test set), and the English system nearly reaches 44% (compared to 13.3% on a broadcast speech test). The enhanced English system was also tested on this dataset, resulting in a 39% WER (11.5% relative gain compared to the baseline).

These results, which can in part be attributed to the difference between the target and and training data, highlight the difficulty of the task at hand.

Some challenging aspects of the terrorist propaganda audio were noticed across all languages. The speech partitioning is perturbed by the strong presence of chanting and preaching that can easily be mistaken for speech, as well as a wide range of background noises. Many files have a relatively low audio quality: the microphones are often placed far from the speakers, sometimes bringing environmental noise to the foreground instead of the speech. In addition, the ASR language models and lexicons are not adapted to this data, the vocabulary and formulations being quite different from those of the training data. For the English speech in particular, strong accents of non-native speakers are sources of many errors. The speech also contains many hesitations and grammatical errors that do not match well with the language models. CS with Arabic is also omnipresent, and over 8% of the words in the reference transcripts are not in the ASR lexicon. As shown in Table 2, even words of Arabic origin that are now commonly used in English are often missed as their Arabic pronunciations can be very different from those in the English lexicon.

Table 2. Common Arabic words with their English and Arabic pronunciations (mapped to the English phone set). Differences are shown in color.

Word	Occurences	Recognized	English pron	Arabic pron
Jihad	36	24	JIhad JIh@d Jihad Jih@d	Zihad
Allah	169	3	@lx	alah
Mujahideen	24	11	myuZxhxdin muZxhxdin myuJxhxdin muJxhxdin	muZahidin

5 Acoustic Event Detection

Sounds carry a large amount of information about our environment and the physical events that take place in it. Humans naturally perceive the sound scene around them (busy street, office, etc.), and can recognise individual sound sources (car passing by, footsteps, etc.). For decades researchers have been fascinated with the idea of machines that could hear and understand audio content just like humans do, referred to as 'machine listening'. Developing signal processing methods to automatically extract this information has huge potential in several applications. The goal of AED is to label temporal regions within an audio recording, determining the start, end and the nature of sound instances. The output can be exploited jointly with other technologies, such as image or video recognition services, bringing valuable complementary information to the table.

Interest in AED has been increasing over recent years, with public challenges, such as DCASE (http://dcase.community), helping to boost research in the field. Unfortunately, most benchmarks and available datasets are not very relevant to this project. In addition, published detection and classification performances on similar tasks are still quite low. Even when only trying to detect a few categories of events, performance remains relatively low (compared to what is seen nowadays with ASR). This illustrates the difficulty of the task and the progress that is still to be made in order to reliably recognise sounds in realistic soundscapes, where multiple sounds are present, often simultaneously, and distorted by the environment. It is important to note that most challenges primarily address classification of events, eliminating altogether the detection stage which adds another level of difficulty. The closest work to ours is that of Google AudioSet described in [21].

5.1 System Description

Neural Networks have proven to be very efficient for speech processing activities, recently resulting in a significant leap in system accuracy. But for AED, the trend to use Deep Convolutional Neural Networks [22] has shown less convincing results in the 2017 DCASE challenge (http://www.cs.tut.fi/sgn/arg/dcase2017/challenge/index) [23]. This is probably due, in part, to the lack of well-annotated data to work with, and of course, to the inherent complexity of the task. In order to incorporate the AED system as shown in Fig. 1, implementing CNN-based models would have required major modifications to the structure of the partitioner. Therefore, for initial experiments, the same acoustic feature extraction methods as for speech were used, allowing a simpler incorporation of new events into the existing technology.

Sounds of interest were selected in collaboration with law enforcement partners, and further narrowed down according to their availability in publicly available datasets. Out of 15 corpora inventoried, of various sizes and containing many sub-corpora, only a few covered the audio events of interest, and Google AudioSet (https://research.google.com/audioset) was the only one to cover all of them. It contains over 2 million semi-automatically labeled 10-second sound clips drawn from YouTube videos with a hierarchical ontology [21], partially validated by humans.

Given the large disparities in the available data (both in quantity and quality), only a few events of critical importance were experimented with in a first validation stage. In addition to speech, four acoustic events were focused on: explosions, shootings (gunshots and machine guns), and Nasheed (singing). The Nasheed is a work of vocal music that usually makes reference to Islamic beliefs, and is meant to inspire Muslims to practice Jihad. This type of singing, shown on the left of Fig. 4, having formant structure similar to speech, is often present in terrorist propaganda recordings and was designated as an important sound to detect by the law enforcement agencies.

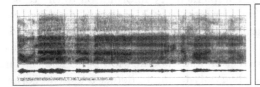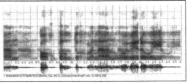

Fig. 4. Spectrograms of singing with background music (left) and preaching (right).

In order to be seamlessly integrated in the audio partitioner, GMMs were used to model the acoustic events. The GMMs for the audio segmentation and labelling procedure use basically the same acoustic feature vector as what is typically used for ASR with the exception that it does not include the energy, but does use the delta energy parameters. For speech and general music, we used the MUSAN music, speech and noise corpus [24], composed of 109 h of precisely annotated audio. GMMs for the other acoustic events were trained using data extracted from the Google Audioset corpus. Finally, the model for the Nasheed was trained on manually annotated data from real terrorist propaganda videos, since it was not included in the AudioSet ontology.

5.2 Experimental Results

Table 3 gives the results of a manual validation of a randomly selected subset of the acoustic events detected in 100 h of audio from the propaganda corpus.

It can be seen that the number of correct detections (validated) is highest for singing, for which carefully annotated training segments were used. There are more false alarms than correct detections for the other 3 categories, with the largest number of false alarms on gunshots. One explanation may be that since these models were trained on 10-second AudioSet samples, there can be other sounds in the segment, which may impact shorter events more than longer ones.

Figure 5 shows a spectrogram of an audio segment classified as machine gunfire. While the regular burst seen in the signal and the spectrogram correspond to machine gunfire, the three darker, longer bursts are explosions overlapping with

Table 3. Manual validation of a random subset of approximately 400 automatically detected acoustic events. The numbers correspond to the total number of detections, the correct/incorrect/unclear detections (Validated/False Alarms).

Acoustic event	Detected	Validated	False alarm	Unclear
Explosion	1564	95	149	63
Gunshot	1207	36	402	22
Machine gun	927	71	293	27
Singing	4745	154	143	11

the gunfire. There are many other polyphony instances, with impulsive acoustic events overlapping other continuous or repetitive events such as singing, wind, speech, steps, etc. Many of these sounds are difficult even for humans to distinguish, for example machine gunfire can sound like fireworks or a loud engine.

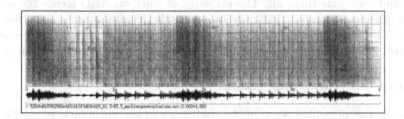

Fig. 5. Spectrogram illustrating explosions alternating with machine gunfire.

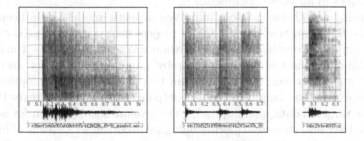

Fig. 6. Spectrograms of single and multiple gunshots (left, middle) and a clang (right).

5.3 Challenges

Some major challenges are still to be tackled. First and foremost, data annotation needs to be improved. The study of the different corpora on AED, and the manual annotation process that was begun show that, even for humans, annotating sounds is a very difficult task. When one is actually within an environment, many sources of information are received about what is happening, but when listening to audio a posteriori without knowing the context, it is difficult for the human ear to distinguish between similar sounds (as shown by the last column in Table 3). This is also illustrated in Fig. 6 which shows spectrograms of a single and multiple gunshots (left, middle) and a clang that was mistakenly detected as a gunshot. Many acoustic events can easily be confused, and have almost identical spectral features. For example a 'bang' can be an explosion, a gunshot, thunder, a firecracker, etc. A first step in future works will need to be the careful selection of events to annotate, the definition of exactly how they should be annotated and the use of as much context as possible to annotate them (exploiting the video images, for example, when available).

A second major difficulty for AED tasks is the issue of polyphony. Unlike speakers who usually try to take turns speaking, there can be an infinite number of overlapping sound events and it is therefore nearly impossible to try to detect and recognize them all. The majority of work on AED treats the sound as monophonic, assuming that only one event is detectable at a time, but, in most real-world situations, sounds overlap and events of interest can co-occur (as shown in Fig. 5 which has explosions overlapping with machine gunfire).

6   Summary and Discussion

This paper has presented some of the challenges in the automatic processing of terrorist-related audio data found on the Web and some of the initial progress made in addressing these challenges. Concerning language identification and code switching, phonotactic and i-vector methods have been explored, and improved decoders developed. Segment-cluster based LID was introduced to handle multiple languages in an audio document.

Concerning speech recognition, improved acoustic models have been developed for the 6 languages of interest in the project using the latest acoustic modelling techniques. Acoustic data augmentation was used to increase the amount and variability of the training data thereby improving genericity and reducing the mismatch between the training and test data. Future developments will address improving the language model components by locating texts that are close to the targeted data, and improving the pronunciation lexicon for accented speech. We have also started exploring bilingual decoding as a means of handling code-switching, where two ASR systems process the data in parallel, allowing a language switch at each word.

It is interesting to note that it was considered a huge challenge when the National Institute of Standards and Technology (https://www.nist.gov/itl/iad/mig/rich-transcription-evaluation) first proposed the task of automatically transcribing broadcast news data back in the 90's. Until that time ASR had mainly addressed processing of read speech, dictation or simple constrained tasks that did not need to deal with heterogeneous data, multiplicity of speakers and acoustic conditions, speech in the presence of music, etc. Today the transcription of broadcast news data is considered a relatively simple task compared to less formal data types such as conversational speech, amateur youtube videos and multiparty meetings [25]. Therefore, we can hope that similar progress will be made in the future at transcribing challenging terrorist-related audio.

Acoustic event detection is still in its early stages, but research on comparable problems such as object detection in images has recently shown astonishing results. The polyphony issue is still a long way from being solved, and is one of the reasons why AED is considered by many specialists as a very difficult task. However, with a better annotation process, machine performance is expected to improve. A semi-supervised method relying both on automatic recognition and human validation at a finer scale than was used for the AudioSet labels could be the key.

References

1. Vu, N.T. et al.: A first speech recognition system for Mandarin-English code-switch conversational speech. In: IEEE ICASSP (2012)
2. Gauvain, J.L., Lamel, L., Adda, G.: Audio partitioningt and transcription for broadcast data indexation. Multimed. Tools Appl. **14**, 187–200 (2001)
3. House, A.S., Neuburg, E.P.: Toward automatic identification of the language of an utterance. I. Preliminary methodological considerations. JASA **62**(3), 708–713 (1977)
4. Gauvain, J.L., Lamel, L.: Identification of non-linguistic speech features. In: Human Language Technology (HLT 1993), pp. 96–101. ACL (1993)
5. Lamel, L., Gauvain, J.L.: A phone-based approach to non-linguistic speech feature identification. Comput. Speech Lang. **9**(1), 87–103 (1995). https://doi.org/10.1006/csla.1995.0005
6. Zissman, M.: Comparison of four approaches to automatic language identification of telephone speech. IEEE Trans. Speech Audio **4**, 31–44 (1996)
7. Benzeghiba, M. Gauvain, J.L., Lamel, L.: Improved n-gram phonotactic models for language recognition. In: Interspeech (2010)
8. Kadambe, S., Hieronymus, J.: Language identification with phonological and lexical models. In: IEEE ICASSP (1995)
9. Gauvain, J.L., Messaoudi, A., Schwenk, H.: Language recognition using phone lattices. In: ICSLP, pp. 1283–1286, Jeju Island (2004)
10. Dehak, N. et al.: Language recognition via i-vectors and dimensionality reduction. In: Interspeech, pp. 857–860, Florence (2011)
11. Martinez, D. et al.: Language recognition in iVectors space. In: Interspeech (2011)
12. Hinton, G., et al.: Deep neural networks foracoustic modeling in speech recognition. IEEE Signal Process. Mag. **29**(6), 82–97 (2012)
13. Weinreich, U.: Languages in Contact. Mouton, The Hague (1953)
14. Demby, G.: How code-switching explains the world (2013)
15. Amazouz, D., Adda-Decker, M, Lamel, L.: Addressing code-switching in French/Algerian Arabic speech. In: Proceedings of Interspeech 2017, pp. 62–66 (2017)
16. Jelinek, F.: Continuous speech recognition by statistical methods. Proc. IEEE **64**, 532–556 (1976)

17. Schwartz, R. et al.: Improved hidden Markov modeling of phonemes for continuous speech recognition. In: IEEE ICASSP, vol. 3, pp. 35.6.1–35.6.4 (1984)
18. Peddinti, V., Povey, D., Khudanpur, S.: A time delay neural network architecture for efficient modeling of long temporal contexts. In: Interspeech (2015)
19. Cui, X., Goel, V., Kingsbury, B.: Data augmentation for deep neural network acoustic modelling. In: IEEE ICASSP, pp. 5619–5623 (2014)
20. Ragni, A., et al.: Data augmentation for low resource languages. In: Interspeech, pp. 810–814, Singapore (2014)
21. Gemmeke, J.F., et al.: Audio set: an ontology and human-labeled dataset for audio events. In: IEEE ICASSP, pp. 776–780 (2017)
22. Hershey, S. et al.: CNN architectures for large-scale audio classification. In: IEEE ICASSP, pp. 131–135 (2017)
23. Takahashi, N. et al.: Deep convolutional neural networks and data augmentation for acoustic event detection, arXiv preprint arXiv:1604.07160 (2016)
24. Snyder, D., Chen, G., Povey, D.: MUSAN: a music, speech, and noise corpus, CoRR abs/1510.08484 (2015). http://arxiv.org/pdf/1510.08484v1.pdf
25. Martin, A. Garofolo, J.: NIST speech processing evaluations: LVCSR, speaker recognition, language recognition. In: IEEE Workshop on Signal Processing Applications for Public Security and Forensics, pp. 1–7 (2007)

Identifying Terrorism-Related Key Actors
in Multidimensional Social Networks

George Kalpakis[(✉)], Theodora Tsikrika, Stefanos Vrochidis,
and Ioannis Kompatsiaris

Information Technologies Institute, Centre for Research and Technology Hellas,
Thermi, Thessaloniki, Greece
{kalpakis,theodora.tsikrika,stefanos,ikom}@iti.gr

Abstract. Identifying terrorism-related key actors in social media is of
vital significance for law enforcement agencies and social media organizations in their effort to counter terrorism-related online activities. This
work proposes a novel framework for the identification of key actors in
multidimensional social networks formed by considering several different types of user relationships/interactions in social media. The framework is based on a mechanism which maps the multidimensional network to a single-layer network, where several centrality measures can
then be employed for detecting the key actors. The effectiveness of the
proposed framework for each centrality measure is evaluated by using
well-established precision-oriented evaluation metrics against a ground
truth dataset, and the experimental results indicate the promising performance of our key actor identification framework.

Keywords: Multidimensional social networks · Key actors
Centrality measures · Online terrorism

1 Introduction

Social media have gained an important role over the past years for the everyday communication of people around the world, by overcoming the barrier of
distance and allowing for the direct and instantaneous connection and exchange
of information among individuals. The popular social media platforms, such as
Twitter, have provided the ground for the development of online social networks
among users sharing common ideas or interests. A key property of these networks
is their potential to facilitate the diffusion of information among their members.
However, their immense social influence has also proven very useful for terrorist
groups aiming at spreading their propaganda or recruiting new members [17].

In this context, social media networks are of great interest to Law Enforcement Agencies (LEAs) and social media organizations in their efforts to counter
terrorism online. Their focus is on monitoring terrorism-related activities on
social networks towards the identification of their most influential members (*key
actors*) who play a significant role in the connectivity of the entire network and

© Springer Nature Switzerland AG 2019
I. Kompatsiaris et al. (Eds.): MMM 2019, LNCS 11296, pp. 93–105, 2019.
https://doi.org/10.1007/978-3-030-05716-9_8

facilitate the diffusion of terrorism-related information to large audiences. Such social networks, including Twitter-based networks [1], exhibit a *scale-free* topology [3,14] making them extremely vulnerable, in terms of their connectivity, when targeted attacks are performed on their most central nodes. As a result, the detection and potential suspension of their (terrorism-related) key actors is of vital significance for all interested stakeholders.

A social media network is formed by capturing the interactions taking place either directly between social media users, or indirectly between users and social media posts (typically published by other users). Social media platforms offer a variety of interaction types to their users, each serving a different purpose. For instance, a Twitter user may *mention*[1] other users within their social media posts (*tweets*), *reply* to or *retweet*[2] tweets of interest, and may also have a *follower* and/or a *following* relationship[3] with other users. This entails that each network user may exhibit multiple links to other users, where each connection represents a different relationship type. In this context, a social media network is defined as a multidimensional network [4,9], so as to better reflect the impact each relationship type has on the overall structure.

This work aims at detecting the most influential user accounts in a social media network which is formed by considering multiple relationship types among its users, and focuses on the particular case of terrorism-related social media networks. In particular, the main contribution of this paper is the development of a novel framework for the identification of (terrorism-related) key actors in multidimensional social networks that have the ability to represent multiple relationship types between network nodes. The key actor identification is performed based on centrality measures for detecting the social network members who play a central role for the diffusion of information. For estimating the centrality measures, the original multidimensional network is mapped to a number of different simple (*single-layer*) weighted networks, each representing the original (*multidimensional*) network through a different weighting scheme.

The evaluation of our framework is performed on a social media network formed by Twitter accounts based on three different types of user relationships: (i) retweets, (ii) replies, and (iii) mentions. The accounts and their relationships have been extracted from a dataset collected from Twitter using terrorism-related Arabic keywords provided by LEAs and domain experts. We assessed the effectiveness of the proposed framework for each centrality measure by using as ground truth the suspension of the retrieved accounts by Twitter.

The remainder of the paper is structured as follows. Section 2 discusses related work. Section 3 presents the proposed multidimensional key actor detection framework. Section 4 presents the evaluation experiments and their results. Finally, Sect. 5 concludes this work.

---

[1] A *mention* represents a simple reference to a user within a tweet.

[2] A *retweet* is a re-post of a tweet.

[3] Twitter followers are users who follow or subscribe to another user's tweets. A user's *following* list contains all the users they follow on Twitter, whereas their *followers* list contains the users who follow them.

2   Related Work

Several research efforts have been conducted over the past few years for detecting the most influential actors of multidimensional social networks. One of the early attempts identified influential users in a Twitter-based multidimensional network composed by following, retweeting, and mentioning interactions based on three link analysis algorithms [13]. In another research effort, the influence of the Twitter users was measured based on random walks in a multidimensional network taking into account several relationship markers [18]. Furthermore, a work on a Twitter-based social network detected the most influential candidates of the European Elections 2014 based on belief functions theory after combining different interaction types [2].

Moreover, various efforts have focused on identifying key actors in terrorism-related social networks. A survey on social network analysis in counter-terrorism provided a comparison of tools which perform key actor identification on single-layer networks based on centrality measures [8]. Additionally, a work on key actor identification in terrorism-related social networks resulted in the development of an entropy-based centrality measure, namely *Mapping Entropy Betweenness*, which has shown good performance when compared with well-established centrality measures [12]. Finally, another research effort focused on uncovering *key communities*, i.e., social media users belonging to the same community as key actors of interest [11]. Contrary to the aforementioned research efforts, this work focuses on identifying (terrorism-related) key actors in multidimensional networks after taking into account several different types of user interactions.

3   Multidimensional Key Actor Detection Framework

This work employs centrality measures so as to identify the key actors in a multidimensional [4,9] terrorism-related social network. Our framework is illustrated in Fig. 1, where a keyword-based search on a social media platform provides a dataset of social media posts and users. Next, a weighted multidimensional network of users is created by exploiting several relationship types derived from either user-to-user or user-to-post interactions; in the latter case, a user-to-post interaction is transformed into a user-to-user relationship based on the owner of the respective post. In the resulting network, each user is represented by a node, while an edge (n_i, n_j, d_k, w_{ijk}) is created between two users n_i, n_j for a given relationship type (*dimension*) d_k, if one or more interactions of the relationship type d_k has been captured within the dataset, and w_{ijk} reflects the edge weight. Then, the multidimensional network is mapped to a weighted single-layer network based on one of the proposed mapping functions. Finally, a centrality measure is applied on the derived simple network and the key actors are ranked in descending order of their respective centrality score.

In the following, we first describe the mapping of the multidimensional network to a weighted single-layer network (Sect. 3.1) and then present the centrality measures employed in our framework (Sect. 3.2).

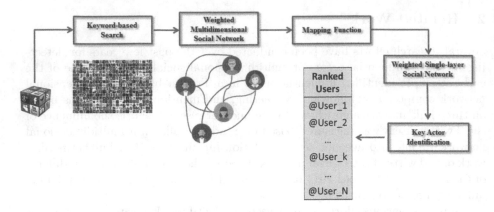

Fig. 1. Multidimensional key actor detection framework

3.1 Multidimensional to Single-Layer Network Mapping

Given that our framework considers multidimensional social media networks, we use weighted edge-labeled multigraphs for modeling their properties. Let $G = (N, E, D)$ denote a weighted edge-labeled undirected multigraph [4], where the set of nodes N represents the network actors, the set of labels D reflects the dimensions (i.e., relationship types) considered, and the set of edges E represents the links between the actors. This multigraph can then be represented by a set of quadruples (n_i, n_j, d_k, w_{ijk}) where $n_i, n_j \in N$ are the edge nodes, w_{ijk} is the weight of the relationship (e.g., reflecting its strength) between these two nodes, and $d_k \in D$ is the edge label. A node appears in a given relationship type d_k, if it is part of at least one edge labeled with d_k adjacent to it, and an edge belongs to a given relationship type d_k, if its label is d_k. It is assumed that for any given pair of nodes $n_i, n_j \in N$ and a label $d_k \in D$, there may exist only one edge.

Given that the centrality measures employed in our framework require single-layer networks for their computation, we propose a set of five mapping functions for transforming the weighted edge-labeled multigraph into a weighted single-layer graph. The goal of the mapping functions is to consider the multigraph structure for producing weighted single-layer equivalents capable of representing the original information captured in the multidimensional structure. The five mapping functions are applied on a weighted edge-labeled multigraph $G = (N, E, D)$, where the weighted adjacency matrix w is projected to a 3-dimensional space (i.e., w_{ijk} represents the weight of the edge between nodes n_i and n_j for relationship type d_k), and produce a weighted undirected network $G' = (N', E')$, where $N' = N$ (i.e., the multigraph and the derived single-layer network contain the same nodes) and w' represents an adjacency matrix of the weighted graph (i.e., w'_{ij} is the weight of the edge between nodes n'_i and n'_j).

The original multigraph is formed based on two different weighting schemes: (i) WS_1 considers that $w_{ijk} = 1$ if node n_i has interacted at least once with node n_j for a given relationship type d_k, whereas (ii) WS_2 considers that w_{ijk} is equal to the number of interactions between nodes n_i and n_j for each relationship type (e.g., if n_i has interacted 10 times with n_j for a given relationship type d_k, then $w_{ijk} = 10$). The proposed mapping functions are listed below:

Mapping Function M_1 (Merged Network): This mapping is applied on a weighted multigraph formed using WS_1 and produces a single-layer network where n'_i is linked to n'_j with $w'_{ij} = 1$, if there exists at least one edge $w_{ijk} = 1$ between n_i and n_j in the original multigraph, regardless of relationship type d_k.

Mapping Function M_2 (Weighted Network Using Relationship Type): M_2 also requires a multigraph formed using WS_1. It considers the number of the different dimensions for each edge between n_i and n_j, and produces a weighted single-layer network where n'_i is linked to n'_j with a weight $w'_{ij} = w_{ij1} + w_{ij2} + \ldots + w_{ijm}$ (i.e., equal to the sum of the edge weights for all the relationship types between n_i and n_j, where an existing relationship type for a given edge has $w_{ijk} = 1$). This entails that w'_{ij} is equal to the number of the existing relationship types for each pair (n_i, n_j) of the multigraph and cannot be greater than the actual number of the relationship types supported by the multigraph.

Mapping Function M_3 (Weighted Network Using Relationship Type Occurrence): M_3 is applied on a weighted multigraph following WS_2. It considers the weight w_{ijk} of each dimension d_k for each edge between n_i and n_j and generates a single-layer weighted network where n'_i is linked to n'_j with a weight $w'_{ij} = w_{ij1} + w_{ij2} + \ldots + w_{ijm}$ (i.e., equal to the sum of the edge weights for all the relationship types between n_i and n_j, where an existing relationship type for a given edge has $w_{ijk} >= 1$). The main difference between M_3 and M_2 lies in the weighting scheme used on the multigraph, which affects the edge weights in the derived single-layer network.

Mapping Function M_4 (Weighted Network Using Relationship Type Importance): This mapping first estimates the importance of each dimension d_k in the multigraph based on two different approaches: (i) the importance of a relationship type, im_k (with $0 \leq im_k \leq 1$), is a fraction of its total weight among all the multigraph edges when compared with the total weight of all the multigraph edges for all the relationship types; i.e., for each relationship type, it takes into account the number of interactions between any given pair of nodes, based on the assumption that the occurrence frequency of a relationship type within the multigraph entails a stronger link between the respective nodes, and (ii) the importance of a relationship type im_k is the inverse fraction of the former approach, meaning that the most significant relationship type is the one exhibiting the less frequent occurrence within the multigraph edges, based on the assumption that the occurrence frequency of a relationship type is inversely proportional to the relationship strength. M_4 requires a weighted multigraph formed using WS_1 and generates a single-layer weighted network where n'_i is linked to n'_j with a weight $w'_{ij} = im_1 \times w_{ij1} + im_2 \times w_{ij2} + \ldots + im_k \times w_{ijm}$, where an existing relationship type for a given edge on the multigraph has $w_{ijk} = 1$.

Mapping Function M_5 (Weighted Network Using Relationship Type Importance and Occurrence): This mapping function exploits the importance of each relationship type based on the two approaches presented in M_4. M_5 is applied on a multigraph created with WS_2 and generates a single-layer weighted network where n_i' is linked to n_j' with a weight $w_{ij}' = im_1 \times w_{ij1} + im_2 \times w_{ij2} + ... + im_k \times w_{ijm}$, with an existing relationship type for a given edge on the multigraph having $w_{ijk} >= 1$. M_5 and M_4 are conceptually similar, however, their difference lies in the weighting scheme used on the input multigraph.

3.2   Centrality-Based Key Actors

This section describes the seven state-of-the-art centrality measures employed for the key actor identification; for the latter two, it also expands their definitions, so that they can be applied on weighted single-layer networks.

The degree of a node is equal to the number of its adjacent nodes, i.e., the number of nodes that a node is linked to [10]. In weighted networks, the degree has been extended so as to reflect the sum of the weights of the adjacent nodes and has been defined as node *strength* [16]. Given a weighted undirected network $G = (N, E)$ where N is the set of nodes and E is the set of edges, the strength of a node $n_i \in N$, $strength(n_i)$, is the sum of the weights of its adjacent edges:

$$strength(n_i) = \sum_{j}^{N} w_{ij} \tag{1}$$

where w is a *weighted adjacency matrix* in which $w_{ij} > 0$, if n_i is connected to n_j, and the value reflects the weight of the edge. In a weighted undirected network, the **Degree Centrality** (DC) of a node equals to its strength.

Besides Degree Centrality which simply sums the weights of adjacent edges and is not affected by the position of a node in the network, our framework also employs Betweenness Centrality which quantifies the number of times a node acts as a bridge along the shortest path between two other nodes [10]. We define a *path* from $n_i \in N$ to $n_j \in N$ as a sequence of nodes and edges which begins by n_i and ends in n_j, such that each edge connects its preceding with its succeeding node. In a weighted undirected network, the *path length* is defined as the sum of the weights of all its edges, and the *shortest path* is the path with the minimum length connecting n_i and n_j. In this context, the **Betweenness Centrality** (BC) of a node n_k is based on the number of shortest paths from node n_i to node n_j that pass through node n_k, divided by the number of all shortest paths from node n_i to node n_j [6]:

$$BC_k = \sum_{n_i \neq n_j \neq n_k \in N} \frac{\sigma_{n_i n_j}(n_k)}{\sigma_{n_i n_j}} \tag{2}$$

where $\sigma_{n_i n_j}$ is total number of shortest paths from node n_i to node n_j and $\sigma_{n_i n_j}(n_k)$ is the number of those paths that pass through n_k.

Our framework also employs **Closeness Centrality** (CC) which is based on the inverse of the average distance to all other nodes of a network [10], the **Eigenvector Centrality** (EC) which considers that a node is more influential if it is connected to many nodes who themselves have high scores and corresponds to the largest eigenvalue of the adjacency matrix [5], and **PageRank** (PR) which (motivated by estimating the importance of Web pages in the Web graph) corresponds to the principal eigenvector of the normalized adjacency matrix [7].

Furthermore, our framework employs two entropy-based centrality measures, **Mapping Entropy** (ME) [15] and **Mapping Entropy Betweenness** (MEB) [12], which take into account the neighborhood $\mathcal{N}(n_k)$ of a node n_k for identifying the key actors. ME and MEB consider the information that is communicated through nodes which act, respectively, as a hubs or bridges, i.e. those with high values of Degree or Betweenness Centrality between any two members, respectively. We expand the definitions of ME and MEB which have been originally applied in unweighted networks [12,15], so as to also consider their computation in weighted networks. To this end, the weighted ME and MEB definitions take advantage of the Eqs. (1) and (2), so as to rely on the weighted computation of the Degree and the Betweenness Centrality, respectively:

$$ME_k = -DC_k \sum_{n_i \in \mathcal{N}(n_k)} \log DC_i \tag{3}$$

$$MEB_k = -BC_k \sum_{n_i \in \mathcal{N}(n_k)} \log BC_i \tag{4}$$

The evaluation of the different mapping functions and corresponding networks is performed by comparing the effectiveness of the centrality measures under consideration: Degree Centrality (DC), Betweenness Centrality (BC), Closeness Centrality (CC), Eigenvector Centrality (EC), PageRank (PR), Mapping Entropy (ME), and Mapping Entropy Betweenness (MEB), as discussed next.

4 Evaluation Experiments

This section first describes and analyses the dataset used in our experimental evaluation (Sect. 4.1) and then presents the evaluation setup and discusses the experimental results (Sect. 4.2).

4.1 Dataset

Our experiments were performed on a social media network formed by data collected from Twitter within a 16-month period (February 9, 2017 to June 8, 2018) using a set of Arabic keywords related to terrorism, provided by LEAs and domain experts. The dataset consists of 65,511 tweets posted by 35,718 users.

Three user interaction types were examined: *retweets*, *replies* and *mentions*. Moreover, two variations of a weighted multidimensional social network were developed based on the two weighting schemes of our framework, respectively,

(i) a multigraph using WS_1 which consists of 33,946 retweets, 4,411 replies, and 8,062 mentions, while the total weight per relationship type is equal to the number of edges (given that all the edge weights are equal to 1), and (ii) a multigraph using WS_2 which contains the exact same number of edges per relationship type as above, while the total weight of retweets, replies and mentions is 57,541, 9,926, and 16,546, respectively (i.e., each edge is assigned a weight based on the number of interactions per relationship type for any given pair of nodes).

Next, seven weighted single-layer networks (having 35,718 nodes each) were produced after applying the proposed five mapping functions and their variations (see Sect. 3.1). For M_4 and M_5, the importance rate for retweets, mentions, and replies was estimated as 0.68, 0.20, and 0.12, respectively, whereas the inverse important rate was estimated as 1.47, 5.00, and 8.33, respectively.

In addition, three single-layer networks were also created (one for each relationship type), so as to be used as a baseline for our evaluation. To examine the behavior of the three baseline single-layer networks, we simulated targeted attacks on the Largest Connected Component (LCC, i.e., the largest subgraph in which any two nodes are connected to each other by paths) of each network, by sequentially removing its most central node(s) based on each of the centrality measures under consideration with the goal to determine which dissolves the network structure faster and affects its robustness.

Before initiating the attacks to the three baseline networks, we examined their scale-free property, so as to gauge their vulnerability to targeted attacks towards their central nodes. To this end, we examined the power-law behavior of the degree distribution for the networks under consideration, so as to identify the vulnerability of the LCC to targeted attacks. For the retweet-based single-layer network, the power-law exponent is estimated to be 3.288 and is statistically significant, as stated by the Kolmogorov-Smirnov hypothesis test with p-value $0.644 > 0.05$, which confirms the scale-free character of the network, therefore allowing for performing targeted attacks on the most central nodes. Similarly, the reply-based network is also scale-free, with Kolmogorov-Smirnov's test p-value $0.851 > 0.05$ and a power-law exponent estimated to be 2.606. Finally, the mention-based network also complies with the scale-free assumption. The power-law exponent is estimated to be 3.0951 and is statistically significant, as confirmed by the Kolmogorov-Smirnov hypothesis test with p-value $0.524 > 0.05$.

For the retweet-based network, the LCC contains 15,577 nodes and 23,105 edges; for the reply-based network, 3,221 nodes and 3,773 edges; and for the mention-based network, 3,953 nodes and 5,078 edges. Figures 2, 3 and 4 illustrate the decay of the LCC on the three networks under consideration. Betweenness Centrality achieves faster removal of the LCC nodes for all networks, while Closeness Centrality and MEB are in the second and third place, respectively. The decomposition of the reply-based network is performed relatively faster when compared with the other two networks, after taking into account both the original size of the LCC and the number of the attacks required until the network is decomposed; 52 nodes on average are removed at each iteration of the attack process on the reply-based network for the best performing centrality measure, whereas 39.53 and 22.77 nodes are removed on average on the mention-based and the retweet-based network, respectively. This entails that the Betweenness Centrality is capable of identifying highly central nodes at earlier stages of the attack process when exploiting the reply-based interactions.

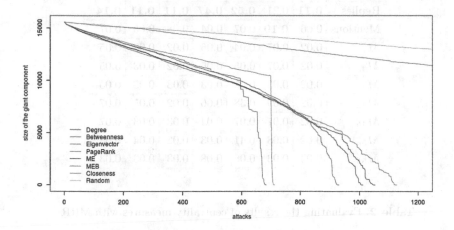

Fig. 2. Decay of the largest component for the retweet-based network

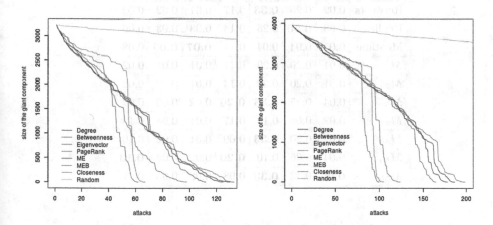

Fig. 3. Decay of the largest component for the reply-based network

Fig. 4. Decay of the largest component for the mention-based network

4.2   Evaluation Results

The evaluation of our framework is performed by comparing the seven centrality measures under consideration for the different generated networks, i.e., the three baseline relationship-based networks and the seven weighted networks produced through the mapping functions. In our experiments, we extract the top 100 key

Table 1. Evaluating the results of centrality measures with P@100

Network	Centrality measure						
	DC	BC	CC	EC	PR	ME	MEB
Retweets	0.02	0.06	0.04	0.06	0.03	0.02	0.04
Replies	**0.11**	0.21	**0.52**	**0.47**	**0.11**	**0.11**	**0.14**
Mentions	0.06	**0.10**	0.07	0.04	0.08	0.05	0.07
M_1	0.02	0.07	0.04	0.06	0.02	0.02	0.05
M_2	0.02	0.07	0.05	0.06	0.02	0.03	0.05
M_3	0.02	0.03	0.05	0.03	0.03	0.03	0.05
M_{4a}	0.02	0.09	0.38	0.06	0.02	0.05	0.07
M_{4b}	0.02	0.07	0.07	0.04	0.03	0.03	0.07
M_{5a}	0.02	0.08	0.41	0.03	0.02	0.04	0.08
M_{5b}	0.03	0.03	0.06	0.08	0.03	0.03	0.03

Table 2. Evaluating the results of centrality measures with MRR

Network	Centrality measure						
	DC	BC	CC	EC	PR	ME	MEB
Retweets	0.02	0.25	**0.33**	0.17	0.01	0.02	0.02
Replies	0.03	**0.50**	0.25	0.14	0.03	0.03	0.06
Mentions	0.05	0.04	0.04	0.11	**0.07**	**0.05**	0.08
M_1	0.01	0.20	0.20	0.17	0.01	0.01	0.02
M_2	0.01	0.20	0.20	0.14	0.01	0.02	0.02
M_3	0.04	0.25	**0.33**	**0.20**	0.02	0.03	0.02
M_{4a}	0.02	0.05	0.14	0.17	0.01	0.03	0.10
M_{4b}	0.02	0.20	**0.33**	0.09	0.01	0.02	0.10
M_{5a}	0.04	0.06	0.10	**0.20**	0.02	0.04	**0.13**
M_{5b}	**0.06**	0.33	**0.33**	0.08	0.02	0.03	0.01

actors returned by the employed centrality measures and evaluate them against ground-truth which we consider to correspond to the suspension of a Twitter account. Given that the suspension process is applied when an account violates Twitter rules by exhibiting abusive behavior, including posting content related to violent threats and hate speech, we consider that the suspended accounts in our dataset are likely to have exhibited such behavior. We assess the performance of the centrality measures based both on set-based and rank-based metrics. In particular, **Precision at k (P@k)** is employed as a set-based metric, whereas the **Mean Reciprocal Rank (MRR)** and the **Mean Average Precision at k (MAP@k)** are used for evaluating the ranking of the returned accounts.

Table 3. Evaluating the results of centrality measures with MAP@100

Network	Centrality measure						
	DC	BC	CC	EC	PR	ME	MEB
Retweets	0.02	0.10	0.23	0.12	0.02	0.02	0.03
Replies	**0.08**	**0.21**	**0.46**	**0.48**	**0.08**	**0.08**	**0.13**
Mentions	0.06	0.09	0.06	0.06	0.07	0.05	0.09
M_1	0.02	0.08	0.20	0.10	0.02	0.02	0.03
M_2	0.02	0.09	0.17	0.09	0.02	0.03	0.03
M_3	0.04	0.11	0.23	0.09	0.02	0.03	0.05
M_{4a}	0.02	0.07	0.37	0.11	0.02	0.05	0.10
M_{4b}	0.02	0.09	0.16	0.06	0.02	0.03	0.10
M_{5a}	0.03	0.07	0.37	0.09	0.02	0.04	0.08
M_{5b}	0.04	0.14	0.19	0.08	0.02	0.04	0.02

Tables 1, 2 and 3 present the performance of the centrality measures in terms of P@100, MRR, MAP@100, respectively. Overall, the reply-based network achieves better results in identifying suspended Twitter accounts within the top 100 key actors detected by all the centrality measures. This indicates that relying on the reply-based interactions helps uncover a large number of suspicious accounts. On the other hand, given that a single baseline network does not include all the potential information reflected by the different relationship types, we consider that the aggregation of additional such types could be beneficial.

With regards to the weighted networks derived by the proposed mapping functions, M_{5a} and M_{4a} exhibit the best performance for P@100 and MAP@100 when combined with CC, whereas the remaining mapping functions identify smaller numbers of suspended accounts. On the other hand, given that MRR focuses only on the highest ranked suspended account, an approach that detects less suspended key actors may have a larger MRR value, if a suspended account is encountered in the first ranks of the top 100. In terms of MRR, the reply-based network exhibits the best performance for BC, given that it manages to detect a suspended account at the second rank, whereas the retweet-based network, and the generated networks M_3, M_{4b}, and M_{5b} follow when combined with CC. The remaining mapping functions also manage to identify the first suspended account within their top 10 key actors for at least one centrality measure.

When examining the centrality measures of our framework, CC is the top performing metric and provides better results in terms of P@100 for replies, M_3, M_{4a}, M_{4b}, and M_{5a}. In terms of MAP@100, CC exhibits the best results for all the mapping functions and the retweet-based network. In terms of MRR, we observe a similar pattern. CC is the top performing centrality measure followed by BC and EC. In general, 13 combinations of mapping functions and centrality measures in total identify a suspended account at the top five key actor positions.

5   Conclusions

This work addressed the key actor identification task in a terrorism-related multidimensional social media network. The proposed framework employs a set of mapping functions for transforming the original multidimensional network to an equivalent weighted single-layer network, and then it applies a centrality measure for detecting the key actors on the derived network. The evaluation of our framework shows its potential to assist towards the discovery of key actors based on a number of different user interactions.

Acknowledgements. This work was supported by the TENSOR (H2020-700024) and the PROPHETS projects (H2020-786894), both funded by the European Commission.

References

1. Aparicio, S., Villazón-Terrazas, J., Álvarez, G.: A model for scale-free networks: application to twitter. Entropy **17**(8), 5848–5867 (2015)
2. Azaza, L., Kirgizov, S., Savonnet, M., Leclercq, E., Faiz, R.: Influence assessment in twitter multi-relational network. In: 2015 11th International Conference on Signal-Image Technology & Internet-Based Systems (SITIS), pp. 436–443. IEEE (2015)
3. Barabási, A.L., Albert, R.: Emergence of scaling in random networks. Science **286**(5439), 509–512 (1999)
4. Boccaletti, S., et al.: The structure and dynamics of multilayer networks. Phys. Rep. **544**(1), 1–122 (2014)
5. Bonacich, P., Lloyd, P.: Eigenvector-like measures of centrality for asymmetric relations. Soc. Netw. **23**(3), 191 (2001)
6. Brandes, U.: A faster algorithm for betweenness centrality. J. Math. Sociol. **25**(2), 163–177 (2001)
7. Brin, S., Page, L.: Reprint of: the anatomy of a large-scale hypertextual web search engine. Comput. Netw. **56**(18), 3825–3833 (2012)
8. Choudhary, P., Singh, U.: A survey on social network analysis for counter-terrorism. Int. J. Comput. Appl. **112**(9), 24–29 (2015)
9. Coscia, M.: Multidimensional network analysis. Ph. D. thesis, Universitá Degli Studi Di Pisa, Dipartimento di Informatica (2012)
10. Freeman, L.C.: Centrality in social networks conceptual clarification. Soc. Netw. **1**(3), 215–239 (1978)
11. Gialampoukidis, I., Kalpakis, G., Tsikrika, T., Papadopoulos, S., Vrochidis, S.: Kompatsiaris, I.: Detection of terrorism-related twitter communities using centrality scores. In: Proceedings of the 2nd International Workshop on Multimedia Forensics and Security, pp. 21–25. ACM (2017)
12. Gialampoukidis, I., Kalpakis, G., Tsikrika, T., Vrochidis, S., Kompatsiaris, I.: Key player identification in terrorism-related social media networks using centrality measures. In: 2016 European Intelligence and Security Informatics Conference (EISIC), pp. 112–115. IEEE (2016)
13. Jabeur, L.B., Tamine, L., Boughanem, M.: Active microbloggers: identifying influencers, leaders and discussers in microblogging networks. In: Calderón-Benavides, L., González-Caro, C., Chávez, E., Ziviani, N. (eds.) SPIRE 2012. LNCS, vol. 7608, pp. 111–117. Springer, Heidelberg (2012). https://doi.org/10.1007/978-3-642-34109-0_12

14. Li, L., Alderson, D., Doyle, J.C., Willinger, W.: Towards a theory of scale-free graphs: definition, properties, and implications. Internet Math. **2**(4), 431–523 (2005)
15. Nie, T., Guo, Z., Zhao, K., Lu, Z.M.: Using mapping entropy to identify node centrality in complex networks. Phys. A Stat. Mech. Appl. **453**, 290–297 (2016)
16. Opsahl, T., Agneessens, F., Skvoretz, J.: Node centrality in weighted networks: generalizing degree and shortest paths. Soc. Netw. **32**(3), 245–251 (2010)
17. Thompson, R.L.: Radicalization and the use of social media. J. Strat. Secur. **4**(4), 167 (2011)
18. Zhaoyun, D., Yan, J., Bin, Z., Yi, H.: Mining topical influencers based on the multi-relational network in micro-blogging sites. China Commun. **10**(1), 93–104 (2013)

Large Scale Audio-Visual Video Analytics Platform for Forensic Investigations of Terroristic Attacks

Alexander Schindler[1(✉)], Martin Boyer[1], Andrew Lindley[1], David Schreiber[1], and Thomas Philipp[2]

[1] Center for Digital Safety and Security, AIT Austrian Institute of Technology GmbH, 1210 Vienna, Austria
alexander.schindler@ait.ac.at,
http://ait.ac.at
[2] LIquA - Linzer Institut für qualitative Analysen, 4020 Linz, Austria
thomas.philipp@liqua.net,
http://liqua.net

Abstract. The forensic investigation of a terrorist attack poses a huge challenge to the investigative authorities, as several thousand hours of video footage need to be spotted. To assist law enforcement agencies (LEA) in identifying suspects and securing evidences, we present a platform which fuses information of surveillance cameras and video uploads from eyewitnesses. The platform integrates analytical modules for different input-modalities on a scalable architecture. Videos are analyzed according their acoustic and visual content. Specifically, Audio Event Detection is applied to index the content according to attack-specific acoustic concepts. Audio similarity search is utilized to identify similar video sequences recorded from different perspectives. Visual object detection and tracking are used to index the content according to relevant concepts. The heterogeneous results of the analytical modules are fused into a distributed index of visual and acoustic concepts to facilitate rapid start of investigations, following traits and investigating witness reports.

Keywords: Audio event detection · Audio similarity
Visual object detection · Large scale computing · Ethics of security
Ethics of technology

1 Introduction

The presented platform is a result of the project *Flexible, semi-automatic Analysis System for the Evaluation of Mass Video Data (FLORIDA)* and is further developed in the project *VICTORIA*. The aim of these projects is to facilitate the work of investigators after a terrorist attack. In such events investigating video data is a major resource to spot suspects and to follow hints by civilian witnesses. From past attacks it is known that confiscated and publicly provided

© Springer Nature Switzerland AG 2019
I. Kompatsiaris et al. (Eds.): MMM 2019, LNCS 11296, pp. 106–119, 2019.
https://doi.org/10.1007/978-3-030-05716-9_9

video content can sum up to thousands of hours (e.g. more than 5.000 h at the *Boston marathon bombing* attack). Being able to promptly analyze mass video data with regards to content is increasingly important for complex investigative procedures, especially for those dealing with crime scenes. Currently, this data is analyzed manually which requires hundreds or thousands of hours of investigative work. As a result, extraction of first clues from videos after an attack takes a long time. Additionally, law enforcement agencies (LEA) may not be able to process all the videos, leaving important evidence and clues unnoticed. This effort continues to increase when evidence videos of civilian witnesses are uploaded multiple times. The prompt analysis of video data, however, is fundamental – especially in the event of terrorist attacks – to prevent immediate, subsequent attacks. The goal of this platform is to provide legally compliant tools for LEAs that will increase their effectiveness in analyzing mass video data and speed up investigative work. These tools include modules for acoustic and visual analysis of the video content, where especially the audio analysis tools provide a fast entry point to an investigation because most terroristic attacks emit characteristic sound events. An investigator can start viewing videos at such events and then progress forward or backward to identify suspects and evidences.

The remainder of this work is structured as follows: Sect. 2 provides an overview of related work, Sect. 3 details the audio analysis, Sect. 4 the video analysis module and Sect. 5 the scalable platform. Section 6 summarizes the accompanying ethical research before we provide conclusions and an outlook to future work in Sect. 7.

2 Related Work

Audio Analysis: The audio analysis methods of the presented platform include modules for Audio Event Detection and Audio Similarity Retrieval. *Audio Event Detection (AED)* systems combine detection and classification of acoustic concepts. Developments in this field have recently been driven by the annual international evaluation campaign *Detection and Classification of Acoustic Scenes and Events* and its associated workshop [1]. Most recent AED approaches are based on deep convolutional neural networks [2], or recurrent convolutional neural networks [3] which can also be efficiently trained on weakly labeled data [4]. Such an approach is also taken for the AED module described in Sect. 3. *Audio Similarity* has been extensively studied especially in the research field of Music Information Retrieval (MIR) [5]. Similarity estimations are generally based on extracting audio features from the audio signal and calculating feature variations using a metric function [6]. A similar approach is followed in Sect. 3. Recent attempts to learn audio embeddings and similarity functions with neural networks has shown promising results [7].

Video Analysis: Video analytics software makes surveillance systems more efficient, by reducing the workload on security and management authorities. Computer vision problems such as image classification, object detection and object tracking have traditionally been approached using hand-engineered features and machine learning algorithms design, both of which were largely independent [8]. Over the last recent years, Deep Learning methods have been shown to out-perform previous state-of-the-art machine learning techniques, with computer vision one of the most prominent cases [9]. In contrast to previous approaches, deep neural networks (DNN) learn automatically the features required for tasks such as object detection and tracking. Among the various network architectures that were discovered and employed for computer vision tasks, the convolutional neural network (CNN) and recurrent neural network (RNN) were found to be best suitable for object classification, detection and tracking [8,9].

Large Scale Workflow Management and Information Fusion: A comprehensive overview of early work-flow management (WfMS) and business process management (BPM) systems is provided by [10]. BPM is generally concerned with describing and controlling the flow of inter-dependent tasks whereas WfMSs aim at facilitating fully automated data flow oriented work-flows which can be described through a Directed Acyclic Graph (DAG). State-of-the-art implementations of scientific DAG work-flow systems, designed to run computationally intensive tasks on large, complex and heterogeneous data, are *Taverna*[1], *Triana*[2], or *Kepler*[3]. Popular systems are *Pegasus*[4] due to its direct relation to Grid- and Cloud Computing, *Kepler* due its *Hadoop* integration as well as *Hadoop* itself. Recent developments in this area are domain specific languages, such as the functional language Cuneiform [11] offering deep integration with Apache *Hadoop* and a high flexibility in connecting with external environments. Further frameworks (languages and execution engine) derived from a Big Data context are *Pig Latin* [12] (part of the *Hadoop* Ecosystem) and Apache Spark [13] (in-memory processing framework). They are widely used in the scientific and commercial context to create work-flows for processing large data sets, but they are general purpose data analysis frameworks rather than specifically built to model work-flows. Table 1 provides an overview on selected open source DAG frameworks, classified by high level requirements that are of major importance specifically regarding audio-visual content management and archiving [14]. The fusion of heterogeneous sensor data and multi-modal analytical results is still underrepresented in literature. A system combining results from various visual-analytical components for combined visualization is presented in [15].

3 Audio Analysis

Audio analysis is one of the key components of this platform. Due to the destructive intention of a terroristic act, this often emits one or more loud acoustic events which are captured from microphones disregarding the direction the sound originates from. Besides the higher perceptive field of acoustic information, many

---

[1] https://taverna.incubator.apache.org/.
[2] http://www.trianacode.org/.
[3] https://kepler-project.org/.
[4] https://pegasus.isi.edu/.

Table 1. Overview of open source DAG work-flow systems

	Airflow[a]	Mistral[b]	Score[c]	Spiff[d]	Oozie[e]	Pinball[f]	Azkaban[g]	Luigi[h]
Workflow description language	Python, Jinja	YAML DSL	YAML	XML, JSON, Python	XML	Python	Built-in Job types, custom jobs	Python
Flow control and conditionals	NO	YES	YES	YES	NO	Minimum	NO	NO
Distributed task execution	YES	YES	YES	NO	NO	NO	NO	NO
Reliability and fault tolerance	YES	YES	YES	NO	YES	YES	YES	YES
Hadoop integration	NO	NO	NO	NO	YES	YES	YES	YES
Extensibility and integration	Utilities	Python	Python, Java	NO	NO	Pluggable Templates	Plugins	CLI integration
Planning and scheduling	YES	YES	NO	NO	YES	YES	YES	NO
Monitoring and visualization	Web-UI	NO	NO	NO	Web-UI	Web-UI	Web-UI	WF graph visualizer

[a] https://github.com/airbnb/airflow
[b] https://wiki.openstack.org/wiki/Mistral
[c] https://github.com/CloudSlang/score
[d] https://github.com/knipknap/SpiffWorkflow/wiki
[e] http://oozie.apache.org
[f] https://github.com/pinterest/pinball
[g] https://azkaban.github.io
[h] https://github.com/spotify/luigi

relevant events are non-visual or happen too fast to be captured by standard cameras (e.g. alarms, screams, gunshots). Thus, we apply audio analysis to index the video content according audible events and to provide an entry point for the investigations (Fig. 1).

Audio Event Detection: The Audio Event Detection (AED) and recognition module is intended to be one of the primary entry points for investigations. Reports by civilian witnesses often refer to acoustic events (e.g. 'there was a loud noise and then something happened'). By indexing loud noises such as explosions, investigators can immediately pre-select videos where explosions are detected. This can be extended to the type of weapon used in the attack such as gunshots emitted by firearms and horns by trucks. The developed audio event detection and recognition method is based on deep neural networks. More specifically, the approach is a combination of the models we have developed and successfully evaluated in the *Detection and Classification of Acoustic Scenes and Events (DCASE)* [16] international evaluation campaign [2,17,18], and the approach presented in [19]. The applied model uses Recurrent Convolutional Neural Networks with an attention layer. In a first step, the audio signal is extracted from the video containers, decoded and re-sampled to 44.100 Hz single channel audio. 437.588 samples (9.92 s) are used as input, which are transformed to log-scaled Mel-Spectrograms, using 80 Mel-bands and a Short-Term Fourier transformed (STFT) window size of 2048 samples with 1024 samples hop length. This preprocessing is directly performed on the GPU using the *Kapre* signal processing layer [20].

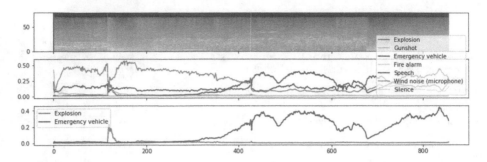

Fig. 1. Audio Event Detection example result (Bombing at Boston Marathon 2013). Top chart: Log-scaled Mel-Spectrogram of the audio signal. Middle chart: Probabilities for different acoustic events. Bottom chart: Explosion of the bomb on the left side, arrival of emergency vehicles from the center to the right of the chart.

The normalized, decibel transformed input I is processed by a rectified linear convolution layer with 240 filter kernels of shape 30×1. Using global average pooling on the feature maps, audio embeddings with 240 dimensions are learned. This transformation is applied sequentially along the temporal axis of the Mel-Spectrogram, resulting in 428 audio embeddings (one for each STFT window). This 428×240 embedding space E is used as input for a stack of three bi-directional Gated Recurrent Units (GRU) [21] followed by a rectified linear fully connected layer as well as a sigmoid fully connected layer with the number of units corresponding to the number of the to be predicted classes. A sigmoid scaled attention layer was further applied to each input frame of I which was multiplied with E as well as with the final prediction f the model. The final output of the model are probabilities for the presence for each of nine predefined sound events including *Gunshot, Explosion, Speech, Emergency vehicle* and *Fire Alarm* (see Fig. 2a). The model was trained on a preprocessed subset of the *Audioset* dataset [22]. Preprocessing contained flattening of ontological hierarchies, resolving semantic overlaps, removing out-of-context classes (e.g. Music), re-grouping of classes and a final selection of task-relevant classes.

Audio Similarity Search: Indexing videos according to predefined categories provides a fast way to start an investigation but it is limited by the type and number of classes defined and undefined events such as *train passing* cannot be detected. To overcome this obstacle and to facilitate the search for any acoustic pattern, an acoustic similarity function is added to search for videos with similar audio content. The approach to estimate the audio similarity is based on [23] where audio features are extracted, including *Statistical Spectrum Descriptors* and *Rhythm Patterns* [24], and distances are calculated between all extracted features using late fusion to merge the results. For this system, these features are extracted for each 6 s of audio content of every video file and the distances are calculated between all these features, facilitating a sub-segment similarity search. Further differences to [23] include omitting normalization by grouping features by their unit as well as using correlation distance for the *Rhythm Patterns* feature-set, which showed better performance in preceding experiments. The audio similarity search serves several goals. First, if a suspect cannot be identified in a certain video, this function can be applied to identify video segments with similar acoustic signatures such as an emergency vehicle passing by, but any other sequence of sounds could be significant as well. Further, the recorded audio signal can be used for instant localization. Similar sound patterns have been recorded in near proximity to the emitting sources and thus the result of a similarity search provides video results for a referred location (see Fig. 2a–c).

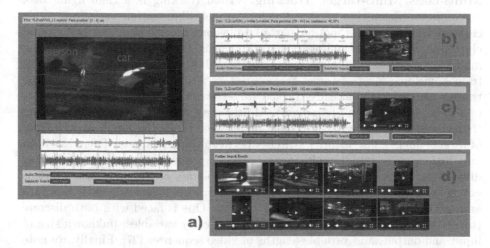

Fig. 2. Audio-visual analysis results example: (a) reference video with detected audio events *Gunshots* (green) and visual objects *Person, Car* (red bounding-box) and segment selected for similarity search (orange). (b) video containing most similar audio sequence (orange) (c) Second most similar sounding video segment (orange). (d) further relevant videos ranked by audio similarity. (Color figure online)

4   Video Analysis

Generic Object Detection and Classification. Object detection and classification identifies semantic concepts in video frames, including segmentation of the identified regions with bounding boxes and their labeling with the classified category such as *car* or *person*. This enables fast search queries that help identify specific scene content and therefore reduce the workload on law enforcement authorities. In recent years, Deep Neural Networks (DNNs) have shown outstanding performance on image detection and classification tasks, replacing disparate parts such as feature extraction, by learning semantic representations and classifiers directly from input data, including the capability to learn more complex models than traditional approaches, and powerful object representations, without the need to hand design features [9, 25]. YOLO (You Only Look Once) detector [25] is one of the most popular CNN based detection algorithms, trained on over 9000 different object categories and real-time performance capacity [25]. Evaluating different DNN based object detectors, we concluded that YOLO provides the best trade-off between accuracy and runtime behavior. The object detection module developed for the scalable forensic platform is based on the YOLO detector. It has been optimized to fit into the distributed environment and to store the results in the distributed database index. Figure 2 provides example outputs of this module.

Multi-class Multi-target Tracking. Visual tracking is a challenging task in computer vision due to target deformations, illumination variations, scale changes, fast and abrupt motion, partial occlusions, motion blur, and background clutter [26]. The task of multi-target tracking consists of simultaneously detecting multiple targets at each time frame and matching their identities in different frames, yielding a set of target trajectories over time. Given a new frame, the tracker associates the already tracked targets with the newly detected objects ("tracking-by-detection" paradigm). Multi-target tracking is more challenging than the single target case, as interaction between targets and mutual occlusions of targets might cause identity switches between similar targets. There has been only little work related to multi-target tracking, presumably due to the following difficulties: First, deep models require huge amounts of training data, which is not yet available in the case of multi-target tracking. Second, both the data and the desired solution can be quite variable. One is faced with both discrete (target labels) and continuous (position and scale) variables, unknown size of input and output, and variable lengths of video sequences [27]. Finally, we note that no neural network based trackers were yet published which handle the general multi-class multi-target case.

DNN based multi-target trackers are trained either on appearance features [26–28], or on some combination of appearance, motion and interaction features [29]. In [28], appearance-based association between targets and new objects is learned by CNNs, based on single frames. More robustly, appearance features are first learned on single frames using CNNs, and then, the long-term temporal dependencies in the sequence of observations are learned by RNNs, more precisely by Long-Short-Term-Memory (LSTM) networks [26, 29]. The jointly trained neural networks then compute the association probability for each tracked target and newly detected object. Finally, an optimization algorithm is used to find the optimal matching between targets and new objects [26, 29]. The developed system is an approach to a real-time multi-class multi-target tracking method, trained and optimized on the specific object categories needed in a forensic crime-scene and post-attack scenario investigation. Currently we employ an appearance based tracker as in [28]. Additional work in progress aims to add additional features such as targets motion and mutual interaction [29], as well as learning temporal dependencies as in [26, 29]. Due to various difficulties mentioned earlier in this section, we currently do not attempt to build and train one network for multi-class multi-target tracking. Rather, for each class, a multi-target tracker as in [28] is trained separately. During run-time, one tracker instance per class is activated, where all trackers are running in parallel. Figure 3) shows exemplary detection/tracking results for person and car classes in various typical criminal/terror scenes.

Integration within the Connected Vision Framework. The generic object detection and multi-class multi-target tracking methods are integrated in a novel framework developed by AIT, denoted as Connected Vision [30], which provides a modular, service-oriented and scalable approach allowing to process computer vision tasks in a distributed manner. The objective of Connected Vision is to create a video computation toolbox for rapid development of computer vision applications. To solve a complex computer vision task, two or more modules are combined to build a module chain. In our case, the modules are (i) video import, (ii) generic object detector, and (iii) multiple instances of a multi-target tracker, one module for each class of objects. Each Connected Vision module is an autonomous web-service that communicates via a Representational State Transfer (REST) interface, collects data from multiple sources (e.g. real-world physical sensors or other modules' outputs), processes the data according to its configuration, stores the results for later retrieval and provides them to multiple consumers. The communication protocol is designed to support live (e.g. network camera) as well as archived data (e.g. video file) to be processed.

Fig. 3. Exemplary visual detection/tracking results for person and car classes in various typical criminal/terror scenes)

5 Scalable Analysis Platform

Two of the main goals of the developed platform are (a) in the case of an attack scenario, it should be possible to probe the provided video media material (mass data) as quickly as possible and (b) Law Enforcement Agency (LEAs) investigators should gain better insight by screening the most essential material from different perspective and by focusing on specific events through the help of an integrated Scalable Analysis Platform (SAP). The FLORIDA SAP integrates the developed advanced analysis modules and performs the tasks *video data inges-tions, data preparation and preprocessing, feature extraction* and *model fitting*. These fitted analysis models are then applied to the preprocessed video content. This is implemented on an Apache Hadoop[5] platform. The analysis results are stored in an Apache HBASE[6] database with an GraphQL[7] layer on top to provide dynamic access for the clients and the visualization of the calculated results. The hardware cluster consists of seven compute nodes and a name node which acts as the orchestrator of the Cloudera Hadoop platform. The underlying commodity hardware (HW) consists of Dell R320 rack servers, Xeon® CPU, E5-2430, 2.2 GHz with 6 cores/12 threads each and about 63 GB of available RAM and a storage capacity of 11TB of disk space (HDD) per data node. Server administration, cluster configuration, update management as well as software distribution on the nodes is automated via Ansible[8]. Tasks for rolling out the Zookeeper, Hive or HBASE configuration, distributing the /etc/hotsts files as well as installing the audio and video feature extraction tools and their software dependencies (such as Python scripts, Linux packages as ffmpeg and libraries as TensorFlow) are specified in the YAML syntax. ToMaR [31] is a generic MapReduce wrapper for third-party command-line and Java applications that were not originally designed for the usage in an HDFS environment. It supports tools that read input based on local file pointers or stdin/stdout streams uses control-files to specify individual jobs. The wrapper integrates the applications in such a way that the required files for execution on the respectively integrated worker nodes (nodes 0..5) are locally copied into the Hadoop cache from HDFS and the application can thus be executed in parallel to the number of active nodes and the results are then written back to HDFS. The individual components (ToMaR jobs, shell scripts for import of JSON data into and generation of HBASE tables via HIVE, etc.) are combined into master workflows using Apache Oozie Workflow Scheduler for Hadoop[9] and event triggers. (see Fig. 4) This requires the setup of ZooKeeper for handling failover or orchestration of the components. In order to execute Hive and HBase in a distributed environment, Hadoop must be executed in Fully Distributed Mode and requires the setup a so-called metastore for state information on Hive and Oozie for Hadoop. ZooKeeper is set up in the SAP as ZooKeeper ensemble on node node2, node5, and the master name node.

6   Accompanying Ethical Research

The FLORIDA project is part of KIRAS, an Austrian research promotion program managed by the Austrian Research Promotion Agency (FFG), the national funding agency for industrial research and development in Austria. In KIRAS

---

[5] http://hadoop.apache.org/.
[6] https://hbase.apache.org/.
[7] https://graphql.org/.
[8] Ansible https://www.ansible.com/.
[9] http://oozie.apache.org/.

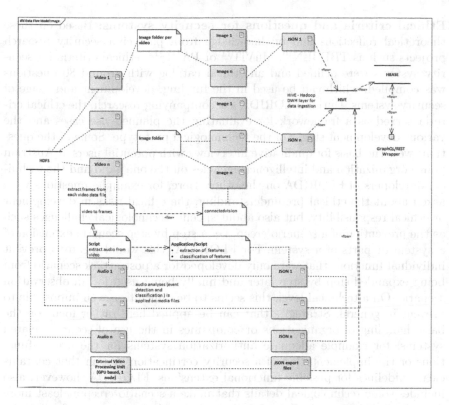

Fig. 4. Data flow model of the FLORIDA scalable analytics platform

projects, an integrative approach is mandatory, which is based not only on technological solutions but also on a social science and humanities approach. For this reason, in FLORIDA accompanying ethical research are conducted.

Ethics of security and ethics of technology: On the background of fundamental ethical principles, analyses in FLORIDA primarily focus on ethics of security and ethics of technology, but also include other ethical subdivisions, e.g. data, information, Internet and media ethics. In the context of security ethics questions about the 'right' or 'wrong' use of a certain security technology are reflected upon, for example by asking about the concept of security used, by linking security actions back to the question of 'good living' and by pointing out alternative options for actions that include comprehensive social and societal responsibility. [32] By taking technical ethics into account the focus is directed to the ethical reflection of conditions, purposes, means and consequences of technology and scientific-technical progress. [33] This leads to questions relating to fundamental ethical principles such as security or freedom, but also to the choice, responsibility or compatibility of used technology: 'Is the chosen technology good?', 'Is the chosen technology safe?' or 'What are the consequences of using this technology?'

Ethical criteria and questions for security systems: Based on these theoretical reflections and on knowledge from past civil security research projects such as THEBEN[10], MuViT[11] or PARIS[12], ethical criteria for security systems were defined and an ethical catalog with around 80 questions was compiled, which can be used in the funding, development and usage of security systems. During FLORIDA's accompanying research, the ethical criteria served as a framework for evaluating the planned use cases and the various development stages of the technological prototype. Some of the questions were the basis for qualitative interviews with potential users at Austrian police organization and intelligence agencies on the one hand and the technical developers of FLORIDA on the other. Here, for example, questions were asked about the ethical pre-understanding, the ethical risks in development or ethical responsibility, but also about specific technological challenges such as the prevention of a scenario creep, i.e. a step by step scenario extension of a system or parts of a system. For FLORIDA, this would mean to prevent individual functions that were only developed for a post-attack scenario from being expanded step by step later and finally being used for an observation scenario. On a technical level, this seems to be difficult or even impossible to prevent in general. Strategies that can be applied here rather focus on the basic handling of organizations or companies in the use of security-related systems, for example adequate authorization systems for the use of functions or the implementation of a security certification system that contains clear guidelines for possible functional extensions. FLORIDA, however, also includes some technological details that make a scenario creep at least more difficult. To give an example: In the audio analysis only predefined audio events are classified and implemented that can occur during attacks (e.g. shots, sirens or detonations) and the system is trained with them. This function of FLORIDA is therefore useful for a specific scenario like terror attacks, while it remains largely useless in other scenarios like an observation. Moreover, subsequent adaptations are difficult to carry out because complex and time-consuming learning processes are what make the functionality of audio analysis possible here.

---

[10] THEBEN (Terahertz Detection Systems: Ethical Monitoring, Evaluation and Determination of Standards) was a research project 10-2007 to 12-2010) within the framework of the program for civil security research in Germany: https://www.uni-tuebingen.de/en/11265.

[11] MuViT (Mustererkennung und Video-Tracking) was a research project (10-2007 to 12-2010) within the framework of the program for civil security research in Germany: http://www.uni-tuebingen.de/de/49647.

[12] PARIS (PrivAcy pReserving Infrastructure for Surveillance) was a research project (01-2013 to 02-2016) with partners from France, Belgium and Austria, funded by the 7th Framework Program for Research and Technological Development: https://www.paris-project.org/.

7   Conclusions and Future Work

The described platform integrates audio-visual analysis modules on a scalable platform and enables a fast start and rapid progress of investigations with the audio event detection module serving as a fast entry point. From these events, investigators can navigate through the video content, by either using the visual tracking modules on identified persons or objects, or use the audio similarity search to find related video content, increasing the chances for identification.

As part of future work we intend to focus on *Audio Synchronization,* because time information provided with video meta-data can not be considered accurate if the capturing equipment is not synchronized with a unified time-server. Personal cameras for example commonly reset their internal clock to a hard-coded time-stamp after complete battery drain. To align video content with unreliable time information, audio synchronization is applied. Audio features sensitive to peaking audio events are applied to extract patterns which are significant for a recorded acoustic scene. These patterns are then matched by minimizing the difference of their feature values over sliding windows. To find clusters of mutually synchronous videos, audio similarity retrieval is combined with audio synchronization. Finally, mutual offsets are calculated between the videos of a cluster which are used to schedule synchronous playback of the videos.

Acknowledgements. This article has been made possible partly by received funding from the European Union's Horizon 2020 research and innovation program in the context of the VICTORIA project under grant agreement no. SEC-740754 and the project FLORIDA, FFG Kooperative F&E Projekte 2015, project no. 854768.

References

1. Giannoulis, D., Benetos, E., Stowell, D., Rossignol, M., Lagrange, M., Plumbley, M.D.: Detection and classification of acoustic scenes and events: An IEEE AASP challenge. In: 2013 IEEE Workshop on Applications of Signal Processing to Audio and Acoustics (WASPAA), pp. 1–4. IEEE (2013)
2. Thomas, L., Schindler, A.: CQT-based convolutional neural networks for audio scene classification. In: Proceedings of the Detection and Classification of Acoustic Scenes and Events 2016 Workshop (DCASE 2016), pp. 60–64, September 2016
3. Adavanne, S., Parascandolo, G., Pertilä, P., Heittola, T., Virtanen, T.: Sound event detection in multichannel audio using spatial and harmonic features. Technical report, DCASE2016 Challenge, September 2016
4. Kukanov, I., Hautamäki, V., Lee, K.A.: Recurrent neural network and maximal figure of merit for acoustic event detection. Technical report, DCASE2017 Challenge (2017)
5. Knees, P., Schedl, M.: Music Similarity and Retrieval: An Introduction to Audio- and Web-based Strategies, vol. 36. Springer, Heidelberg (2016). https://doi.org/10.1007/978-3-662-49722-7
6. Pampalk, E., Flexer, A., Widmer, G., et al.: In: Improvements of audio-based music similarity and genre classificaton. In: ISMIR, London, UK, vol. 5, pp. 634–637 (2005)

7. Kim, J., Urbano, J., Liem, C., Hanjalic, A.: One deep music representation to rule them all?: A comparative analysis of different representation learning strategies. arXiv preprint arXiv:1802.04051 (2018)
8. Srinivas, S., Sarvadevabhatla, R.K., Mopuri, K.R.: A taxonomy of deep convolutional neural netwprks for computer vision (2016)
9. Voulodimos, A., Doulamis, N., Doulamis, A., Protopapadakis, E.: Deep learning for computer vision: a brief review. Comput. Intell. Neurosci. **2018**, 1–13 (2018). Article ID 7068349
10. Xu, L.D.: Enterprise systems: state-of-the-art and future trends. IEEE Trans. Ind. Inform. **7**(4), 630–640 (2011)
11. Brandt, J., Bux, M., Leser, U.: Cuneiform: a functional language for large scale scientific data analysis. In: EDBT/ICDT Workshops (2015)
12. Olston, C., Reed, B., Srivastava, U., Kumar, R., Tomkins, A.: Pig latin: a not-so-foreign language for data processing. In: Proceedings of International Conference on Management of Data (SIGMOD 2008), pp. 1099–1110. ACM (2008)
13. Zaharia, M., Mosharaf Chowdhury, N.M., Franklin, M., Shenker, S., Stoica, I.: Spark: cluster computing with working sets. Technical Report UCB/EECS-2010-53, EECS Department, University of California, Berkeley, May 2010
14. Nadarajan, G., Chen-Burger, Y.-H., Malone, J.: Semantic-based workflow composition for video processing in the grid. In: 2006 IEEE/WIC/ACM International Conference on Web Intelligence (WI 2006 Main Conference Proceedings) (WI 2006), pp. 161–165 (2006)
15. Fan, C.T., Wang, Y.K., Huang, C.R.: Heterogeneous information fusion and visualization for a large-scale intelligent video surveillance system. IEEE Trans. Syst. Man Cybern. Syst. **47**(4), 593–604 (2017)
16. Mesaros, A., Heittola, T., Virtanen, T.: Tut database for acoustic scene classification and sound event detection. In: 24th European Signal Processing Conference (EUSIPCO) (2016)
17. Schindler, A., Lidy, T., Rauber, A.: Comparing shallow versus deep neural network architectures for automatic music genre classification. In: 9th Forum Media Technology (FMT 2016), vol. 1734, pp. 17–21. CEUR (2016)
18. Schindler, A., Lidy, T., Rauber, A.: Multi-temporal resolution convolutional neural networks for acoustic scene classification. In: Detection and Classification of Acoustic Scenes and Events Workshop (DCASE 2017), Munich, Germany (2017)
19. Xu, Y., Kong, Q., Huang, Q., Wang, W., Plumbley, M.D.: Attention and localization based on a deep convolutional recurrent model for weakly supervised audio tagging. arXiv preprint arXiv:1703.06052 (2017)
20. Choi, K., Joo, D., Kim, J.: Kapre: On-GPU audio preprocessing layers for a quick implementation of deep neural network models with keras. In: Machine Learning for Music Discovery Workshop at 34th International Conference on Machine Learning. ICML (2017)
21. Chung, J., Gulcehre, C., Cho, K., Bengio, Y.: Empirical evaluation of gated recurrent neural networks on sequence modeling. arXiv preprint arXiv:1412.3555 (2014)
22. Gemmeke, J.F., et al.: Audio set: an ontology and human-labeled dataset for audio events. In: 2017 IEEE International Conference on Acoustics, Speech and Signal Processing (ICASSP), pp. 776–780. IEEE (2017)
23. Schindler, A., Gordea, S., van Biessum, H.: The europeana sounds music information retrieval pilot. In: Ioannides, M., et al. (eds.) EuroMed 2016. LNCS, vol. 10059, pp. 109–117. Springer, Cham (2016). https://doi.org/10.1007/978-3-319-48974-2_13

24. Lidy, T., Rauber, A., Pertusa, A., Quereda, J.M.I.: Improving genre classification by combination of audio and symbolic descriptors using a transcription systems. In: Proceedings of International Conference on Music Information Retrieval (2007)
25. Redmon, J., Farhadi, A.: YOLO9000: better, faster, stronger. In Proceedings of the IEEE Conference on Computer Vision and Pattern Recognition (CVPR), July 2017
26. Ning, G., Zhang, Z., Huang, C., He, Z., Ren, X., Wang, H.: Spatially supervised recurrent convolutional neural networks for visual object tracking (2016)
27. Milan, A., Rezatofighi, S.H., Dick, A., Reid, I., Schindler, K.: Online multi-target tracking using recurrent neural netwroks (2016)
28. Wojke, N., Bewley, A., Paulus, D.: Simple online and realtime tracking with deep association metric (2017)
29. Wojke, N., Bewley, A., Paulus, D.: Tracking the untrackable: learning to track multiple cues with long-term dependencies. In: CVPR (2017)
30. Boyer, M., Veigl, S.: A distributed system for secure, modular computer vision. In: Proceedings of Future Security 2014 9th Future Security Security Research Conference, Berlin, 16–18 September 2014, pp. 696–699 (2014)
31. Schmidt, R., Rella, M., Schlarb, S.: ToMaR–a data generator for large volumes of content. In: 14th IEEE/ACM International Symposium on Cluster, Cloud and Grid Computing, pp. 937–942 (2014)
32. Rampp, B.: Zum Konzept der Sicherheit. In: Ammicht Quinn, R. (ed.) Sicherheit-sethik. Studien zur Inneren Sicherheit, vol. 16, pp. 51–61. Springer VS, Wiesbaden (2014). https://doi.org/10.1007/978-3-658-03203-6_2
33. Grunwald, A.: Einleitung und Überblick. In: Grunwald, A., Simonidis-Puschmann, M. (eds.) Handbuch Technikethik, pp. 1–11. J.B. Metzler, Stuttgart (2013). https://doi.org/10.1007/978-3-476-05333-6_1

A Semantic Knowledge Discovery Framework for Detecting Online Terrorist Networks

Andrea Ciapetti[1], Giulia Ruggiero[1], and Daniele Toti[1,2(✉)] (iD)

[1] Innovation Engineering S.r.l., Rome, Italy
{a.ciapetti,g.ruggiero,d.toti}@innovationengineering.eu
[2] Department of Sciences, Roma Tre University, Rome, Italy

Abstract. This paper presents a knowledge discovery framework, with the purpose of detecting terrorist presence in terms of potential suspects and networks on the open and Deep Web. The framework combines information extraction methods and tools and natural language processing techniques, together with semantic information derived from social network analysis, in order to automatically process online content coming from disparate sources and identify people and relationships that may be linked to terrorist activities. This framework has been developed within the context of the DANTE Horizon 2020 project, as part of a larger international effort to detect and analyze terrorist-related content from online sources and help international police organizations in their investigations against crime and terrorism.

Keywords: Natural language processing · Knowledge discovery
Group discovery · Ontology building · Named entity recognition

1 Introduction

Nowadays, terrorists and criminal organizations have been increasingly taking advantage of the Internet in order to spread their message and gain support all over the world, by indeed using the Web as their main communication tool for a variety of purposes, ranging from recruitment and propaganda, to disinformation, fund raising, management, planning, and so forth. In the latest years, terrorist groups like Al-Qaeda and its affiliates, as well as other terrorist organizations, have rapidly moved their online presence to public portals and social networks like YouTube, Twitter, Facebook, Instagram and similar social media, either on the surface Web or on the Deep Web and Dark nets. On one hand, this poses novel and additional challenges to agencies devoted to counter terrorism, given the huge, widespread, and often uncontrollable nature of these online places. On the other hand, however, this may also bring about further opportunities to detect and monitor criminals, by resorting to methodological and technological advancements in the research fields of computer science tackling the processing and analysis of Big Data and the social networks themselves.

© Springer Nature Switzerland AG 2019
I. Kompatsiaris et al. (Eds.): MMM 2019, LNCS 11296, pp. 120–131, 2019.
https://doi.org/10.1007/978-3-030-05716-9_10

   As a matter of fact, in order to promptly address such challenges, it has become urgent and paramount to put appropriate countermeasures in place, so that to enable Law Enforcement Agencies (LEAs) and intelligence officials to continuously monitor in near real-time the relevant online communications and contents, both in the open/surface Web and in the Deep Web; within the latter, there is a deluge of data (estimates tell that they amount to more than 95% of the available data on the whole Internet) not always indexed by automated search engines, but potentially providing useful contents and information for detecting and fighting criminal activities. Indeed, significant sections of the WWW 2.0 and WWW 3.0 contents are often protected by registration and thus not indexed by search engines.

   This work describes a knowledge discovery framework aimed at detecting potential suspects, groups and their affiliates by processing and analyzing the information coming from the interactions taking place within the context of social networks. This framework combines Natural Language Processing methods and techniques meant to find relevant mentions of people (potentially under scrutiny by LEAs) among textual content published and shared online, with mechanisms to crawl and analyze their corresponding social network accounts in order to detect the relationships between those people and other users according to their mutual online interactions. This is a component making up a larger framework for detecting and analyzing terrorist and crime-related online content that is being developed within the context of the EU-funded DANTE Horizon 2020 project, and has the purpose of discovering either new terrorist/criminal subjects/groups or people who are about to be radicalized and to become as such.

   This paper is structured as follows. In Sect. 2, related work is discussed and the DANTE project is introduced. Section 3 describes the knowledge discovery framework with its two main components, namely the Natural Language Processing pipeline and the Group Discovery module. Section 4 reports the application scenario within which the framework has been used so far. Finally, in Sect. 5, conclusions are drawn.

2   Context and Related Work

Several research studies have shown that Complex Networks modeling real-world phenomena are characterized by striking properties: (i) they are organized according to community structure, and (ii) their structure evolves over time. Many researchers have worked on methods that can effectively unveil substructures in complex networks, giving birth to the field of community and group discovery. A novel and fascinating problem has recently begun to capture the researchers' interest: the identification of evolving communities. Dynamic networks can be used to model the evolution of a system: nodes and edges are mutable and their presence, or absence, deeply affects the community structure that makes them up. This work has the purpose of presenting the distinctive features and challenges of dynamic group discovery, using state-of-the-art methodologies. Complex Networks [8] are popular tools—both theoretical and analytical—commonly used to describe and analyze interaction phenomena that occur in the real world. Socialites formation, face-to-face communication, or the unfolding of human mobility are a few examples of observable events that are often investigated using instruments borrowed from Graph Theory. A major issue to address while studying such real-world events lies in the identification of meaningful substructures hidden within the overall complex system. How to partition a complex network into communities is a widely studied problem [4,5]: several works, from a broad set of disciplines, proposed different community definitions and approaches able to retrieve such structures automatically. The magnitude of papers that cover this fascinating topic highlights its ubiquity: communities can capture groups of strongly connected online documents, individuals sharing a social environment as well as products being frequently purchased together. Most of the scientific literature dedicated to the community discovery problem start from a very stringent assumption: real-world phenomena can be modeled with static networks, *i.e.*, mathematical objects "frozen" in time. Unfortunately, such simplified scenario does not fit the evolving nature of the world we live in and the specific challenge faced in the DANTE project to reconstruct only occasionally connected and often elusive terrorist groups.

DANTE (Detecting and ANalysing TErrorist-related online contents and financing activities - project id: 700367) is an ongoing innovation project funded by the European Community under the Horizon 2020 grant framework (H2020-FCT-2015 call). DANTE's ultimate goal is to discover, analyze and monitor potential terrorist-related activities and people, with a focus on online fund raising, propaganda, training and communication/interaction activities.

Indeed, one of the key features that characterize interaction phenomena is that they naturally unfold through time: social interactions evolve and explicit group affiliation changes as time goes by. The temporal dimension conveys highly valuable information that an analyst needs to exploit to better understand the observed reality. The need to include such knowledge in the tools offered by graph theory has been one of the linchpins in an entirely new field of investigation that emerged in the last decade: dynamic network analysis. Several formalisms have been proposed to represent evolving networks without loss of information: Temporal Networks [6], Time-Varying Graphs [2], Interaction Networks [9], Link Streams and Stream graphs [7,13], to name the most popular. The perfect Community Discovery algorithm probably does not exist. In DANTE, an algorithm has been chosen that performs better on the specific declination of the general problem of interest: the representation of loosely coupled communities on dynamic graphs, which is very effective to make the interactions between each member of the group and the lifecycle of the community clear.

3   Knowledge Discovery Framework

This section describes the knowledge discovery framework for detecting potential suspects and groups from social media interactions, thus meant to bring about a dynamic community graph upon which a number of subsequent operations and reasoning could be applied.

This framework, as briefly mentioned earlier, is made up of two major components: a Natural Language Processing pipeline, meant to detect social mentions within textual contents, and a Group Discovery module, whose purpose is to detect corresponding relationships between the people mentioned and those with whom they interact across social media. Figure 1 shows the overall architecture of the framework, displaying these two components with all of their sub-modules. Further details about the latter can be found in the next paragraphs.

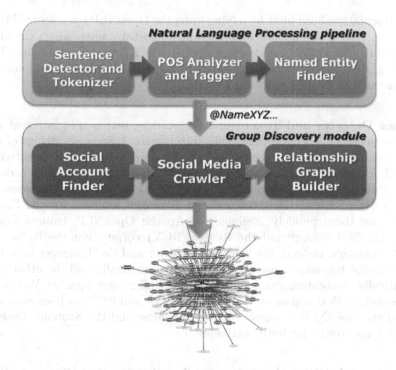

Fig. 1. Architecture of the knowledge discovery framework.

3.1 Natural Language Processing Pipeline

The very first step in order to perform a group discovery process is the retrieving of a social mention in textual snippets extracted from the Social Media (Facebook, Twitter and Google+ mainly).

The Social Media mentions and hashtags detector is specifically designed to identify mentions and hashtags by applying natural language analyses combined with appropriate regular expressions to the selected text. A set of statistical NLP (Natural Language Processing) analyzers, based on Maximum Entropy and Hidden Markov models, is employed in order to provide various types of semantic analysis on textual contents. The statistical NLP module is a machine learning based toolkit that supports the most common NLP tasks, such as tokenization, sentence segmentation, Part-of-Speech tagging, named entity extraction, chunking, parsing, and coreference resolution.

The pipeline used for this task is made up of the following modules, whose details are reported in the following paragraphs:

- Sentence Detector and Tokenizer;
- Part-Of-Speech (POS) Analyzer and Tagger;
- Named Entity Finder.

Such a pipeline has been built by relying upon the OpenNLP open source library by Apache [1]. The library has been used as a substrate upon which the aforementioned modules have been developed, where the former's functionalities have been integrated into custom algorithms and rules to complement and enhance them for the framework's purposes accordingly.

Sentence Detector and Tokenizer. The starting text is split into sentences and every sentence is subsequently split into tokens. Tokens are strings of contiguous characters between two spaces, or between a space and punctuation marks. A learnable Tokenizer based on maximum entropy is used in order to detect token boundaries according to a probability model. The corresponding models for the Sentence Detector and the Tokenizer modules for the English language are those publicly available for Apache OpenNLP, trained against the CoNLL 2003 dataset and the Reuters RCV1 corpus. For the Italian and Spanish languages, instead, the Sentence Detector and the Tokenizer have been trained against two large annotated corpora, one manually and the other semi-automatically annotated, extracted from the Italian and Spanish Wikipedia, each containing 1500 sentences. A precision of 99% and 98% has been estimated by using the OpenNLP evaluator for the Tokenizer and the Sentence Detector modules, respectively, for both languages.

Part Of Speech (POS) Analyzer and Tagger. The Part-Of-Speech (POS) Analyzer and Tagger marks tokens with their corresponding word type based on the token itself and the context of the token. To train the POS Analyzer and Tagger model a tag dictionary has been defined, fit for the Italian language, which is a subset of the Tanl tag dictionary, *i.e.* a standard tag set implementation compliant with the EAGLES international standards. To test the accuracy of the POS Analyzer and Tagger model for the Italian and Spanish languages, a "uniform" test corpus has been used, taken from the corresponding versions of Wikipedia (but completely unrelated to the training corpus). An accuracy of 97.6% and 97.3% has been estimated for the POS Analyzer and Tagger by using the OpenNLP evaluator for the Italian and Spanish languages, respectively.

Named Entity Finder. The Named Entity Finder module is able to detect named entities (persons or organizations) and places or locations inside the text. To be able to detect entities the Named Entity Finder module has been trained on large collections of textual snippets containing names of well-known places and persons for each language to support (English, Italian and Spanish are currently fully supported by the analyzers) and entity type to detect. Furthermore, specific dictionaries featuring names of known criminals or terrorists have been included as well. The experimentation has been carried out against the `eng.testb` set of the CoNLL 2003 corpus. This corpus is mainly made up of news articles related to sports, economics and international conflicts. The results of such an experimentation is reported in Table 1. Additional named entities not featured in the original annotations but found by the module are reported in Table 2.

Table 1. Results for the Named Entity Finder against the CoNLL 2003 corpus.

	Recall	Precision	F-measure	# recall	# precision
LOC	80.92%	88.83%	84.65%	1553	1378
PER	97.25%	94.03%	95.61%	2697	2536
ORG	51.10%	41.00%	45.55%	1273	522

Table 2. Additional named entities found by the Named Entity Finder with respect to the CoNLL 2003 corpus.

LOC	89
PER	124
ORG	233

The standard Named Entity Finder has been extended to make it able to find social media mentions and hashtags. Every token marked with a specific POS tag is checked under an appropriate set of regular expressions and, in case of a positive match, the result is used to extend the NER span. For this additional function a precision of about 98% has been detected.

3.2   Group Discovery Module

Social Account Finder. By relying upon the results of the Natural Language Processing pipeline in terms of a number of entities (mentions), the first sub-module of the Group Discovery module retrieves additional information related to each of the mentions. This information may include the full name of the person mentioned, as well as a number of social profiles on a number of social networks associated with it.

Social Media Crawler. This sub-module is responsible of retrieving public posts and messages from the social network accounts/profiles as detected by the Social Account Finder for a given person mentioned, via the APIs of their corresponding social networks.

Relationship Graph Builder. Once the information coming from the given social networks is retrieved by the aforementioned sub-modules and is available for processing, the Relationship Graph Builder sub-module comes into play. This component is in fact responsible of gathering the information retrieved for a given person (in terms of people/users who mentioned him/her, who commented on his/her posts, placed some "likes" or similarly reacted to those posts, shared or forwarded them, etc.) and use it to build a semantic graph representing the explicit relationships between such a person and other social network subscribers.

In this regard, this semantic graph is an ontological instance defined via the RDF/RDFS/OWL formalisms [14–16] and possesses the following characteristics:

- the `owl:Class` is used to represent the concepts of Person and User;
- the given person whose relationships are to be detected is represented as an instance of `owl:Thing` and is the central node of the ontological graph;
- users/people connected to the person under scrutiny are represented as instances of `owl:Thing` as well;
- relationships linking together those users with the given person are represented as specific properties (*e.g.*, `hasBeenMentionedBy`, `hasBeenLikedBy`, etc.). A single edge is produced for each user and each kind of relationship (*e.g.*, if User A has mentioned Person X a certain number of times, one `hasBeenMentionedBy` relationship is produced from Person X to User A).
- the "strength" of those relationships, *i.e.*, how many times a user has liked, commented, mentioned, etc. the person under scrutiny, given the representation as single edges chosen above, is described via the reification mechanism with the `rdf:Statement` constructs, allowing the assignment of attributes to the produced properties.

The ontological graph defined as above is produced via a mechanism derived from the construction of the semantic graph featured in [12], and is then visualized via the Cytoscape library [3] used for the same purposes both in [12] and [11]. Examples of the output can be found in Sect. 4.

In this regard, the choice of representing dynamic community graphs as full-fledged ontologies as described so far is at least two-fold. On one hand, in fact, the simplicity and expressiveness of the ontological formalism employed enables these graphs to be effectively used as conceptualization models that are clearly understandable by real-world users; on the other hand, their intrinsic, standards-compliant characteristics allows them to be easily processed by unmanned systems. Besides, due to their very nature, they can be mutually interconnected or extended by interlinking them with other semantic models, and a wide range of graph theory-based and reasoning algorithms can be applied upon them to discover additional and potentially hidden knowledge behind them (including those from recently-arisen research fields like semantic social network analysis for people and organizations).

4 Application Scenario

An essential part of terrorist practices that is paramount for further developing their activities is indeed training. In this regard, it is imperative for LEAs to detect training and knowledge sharing activities from online sources. As a matter of fact, one of DANTE's ultimate objectives lies in the monitoring, detection and identification of the training activities that take place within terrorist organizations. Since online sites are becoming increasingly popular for terrorists in order to demonstrate their skill set and to introduce new radicalized persons into the practices of their organizations, there is a high level of difficulty in detecting those actions online. Training content often lies in Dark Nets and Deep Web (aside from the content already publicly available on the Open Web), and it is indeed a challenging task to detect the organizations posting the training content, as well as to identify the terrorists involved behind the published training material. The knowledge discovery framework described in Sect. 3 has been experimented upon within this context, with the purpose of helping address the difficulties regarding the source and group discovery behind the online presence of people and the content they share or discuss on social networks.

4.1 The Lone Wolf

As known to everyone, after the defeat of the ISIS organization on the field, the episodes of international terrorism have been changing their nature and character, turning from events planned by very organized groups of terrorist cells, infiltrated in the European countries and throughout the West, into episodes in which even a single person, often not tied to specific groups or known cells, organizes an attack using improvised weapons and means. Usually, those so-called "lone wolves" do not try to hit specific targets, politicians or symbolic places, but masses and groups of people, often during public events with many participants. This transformation, if on one hand often leads to face individual people or groups of aggressors much less organized, on the other hand becomes even more difficult to prevent with actions of intelligence and pre-emptive intervention. In fact, the typical figure to be faced now for the counter-terrorism organizations is the very one mentioned above, the "lone wolf", a person who, due to strong social or personal unease or discomfort, has progressively or even suddenly approached extremist propaganda contents and materials on the Internet and has been "captured" by their instigations to revenge against the so-called unbelievers. Typically, after that, the "early radicalized" person obsessively seeks and finds training contents—on public sources (Open Web) or on forums and other private chats or discussion groups (Deep Web), or even on private nets, not publicly accessible (Dark Nets)—which teach how to find funds and materials, in order to organize terrorist acts in the simplest possible way, like homicidal actions or devastations, involving as many people as possible. It is therefore extremely important for the LEAs, in trying to prevent such dramatic situations, to identify such online documents (or real guides, as is the case of the *"How To Survive in the West"* handbook or of the *"Manual of the Terrorist"*).

The difficulty here is that various copies of the same contents exist and have been spread on the Internet. Thus, the LEAs need a tool able to monitor access to these contents by users or social accounts, in order to quickly discover people that are in the phase of "early radicalization", track them and their contacts on social networks and act promptly with repressive actions, so as to prevent the occurrence of the planned terrorist attacks.

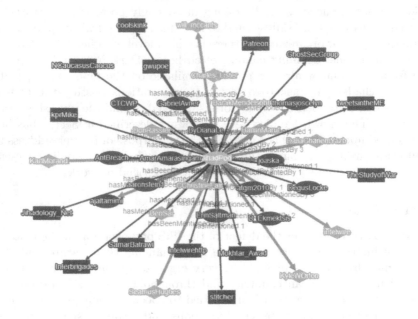

Fig. 2. Graph produced from the analysis of a known Twitter account potentially spreading Jihad-related messages over the Web. The thickness of the edges reflect their importance in terms of the number of times the corresponding action has been performed by the user (# times commented, # times mentioned, etc.), with a color emphasis ranging from blue (minimum) to red (maximum). The person under scrutiny is represented as the grey central node of the graph, whereas users who commented on his Tweets are represented as purple ellipses, users who mentioned him are depicted as cyan rhombi, and users who have been mentioned by him are depicted as red rectangles; users who both commented and mentioned are represented as purple ellipses (comments have priority in this representation). (Color figure online)

4.2   The Role of the Knowledge Discovery Framework

In this application scenario, obviously, the knowledge discovery framework plays a fundamental role for the LEAs, as it allows the investigators to view and discover with an almost completely automated tool the relationships that exist among suspicious users or accounts on the current social networks, ranging from Twitter to Facebook, or on the most popular messaging tools of the moment,

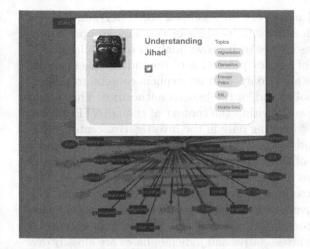

Fig. 3. The card showing the details of a given user, named "Understanding Jihad", including its social profiles and related topics.

Fig. 4. Picture posted as part of the #We_Are_Coming_O_Rome 2015 Twitter campaign.

namely Telegram. The contents examined by the framework include publicly available resources, in PDF or HTML format, like the manuals and handbooks cited previously (Open Web), the public and private posts downloaded from specific social accounts (Deep Web) and some resources, collected from Freenet and other private nets, with appropriate crawlers (Dark nets).

Through an intelligent usage of the underlying sub-modules described in Sect. 3, the framework attempts to identify the social relationships existing between a suspected individual or group, perhaps the author of one or more training contents for "aspiring" terrorists, and the network of contacts gravitating around the given account. The existence of links and correlations are examined within a specified time interval, and the resulting graph takes into account the variability over time of the relationships, showing with a different thickness and color the edges of the stronger and more persistent relationships. Very interesting for the investigators is the ability of the framework to show a graphical representation of this networks in a graph format, with different colored shapes for each type of existing connection (see Fig. 2), and to enable an intuitive navigation of the graph itself. In fact, it is possible to move from a potentially suspicious account to another; in addition, the analysis carried out in background enables the framework to present, for each node, a sheet containing the list of accounts detected for the same person on other social networks, as well as a photo of the given person. Furthermore, a list of "topics" representing the concepts featured with greater frequency in the person's social posts is also provided. Figure 3 shows the "social" card and the photo of a social account named "*Understanding Jihad*" (a public Twitter account) and its social relationships with other users who have expressed appreciation for the posts published by this account, have mentioned it in some messages or were mentioned by it somewhere. On different social network, *e.g.*, Facebook and Telegram, different correlations are examined, such as likes, friendships or common groups.

Obviously, for enabling these types of invasive analysis on a social profile, an exception to the principles of privacy protection of the individuals is needed and this derogation can be obtained only with an explicit consent to proceed provided by the investigative police and/or the judicial authorities. That is why the knowledge discovery framework, within the context of the DANTE project, is currently undergoing advanced testing only in the investigative centers of the "Ayuntamiento de Madrid" and of the Portuguese "Policia Judiciaria", and it is not possible for the authors of this paper to access details or statistics of the social profiles examined with this instrument or of the success rate achieved in the identification of suspects or persons connected to known terrorist accounts. This is especially true for ongoing investigations, whose progresses and partial results are accessible only to investigators. For this reason, the example presented below is related to a past event whose investigative and judicial phases are already over and have been archived.

Twitter Propaganda. In 2015, the Twitter account @OmarJohnDeep506 was opened by two people without any criminal records who had been living in Italy for the past eight years, Muhammad Waqas and Lassaad Briki. This account posted 230 tweets; it was closed afterwards. Then, another account, @homar_moktar2 was opened, and posted around 50 tweets. From the analysis of the network of the latter via the knowledge discovery framework, a Twitter account named @Islamic_State_in_Rom was found. From this account the #We_Are_Coming_O_Rome campaign was launched, posting several photos that included messages such as "*We are in your streets. We are everywhere. We are localizing the objectives, waiting for the zero hour*" and similar contents (*e.g.*, Fig. 4) were published. They were written in slips of paper (in Arabic, French and Italian) with the background of typical Italian places or points of interest (mostly from Rome and Milan). 18 tweets were posted by 15 users in response to the campaign immediately after its launch; such users were discovered by the knowledge discovery framework as part of the account's contact network and thus deemed related to terrorist propaganda activities. Eventually, the two original users were arrested and sentenced to six years in prison and subsequent expulsion from Italy.

5 Conclusion

This paper presented a knowledge discovery framework for detecting potential terrorist and criminal suspects from their interactions on online social networks with people of interest or under scrutiny by Law Enforcement Agencies. This framework has been developed within the DANTE project and is being currently tested by two Law Enforcement Agencies as a support tool in their investigations against crime and terrorism. Potential enhancements of this framework that are being considered include the possibility of using further natural language processing techniques (exploiting for instance the methods described in [10,12]) in order to conceptualize textual messages and documents exchanged online and use the corresponding results to detect non-explicit, hidden relationships among online users. Besides, the approach implemented in this framework could be in principle applied to other application scenarios, including those related to the identification of hate-speech and hate spreaders over the Web.

Acknowledgments. The work presented in this paper was supported by the European Commission under contract H2020-700367 DANTE.

References

1. Apache: Open NLP (2018). https://opennlp.apache.org/
2. Casteigts, A., Flocchini, P., Quattrociocchi, W., Santoro, N.: Time-varying graphs and dynamic networks. Int. J. Parallel Emergent Distrib. Syst. **27**, 387–408 (2012)
3. Cytoscape Consortium: Cytoscape JS (2016). http://js.cytoscape.org/
4. Coscia, M., Giannotti, F., Pedreschi, D.: A classification for community discovery methods in complex networks. Stat. Anal. Data Min. ASA Data Sci. J. **4**, 512–546 (2011)
5. Fortunato, S.: Community detection in graphs. Phys. Rep. **486**, 75–174 (2010)
6. Holme, P., Saramaki, J.: Temporal networks. Phys. Rep. **519**, 97–125 (2012)
7. Latapy, M., Viviard, T., Magnien, C.: Stream graphs and link streams for the modeling of interactions over time. arXiv preprint arXiv:1710.04073 (2017)
8. Newman, M.: The structure and function of complex networks. SIAM Rev. **45**, 167–256 (2003)
9. Rossetti, G., Guidotti, R., Pennacchioli, D., Pedreschi, D., Giannotti, F.: Interaction prediction in dynamic networks exploiting community discovery. In: Proceedings of the IEEE/ACM International Conference on Advances in Social Networks Analysis and Mining (ASONAM), pp. 553–558 (2015)
10. Toti, D., Atzeni, P., Polticelli, F.: Automatic protein abbreviations discovery and resolution from full-text scientific papers: the PRAISED framework. Bio-Algorithms Med-Syst. **8** (2012). https://doi.org/10.2478/bams-2012-0002
11. Toti, D., Longhi, A.: SEMANTO: a graphical ontology management system for knowledge discovery. J. Ambient. Intell. Humaniz. Comput. **online first** (2017). https://doi.org/10.1007/s12652-017-0518-0
12. Toti, D., Rinelli, M.: On the road to speed-reading and fast learning with CONCEPTUM. In: IEEE INCoS 2016 Proceedings - 2016 International Conference on Intelligent Networking and Collaborative Systems, pp. 357–361 (2016). https://doi.org/10.1109/INCoS.2016.30
13. Viard, T., Latapy, M., Magnien, C.: Computing maximal cliques in link streams. Theor. Comput. Sci. **609**, 245–252 (2016)
14. W3C: Web Ontology Language (OWL) (2012). https://www.w3.org/OWL/
15. W3C: RDF Resource Description Framework (2014). http://www.w3.org/RDF/
16. W3C: RDF Schema (2014). http://www.w3.org/TR/rdf-schema/

A Reliability Object Layer for Deep Hashing-Based Visual Indexing

Konstantinos Gkountakos[(✉)], Theodoros Semertzidis, Georgios Th. Papadopoulos, and Petros Daras

Information Technologies Institute, Centre for Research and Technology Hellas, Thessaloniki, Greece
{gountakos,theosem,papad,daras}@iti.gr

Abstract. Nowadays, time-efficient search and retrieval of visually similar content has emerged as a great necessity, while at the same time it constitutes an outstanding research challenge. The latter is further reinforced by the fact that millions of images and videos are generated on a daily basis. In this context, deep hashing techniques, which aim at estimating a very low dimensional binary vector for characterizing each image, have been introduced for realizing realistically fast visual-based search tasks. In this paper, a novel approach to deep hashing is proposed, which explicitly takes into account information about the object types that are present in the image. For achieving this, a novel layer has been introduced on top of current Neural Network (NN) architectures that aims to generate a reliability mask, based on image semantic segmentation information. Thorough experimental evaluation, using four datasets, proves that incorporating local-level information during the hash code learning phase significantly improves the similar retrieval results, compared to state-of-art approaches.

Keywords: Deep hashing · Hash codes · Deep learning
Image segmentation · Neural networks

1 Introduction

Over the recent years, the amount of visual content that is generated on a daily basis grows exponentially, mainly due to the widespread use of portable devices (e.g. smart-phones, tablets, etc.) that typically feature high-quality camera sensors. This results in the generation of extremely large visual databases, where the tasks of accurate and time-efficient search/retrieval comprise a great challenge. To address this, hashing methods have been proposed, in order to realize an efficient way of visually relevant information retrieval, in terms of both retrieval accuracy and computational time. Generally, hashing methods have very low

The work presented in this paper was supported by the European Commission under contract H2020-700367 DANTE.

I. Kompatsiaris et al. (Eds.): MMM 2019, LNCS 11296, pp. 132–143, 2019.
https://doi.org/10.1007/978-3-030-05716-9_11

storage requirements and exhibit fast responses, compared to other traditional retrieval approaches (e.g. image descriptors). The merits of hashing methods stem out from the efficient mapping of high dimensional feature vectors to corresponding significantly low dimensional binary codes, which are subsequently used for 'query-by-example' image retrieval [18]. These mappings are also known as 'hash functions' and the generated binary vectors are typically termed 'hash codes'.

Different hashing methods have been proposed so far that can generally be divided in two main categories, namely data-independent and data-dependent ones [18,28], as presented in Fig. 1. Data-independent approaches are not taking into account a training dataset sampled from the target data and thus apply generic approaches to learn or randomly select a mapping of the high dimensional input feature space to a lower dimensional one. In the next step, quantization is applied for generating a compact binary vector that robustly encodes the original one [22,30]. Indicative approaches of this category are the Locality Sensitive Hashing (LSH) method [6] and its variants, which are selecting projection matrices to lower-dimensional spaces and threshold the vectors to compute binary codes. On the contrary, data-dependent methods aim at learning hash functions from the target dataset to generate more efficient mappings of the input data to the new hamming space [24]. Representative data-depended methods are Spectral Hashing (SH) [23], Binary Reconstructive Embedding (BRE) [14] and Iterative Quantization (ITQ) [7].

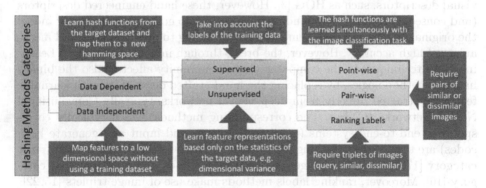

Fig. 1. A visual representation of the different hashing methods categories.

Data-dependent methods can generally be divided into two sub-categories namely supervised and unsupervised ones (Fig. 1). Unsupervised approaches aim at learning feature representations based only on pure statistics of the target data, e.g. the variance of the values in each dimension or their cardinality [20]. In other words, unsupervised methods do not take into account semantic information [22]. For instance, Iterative Quantization (ITQ) aims at preserving the locality structure of the projected data that have been processed using Principal Component Analysis (PCA), by performing rotation so as to minimize the discretization error [7]. Additionally, Isotropic Hashing (IsoHash) learns projection functions, which can produce dimensions with isotropic variance [11]. Further-more, Spectral Hashing (SH) initially applies PCA on the original data, then calculates the analytical Laplacian eigenfunctions along the principal directions and eventually hash codes are generated based on the projections of these eigen-functions [23].

On the contrary, supervised methods make use of semantic information dur-ing the hash functions learning phase. The advantage of using labeled data to guide the learning process enables supervised methods to generate hash codes that represent more accurately the original data and with fewer bits (i.e. smaller hash code length), compared to the ones obtained by the application of unsu-pervised techniques. Small hash code length is desirable for building efficient image retrieval frameworks, with respect to the required computational resources [15, 22]. Supervised information is typically considered in three different forms, namely point-wise, pair-wise and ranking labels [16] (Fig. 1). When point-wise information is used, the model simultaneously handles both the problems of hash functions and image classification learning. Methods that make use of pair-wise information generally require pairs of similar or dissimilar images for learning hash codes. Moreover, methods that make use of information in the form of ranked labels are typically generate triplets of images based on their estimated classification labels, where one image constitutes the query and the remaining two are similar/dissimilar to the query, such as DBC [19].

The above-mentioned hashing methods make use of traditional hand-crafted visual descriptors, such as HOG [3]. However, these hand-engineered descriptors (and consequently the corresponding hash codes) do not always efficiently model the original images and their semantics; thus, failing to provide a retrieval mech-anism of high accuracy. However, the break-through introduced by Deep Learn-ing (DL) techniques in the computer vision community affected also the binary hashing methodologies, by replacing the hand-crafted descriptors with learnable features extracted directly from deep neural networks, typically Convolutional Neural Networks (CNNs). The corresponding methods, which typically corre-spond to end-to-end systems (i.e. receive images and input and generate hash codes) are termed deep hashing. Point-wise methods is the most commonly met category [17, 26]. Pairs of images are used by methods under the pairwise cate-gory [16]. Moreover, ranking labels methods make use of image triplets [15, 22].

In this paper, a novel deep hashing framework for fast image retrieval is proposed, which takes into account the reliability of the objects that appear in an image. In particular, semantic segmentation masks are used to determine the object. Then a novel layer is introduced, which penalizes image regions where objects are not detected with high confidence. The main contributions of this work are as follows:

– The fusion of semantic information in the form of image segmentation masks, in order to generate more expressive and robust hash codes that will com-bine image-level features with discriminative object-level information cues. Current deep hashing techniques are only limited to image-level analysis.

– The introduction of a Reliability Object Layer (ROL), which generates a binary mask, denoting image pixels that correspond to an object with high degree of confidence.

The remainder of the paper, is organized as follows: Related work, is discussed in Sect. 2. In Sect. 3 the proposed method is detailed while experimental results are presented in Sect. 4. Finally, conclusions are drawn in Sect. 5.

2 Related Work

In this section, analysis regarding the state-of-the-art of deep-hashing techniques is provided. As already described in Sect. 1, supervised methods generate more efficient and accurate respective hash functions, compared to the unsupervised techniques.

Point-wise deep hashing methods do not make use of data augmentation techniques and can resolve the hashing problem in conjunction with the classification one. In [17] a method which learns the hash functions and the classification layer at the same time is proposed. Specifically, a latent layer, placed before the classification one, learns both image features and the corresponding hash code in an end-to-end fashion. The latent layer is added between the last fully connected layer (classification layer) and after the semi-final fully connected layer that consists of 4096 hidden nodes. The authors also propose a two-step retrieval framework. In the first step, termed coarse-level search, the framework is fed with a query image and retrieves the top-k similar images calculating the hamming distances for the whole dataset. In the next step, (namely fine-level search), the ranked list of similar retrieved images is computed, while calculating the Euclidean distance from the candidate images of the previous step. An extension of the aforementioned method is proposed from Yang et al. [26], termed Supervised Semantics-preserving Deep Hashing (SSDH). The SSDH method also learns the hash codes and the image representation at the same time. In order to generate more efficient hash codes, the loss function has been enriched, by adding two more functionalities. Specifically, a mechanism forcing the outputs to be 0 or 1 is applied after the latent layer. This enables the model to minimize the quantization error. Additionally, a component that fires at each bit location with probability equal to 0.5 is included. The latter leads to the production of more discriminative hash codes.

Deep hashing methods comprising the pair-wise category have also been widely investigated. An indicative method is the so called Deep Pairwise - Supervised Hashing (DPSH) [16]. Specifically, DPSH learns hash codes in a pairwise manner within an end-to-end framework. Initially, a pair is defined as similar if both input images belong to the same class, otherwise it is defined dissimilar. Then, a siamese network architecture is implemented, in order to pass pairs of images simultaneously across the network. It is worth noting, that the two CNNs have the same structure and share the same weights. A latent layer is added on top of the network, as a common practice in deep hashing approaches, so as to be able to learn the hash functions. Eventually, the framework also takes into account if an input pair is similar or dissimilar. More specifically, the loss function aims to minimize the distance of the real-valued vectors for similar pairs or to maximize this distance for pairs that are dissimilar, respectively. Moreover, Cao et al. [2] have introduced the so called 'HashNet'. The method relies on an architecture which exhibits improved performance in imbalanced datasets. More specifically, a weighted pairwise cross-entropy loss function is used, in order to learn similarity/dissimilarity scores between pairs of images from sparse data. For preventing the vanishing gradient problem, the tanh activation function is applied.

The ranking labels category refers to the methods that employ triplets of images. In particular, these approaches almost always receive as input three images, namely a query image a similar and a dissimilar one. Lai et al. [15] propose a triplet-based deep hashing method, in order to learn more discriminative hash codes. In more details, a divide-and-encode module that splits each image (query, positive, negative) feature representation into parts is included. In particular, the transformation from long length real vectors to short binary codes is performed by adding one node for each binary bit after an average pooling layer. Also a triplet ranking loss function is implemented that aims to regularize the distance between similar/dissimilar images from the query one to a minimum/maximum, respectively. Additionally, Zhang et al. [27] propose the framework where the binary codes are scalable. The size of hash code is generated by the addition of a new layer that learns the weight of each bit. During the test phase, the bits which contribute more are taken into account to extract the binary vector.

In all cases of supervised learning, the use of supervised information is advantageous towards learning robust hash functions, with the cost of depending on labeled data that are not always available. Additionally, the recent trend of simultaneously learning both hash functions and classification labels has also resulted into significantly improved retrieval results. However, explicitly incorporating object-level information in deep hashing schemes has not been investigated so far, while it is very likely to further reinforce the expressiveness and the discriminative power of the estimated hash codes. Regarding implementation complexity, the methods of the point-wise category are easier to be materialized, as a result of lack of data augmentation requirements. However, the possible merits of using local-level information can favor both pair-wise and ranking labels approaches.

3   Proposed Method

In this section, the proposed framework is explained in details. In particular, the developed architecture consists of three main components: (a) The classification stream that learns the hash functions while also solving the classification problem. (b) The object level stream that handles the pixel-wise classification problem, based on the use of image segmentation masks. (c) The Reliability Object Layer that penalizes pixel areas that are not associated with object classification decisions with high confidence.

3.1   Classification Stream

The fundamental consideration of the proposed framework is to reinforce features that correspond to certain semantic object categories (with a relatively high degree of confidence) during the hash code learning phase. For achieving this, the RGB input image is fed into a two stream architecture, as presented in Fig. 2. The output of the bottom stream corresponds to a semantic segmentation mask of the input image, while the upper stream handles the classification problem. As can be seen in Fig. 2 (top) the classification stream of the proposed architecture comprises of a Neural Network pre-trained using the ImageNet dataset [13]. In the current work, this base network is selected to be the VGG network with configuration 'C' [21], which consists of a total of 16 layers. The primary goal of this work, as already discussed, is not to focus on particular base network architectures, but it is on directly using semantic segmentation information, in order to generate more efficient hash codes. To this end, different well-known base network architectures, such as ResNet [9] or VGG with different configurations, can be utilized.

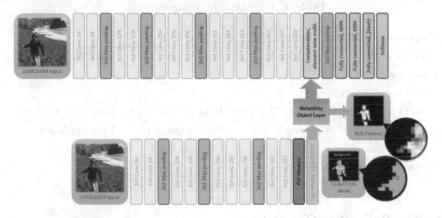

Fig. 2. Proposed deep hashing framework for directly incorporating local-level information in the form of a semantic segmentation mask using a reliability object layer.

3.2   Local-Level Stream

The lower part of the architecture in Fig. 2 is responsible for incorporating semantic segmentation related information. It is worth noting that local-level information in the form of segmentation masks can be encoded using a variety of different implementations, such as [1,8,10]; however, the aim of this work is not excessively evaluating the different available implementations, but to investigate the usefulness of incorporating semantic segmentation information during the hash code learning phase. For that purpose, the well-known Pyramid Scene Parsing (PSP) network [29], which exhibits satisfactory segmentation performance and relatively decreased module integration requirements, is incorporated. Specifically, the PSP architecture receives as input the feature map of the semifinal VGG convolution layer. Then, average pooling layers of different sizes are applied. Subsequently, convolution layers with kernel size 1×1 are used, followed by corresponding up-sampling layers. Eventually, the generated features are stacked with the original ones. Information for supervised training of this part of the network is given in the form of an image segmentation mask. As mentioned in Table 1, the PSP module receives as input a feature map of size $28 \times 28 \times 512$. Then, four average pooling layers with bin size 28×28, 14×14, 9×9 and 7×7 are applied. Each pooling layer is followed by a convolution layer with kernel size 1×1 and outputs $N/4$ features, where N is the number of features in the input feature map. Sequential application of batch normalization, Rectied Linear Unit (ReLU) activation and up-sampling layers over each pooling stream enables the reconstruction of the input feature map. The original feature map and the four reconstructed ones are then stacked. Subsequent activation of convolutional, non-linear and up-sampling layers lead to the restoration of the original (ground truth) image segmentation mask dimensions.

Table 1. PSP module configuration.

Vgg16 semi-final conv. layer output : $28 \times 28 \times 512$			
Pool 28×28	Pool 14×14	Pool 9×9	Pool 7×7
Conv 1×1, 128			
Batch normalization			
Relu ($1 \times 1 \times 128$)	Relu ($2 \times 2 \times 128$)	Relu ($3 \times 3 \times 128$)	Relu ($4 \times 4 \times 128$)
Up-sample $\times 28$	Up-sample $\times 2$	Up-sample $\times 10$	Up-sample $\times 4$
-	-	Crop2D 1×1	-
Stacked $28 \times 28 \times 1024$			

3.3   The Reliability Object Layer

In this sub-section, the functionality of the proposed reliability object layer is discussed. The developed layer aims to penalize the regions of the objects that appear in the image, taking into account the predicted segmentation masks. In particular, the generated segmentation mask is actually composed of a set of binary masks, one for each semantic object class. For each pixel, a probability is computed that denotes how possible is a certain pixel to belong to a given class. The probability corresponding to the class 'background' is neglected. Thus, the generated gray-scale segmentation mask contains pixel-level object classification information for all classes, with values close to 1 to be considered more reliable and values close to 0 to be less reliable. Specifically, let $M = \{x_1, x_i, ..., x_N\}$ be the set of the N predicted binary segmentation masks for a given image. Initially, class 'background' is removed from M; hence, $M' = \{x_1, x_i, ..., x_{N-1}\}$ includes the pixel-level predicted probabilities for all classes except the background one. Then, the highest probability for each pixel is considered, resulting to the 2D probability matrix R. As already mentioned, the aim of integrating local-level information is to boost visual features that are selected taking into account semantic information, i.e. object classification decisions. For achieving this, element-wise multiplication is applied between the last feature map of the classification stream and matrix R.

4   Experimental Results

4.1   Employed Datasets

In order to evaluate the performance of the proposed approach in different domains and scales, the following datasets were used:

Terrorist related dataset that has been generated using visual content of the highly challenging domain of on-line terrorist propaganda videos. Specifically, the collected dataset consists of 9191 annotated images, divided into training, gallery and test sets that comprise 5000, 7407 and 1784, respectively.

PASCAL-VOC2012 [5] dataset is used in order to train the semantic segmentation architecture (Fig. 2). This dataset contains approximately 2912 images with pixel-level ground truth annotation and supports 20 semantic classes (plus one for background). It was selected on the basis that the defined semantic classes correspond to commonly met real-world object categories, such as person, car, TV/monitor, etc. In the hash code learning phase, the labeled images of the training and validation sets are used. In order to maintain a fair comparison, images that have been used to train the PSP module have now been excluded. In particular, the dataset consists of 9267 images in total; 5000 of them are used in the training set, 1000 are randomly selected as query images and the gallery set contains 8267 instances.

CIFAR-10 [12] dataset is also used. This dataset consists of approximately 60000 images. 5000 images are randomly selected (500 per class) for defining the training set. The query set consist of 1000 images (100 per class) while the gallery set consists of 59000 images.

AWA2 [25] dataset consists of a total of 37322 images, belonging to 50 classes is used. The framework was trained using a set of 10000 images and 1000 images were selected for the query set; the gallery set consists of 36322 images.

4.2   Implementation Details

For training the semantic segmentation stream (Fig. 2), the AdaGrad optimizer [4] was used. The total number of epochs was set to 40 and the defined batch size was set to 64. For the classification stream (Fig. 2), the negative log-likelihood criterion was used during training, along with Stochastic Gradient Descent (SGD) for implementing back-propagation with momentum equal to 0.9. The learning rate was initially selected equal to 10^{-3} and was subsequently decreased to 10^{-4} after 20 epochs. The total number of epochs was set to 40 and the defined batch size was set equal to 40. All input images were resized to 256×256 and then were cropped to 224×224, using a square window placed at the center of the image.

All implementation activities were carried out using the Keras[1] framework and a Nvidia GTX 1070 GPU with 8GB memory.

4.3   Evaluation Results

For evaluation, the metric defined in [17] was adopted. In particular, a ranking Mean Average Precision (MAP) value was estimated for each query image. For the calculations, the retrieved images that belonged to the same semantic class with the query image were considered relevant. MAP values were computed for the top-1000 retrieved images.

The SSDH method was selected in order to have a comparison between the proposed architecture and the state-of-art approaches. It should be noted that the SSDH method not only exhibits state-of-art results, but also it is characterized by relative implementation simplicity. Table 2 illustrates the obtained retrieval results from the application of the proposed method in each dataset, while the performance of the SSDH approach is also given. Additionally, different hash code length experiments are also given. Specifically, experiments with hash code length equal to 12, 24, 32 and 48 bits have been carried out. From the obtained results, it can be seen that the proposed method outperforms the SSDH one in most cases. In particular, the proposed method outperforms significantly the SSDH approach when the length of the hash code is 12 bits.

Indicative retrieval results of the 12 bits experiments for the AWA2 and PASCAL-VOC2012 datasets are shown in Fig. 3. From a detailed examination of the provided results, it can be seen that the proposed method exhibits significantly better results when the visual content of the images needs to be compressed in few bits. It is worth noting here that the CIFAR-10 dataset consists of tiny images that contain single objects; so, the proposed architecture acts like a background removal algorithm, aiming at focusing on a single object. Moreover, a significant improvement is shown (in Table 2) when the AWA2 dataset is used. Since, the predicted segmentation masks and consequently the binary masks, which have been generated from the ROL ones, typically contain animals (such as 'cat', 'dog', 'bird', 'cow', 'horse', 'sheep', etc), it is obvious that the respective ROL masks would exhibit high confidence scores (i.e. robust object classification decisions). This is mainly due to multiple animal classes are also present during the local-level information (segmentation) learning phase. In other words, the semantic classes of this particular dataset coincide with classes of the PASCALVOC-2012 one; hence, more accurate ROL masks can be generated. This suggests that incorporating local-level information (semantic segmentation) in the hash code learning phase and boosting features that correspond to objects with high classification confidence can also improve the retrieval performance of a deep hashing framework.

In order to provide a deeper insight on the obtained results, Fig. 3 (top) shows the top-10 retrieved images for both the SSDH and the proposed method, when the same image is used as query. Additionally, similar obtained results

---

[1] https://github.com/fchollet/keras.

Table 2. Comparative evaluation results using the MAP@1000 metric

Hash code length	Method	Dataset			
		Terrorist related dataset	PASCAL-VOC2012	CIFAR-10	AWA2
12 bits	SSDH	55.93%	56.83%	40.25%	57.16%
	Proposed	**60.16%**	**62.44%**	**51.95%**	**60.80%**
24 bits	SSDH	68.00%	**66.27%**	69.27%	73.83%
	Proposed	**68.71%**	64.36%	**70.80%**	**77.30%**
32 bits	SSDH	69.05%	**70.30%**	**76.46%**	79.08%
	Proposed	**70.94%**	68.98%	75.60%	**81.11%**
48 bits	SSDH	69.13%	69.55%	76.59%	**83.91%**
	Proposed	**72.13%**	**71.65%**	**78.48%**	83.71%

are given for the case of the PASCALVOC-2012 dataset (Fig. 3, bottom). From the illustrated results, the superior performance of the proposed approach is demonstrated. It needs to be highlighted that for both queries, not only the number of relevant returned images, but also their ranking, is improved for the case of the proposed approach. This is mainly due to the proposed method paying more attention to the objects of the image, such as animals and airplanes, while providing decreased importance to the features of that belong to the background.

Fig. 3. Indicative retrieval results in AWA2 (top) and PASCAL-VOC2012 (bottom) datasets. The query image, for each dataset, is shown on the left and the top-10 retrieved images (for both the SSDH and the proposed method) are illustrated on the right.

5   Conclusions

In this work, a novel deep learning layer was proposed in order to construct binary hash codes which take into account local-level semantic information. The proposed framework was evaluated in four different and diverse datasets. The proposed architecture exhibited significantly improved performance, compared to the baseline approach (SSDH) that makes use of only image level information. The experimental results also demonstrated that boosting local-level features using local semantic information, in the form of ROL 2D masks is advantageous. Future work includes the investigation of alternative ways of using local-level information for generating more expressive ROL masks, which will consequently be used in deep hashing schemes.

References

1. Badrinarayanan, V., Kendall, A., Cipolla, R.: Segnet: a deep convolutional encoder-decoder architecture for image segmentation. IEEE Trans. Pattern Anal. Mach. Intell. **39**(12), 2481–2495 (2017)
2. Cao, Z., Long, M., Wang, J., Yu, P.S.: Hashnet: Deep learning to hash by continuation. arXiv preprint arXiv:1702.00758 (2017)
3. Dalal, N., Triggs, B.: Histograms of oriented gradients for human detection. In: IEEE Computer Society Conference on Computer Vision and Pattern Recognition, 2005, CVPR 2005, vol. 1, pp. 886–893. IEEE (2005)
4. Duchi, J., Hazan, E., Singer, Y.: Adaptive subgradient methods for online learning and stochastic optimization. J. Mach. Learn. Res. **12**(Jul), 2121–2159 (2011)
5. Everingham, M., Van Gool, L., Williams, C.K.I., Winn, J., Zisserman, A.: The PASCAL Visual Object Classes Challenge 2012 (VOC2012) Results (2012). http://www.pascal-network.org/challenges/VOC/voc2012/workshop/index.html
6. Gionis, A., Indyk, P., Motwani, R., et al.: Similarity search inhigh dimensions via hashing. In: VLDB, pp. 518–529 (1999)
7. Gong, Y., Lazebnik, S., Gordo, A., Perronnin, F.: Iterative quantization: a procrustean approach to learning binary codes for large-scale image retrieval. IEEE Trans. Pattern Anal. Mach. Intell. **35**(12), 2916–2929 (2013)
8. He, K., Gkioxari, G., Dollár, P., Girshick, R.: Mask r-cnn. In: 2017 IEEE International Conference on Computer Vision (ICCV), pp. 2980–2988. IEEE (2017)
9. He, K., Zhang, X., Ren, S., Sun, J.: Deep residual learning for image recognition. In: Proceedings of the IEEE Conference on Computer Vision and Pattern Recognition, pp. 770–778 (2016)
10. Hong, S., Noh, H., Han, B.: Decoupled deep neural network for semi-supervised semantic segmentation. In: Advances in Neural Information Processing Systems, pp. 1495–1503 (2015)
11. Kong, W., Li, W.J.: Isotropic hashing. In: Advances in Neural Information Processing Systems, pp. 1646–1654 (2012)
12. Krizhevsky, A., Hinton, G.: Learning multiple layers of features from tiny images (2009)
13. Krizhevsky, A., Sutskever, I., Hinton, G.E.: Imagenet classification with deep convolutional neural networks. In: Advances in Neural Information Processing Systems, pp. 1097–1105 (2012)

14. Kulis, B., Darrell, T.: Learning to hash with binary reconstructive embeddings. In: Advances in Neural Information Processing Systems, pp. 1042–1050 (2009)
15. Lai, H., Pan, Y., Liu, Y., Yan, S.: Simultaneous feature learning and hash coding with deep neural networks. arXiv preprint arXiv:1504.03410 (2015)
16. Li, W.J., Wang, S., Kang, W.C.: Feature learning based deep supervised hashing with pairwise labels. arXiv preprint arXiv:1511.03855 (2015)
17. Lin, K., Yang, H.F., Hsiao, J.H., Chen, C.S.: Deep learning of binary hash codes for fast image retrieval. In: 2015 IEEE Conference on Computer Vision and Pattern Recognition Workshops (CVPRW), pp. 27–35. IEEE (2015)
18. Liong, V.E., Lu, J., Wang, G., Moulin, P., Zhou, J., et al.: Deep hashing for compact binary codes learning. In: CVPR, vol. 1, p. 3 (2015)
19. Rastegari, M., Farhadi, A., Forsyth, D.: Attribute discovery via predictable discriminative binary codes. In: Fitzgibbon, A., Lazebnik, S., Perona, P., Sato, Y., Schmid, C. (eds.) ECCV 2012. LNCS, vol. 7577, pp. 876–889. Springer, Heidelberg (2012). https://doi.org/10.1007/978-3-642-33783-3_63
20. Semertzidis, T., Rafailidis, D., Strintzis, M.G., Daras, P.: The influence of image descriptors' dimensions' value cardinalities on large-scale similarity search. Int. J. Multimedia Inf. Retr. 4(3), 187–204 (2015)
21. Simonyan, K., Zisserman, A.: Very deep convolutional networks for large-scale image recognition. arXiv preprint arXiv:1409.1556 (2014)
22. Wang, X., Shi, Y., Kitani, K.M.: Deep supervised hashing with triplet labels. In: Lai, S.-H., Lepetit, V., Nishino, K., Sato, Y. (eds.) ACCV 2016. LNCS, vol. 10111, pp. 70–84. Springer, Cham (2017). https://doi.org/10.1007/978-3-319-54181-5_5
23. Weiss, Y., Torralba, A., Fergus, R.: Spectral hashing. In: Advances in neural information processing systems, pp. 1753–1760 (2009)
24. Xia, R., Pan, Y., Lai, H., Liu, C., Yan, S.: Supervised hashing for image retrieval via image representation learning. In: AAAI, vol. 1, p. 2 (2014)
25. Xian, Y., Lampert, C.H., Schiele, B., Akata, Z.: Zero-shot learning-a comprehensive evaluation of the good, the bad and the ugly. arXiv preprint arXiv:1707.00600 (2017)
26. Yang, H.F., Lin, K., Chen, C.S.: Supervised learning of semantics-preserving hash via deep convolutional neural networks. IEEE Trans. Pattern Anal. Mach. Intell. 40(2), 437–451 (2018)
27. Zhang, R., Lin, L., Zhang, R., Zuo, W., Zhang, L.: Bit-scalable deep hashing with regularized similarity learning for image retrieval and person re-identification. IEEE Trans. Image Process. 24(12), 4766–4779 (2015)
28. Zhao, F., Huang, Y., Wang, L., Tan, T.: Deep semantic ranking based hashing for multi-label image retrieval. In: 2015 IEEE Conference on Computer Vision and Pattern Recognition (CVPR), pp. 1556–1564. IEEE (2015)
29. Zhao, H., Shi, J., Qi, X., Wang, X., Jia, J.: Pyramid scene parsing network. In: IEEE Conference on Computer Vision and Pattern Recognition (CVPR), pp. 2881–2890 (2017)
30. Zhong, G., Xu, H., Yang, P., Wang, S., Dong, J.: Deep hashing learning networks. In: 2016 International Joint Conference on Neural Networks (IJCNN), pp. 2236–2243. IEEE (2016)

Spectral Tilt Estimation for Speech Intelligibility Enhancement Using RNN Based on All-Pole Model

Rui Zhang[1,2], Ruimin Hu[1,2(✉)], Gang Li[1,2], and Xiaochen Wang[1,3]

[1] National Engineering Research Center for Multimedia Software,
School of Computer Science, Wuhan University, Wuhan, China
`{ruizhang1216,hrm,ligang10,clowang}@whu.edu.cn`
[2] Hubei Key Laboratory of Multimedia and Network Communication
Engineering, Wuhan University, Wuhan, China
[3] Collaborative Innovation Center of Geospatial Technology, Wuhan, China

Abstract. Speech intelligibility enhancement is extremely meaningful for successful speech communication in noisy environments. Several methods based on Lombard effect are used to increase intelligibility. In those methods, spectral tilt has been suggested to be a significant characteristic to produce Lombard speech that is more intelligible than normal speech. All-pole model computed by some methods has been used to capture the accurate spectral tilt of high-quality speech, but they are not appropriate for the spectral tilt estimation of telephone speech. In this paper, recurrent neural networks (RNNs) are used to estimate the tilt of telephone speech in German and English. RNN-based spectral tilt estimation show the robustness on the change of the all-pole model order and phonation type for narrow and wideband speech. Mean squared error (MSE) of spectral tilt estimation using RNN-based method is increased by about 26.20% in narrow speech and 19.49% in wideband speech comparing to the DNN-based measure.

Keywords: Spectral tilt · All-pole model · RNN

1 Introduction

With the widespread of mobile communication devices, modern communication is extensively applied in our society as a sort of multimedia communication. Therefore, in the daily living environments, such as subway, curbside, airport and so on, it is inevitable for the public to communicate with others through cellphone, which means that people will be accompanied by more noise in the processing of speech communication. So, it is particularly significant to increase speech intelligibility for the cellphone users who located in noisy environments.

According to the transmitting and receiving terminal of speech communication systems, two different scenarios (see Fig. 1) are generally distinguished, referred to as the far-end scenario and the near-end scenario. Many researchers have focused on noise cancellation in the far-end scenario to remove noise from noisy speech. However, assuming that the listener in a noisy environment receives the clean speech from the

I. Kompatsiaris et al. (Eds.): MMM 2019, LNCS 11296, pp. 144–156, 2019.
https://doi.org/10.1007/978-3-030-05716-9_12

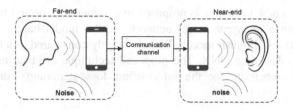

Fig. 1. A diagram of a speech communication system.

loudspeaker of smartphone, the clean speech will still be masked by noise, causing degradation of speech intelligibility. In recent years, several methods of speech intelligibility enhancement (IENH) are proposed to solve this problem [1], and are also named as near-end listening enhancement (NELE).

Several IENH methods are based on the speech intelligibility index (SII) optimization [2, 3] or band-energy reallocation [4, 5]. SII optimization measures are noise-dependent, and tend to degrade the quality of speech. When available gain is limited, the performance of this technique decreases apparently, so it is difficult to implement them in real-time speech communication. Band-energy reallocation measures modify the band-energy on the basis of noise and the quantified relationship between the signal band-energy under the total signal energy constraint. They improve the intelligibility a lot, but they also reduce the naturalness of speech and subjective listening comfort.

Some researchers focus on the IENH methods based on human speech production mechanism [6–10]. In noisy scenario, speakers are prone to modify the speaking style instinctively under the stress of ambient noise, which named as Lombard effect [11]. Previous researches demonstrate that Lombard speech is typically more intelligible than normal speech produced in quiet scene, even with different languages [12–14], which is attributed to some changes of features: the flattening of spectral tilt, the reduction of speech rate and the rise of vocal intensity. Among them, it is illustrated that spectral tilt is the most significant factor for intelligibility enhancement in previous study [6–10].

Zorilâ proposes the IENH technique based on spectral shaping and dynamic range compression (SSDRC) in 2012 [6]. SSDRC algorithm uses the feature of Lombard effect that the flattening of spectral tilt can markedly improve the speech intelligibility. Under the frame-based energy constraint, it shapes the spectral tilt according to Lombard effect and reallocates energy by using dynamic range compression (DRC) in time-domain. It enhances the intelligibility, but with the decline of speech quality.

Jokinen proposes a complete IENH system based on the normal-Lombard conversion of the spectral tilt all-pole model by using Gaussian process regression (GPR) for narrow telephone speech in 2017 [8]. This system has four parts: spectral tilt estimation, the train of GPR mapping, all-pole model conversion and gain control. It is very important for this system to estimate the spectral tilt all-pole model of telephone speech by using a deep neural network (DNN) that is described in detail in [15]. However, this DNN-based spectral tilt estimation measure is barely suitable to the Finish speech, which means that this method couldn't be applied in telephone speech with other languages.

In this paper, a new technique is proposed to estimate the spectral tilt of telephone speech by training a recurrent neural network (RNN) model based on the all-pole model for German and English speech. RNN is largely considered as a better model to process sequence data than DNN. The proposed technique estimate more accurately spectral tilt to compensate for the information loss stemming from coding and decoding.

2   All-Pole Model for Spectral Tilt Estimation

The all-pole model is used to estimate spectral tilt of speech signal, and there are different methods that could compute the all-pole model of spectral tilt.

2.1   Linear Prediction Analysis

Linear prediction (LP) analysis is a traditional method in the multimedia field, and can be used to estimate the spectral envelope and vocal tract resonance as the all-pole model in speech signal processing [16, 17]. Its most common equation in time-domain is:

$$\hat{X}_n = \sum_{i=1}^{p} a_i \cdot X_{n-i}, 1 \le i \le p \tag{1}$$

where $\hat{X}_n$ denotes the prediction value of speech wave, $\{X_{n-i}\}_{i=0}^{p}$ denotes the previous observed value, $\{a_i\}_{i=0}^{p}$ is the prediction parameters, and is also named as the all-pole coefficients, p is the order of LP model. The prediction error e_n is formulated as:

$$e_n = X_n - \hat{X}_n \tag{2}$$

where X_n is the true value of speech wav. LP method optimizes a_i by minimizing the total squared prediction error E:

$$E = \sum_n e_n^2 \tag{3}$$

where E denotes the cost function of LP. For the assurance that E reaches the minimum, the derivate of E should meet the condition $(\partial E/\partial a_i = 0)$, then the result of the linear prediction coefficients $\{a_i\}$ are computed by the following equations:

$$\sum_n a_i \cdot \phi_{k,i} = \phi_{k,0}, 1 \le i \le p, \quad \text{Where } \phi_{k,i} = \sum_n X_{n-k}X_{n-i} \tag{4}$$

The all-pole model computed by LP can estimate the spectral tilt of speech, but it needs higher order to estimate the spectral tilt and is vulnerable to the effect of fundamental frequency (F0) and harmonics of speech.

2.2   Weighted Linear Prediction

Weighted linear prediction (WLP) is proposed to get more robust all-pole models for reducing the impact of F0 and harmonics of the speech signal as a medication of LP analysis [18, 19], WLP is distinguished from LP by improving the cost function:

$$E_w = \sum_n E \cdot W_n \tag{5}$$

Where W_n denotes the temporal weight function in time-domain with respect to the prediction error e_n. It is extremely significant to realize that W_n works on the prediction error instead of being similar to the conventional window function (e.g., Hamming) that works on original input speech signal for reducing spectrum leakage and fence effect due to the signal truncation. On condition $(\partial E_w / \partial a_i = 0, 1 \leq i \leq p)$ the result linear equation is slightly adjusted to compute the coefficients $\{a_i, 1 \leq i \leq p\}$:

$$\sum_n a_i \cdot \beta_{k,i} = \beta_{k,0}, \quad \text{Where } \beta_{k,i} = \sum_n X_{n-k}X_{n-i} \cdot W_n \tag{6}$$

The short-time energy (STE) weight function is a popular kind of previous temporal weight function [21], STE function is shown as:

$$W_n = \sum_{i=0}^{M-1} X_{n-i-1}^2 \tag{7}$$

Where M is length of the STE window. STE function is computed without iterative operation, and gives more energy to the closed phase regions of the glottal cycle by setting higher weight, which makes sure that stable all-pole model filter is produced. However, STE function suppresses the open phase regions of the glottal cycle and the main excitation strongly, and it is not necessary to restrain them completely so that this technique cannot estimate accurate spectral tilt.

2.3   Quasi Closed Phase

Quasi closed phase (QCP) is a variant of WLP by using AME weighting function in [20, 21]. AME weight function based on glottal closure instant (GCI) is different from conventional weighting function via being focus on the closed phase domain. It is computed via glottal flow derivative that is given by the speech signal after glottal inverse filtering (GIF). The algorithm of GCI detection is derived from the study in [22].

The AME weight function has different amount of duplicate cycles due to different amount of GCI. A cycle of AME function consists of three main parameters showed in Fig. 2: position quotient, duration quotient, and ramp duration.

Where T is the period of two adjacent GCI, a non-zero value $d = 10^{-5}$ is set up to avert the singularities for weighted autocorrelation matrices. $L_p = T_p/T$ is the length of position quotient, $L_d = T_d/T$ is the length of duration quotient, $L_r = 2T_r/T$ is the length of ramp duration. They are used to reduce the weight of the closed phase region to get more accurate spectral tilt for studio-quality speech particularly. In QCP technique, GIF is contained in the post-processing of the WLP with AME weight function.

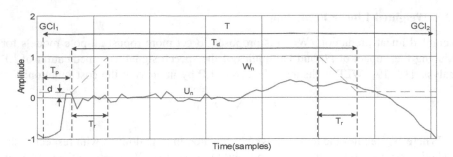

Fig. 2. AME weighting function W_n used in QCP together with a glottal flow derivate U_n computed by glottal inverse filtering (GIF) for a cycle period, W_n is computed by $L_p = 0.1$, $L_r = 0.7$ and $L_d = 7$ in this study.

It is worth noting that there are two different views on how to use QCP to estimate the spectral tilt in [15, 23, 24], one considers that GIF is unnecessary, and the other thinks that GIF is needed. More researchers trended to recognize the latter [15, 24], QCP with GIF is a more effective method to estimate the spectral tilt comparing to the QCP without GIF in our datasets.

The all-pole model computed by a glottal flow derivative from QCP is a most accurate measure to estimate spectral tit currently. However, QCP cannot apply to the spectral tit estimation of telephone speech directly owing to the reduction of speech quality that causes the failure of GCI detection algorithm.

3   RNN Model for Spectral Tilt Estimation

A recurrent neural network (RNN) model is used to predict the all-pole model of the spectral tilt of telephone speech in German and English by contrasting with the DNN-based spectral tilt estimation measure.

3.1   DNN-Based Spectral Tilt Estimation

The all-pole model of QCP can estimate the spectral tilt for high-quality speech, however it is not suitable for telephone speech. In [15] DNN-based method is designed to solve this problem for applying spectral tilt estimation in real-time Multimedia speech communication.

In German and English datasets, the original studio-quality speech is resampled at 8 kHz and 16 kHz sampling rates to get Narrow speech (8k) and wideband speech (16k) telephone speech are achieved by the same processing of encoding and decoding in [15] for 8 kHz and 16 kHz original speech at AMR codec. The input of DNN is the logarithmic spectrum amplitude computed by telephone speech. Speech frame with Hamming window uses 512-point fast Fourier transform (FFT). 257 points from first half of the FFT are chosen as the input vector of DNN, which is different from the 255 points in [15]. Two points in the Symmetric axis of FFT is also included in our study.

The output of DNN is the all-pole model of the glottal source from QCP glottal flow by LP instead of cascading two of 4 order power-law modified linear prediction (LP-α) where $\alpha = 1/2$ in [15]. LP is the most likely to rescue more information of spectral tilt than LP-α for the reason that energy of spectral tilt is preserved more completely in LP. The output vectors are line spectrum frequencies (LSFs) by parameterizing the all-pole model computed by using QCP for high-quality speech frame. DNN model use sigmoid activation function for hidden layers, 500 epochs, four hidden layers units [150, 100,100, 50] for narrow speech and [100, 100, 50, 50] for wideband speech.

DNN-based tilt estimation can estimate the spectral tilt of telephone speech, but DNN-based measure does not show strong robustness on change of the all-pole model order and phonation type.

3.2 RNN-Based Spectral Tilt Estimation

RNN is a kind of prevailing artificial neural work for sequence data because it could exhibit dynamic temporal process for a time sequence. In RNN model, there is a directed cycle graph for each hidden layer. Therefore, RNN can make use of their internal state to process sequence data. A simple RNN model [25] is utilized to capture precise spectral tilt of telephone speech for German and English both. The structure of RNN-based spectral tilt estimation is shown in Fig. 3.

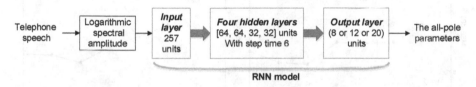

Fig. 3. The schematic diagram of RNN-spectral tilt estimation method, the units of output layer changes in 8, 12 and 20 according to the difference of the all-pole model order, the all-pole computed by this method can estimate the spectral tilt of the telephone speech.

Input and output of RNN-based method are similar to the one of DNN-based method for spectral tilt estimation. The incoming speech signals need several pre-processing that they were processed in 20-ms per frame, simultaneously with 50% overlap between constant frames, then windowed with Hamming window for each frame. Since this technique just focus on voiced speech frames, it is significant to distinguish the voiced frame and unvoiced frame by computing the energy of each frame and setting reasonable threshold. The input feature is 257-dimensional vector with logarithmic spectral amplitude from 512-point FFT of each speech frame where half of FFT of discrete signal could represent the spectrum amplitude due to the periodic conjugate symmetry of discrete Fourier transform (DFT).

The output feature stems from the studio-quality speech without AMR codec processing. QCP is used to calculate spectral tilt of high-quality speech frames where the content of telephone speech frames is the same as the one of high-quality speech frames, then GIF is used to catch more accurate the spectral tilt because the impact of vocal tract resonance is reduced after GIF. The output vectors consist of an all-pole model by using LP (8th-order, 12th-order and 20th-order) to compute glottal flow of spectral tilt. The output of RNN is linear prediction coefficients (LPCs) of glottal of spectral tilt instead of LSFs, because the spectral range of datasets probably from −50 dB to 50 dB, LSFs ranges from −1 to 1, the value of spectrum is about 300 times the value of LSFs, the times is too large to increase the accuracy of spectral tilt estimation.

The input vectors and output vectors are normalized for ensuring training data in a reasonable range to increase the convergence rate of the neural network. Two datasets with German and English are used in our study. In two different datasets, RNN models are trained for narrow speech and wideband speech separately under different dimensions (8, 12 and 20). Neural networks in this study are all trained by using sigmoid activation functions in hidden layers and setting 500 epochs. In both German and English datasets, the units of four hidden layers are [64, 64, 32, 32] and step time is 6 for RNN models under the different dimensions of the output for narrow and wideband speech. Units of RNN output layer are the same as the order of all-pole model.

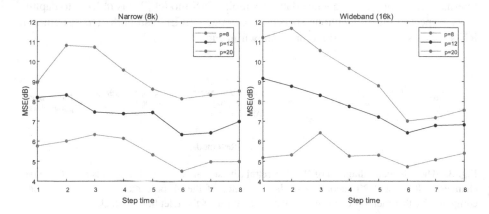

Fig. 4. Performance of RNNs with step times is evaluated by MSE.

Step time is set as 6 according to the results of experiment. RNNs all use the hidden layers sizes [64, 64, 32, 32]. Then RNNs with different step time are respectively trained using different all-pole model order. Mean squared error (MSE) is used to evaluate the performance of RNNs with different step time for narrow and wideband speech. The results in English test set are presented in Fig. 4.

3.3   Training Data

Two speech corpora with different languages (English and German) are used in spectral tilt estimation based on RNN in this study. The German speech corpus consists of normal and Lombard speech from 8 speakers (3 females, 5 males) recorded in anechoic chamber [26]. Each speaker utters same 40 sentences (6–10 s per sentence). Normal speech is recorded in quiet scenario, what's more, Lombard speech including two parts that they are separately recorded in 55 dB and 77 dB noisy cases. The text of normal and Lombard speech is same, which named as parallel normal and Lombard data.

A single male native British-English speaker recorded the English dataset [27] including three parts: Harvard sentences, Modified Rhyme Test (MRT), news sentences in quiet environment or wearing the headphone with 84 dB ICRA noise. In this database, only Harvard set and MRT set are used in RNN-based spectral tilt estimation. Harvard set is made up of double 720 sentences (2–3 s per sentence) recorded in quiet and noisy scene respectively, and the text of it stems from the study in [28]. MRT sentences are composed of double 300 sentences (1–2 s per sentence) in same different scenes. In two datasets, 95% of parallel normal and Lombard speech is used to train neural networks, 5% of the data is used for testing.

4 Evaluation

Performance of RNN-based spectral tilt estimation is evaluated by waveform and mean squared error (MSE) comparing to the DNN-based method. In experiments, when DNN-based measure uses LSFs of spectral tilt as the output of network like [15], MSE of tilt estimation for 12th-order all-pole is approximately 20 dB. It's found that the output of DNN-based measure uses LPCs of spectral tilt could improve the accuracy of tilt estimation, so we use LPCs as the output of DNN like as RNN-based measure.

4.1 Waveform Analysis

The accuracy of RNN-based spectral tilt estimation is evaluated by comparing with DNN-based spectral tilt estimation. In the training of neural networks, the input and output of RNN-based method are the same as the input and output of DNN-based method. An example of RNN-based and DNN-based spectral tilt estimation is illustrated in Fig. 2 for narrow and wideband voiced speech in test dataset using the all-pole model with different orders. Because of the limitation of paper space, the figure just shows the performance of an English speech frame with different sampling rates and orders of all-pole models (Fig. 5).

The spectral tilt curve of RNN-based method is more closer to the reference curve computed by QCP from high-quality original speech comparing with DNN-based method for both narrow and wideband speech under different all-pole model orders.

4.2 Mean Squared Error Analysis

Mean squared error (MSE) is a basic statistical measure, which is used to evaluate the performance of the RNN-based spectral tilt estimation method comparing to the DNN-based spectral tilt estimation method as an objective method.

$$\text{MSE} = \frac{1}{n}\sum\nolimits_{i-1}^{n}\left(Y_i - \hat{Y}_i\right)^2 \tag{8}$$

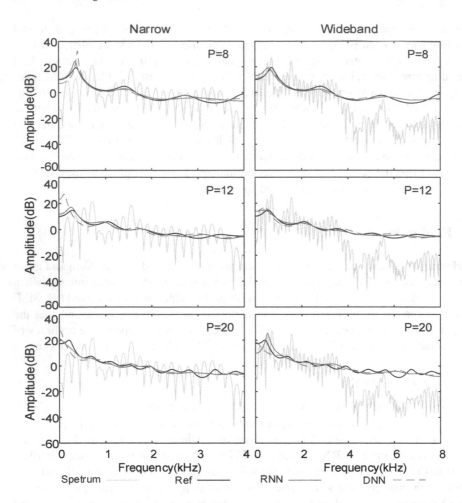

Fig. 5. Diagrams show the performance of RNN-based spectral tilt estimation of an English voiced frame comparing with DNN-based spectral tilt estimation under different orders of the all-pole model for both narrow speech and wideband speech. Spectrum denotes the spectrum of incoming speech (coded) frame. Ref is the spectral tilt computed by QCP from high-quality original speech. DNN and RNN represent the spectra of two different spectral tilt measures (DNN-based and RNN-based methods).

Where $\hat{Y}_i$ is the estimated value (in dB) of spectral tilt from neural networks for telephone speech frames, Y_i is the expected value (in dB) of spectral tilt computed from parallel studio-quality speech frames.

In Germen test corpus, there were three phonation types (normal phonation type, 55 dB pressed phonation type and 70 dB pressed phonation type) used to measure the performance of spectral tilt estimation. According to density of noise used in recording Lombard speech dataset, pressed phonation type is divided into 2 classes for inquiring the effect of different pressed phonation types on spectral tilt estimation. Because there

Table 1. MSE (in dB) of two different spectral tilt estimation methods (DNN, RNN) are shown for the narrow speech frames with three phonation types in German test set, the order of all-pole model is also considered and set as 8, 12 and 20. N denotes normal speech frames, L (55 dB) denotes pressed speech produced in 55 dB noise condition, L (70 dB) denotes pressed speech produced in 70 noise condition. p denotes the order of the all-pole model used to computed the output of the neural networks. Narrow (8k) denotes narrow speech. Wideband denotes (8k) wideband speech.

		Narrow (8k)			Wideband (16k)		
		N	L(55 dB)	L(70 dB)	N	L(55 dB)	L(70 dB)
p = 8	RNN	3.47	3.91	5.20	3.62	3.76	4.74
	DNN	4.43	4.95	6.31	4.25	4.33	5.61
Improvement (%)		*21.67*	*21.01*	*17.59*	*14.82*	*13.16*	*15.51*
p = 12	RNN	4.96	5.30	6.78	4.44	4.59	6.23
	DNN	7.55	7.96	9.32	6.14	6.30	8.16
Improvement (%)		*34.30*	*33.42*	*27.25*	*27.69*	*27.14*	*23.65*
p = 20	RNN	5.91	6.30	7.12	5.54	5.88	7.67
	DNN	8.18	8.37	9.56	6.23	6.49	8.17
Improvement (%)		*27.75*	*24.73*	*25.52*	*11.07*	*9.40*	*6.12*

Table 2. MSE (in dB) under various circumstances is shown for narrow and wideband speech in Harvard and MRT English test set. N is normal speech and L is Lombard speech.

		Narrow (8k)				Wideband (16k)			
		Harvard		MRT		Harvard		MRT	
		N	L	N	L	N	L	N	L
p = 8	RNN	5.51	4.01	4.35	4.13	5.80	4.24	5.59	4.11
	DNN	6.70	5.58	5.44	5.42	7.56	6.43	6.42	5.81
Improvement (%)		*17.76*	*28.14*	*20.04*	*23.80*	*23.28*	*34.06*	*10.98*	*29.26*
p = 12	RNN	7.53	6.13	6.20	5.46	8.83	6.82	7.68	6.13
	DNN	10.10	8.74	8.79	8.10	10.32	8.70	9.36	8.36
Improvement (%)		*25.44*	*29.86*	*29.47*	*32.59*	*14.44*	*21.61*	*16.28*	*26.67*
p = 20	RNN	9.72	7.14	8.31	7.35	11.12	7.57	8.82	7.33
	DNN	12.23	11.07	11.86	9.87	13.76	10.58	11.70	9.69
Improvement (%)		*20.52*	*35.50*	*29.26*	*25.53*	*19.19*	*28.45*	*20.93*	*24.43*

is only Lombard speech recorded in 84 dB noise scene for English dataset, it just consists of two phonation types. For English test set, the MSEs of two methods are separately computed in Harvard and MRT set. The order of all-pole models is also regarded as a factor to be considered in this study. The results of objective measures in German and English test sets are respectively indicated in Tables 1 and 2.

The results indicate that RNN-based tilt estimation shows the robustness for resisting on the change of the all-pole model order and phonation type for narrow and wideband speech. DNN-based tilt estimation is not stable enough facing these changes. Comparing with DNN-based method, the accuracy of spectral tilt estimation using RNN-based method is increased by about 26.20% in narrow speech and 19.49% in wideband speech. The improvement in narrow speech is apparently higher than the one in wideband speech since the DNN-based method cannot accurately estimate the spectral tilt of narrow speech. DNN-based method is vulnerable to the change of the phonation type, but RNN-based method can precisely estimate the spectral tilt of both normal speech and Lombard speech.

5 Conclusion

The spectral tilt is an essential feature for producing Lombard speech to enhance the speech intelligibility. The all-pole model computed by different techniques is utilized to model the spectral tilt, and QCP is a state-of-the-art technique to the all-pole model of spectral tilt from high-quality speech among them. However, QCP cannot be fit to the tilt estimation of telephone speech.

The proposed RNN-based spectral tilt estimation measure shows the robustness on the rise of the all-pole model order and the change of phonation type for German and English speech both. In addition, RNN-based spectral tilt estimation is more accurate than DNN-based spectral tilt estimation for narrow and wideband speech. So RNN-based tilt estimation method proposed in this study has possessed the robustness and the accuracy to estimate the spectral tilt of telephone speech in German and English, which will promote the study of speech intelligibility enhancement based on Lombard effect.

Acknowledgment. This work is supported by National Key Program of China (No. 2017YFB1002803) and National Nature Science Foundation of China (No. U1736206, No. 61801334, No. 61762005).

References

1. Kleijn, W.B., Crespo, J.B., Hendriks, R.C., et al.: Optimizing speech intelligibility in a noisy environment: a unified view. IEEE Signal Process. Mag. **32**(2), 43–54 (2015)
2. Sauert, B., Vary, P.: Near end listening enhancement optimized with respect to speech intelligibility index. In: 17th European Signal Processing Conference, pp. 1844–1848. IEEE (2009)
3. Schepker, H., Rennies, J., Doclo, S.: Improving speech intelligibility in noise by SII-dependent preprocessing using frequency-dependent amplification and dynamic range compression. In: Proceedings of Interspeech, pp. 3577–3581. ISCA, Lyon (2013)

4. Petkov, P.N., Kleijn, W.B.: Spectral dynamics recovery for enhanced speech intelligibility in noise. IEEE/ACM Trans. Audio Speech Lang. Process. **23**(2), 327–338 (2015)
5. Petko, P.N., Stylinaou, Y.: Adaptive gain control and time warp for enhanced speech intelligibility under reverberation. In: IEEE International Conference on Acoustic, Speech and Signal Processing (IASSP), New Orleans, pp. 691–695. IEEE (2017)
6. Zorilâ, T.C., Kandia, V., Stylianou, Y.: Speech-in-noise intelligibility improvement based on spectral shaping and dynamic range compression. In: Proceedings Interspeech, pp. 635–638. ISCA, Portland (2012)
7. Zorilâ, T.C., Stylianou, Y., Ishihara, T., et al.: Near and far field speech-in-noise intelligibility improvements based on a time-frequency energy reallocation approach. IEEE Trans. Audio Speech Lang. Process. **24**(10), 1808–1818 (2016)
8. Jokinen, E., Remes, U., Takanen, M., et al: Spectral tilt modelling with GMMs for intelligibility enhancement of narrowband telephone speech. In: Proceedings of Interspeech, pp. 2036–2040. ISCA, Singapore (2014)
9. Jokinen, E., Remes, U., Alku, P.: The use of read versus conversational Lombard speech in spectral tilt modeling for intelligibility enhancement in near-end noise conditions. In: Proceedings of Interspeech, pp. 2771–2775. ISCA, San Francisco (2016)
10. Jokinen, E., Remes, U., Alku, P.: Intelligibility enhancement of telephone speech using gaussian process regression for normal-to-lombard spectral tilt conversion. IEEE Trans. Audio Speech Lang. Process. **25**(10), 1985–1996 (2017)
11. Summers, W.V., Pisoni, D.B., Bernacki, R.H., et al.: Effects of noise on speech production: acoustic and perceptual analyses. J. Acoust. Soc. Am. **3**(84), 917–928 (1988)
12. Bronkhorst, A.W.: The cocktail party phenomenon: a review of research on speech intelligibility in multiple-talker conditions. Acta Acust. United Acust. **86**(1), 117–128 (2000)
13. Lu, Y., Cooke, M.: The contribution of change in F0 and spectral tilt to increased intelligibility of speech produced in noise. Speech Commun. **51**(12), 1253–1262 (2009)
14. Cooke, M., Lu, Y.: Spectral and temporal changes to speech produced in the presence of energetic and informational masker. J. Acoust. Soc. Am. **128**(4), 2059–2069 (2010)
15. Jokinen, E., Alku, P.: Estimating the spectral tilt of the glottal source from telephone speech using neural network. J. Acoust. Soc. Am. Express Lett. **141**(4), 327–330 (2017)
16. Makhoul, J.: Linear prediction: a tutorial review. Proc. IEEE **63**(4), 561–580 (1975)
17. El-Jaroudi, A., Makhoul, J.: Discrete all-pole modeling. IEEE Trans. Signal Process. **39**(2), 411–423 (1991)
18. Ma, C., Kamp, Y., Willems, L.F.: Robust signal selection for linear prediction analysis of voiced speech. Speech Commun. **12**(1), 69–81 (1993)
19. Magi, C., Pohjalainen, J.: Stabilised weighted linear prediction. Speech Commun. **51**(5), 401–411 (2009)
20. Airaksinen, M., Story, B., Alku, P.: Quasi closed phase analysis for glottal inverse filtering. In: 14th Annual Conference of the International Speech Communication Association, pp. 143–147. ISCA, Lyon (2013)
21. Airaksinen, M., Raitio, T., Story, B., et al.: Quasi closed phase glottal inverse filtering analysis with weighted linear prediction. IEEE Trans. Audio Speech Lang. Process. **22**(3), 596–607 (2014)
22. Drugman, T., Thomas, M., Gudnason, J., et al.: Detection of glottal closure instants from speech signal: a quantitative review. IEEE Trans. Audio Speech Lang. Process. **20**(3), 994–1006 (2012)
23. Sofoklis, K., Okko, R., Pavvo, A.: Evaluation of spectral tilt measures for sentence prominence under different noise conditions. In: Proceedings of Interspeech, pp. 3211–3215. ISCA, Stockholm (2017)

24. Lopez, A.R., Seshadri, S., Juvela, L., et al.: Speaking style conversion from normal to Lombard speech using a glottal vocoder and Bayesian GMMs. In: Proceedings of Interspeech, pp. 1363–1367. ISCA, Stockholm (2017)
25. Tsoi, A.C., Back, A.: Discrete time recurrent neural network architectures: a unifying review. Neurocomputing **15**(3–4), 183–223 (1997)
26. Sołoducha, M., Raake, A., Kettler, F., Voigt, P.: Lombard speech database for German language. In: Proceedings of DAGA, Aachen (2016)
27. Cooke, M., Mayo, C., Valentini-Botinhao, C., et al.: Evaluating the intelligibility benefit of speech modifications in known noise conditions. Speech Commun. **55**(4), 572–585 (2013)
28. Rothauser, E.H.: IEEE recommended practice for speech quality measurements. IEEE Trans. Audio Electroacoust. **17**, 225–246 (1969)

Multi-channel Convolutional Neural Networks with Multi-level Feature Fusion for Environmental Sound Classification

Dading Chong[1], Yuexian Zou[1,2(✉)], and Wenwu Wang[3]

[1] ADSPLAB, School of ECE, Peking University, Shenzhen, China
zouyx@pkusz.edu.cn
[2] Peng Cheng Laboratory, Shenzhen, China
[3] Centre for Vision, Speech and Signal Processing, University of Surrey,
Guildford, UK

Abstract. Learning acoustic models directly from the raw waveform is an effective method for Environmental Sound Classification (ESC) where sound events often exhibit vast diversity in temporal scales. Convolutional neural networks (CNNs) based ESC methods have achieved the state-of-the-art results. However, their performance is affected significantly by the number of convolutional layers used and the choice of the kernel size in the first convolutional layer. In addition, most existing studies have ignored the ability of CNNs to learn hierarchical features from environmental sounds. Motivated by these findings, in this paper, parallel convolutional filters with different sizes in the first convolutional layer are designed to extract multi-time resolution features aiming at enhancing feature representation. Inspired by VGG networks, we build our deep CNNs by stacking 1-D convolutional layers using very small filters except for the first layer. Finally, we extend the model using multi-level feature aggregation technique to boost the classification performance. The experimental results on Urbansound 8k, ESC-50, and ESC-10 show that our proposed method outperforms the state-of-the-art end-to-end methods for environmental sound classification in terms of the classification accuracy.

Keywords: Environmental sound classification
Multi-channel deep convolutional neural networks · End-to-end
Multi-level feature fusion

1 Introduction

Environmental sound classification (ESC) is an important research area in human-computer interaction with a variety of applications such as abnormal sound detection in security surveillance. There are many research outcomes of ESC in the last decade [1]. However, with the limit amount of publicly available research datasets, ESC is still an open and difficult challenge.

Traditional ESC methods are based on hand-craft features, such as zero-crossing, mel-frequency cepstral coefficients (MFCCs) [2], and mel-filterbank features [3], and traditional classifiers such as Random forest, support vector machines, and Gaussian

I. Kompatsiaris et al. (Eds.): MMM 2019, LNCS 11296, pp. 157–168, 2019.
https://doi.org/10.1007/978-3-030-05716-9_13

mixture models [4–7]. However, the performance of all the feature based methods highly depends on the representation ability of these hand-craft features. In recent years, deep learning has gained incredible popularity [8–10]. Among them, the convolutional neural network is regarded as a powerful method, due to its ability in learning hierarchical high-level representations from sound data. CNNs have been applied to sound event recognition in two different ways. The first approach is to use the CNNs as the classifier with MFCCs or log-mel features as the input [3, 11–14]. The second approach use CNNs to extract salient and discriminative features from raw wave signals for ESC [6, 15–17].

Current approaches have the following limitations. (1) Since most of the features were originally designed for Automatic Speech Recognition (ASR) rather than for the ESC task, it may fail to capture the intrinsic information from the environmental sounds that may be critical for classification; (2) The feature extraction stage is separated from classification stage, as a result, the designed feature may not be optimal for the classification task. (3) The existing CNN models often use 2D convolution which involves more parameters as compared with 1D convolution. (4) The feature extracted from 1-D convolutional layer with a fixed size might be insufficient for building high-level discriminative representations.

In this study, we present a multi-scale deep convolutional neural network architecture for ESC that is able to address these issues. Our architecture allows one to develop much deeper and more "complex" structure while using a model of small size. The proposed method consists of ten 1-D convolutional layers and multiple filters with different sizes in the first 1-D convolutional layer which are learned simultaneously. Finally, multi-level feature fusion is proposed to make full use of hierarchical features extracted from deep CNNs.

Our main contribution can be summarized as follows:

- We propose an end-to-end accurate and efficient methods for ESC based on deep convolutional neural networks.
- We design parallel CNNs to learn richer representation from raw waveforms.
- Comparatively studies are conducted to demonstrate the effect of multi-level features on the classification performance.
- Without full connection layers, our proposed method reaches comparable classification performance but with a much smaller model size and much faster speed for environmental sound classification.

The paper is organized as follows. In the next section, related works are introduced briefly for presentation clarity. Problem definition and the proposed ESC system and its subsystems with implementation details are given in Sect. 3. Experimental setup and results will be shown in Sect. 4 and conclusion is drawn in Sect. 5.

2   Related Work

In recent years, CNNs have led to impressive results in ESC tasks, thanks to its ability in automatically learning complex feature representations with its convolutional layers. Conventional feature, such as spectrograms, MFCCs [2], mel-filterbank features [3], are the most commom inputs for CNN-based architectures. This method was firstly proposed by Piczak [3] for ESC task. Where log-mel and delta log-mel (i.e. first temporal derivative) features are extracted in each frame. Then, the two-dimensional feature map constituted by static log-mel and delta log-mel is fed into a two-channel CNNs for classification. This increased the classification accuracy over the traditional methods by 13% on the ESC-50 dataset.

Meanwhile, motivated by Hoshen et al. [18], where the first 1-D convolutional layer is taken as a finite impulse response filter bank, many attempts have been made to learn features automatically from raw waveforms for ESC. Tokozume and Harada [15] proposed an end-to-end ESC method using two convolution layers to classify environmental sound. The accuracy of their method was 5.1% higher than the model using log-mel features. Based on this research, Dai et al. [17] proposed to use deep convolutional neural networks (DCNNs) to extract more discriminative features, and the DCNN model was shown to outperform the shallow convolutional neural network model.

Inspired by recent advance in end-to-end ESC methods, we proposed an end-to-end method based on multi-channel deep convolutional neural networks (MC-DCNNs) to further improve the performance of ESC task. Below we present our method in detail.

3   Methodology

We formally define the aforementioned ESC problem. Then the pipeline and algorithms of our proposed methods are described in detail. Our MC-DCNNs ESC model is shown in Fig. 1. In Sect. 3.1, we gave a brief discussion on the problem formulation of the ESC task. In Sect. 3.2, we show the architecture of multi-channel CNNs used in our system. In Sect. 3.3, a multi-level feature fusion module is proposed to enhance the feature representation. The architecture and parameter settings are detailed in Sect. 3.4.

3.1   Problem Definition

Recognition of environmental sound from raw waveform can be considered as a classical learning problem of estimating an unknown relationship between the elements from input feature space to the corresponding elements in the target space. A time series is a sequence of real-valued data points with timestamps. In this paper, we define $S = \{(X_i, Y_i)|X_i \in R_l, Y_i \in Z; i = 1, \cdots, N\}$ with $X_i = [X_l, \cdots, X_i]^T$ as input vector formulated by considering the raw waveform that belongs to different environmental sounds; l is the length of the environmental sound. The elements in target space are the class labels to which the corresponding elements input feature space $X = [x_1, x_2, \cdots, x_N]$. The ESC problem is to build a classification model to predict a class label $y \in Y_i$ given an input sound data X.

3.2   Multi-channel Convolution Operation

Convolution has been a well-established method for modeling time series signals [19]. Suppose the waveform signal $w(i)$ is convolved with filters $h_{(s)}$ at different scales. The results of $x_j^{(s)}(n)$ are given by

$$x_j^{(s)}(n) = f(\sum_{i=0}^{N-1} w(i)h_j^s(n-i) + b_j^s)$$

where f is an activation function, N is the length of $w(i)$, and b_j is an additive bias.

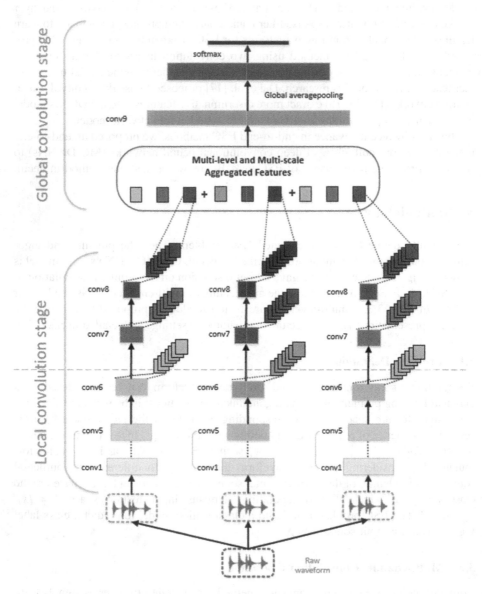

Fig. 1. The overall framework of the multi-channel deep convolutional neural networks environmental sound classification system

Using filters of different size, the convolution is capable of extracting multi-temporal resolution features from the raw waveform. For example, 40, 80 and 160 samples correspond to 2.5, 5 and 10 ms at 16 kHz sampling rate. In our proposed method, three different kernel sizes with same stride are chosen representatively in the first 1-D convolution layer to learn multi-temporal resolution features with the same dimension. Each convolutional layer with filters is functionally similar to a bandpass filter bank. Each layer has 64 filters, generating 64 one-dimensional vectors. The receptive field is different due to different kernel size used in the first convolution layers, and the stride is set as 8 in time series. The filter size is set according to the experimental results of DCNNs [17], which demonstrated that the CNN model can extract local features of various time scales hierarchically by using parallel convolutional layers. The input shape and the parameters of the first convolutional layers are as in Table 1.

Table 1. Parameters of the first 1-D convolutional layer in MC-DCNNs

Layers	Input shape	Filter	Kernel size	Stride	Output shape
Conv1	[1,64000,1]	64	[40], [80], [160]	8	[1,8000,64]
Pool	[1,8000,1]	–	Pooling size = 4	4	[1,2000,64]

We apply no-overlapping max pooling to the output of these parallel three convolutional layers with a pooling size of 4. Then, the three outputs of the pool matrix is of size $1 \times 2000 \times 64$. Finally, these vectors are fed into the multi-channel convolutional filters to extract local features.

3.3 Multi-scale and Multi-level Feature Fusion

Using a single CNN model, different levels of features can be extracted, therefore, we establish parallel CNNs with different kernel sizes to extract multi-level and multi-scale features. Benefiting from the structure, we can extract multi-temporal resolution and multi-level features. To further enhance the convolutional features and improve the performance of the ESC task, we generate a global representation by aggregating the multi-level features from single CNNs into a single large feature vector. Empirically, for the ESC task, when the neural network goes deeper, its ability in catching global information will get better. We also noted that the features in lower layers tend to focus more on detailed information which can be beneficial for short environmental sounds. Meanwhile, the higher layers tend to contain more abstract semantic information which would be useful for capturing global information related to acoustic scenes. Therefore, we design a multi-level feature fusion module to balance the local and global information captured by features in lower and higher layers in the MC-DCNNs.

3.4 Architecture of MC-DCNNs

According to the above discussion, we propose the multi-scale deep convolutional neural network with feature fusion as shown in Fig. 1.

Firstly, we apply the parallel convolutional operation with different size of convolutional kernels on the input waveform. Three sizes are chosen as small receptive field model (SRF), middle receptive field model (MRF), and large receptive field model (LRF). Then we progressively reduce the temporal resolution to 2000 with a non-overlapping max pooling layer to each feature map. Three channel CNNs are applied on the three kinds of features. In the local convolutional stage, the raw waveform is provided to 1-D local convolution filters followed by max pooling to extract the local and independent features. The filter has the same size for local convolution in MC-DCNNs. By selecting the same filter size and performing down sampling with Maxpooling, each channel CNNs in local convolution stage captures features from different receptive fields. We also adopt batch normalization (BN) [20] after each convolutional layer. In the global convolutional stage, features extracted from each channel are locally and globally concatenated. Finally, similar to local convolution stage, 1-D convolutions is performed followed by the Global average pooling. The features obtained after the global convolution stage are provided to Softmax to predict the labels. In this work, we adopted the deep concatenation technique in [21] to concatenate all the feature maps vertically. The details of parameters are summarized in Table 2.

Table 2. Detailed parameters of proposed fully convolutional network for time-domain waveform inputs. [40/8, 64] denotes a convolutional layer with receptive field 40 and 64 filters, with stride 8. [...] × k denotes k stacked layers. Output size after each pooling is written as $m \times n$ where m is the size in time-domain and n is the number of feature maps. Maxpooling is also done with the feature get from conv6-7 to get the same dimension.

MC-DCNNs model for ESC		
Input: 64000 Samples(4s) as Inputs (e.g. Urbansound 8k)		
Conv1 [40/8,64]	Conv1 [80/8,64]	Conv1 [160/8,64]
Maxpooling: 4 × 1 (output: 2000 × 64)	Maxpooling: 4 × 1 (output: 2000 × 64)	Maxpooling: 4 × 1 (output: 2000 × 64)
Conv2-3 [3/1,64] ×2	Conv2-4 [3/1,64] ×2	Conv2-4 [3/1,64] ×2
Maxpooling: 4 × 1 (output: 500 × 64)	Maxpooling: 4 × 1 (output: 500 × 64)	Maxpooling: 4 × 1 (output: 500 × 64)
Conv4-5 [3/1, 128] ×2	Conv4-5 [3/1, 128] ×2	Conv4-5 [3/1, 128] ×2
Maxpooling: 4 × 1 (output: 125 × 128)	Maxpooling: 4 × 1 (output: 125 × 128)	Maxpooling: 4 × 1 (output: 125 × 128)
Conv6-7 [3/1, 256] ×2	Conv6-7 [3/1, 256] ×2	Conv6-7 [3/1, 256] ×2
Maxpooling: 4 × 1 (output: 32 × 256)	Maxpooling: 4 × 1 (output: 32 × 256)	Maxpooling: 4 × 1 (output: 32 × 256)
Conv8 [3/1, 512] ×1	Conv8 [3/1, 512] ×1	Conv8 [3/1, 512] ×1
Conv6-8concat (output: 32 × 1024)	Conv6-8Concat (output: 32 × 1024)	Conv6-8Concat (output: 32 × 1024)
Global concat (output: 32 × 3072)		
Conv9 [3/1, 512] ×1 (output: 32 × 512)		
Globalaverage pooling (1 × 512)		
Softmax		

4   Experiments and Discussion

In this section, we first provide a brief description about the Urbansound 8K [22], ESC-50 [23], and ESC-10 [23] datasets and the implementation procedure for the evaluation of MC-DCNNs. Performance comparison will also be provided in this section.

4.1   Datasets

Urbansound 8K contains of 10 types of environmental sounds in urban areas, such as engine idling, street music, and children playing. The dataset consists of 8732 audio clips of 4 s or less, in total 9.7 h. We use the official fold 10 to be our test set, and the remaining folds for training.

ESC-50 consists of 50 environmental sounds categories that are allocated into 5-folds with 40 samples per category. The 50 classes can be divided into 5 major groups: animals, natural soundscapes and water sounds, human non-speech sound, interior/domestic sounds, and exterior/urban noises. The dataset provides an exposure to a variety of sound sources, some very common (laughter, cat meowing, dog barking), some quite distinct (glass breaking, brushing teeth) and then some where the differences are more nuanced (helicopter and airplane noise). We use the official fold 5 to be our test set, and the remaining folds for training.

ESC-10 dataset is a subset of ESC-50, which contains 400 recordings divided equally into 10 categories: dog barking, rain, sea waves, baby crying, clock ticking, person sneezing, helicopter, chainsaw, rooster, and file crackling. We use the official fold 5 to be our test set, and the remaining folds for training.

4.2   Data Preparation and Implementation Details

We convert all sound files to monaural wav files with a sampling rate of 16 kHz. Differently from other standard methods, we did not remove the silent section from the whole 5s sound to preserve the integrity of the original audio in ESC-50 and ESC-10 datasets. All data are normalized to zero mean and unit variance in Urbansound 8k ESC-50 and ESC-10. The length of each sound segment is 40000 samples (corresponding to 2.5s raw waveform) in ESC-50 and ESC-10. We take the 64000 samples (corresponding to 4s raw waveform) as inputs in Urbansound 8k. In the training stage, we randomly select these segments from the original training audio and input them into the prediction models. In the test phase, we perform a majority voting of the output prediction results for classification.

Hyper parameters selection: The list of MC-DCNNs hyper parameters and the initialization used in this work are listed in Table 3.

4.3   Results

We compared our MC-DCNNs model with existing log-mel-CNN models and end-to-end based models such as reported by Piczak [3], Tokozume and Harada [15] and Dai

Table 3. The MC-DCNNs hyper parameters and their initialization

Parameter	Initialization values
Activation function	Leakyrelu ($\alpha = 0.2$) [24]
Optimizer	Adam [25]
Learning rate	0.001 with weight decay
Batch-size	32
Regularization	L2 regularization with coefficient 0.0001
Parameter initialization	He initialization
Epochs	400
Loss function	Categorical cross-entropy

et al. [17], Salamon and Bello [22]. Table 4 shows the results of the proposed MC-DCNNs on three datasets with previous state-of-the-art published methods.

First of all, with the ESC-50 dataset, our model achieves 73.5% classification accuracy, which is much higher than other end-to-end based ESC models and a little higher than the static-delta log-mel-CNN+BN methods proposed by Tokozume and Harada [15]. On the ESC-10 dataset, the classification accuracy of MC-DCNNs reaches 87.5%, which is 9.7% and 3.5% higher than the other two end-to-end based method respectively. Finally, we evaluated the algorithms on the Urbansound 8k dataset.

Table 4. Comparison of classification accuracy with other models on evaluated datasets.

Accuracy (%) on Dataset					
Model	Feature	Fusion	ESC-50	ESC-10	Urbansound 8k
Logmel-EnvNet [15]	log-mel	–	66.9 ± 3.1	79.8 ± 1.7	–
SB-CNN [26]	log-mel	–	71.0 ± 1.4	–	73.9 ± 0.4
Logmel+CNN [3]	log-mel	–	64.5 ± 0.9	81.5 ± 1.3	–
Logmel+CNN +BN [15]	log-mel	–	72.4 ± 1.7	–	72.7
D-CNNs [13]	log-mel	–	68.0 ± 1.4	84.6 ± 2.1	–
EnvNet [15]	Raw waveform	–	64.0 ± 2.4	77.6 ± 2.3	69.2 ± 0.8
EnvNet2 [16]	Raw waveform	–	71.6 ± 2.7	83.2 ± 1.5	74.2 ± 1.5
M18 [17]	Raw waveform	–	–	–	71.68
MC-DCNNs (this paper)	Raw waveform	–	71.1 ± 0.8	84.1 ± 0.7	73.6 ± 0.8
MC-DCNNs (this paper)	Raw waveform	Multi-level fusion	73.1 ± 1.1	87.6 ± 1.3	75.1 ± 0.6

The accuracy of our proposed methods is 75.1%, much higher than the 71.68% accuracy achieved by Dai et al. [17] using the DCNNs based methods. These results on these three datasets indicate that our multi-channel deep convolutional neural networks with multi-level feature fusion have achieved significant improvement in environmental sound classification with the raw waveform as input, offering state-of-the-art performance in environmental sound classification.

Furthermore, we did a comparative experiment, as shown in Fig. 2. It can be seen that the multi-channel model consistently outperforms the single-channel model. It confirms the effectiveness of our proposed multi-channel model.

We further compared the accuracy of the MC-DCNNs with or without multi-level feature fusion on ESC-50. We noticed that the classification accuracy of the combination model increases on short duration environmental sounds compared with D-CNNs and human non-speech in contrast with log-mel feature based methods. The D-CNN model may lose detailed information while extracting global information. However, in our MC-DCNNs method, benefiting from the features extracted from former layers, the classification accuracy increased significantly. Similarly, for human non-speech sound, the accuracy has been improved, which indicates that some features in the human non-speech sound can be ignored by log-mel features. Using the MC-DCNNs, we can make full use of features learned from raw waveform, so that the classification accuracy can be improved via multi-level information fusion.

At the same time, benefited from the peculiarity of FCNs, the model size of MC-DCNNs is only 1.8M. Besides, our MC-DCNNs can classify two minutes of audio per second on NVIDIA GTX 1080, which is able to perform real-time environmental sound classification and is of great value in practical applications.

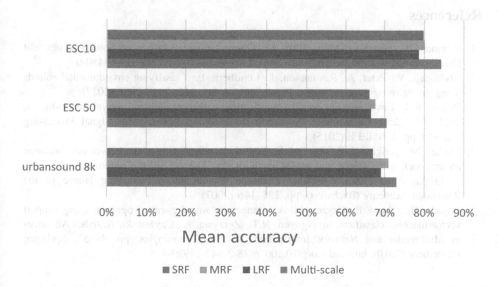

Fig. 2. Effectiveness of multi-channel models. We compare multi-channel with single-channel with SRF, MRF, LRF on ESC-10, ESC-50 and Urbansound 8K, The classification of Multi-channel models are superior to single-channel.

5 Conclusion

We presented a new end-to-end environmental sound classification system MC-DCNNs, which is composed of three channel stacked convolutional neural networks, trained on raw waveform as input. Each channel is composed of eight 1-D convolutional layers with batch normalization [20]. Three public datasets, Urbansound 8K, ESC-50, and ESC-10, are used to evaluate the classification performance of the MC-DCNNs model. The classification accuracy of the MC-DCNNs is 75.1%, 73.5%, 87.5%, on Urbansound 8K, ESC-50, and ESC-10, respectively, which is 1.1%, 6%, and 2.4% higher than existing log-mel feature based methods. It is also 1.5%, 4.4%, and 0.9% higher than the state-of-the-art end-to-end methods. These results showed that our MC-DCNNs are more effective for environmental sound classification due to the exploitation of both global and local features. While we have achieved excellent classification accuracy, our method also has the advantage in small model size and real-time classification performance. Future work will consider different structures of convolution neural networks for ESC task, such as convolutional recurrent neural networks. We will also consider applying the MC-DCNNs to time-series signal other than environmental sounds.

Acknowledgment. This project was partially supported by Shenzhen Science & Technology Fundamental Research Programs (No: JCYJ20170817160058246 and JCYJ20170306165153653) & Shenzhen Key Laboratory for Intelligent Multimedia and Virtual Reality (ZDSYS20170 3031405467). Special acknowledgements are given to Aoto-PKUSZ Joint Research Center of Artificial Intelligence on Scene Cognition & Technology Innovation for its support.

References

1. Virtanen, T., Plumbley, M.D., Ellis, D.: Computational Analysis of Sound Scenes and Events. Springer, Heidelberg (2018). https://doi.org/10.1007/978-3-319-63450-0
2. Boddapati, V., Petef, A., Rasmusson, J., Lundberg, L.: Classifying environmental sounds using image recognition networks. Proc. Comput. Sci. **112**, 2048–2056 (2017)
3. Piczak, K.J.: Environmental sound classification with convolutional neural networks. In: 2015 IEEE 25th International Workshop on Machine Learning for Signal Processing (MLSP), pp. 1–6. IEEE (2015)
4. Vacher, M., Serignat, J.-F., Chaillol, S.: Sound classification in a smart room environment: an approach using GMM and HMM methods. In: The 4th IEEE Conference on Speech Technology and Human-Computer Dialogue (SpeD 2007), Publishing House of the Romanian Academy (Bucharest), pp. 135–146 (2007)
5. Łopatka, K., Zwan, P., Czyżewski, A.: Dangerous sound event recognition using support vector machine classifiers. In: Nguyen, N.T., Zgrzywa, A., Czyżewski, A. (eds.) Advances in Multimedia and Network Information System Technologies, pp. 49–57. Springer, Heidelberg (2010). https://doi.org/10.1007/978-3-642-14989-4_5

6. Su, F., Yang, L., Lu, T., Wang, G.: Environmental sound classification for scene recognition using local discriminant bases and HMM. In: Proceedings of the 19th ACM International Conference on Multimedia, pp. 1389–1392. ACM (2011)
7. Saki, F., Kehtarnavaz, N.: Background noise classification using random forest tree classifier for cochlear implant applications. In: 2014 IEEE International Conference on Acoustics, Speech and Signal Processing (ICASSP), pp. 3591–3595. IEEE (2014)
8. Sainath, T.N., Mohamed, A.-R., Kingsbury, B., Ramabhadran, B.: Deep convolutional neural networks for LVCSR. In: 2013 IEEE International Conference on Acoustics, Speech and Signal Processing (ICASSP), pp. 8614–8618. IEEE (2013)
9. Abdel-Hamid, O., Mohamed, A.-R., Jiang, H., Deng, L., Penn, G., Yu, D.: Convolutional neural networks for speech recognition. IEEE/ACM Trans. Audio Speech Lang. Process. **22**, 1533–1545 (2014)
10. Kong, Q., Sobieraj, I., Wang, W., Plumbley, M.: Deep neural network baseline for DCASE challenge 2016. In: Proceedings of DCASE 2016 (2016)
11. Cotton, C.V., Ellis, D.P.: Spectral vs. spectro-temporal features for acoustic event detection. In: 2011 IEEE Workshop on Applications of Signal Processing to Audio and Acoustics (WASPAA), pp. 69–72. IEEE (2011)
12. Zhang, H., McLoughlin, I., Song, Y.: Robust sound event recognition using convolutional neural networks. In: 2015 IEEE International Conference on Acoustics, Speech and Signal Processing (ICASSP), pp. 559–563. IEEE (2015)
13. Zhang, X., Zou, Y., Shi, W.: Dilated convolution neural network with LeakyReLU for environmental sound classification. In: 2017 22nd International Conference on Digital Signal Processing (DSP), pp. 1–5. IEEE (2017)
14. Medhat, F., Chesmore, D., Robinson, J.: Masked conditional neural networks for audio classification. In: Lintas, A., Rovetta, S., Verschure, P.F.M.J., Villa, A.E.P. (eds.) ICANN 2017. LNCS, vol. 10614, pp. 349–358. Springer, Cham (2017). https://doi.org/10.1007/978-3-319-68612-7_40
15. Tokozume, Y., Harada, T.: Learning environmental sounds with end-to-end convolutional neural network. In: 2017 IEEE International Conference on Acoustics, Speech and Signal Processing (ICASSP), pp. 2721–2725. IEEE (2017)
16. Tokozume, Y., Ushiku, Y., Harada, T.: Learning from between-class examples for deep sound recognition. arXiv preprint arXiv:1711.10282 (2017)
17. Dai, W., Dai, C., Qu, S., Li, J., Das, S.: Very deep convolutional neural networks for raw waveforms. In: 2017 IEEE International Conference on Acoustics, Speech and Signal Processing (ICASSP), pp. 421–425. IEEE (2017)
18. Hoshen, Y., Weiss, R.J., Wilson, K.W.: Speech acoustic modeling from raw multichannel waveforms. In: 2015 IEEE International Conference on Acoustics, Speech and Signal Processing (ICASSP), pp. 4624–4628. IEEE (2015)
19. Zhao, B., Lu, H., Chen, S., Liu, J., Wu, D.: Convolutional neural networks for time series classification. J. Syst. Eng. Electron. **28**, 162–169 (2017)
20. Ioffe, S., Szegedy, C.: Batch normalization: accelerating deep network training by reducing internal covariate shift. arXiv preprint arXiv:1502.03167 (2015)
21. Lee, J., Nam, J.: Multi-level and multi-scale feature aggregation using pretrained convolutional neural networks for music auto-tagging. IEEE Signal Process. Lett. **24**, 1208–1212 (2017)
22. Salamon, J., Jacoby, C., Bello, J.P.: A dataset and taxonomy for urban sound research. In: Proceedings of the 22nd ACM International Conference on Multimedia, pp. 1041–1044. ACM (2014)

23. Piczak, K.J.: ESC: dataset for environmental sound classification. In: Proceedings of the 23rd ACM International Conference on Multimedia, pp. 1015–1018. ACM (2015)
24. Maas, A.L., Hannun, A.Y., Ng, A.Y.: Rectifier nonlinearities improve neural network acoustic models. In: Proceedings of ICML, p. 3 (2013)
25. Kingma, D.P., Ba, J.: Adam: a method for stochastic optimization. arXiv preprint arXiv: 1412.6980 (2014)
26. Salamon, J., Bello, J.P.: Deep convolutional neural networks and data augmentation for environmental sound classification. IEEE Signal Process. Lett. **24**, 279–283 (2017)

Audio-Based Automatic Generation of a Piano Reduction Score by Considering the Musical Structure

Hirofumi Takamori[1]([📧]), Takayuki Nakatsuka[1]([📧]), Satoru Fukayama[2]([📧]), Masataka Goto[2]([📧]), and Shigeo Morishima[3]([📧])

[1] Department of Pure and Applied Physics, Waseda University, Tokyo, Japan
{tkmrkc1290,t59nakatsuka}@gmail.com
[2] National Institute of Advanced Industrial Science and Technology (AIST), Ibaraki, Japan
{s.fukayama,m.goto}@aist.go.jp
[3] Waseda Research Institute for Science and Engineering, Tokyo, Japan
shigeo@waseda.jp

Abstract. This study describes a method that automatically generates a piano reduction score from the audio recordings of popular music while considering the musical structure. The generated score comprises both right- and left-hand piano parts, which reflect the melodies, chords, and rhythms extracted from the original audio signals. Generating such a reduction score from an audio recording is challenging because automatic music transcription is still considered to be inefficient when the input contains sounds from various instruments. Reflecting the long-term correlation structure behind similar repetitive bars is also challenging; further, previous methods have independently generated each bar. Our approach addresses the aforementioned issues by integrating musical analysis, especially structural analysis, with music generation. Our method extracts rhythmic features as well as melodies and chords from the input audio recording and reflects them in the score. To consider the long-term correlation between bars, we use similarity matrices, created for several acoustical features, as constraints. We further conduct a multivariate regression analysis to determine the acoustical features that represent the most valuable constraints for generating a musical structure. We have generated piano scores using our method and have observed that we can produce scores that differently balance between the ability to achieve rhythmic characteristics and the ability to obtain musical structures.

Keywords: Piano reduction · Multivariate regression analysis · Musical structure · Acoustic feature · Self-similarity matrix

Supported by JST ACCEL, Japan (grant no. JPMJAC1602).

I. Kompatsiaris et al. (Eds.): MMM 2019, LNCS 11296, pp. 169–181, 2019.
https://doi.org/10.1007/978-3-030-05716-9_14

1   Introduction

One way to enjoy music is by playing an instrument yourself, which brings a different joy as compared to merely listening to music. The piano is the instrument that can simultaneously play multiple roles, including the melody line, harmony, and rhythm. For genres such as popular music, comprising a main vocal melody and an accompaniment played using various instruments, the piano is a suitable instrument for an individual to play his or her favorite songs. Herein, we focus on generating a piano reduction score for popular music.

Piano scores for several popular songs have been written by professional music arrangers. However, it is often necessary for a player to create a piano score from scratch because there is no guarantees that the desired song will be available as a piano score. Creating a piano reduction requires carefully working out how all parts of the original music can be expressed using a playable piano score. To address this issue, our method automatically generates a piano reduction score. It considers the audio signals from a pop song as the input and outputs a score suitable a piano.

The goal of this study is to automatically generate piano scores from audio signals. To achieve this goal, we adopt the approach proposed in paper [1]. The previous approach generates piano scores for each bar based on musical elements; melody, rhythm, chords, and number of notes. These elements are obtained from original scores. However, directly adopting this score-based method in audio-based applications is problematic since audio-based feature extraction is not always accurate, and it causes a lack of overall coherence. Hence, structural considerations are necessary for audio-based piano reduction.

In this study, we present a piano reduction method while considering the structure of the music. Our piano reduction method follows three stages: (a) analysis of the musical structure; (b) determination of the structure of the audio signal; and (c) score composition. Figure 1 shows the schematic of the proposed method. The main contribution of our study is twofold: First, we have generated piano scores that reflect both the rhythmic and structural features of the input audio signals. Second, we have determined self-similarity matrices (SSMs) for seven different acoustical features, which represent the structure of the piano performance. As the limitations of our method, we treat only popular songs in quadruple time, and the minimum resolution of generating the score is limited to a semiquaver note.

2   Related Work

Several studies have attempted to generate piano scores from original scores involving the usage of multiple instruments. Fujita et al. [2] generated a piano score from an ensemble score by extracting the melody and bass part and using them to develop the piano reduction. Chiu et al. [3] have considered five roles of the piano in music, which are the lead, foundation, rhythm, pad, and fill that were originally proposed by Owsinski [4]. By analyzing an original score, Chiu et al.

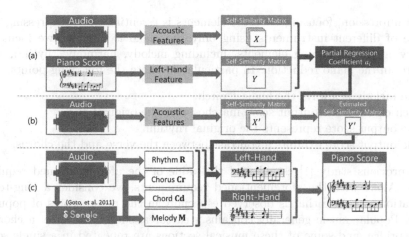

Fig. 1. Overview of our proposed method. (a) Using multivariate regression analysis, we analyze the correlation between the SSMs of the acoustical features and the SSM of the left-hand part of a manually arranged score. (b) We determine the SSM for a sample song using partial regression coefficients obtained in (a). (c) We generate a piano score with both the right- and left-hand parts using the extracted musical elements and structural feature estimated as SSM in (b).

associated each phrase in the score with a weighted importance value. They proposed a phrase-selection algorithm that maximized the importance value while considering the score's playability. Nakamura et al. [5] generated a piano reduction from an ensemble score using a fingering model. They focused both on the preservation of the sounds and on playability as constraints, where playability can be separately controlled by the respective difficulty parameters observed in case of the right- and left-hand parts. A common thread in these previous studies has been the reduction and selection of notes from an original score using either the original notes directly or through octave shifts. These are valid approaches that preserve the original impression of the music without generating any dissonance.

Methods exist that do not completely transcribe a score from an audio signal, but that can extract musical elements from an audio signal to generate an arrangement. For example, Percival et al. [6] have presented Song2Quartet, a system for generating string-quartet versions of popular music from audio recordings without requiring pitch determinations for all parts. This method can extract musical elements from an original piece, including the melodies, rhythms, chords, and number of notes. We emphasize the consideration of the constraints involved in piano reduction.

3   Piano Reduction of Popular Music

Melody, harmony, rhythm, timbre, and texture are deemed essential elements of music [7], and play important roles in musical expression. To preserve the original song's impression, focusing on these elements is essential. Since expressing the timbre of different instruments using only the piano is difficult, we focus on preserving the remaining elements, including melody, harmony, rhythm, and texture, in the piano reduction. In particular, we note the following points:

- The melody is always the highest pitch.
- Each chord in the output score matches with the original one.
- The output score represents the original rhythm.
- The output score exhibits a contrast between the verse and the chorus.

A previous study [1] established the value of the aforementioned requirements. Along with the aforementioned requirements, we consider a long-term correlation structure that is observed especially in the piano scores of popular music. Popular music generally contains structures, such as a verse, a chorus, and a bridge, and some of these musical sections are repeated in a single song [8]. Hence, it is important to reflect these repetitive structures in the generated piano scores. Thus, we impose an additional requirement to express the structural features of popular music as follows:

- The left-hand part should exhibit similar accompaniment patterns within the same section.

In this study, we perform piano reduction by considering the five aforementioned requirements.

4   Analysis of the Structure of the Music

In this section, we explain the analysis stage illustrated in Fig. 1(a) and outlined in Fig. 2. We have initially prepared a dataset containing 27 popular songs that include both the audio data and the corresponding piano scores. These audio data are acquired from the Internet, and these piano scores are manually produced.[1,2,3]

4.1   Feature Extraction

As acoustic features, we use chromagrams, Mel-frequency cepstrum coefficients (MFCCs), onsets, root-mean-square (RMS) energy, spectral centroid, spectral flatness, and zero-crossing rates (ZCRs). The audio signals are monaural and their sampling frequencies are 44.1 kHz. The window length during analysis is 1024, with an overlap of 256. We also set the number of channels of the Mel-scale filter bank at 20, and we use the 12 low dimensions. Especially for onsets detection, the methodology is inspired by Böck et al. [10].

---

[1] Bokaro Kamikyoku Daishugo Best 30, Depuro MP, Japan (2016).
[2] Jokyu Piano Grade Bokaro Meikyoku Piano Solo Concert, Depuro MP, Japan (2015).
[3] Print Score, https://www.print-gakufu.com/.

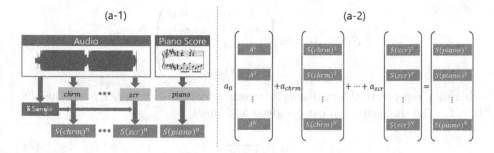

Fig. 2. Overview of the analysis of the musical structure. (a-1) Feature extraction from an audio recording and a score. We use *Songle* [9] to acquire the beats data. (a-2) Multivariate regression analysis of all songs in the dataset. The quantity, **A**, represents a matrix whose complete list of entries are 1. The quantity, $S(\cdot)$, represents the SSM of acoustic features or of a piano feature, and a_i represents a partial regression coefficient.

In this study, we extract the aforementioned seven features for each bar. *Songle* [9], a web service for active music listening, is used to get the start time of each bar in a song. This allows us to work out how the times (frames) of the audio signal correspond to the bars. Each feature of the mth bar can be represented as follows: $\mathbf{chr}_m \in \mathbb{R}^{12 \times 16}$ for the chromagram, $\mathbf{mfcc}_m \in \mathbb{R}^{12 \times 16}$ for the MFCCs, $\mathbf{onset}_m \in \mathbb{Z}^{1 \times 16}$ for the onsets, $\mathbf{rms}_m \in \mathbb{R}^{1 \times 16}$ for the RMS energy, $\mathbf{cent}_m \in \mathbb{R}^{1 \times 16}$ for the spectral centroid, $\mathbf{flat}_m \in \mathbb{R}^{1 \times 16}$ for the spectral flatness, and $\mathbf{zcr}_m \in \mathbb{R}^{1 \times 16}$ for the ZCR, respectively. Row-wise represents the time direction of a bar which is divided into segments with length of 16th note. For example, the first column represents the one-dimensional feature for the first 16th note in a bar. Acoustic features, excluding the $\mathbf{onset}_m$, are projected onto each segment with length of a 16th note by considering the mean between the current and subsequent beats. The jth column value of $\mathbf{onset}_m$ is set to unity if there is a peak between the current and subsequent beats or is set to zero if there is none.

Considering the features of a piano score, we extract the positions and numbers of the notes from the left-hand part and described them for each bar. We denote the mth bar's feature of a piano score by $\mathbf{piano}_m \in \mathbb{Z}^{1 \times 16}$. Row-wise again represents the time direction. The values of the jth column of $\mathbf{piano}_m$ are the numbers of notes positioned at the jth beat.

4.2 Multivariate Regression Analysis of the Self-Similarity Matrices

SSMs are calculated for both acoustic features and the features of a piano score by the procedures described in Sec. 4.1. The SSM indicates the structural similarity between the bars included in a song. For the feature sequence of a song, $\mathbf{f} = \{\mathbf{f}_1, \mathbf{f}_2, \cdots, \mathbf{f}_M\}$, the SSM, $\mathcal{S}(\mathbf{f}) \in \mathbb{R}^{M \times M}$, can be defined as follows:

$$S(\mathbf{f}) = [s_{ij}] = \begin{pmatrix} 1 & s_{12} & \cdots & s_{1M} \\ s_{21} & 1 & \cdots & s_{2M} \\ \vdots & \vdots & \ddots & \vdots \\ s_{M1} & s_{M2} & \cdots & 1 \end{pmatrix} \tag{1}$$

where s_{ij} represents the similarity between a feature's i^{th} bar, $\mathbf{f}_i$, and the jth bar, $\mathbf{f}_j$. The similarity, s_{ij}, can be given as follows:

$$s_{ij} = \frac{1}{1 + d_{ij}} \tag{2}$$

$$d_{ij} = \|\mathbf{f}_i - \mathbf{f}_j\| \tag{3}$$

where d_{ij} represents the distance between $\mathbf{f}_i$ and $\mathbf{f}_j$, which can be obtained by computing the Frobenius norm. The values of s_{ij} lie in the range $(0, 1]$, where $s_{ij} = 1$ indicates that the two features being compared are identical. Conversely, s_{ij} exhibits a low value if the two features being compared are unidentical.

We further perform multivariate regression analysis on the SSM. We assign the explanation variable, $\mathbf{X}$, and the objective variable, $\mathbf{Y}$, as follows:

$$\mathbf{X}_f = \{S(\mathbf{f})^1, S(\mathbf{f})^2, \cdots, S(\mathbf{f})^N\}$$

$$\mathbf{Y}_{piano} = \{S(\mathbf{piano})^1, S(\mathbf{piano})^2, \cdots, S(\mathbf{piano})^N\},$$

where $\mathbf{f}$ represents a sequence of each acoustic feature. The quantity, $S(\cdot)^n$, represents the SSM of the dataset's n^{th} song. We denote the formula to perform multivariate regression analysis as follows:

$$a_0 \mathbf{A} + \sum_{\gamma} a_{f_\gamma} \mathbf{X}_{f_\gamma} = \mathbf{Y}_{piano} \tag{4}$$

where a_0 represents the intercept and a_f denotes the acoustic features' partial regression coefficient. The quantity, $\mathbf{A}$, denotes a list of the matrices whose complete list of entries include 1, and it is introduced to match the matrix dimensions. The subscript, f_γ, represents one of the seven acoustic features used in this study. Eq. (4) is schematically depicted in Fig. 2(a-2). According to Eq. (4), we determine the intercept a_0 and the partial regression coefficients a_f.

5   Structural Segmentation

In this section, we explain the approach used to determine the structure of a piano score from the audio signals (Fig. 1(b)). The structure of a piano score is determined by segmenting SSM, which is estimated from acoustic features by using Eq. (4) with the partial regression coefficient obtained by multivariate regression described in Sect. 4.2. To segment a song into several musical sections, we adopt novelty detection [11]. We perform novelty detection by identifying the peaks of the novelty scores, obtained by multiplying the checkerboard kernel, $\mathbf{C}$, along the SSM's diagonal.

$$\mathbf{C} = \begin{pmatrix} 1 & -1 \\ -1 & 1 \end{pmatrix} \tag{5}$$

In our methodology, we calculate five kinds of novelty scores having checkerboard kernel sizes of (2×2), (4×4), (6×6), (8×8), and (10×10), respectively. We further consider the mean of the five novelty scores and normalize them to $[0, 1]$ range. Additionally, we perform peak detection for the novelty scores by introducing a second-order differential threshold, $th = 0.00$, -0.05, -0.07, -0.10, -0.15. The peak position is set to one at which the first-order differentiation turns from positive to negative and at which the second-order differentiation is less than th. We further obtain the musical structures' boundaries according to the peaks of the novelty scores. The musical structure is represented by lists of bars that mark the boundaries between various segments. Bars located between the acquired boundaries are considered to belong to the same segment.

6 Score Composition from Audio Signals

In this section, we explain the architecture for generating a piano score from the audio signals (Fig. 1(c)). First, we focus on the accompaniment database constructed beforehand. Further, we discuss the extraction of musical elements from the audio signals. We obtain the chorus, chord, and melody using *Songle* [9], while rhythm is obtained by detecting the onsets of spectral flux. Finally, we generate a piano score for both left- and right-hand parts based on the extracted elements.

6.1 Accompaniment Database

We construct the accompaniment database, **DB**, based on the existing piano scores [1]. The accompaniment database comprises accompaniment matrices. An accompaniment matrix represents a bar of the left-hand part as an 88×16 matrix, where 88 is the number of piano keys and 16 is set to match the length of a semiquaver. The matrix is generated after being transposed so that the root becomes C. In case of the matrix elements, the note value is stored in the places at which the note exists; zero is stored if there is no note. This allows the system to record the relative pitch transition and the rhythm of the original piano score. In this study, $\mathbf{DB}_n \in \mathbb{Z}^{88 \times 16}$ denotes the nth accompaniment matrix; it contains the 16-dimensional vector, $\mathbf{DBR}_n$, that represents the rhythm. When a non-zero value is stored in the jth column of $\mathbf{DB}_n$, the value 1 is stored in the jth element of $\mathbf{DBR}_n$. If only zeros are stored in the jth column of $\mathbf{DB}$, the value zero is also stored in the jth element of $\mathbf{DBR}_n$.

6.2 Extraction of Musical Elements from Audio Signals

We extract musical elements, including the melody $\mathbf{M}$, chord $\mathbf{Cd}$, chorus $\mathbf{Cr}$, and rhythm $\mathbf{R}$. We acquire $\mathbf{M}$, $\mathbf{Cd}$, and $\mathbf{Cr}$ from *Songle* [9], while we extract $\mathbf{R}$ by onset detection of the spectral flux, as described in Sect. 4.1. We obtain the following analysis results for each element from *Songle Widget* [4]:

---

[4] http://widget.songle.jp/.

Beat: index, start time, position
Chord: index, start time, duration, chord name
Melody: index, start time, duration, MIDI note number
Chorus: index, start time, duration

The index denotes the number of beats, chords, or notes of melody observed from the beginning of a song; start time represents the time at which each event starts; the position specifies the number of beats in each bar; duration denotes the length of the event; chord name shows the root note and the chord type; and the MIDI note number is the value that indicates the pitch. From these information, the melody and the chords can be described for each bar, and we also obtain the bar number, which is in the chorus section. For $\mathbf{M}$, $\mathbf{Cd}$, $\mathbf{Cr}$ and $\mathbf{R}$, the subscript, m, indicates the mth bar of the score. The quantity, $\mathbf{M}_m \in \mathbb{Z}^{88 \times 16}$, provides the pitch, note values, and position in the score for each bar. The number of rows corresponds to the number of keys on the keyboard, whereas the number of columns corresponds to the time resolution (16th note). The chord notes are represented in $\mathbf{Cd}_m$ for each beat as a set of MIDI note numbers. For Cr_m, the value is set to unity if the mth bar is in the chorus and is set to zero otherwise. The rhythm, $\mathbf{R} \in \mathbb{Z}^{1 \times 16}$, is acquired in the same manner as the onset, as explained in Sect. 4.1.

6.3   Generation of the Right-Hand Part

We allocate the melody, $\mathbf{M}$, to the right-hand part, $\mathbf{RH}$, as follows:

$$\mathbf{RH}_m = \begin{cases} \mathbf{Add}(\mathbf{M}_m, \mathbf{R}_m, \mathbf{Cd}_m) & Cr_m = 1 \\ \mathbf{M}_m & \text{otherwise} \end{cases} \tag{6}$$

The quantity, $\mathbf{RH}_m \in \mathbb{Z}^{88 \times 16}$, represents the mth bar of $\mathbf{RH}$. If the mth bar is in a chorus section, $\mathbf{Add}_m$ attaches additional chord notes to each note in the melody, $\mathbf{M}_m$, where a component of the rhythm, $\mathbf{R}_m$, is unity. The chord notes at each beat are obtained from $\mathbf{Cd}_m$ and are considered to be lower in pitch than the melody and more than four semitones away.

6.4   Generation of the Left-Hand Part

The left-hand part, $\mathbf{LH}$, of the piano score can be generated by selecting from the accompaniment database, $\mathbf{DB}$. First, we select an accompaniment for which the rhythm is similar to that of the audio signal, $\mathbf{R}$, for each bar. This accompaniment list is defined as $\mathbf{LH'}$, which represents the accompaniment list by considering only the rhythm. Further, we reflect the features of the musical structure, as determined in Sec. 5. We reduce the kinds of accompaniments that appeared in the same musical section so that they exhibit similar rhythmic patterns. The result of this reduction is designated as $\mathbf{LH}$. The mth bar of $\mathbf{LH'}$ is denoted by $\mathbf{LH'}_m$. We define the parameter, λ, to be the number of kinds of accompaniments in the same musical section. This process is described by the following formula:

$$LH = FuncS(\mathbf{LH'}, \lambda, th) \tag{7}$$

$$\mathbf{LH'}_m = \arg\min \; CostR(\mathbf{DB}, \mathbf{R}_m) \tag{8}$$

$$CostR(\mathbf{DB}, \mathbf{R}_m) = \sum_n ||\mathbf{DBR}_n - \mathbf{R}_m|| \tag{9}$$

Here, $FuncS(\cdot)$ reduces the kinds of accompaniments by changing the accompaniment patterns with a low appearance frequency to form accompaniments with a high appearance frequency. This reduction continues until the number of kinds of accompaniments became less than λ for each musical section. The value, $\lambda = 1$, indicates that only one kind of accompaniment is selected in each musical section, and $\lambda = \infty$ indicates that the musical structure is not considered. $\mathbf{LH'}$ is a candidate accompaniment list selected on the basis of $CostR(\cdot)$, where $CostR$ is introduced to select accompaniments with high similarities in audio rhythms. Finally, to ensure that the sound of $\mathbf{LH}_m$ reflects $\mathbf{Cd}_m$ we shift $\mathbf{LH}_m$ to the nearest chord notes for each bar.

7   Results and Evaluation

As the result of the multivariate regression analysis described in Sect. 4, the partial regression coefficients and t-values of them are presented in Table 1.

Table 1. The result of multivariate regression analysis.

	a_0	a_{chr}	a_{mfcc}	a_{onset}	a_{cent}	a_{flat}	a_{rms}	a_{zcr}
coefs	−0.0373	0.4439	−0.0329	0.1403	0.2224	0.3153	0.0494	−0.1175
t-value	−8.974	74.50	−8.863	74.88	111.3	87.47	27.87	−34.95

Here, a_0 represents the intercept and a_f represents each acoustic feature's partial regression coefficient. The t-value in linear regression analysis is commonly considered to be a value that indicates the similarity of the explanation value with the objective value. The t-value can be derived by dividing a coefficient with its standard error. A large absolute t-value indicates that the explanation value exhibits large effectiveness in determining the objective. We also calculate p-values and an adjusted coefficient of determination R^2_{adj}. The p-value represents the probable significance of the explanation value. Generally, an explanation value is effective when the p-value is lower than 0.05. The results of all the p-values of the coefficients are lower than the order of 10^{-18}. R^2_{adj} is an indicator of multivariate regression analysis' accuracy, and can be defined as follows:

$$R^2_{adj} \equiv 1 - \frac{\sum_i (y_i - y'_i)^2/(N - p - 1)}{\sum_i (y_i - \overline{y}_i)^2/(N - 1)} \tag{10}$$

where y is the true data; $\bar{y}$ is the mean of y; y' is the predicted data; N is the sample size; and p is the number of explanation values. Unity is achieved when there is no residual relative to the predicted data, and unity decreases as the residual increases. The obtained R^2_{adj} in our model was 0.1590.

We output the piano score for each of the 27 popular songs included in the dataset. To verify the effectiveness of our method, we conduct leave-one-out cross-validation for the SSMs of all the songs in the dataset. Each SSM is calculated from a left-hand part of each score.

First, we select one song as test data and generate a piano score of this song using the partial regression coefficients derived from the remaining 26 songs. Finally, we obtain the residuals by calculating the Frobenius norm of the difference between the SSM of the generated and manually created piano scores. We calculate the residuals for each of the seven different values of λ, which denotes the number of types of accompaniments in one musical section, and for five different block thresholds, th. Table 2 presents the result of this cross-validation.

Table 2. The result of leave-one-out cross-validation. $(\times 10^{-3})$

threshold th	The number of kinds of accompaniments λ						
	1	2	3	4	5	6	∞
0.00	3.550	3.630	3.674	3.685	3.714	3.730	3.760
−0.05	3.535	3.612	3.684	3.708	3.738	3.742	3.760
−0.07	3.277	**3.357**	3.452	3.522	3.591	3.647	3.760
−0.10	**3.257**	3.451	**3.413**	**3.430**	**3.460**	**3.506**	3.760
−0.15	3.311	3.503	3.538	3.535	3.564	3.560	3.760

All the values are normalized by dividing with the size of the matrix. We calculate the residuals for all songs in the dataset and estimate the mean value. The values represent how closely the generated scores' accompaniments resemble those of manually-produced scores in their structure. Figure 3 depicts the variation of the SSM structure with λ for the cases in which $th = -0.07, -0.10$. We selected three songs[5,6,7] where the SSMs of these songs clearly changed by trying different values for λ. We also test our method using one song from the RWC Music Database [12] (RWC-MDB-P-2001 No. 7).[8]

8   Discussion

Table 1 shows that the t-values of the spectral centroid, spectral flatness, onset, and chromagram exhibit comparably high values, indicating that these acoustic

---

[5] *Mosaic Roll* (DECO*27), https://www.nicovideo.jp/watch/sm11398357.

[6] *Ghost Rule* (DECO*27), https://www.nicovideo.jp/watch/sm27965309.

[7] *Irohauta* (Ginsaku), https://piapro.jp/t/0D18/20100223020519.

[8] The generated results is available at https://youtu.be/Yx9c0LnEyyE.

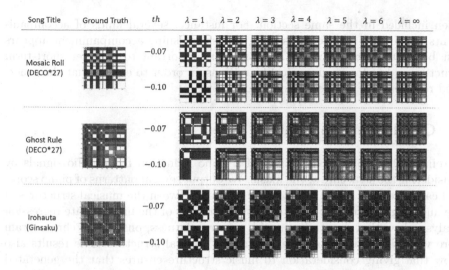

Fig. 3. Comparison of the SSMs with the ground truth about three songs.

features effectively determine the structure of the piano performance. The spectral centroid, spectral flatness, and chromagram are features related to the pitch of the sound and harmony. Hence, the registers, melodies, and chords are deemed important for structural determination. The onset is a rhythmic feature; hence, focusing on the sounds that correspond to beats or rhythm is also important.

Conversely, the t-values for MFCC, RMS, and ZCR exhibit comparably low values, indicating that the features related to timbre and texture are not as effective as the aforementioned harmonic and rhythmic features. Obviously, timbre and texture change during a song. However, repetitive structures of these features are not as well-correlated with the structure of the piano performance. In this study, the left-hand part of the piano score represents the structure of the piano score. We conclude that the timbre and texture of the sounds are expressed in the piano score by other elements such as musical symbols and the number of notes. Hence, the structure of the piano score generated by our method is not sufficient to express the structure of timbre and texture, resulting in low t-values for MFCC, RMS, and ZCR.

R_{adj}^2 is below unity, which is the maximum value of R_{adj}^2. Several possible variations of piano scores exist for a given song depending on the arranger. Therefore, R_{adj}^2 inevitably exhibits low values owing to these fluctuations. However, a determination of the musical structure from the acoustic features is possible to some extent because R_{adj}^2 exhibits a positive value.

Table 2 shows that the SSMs of the generated piano scores exhibit low residuals when λ is small and when th is -0.07 and -0.10. This indicates that segmenting the music with moderate roughness and selecting fewer kinds of accompaniments in the segmented sections produces results closer to the ground truth. However, in a piano score by an arranger, several kinds of accompaniments are often included in the same section. For instance, several kinds of accompaniments may be alternatively observed, or distinguishing accompaniment appears just before the next phrase. Therefore, it is important to consider short-term structure and to focus on musical transitions, in order to ensure that the generated result is close to the original piano score.

9   Conclusions and Future Work

Herein, we have proposed method of a piano reduction from audio signals by considering the structure of the music. We output several patterns of piano scores and calculated the SSMs to verify the relation between the musical structures of the audio signals and the piano scores. The results of the multivariate regression analysis show that spectral centroid, spectral flatness, onset, and chromagram were valuable features for determining the musical structure. The results also show that giving consideration to music structure ensures that the generated piano structure will be close to one written by an arranger. In future studies, we aim to augment the music database and reselect acoustic features that are more valuable for generating a piano reduction score.

References

1. Takamori, H., Sato, H., Nakatsuka, T., Morishima, S.: Automatic arranging musical score for piano using important musical elements. In: Proceedings of the 14th Sound and Music Computing Conference, Aalto, Finland, pp. 35–41 (2017)
2. Fujita, K., Oono, H., Inazumi, H.: A proposal for piano score generation that considers proficiency from multiple part. In: IPSJ SIG Technical reports, pp. 47–52 (2008)
3. Chiu, S., Shan, M., Huang, J.: Automatic system for the arrangement of piano reductions. In: Proceedings of the 11th IEEE International Symposium on Multimedia, pp. 459–464 (2009)
4. Owsinski, B.: The Mixing Engineer's Handbook. Thomson Course Technology (1999)
5. Nakamura, E., Sagayama, S.: Automatic piano reduction from ensemble scores based on merged-output Hidden Markov model. In: Proceedings of the 41st International Computer Music Conference (ICMC), pp. 298–305 (2015)
6. Percival, G., Fukayama, S., Goto, M.: Song2Quartet: a system for generating string quartet cover songs from polyphonic audio of popular music. In: Proceedings of the International Symposium Music Information Retrieval, pp. 114–120 (2015)
7. Schmidt-Jones, C.: The Basic Elements of Music (2014). Lulu.com
8. Doll, C.: Rockin' out: expressive modulation in verse-chorus form. J. Soc. Music Theory 17(3), 1–10 (2011)

9. Goto, M., Yoshii, K., Fujihara, H., Mauch, M., Nakano, T.: Songle: a web service for active music listening improved by user contributions. In: Proceedings of the International Symposium on Music Information Retrieval, pp. 311–316 (2011)
10. Böck, S., Florian, K., Markus, S.: Evaluating the online capabilities of onset detection methods. In: Proceedings of the International Symposium on Music Information Retrieval, pp. 49–54 (2012)
11. Jonathan, F.: Automatic audio segmentation using a measure of audio novelty. In: Proceedings of the 2000 IEEE International Conference on Multimedia and Expo, vol. 1, pp. 452–455 (2000)
12. Goto, M.: Development of the RWC music database. In: Proceedings of the 18th International Congress on Acoustics (ICA 2004), vol. 1, pp. 553–556 (2004)

Violin Timbre Navigator: Real-Time Visual Feedback of Violin Bowing Based on Audio Analysis and Machine Learning

Alfonso Perez-Carrillo(✉)

Music Technology Group, Department of Information and Communication Technologies, Universitat Pompeu Fabra, Barcelona, Spain
alfonso.perez@upf.edu

Abstract. Bowing is the main control mechanism in sound production during a violin performance. The balance among bowing parameters such as acceleration, force, velocity or bow-bridge distance are continuously determining the characteristics of the sound. However, in traditional music pedagogy, approaches to teaching the mechanics of bowing are based on subjective and vague perception, rather than on accurate understanding of the principles of movement bowing. In the last years, advances in technology has allowed to measure bowing parameters in violin performances. However, sensing systems are generally very expensive, intrusive and require for very complex and time consuming setups, which makes it impossible to bring them into a classroom environment. Here, we propose an algorithm that is able to estimate bowing parameters from audio analysis in real-time, requiring just a microphone and a simple calibration process. Additionally, we present the *Violin Palette*, a prototype that uses the reported algorithm and presents bowing information in an intuitive way.

Keywords: Audio analysis · Violin bowing · Machine learning

1 Introduction

Playing a musical instrument is a highly complex sensory-motor activity that requires a long learning trajectory. Traditional music pedagogy is mostly based on a master-apprentice model in which the student observes and imitates the teacher, and the teacher provides verbal feedback on the performance of the student. In addition, the student engages in long periods of self-study without teacher supervision. First, verbal feedback is based on subjective and vague perception and is often susceptible to ambiguous interpretation [3] and second, such a feedback is dissociated from the online proprioceptive and auditory sensations accompanying the performance [23]. In this work we propose method for

This work has been sponsored by the European Union Horizon2020 Research and Innovation program under grant agreement No. 688269 (TELMI project).

© Springer Nature Switzerland AG 2019
I. Kompatsiaris et al. (Eds.): MMM 2019, LNCS 11296, pp. 182–193, 2019.
https://doi.org/10.1007/978-3-030-05716-9_15

the acquisition of bowing parameters in violin performances based on audio analysis and an enhanced feedback system that is able to present bowing information in an intuitive way in real-time.

Bowing is the main control mechanism in sound production during a violin performance. The balance among bowing control parameters such as acceleration, force, velocity or bow-bridge distance are continuously determining the characteristics of the sound [4,7,19]. During note sustains the three major bowing parameters that determine the characteristics of the sound are the bowing force (*force*), the bowing distance to the bridge (*bbd*) and the bowing velocity (*velocity*). The ratio of bow velocity and bow-bridge distance is logarithmically proportional to sound energy (independent of frequency), increasing force boosts high harmonics and the main role of *bbd* is to control the balance between *force* and *velocity*, usually represented by Schelleng's Diagram [19].

There exist a variety of sensors and methods to acquire musical gestures adapted to different specific needs. In the context of our study, music practice, the ideal characteristics for a system to measure bowing, are high accuracy, high sampling rate, real-time capabilities, non-intrusiveness, user-friendliness, and low price. The majority of the existing methods are based on the use of sensors on the instrument or on the performer. Regarding the violin, the main reported techniques are: with electrified strings and bow [2]; based on capacitive sensing [20,24]; with accelerometers [18] to measure bow acceleration; using strain gages to measure bowing pressure [5,6]; based on electro-magnetic field (EMF) sensors [11]; and by means of high-speed infrared cameras systems detecting the position of small reflecting markers [10,21]. These techniques are in general accurate, allow for high sampling rates and in most cases bowing features can be computed in real-time. However they usually involve the use of expensive sensing systems and complex setups that are generally intrusive in practice and they are therefore not adapted to a classroom scenario.

An alternative to *direct* acquisition are low-cost systems based on the analysis of audio or video signals recorded in performance [9,13,17]. So called *indirect acquisition* [22] has many advantages in a classroom context, including low-cost, real-time capabilities, and non-intrusive nature. In this work we use simple microphones (or pickups) as measuring devices. The main challenge is that of designing robust detection algorithms that can compete with the *direct* approaches.

There can be found in the literature *indirect acquisition* methods that are able to extract bowing from audio analysis based on Hidden Markov Models [13] and Convolutional Networks [16]. These methods are specifically adapted to the same violin and recording setup they were trained with. We refer to these approaches as *Super-fitted* methods. In our case, we are interested in general solutions that can be applied to any violin and any recording setup and we call these solutions *Generalized* methods. While *Super-fitted* models provide high accuracy (95%) they can only be used with the precise trained violin and recording setup, they require expensive measuring systems and complex setups and they are also intrusive. Instead, *Generalized* models are less accurate but they have the clear advantage that they can be easily applied to any violin and low-cost recording device such as an off-the-shelf microphone.

In this work we propose *indirect acquisition* method for the acquisition of bowing parameters in violin performances based on audio analysis. The method lays in the category of a *Generalized* methods, which can be applied to any violin and recording setup after a simple audio calibration. We use machine learning models to estimate bowing from analysis of the audio signal (Sect. 3). The models need first to be trained with a database that contains synchronized audio and bowing parameters from violin performances (Sect. 2) and once the models are trained we can use them to predict bowing from audio analysis.

2   Data Acquisition and Feature Extraction

2.1   Training Database

Models are trained using the database built by [15], which contains synchronized streams of audio signals and bowing controls. Audio was captured with two recording devices, a microphone and a vibration transducer mounted in the violin bridge, and bowing was measured with the system described in [11] and [6]. The musical corpus contained in the database consists of a set of musical scores designed with the aim of covering the most common violin playing contexts by means of a semiautomatic algorithm described in [15]. The duration of the recordings is around 45 min per recording device (making a total of 90 min).

2.2   Audio Descriptors

A key characteristic of *Generalized* models is the computation of spectral features that characterize the general shape of an audio spectrum opposed to *Super-fitted* methods that are trained with features that describe in much more detail the spectrum. This abstraction of the spectral shape makes that *Generalized* models be more smoothed but also much more stable and robust to different violins, recording devices and acoustic environments. For instance, the spectral centroid indicates where the "center of mass" of the spectrum is located and perceptually, it has a robust connection with the impression of "brightness" of a sound.

The used features are listed below and computed as described in [12]:

- Root-mean-squared Energy (E_{RMS}) in dB. It is an energy measure that is very related to the perception of sound pressure. It is computed in time domain.
- Spectral Moments: *Centroid, Spread, Skewness* and *Kurtosis*. Statistical moments that indicate how the energy is distributed in the spectrum. The 1st moment (the average) is the *Spectral Centroid* and indicates the barycenter of the spectrum. The second moment (the variance) is called the *Spectral Spread* and indicates the spread of the spectrum around the centroid. The 3rd moment is the *Spectral Skewness* and gives a measure of asymmetry around the centroid (negative indicates more energy to the right and positive to the left). And the 4th moment is the *Spectral Kurtosis*, which gives a measure of the flatness of the spectrum.

- Spectral Tristimulus $(T0, T1, T2)$. Analogously to the field of image where color can be described as a combination of three primary colors, the musical tristimulus is a specification of timbre that measures the mixture of harmonics in a given sound, grouped into three sections. The first tristimulus measures the relative weight of the first harmonic; the second tristimulus measures the relative weight of the second, third, and fourth harmonics taken together; and the third tristimulus measures the relative weight of all the remaining harmonics.
- Spectral Roll-off, is the frequency below which 95% of the signal energy is contained.
- Spectral Slope, computed in dB, represents the amount of decreasing energy in the spectrum.
- Spectral Decrease, is very similar to the spectral slope, but it is more correlated to human perception.
- High-frequency content (hfc), is the sum of spectral energy content in high frequency bands.
- Spectral Flux, represents the amount of variation of the spectral along time.
- Spectral Flatness, computed in dB, is a measure of noisiness (flatness) of a spectrum. For tonal signals, it is close to 0, for noisy signals it is close to 1.
- Spectral Crest is a perceptually similar measure to the spectral flatness.
- Pitch is the fundamental frequency of a tone. Is just used fro the *string* detection models.

2.3 Bowing Parameters

The computed bowing parameters are the played string (*string*), the bowing speed (also called bowing *velocity*), the bowing pressure (also called bowing *force*) and the point of contact (also called *bow-bridge distance*). The bowing parameters include the main bowing controls appearing in the classic literature about bowed strings [1,4,19]. They are computed as described in [14].

3 Models for Bowing Estimation

This section presents and compares several machine learning methods for the estimation of bowing. We start with a *baseline* model (Subsect. 3.1) based on intuitions from observations and knowledge about the mechanic-acoustical properties of sound production. Later, we present regression models (Subsect. 3.2) and classification models (Subsect. 3.3) and finally, we describe the models used for the parameter *string* (Subsect. 3.4), which is modelled differently as it is a categorical variable.

3.1 Baseline Models

A baseline model is the most basic model that can be found in order to have a very stable estimate of the bowing parameters independently of the violin and recording setup. The most trivial model for each bowing parameter, is a linear regression with a single (univariate) input parameter.

In order to find the best correspondence between input and output variables, we apply a univariate linear feature selection algorithm. The algorithm examines each audio feature individually to determine the strength of its relationship with the bowing variable based on the *Pearson Statistical Test*, which measures linear correlation between two variables. Based on these results we take the following estimators as baseline models:

$$velocity = \quad 0.8E_{RMS}, \tag{1}$$
$$force = 0.4centroid, \tag{2}$$
$$beta = 0.25decrease, \tag{3}$$

where the values are the linear regression coefficients after normalization of the variables. In Fig. 1, we can see examples of data streams of the bowing parameters and their correlation with the selected baseline variables.

Regarding the parameter *string*, it is a categorical variable and therefore a linear regression makes no sense. In this case, we take the pitch [Hz] as baseline estimator and propose a simple model based on the fundamental frequencies of the open (freely-vibrating) strings: $G_0 = 196\,\text{Hz}$, $D_0 = 294\,\text{Hz}$, $A_0 = 440\,\text{Hz}$, $E_0 = 659\,\text{Hz}$:

$$if(G_0 <= pitch < D_0)string = 4$$
$$elseif(D_0 <= pitch < A_0)string = 3$$
$$elseif(A_0 <= pitch < E_0)string = 2$$
$$elseif(pitch => E_0)string = 1$$

In the following Sects. (3.2 and 3.3) we present two modeling approaches to improve the estimation from the baseline models. The first approach is based on regression and the second on clustering and classification.

3.2 Regression Models

Linear Regression. Linear regression is particularly suited for purely linear relationships between features and the response variable, and no correlations between features, but when there are multiple correlated features (as it is our case) the model becomes unstable, meaning that small changes in the data can cause large changes in the model, making model interpretation very difficult.

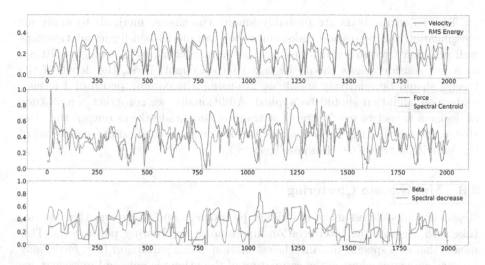

Fig. 1. Measured streams of *velocity, force* and *beta* and corresponding baseline variables (normalized), which allows to observe data correlation in a real data stream. We can observe how *velocity* is highly correlated to E_{RMS} *force* is moderately correlated to the *centroid*; and beta is very lowly correlated with the *decrease*. We do not show the *string* because it is a categorical variable and therefore no clear observations can be extracted with such a representation.

In order to prevent overfitting and improve generalization we also make use of the *Regularized* linear regression, i.e. *lasso (L1)* and *ridge(L2)*. The effect of this is that models are much more stable (coefficients do not fluctuate on small data changes). The resulting linear regressions are:

$$velocity_{LR} = 20.36skewness + 18.84kurtosis + 5.31spread,$$
$$velocity_{L1} = 0.8E_{RMS} + 0.28spectral.slope,$$
$$velocity_{L2} = 0.52E_{RMS} + 0.38slope - 0.25decrease,$$
$$force_{LR} = 35.44skewness + 21.63kurtosis + 17.6spread,$$
$$force_{L1} = -0.48flatness + 0.46E_{RMS} + 0.30centroid$$
$$force_{L2} = 0.39centroid + 0.38E_{RMS} - 0.34flatness$$
$$beta_{LR} = 45skewness, +38kurtosis + 15spread$$
$$beta_{L1} = -0.45centroid - 0.31flatness - 0.26kurtosis$$
$$beta_{L2} = -0.53centroid - 0.47flatness - 0.45kurtosis$$

Non-linear Regression. In this study we propose the use of Support Vector Regression (SVR) and Tree-based methods. In the case of SVR, we compare the following kernel functions: linear, polynomial (2nd and 3nd degree) and radial basis functions (RBF).

Tree based methods are probably among the easiest methods to apply for classification and regression tasks, since they can model non-linear relationships well and don't require much tuning. The main concern is to avoid overfitting, so a few considerations should be taken into account. First, the depth of the tree(s) should be relatively small (we are using a maximum depth of 4 levels), and cross-validation should be applied. Additionally, we construct a multitude of decision trees (we use 20 trees) at training time and take as output the class that is the mode of the classes (classification) or mean prediction (regression) of the individual trees (i.e. Random Trees [8]).

3.3   Multivariate Clustering

Regression models estimate individual parameters and therefore, they do not take into account the inter-relationships among the bowing parameters. This means that at a specific instant, the estimation of one parameter (e.g. *force*) may be very accurate, whereas the estimation of the others is not, and moreover, we may find combinations of the estimated bowing parameters that are impossible in practice. We propose an alternative method to overcome this unwanted aspect. The approach consists of dividing the n-dimensional bowing parameter space into n-clusters and then, train models to classify input sound features into one of the clusters. Using a high number of clusters ($n = 1000$), we reach a high resolution in the predicted values, so that such classification becomes, in fact, very close to a regression solution. For the clustering we use a *K-means* algorithm, and for the training, we use *SVM* with *RBF* kernel functions to capture non-linearities among the sound features. We denote this novel method as *MVClustering*.

3.4   *String* Model

In very similar manner as its baseline model, we propose to have four different *string* detection models. Depending on the region of detected *pitch*, one model or another will be activated (see Fig. 2). For instance, if $G_0 < pitch < D_0$, then the model $string_{m1}$ would be applied. This model is trivial, as in that range of pitches, we can be sure that the played string is the G-string and therefore, this model will always predict G with a 100% of accuracy. In the case that $D_0 < pitch < A_0$, then model $string_{m2}$ would be applied. In this model, the only possible output categories are G and D. And so forth with the other models. Each of the four $string_{mi}$ models solves a classification problem and therefore classifiers should be used instead of regressors. However, we apply the same regressors as for the other parameters and at the end of the estimation pipe we round the resulting values to the closest integers, obtaining values in the subset $[1, 2, 3, 4]$, which correspond to the string labels [E, A, D, G] respectively.

An additional concern is that of stability. Even with classification rates over the 99%, the models can be unstable specially during note transients. This would result in sudden changes in the prediction, which are not possible in reality.

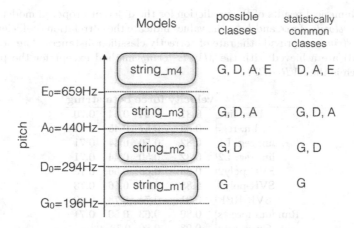

Fig. 2. We propose four *string* models, one per *pitch* interval (using the *pitch* divisions given by the open strings). The advantage of proceeding this way, is that for lower pitches, the possible classes are restricted, so we are avoiding many possible errors.

In order to avoid this artifact and provide the system with stability, we apply to the *string* prediction a hysteresis function, which allows a change in the prediction only if the last n frames had the same value, obtaining very good results with $n = 5$.

4   Results

We present numerical results to give an insight of the performance of the different algorithms against the baseline models (Subsect. 4.1) and then we present the *Violin Palette* (Subsect. 4.2), a prototype that uses the presented algorithms and allows for self-monitoring and exploration of timbre in violin practice by providing enhanced visual feedback in real-time.

4.1   Numerical Results

The metric used to compare the different models is the *Pearson Correlation Coefficient (c_C)*. The algorithms are evaluated by 10-fold cross-validation. In the case of the *string*, as it is a classification problem, the evaluation metric is the rate of correctly classified instances. The results of the evaluation are shown in Table 1 as the average value across all four strings. In general, the best performing algorithm is *Clustering*, followed by *SVR-RBF*, then *Random Forests*, then *SVR* methods with polynomial kernels, then *linear regressions* and finally the *baseline* model. The degree of the polynomial in *SVR* methods, does not seem to be an important parameter. Regarding the *linear regressions*, accuracy is slightly higher without applying regularization (*L1, L2*), however as explained in Subsect. 3.2, it is preferred L2 as it is much more stable against changes in input variables. The presented results are the average across all four strings.

Table 1. Numerical results of the prediction for the different proposed models. For the parameters *velocity*, *force* and *beta*, the values indicate the correlation coefficient. In the case of the *string*, we provide the rate of correctly classified instances. The best results (highlighted) are achieved with the *MVClustering* method except for the parameter *string*, which is the *SVR-RBF*.

	velocity	force	beta	string
base-line	0.81	0.24	0.44	0.70
lin. reg.	0.83	0.57	0.45	0.72
lin. reg. L1	0.82	0.50	0.44	0.71
lin. reg. L2	0.82	0.50	0.44	0.71
SVR-poly2	0.88	0.63	0.56	0.73
SVR-poly3	0.88	0.64	0.56	0.73
SVR-RBF	0.91	0.74	0.78	0.99
Random forests	0.80	0.63	0.50	0.71
Clustering	0.93	0.80	0.78	–

4.2   The Violin Palette

We present the *Violin Palette*, a prototype that allows self-monitoring and exploration of timbre in violin practice by providing enhanced visual feedback in real-time. As an analogy to a paint palette, the *Violin Palette* shows in real-time the *position* of the sound (i.e. timbre) of the performance. A specific timbre in represented as a point in a 3D-space with axes the three main bowing parameters (*force*, *velocity* and *beta*). We call such parameter space, the *bowing control space* (*BCS*).

The visualizations of the *Violin Palette* consist of bowing control trajectories navigating inside the *BCS*. As 3D visualizations are complicated to understand in a computer screen, 2D projections using two of the main axes, are preferred. The bowing parameters are estimated using the presented methods and therefore there is no need of specific equipment other than a microphone.

In order to show the potential of the *Violin Palette* a set of semantic label-pairs (the pair of labels are a timbre description and its opposite) representing different violin timbres was proposed based on surveys among professional violinists. The resulting pairs are: bright/dark, closed/open, cold/warm, coarse/smooth, dry/resonant, grainy/pure, harsh/sweet, restricted/free, soft/heavy, thin/broad. In Fig. 3 we can observe 2D trajectories of *velocity* and *force* for a G-major scale played having in mind those semantic labels. We show in the same plot the trajectories corresponding to each of the label-pairs. As expected, the region of the used 2D palette for each of the opposite labels is located in different parts of the space.

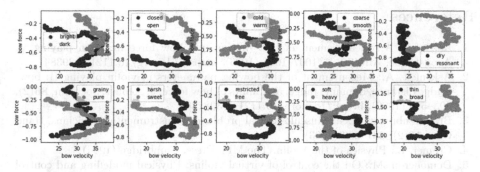

Fig. 3. 2D trajectories of *velocity* and *force* for a G-major scale played following different semantic label-pairs. As expected, the region of the used 2D palette for each of the opposite labels is located in different parts of the space.

5   Discussion

This research presents a novel algorithm for the real-time acquisition of bowing parameters from the analysis of audio in violin performances and a prototype, *The Violin Palette*, that makes use of the algorithm to give feedback of the bowing parameters to the user. Although there exists previous works that propose similar algorithms [14], they are over-fitted to a specific violin and recording device. In this work, the main interest is to build tools that can be used in a classroom scenario, which requires that the methods be user-friendly, non-intrusive and low-cost and more important, we need a system that is general and robust to any violin and recording situation. The main contribution of this work is therefore that of *Generalization* of the algorithms, which can be applied with similar results to any violin and recording setup with very reduced requirements. It is just necessary to carry out a calibration of the recording levels at the beginning of the session and also, the performer can not move substantially from its original position, otherwise a new calibration would be necessary.

The numerical results show a very high rate of *string* detection (99%). The other parameters achieve lower correlation values. Although they are statistically less accurate, they provide in fact, a very robust and rigorous feedback, specially for the parameter *velocity*. There are two reasons for this precise perception, first, the audio features describe the spectrum in general terms, and therefore, the predictions are very stable, and second, the visualizations do not require a very high accuracy, as we are not interested in the exact values but on representations of the gesture and the area of the performed timbre.

The presented models are used in the *Violin Palette*, an application that allows for real-time navigation through the *BCS* and can also superimpose the user's parameters with coloured regions corresponding to different *timbres*. We have shown the potential of such interaction as pedagogical tool in violin practice and in the future, we will evaluate the effectiveness of such self-monitoring tools in violin learning.

References

1. Askenfelt, A.: Measurement of bow motion and bow force in violin playing. J. Acoust. Soc. Am. **80**(4), 1007–1015 (1986). https://doi.org/10.1121/1.393841
2. Askenfelt, A.: Measurement of the bowing parameters in violin playing II: bow-bridge distance, dynamic range, and limits of bow force. J. Acoust. Soc. Am. **86**(2), 503–516 (1989). https://doi.org/10.1121/1.398230
3. Brandfonbrener, A.G.: Musculoskeletal problems of instrumental musicians. Hand Clin. **19**(2), 231–239 (2003)
4. Cremer, L.: Physics of the Violin. The MIT Press, Cambridge (1984)
5. Demoucron, M.: On the control of virtual violins: Physical modelling and control of bowed string instruments. Ph.D. thesis, Universite Pierre et Marie Curie (Paris, France) and the Stockholm Royal Institute of Technology (Stockholm, Sweden) (2008)
6. Guaus, E., Bonada, J., Maestre, E., Perez, A., Blaauw, M.: Calibration method to measure accurate bow force for real violin performances. In: International Computer Music Conference, Montreal, Canada, pp. 251–254, August 2009
7. Guettler, K., Askenfelt, A.: On the creation of the Helmholtz motion in bowed strings. Acust. Acta Acust. **88**(6), 970–985 (2002)
8. Ho, T.K.: Random decision forests. In: Proceedings of the 3rd International Conference on Document Analysis and Recognition, Montreal, QC, vol. 14-16, pp. 278–282, August 1995
9. Kristis, K., Pérez-Carrillo, A.: Gesture recognition for musiclearning assesment. Master's thesis, Universitat Pompeu Fabra, Barcelona, Spain (2016)
10. Maestre, E., et al.: Enriched multimodal representations of music performances: online access and visualization. IEEE MultiMedia Mag. **24**(1), 24–34 (2017)
11. Maestre, E., Bonada, J., Blaauw, M., Pérez, A., Guaus, E.: Acquisition of violin instrumental gestures using a commercial EMF device. In: International Computer Music Conference, Copenhagen, Denmark (2007)
12. Peeters, G.: A large set of audio features for sound description (similarity and classification) in the cuidado project. Technical report, IRCAM, Paris, France (2004)
13. Pérez, A., Wanderley, M.M.: Indirect acquisition of violin instrumental controls from audio signal with Hidden Markov models. IEEE/ACM Trans. Audio Speech Lang. Process. **23**(5), 932–940 (2015). https://doi.org/10.1109/TASLP.2015.2410140
14. Perez-Carrillo, A., Bonada, J., Maestre, E., Guaus, E., Blaauw, M.: Performance control driven violin timbre model based on neural networks. IEEE Trans. Audio Speech Lang. Process. **20**(3), 1007–1021 (2012). https://doi.org/10.1109/TASL.2011.2170970
15. Perez-Carrillo, A.: Enhancing spectral synthesis techniques with performance gestures using the violin as a case study. Ph.D. thesis, Universitat Pompeu Fabra (2009). http://www.mtg.upf.edu/static/media/Perez-Alfonso-PhD-2009.pdf
16. Perez-Carrillo, A.: Statistical models for the indirect acquisition of violin bowing controls from audio analysis. In: Proceedings of Meetings on Acoustics 172ASA. vol. 29, p. 035003. ASA (2016)
17. Pérez-Carrillo, A., Wanderley, M.: Learning and extraction of violin instrumental controls from audio signal. In: In proc. of the MIRUM Workshop, ACM Multimedia Conference, Nara, Japan, November 2012
18. Rasamimanana, N.: Gesture analysis of bow strokes using an augmented violin. Master's thesis, IRCAM, Paris, France (2003)

19. Schelleng, J.: The bowed string and the player. J. Acoust. Soc. Am. **53**(1), 26–41 (1973)
20. Schoner, B.: Probabilistic characterization and synthesis of complex driven systems. Ph.D. thesis, MIT Media Lab, Cambridge, Massachusetts, USA (2000)
21. Schoonderwaldt, E., Demoucron, M.: Extraction of bowing parameters from violin performance combining motion capture and sensors. J. Acoust. Soc. Am. **126**(5), 2695–2708 (2009). https://doi.org/10.1121/1.3227640. http://link.aip.org/link/?JAS/126/2695/1
22. Wanderley, M.M., Depalle, P.: Gestural control of sound synthesis. In: Proceedings of the IEEE, pp. 632–644 (2004)
23. Welch, G.F.: Variability of practice and knowledge of results as factors in learning to sing in tune. In: Bulletin of the Council for Research in Music Education, pp. 238–247 (1985)
24. Young, D.S.: Wireless sensor system for measurement of violin bowing parameters. In: Proceedings of the Stockholm Music Acoustics Conference, Stockholm, Sweden (2003)

The Representation of Speech in Deep Neural Networks

Odette Scharenborg[1,2], Nikki van der Gouw[2], Martha Larson[1,2(✉)],
and Elena Marchiori[2]

[1] Multimedia Computing Group,
Delft University of Technology, Delft, The Netherlands
{o.e.scharenborg,m.a.larson}@tudelft.nl
[2] Radboud University, Nijmegen, The Netherlands

Abstract. In this paper, we investigate the connection between how people understand speech and how speech is understood by a deep neural network. A naïve, general feed-forward deep neural network was trained for the task of vowel/consonant classification. Subsequently, the representations of the speech signal in the different hidden layers of the DNN were visualized. The visualizations allow us to study the distance between the representations of different types of input frames and observe the clustering structures formed by these representations. In the different visualizations, the input frames were labeled with different linguistic categories: sounds in the same phoneme class, sounds with the same manner of articulation, and sounds with the same place of articulation. We investigate whether the DNN clusters speech representations in a way that corresponds to these linguistic categories and observe evidence that the DNN does indeed appear to learn structures that humans use to understand speech without being explicitly trained to do so.

Keywords: Deep neural networks · Speech representations · Visualizations

1 Introduction

Recently, Deep Neural Networks (DNNs) have achieved striking performance gains on multimedia analysis tasks involving processing of images [1], music [2], and video [3]. DNNs are inspired by the human brain, which the literature often suggests to be the source of their impressive abilities, e.g. [4]. Although DNNs resemble the brain at the level of neural connections, little is known about whether they actually solve specific tasks in the same way the brain does. In this paper, we focus on speech recognition, which was one of the first multimedia processing areas to see remarkable gains due to the introduction of neural networks. We investigate whether a generic DNN trained to distinguish high-level speech sounds (vowels and consonants) naturally learns the underlying structures used by human listeners to understand speech. Speech is a uniquely useful area for such an investigation since decades of linguistic research in the area of phonetics provide us with a detailed and reliable inventory of the abstract categories of sounds with which human listeners conceptualize speech.

© Springer Nature Switzerland AG 2019
I. Kompatsiaris et al. (Eds.): MMM 2019, LNCS 11296, pp. 194–205, 2019.
https://doi.org/10.1007/978-3-030-05716-9_16

This paper is an exploratory study, and its contribution lies in the larger implications of its findings. Here, we mention two of these implications explicitly. First, insights into the extent to which neural networks learn human conceptual categories without being taught these categories may extend to other areas of multimedia, such as image or video, for which we lack the detailed structural characterization we have for speech. Second, insight into the ways in which neural networks fail to learn the same underlying categories used by humans could potentially point us to ways of improving speech recognition systems. Such insight is particularly valuable. Although today's automatic speech recognition systems have achieved excellent performance, they still perform much worse than human listeners when listening conditions are more difficult, e.g., when background noise is present or when speakers are speaking with an accent (cf. [5]).

The design of our investigation is straightforward. First, we train a naïve, generic feed-forward DNN on the task of vowel/consonant classification. We chose this task because it is a relatively simple and well understood task and will allow us to focus on what exactly a generic DNN learns when it is faced with the large variability of the speech sounds in the speech stream. Subsequently, we visualize the clusters of speech representations at the different hidden layers and observe the patterns that are formed. In analogy to visualization techniques used in the field of vision, e.g., [6, 7], we need to reduce the data to a lower dimension. We adopt the t-distributed neighbor embedding (t-SNE) algorithm in order to visualize the high-dimensional speech signal, typically two or three dimensions are used [8]. We choose t-SNE because of its previously shown usefulness for related tasks. For example, in [9], it has been successfully used to visualize the similarities between Mel feature cepstral coefficient (MFCC) feature and filterbank feature vectors created by deep belief neural networks (DBNs) to determine the most suitable feature vector as input representation for the DBN. The closest work to our own is [10], which visualizes how phoneme category representations in the hidden layers of a feed-forward network adapt to ambiguous speech. Our work is different in that we are not interested in individual phoneme categories, but rather train the network to distinguish vowels and consonants and observe the structures with which they emerge. The authors of [10] also visualize with principle component analysis (PCA) rather than t-SNE.

The paper is structured as follows. Section 2 describes the experimental framework including the data, the DNN architecture, as well as our t-SNE visualization. Section 3 presents the vowel/consonant classification results and the analysis of the speech representations learned by the DNN. Finally, Sect. 4 provides a brief discussion and our conclusions.

2 Experimental Framework

2.1 Speech Data and Labels

The DNN was trained using a selected subset of the Spoken Dutch Corpus (Corpus Gesproken Nederlands, CGN, [11]), which is a dataset containing nearly 9 M words of Dutch spoken in the Netherlands and in Flanders (Belgium) in 14 different speech styles. For the experiments reported here, we only used the read speech material from the Netherlands, and only the part from the so-called core corpus, which has a manual phonetic transcription of the speech signal. In total, our dataset contains 135,071 spoken words. The speech signal was transformed into 24 dimensional Mel Filterbank acoustic features calculated for every 10 ms.

The CGN uses 46 different phonemes for Dutch. Some phonemes only occur rarely in Dutch due to only being part of loan words. Since not enough training material is available for these phonemes, we mapped these rare phonemes onto similar Dutch phonemes. Such a mapping is common practice in automatic speech recognition. Table 1 lists all Dutch phonemes and their manner and place of articulation/tongue position. The phoneme label indicates the sound that is spoken.

Table 1. The phonemes of Dutch in the CGN with their manner and place of articulation label. Multiple phonemes in one cell are all mapped onto the first phoneme of that cell. Consonants are on the left-side and vowels are on the right-side of the table.

Phoneme	Manner of articulation	Place of articulation	Phoneme	Manner of articulation	Tongue position
p	Plosive	Bilabial	I	Short vowel	Front
b	Plosive	Bilabial	E, E~, E:	Short vowel	Front
t	Plosive	Alveolar	A, A~	Short vowel	Central
d	Plosive	Alveolar	O, O~, O:	Short vowel	Back
k	Plosive	Velar	Y, Y~, Y:	Short vowel	Front
g	Plosive	Velar	i	Long vowel	Front
f	Fricative	Labiodental	y	Long vowel	Central
v	Fricative	Labiodental	e	Long vowel	Front
s	Fricative	Alveolar	2	Long vowel	Central
z, Z	Fricative	Alveolar	a	Long vowel	Back
S	Fricative	Palatal	o	Long vowel	Back
x	Fricative	Glottal	u	Long vowel	Back
G	Fricative	Glottal	@	Long vowel	Central
h	Fricative	Glottal	E+	Diphthong	Front
N	Nasal	Glottal	Y+	Diphthong	Central
m	Nasal	Bilabial	A+	Diphthong	Back
n	Nasal	Alveolar			
l	Approximant	Alveolar			
r	Approximant	Labiodental			
w	Approximant	Labiodental			
j, J	Approximant	Palatal			

The manner and place of articulation are acoustic/phonological descriptions of the articulations of the phoneme. Vowels and consonants differ in the way they are produced primarily by the absence and presence, respectively, of a constriction in the vocal tract. In consonants, constriction can occur in various ways, such as, a full closure of the vocal tract followed by an audible release in the case of plosives (e.g., the /p/ in pot), or a narrowing of the vocal tract which results in an audible frication noise (e.g., the /s/ in stop). The amount of closure of the vocal tract in consonants determines the manner of articulation. Vowels are produced without a constriction in the vocal tract. Since Dutch has both long and short vowels, as well as diphthongs, rather than having one vowel class, we specified three vowel classes. The place of articulation indicates the location of the constriction in consonants. Since vowels do not have a place of constriction, we use position of the tongue to specify place of articulation, or rather tongue position on the front-back plane.

It is important to understand why we refer to manner and place of articulation as acoustic/phonological descriptions of speech sounds. They are acoustic in that manner and place of articulation do have a defining impact on the acoustic properties of the signal (i.e., its dominant frequencies). However, speech is highly variable, and acoustic properties are far from being unique to specific categories. When learning their first language, human listeners learn to associate certain acoustic variability with certain conceptual categories, in other words, phonological categories, e.g., an English native speaker will learn that the /ε/ (as in 'bed') and the /æ/ (as in 'bad') are different phonological categories, while a Dutch person will map the acoustic signal associated with both these categories onto a single category, /ε/, as Dutch does not have the /æ/ category. We expect a DNN to learn to leverage acoustics. The goal to our investigation is to start to understand whether a DNN also learns phonological categories similar to those used by human listeners.

2.2 Deep Neural Networks

The model used in the experiments is a feed-forward deep neural network, based on the architecture used in [12], but without the pre-training used in [12]. Another difference is that we used ReLU functions (following the rationale in [13]). The DNN consists of 3 fully connected hidden layers, each containing 1024 units with ReLU. The network is trained to optimize a cross entropy loss function for 20 epochs with batches of size 128 and an Adam optimizer with learning rate 0.0001. No dropout was applied.

The input to the DNN is a frame of 10 ms duration in a context of its five preceding and succeeding frames. The output layer consists of two units (consonant and vowel) with soft-max activation functions. Our CGN dataset was randomly split into 80% training set and 20% test set. Training was carried out 5 times with different random splits of the training and test set. Classification results are reported in terms of percentage of correctly classified frames, the frame accuracy rate (%FAR).

2.3 Visualizations

For the visualizations, we use the t-distributed neighbor embedding (t-SNE) algorithm to reduce the high-dimensional into two dimensions [8]. T-SNE places data points that are highly similar close to one another while placing data points that are less similar further apart. In the input layer, the activations are directly related to the input features. We therefore expect any clusters in the input layer to be directly related to the input features. In later (hidden) layers, we expect this relationship between input features and clustering to become less strong and rather more abstract. We hypothesize that these clusters, instead, relate to the linguistic categories, specifically, phonemes and manner and/or place of articulation categories, and that clusters of these categories can be observed without the network having been specifically trained to recognize them.

To implement the visualizations, we randomly selected 1024 frames from our test set. To create the t-SNE visualizations, a learning rate of 10 and a perplexity of 25 were used. The algorithm iterated until no further changes were observed.

3   Results

3.1   Frame Accuracy Rates

The five trained networks had an average frame accuracy of 85.5% (SD = .003). The low SD shows that the randomly created training sets yield similar performance of the trained network. Looking at the two classes of the vowel/consonant classification task individually: 85.19% of the frames with the consonant label were classified correctly, and 86.69% of the frame with the vowel label. As automatic speech recognition systems typically recognize phonemes or words, we cannot directly compare our results to existing results. Nevertheless, we should note that these recognition rates are reasonable and as to be expected. The discussion that follows includes information on the reasons that certain errors occur.

We then calculated the frame accuracies per phoneme label and per manner and place of articulation label by labelling all correctly and incorrectly classified frames with their appropriate phoneme, manner of articulation and place of articulation label. Table 2 shows the results per phoneme label. Generally, all phonemes were well classified, with the exception of /j/ and /r/ and to a lesser extent /l/, although for these phonemes classification performance was still well above chance. These sounds all belong to the manner of articulation category approximant. As Table 3 shows approximants are the manner of articulation category which have the lowest frame accuracy. This is not surprising as another word for approximants is half-vowels. The articulation, i.e., no clear constriction in the vocal tract, and consequently the spectral mark-up of approximants, or half-vowels, is very close to that of vowels. From a linguistic point of view, however, approximants cannot be the nucleus of syllables or stand-alone syllables where vowels can be, they are consonants. It is thus not surprising that approximants are relatively often misclassified as vowels.

Regarding the place of articulation/tongue position categories, the frames with the palatal label are most often misclassified in the vowel/consonant classification task. Most likely this is explained by the fact that this category only consists of two phonemes, one of which is the /j/ which, as we saw earlier, is not so well classified. Overall, the misclassifications in the vowel/consonant classification task seem to be

Table 2. The frame accuracy rates per phoneme label.

Phoneme	Accuracy (%)	Phoneme	Accuracy (%)	Phoneme	Accuracy (%)
P	90.69	h	69.82	I	88.03
B	93.00	N	81.02	i	87.81
T	93.71	m	90.77	y	73.16
D	86.66	n	84.07	e	95.24
K	89.52	l	65.73	2	89.34
G	78.10	r	59.52	a	93.20
F	93.75	w	77.97	o	91.69
V	92.19	j, J	53.84	u	78.00
S	97.50	A, A~	90.14	@	75.34
Z, Z	92.37	O, O~, O:	88.59	E+	93.12
S	89.52	Y, Y~, Y:	83.03	Y+	90.39
X	93.91	E, E~, E:	86.31	A+	92.75
G	89.38				

Table 3. The frame accuracy rates per manner and place of articulation/tongue position label.

Manner of articulation	Accuracy (%)	Place of articulation/tongue position	Accuracy (%)
Plosive	91.00	Bilabial	91.11
Fricative	92.06	Alveolar	84.19
Nasal	85.67	Labiodental	87.96
Approximant	63.82	Velar	90.29
Short vowel	82.52	Glottal	69.82
Long vowel	90.89	Palatal	58.38
Diphthong	92.50	Front (vowel)	90.48
		Central (vowel)	80.28
		Back (vowel)	90.50

fairly evenly distributed over the different phonemes and manner and place of articulation categories.

3.2 Visualizations

Vowel/Consonant Classification. We first investigated the clustering of the speech sounds in the input and the three hidden layers, and the relationship with the vowel and consonant labels, i.e., the task on which the DNN was trained. Figure 1a shows the representation of the original input of the network, with the blue dots corresponding to frames with the vowel label and the orange dots corresponding to the frames with the consonant label. We can observe a slight clustering structure in the representation of the vowels and consonants, with most of the consonants on the left side of the figure and most of the vowels on the right side. The clusters are however not well separated. Figure 1b–d visualize the representations at the first, second, and third hidden layers of the DNN, respectively. As expected, in later layers the clusters become more compact and more distinct, reflecting that the model is learning to create representations of the speech signal which abstract away the high variability of the speech signal. This is especially evident in the third layer, with one fairly well-defined vowel cluster and two consonant clusters, one of which is highly homogeneous and far removed from the rest.

a

b

•: vowels   ·: consonant

c

d

Fig. 1. Representation of the input frames at different layers of the model: (a) input layer; (b) hidden layer 1; (c) hidden layer 2; (d) hidden layer 3.

The intrusion of vowel labels in the consonant clusters and vice versa raise the question whether some of these frames are incorrectly classified. Figure 2 shows the third hidden layer of the model again but now the correctly and incorrectly classified frames are indicated. The results clearly show that few of the frames in the cluster in the top right corner of the figure are misclassified. More errors are observed for the vowel and consonant clusters in the bottom of the figure, where indeed a number of the vowel frames which appeared in the consonant cluster are misclassified as consonant and vice versa.

Phoneme Classification. Figure 3 shows the third hidden layer of the model with the frames labeled with their ground-truth phoneme identity. Inspection of this figure sheds light onto the question how the network is learning. Despite the fact that the model was

∘: correctly classified consonant   ∘: correctly classified vowel
•: incorrectly classified consonant   •: incorrectly classified vowel

Fig. 2. Representation of the correctly and incorrectly classified vowel and consonant frames in the third layer of the model.

trained on the task of vowel/consonant classification, the network is implicitly learning clusters that are related to the way in which humans conceptualize speech. Specifically, we see that the phonemes are not randomly distributed within a larger cluster, but rather frames with the same phoneme label are clustered together. The cluster in the top right corner mainly consists of /p, t, k, z, s/. However, also in the larger cluster at the bottom of the figure, smaller clusters can be observed, with more consonants on the right of the big cluster and more vowels on the left of the big cluster. Three of these vowel clusters are indicated in the figure.

Manner of Articulation. Figure 4 shows a visualization of the representations of the consonants (Fig. 4a) and vowels (Fig. 4b) at the third layer of the model. Each point represents a frame, and is color coded with the manner of articulation of that frame. Some of the frames are not correctly classified, but the numbers are relatively low (see Table 3), and we do not visualize the difference between correct and incorrectly classified frames in the figure.

The global picture arising in Fig. 3 regarding the smaller clusters in the larger cluster is confirmed by the visualization of the activations in the third hidden layer in terms of manner of articulation. With regards to the consonants in Fig. 4a, the frames in the right cluster almost exclusively belong to the fricative and plosive categories. From a linguistic perspective, these categories are clearly distinct in their production from the manner of articulation categories of the frames in the left cluster. Interestingly, within the plosive-fricative cluster on the right, there is a clear separation between the plosive (blue) and fricative (red) frames. So, even though the task of the DNN was to classify vowels and consonants, underlyingly it represented the speech signal in similar speech clusters. We note that approximants and nasals share some vowel-like properties, and it is not surprising that they are less well separated than the consonants.

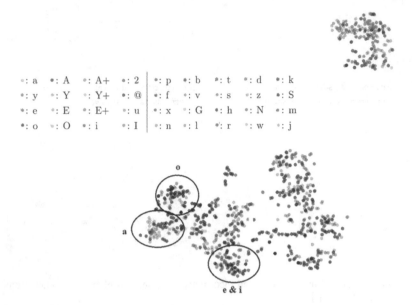

Fig. 3. Representation of the input frames labeled with their phoneme labels in the third hidden layer of the model.

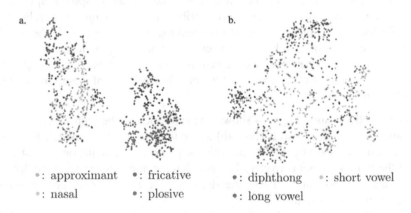

•: approximant   •: fricative   •: diphthong   •: short vowel

•: nasal   •: plosive   •: long vowel

Fig. 4. Representation in the third hidden layer of the model of the input frames labeled with *manner of articulation*. Consonants are shown in (a) and vowels in (b). (Color figure online)

With regards to the vowels in Fig. 4b, we see that short and long vowels are not evenly distributed, but rather also have a tendency to group together. Diphthongs, however, show no particular pattern. Since diphthongs can be understood as a long vowel composed of a combination of two short vowels, their distribution is not surprising.

Place of Articulation. Figure 5 shows another visualization of the representations of the consonants (Fig. 5a) and vowels (Fig. 5b) at the third layer of the model. Each point represents a frame, and, this time, is color coded with the place of articulation of that frame. Compared to the labeling in terms of manner of articulation in Fig. 4a, fewer clear clusters can be observed for the consonants in Fig. 5a. This plot suggests that we cannot expect the DNN to learn all consonantal place distinctions that are relevant for human listeners. A human effortlessly distinguishes consonants that differ with respect to place of articulation. The DNN can achieve a relatively high classification rate for phonemes and place of articulation, while this is at the same time not well reflected in distinct clustering structure of the speech representations in the third hidden layer. In Fig. 5b we see that the situation is different for vowels. Clusters corresponding to the back vowels (orange), the front vowels (red), and the central vowels (blue) are visible. Taking the analyses in terms of manner and place of articulation together, the visualizations seem to suggest that the model pays more attention to spectral information than to other information.

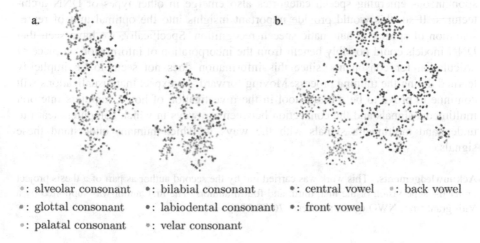

•: alveolar consonant	•: bilabial consonant	•: central vowel	•: back vowel
•: glottal consonant	•: labiodental consonant	•: front vowel	
•: palatal consonant	•: velar consonant		

Fig. 5. Representation in the third hidden layer of the model of the input frames labeled with *place of articulation*. Consonants are shown in (a) and vowels in (b). (Color figure online)

4 Discussion and Conclusion

In this paper, we investigated whether a naïve, generic deep neural network-based ASR system can learn to capture the underlying speech representations by relating these speech representations to categories as defined in linguistics through the visualization of the activations of the hidden nodes. We trained a naïve feed-forward DNN on the task of vowel/consonant classification. Subsequently, we used different linguistic labels to visualize and investigate the clusters of speech representations at the different hidden layers.

There are two main findings. First, we established that our DNN was learning as we expected with the observation that the speech category representations became more abstract deeper into the model. So, like human listeners have been found to do [14], rather than storing all variation in the speech signal in the hidden layers, the variation was progressively abstracted away at subsequent higher hidden layers. Second, we moved beyond looking at categories that the DNN had been explicitly trained to recognize, to investigate whether the DNN would cluster the speech signal into linguistically-defined speech category representations (despite not explicitly having been taught to do so) that are used during human speech processing. Indeed, under-lyingly the model represented the speech signal in similar speech clusters, mostly grouping together consonants that have the same manner of articulation, while for vowels, place of articulation seemed to be a good descriptor or explicator of the clusters.

A naïve DNN is thus not only able to deal with the large variability of the speech sounds in the speech stream but it does so by capturing the structure in the speech. In the future, we will move towards less naïve models to investigate whether these spontaneous emerging speech categories also emerge in other types of DNN archi-tectures. If so, this would provide important insights into the optimal unit of repre-sentation of speech in automatic speech recognition. Specifically, we have seen that DNN models could possibly benefit from the incorporation of information on place of articulation for consonants, since this information does not seem to be implicitly learned during the training process. Moving forward, we expect that visualizations will continue to prove to be a useful tool in the investigation of how computers interpret multimedia signals and the connection between the ways in which computers learn to understand multimedia signals with the ways in which humans understand these signals.

Acknowledgements. This work was carried out by the second author as part of a thesis project under the supervision of the first, third, and fourth authors. The first author was supported by a Vidi-grant from NWO (grant number: 276-89-003).

References

1. Krizhevsky, A., Sutskever, I., Hinton, G.E.: ImageNet classification with deep convolutional neural networks. In: 25th International Conference on Neural Information Processing Systems (NIPS 2012), vol. 1, pp. 1097–1105 (2012)
2. van den Oord, A., Dieleman, S., Schrauwen, B.: Deep content-based music recommenda-tion. In: 26th International Conference on Neural Information Processing Systems (NIPS 2013), vol. 2, pp. 2643–2651 (2013)
3. Karpathy, A., Toderici, G., Shetty, S., Leung, T., Sukthankar, R., Fei-Fei, L.: Large-scale video classification with convolutional neural networks. In: 2014 IEEE Conference on Computer Vision and Pattern Recognition (CVPR 2014), pp. 1725–1732 (2014)
4. Wan, J., et al.: Deep learning for content-based image retrieval: a comprehensive study. In: 22nd ACM International Conference on Multimedia (MM 2014), pp. 157–166 (2014)
5. Juneja, A.: A comparison of automatic and human speech recognition in null grammar. J. Acoust. Soc. Am. **131**(3), EL256–EL261 (2012)

6. Zeiler, M.D., Fergus, R.: Visualizing and understanding convolutional networks. In: Fleet, D., Pajdla, T., Schiele, B., Tuytelaars, T. (eds.) ECCV 2014. LNCS, vol. 8689, pp. 818–833. Springer, Cham (2014). https://doi.org/10.1007/978-3-319-10590-1_53
7. Rauber, P.E., Fadel, S.G., Falcão, A.X., Telea, A.C.: Visualizing the hidden activity of artificial neural networks. IEEE Trans. Vis. Comput. Graph. 23(1), 101–110 (2017)
8. Van der Maaten, L., Hinton, G.: Visualizing data using t-SNE. J. Mach. Learn. Res. 9, 2579–2605 (2008)
9. Mohamed, A.-R., Hinton, G., Penn, G.: Understanding how deep belief networks perform acoustic modelling. In: 2012 IEEE International Conference on Acoustics, Speech and Signal Processing (ICASSP 2012), pp. 4273–4276 (2012)
10. Scharenborg, O., Tiesmeyer, S., Hasegawa-Johnson, M., Dehak, N.: Visualizing phoneme category adaptation in deep neural networks. In: Interspeech (2018)
11. Oostdijk, N.H.J., et al.: Experiences from the spoken Dutch corpus project. In: Third International Conference on Language Resources and Evaluation, (LREC 2002), pp. 340–347 (2002)
12. Mohamed, A.-R., Dahl, G.E., Hinton, G.: Acoustic modeling using deep belief networks. IEEE Trans. Audio Speech Lang. Process. 20, 14–22 (2012)
13. Zeiler, M.D., et al.: On rectified linear units for speech processing. In: 2013 IEEE Acoustics, Speech and Signal Processing (ICASSP 2013), pp. 3517–3521 (2013)
14. McQueen, J.M., Cutler, A., Norris, D.: Phonological abstraction in the mental lexicon. Cogn. Sci. 30(6), 1113–1126 (2006)

Realtime Human Segmentation in Video

Tairan Zhang[1(✉)], Congyan Lang[1], and Junliang Xing[2]

[1] School of Computer Science and Technology,
Beijing Jiaotong University, Beijing 100044, People's Republic of China
{zhangtairan,cylang}@bjtu.edu.cn
[2] National Laboratory of Pattern Recognition, Institute of Automation,
Chinese Academy of Sciences, Beijing 100190, People's Republic of China
jlxing@nlpr.ia.ac.cn

Abstract. Human segmentation from a single image using deep learning models has obtained significant performance improvements. However, when directly adopting a deep human segmentation model on video human segmentation, the performance is unsatisfactory due to some issues, e.g., the segmentation results of video frames are discontinuous, and the speed of segmentation process is slow. To address these issues, we propose a new real-time video-based human segmentation framework which is designed for the single person from videos to produces smoothing, accurate and fast human segmentation results. The proposed framework for video human segmentation consists of a fully convolutional network and a tracking module based on a level set algorithm, where the fully convolutional network segments the human part in the first frame of the video sequence, and the tracking module obtains the segmentation results of other frames using the segmentation result of the last frame as the initial segmentation. The fully convolutional network is trained using human images datasets. To evaluate the proposed framework for video human segmentation, we have created and annotated a new single person video dataset. The experimental results demonstrate very accurate and smoothing human segmentation with very higher speed only using a deep human segmentation model.

Keywords: Human segmentation · Video segmentation
Deep learning · Level set

1 Introduction

Human segmentation in images and videos is a very important and challenging computer vision task. It has been applied to a lot of computer vision applications such as human pose estimation [8], video surveillance [31], and 3D modeling [11]. Human segmentation is also the fundamental of human parsing, which segments a human image into multiple regions of body parts or clothing items [17]. Although a lot of hand-crafted models have been proposed and have achieved good performance in some specific problems [1, 4–6, 10, 14, 15, 23, 24, 28], however,

© Springer Nature Switzerland AG 2019
I. Kompatsiaris et al. (Eds.): MMM 2019, LNCS 11296, pp. 206–217, 2019.
https://doi.org/10.1007/978-3-030-05716-9_17

it is still very complicated due to many factors such as pose of human body, human clothing and human image background that affect the performance.

Recently, with the rapid development of the deep learning models, the accuracy and speed of human segmentation have been greatly improved, and fully automatic human segmentation methods have been proposed [25,27]. Nowadays, deep learning models have achieved state-of-the-art performance in many computer vision tasks such as object classification, object detection, and human segmentation problem. With the adoption of deep convolutional neural networks (CNN) and fully convolutional networks (FCN) [19], many deep learning semantic segmentation models have been proposed [3,20,21,29], and some can be applied to human segmentation problem.

Many researches on human segmentation based on deep learning focus more on accuracy. Although there are some approaches which achieve very fast speed on human segmentation, there is still no good balance between accuracy and speed. Recently, with a lot of deeper neural networks proposed, higher accuracy on semantic segmentation can be achieved. However, with more layers in deep neural networks, the computation needs more computing units of the hardware, more memory to store the parameters of the networks, and more time to compute. Besides, the resolution of images also matters. With more pixels of the image, there will be more memory needed for the deep learning model and more time to do inference. With the rapid development of the hardware such as GPU, the computer can do faster inference than before. However, it is still hard to meet the requirements of real-time video segmentation. In addition, video is known for its temporal information which makes videos more complex than images. Due to some limitations in the hardware and software of the video capture devices, there is some unexpected noise in the video frames which may cause the network to generate quite different results among frames. As we all know, there is no much difference between two adjacent frames. Therefore, the segmentation mask of the previous frame can be partially used in the segmentation of the next frame. Consequently, our framework should address these issues: on one hand, improving the speed as much as possible under the premise of high accuracy, and on the other hand, improving continuity of the segmentation results among video frames.

Towards this end, this work presents a novel real-time human segmentation framework which is specifically designed for the single person video sequences task. The whole framework consists of two parts: a deep learning model which segments the human in the specified frames of the video sequence, and a tracking system which obtains the segmentation results of the rest frames. The flow chart of our proposed framework is shown in Fig. 1. For every N frames, the first frame is segmented by the deep learning model to acquire the segmentation results as accurately as possible. For the rest frames, each frame with the segmentation results of its corresponding previous frame are passed together to the tracking system to acquire the segmentation results as quickly as possible. We use an FCN-based network which is extended from [25] as our deep learning model due to the great successes of FCN on the semantic segmentation task and its capability of predicting dense outputs from arbitrary-sized inputs [19].

Due to the lack of publicly available datasets for single person video human segmentation and to test the accuracy as well as speed of our framework, we have built a new single person video dataset which contains 5 video sequences. Each sequence has around 200 frames and there are about 1000 frames in total. All the frames have its corresponding pixel-level annotation.

The main contributions of our approach can be summarized as follows.

1. We extend the PortraitFCN and PortraitFCN+ models proposed in [25] so that we can segment both portrait and full-body human images with high accuracy.
2. We propose a new real-time human segmentation framework which combines deep learning model and visual tracking method to achieve better balance between accuracy and speed.
3. We have built a new single person video dataset for our framework testing.

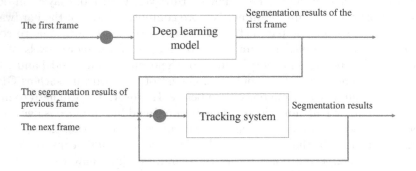

Fig. 1. The flow chart of our proposed framework for every N frames.

2   Related Work

Human Segmentation Approaches: Recently, various human segmentation approaches have been proposed and some attempts have achieved satisfying segmentation accuracy. Wu et al. [30] introduced an early hierarchical context model which obtains the inputs of CNN by combining multiple context patches of different scales where short range contexts describe the local details and long range contexts capture the object-scene relationships in an image. Kohli et al. [13] applied a model named as PoseCut to integrated segmentation and 3D pose estimation of a human body from multiple views and this model use all the data in the image with no need for a feature extraction step. Gu et al. [4] proposed a human segmentation approach based on disparity map and GrabCut which can automatically segment humans in a still image by giving a rectangular selection box without using background subtraction and motion estimation algorithms. Lee et al. [15] combined Random Walk algorithm with human shape prior adaption to propose an automatic human segmentation method for video conferencing applications. Kim et al. [10] applied support vector machine (SVM) to a non-parametric framework to achieve human segmentation. Song et al. [27] proposed a very fast human segmentation method with convolutional neural networks although the accuracy of the method is less than 90%. With the development of fully convolutional networks (FCN), Shen et al. [25] applied portrait-specific knowledge to an FCN network to propose an automatic portrait segmentation method which achieves very high accuracy of segmentation.

Level Set Methods: With the proposal of the level set method by Osher and Sethian [22], many level-set-based methods have been proposed and can be used in segmentation and tracking problems. Chopp introduced the Narrow Band Approach [2] which improves the speed of level-set-based curve evolution. It limits the solution of the level set PDE by dealing only with pixels which are close to the zero level-set contour. Li et al. [16] proposed a variational method for geometric active contours which forces the level set function to be close to a signed distance function and reduces the need of re-initialization process. Although the Narrow Band Approach has reduced the computation of partial differential equations, the process of solving PDE is still time-consuming. Thus, Shi et al. [26] proposed a real-time level-set-based tracking method which implements the evolution of the curve by simple operations such as switching elements between two linked lists and eliminates the process of solving partial differential equations.

3 Proposed Framework

In this paper, the combination of the deep learning model and a visual tracking approach is implemented to segment human in single person video sequences. Deep learning model is the fundamental of high accuracy in our framework, while the adoption of the visual tracking approach improves the speed effectively. After segmenting certain quantity of frames using the tracking approach, the deep learning model is used again to segment the next frame to further improve segmentation accuracy. The segmentation result of the last frame from the deep learning model is then passed to the tracking system, and the entire procedure of our framework loops until the end of the video sequence. In this section, we first introduce the deep learning model and then briefly describe the level-set-based tracking approach in our proposed framework.

3.1 Deep Learning Model

Nowadays, many semantic segmentation models are based on the fully convolutional network (FCN) [19] which outperforms the conventional convolutional neural network (CNN) in accuracy. Considering the advantages of FCNs, we build our deep learning model based on the PortraitFCN and PortraitFCN+ models proposed in [25] which are based on the FCN-8s model [19] and designed for automatic portrait segmentation. We start with a brief description of the PortraitFCN and PortraitFCN+ models.

The PortraitFCN model is fine-tuned with the portrait dataset from [25] and reduced to two output channels. The PortraitFCN+ model which extends the PortraitFCN model injects spatial information extracted from the portrait image to the input of the FCN network. To leverage portrait-specific knowledge, [25] introduces auxiliary position and shape input channels. These channels are then appended as inputs along with the image color channels into the first convolutional layer of the network.

The position channels encode the pixel positions relative to the face with the origin of coordinate at the face center in the image. There are two channels referred to as position channels, the *normalized* x and y channels where x and y are the coordinates of pixels. A face detector is used to detect facial feature points and a homography transform T between the detected features and a canonical pose is estimated. Then the transform T is applied to the position channels. Finally, the position of each pixel is in a coordinate system centered on the face and scaled according to the image size.

The shape channel explicitly provides the shape feature to the network which should be an approximate estimation. To generate the shape channel, the transform T mentioned above is applied to the mean mask provided by [25] which has been aligned to a canonical pose and the channel is cropped according to the image size.

Our deep learning model adopts the network structures of the PortraitFCN+ model and takes the inputs of image color, additional position and shape channels as the PortraitFCN+ does. To segment both portrait and full-body human images with high accuracy, we train the model using the datasets with enormous human images. We combine the training sets of ATR [18] dataset and the portrait dataset from [25] as a dataset for training. The ATR [18] dataset is a human parsing dataset with 16,000 training images, 700 validation images and 1,000 testing images. We convert the annotations of the ATR dataset to fit the human segmentation problem. The portrait dataset is collected and annotated by [25] which provides the corresponding mask and coordinates of facial feature points of the cropped images. Finally, we have downloaded 1,148 training images and 278 testing images of the portrait dataset.

For facial detection, we use the Dlib library [12] which implements a face alignment algorithm [9] and provides a trained model as our face detector. We select 49 points of facial landmarks for keeping compatible with the portrait dataset. For keeping consistent with the portrait dataset, the shape channel takes effect on the upper body of the human images. The facial feature points detected from the face are used to generate the additional position and shape channels of the input image as the PortraitFCN+ model does. If the face detector fails, the three channels are filled with all zeros.

After the combination of two training sets, we obtain a training dataset which contains 17,148 images. Our deep learning model trained using this training dataset will be referred to as ATRportrait model for 3 channels inputs and ATRportrait+ model for 6 channels inputs in this paper. Our deep learning model is shown in Fig. 2.

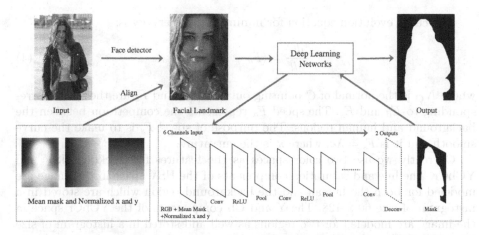

Fig. 2. The pipeline of our deep learning model.

3.2 Level Set Tracking

As mentioned before, we use the visual tracking approach to speed up the segmentation of the video sequence. The tracking results of video frames can be used as segmentation results. Tracking the object boundary can be considered as a kind of curve evolution and the level set method is an efficient way to do so. It represents the boundary implicitly as the level set of a higher dimensional function. The main advantage of level set method is its ability to automatically handle the topological changes such as the merging and splitting of object regions. Generally, the boundary curve of the object is represented by the zero level-sets $C_j = \{\mathbf{x}|\Phi_j(\mathbf{x}) = 0\}$ where $\Phi_j(\mathbf{x})$ is the level set function. In this paper, we implement a fast level-set-based two-cycle tracking algorithm proposed in [26] and construct a visual tracking system based on it in C++ and MATLAB.

We assume that the scene of every video sequence consists of a background region Ω_0 and a human region Ω_1. The boundary of the human region is denoted as C. We model each region with a feature distribution $p\left(v(\mathbf{x})|\Omega_m\right)(m = 0, 1)$, where $v(\mathbf{x})$ is the feature vector defined at each pixel. The segmentation is done by minimizing the follow energy function:

$$E = E_d + E_s \tag{1}$$

$$E_d = -\sum_{m=0}^{1} \int_{\Omega_m} \log p\left(v\left(x\right)|\Omega_m\right) dx \tag{2}$$

$$E_s = \lambda \int_C ds \tag{3}$$

where E_d is the data fidelity term for the likelihood of the current scene, E_s is smoothness regularization term which is proportional to the length of the boundary curve, and λ is a non-negative regularization parameter.

The curve evolution equation for minimizing the energy is:

$$\frac{dC}{dt} = (F_d + F_s)\overrightarrow{N}_C \tag{4}$$

where $\overrightarrow{N}_C$ is the normal of C pointing outward, F_d and F_s are the speed corresponding to E_d and E_s. The speed F_d represents the competition between the background and human regions. The purpose of speed F_s is to make the curve smooth and it is $F_s = \lambda\kappa$, where κ is the curvature.

Currently we use two color spaces as the features for tracking, HSV and YCbCr. The hue and saturation components of the HSV space in the image are modeled for both the human and the background region which are stored in a histogram of size 60×128. The Y and Cb components of the YCbCr space in the image are modeled for two regions as well and stored in a histogram of size 64×128. We calculate the speed F_d as follows:

$$F_d = \alpha F_{d\_HSV} + \beta F_{d\_YCbCr} \quad (\alpha + \beta = 1 \text{ and } \alpha, \beta \in [0,1]) \tag{5}$$

$$F_{d\_color} = log[p_{color}\left(v\left(x\right)|\Omega_1\right)/p_{color}\left(v\left(x\right)|\Omega_0\right)] \quad (color = \text{HSV, YCbCr}) \tag{6}$$

where $\alpha = 0.57$ can be a good balance between HSV and YCbCr color spaces according to extensive experiments. The tracking system can achieve fast segmentation without the need of solving PDEs.

4   Experiments and Results

In this section, we first introduce our human video dataset and training schemes of our deep learning model. Then, we present the accuracy of our deep learning models on the testing sets of ATR and the portrait datasets. Finally, we show the results of our proposed framework on our annotated human video dataset. The device which we conduct training and testing is a deep learning computing server with Intel(R) Xeon(R) CPU E5-2630 v4 which is a 20 cores CPU, 62 GB main memory and Nvidia Titan Xp GPU.

4.1   Human Video Dataset

To evaluate the performance of our proposed framework, we have built our own single person video dataset. We downloaded 4 single person videos from the Internet where all videos are in the indoor environment and there is no subtitle in the video frames. The resolution of all videos is 1280×720 which can be considered as high definition. Then, we trimmed 5 video sequences from these videos. Each video sequence has around 200 frames which lasts about 8 s. There are 1000 frames in total with each frame annotated manually by ourselves using a segmentation annotation tool. Finally, we get our human video dataset which contains 1000 frames with its corresponding pixelwise annotation file.

4.2   Deep Learning Model Training

We leverage Caffe [7] as the training and testing framework of our deep learning model. We use a stochastic gradient descent (SGD) solver with SoftMax loss function. We start training the model with an FCN-8s model pre-trained on the PASCAL VOC 2010 20-class object segmentation dataset provided by [25]. Since the pre-trained model does not contain weights for the additional three channels of input in the first convolutional layer, we fine-tune the network by initializing these unknown weights with random values and setting the base learning rate to 10^{-4}. Due to enormous GPU memory consuming with the FCN-based network, we set the batch size parameter to 4 in the network definition file. For other hyper-parameters in the Caffe solver, we set the momentum to 0.999, weight decay to 5×10^{-5}, and *iter_size* to 4. The training process of our deep learning model requires several days to learn a good model with about 310,000 Caffe SGD iterations.

4.3   Testing on Human Image Datasets

The segmentation accuracy is measured by the overlap accuracy, also known as the Intersection-over-Union (IoU) accuracy which is computed as the area of the intersection of the predicted output and the ground truth divided by the area of the union of the two parts. IoU accuracy can be defined as follows.

$$IoU = \frac{Area(\text{predicted output} \cap \text{ground truth})}{Area(\text{predicted output} \cup \text{ground truth})} \qquad (7)$$

The accuracy testing results of the deep learning models on the testing sets of both ATR and the portrait datasets is shown in Table 1. Most images in the ATR dataset are full-body human images. Although the PortraitFCN and PortraitFCN+ models achieve very high IoU accuracy on the portrait dataset, they fail to achieve high IoU accuracy on ATR dataset. ATRportrait+, on the other hand, achieves high IoU accuracy on both ATR and the portrait datasets, which means our deep learning models outperform PortraitFCN+ in full-body human images.

Table 1. Accuracy of deep learning models on the testing sets of human image datasets.

Models	Mean IoU (ATR)	Mean IoU (portrait)
PortraitFCN [25]	30.7787%	94.9782%
PortraitFCN+ [25]	21.9822%	**95.6353%**
ATRportrait	92.8386%	94.3679%
ATRportrait+	**94.4937%**	95.513%

4.4   Testing on Human Video Dataset

The testing accuracy of segmentation on our human video dataset is measured by IoU accuracy. For testing the speed of our framework, we record the frame rate of every video sequence for 10 times and calculate the average frame rate. The results of accuracy testing of our framework and deep learning models on our human video dataset is shown in Table 2. Currently, the deep learning model is used to segment the first frame in every 20 frames.

Table 2. IoU accuracy of our framework and deep learning models on 5 video sequences of our human video dataset. Our 3 channels represent the deep learning model of our framework takes input of only 3 color channels input, while our 6 channels represent the deep learning model takes input of 3 color channels as well as additional position and shape channels.

Methods	Sequence 1	Sequence 2	Sequence 3	Sequence 4	Sequence 5
PortraitFCN [25]	66.3696%	68.4933%	77.6552%	77.3054%	68.1368%
PortraitFCN+ [25]	63.257%	82.8907%	78.0654%	77.8603%	71.3218%
ATRportrait	**95.779%**	60.6008%	98.0532%	97.9722%	88.9662%
ATRportrait+	93.5179%	**96.9972%**	98.1729%	98.0924%	**98.4788%**
Our 3 channels	92.5396%	59.5837%	98.5814%	98.4561%	84.361%
Our 6 channels	92.9613%	92.2457%	**98.9077%**	**98.7911%**	93.9467%

Table 3. Speed results of our framework and deep learning models on 5 video sequences of our human video dataset in frame per second (FPS).

Methods	Sequence 1	Sequence 2	Sequence 3	Sequence 4	Sequence 5
ATRportrait	4.89	4.86	4.87	4.90	4.84
ATRportrait+	1.30	1.27	1.24	1.24	1.27
Our 3 channels	**11.50**	4.20	**14.76**	**14.01**	**12.78**
Our 6 channels	9.12	**7.06**	10.12	10.02	8.69

Our deep learning model trained using the combined training dataset achieves significant improvement and outperform PortraitFCN+ in IoU accuracy. Figure 3 shows segmentation results of some video frames in our human video dataset. The results of speed testing of our framework and deep learning models on our human video dataset is shown in Table 3.

Although the accuracy of our framework is slightly worse than the deep learning model trained using the combined training dataset, our framework can achieve faster segmentation than the deep learning model and can restore high accuracy when using the deep learning model.

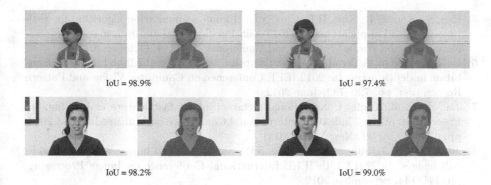

IoU = 98.9%   IoU = 97.4%

IoU = 98.2%   IoU = 99.0%

Fig. 3. Segmentation results of some video frames with IoU accuracy attached. Row 1 shows some frames in video sequence 1 where a 6-year-old boy is presented. Frame 1, 69 are shown in row 1. Row 2 shows some frames in video sequence 3 where a 27-year-old woman is presented. Frame 1, 57 are shown in row 2. Each frame is on the left side with its corresponding segmentation result on the right side.

5 Conclusions

In this paper, we propose a new real-time video-based human segmentation framework. The framework is built upon a deep learning model and a visual tracking system. The deep learning model in our framework which extends PortraitFCN+ [25] achieves high accuracy on both portrait and full-body human images, which means our framework can process more situations. To effectively evaluate the proposed framework for video human segmentation, we have built a new single person video dataset with manual annotations. The experiment results show better balance between segmentation accuracy and speed of our framework. Our framework maybe fails when the background is complicated which is a limitation of our approach. In the future, we will improve our framework for higher accuracy as well as speed and achieve better robustness for the complicated background.

References

1. Bi, S., Liang, D.: Human segmentation in a complex situation based on properties of the human visual system. In: 2006 6th World Congress on Intelligent Control and Automation, vol. 2, pp. 9587–9590 (2006)
2. Chopp, D.L.: Computing minimal surfaces via level set curvature flow. J. Comput. Phys. **106**, 77–91 (1993)
3. Dai, J., He, K., Sun, J.: Boxsup: Exploiting bounding boxes to supervise convolutional networks for semantic segmentation. In: 2015 IEEE International Conference on Computer Vision (ICCV). pp. 1635–1643, December 2015
4. Gu, D., Zhao, Y., Yuan, Y., Hu, G.: Human segmentation based on disparity map and grabcut. In: 2012 International Conference on Computer Vision in Remote Sensing, pp. 67–71, December 2012

5. Heo, S., Koo, H.I., Kim, H.I., Cho, N.I.: Human segmentation algorithm for real-time video-call applications. In: 2013 Asia-Pacific Signal and Information Processing Association Annual Summit and Conference, pp. 1–4, October 2013
6. Hernandez-Vela, A., et al.: Graph cuts optimization for multi-limb human segmentation in depth maps. In: 2012 IEEE Conference on Computer Vision and Pattern Recognition, pp. 726–732, June 2012
7. Jia, Y., et al.: Caffe: Convolutional architecture for fast feature embedding. In: Proceedings of the 22nd ACM International Conference on Multimedia. MM 2014, pp. 675–678. ACM, New York (2014)
8. Junior, J.C.S.J., Jung, C.R., Musse, S.R.: Skeleton-based human segmentation in still images. In: 2012 19th IEEE International Conference on Image Processing, pp. 141–144, September 2012
9. Kazemi, V., Sullivan, J.: One millisecond face alignment with an ensemble of regression trees. In: 2014 IEEE Conference on Computer Vision and Pattern Recognition, pp. 1867–1874, June 2014
10. Kim, K., Oh, C., Sohn, K.: Non-parametric human segmentation using support vector machine. In: 2016 IEEE International Conference on Consumer Electronics (ICCE), pp. 131–132, January 2016
11. Kim, Y.S., Yoon, J.C., Lee, I.K.: Real-time human segmentation from RGB-d video sequence based on adaptive geodesic distance computation. In: Multimedia Tools and Applications, November 2017
12. King, D.E.: Dlib-ml: a machine learning toolkit. J. Mach. Learn. Res. **10**, 1755–1758 (2009)
13. Kohli, P., Rihan, J., Bray, M., Torr, P.H.: Simultaneous segmentation and pose estimation of humans using dynamic graph cuts. Int. J. Comput. Vision **79**(3), 285–298 (2008)
14. Kumar, R., Kumar, R., Gopalakrishnan, V., Iyer, K.N.: Fast human segmentation using color and depth. In: 2017 IEEE International Conference on Acoustics, Speech and Signal Processing (ICASSP), pp. 1922–1926, March 2017
15. Lee, Y.T., Su, T.F., Su, H.R., Lai, S.H., Lee, T.C., Shih, M.Y.: Human segmentation from video by combining random walks with human shape prior adaption. In: 2013 Asia-Pacific Signal and Information Processing Association Annual Summit and Conference, pp. 1–4, October 2013
16. Li, C., Xu, C., Gui, C., Fox, M.D.: Level set evolution without re-initialization: a new variational formulation. In: 2005 IEEE Computer Society Conference on Computer Vision and Pattern Recognition (CVPR 2005) (CVPR), vol. 01, pp. 430–436, June 2005
17. Li, J., et al.: Multiple-Human Parsing in the Wild. ArXiv e-prints, May 2017
18. Liang, X., et al.: Human parsing with contextualized convolutional neural network. In: 2015 IEEE International Conference on Computer Vision (ICCV), pp. 1386–1394, December 2015
19. Long, J., Shelhamer, E., Darrell, T.: Fully convolutional networks for semantic segmentation. In: 2015 IEEE Conference on Computer Vision and Pattern Recognition (CVPR), pp. 3431–3440, June 2015
20. Mostajabi, M., Yadollahpour, P., Shakhnarovich, G.: Feedforward semantic segmentation with zoom-out features. In: 2015 IEEE Conference on Computer Vision and Pattern Recognition (CVPR), vol. 00, pp. 3376–3385, June 2015
21. Noh, H., Hong, S., Han, B.: Learning deconvolution network for semantic segmentation. In: 2015 IEEE International Conference on Computer Vision (ICCV), vol. 00, pp. 1520–1528, December 2015

22. Osher, S., Sethian, J.A.: Fronts propagating with curvature-dependent speed: algorithms based on hamilton-jacobi formulations. J. Comput. Phys. **79**, 12–49 (1988)
23. Park, S., Yoo, J.H.: Human segmentation based on grabcut in real-time video sequences. In: 2014 IEEE International Conference on Consumer Electronics (ICCE), pp. 111–112, January 2014
24. Ramadan, H., Tairi, H.: Automatic human segmentation in video using convex active contours. In: 2016 13th International Conference on Computer Graphics, Imaging and Visualization (CGiV), pp. 184–189, March 2016
25. Shen, X., et al.: Automatic portrait segmentation for image stylization. In: Proceedings of the 37th Annual Conference of the European Association for Computer Graphics (2016)
26. Shi, Y., Karl, W.C.: Real-time tracking using level sets. In: 2005 IEEE Computer Society Conference on Computer Vision and Pattern Recognition (CVPR 2005), vol. 2, pp. 34–41, June 2005
27. Song, C., Huang, Y., Wang, Z., Wang, L.: 1000fps human segmentation with deep convolutional neural networks. In: Pattern Recognition, pp. 474–478 (2016)
28. Tan, Y., Guo, Y., Gao, C.: Background subtraction based level sets for human segmentation in thermal infrared surveillance systems. Infrared Phys. Technol. **61**(5), 230–240 (2013)
29. Wu, X., Du, M., Chen, W., Li, Z.: Exploiting deep convolutional network and patch-level CRFs for indoor semantic segmentation. In: 2016 IEEE 11th Conference on Industrial Electronics and Applications (ICIEA), pp. 150–155, June 2016
30. Wu, Z., Huang, Y., Yu, Y., Wang, L., Tan, T.: Early Hierarchical Contexts Learned by Convolutional Networks for Image Segmentation. In: Proceedings of the 22nd International Conference on Pattern Recognition, pp. 1538–1543. IEEE (2014)
31. Zhao, T., Nevatia, R.: Stochastic human segmentation from a static camera. In: Proceedings of the Workshop on Motion and Video Computing, pp. 9–14, December 2002

psDirector: An Automatic Director for Watching View Generation from Panoramic Soccer Video

Chunyang Li[1,2], Caiyan Jia[1(✉)], Zhineng Chen[2], Xiaoyan Gu[3],
and Hongyun Bao[2]

[1] School of Computer and Information Technology, Beijing Jiaotong University,
Beijing, China
3080922310qq.com, cyjia@bjtu.edu.cn
[2] Institute of Automation, Chinese Academy of Sciences, Beijing, China
{zhineng.chen,hongyun.bao}@ia.ac.cn
[3] Institute of Information Engineering, Chinese Academy of Sciences, Beijing, China
guxiaoyan@iie.ac.cn

Abstract. Watching TV or Internet video is the most common way for people perceiving soccer matches. However, it is immature to generalize this mean to amateur soccer, as it is expensive to direct a match professionally by human. As an alternative, using multiple cameras to generate a panoramic video can faithfully record the match, but with bad watching experience. In this work, we develop a psDirector system to address this dilemma. It takes the panoramic soccer video as input and outputs a corresponding watching view counterpart, which continuously focuses on attractive playing areas that people are interested in. The task is somewhat unique and we propose a novel pipeline to implement it. It first extracts several soccer-related semantics, i.e., soccer field, attractive ROI, distribution of players, attacking direction. Then, the semantics are reasonably utilized to produce the outputted video, where important match content, camera action as well as their consistency along the time axis are carefully considered to ensure the video quality. Experiments on school soccer videos show rationality of the proposed pipeline. Meanwhile, psDirector generates video with better watching experience than an existing commercial tool.

Keywords: Panoramic video · Video directing · Amateur soccer
Deep learning

1 Introduction

As the world's most popular sport, soccer has been enjoyed by people all over the world. An important soccer match always attracts a large number of audience, mostly by watching TV or Internet video. In both scenarios, the match is generally provided by agencies from a so called *watching view* for better viewing

I. Kompatsiaris et al. (Eds.): MMM 2019, LNCS 11296, pp. 218–230, 2019.
https://doi.org/10.1007/978-3-030-05716-9_18

via TV or other displays, where at each moment, only the attractive playing area is sampled from the match. To determine the area, several to dozens of cameras are used to record the match from different angles and visual fields. Simultaneously, professional directors manually operate the cameras by movement, zooming in/out, etc., and dynamically select the most appropriate area as the view.

Despite accepted by the professional community for years, this mean is unaffordable for amateur soccer (e.g., campus soccer), as expense of the directing such as cameras and labour cost is a kind of heavy burden. However, amateur soccer also has its specific audience. There is an emerging trend to develop novel solutions to capture and analyze these matches. For example, *Pixellot*[1] has devised a dedicated panoramic camera for amateur soccer. After a few venue-related configurations, panoramic picture covering the whole soccer field can be obtained, as depicted in the left of Fig. 1. As can be seen, although faithfully recording the match, the panoramic soccer video is not optimal with respect to audience in watching experience, due to reasons such as the camera is too far away such that many non-field areas are also captured. The camera is fixed without any movement, zooming in/out, etc. It is evident that the video could be further analyzed to provide better watching experience, which is a field that less studied previously. To our knowledge, only *Pixellot* had done some pioneering work on this direction, in the form of developing a tool that samples an appropriate watching view video from the panoramic soccer video. However, its technical details have not been reported so far. Meanwhile according to our observation, *Pixellot*'s solution is hard to say perfect and there are still rooms for further improvement.

Fig. 1. An illustrative frame extracted from the panorama video (left) and its watching view generated by the proposed psDirector (right).

Motivated by this, in this work we investigate this interesting task and develop a novel system, termed as psDirector, for automatic watching view video generation. Specifically, given a panoramic soccer video, we first determine the soccer field offline by color analysis. Then, an *attractive ROI* of fixed resolution is derived by leveraging the soccer field and motion information. It is a relative large area deemed to cover the desired watching view. To this end, several soccer-related semantics, i.e., distribution of players, playing region, attacking

---

[1] http://www.pixellot.tv/.

direction are dynamically extracted and evaluated in the ROI, from which a smaller but more suitable view at each moment are determined. To avoid irrational view movement alone the time axis, we first divide the video into consecutive short clips. The frame-level results are aggregated to generate camera actions (e.g., unchange, move to a certain direction, zoom in/out) of each clip. Then the clips are concatenated sequentially to produce the final watching view video. By applying the pipeline, psDirector produces video analogous to human directed, but without any human intervention, as snapshotted in the right of Fig. 1. We have carried out experiments on school soccer videos captured from different venues. The results show that our psDirector can reasonably integrate the semantics and produce a satisfactory result video, whose watching experience outperforms the video generated by *Pixellot*. Main contributions of this work are:

- We propose a novel psDirector system to generate watching view from the panoramic amateur soccer video. In the implementation, low-level features and deep learning models are both leveraged to extract soccer-related semantics and integrate them smoothly. To our knowledge, our work is the first study revealing technical detail on this task.
- Experiments are carried out to demonstrate rationality of the sampled watching view. User-based studies also show that psDirector outperforms the existing *Pixellot* by a large margin.

2   Related Work

Soccer video analysis is a longstanding research topic with fruitful research results in the past years. According to the tasks focused on, we can broadly categorize related studies into video highlight and semantic parsing.

Video Highlight. Highlight extraction or summarization technologies have been studied widely in soccer video analysis. For example in [3], Gong et al. proposed a method by using domain knowledge to summarize a soccer video. Zhao et al. [13] proposed a highlight detection method based on goalmouth frame detection and audio energy ranking. Another work of them shown that replay detection is also useful for highlight detection [14]. Zawbaa et al. [12] presented a machine learning based summarization system for soccer videos. Wang et al. [10] developed a novel highlight extraction approach based on affection arousal analysis. These methods performed well on professional soccer such as World Cup or European Cup, partially attributed to the exploration of semantics conveyed by common soccer directing actions, e.g., when to use replay.

Semantic Parsing. Semantic parsing aims at understanding what happened in the match at when, usually in the form of assigning short video clips each with an event tag or a text description about player and ball actions. For example, Ekin et al. [2] proposed a framework for soccer event detection. It utilizes both low-level features (e.g., dominant color region, shot boundary, shot classification) and higher-level semantics (e.g., goal and referee location, the appearance of penalty box) for event inference. Wang et al. [9] devised an approach that synchronizes video event to text description with coarse time constraints. Bertini et al. [1] presented an automatic system that was able to forecast soccer highlight clips based on MPEG feature.

For player and ball analysis, Intille and Bobickd [4] used the field lines, motion and visual features in the soccer field to implement player detection and tracking. Yao et al. [11] also proposed a player tracking method based on the combination of particle filtering and person detection. Khatoonabadi et al. [5] proposed an algorithm to track soccer players on the scoring scene by analyzing their movements with respect to the field lines. Gong et al. [3] and Tong et al. [8] proposed to use color and shape features to detect and track the soccer ball. Seo et al. [7] investigated ball tracking and positioning based on Kalman filtering.

Despite with aforementioned progresses, we argue that existing studies mainly focus on professional soccer, while advanced deep models are seldom utilized. This work focuses on amateur soccer. It aims at automatic watching view generation from the panoramic video, which is a somewhat unique task and the research outcome would be a meaningful supplement to existing studies.

3 The Proposed Method

3.1 Overview

In this section, we introduce the proposed psDirector System in detail. As illustrated in Fig. 2, psDirector consists of seven modules. Given a panoramic soccer video, a *soccer field determination* module is employed to extract the soccer field from the panoramic view offline by leveraging some evenly sampled frames. Then, a *motion extraction* module calculates motion information based on differences among consecutive frames of soccer fields. Based on it, an *attractive ROI positioning* module is performed to obtain a large-sized area that roughly navigates the view selection. A *deep player detection* module is applied to the *attractive ROI* to perform player detection, with a *frame-level view generation* module behind to infer the appropriate watching view at the frame-level. At the same time, a *attracting direction inference* module is employed to determine the attracting direction of a few seconds. Based on these semantics, a *video-level view generation* module is applied to generate the outputted watching view video. We will elaborate these modules in the rest of this section.

3.2 Module Elaboration

Soccer Field Determination. As shown in Fig. 1, the panoramic picture provides a wide view of the whole soccer field, where irrelevant objects like buildings, the running track are also included. Since we only concern what happened in the soccer field, it is a prerequisite to eliminate the influence of those objects.

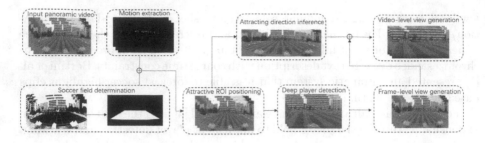

Fig. 2. An illustrative flowchart of psDirector. It takes a panoramic soccer video as input and outputs a watching view video in accordance with human perception.

Motivated by [2] that HSI color space provides a more obvious separation of soccer field and other objects in professional soccer, we develop a heuristic to determine the soccer field as follows.

Specifically, given a panoramic picture, we firstly transform it from RGB to HSI color space, in which the image is represented by three channels, i.e., H, S, I. Then, we get histograms of the three channels. Based on the histograms, we can calculate peak regions of the three channels by using

$$\begin{cases} i^j_{min} \geq K \times peak_j \\ i^j_{min} - 1 < K \times peak_j \\ i^j_{max} \geq K \times peak_j \\ i^j_{max} + 1 < K \times peak_j \end{cases} \tag{1}$$

$$subject\ to: i^j_{min} \leq i^j_{peak},\ \ i^j_{max} \geq i^j_{peak},\ \ i \in [0, 255],\ \ j \in [H, S, I]$$

where $peak_j$ is the peak value of the j-th histogram, i^j_{peak} is its bin number, $[i^j_{min}, i^j_{max}]$ is the obtained peak region. K is empirically set to 0.2. We further calculate $H_{mean}, S_{mean}, I_{mean}$, the average values of pixels falling into the peak regions. With these parameters, we can segment the soccer field by using cylindrical projection [2] described as follows and a threshold T.

$$\begin{cases} \Delta(j) = |H_j - H_{mean}| \\ \theta_j = \begin{cases} \Delta(j) & \Delta(j) < 180° \\ 360° - \Delta(j) & others \end{cases} \\ d_{intensity}(j) = |I_j - I_{mean}| \\ d_{chroma}(j) = \sqrt{S_j^2 + S_{mean}^2 - 2 S_j S_{mean} \cos(\theta_j)} \\ d_{cylindrical}(j) = \sqrt{(d_{intensity}(j))^2 + (d_{chroma}(j))^2} \end{cases} \tag{2}$$

where H_j denotes the value of j-th pixel in the H channel. Once the cylindrical distance $d_{cylindrical}(j) < T$, this pixel is recognized as a foreground pixel (i.e., soccer field). T empirically set to 0.45 in the implementation.

The soccer field segmented based on a single frame is often noisy, due to motion on the field and parameter sensitivity. To address this problem, we evenly sample a few frames from the panoramic video, calculate their respective soccer fields and employ pixel level union to obtain the final field, usually 10 frames is suffice to achieve pretty good performance. Besides, morphological operations is also applied to fill small holes and eliminate the field lines. A derived soccer field mask is given in the bottom left of Fig. 2.

Motion Extraction and Attractive ROI Positioning. We develop a novel scheme to gradually produce the final watching view. The first step is motion extraction on the whole picture, which uses motion feature to determine an *attractive ROI*, a relative large-sized area that roughly localizes the view. Then, we employ two modules, namely *deep player detection* and *frame-level view generation* on top of the attractive ROI, where high-level semantics are extracted and analyzed to navigate a smaller watching view selection. By using this gradual confirmation scheme, both speed and accuracy are well balanced.

As for the motion extraction, player and ball movements are important indicators to the area that people are interested in. We use frame difference to capture this information, where panoramic frames are evenly sampled with a fixed *stepsize* = 5 and differences between adjacently sampled frames are computed pixel-by-pixel. To this end, motion images of the same resolution are obtained continuously and whose pixels denote the motion intensities at a moment, as illustrated in Fig. 2.

It is observed that in the motion image, different pixels are with different motion intensities, due to their distance differences with respect to the camera. General speaking, pixels on the top or side of an image are even far from the camera. They contain more information compared to those nearby ones. Thus, we first apply the AND operation on the soccer field mask image and motion image to elimination irrelevant motion. Then, we use the following linear function to weight different pixels as follows.

$$\begin{cases} i_w = \alpha_w * |i - w/2| \\ j_h = \alpha_h * |j - h| \end{cases} \tag{3}$$

where w and h are width and height of the panoramic frame. i_w and j_h are weighted indexes on x and y axis, respectively. α_w and α_h are two hardware-related parameters. They are obtained once settings of the camera and venue are given. With the weighting, we can use the following formulas to localize the attractive ROI.

$$\max_y \sum_{j=y}^{y+boxH} \sum_{i=0}^{w} sgn(I(i,j))(i_w + j_h) \tag{4}$$

$$\max_x \sum_{i=x}^{x+boxH} \sum_{j=y}^{y+boxW} sgn(I(i,j))(i_w + j_h) \tag{5}$$

where $boxH$ and $boxW$ are the height and width of the attractive ROI given in advance, I is the motion image and $I(i,j)$ is the value of pixel locating at (i,j). $sgn(\cdot)$ is an indicator function that equals to 1 if the contained condition satisfies (i.e., not zero), and 0 otherwise. Usually, $boxH$ and $boxW$ are relative large in order to avoid missing possible interesting match content. The equations use a column-first greedy algorithm to quickly recognize the motion-intensive region as the attractive ROI.

Deep Player Detection and Frame-Level View Generation. With the attractive ROI, we further utilize high-level semantics to derive the final view for better watching experience. Specifically, we use the popular deep model YOLOv3 [6] to detect players in the ROI. The off-the-shelf YOLOv3 has a detector for *person* that is proved to perform well on our panorama school soccer picture. Therefore, we directly use it and design a two-step procedure to determine the view at the frame-level. First, we take the whole attractive ROI as input and employ YOLOv3 to get the detection results, in the form of $P = \{p_1, p_2, ..., p_n\}$, where $p_i = \{x_i, y_i, w_i, h_i\}$ are coordinates of central point and its radii in the x and y directions. With these bounding boxes, we can obtain a refined area of $V_{ref} = (x_{min}, y_{min}, x_{max}, y_{max})$, where

$$\begin{cases} x_{min} = \min_i(x_i - w_i/2) \\ x_{max} = \max_i(x_i + w_i/2) \\ y_{min} = \min_i(y_i - h_i/2) \\ y_{max} = \max_i(y_i + h_i/2) \end{cases} \tag{6}$$

The area is smaller but contains all the players. It is again fed into the YOLOv3 detector and new detections $P = \{\hat{p}_1, \hat{p}_2, ..., \hat{p}_m\}$ are obtained. Usually, the result is more accurate as players are fed into with a more focused resolution.

With the re-detected results, we first calculate their central point by $x_{cent} = \frac{1}{m}\sum_{i=1}^{m} x_i$ and $y_{cent} = \frac{1}{m}\sum_{i=1}^{m} y_i$. Then, we compute the distances between players and the central point and rank them in a descending order. We define a basic view as the minimum area that covers T_p players nearest to the central point, where T is empirically set to $max(m-4, 4)$. Although the basic view is decent in most cases, we observe that for human directing, focused view is utilized when players are gathered, while larger view is used when they are apart. Therefore, a view enlarging scheme is designed for this purpose. Specifically, we calculate the standard deviation std of the obtained distances, then proportionately enlarge the basic view if it is larger than a predefined threshold T_d, i.e.,

$$std = \sqrt{\frac{\sum_{i-1}^{m}((x_i - x)^2 + (y_i - y)^2)}{m}} > T_d = (\frac{2}{3}\sqrt{(w_v/2)^2 + (h_v/2)^2}) \tag{7}$$

where w_v and h_v are the width and height of the basic view. Note that T_d grows with the increase of w_v and h_v. Thus, the enlarging process is terminated when

$std = T_d$ or it reaches the size of V_{ref}. When terminated, to avoid splitting on players, we further enlarge the view by $0.01 * w$ and $0.03 * h$, respectively along the x and y axis, which produce the view result at the k-th frame, i.e., $V_{frame}^k = (x_v^k, y_v^k, x_v^k, y_v^k)$. It is deemed to best capture the attractive area at this moment.

We also use a few rules to handle occasionally special cases to ensure the watching experience. They are: (1) When at least a third of the goalmouth is visible, we proportionally enlarge the view to cover the whole goalmouth; (2) When the view invades the two near corners, we proportionally enlarge the view to cover the whole corner region.

Attacking Direction Inference and Video-Level View Generation. Attacking direction at a moment is an important clue that decides the view selection along the time axis. Here we directly obtain it by allowing delay of a few seconds. In case that the delay is t seconds, we can simultaneously get all the views in interval $[V_{frame}^k, V_{frame}^{k+r*t}]$, where r is the framerate of the video. Thus, we determine the attacking direction at this time slot by

$$
\begin{cases}
\sum_{i \in \Gamma} sgn(q_v^i - q_v^k) \geq T & direction : right/up \\
\sum_{i \in \Gamma} sgn(q_v^i - q_v^k) \leq -T & direction : left/down \\
others & direction : none
\end{cases}
\tag{8}
$$

where $q \in [x, y]$, Γ is the set of frames evenly sampled from $[k, k+r*t]$ according to the predefined $stepsize = 5$. T is a parameter empirically set to 2.

Once the attacking direction is determined, we select only the frame-level view compatible with the attacking direction and with the maximum summed distance as the target view of this time interval. By using linear interpolation, the view of each frame in it is given by

$$
q_{k+i} = \frac{(r*t - i) * q_k + i * q_{k+r*t}}{r*t}, \quad q \in [x, y, h, w]
\tag{9}
$$

By doing this, the whole video is decomposed to many short clips of t seconds with independent scale and direction variations. A video-level view is obtained by concatenating them sequentially. We empirically set $t = 4$ in the implementation.

4   Experiments

4.1   Dataset

We collect 54 panoramic videos with resolution $3840 * 800$ from 4 different venues as our dataset in the experiment. Each video is a school soccer of nearly 2 h, starting from warming up before the match to end of the match. We have manually record the begin and end times of both the first and second half of a match to extract the valid video segments. Based on the segments, We apply the tool provided by *Pixellot* to obtain their watching view, which is the baseline for performance comparison.

Fig. 3. Panoramic picture and the corresponding attractive ROI (yellow box), frame-level watching view generated by *Pixellot* (blue box) and psDirector (red box). (Color figure online)

4.2 Objective Results and Analysis

We mainly evaluate rationality of the sampled watching view at both the frame and video levels. Generally, a good view should satisfies: sampled on truly attractive area, more focused to players and ball, moved smoothly along the time axis. In the design of the modules above, we have carefully considered these factors. However due to space limitation, we do not quantize them step-by-step and only list a few illustrative view examples and explain them from the three aspects.

To compare the frame-level view sampled by different methods, a panoramic picture, its attractive ROI, its frame-level views generated by *Pixellot* and psDirector are all displayed in Fig. 3. As for our psDirector, the ROI, despite relative large compared to the frame-level view of *Pixellot*, has provided a rough positioning of the attractive area. Together with the follow up analysis, it could generate a correct and more focused view compared to *Pixellot*, clearly indicating that a more suitable watching view has obtained by employing the proposed gradually positioning strategy. Moreover, we observe that more focused view are always produced by using psDirector. Its view is more in accordance with the effect of human directing and thus more easily accepted by audience.

In Fig. 4, we give two examples to further compare the two methods. Each example contains two clips from the same source but generated by *Pixellot* and our psDirector, respectively. As can be seen, in the first example, psDirector provides more reasonable view navigation. It not only moves smoothly, but also successfully catches up the attacking player and ball in an counter attack, while *Pixellot* fails to do this. The second example is a scene about a missed shot. *Pixellot* does not provide an appropriate view, probably because of that people outside the soccer field are not appropriately handled. On the contrary, psDirector generates a much better view. Besides these examples, there are also a few

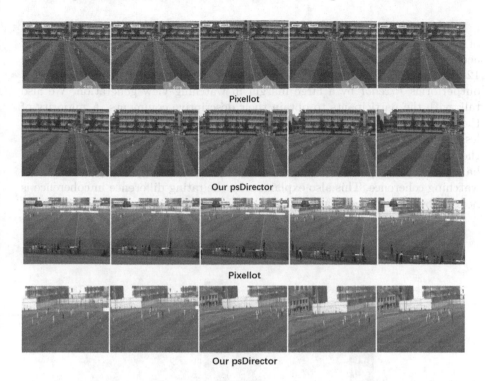

Pixellot

Our psDirector

Pixellot

Our psDirector

Fig. 4. Visualization of video clips generated by *Pixellot* and our psDirector.

cases (e.g., long pass and fast attack, not shown in this work) that both methods are missed, which also highlight the research direction in future.

4.3   User-Based Studies

We conduct user-based studies to subjectively compare the videos generated by our psDirector and *Pixellot*. Specifically, a total of 10 people familiar with soccer are recruited in this study, including 3 females and 7 males. They are all graduate students in computer science and related specialties. Each participant is asked to watch four pairs of video respectively recorded on four venues. Each pair contains three videos: a panoramic video segment of 5 to 10 min, two watching view counterparts generated by psDirector and *Pixellot*, respectively. The participants are asked to watch these videos one-by-one, and provide their judgements separately for each pair in two aspects: accuracy and coherence. The former evaluates whether the generated video accurately capture the real attractive area with appropriate view size. While the latter evaluates the rationality of camera actions along the time axis. To quantitate the judgements, three options are offered: *better, same, worse*, where *better* means that psDirector performs better than *Pixellot* and the rest are explained similarly. To avoid bias in judgement, the videos are given without their generation labels, i.e., coming from psDirector or *Pixellot*.

The evaluation results are given in Fig. 5. As can be seen, 45% and 22.5% of participants rate that psDirector performs better than *Pixellot* in terms of accuracy and coherence, respectively, while their counterpart rates for *worse* are 12.5% and 15%. The results clearly demonstrate that the proposed psDirector outperforms *Pixellot* by a large margin in watching view generation. We also talk with the participants to obtain their descriptive comments. A majority of them say that the view generated by psDirector is often more focused and misses less important shots. Moreover, psDirector always produces better navigation in the two near corners, thus offering better watching experience. On the other hand, most participants agree that both psDirector and *Pixellot* provide decent watching coherence. This also explains why the rating difference in coherence is not as obvious as in accuracy.

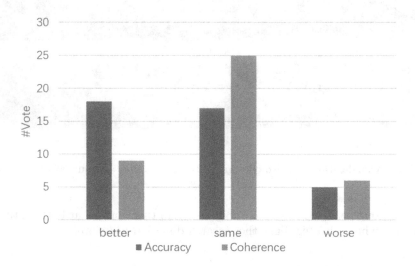

Fig. 5. Comparisons between psDirector and *Pixellot* from the 10 participants.

Drawing from the results above, we come to the conclusion that the proposed psDirector reasonably generate a watching view video from the given panoramic soccer video, who always provide better watching experience when compared to *Pixellot*, an existing commercial solution.

5   Conclusions

Observing that professional manual directing is too expensive to afford for amateur soccer while the panoramic soccer video provides bad watching experience, we have developed the psDirector system for automatic watching view generation. It aims to generate a video from the panoramic video, which is more suitable for people watching on TV or Internet. We have devised a novel pipeline to achieve this goal by reasonably extracting and analyzing soccer-related high-level semantics. The experiments conducted on school soccer basically validate our proposal. Performance improvements are also observed when compared to an existing commercial solution. We also note that the watching experience of psDirector still could be improved. For instance, the view could be more reasonable in a few cases. Thus, we plan to incorporate more semantics such as the trajectory of ball to further enhance the quality of generated video.

Acknowledgements. This research is supported by National Nature Science Foundation of China (Grant No. 61772526, 61876016).

References

1. Bertini, M., Del Bimbo, A., Nunziati, W.: Soccer videos highlight prediction and annotation in real time. In: Roli, F., Vitulano, S. (eds.) ICIAP 2005. LNCS, vol. 3617, pp. 637–644. Springer, Heidelberg (2005). https://doi.org/10.1007/11553595_78
2. Ekin, A., Tekalp, A.M., Mehrotra, R.: Automatic soccer video analysis and summarization. IEEE Trans. Image Process. **12**(7), 796–807 (2003). A Publication of the IEEE Signal Processing Society
3. Gong, Y., Sin, L.T., Chuan, C.H., Zhang, H., Sakauchi, M.: Automatic parsing of TV soccer programs. In: International Conference on Multimedia Computing and Systems, p. 167 (2002)
4. Intille, S.S., Aaron, A., Bobick, F.: Tracking using a local closed-world assumption: tracking in the football domain. In: Proceedings of the SPIE Storage and Retrieval for Image and Video Databases (1994)
5. Khatoonabadi, S.H., Rahmati, M.: Automatic soccer players tracking in goal scenes by camera motion elimination. Image Vis. Comput. **27**(4), 469–479 (2009)
6. Redmon, J., Farhadi, A.: Yolov3: an incremental improvement (2018)
7. Seo, Y., Choi, S., Kim, H., Hong, K.-S.: Where are the ball and players? Soccer game analysis with color-based tracking and image mosaick. In: Del Bimbo, A. (ed.) ICIAP 1997. LNCS, vol. 1311, pp. 196–203. Springer, Heidelberg (1997). https://doi.org/10.1007/3-540-63508-4_123
8. Tong, X.F., Lu, H.Q., Liu, Q.S.: An effective and fast soccer ball detection and tracking method. In: International Conference on Pattern Recognition, vol. 4, pp. 795–798 (2004)
9. Wang, Z., Yu, J., He, Y.: Soccer video event annotation by synchronization of attack-defense clips and match reports with coarse-grained time information. IEEE Trans. Circuits Syst. Video Technol. **27**(5), 1104–1117 (2017)
10. Wang, Z., Yu, J., He, Y., Guan, T.: Affection arousal based highlight extraction for soccer video. Multimed. Tools Appl. **73**(1), 519–546 (2014)
11. Yao, A., Uebersax, D., Gall, J., Gool, L.V.: Tracking people in broadcast sports. In: DAGM Conference on Pattern Recognition, pp. 151–161 (2010)
12. Zawbaa, H.M., El-Bendary, N., Hassanien, A.E., Kim, T.: Machine learning-based soccer video summarization system. In: Kim, T., Adeli, H., Grosky, W.I., Pissinou, N., Shih, T.K., Rothwell, E.J., Kang, B.-H., Shin, S.-J. (eds.) MulGraB 2011. CCIS, vol. 263, pp. 19–28. Springer, Heidelberg (2011). https://doi.org/10.1007/978-3-642-27186-1_3

13. Zhao, Z., Jiang, S., Huang, Q., Ye, Q.: Highlight summarization in soccer video based on goalmouth detection. In: Asia (2006)
14. Zhao, Z., Jiang, S., Huang, Q., Zhu, G.: Highlight summarization in sports video based on replay detection. In: IEEE International Conference on Multimedia & Expo, pp. 1613–1616 (2006)

No-Reference Video Quality Assessment Based on Ensemble of Knowledge and Data-Driven Models

Li Su[1]([⊠]), Pamela Cosman[2], and Qihang Peng[3]

[1] University of Chinese Academy of Sciences, Beijing, China
suli@ucas.ac.cn
[2] University of California at San Diego, San Diego, USA
pcosman@eng.ucsd.edu
[3] University of Electronic Science and Technology of China, Chengdu, China
anniepqh@uestc.edu.cn

Abstract. No-reference (NR) video quality assessment (VQA) aims to evaluate video distortion in line with human visual perception without referring to the corresponding pristine signal. Many methods try to design models using prior knowledge of people's experience. It is challenging due to the underlying complexity of video content, and the relatively limited understanding of the intricate mechanisms of the human visual system. Recently, some learning-based NR-VQA methods were proposed and regarded as data driven methods. However, in many practical scenarios, the labeled data is quite limited which significantly restricts the learning ability. In this paper, we first propose a data-driven model, V-CNN. It adaptively fits spatial and temporal distortion of time-varying video content. By using a shallow neural network, the spatial part runs faster than traditional models. The temporal part is more consistent with human subjective perception by introducing temporal SSIM jitter and hysteresis pooling. We then exploit the complementarity of V-CNN and a knowledge-driven model, VIIDEO. Compared to state-of-the-art full reference, reduced reference and no reference VQA methods, the proposed ensemble model shows a better balance between performance and efficiency with limited training data.

Keywords: No reference video quality assessment · Neural network
Prior knowledge · Spatial and temporal information

1 Introduction

With the rapid development and wide application of digital media devices, the number of video resources is growing at an explosive rate. Video Quality Assessment (VQA) plays an important role in a broad range of applications, e.g., enhancement, reconstruction, compression, communication, display, registration, watermarking and etc., and has drawn increasing attention from researchers in recent years.

Existing VQA methods can be roughly divided into two categories: subjective and objective. Subjective viewing tests are performed according to standard procedures. However, since Mean Opinion Scores (MOS) need to be obtained from a large number

© Springer Nature Switzerland AG 2019
I. Kompatsiaris et al. (Eds.): MMM 2019, LNCS 11296, pp. 231–242, 2019.
https://doi.org/10.1007/978-3-030-05716-9_19

of observers, measuring subjective video quality can be challenging, time-consuming and expensive. Sometimes, trained experts are required for judging.

Therefore, there has been an increasing demand to build intelligent, objective quality measurement models to predict perceived video quality. These models aim to provide similar results to subjective quality assessment, but are based on automatically measured criteria and metrics. According to the availability of the original video signal (generally not compressed), these methods are classified as Full Reference (FR), Reduced Reference (RR) and No-Reference (NR) Methods. FR metrics compute the quality difference between distorted video and lossless reference video. For RR metrics, the reference video is partially available and usually is in the form of a set of extracted features to help evaluate the quality of the distorted video. NR metrics try to assess the quality of a distorted video without any reference to the original one. Recently, NR-VQA is becoming more important because NR metrics have broader applications than FR and RR metrics [1, 2].

Numerous NR-VQA algorithms have been proposed. The majority attempt to predict the quality of videos that suffer specific types of distortion. Caviedes and Oberti [3] compute a set of blocking, blurring, and sharpness features, and other papers measure blocking and packet loss [4], or blockiness, blur and noise [5]. Later work considered blockiness and blurriness on detected regions of interest [6], or measured the distortion of compressed videos using Laplacian pyramid features [7]. In [8], the authors proposed an NR-VQA algorithm that measures spatial distortion between a video block and its motion compensated block in the previous frame, where temporal distortion is computed as a function of the mean of the motion vectors.

The application of those distortion specific methods is restricted because practical distortions are hybrid and complicated. Hence, some distortion non-specific (also called general purpose) NR-VQA methods were put forward recently. Some try to directly predict video quality driven by strong prior knowledge, such as [9], designed according to principles of the human vision system (HVS). The algorithm predicts video quality by modeling subband filter coefficients. Others design learning-based methods, mostly following the approach of first obtaining distortion representation features and then training a regression model. An NR-VQA method was proposed based on natural video statistics in the discrete cosine transform domain by incorporating temporal motion information, then a linear regression model was trained to predict video quality [10]. In [11], the authors proposed a bag-of-words and support vector regression (SVR) model to obtain each frame score, and then a temporal pooling strategy yields the final score for a whole video sequence. In [12], a novel model was based on a 1D convolutional neural network (CNN) and logistic regression. It uses the 3D Shearlet transform to extract features and then puts the features into the CNN and regression sequentially.

There are disadvantages with both the knowledge-driven and learning-based methods. On the knowledge-driven side, video distortions are complicated and people's prior knowledge is limited. The HVS is complex and only partially understood. So, it is difficult to design an algorithm consistent with human perception. Learning-based methods, as a rule, need plenty of data to train a robust model, but existing labeled data is limited and it is expensive to obtain additional labeled video quality data, which restricts the learning ability of these methods.

To tackle these problems, we decide to exploit the complementarity of knowledge-driven methods and learning-based methods. Prediction results of knowledge-driven methods could be more stable because of the model simplicity, whereas learning-based methods could fit the data with better prediction tendency since they use extra data to train models. In this paper, we involve the algorithm in [9] as a representation of knowledge-driven methods. We propose a new learning-based method because existing methods are either too slow or do not learn from the original frames. Our new learning-based method is based on 2D-CNN that learns spatial features from original frames. Then a linear regression is trained to predict video quality incorporating a group of temporal features we devised.

The contributions of the proposed NR-VQA model are summarized as follows:

(1) We exploit the complementarity of knowledge-driven and learning-based methods. The proposed ensemble model achieves a better tradeoff between performance and efficiency with limited training data.
(2) We propose V-CNN, a novel end-to-end learning-based NR-VQA model that adaptively fits distinctive features for universal distortion types.
(3) The proposed V-CNN model is composed of spatial and temporal parts, which benefit the assessment for time-varying video content. The spatial distortion model runs faster than traditional models and fits data well with a shallow neural network. The temporal distortion model is more consistent with human subjective perception by introducing temporal SSIM jitter and hysteresis pooling.

This paper is organized as follows: The two kinds of algorithms are presented in Sect. 2. Experimental results are in Sect. 3 and conclusions in Sect. 4.

2 Algorithm

The framework of the proposed ensemble model is illustrated in Fig. 1. The model is composed of VIIDEO [9], a knowledge-driven method, and our proposed CNN-based algorithm called V-CNN, for the data-driven side.

2.1 Knowledge-Driven Method: VIIEDO

VIIDEO [9] is a representative knowledge-driven algorithm. It is based on the insight that the bandpass filter coefficients of frame differences capture temporal statistical regularities arising from structures such as moving edges. The authors found that such coefficients are more homogeneous for pristine frame differences than for those with distortion. They probe these deviations by analyzing the sample distributions of products of pairs of adjacent coefficients computed along horizontal, vertical and diagonal spatial orientations. The products of neighboring coefficients were shown to be well modeled as following a zero mode asymmetric generalized Gaussian distribution. The model predicts the quality from fine and coarse levels of frame differences.

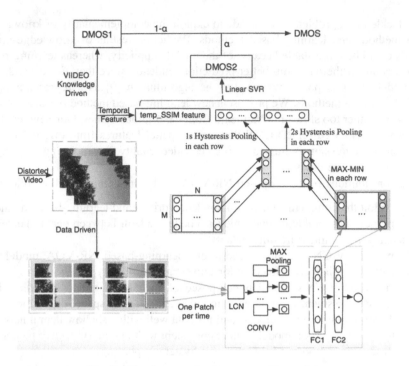

Fig. 1. The framework of our ensemble model.

2.2   Data-Driven Method: V-CNN

In order to adaptively fit the time-varying content of video, the proposed V-CNN algorithm is divided into spatial and temporal parts.

- **Spatial Part**

We reference the network structure of [14], which shows great performance in no-reference image quality assessment (NR-IQA). It has only one convolutional layer (50 kernels of size 7×7) because of speed and because a shallow structure would be stable to fit limited labeled data. Two fully connected layers (FC1 and FC2) both with 1024 nodes are concatenated next. An L1 loss function is used. The input of the network is a 32×32 image patch. Each patch is processed by local contrast normalization to alleviate the saturation problem and make the network robust to illumination and contrast variation. The CNN is pre-trained on the LIVE dataset for image quality assessment (IQA) [15, 16].

When CNN training is complete, we need to organize the patch-level features into video-level features. We select the features of FC1 as the patch-level features. Based on our experiments and those of other papers [11] we first organize patch-level features into frame-level features using the MAX-MIN of local responses, which is beneficial for capturing changes of quality.

- **Temporal Part**

Next, we organize the frame-level features into sequence-level features. Different from conventional linear fusion methods, we propose a temporal pooling strategy to account for the subjective effects.

As discussed in [17], there exists a hysteresis effect in subjective video quality judgment. When a distortion event results in a sharp decrease in video quality, poorer subjective quality scores remain even after the event passes [17]. Hysteresis pooling, shown to be effective for temporal changes of video quality, is used to organize the frame-level features into sequence-level features. With N frames in total, we use $Z(t_c)$ to denote the spatial feature for the t_c^{th} video frame. The pooling feature $a(t_c)$ accounts for the memory effect of the previous T frames. It is a MAX pooling strategy because the worst quality attracts more attention in people's memory. The feature $b(t_c)$ accounts for the propagation effect over the following T frames. To account for the fact that subjects respond strongly to drops in quality, we sort the quality scores in ascending order and combine them using a Gaussian weighting function.

Linear fusion is used to get the weighted feature of the current frame Q_{frame} and the final feature of the whole video Q_{video}. In the following, w_p, w_1, w_2 are empirically-determined parameters controlling the weights.

$$a(t_c) = \begin{cases} Z(t_c), & t_c \leq 1 \\ \max_{t=max(t_c-T,1)}^{t_c} (Z(t)), & t_c \geq 2 \end{cases} \tag{1}$$

$$b(t_c) = w_p \cdot \operatorname*{sort}_{t=t_c}^{min(t_c+T,N)} (Z(t)) \tag{2}$$

$$Q_{frame}(t_c) = w_1 \cdot a(t_c) + w_2 \cdot b(t_c) \tag{3}$$

$$Q_{video} = \frac{1}{N} \sum_{t_c=1}^{N} Score(t_c) \tag{4}$$

Table 1. Performance comparison for introducing different modules in V-CNN

Modules	SROCC	LCC
1s hysteresis pooling	0.587	0.660
2s hysteresis pooling	0.568	0.641
(1s+2s) hysteresis pooling	0.612	0.660
Temp_SSIM	0.260	0.517
1s hysteresis pooling+Temp_SSIM	0.650	0.709
2s hysteresis pooling+Temp_SSIM	0.640	0.697
(1s+2s) hysteresis pooling+Temp_SSIM	**0.671**	**0.713**

Referring to [17], T usually is selected to be two seconds. We believe that the latest memories are more influential. So we add extra one-second hysteresis pooling onto the traditional two-second pooling to emphasize the short-term memory effect. Our experience verified that it further improved the performance, as shown in Table 1.

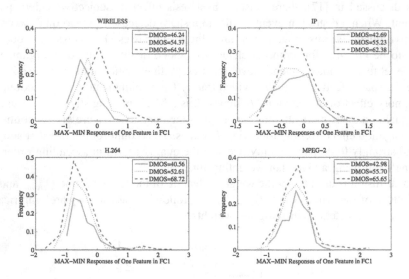

Fig. 2. Example of feature distribution histograms for different types and levels of distortion.

In order to verify the effectiveness of the learned features, we examine distribution histograms for different types and levels of distortions as shown in Fig. 2. We see that the learned features can clearly distinguish the different levels of distortions for universal distortion types.

We also note that local jitter exists in many kinds of temporal distortions. We can model jitter by examining statistics for the motion compensated corresponding blocks across adjacent frames. We divide frames into 16×16 blocks. For each block, a motion vector three-step search algorithm [18] is used to find the reference block. Then we calculate the jitter according to Eq. (5) below.

We devise a group of temporal features based on the idea that the structural similarity index (SSIM) [19] in corresponding blocks across adjacent frames may reflect the temporal quality of a video. The temporal features can be represented as follows:

$$JITTER(t) = Temp\_SSIM\_MAP(t) \tag{5}$$

$$Mean\_M = \frac{1}{N-1} \sum_{t=2}^{N} Mean(JITTER(t)) \tag{6}$$

$$Variance\_M = \frac{1}{N-1} \sum_{t=2}^{N} (Mean(JITTER(t)) - Mean\_M)^2 \tag{7}$$

$$Mean\_V = \frac{1}{N-1} \sum_{t=2}^{N} Variance(JITTER(t)) \qquad (8)$$

$$Variance\_V = \frac{1}{N-1} \sum_{t=2}^{N} (Variance(JITTER(t)) - Mean\_V)^2 \qquad (9)$$

where $Temp\_SSIM\_MAP(t)$ is a matrix whose entries represent the SSIM value of the corresponding blocks across the tth pair of adjacent frames, N is the total number of video frames, and $Mean()$ and $Variance()$ calculate the expectation and variance of a matrix. To predict video quality, a linear support vector regression (SVR) model is trained using the spatial and temporal features.

2.3 Ensemble of Two Kinds of Methods

Although VIIDEO performs well as a knowledge-driven method, it ignores detail information and its prediction accuracy is not good enough to be used in practice. But its prediction results are stable because of its inherent simplicity. Though there are not enough data for V-CNN as a learning-based method, which leads to unstable prediction results, it still shows good prediction tendencies. Thus, the two kinds of methods have complementary advantages and disadvantages when the dataset is limited.

To aggregate their advantages, we propose an ensemble model composed of the two methods. In our ensemble model, we merge their predicted quality scores:

$$QS_{final} = \alpha \times QS_{V-CNN} + (1 - \alpha) \times QS_{VIIDEO} \qquad (10)$$

where QS_{final} is the final predicted video quality score, QS_{V-CNN} and QS_{VIIDEO} are the predicted scores of the proposed V-CNN and VIIDEO respectively, and $\alpha = 0.25$ is an empirically-determined parameter controlling the weight of the two algorithms.

3 Experiments

3.1 Dataset and Evaluation Protocol

Most popular NR-VQA methods such as V-BLIINDS and VIIDEO are tested on the LIVE VQA dataset [20, 21]. For the sake of comparison, we conduct experiments on it as well. The dataset includes 160 videos, with ten uncompressed high-quality videos as reference videos. A set of 150 distorted videos are created from these reference videos (15 distorted videos per reference) using four different distortion types: MPEG-2 compression, H.264 compression, and simulated transmission of H.264 compressed bit-streams through error-prone IP networks and through error-prone wireless networks. The differential mean opinion score (DMOS) in the range from 0 to 100 is used. A higher DMOS denotes worse quality.

Like most VQA research, we employ the linear correlation coefficient (LCC) and Spearman's rank correlation coefficient (SROCC) to evaluate performance. For both, a higher value denotes better performance. There are 10 distinct video contents in the dataset; we used 8 for training and 2 for testing, and there are 45 such combinations. All experiments are repeated 45 times, and the median LCC and SROCC values are presented as final results.

Additionally, since the prediction quality score of VIIDEO is in the range of 0 to 1, and the ground truth score is in the range of 0 to 100, in V-CNN, we first normalize the ground truth score into the range of 0 to 1 as follows:

$$QS_i = (QS_i - QS_{min})/(QS_{max} - QS_{min}) \tag{11}$$

where QS_i denotes the ground truth score of the ith video, and QS_{min} and QS_{max} denote the minimum and maximum scores across all videos.

3.2 Results and Discussion

We first tested on every specific distortion dataset and then on the whole dataset. We compare our algorithm with four FR-VQA methods, one RR-VQA method and two NR-VQA methods: PSNR and SSIM [19] are evaluated for image quality and we use mean pooling across frame scores in our experiment. STMAD [22] and MOVIE [23] are recent VQA methods with top performance. STRRED [24] is a typical RR-VQA method, and V-BLIINDS [10] and VIIDEO [9] are popular NR-VQA methods with state-of-the-art performance.

- **Proposed temporal modules in V-CNN**

As shown in Table 1, by introducing hysteresis pooling and the temporal SSIM jitter module, the proposed V-CNN model fits temporal quality features well and is more consistent with human subjective perception.

Table 2. Median SROCC correlations for different VQA methods on the LIVE database.

Methods		Distortion types				
		Wireless	IP	H.264	MPEG2	Mix
FR	PSNR	0.691	0.600	0.714	0.643	0.677
	SSIM [19]	0.691	0.543	0.881	0.786	0.650
	MOVIE [23]	0.786	**0.771**	0.881	0.905	0.807
	STMAD [22]	**0.810**	**0.771**	**0.952**	**0.929**	**0.834**
RR	STRED [24]	0.762	0.771	0.905	0.905	0.826
NR	V-BLIINDS [10]	0.691	0.600	0.643	0.667	0.735
	VIIDEO [9]	0.548	0.600	0.762	0.571	0.651
	V-CNN	0.690	0.600	0.738	0.738	0.671
	V-CNN+VIIDEO	**0.738**	**0.657**	**0.786**	**0.786**	**0.751**

Table 3. Median LCC correlations for different VQA methods on the LIVE database.

Methods		Distortion types				
		Wireless	IP	H.264	MPEG2	Mix
FR	PSNR	0.798	0.733	0.698	0.696	0.722
	SSIM [19]	0.634	0.726	0.851	0.805	0.625
	MOVIE [23]	**0.920**	0.895	0.919	**0.955**	0.852
	STMAD [22]	0.904	**0.901**	**0.947**	0.942	**0.861**
RR	STRED [24]	0.806	0.816	0.892	0.904	0.725
NR	V-BLIINDS [10]	0.844	0.852	**0.956**	**0.949**	0.790
	VIIDEO [9]	0.740	0.848	0.886	0.872	0.701
	V-CNN	0.808	0.914	0.892	0.871	0.713
	V-CNN+VIIDEO	**0.874**	**0.923**	0.870	0.876	**0.794**

Table 4. Average runtime for different NR-VQA methods on the LIVE database.

Methods	Runtime (s)
STMAD	667.57
V-BLIINDS [10]	709.14
VIIDEO [9]	160.94
V-CNN	175.63
V-CNN+VIIDEO	336.57

- **Proposed NR-VQA model versus state-of-the-art VQA models**

As shown in Tables 2 and 3, both the SROCC and LCC coefficients of our ensemble algorithm are the best among NR-VQA methods and are also better than FR methods PSNR and SSIM on three single distortion subsets and on the whole dataset. Also, the proposed ensemble model runs much faster but achieves comparable performance with all state-of-the-art FR and RR methods, as shown in Table 4.

- **V-CNN versus knowledge-driven NR-VQA methods**

From Tables 2 and 3, we see that V-BLIINDS performs best among all knowledge-driven NR-VQA methods. It even outperforms the proposed data-driven method V-CNN. However, the increased running time for V-BLIINDS is large, as shown in Table 4. That is because the feature extraction of V-BLIINDS references more comprehensive prior knowledge, which contributes to final performance but results in higher runtime.

V-CNN is trained on limited training data, which restricts its learning ability. However, V-CNN fits the data better than the knowledge-driven model VIIDEO and costs similar runtime with a shallow neural network. That is to say, V-CNN achieves comparable results with V-BLIINDS with less runtime.

- **Ensemble versus Separate**

As shown in Tables 2 and 3, the ensemble of data-driven model V-CNN and knowledge-driven model VIIDEO improves the performance dramatically compared to the two algorithms run separately. The ensemble algorithm runs much faster than V-BLIINDS as shown in Table 4. Therefore, the ensemble method keeps better balance between performance and efficiency compared to the state-of-the-art.

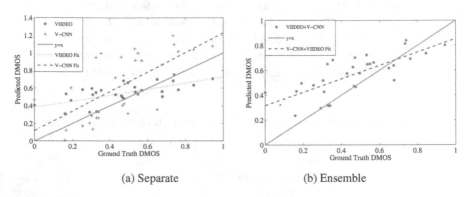

(a) Separate   (b) Ensemble

Fig. 3. The regression tendency of separate two models and the ensemble model on LIVE.

We have conducted another experiment to verify the complementarity of the two methods. As shown in Fig. 3(a), the prediction results of VIIDEO are more stable. It demonstrates the simplicity and universal adaptability. However, V-CNN has better prediction tendency. Figure 3(b) indicates the ensemble method aggregates their advantages and gains better performance. These findings support our ensemble motivation. Figure 4 shows the three algorithms' distributions of absolute residual values between predicted DMOS and ground truth DMOS. The residual values of the ensemble method are smaller. It also indicates that the complementarity of the two methods improves the performance of the ensemble model.

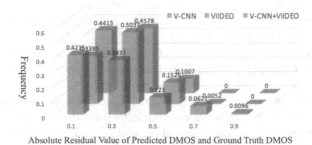

Fig. 4. Distribution of absolute residual value between the predicted DMOS and the ground truth DMOS.

4 Conclusion

In this paper, we propose V-CNN, a learning-based VQA model, and exploited the complementarity of V-CNN and the well-known knowledge-driven model VIIDEO. Experiments show that V-CNN achieves comparable performance and runs fast. The proposed ensemble of two models further improves the performance when there is limited labeled training data. It also keeps a better balance between performance and efficiency compared to state-of-the-art approaches.

Acknowledgement. This work was supported in part by the China Scholarship Council Program and by the National Natural Sciences Foundation of China: 61472389, 61332016 and 61301154.

References

1. Fang, Y., Yan, J., Li, L., Wu, J., Lin, W.: No reference quality assessment for screen content images with both local and global feature representation. IEEE Trans. Image Process. **27**(4), 1600–1610 (2018)
2. Wu, Q., Li, H., Meng, F., Ngan, K.N.: Generic proposal evaluator: a lazy learning strategy toward blind proposal quality assessment. IEEE Trans. Intell. Transp. Syst. **19**(1), 306–319 (2018)
3. Caviedes, J.E., Oberti, F.: No-reference quality metric for degraded and enhanced video. In: Visual Communications and Image Processing, International Society for Optics and Photonics, pp. 621–632 (2003)
4. Babu, R.V., Bopardikar, A.S., Perkis, A., Hillestad, O.I.: No-reference metrics for video streaming applications. In: International Workshop on Packet Video, pp. 10–11 (2004)
5. Farias, M.C., Mitra, S.K.: No-reference video quality metric based on artifact measurements. In: IEEE International Conference on Image Processing, vol. 3, pp. III–141 (2005)
6. Lin, X., Tian, X., Chen, Y.: No-reference video quality assessment based on region of interest. In: 2nd International Conference on Consumer Electronics, Communications and Networks (CECNet), pp. 1924–1927 (2012)
7. Zhu, K., Hirakawa, K., Asari, V., Saupe, D.: A no-reference video quality assessment based on Laplacian pyramids. In: 20th IEEE International Conference on Image Processing (ICIP), pp. 49–53 (2013)
8. Yang, F., Wan, S., Chang, Y., Wu, H.R.: A novel objective no-reference metric for digital video quality assessment. IEEE Signal Process. Lett. **12**(10), 685–688 (2005)
9. Mittal, A., Saad, M.A., Bovik, A.C.: A completely blind video integrity oracle. IEEE Trans. Image Process. **25**(1), 289–300 (2016)
10. Saad, M.A., Bovik, A.C., Charrier, C.: Blind prediction of natural video quality. IEEE Trans. Image Process. **23**(3), 1352–1365 (2014)
11. Xu, J., Ye, P., Liu, Y., Doermann, D.: No-reference video quality assessment via feature learning. In: IEEE International Conference on Image Processing (ICIP), pp. 491–495 (2014)
12. Li, Y., et al.: No-reference video quality assessment with 3D shearlet transform and convolutional neural networks. IEEE Trans. Circ. Syst. Video Technol. **26**(6), 1044–1057 (2016)

13. Mittal, A., Soundararajan, R., Bovik, A.C.: Making a completely blind image quality analyzer. IEEE Signal Process. Lett. **20**(3), 209–212 (2013)
14. Kang, L., Ye, P., Li, Y., Doermann, D.: Convolutional neural networks for no-reference image quality assessment. In: IEEE Conference on Computer Vision and Pattern Recognition (CVPR), pp. 1733–1740 (2014)
15. Sheikh, H.R., Sabir, M.F., Bovik, A.C.: A statistical evaluation of recent full reference image quality assessment algorithms. IEEE Trans. Image Process. **15**(11), 3440–3451 (2006)
16. Wang, Z., Bovik, A.C., Sheikh, H.R., Simoncelli, E.P.: Image quality assessment: from error visibility to structural similarity. IEEE Trans. Image Process. **13**(4), 600–612 (2004)
17. Seshadrinathan, K., Bovik, A.C.: Temporal hysteresis model of time varying subjective video quality. In: IEEE International Conference on Acoustics, Speech and Signal Processing (ICASSP), pp. 1153–1156 (2011)
18. Li, R., Zeng, B., Liou, M.L.: A new three-step search algorithm for block motion estimation. IEEE Trans. Circ. Syst. Video Technol. **4**(4), 438–442 (1994)
19. Wang, Z., Bovik, A.C., Sheikh, H.R., Simoncelli, E.P.: The SSIM index for image quality assessment. MATLAB implementation, vol. 23, p. 66 (2003). http://www.cns.nyu.edu/lcv/ssim
20. Seshadrinathan, K., Soundararajan, R., Bovik, A.C., Cormack, L.K.: Study of subjective and objective quality assessment of video. IEEE Trans. Image Process. **19**(6), 1427–1441 (2010)
21. Seshadrinathana, K., Soundararajanb, R., Bovik, A.C., Cormack, L.K.: A subjective study to evaluate video quality assessment algorithms. In: IS&T/SPIE Electronic Imaging. International Society for Optics and Photonics, p. 75270H (2010)
22. Vu, P.V., Vu, C.T., Chandler, D.M.: A spatiotemporal most-apparent-distortion model for video quality assessment. In: 18th IEEE International Conference on Image Processing (ICIP), pp. 2505–2508 (2011)
23. Seshadrinathan, K., Bovik, A.C.: Motion tuned spatio-temporal quality assessment of natural videos. IEEE Trans. Image Process. **19**(2), 335–350 (2010)
24. Soundararajan, R., Bovik, A.C.: Video quality assessment by reduced reference spatio-temporal entropic differencing. IEEE Trans. Circ. Syst. Video Technol. **23**(4), 684–694 (2013)

Understanding Intonation Trajectories and Patterns of Vocal Notes

Jiajie Dai[✉] and Simon Dixon

Centre of Digital Music, Queen Mary University of London,
Mile End Road, London E1 4NS, UK
{j.dai,s.e.dixon}@qmul.ac.uk

Abstract. Unlike fixed-pitch instruments hold the same pitch over time, the voice requires careful regulation during each note in order to maintain a steady pitch. Previous studies have investigated singing performance which takes single note as an element, such as intonation accuracy, pitch drift while the note trajectory within the notes has hardly been investigated. The aim of this paper is to study pitch variation within vocal notes and ascertain what factors influence the various parts of a note. We recorded data which including five SATB groups (four participants each group) singing two pieces of music in three listening conditions according to whether can hear other participants or not. After extracting fundamental frequency and analysing, we obtained all the notes by relative time and real-time duration, then observed a regular pattern among all the notes. To be specific: (1) There are transient parts in both the beginning and end of a note which is about 15–20% of the whole duration; (2) The shapes of transient parts differ significantly according to adjacent pitch, although all singers tend to have a descending transient at the end of a note.

Keywords: Intonation accuracy · Pitch trajectories · Note pattern

1 Introduction

Singing is our natural instrument, which directly expresses our personalities and emotions. Unlike instruments which have hundreds of years of manufactural development behind it, almost everyone can speak, everyone can sing, so we all have our own idea of what singing actually is [15, p. 1]. Although singing is the most common instrument to all human societies [3], many aspects of singing have not been explored in the research literature. For example, the patterns of, and factors that affect, vocal pitch trajectories have yet to be explained. The motivation of this paper is to determine whether pitch trajectories share common shapes, and what factors influence the transient parts of notes.

Intonation is commonly regarded as an important aspect of music performance [17], which is defined as how a pitch is played or sang in tune [8], and also describeed as the accuracy of pitch in playing or singing [18]. Such accuracy

© Springer Nature Switzerland AG 2019
I. Kompatsiaris et al. (Eds.): MMM 2019, LNCS 11296, pp. 243–253, 2019.
https://doi.org/10.1007/978-3-030-05716-9_20

could be inside or an entirety of a note. For the entirety intonation accuracy, some of the previous studies calculated the mean or median of the fundamental frequency (F0) inside the note (such as [7] and [12]). For the intonation inside a note, some software such as *Tony* [10] could export the pitch information in time series. We measured the intonation as the signed pitch difference compares with the score pitch, labelled in semitones on an equal-tempered scale. The beginning and end parts of the note trajectories which have more pitch variation are called transient parts.

It is very difficult to produce a correct pitch directly without the use of an external reference pitch [19]. Most singers adjust their intonation using auditory feedback to reach the intended pitch [21]. Howard tried to find that just intonation (the frequencies of notes are related by ratios of small whole numbers [9]) causes drift and found out that singers tend to non-equal-tempered tuning and do shift their pitch with modulation [7]. However, Devaney *et al.* reported that singers tended toward equal temperament and did not exhibit a large amount of drift. These evidences show the insatiability of the human tuning.

Our voice organs which produce speech and singing are extremely complex, which makes human are hard to tune. The voice production requires the cooperation of the lungs, vocal folds, larynx, pharynx and mouth [16]. To produce a voice in a particular pitch also require muscle memory and tonal memory [1]. For most people without the perfect pitch (the ability to recognise the pitch of a note or produce any given note), they tune their intonation rely on a recent reference [19]. Therefore, the instrumental accompaniment or reference pitch is very crucial for the tuning. For the circumstance that singers have to produce the performance without instrumental accompaniment.

This paper is a exploratory research to find which factor has an effect on note trajectory. There are many influencing factors which effect on overall intonation accuracy of a note. Such as score information, the individual difference (gender, training background [4]), with or without a accompaniment (instrument or singing ensembles). Some of the factors may have a variable effect, for example, instrumental accompaniment has been shown to enhance the individual learning of a piece [2], it can also reduce pitch accuracy during singing, even when the accompaniment is another singer who sings the exactly the same piece with you [6,14].

Previous studies have explored vocal pitch trajectories for singing voice synthesis, especially for performance modelling [20], and modelled the observed pitch in an imitation task, given a time-varying stimulus pitch [5]. Or modelling the observed pitch with the stimulus pitch which given to the participants to imitate [5]. The paper focuses on more factors which have an effect on note trajectory and pattern, according to the real-time performance.

2   Methodology

2.1   Research Questions

This study of interactive intonation in unaccompanied SATB singing is driven by a number of research questions. Firstly, we wish to know whether there are patterns or regularities in the pitch trajectories of individual notes. We expect to find common trends in the note trajectories, with differences due to context and experimental conditions. The second question is how to characterise the trajectories in terms of the time required for the singer to reach the target pitch. The third questions is what factors influence the tendencies of the transient part. The note trajectories might show significant differences due to context, such as when singing after a higher pitch or a lower pitch. We also wish to determine whether pitch trajectories differ by vocal part or sex. We previously observed significant differences between vocal parts in terms of pitch error [6]. Finally, we would like to see whether the listening condition affects note trajectories. That is, do the shapes of vocal notes differ depending on whether the participants can hear other vocal parts or not?

2.2   Participants

20 adult amateur singers (10 male and 10 female) with choir experience volunteered to take part in the study. They came from the music society and a capella society of the university and a local choir. (There was also a pilot experiment involving four participants from our research group; this data is not used in this paper.) The age range was from 20 to 55 years old (mean: 28.0, median: 26.5, std.dev.: 7.8). Participants were compensated £10 for their participation. The participants were able to sing their parts comfortably and they were given the score and sample audio files at least 2 weeks before the experiment.

Since training is a crucial factor for intonation accuracy, all the participants were given a questionnaire based on the Goldsmiths Musical Sophistication Index [13] to test the effect of training. The participants had an average of 3.3 years of music lessons and 5.8 years of singing experience.

2.3   Materials

Two contrasting musical pieces were selected for this study: a Bach chorale, "Oh Thou, of God the Father" (BWV 164/6) and Leo Mathisen's jazz song "To be or not to be". Both pieces were chosen for their wide range of harmonic intervals: the first piece has 34 unique harmonic intervals between parts and the second piece has 30 harmonic intervals. To control the duration of the experiment, we shortened the original score by deleting the repeats. We also reduced the tempo from that specified in the score, in order to make the pieces easier to sing and compensate for the limited time that the singers had to learn the pieces. The resulting duration of the first piece is 76 s and the second song is 100 s.

The equipment included an SSL MADI-AX converter, five cardioid microphones and four loudspeakers. All the tracks were controlled and recorded by the software Logic Pro 10. The metronome and the four starting reference pitches were also given by Logic Pro. The total latency of the system is 4.9 ms (3.3 ms due to hardware and 1.6 ms from the software).

2.4 Procedure

A pilot experiment with singers not involved in the study was performed to test the experimental setup and minimise potential problems such as bleed between microphones. Then the participants in the study were distributed into 5 groups according to their self-identified voice type, time availability and collaborative experience (the singers from the same music society were placed in the same group). Each group contained two female singers (soprano and alto) and two male singers (tenor and bass). Each participant had at least two hours practice before the recording, sometimes on separate days. They were informed about the goal of the study, to investigate interactive intonation in SATB singing, and they were asked to sing their best in all circumstances.

For each trial, the singers were played their starting notes before commencing the trial, and a metronome accompanied the singing to ensure that the same tempo was used by all groups. Each piece was sung 10 times by each group. The first and the last trial were recorded in the open condition. The partial and closed condition trials, consisting of 8 test conditions, 4 (isolated voice) × 2 (direction of feedback), were recorded in between. The order of isolated conditions was randomly chosen to control for any learning effect. For each isolated condition, the three-to-one condition always preceded the one-to-three condition. We use the performance of the isolated singer in the one-to-three condition as the data for the closed condition.

3 Data Analysis

This section describes the annotation procedure and the measurement of pitch error, melodic interval error, harmonic interval error. These metrics of accuracy are applied to the Sect. 4 for generate and analyse the pattern of note trajectories.

3.1 Annotation

The experimental data comprises 5 (groups) × 4 (singers) × 2 (pieces) × 10 (trials) = 400 audio files, each containing 65 to 116 notes. The software *Tony* [10] was chosen as the annotation tool. *Tony* performs pitch detection using the pYIN algorithm, which outperforms the YIN algorithm [11], and then automatically segments pitch trajectories into note objects, and provides a convenient interface for manual checking and correction of the resulting annotations. The automatic segmentation, based on note energy and pitch changes, provided the note onset and offset times for our data, and rarely needed any correction. Any missing notes were excluded from the analysis.

3.2 Conversion of F0

The *Tony* software segments the recording into notes and silences, and outputs the median fundamental frequency f_0 for each note, as well as the f_0 value for each 5.8 ms frame. The conversion of fundamental frequency to musical pitch p is calculated as follows:

$$p = 69 + 12 \log_2 \frac{f_0}{440}. \tag{1}$$

This scale is chosen such that its units are semitones, with integer values of p coinciding with MIDI pitch numbers, and reference pitch A4 (p = 69) tuned to 440 Hz. After automatic annotation, every single note was checked manually to make sure the tracking was consistent with the data and corrected if it was not.

3.3 Intonation Metrics

To quantify the effects of interaction on intonation, we measure pitch accuracy in terms of pitch error, melodic interval error, harmonic interval error and note stability, defined below.

Pitch Error. Assuming that a reference pitch has been given, *pitch error* can be defined as the difference between observed pitch and score pitch [12]:

$$e_i^p = \bar{p}_i - p_i^s \tag{2}$$

where $\bar{p}_i$ is the median of the observed pitch trajectory of note i (calculated over the duration of an individual note), and p_i^s is the score pitch of note i.

To evaluate the pitch accuracy of a sung part, we use *mean absolute pitch error* (MAPE) as the measurement. For a group of M notes with pitch errors $e_1^p, \ldots, e_M^p$, the MAPE is defined as:

$$\text{MAPE} = \frac{1}{M} \sum_{i=1}^{M} |e_i^p| \tag{3}$$

4 Results

After annotation and half-manually check the segmentation, there are totally 37246 single notes. Every single note has it own pitch trajectories which is 174 sampling points per seconds (default value from the software *Tony*). The score duration is from 0.25 to 5.50 s (mean 0.86, median 0.75) while the observed note duration is from 0.01 s to 5.10 s (mean 0.69, median 0.62), 89.5% of the score duration in the data is less than one seconds. We excluded the notes which has note duration shorter than 0.15 s (4.1%) and MAPE bigger than one semitone (12.0%) for all the results.

4.1   The Pattern of Note Trajectories

To observe regularities in note trajectories across differing note durations, we compared two methods of equalising the time-scale of notes: normalisation and truncation. Normalised pitch trajectories are expressed as a function of the fraction of the note that has elapsed (from 0 to 1), while for the truncated trajectories, only the first 0.4 and last 0.4 s of each note are considered (77% of notes have a duration longer than 0.4 s; shorter notes are aligned with the respective end of the note). For comparing trajectories of different score pitches, we use the pitch error, that is, the deviation from the target (score) pitch.

For the normalisation method, the note trajectories were re-sampled to 100 sampling points with the MATLAB resample function. Then any common shape of vocal notes can be obtained by averaging across notes. Figure 1 plots the resulting note trajectory generated by calculating the mean of all the sampling points.

In Fig. 1 we observe two transient parts at the beginning and end of the note. Based on the slope of this curve, the initial and final transients each comprise about 15–20% of the note's duration. In the following, we take the 15% at the beginning and the end as the transient parts. The length of the two transient parts is approximately the same, and the shape is almost symmetrical, consisting of peaks at both ends of the note, with a relatively stable middle portion. The mean pitch error is negative, reflecting a tendency to sing flat relative to the score pitch.

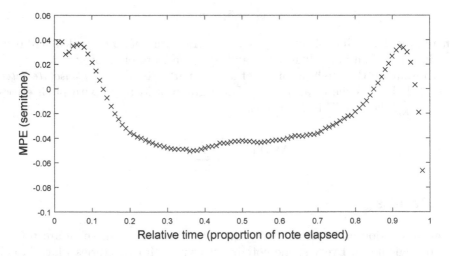

Fig. 1. Mean pitch error across time-normalised notes

An alternative way to combine note trajectories of varying length is to truncate the time series and only consider the initial and final segments of each note. Taking the first 0.4 and last 0.4 s of the notes reveals similar trajectories as for time-normalised notes (Figs. 2 and 3). From these figures, we observe that the first 0.12 and last 0.12 s of each note has the most pitch variance. This corresponds to about 15–20% of the mean note duration (0.69 s). This result is similar to that for normalised trajectories (Fig. 1), where the initial sharp fall and final rise in pitch are not as sharp due to the normalisation of different length notes. The average results hide differences in the proportion and direction of transients which arise due to individual differences, score pitch and vocal part, which will be investigated in the following sections.

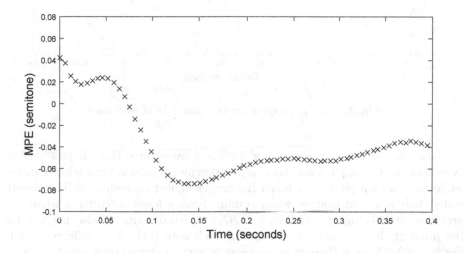

Fig. 2. Mean pitch error for the initial 0.4 s of each note

The appearance of note trajectories is significantly different between singers who have different degrees of musical training. For the trained singers, the note trajectories are smoother, and the two transient parts have a clear direction. For singers with less training, their note trajectories tend to be uneven and have less common shape in the beginning and ending.

In Fig. 2, the first turning point at 0.02 s may be an artefact of the averaging of different pitch trajectory shapes. There are several possible factors that might influence trajectory shapes, such as the pitch of the surrounding notes, vocal part, sex and listening condition, which we now examine.

4.2   Adjacent Pitch

In the previous section, we observed large pitch fluctuations at each end of the note. To test whether these fluctuations are influenced by adjacent pitches in the score, we separate the data for each end of a note into two situations, based on whether the previous (respectively next) pitch is lower or higher than the current pitch. Repeated notes are ignored. An analysis of variance (ANOVA) confirms that the pitch error in relative time is significantly different based on whether

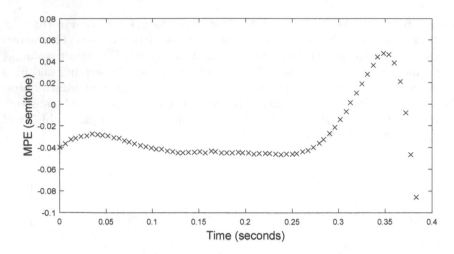

Fig. 3. Mean pitch error for the final 0.4 s of each note

the adjacent pitch is higher or lower. In Fig. 4 we observe that singers tend to overshoot the target pitch and then adjust downward after singing a lower pitch, while after a high pitch they reach the target almost immediately. The steady state pitch is 1 cent sharper when coming from a lower pitch than when the previous pitch is higher ($F(1, 38) = 77.97, p < 0.001$). Singers also prepare for the pitch of the next note at the end of each note ($F(1, 38) = 7.98, p < 0.01$, Fig. 5). In both cases there is an increase in pitch followed by a rapid decrease as the note ends and the vocal cords are relaxed, but the increase in pitch is

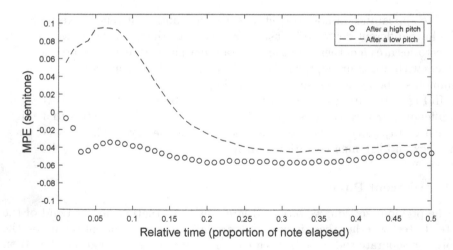

Fig. 4. The effect of singing after a lower or higher pitch: mean pitch error in relative time

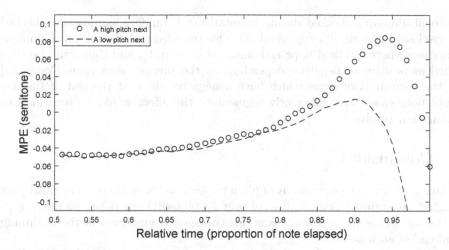

Fig. 5. The effect of singing before a lower or higher pitch: mean pitch error in relative time

much more marked in the case that the succeeding pitch is higher. There are some individual differences between singers in this respect, but most exhibit the average behaviour of being influenced by adjacent notes.

Although the peak might be smaller if the note after a high pitch or has a low pitch adjacent, the slope tendency is still obvious. Some participants have a slope at the beginning while others have a convex in the beginning, there might be more influencing factors rather than the adjacent pitch.

5   Discussion

All notes tend to have a negative slope at the end, regardless of whether the next pitch is higher or lower, or any other factor. This is probably due to the relaxation of the vocal muscles at the end of a note. The listening condition does not influence the shape of the transient parts, but has an effect on the mean pitch error, which correlates with the pitch in middle of the notes.

Besides the music training and adjacent pitches, there are more factors may influence the note pattern. We find that vocal parts and gender also have significant different in note trajectories in terms of transient shape. This may due to the music training of male singers (we observed that bass vocal part has lowest mean pitch error than other three vocal parts in this study). Sopranos have highest marks of musical training background in the Golden Smith questionnaire, while the lowest two singers are in the bass part. More investigation of influencing factors will in future works.

The note segmentation is based on the default settings of the software Tony, which segments the pitch track into notes according to the pitch and energy. Different settings and segmentation strategies may influence the results. The coarse segmentation was checked during annotation. A random sample was checked more closely after results were obtained. This revealed a small fraction of ambiguous cases where the final slope is dominated by vibrato, and thus could be classified as positive or negative, depending on the precise offset time. Compared to the thousands of notes which have a negative slope at the end, if the few ambiguous cases were differently segmented, the effect would be too small to change our results.

6   Conclusions

In this paper, we present a study of pitch trajectories of single notes in multi-part singing. According to our analysis of over 40000 individual notes, we find a general shape of vocal notes which contains transient components at the beginning and end of each note.

The analysis is based on both absolute and relative timing of notes, where the initial and final transients are about 120 ms, or 15–20% of note duration. The results suggest that the adjustment of pitch at the ends of notes is governed by absolute timing, i.e. due to physiological and psychological factors, rather than relative timing, which might imply a musical motivation. The transient components vary according to the individual performer, previous pitch, next pitch.

In conclusion, the main contribution of this paper is the observation, measurement and analysis of the note transient parts by investigating their shapes and influencing factors. Although many further issues remain to be investigated, we hope that the current observations provide a better understanding of the singing voice.

7   Acknowledgements and Data Availability

The study was conducted with the approval of the Queen Mary Research Ethics Committee (approval number: QMREC1560). Many thanks to all of the participants who contributed to this project. We also thank Marcus Pearce, Daniel Stowell and Christophe Rhodes for their advice on experimental design.

The code and the data needed to reproduce our results (note annotations, questionnaire results, score information) are available from:
https://code.soundsoftware.ac.uk/projects/satb-study/repository.

References

1. Alldahl, P.-G.: Choral Intonation. Gehrmans, Stockholm (2008)
2. Brandler, B.J., Peynircioglu, Z.F.: A comparison of the efficacy of individual and collaborative music learning in ensemble rehearsals. J. Res. Music Educ. **63**(3), 281–297 (2015)
3. Brown, D.E.: Human Universals, pp. 1–160. Temple University Press, Philadelphia (1991)

4. Cooper, N.A.: Children's singing accuracy as a function of grade level, gender, and individual versus unison singing. J. Res. Music Educ. **43**(3), 222–231 (1995)
5. Dai, J., Dixon, S.: Analysis of vocal imitations of pitch trajectories. In: 17th International Society for Music Information Retrieval Conference, pp. 87–93 (2016)
6. Dai, J., Dixon, S.: Analysis of interactive intonation in unaccompanied SATB ensembles. In: 18th International Society for Music Information Retrieval Conference, pp. 599–605 (2017)
7. Howard, D.M.: Intonation drift in A Capella soprano, alto, tenor, bass quartet singing with key modulation. J. Voice **21**(3), 300–315 (2007)
8. Kennedy, J.B., Kennedy, M.: The Concise Oxford Dictionary of Music. Oxford University Press, Oxford (2004)
9. Lindley, M.: Just intonation. In: Macy, L. (ed.) Grove Music Online (2001). http://www.grovemusic.com. Accessed 30 Jan 2015
10. Mauch, M., et al.: Computer-aided melody note transcription using the Tony software: accuracy and efficiency, pages 23–30, May 2015
11. Mauch, M., Dixon, S.: PYIN: a fundamental frequency estimator using probabilistic threshold distributions. In IEEE International Conference on Acoustics, Speech and Signal Processing, pp. 659–663 (2014)
12. Mauch, M., Frieler, K., Dixon, S.: Intonation in unaccompanied singing: accuracy, drift, and a model of reference pitch memory. J. Acoust. Soc. Am. **136**(1), 401–411 (2014)
13. Müllensiefen, D., Gingras, B., Musil, J., Stewart, L.: The musicality of non-musicians: an index for assessing musical sophistication in the general population. PLoS ONE **9**(2), e89642 (2014)
14. Pfordresher, P.Q., Brown, S.: Poor-pitch singing in the absence of 'tone deafness'. Music Percept. **25**(2), 95–115 (2007)
15. Potter, J.: Introduction: singing at the turn of the century. In: Potter, J. (ed.) The Cambridge Companion to Singing, pp. 1–5. Cambridge University Press, Cambridge (2000)
16. Sundberg, J.: The acoustics of the singing voice. Sci. Am. **236**(3), 82–91 (1977)
17. Sundberg, J., Lã, F.M.B., Himonides, E.: Intonation and expressivity: a single case study of classical Western singing. J. Voice **27**(3), 391–e1 (2013)
18. Swannell, J.: The Oxford Modern English Dictionary, p. 560. Oxford University Press, USA (1992)
19. Takeuchi, A.H., Hulse, S.H.: Absolute pitch. Psychol. Bull. **113**(2), 345 (1993)
20. Umbert, M., Bonada, J., Goto, M., Nakano, T., Sundberg, J.: Expression control in singing voice synthesis: Features, approaches, evaluation, and challenges, **32**(6), 55–73 (2015)
21. Zarate, J.M., Zatorre, R.J.: Experience-dependent neural substrates involved in vocal pitch regulation during singing. Neuroimage **40**(4), 1871–1887 (2008)

Temporal Lecture Video Fragmentation Using Word Embeddings

Damianos Galanopoulos and Vasileios Mezaris[✉]

Information Technologies Institute/CERTH, 6th Km. Charilaou - Thermi Road,
Thermi-Thessaloniki, Greece
{dgalanop,bmezaris}@iti.gr

Abstract. In this work the problem of temporal video lecture fragmentation in meaningful parts is addressed. The visual content of lecture video can not be effectively used for this task due to its extremely homogeneous content. A new method for lecture video fragmentation in which only automatically generated speech transcripts of a video are exploited, is proposed. Contrary to previously proposed works that employ visual, audio and textual features and use time-consuming supervised methods which require annotated training data, we present a method that analyses the transcripts' text with the help of word embeddings that are generated from pre-trained state-of-the-art neural networks. Furthermore, we address a major problem of video lecture fragmentation research, which is the lack of large-scale datasets for evaluation, by presenting a new artificially-generated dataset of synthetic video lecture transcripts that we make publicly available. Experimental comparisons document the merit of the proposed approach.

Keywords: Lecture video fragmentation · Word embeddings
Video segmentation

1   Introduction

As multimedia based e-learning systems and online video-lecture databases grow rapidly, accessing and searching lecture video content becomes an important and challenging task. A key challenge is enabling fine-grained access to the lectures, i.e. accessing the video fragments that satisfy the needs of the user, rather than entire lectures. This brings up the problem of lecture video fragmentation, i.e. how to segment video lectures in logical and meaningful parts in order to enable easy access. Video lecture fragmentation differs from the classic video segmentation approaches, since in lecture videos the changes in visual content are usually scarce and are not necessarily associated with semantic transitions in the videos.

A typical lecture video includes a speaker in front of a blackboard or a projector display, in which presentation slides are projected while the speaker comments on them. In most cases the camera is static and focuses only on the speaker and possibly also the slides. Camera movements are scarce and mainly smooth.

I. Kompatsiaris et al. (Eds.): MMM 2019, LNCS 11296, pp. 254–265, 2019.
https://doi.org/10.1007/978-3-030-05716-9_21

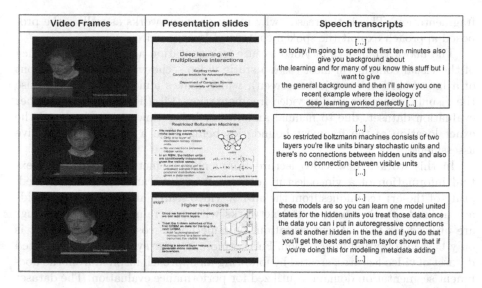

Video Frames	Presentation slides	Speech transcripts
	Deep learning with multiplicative interactions Geoffrey Hinton Canadian Institute for Advanced Research & Department of Computer Science University of Toronto	[...] so today i'm going to spend the first ten minutes also give you background about the learning and for many of you know this stuff but i want to give the general background and then i'll show you one recent example where the ideology of deep learning worked perfectly [...]
	Restricted Boltzmann Machines	[...] so restricted boltzmann machines consists of two layers you're like units binary stochastic units and there's no connections between hidden units and also no connection between visible units [...]
	skip? Higher level models	[...] these models are so you can learn one model united states for the hidden units you treat those data once the data you can i put in autoregressive connections and at another hidden in the the and if you do that you'll get the best and graham taylor shown that if you're doing this for modeling metadata adding [...]

Fig. 1. Example of a typical lecture video where video frames, slides and the corresponding speech transcripts are illustrated.

In most cases the only noteworthy visual changes are the slide transitions. As a general observation, the main subject of a lecture video may often be relatively broad (e.g. "Neural Networks", "Information Retrieval" etc.), but during the lecture a lot of different sub-topics are usually analyzed. It is vital to find an efficient and fast way to fragment lecture videos in parts, in a way that each part corresponds to a different sub-topic that can be indexed and searched efficiently.

Figure 1 illustrates an example of a typical lecture video. The visual content is quite unchanged during the entire video and cannot be associated with the sub-topics that are analyzed in this video. The corresponding slides, if available, could provide hints about the sub-topics; but, in many cases slides are not provided or are not used at all in a lecture. In contrast, speech transcripts can always be easily generated from an ASR system and they contain the key information for lecture video fragmentation, due to the detailed information that they convey.

The majority of state-of-the-art methods in video lecture fragmentation, e.g. [4,14], utilize various video modalities, i.e. visual, audio, SRTs and information based on the presentation slides. However, previous research [10,14] on lecture video fragmentation has shown that the performance of fragmentation methods that use the textual information extracted from lecture videos exceeds the corresponding performance of visual-based methods, when annotated lecture videos that could be used for training a supervised classifier are absent. In most cases, the visual part of a video segment is not associated with the semantic content that this segment deals with. For example, in the illustrated segments of Fig. 1, it is impossible to determine subject transitions from the frame changes, while the information from transcripts and video slides could be used for video fragmentation. This is the reason why many previous works as well as the proposed approach exploit the spoken content of lecture video.

The major challenges in video lecture fragmentation are (i) the consistency of the visual content (in most cases a static video scene with a speaker in front of a blackboard or a projector screen), which makes almost impossible to use the visual content for quality video fragmentation [14], (ii) the lack of a proper evaluation dataset, due to manual annotation being time consuming, and the exact location of the fragment boundaries being often a matter of subjective assessment.

In this work a new video lecture fragmentation method, using only textual information of a video lecture derived from its transcripts, is proposed. State-of-the-art techniques from the ad-hoc video search and text analysis fields are utilized. Furthermore, neural networks with pre-trained word embeddings are utilized for textual representation. Our method is cost-effective, since it is only based on textual information. Furthermore, a large synthetically-generated dataset of video lectures, created by following an approach inspired from the document segmentation domain, is utilized for performance evaluation. The dataset is specifically designed for the temporal video lecture fragmentation problem and is made publicly available. The key contributions of the proposed work are:

- Inspired from state-of-the-art works on ad-hoc video search, new approaches to text analysis for cue extraction are examined.
- Word embeddings instead of traditional bag-of-words approaches are utilized. Taking into consideration the previous literature, this is the first work that exploits word embeddings on the lecture video fragmentation problem.
- A large-scale dataset of artificially-generated lectures, which is made available online, is created, and used for experimentation.

2   Related Work

Several works have been proposed in previous years dealing with lecture video related issues, such as lecture video indexing, retrieval, recommendation and segmentation. In [11] an automated lecture video indexing system is proposed. Boosted deep convolution neural networks are used to correlate lecture slide images with candidate video frames. In [18] slide-based video segmentation combined with OCR and ASR analysis are used for lecture video indexing and video search. Multi-modal language models are proposed in [5] for lecture video retrieval. The co-occurrence of words in the spoken content and the video slides are modeled by latent variable models for efficient multi-modal lecture video retrieval. Recommendation systems for educational videos have also been proposed. In [1] the *Videopedia* system is designed to recommend educational videos using topic extraction from video transcripts as well as from video metadata.

In earlier years a few approaches attempted to address the problem of temporal lecture video fragmentation. Those were based on audio-visual features combined with linguistic analysis methods [13]. [10] address the problem by exploiting textual features. The performance of different types of natural language processing methods are evaluated and their performance is compared. More recently, in [15] a method based on visual and textual analysis is presented. Lecture videos with known fragment boundaries are utilized in order to train SVMs using color histograms of video frames. Moreover, textual cues from the presentation slides and video transcripts are extracted. However, this approach in order to train SVMs requires already annotated (with ground-truth fragmentation information) lecture videos, which are scarce. In [4] a solution which segments lecture video by analyzing its supplementary synchronized slides using an OCR system is presented. Similarly, [17] uses slide transition recognition, text localization and OCR techniques in order to determine fragment boundaries. In [2] a supervised method using visual features along with transcripts is proposed. The authors of [2] trained SVMs in order to find events on a lecture video, e.g. "speaker writing on the blackboard" or "slide presentation". Fragment boundaries were derived from these events. In [14] a method which utilizes Wikipedia articles is presented. Transcript blocks and Wikipedia text are matched w.r.t the topics that a lecture video examines. Additionally, similar to [15] color histograms of the visual content are used for training SVMs.

As the majority of the proposed methods for lecture video segmentation exploits textual information that is extracted from some modality (audio or visual), either exclusively or in combination with visual information, the text-based part of the task could also be approached as a text segmentation problem. Text segmentation is the problem of dividing documents in such way that each part is a self-contained piece of text dealing with a different sub-topic. In [7] GRAPHSEG is presented. This is an unsupervised graph based text segmentation method that exploits word embeddings and the semantic relatedness of text parts to construct a semantic relatedness graph, where each node represents a sentence and each edge is the semantic relatedness between two nodes. Then the maximal cliques of the graph determine the text segments. In contrast to previous text segmentation works, in [9] the task is addressed as a supervised learning problem. Using a large labeled dataset from Wikipedia corpus, an hierarchy model of two LSTN based sub-networks is trained. The first network calculates the text representation, while the second network estimates the segmentation boundaries.

The majority of previous works on lecture video fragmentation require the use of either supplementary materials of the lecture videos (e.g. sideshows), or annotated datasets for supervised training. Furthermore, the evaluation is performed in small datasets whose size ranges from 3 to 20 manually-annotated lecture videos. The method proposed in this work overcomes these problems by exploiting only one audio modality of the lecture video, and requiring no lecture-specific training data. Moreover, the introduction of a large-scale generated lecture video dataset enables the reliable evaluation of the proposed method and its comparison with previous approaches.

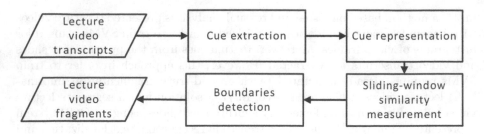

Fig. 2. Block diagram of the proposed temporal lecture video fragmentation method.

3 Proposed Method

We propose a lecture fragmentation method that relies on the transcripts (SRT files) of a video lecture. Video transcripts can be easily generated by any off-the-shelve automatic speech recognition system (ASR); research on speech recognition is not the subject of this work, and therefore will not be further examined. Figure 2 illustrates the pipeline of the proposed method.

A transcript is a sequence of text parts, each one being followed by the start and end time of the corresponding spoken content in the video's audio track. To briefly explain our pipeline, the textual information derived from a transcript is utilized to extract meaningful textual cues, which are phrases or terms that the original text contains. These cues are characteristic of the original text; they capture very concisely the essence and the meaning of that text. The transcript text is used as input to our method, which outputs a set of time boundaries of the video fragments. Transcript textual parts are processed in order to extract meaningful textual cues. Two different methods for cue extraction are examined. The first method is a state-of-the-art work [14] in video lecture segmentation that uses Noun Phrases as cues. The second one is based on the textual analysis and textual decomposition component of an ad-hoc video search system [12]. Then, these cues are vectorized in a way that each textual part is represented as a single vector. Again, two different approaches are examined for transforming the extracted cues in a vector space. Finally, to fragment each lecture video, a sliding-window-based method is used in order to detect time boundaries. These boundaries define the final set of temporal video fragments.

3.1 Text Processing and Cue Extraction

Standard Natural Language Processing (NLP) techniques are used in order to process the SRTs text. Text cleaning methods, such as stop-word removal, punctuation and tag cleaning are applied, followed by text lowercase conversion, in order to reduce vocabulary size. Consequently, the Stanford POS tagger [16] is used for part of speech tag extraction and the Stanford Named Entity Recognizer (NER) [6] for named entity extraction (e.g. names, organizations etc). These tags are used to find cue phases and words that can encapsulate the information of a text part. Two different approaches are examined to this end. The first approach is the method of [14], based on which Noun Phrases (NP) are extracted from the available text. A "noun phrase" is basically a noun, plus all the words that surround and modify the noun, such as adjectives, relative clauses and prepositional phrases. The motivation behind choosing to examine this method is that in [10] the performance of several different textual features was examined, and it was shown that NP performance is better than that of other textual feature extraction methods. The second approach we examine is inspired from the query analysis and decomposition method of an ad-hoc video search (AVS) system [12]. Specifically, in [12] task-specific NLP rules are used in order to extract textual cues from a text part. For example, "Noun-Verb-Noun" sequences are searched for in the text. Such a triad can encapsulate more information than one word by itself. Both the above approaches produce a set of words or phrases $C = [c_1, c_2, \ldots, c_t]$, where t is the number of extracted cues in a textual part, which characterizes this particular part.

3.2   Cue Representation

To represent the extracted cues in a vector space, two different representations are adopted.

First, a Bag-of-words approach with an N-gram language model, which uses the extracted cues as sequences of the model. For a specific part of text, the tf-idf weighting of the cues C extracted form this part of text is calculated, to produce a vector $\mathbf{V}_{BoW}^{C} = [v_{c_1}, v_{c_2}, \ldots, v_{c_d}] \in \mathbb{R}^d$, where d is the total number of distinct cues in the whole transcript, i.e. the dictionary of the language model.

As a cue representation alternative, Word2Vec is utilized, a state-of-the-art neural-network-based word embedding method that transforms words into a semantic vector space. Word2Vec represents every word w_i of a phrase or other piece of text as a continuous vector $\mathbf{V}_{word2vec}^{w_i} = [v_1, v_2, \ldots, v_n]$ in a low dimensional space $\mathbb{R}^n$, which captures lexical and semantic properties of words. As global representation of a text part, $\mathbf{V}_{word2vec}^{C}$, the *average word vector* approach is followed, which averages the vectors of each word of each cue that has been extracted from this text part.

Each one of the aforementioned approaches results in a vector that represents a specific part of text, making the comparison of text parts easy.

3.3   Video Fragmentation

To find meaningful fragments in a video transcript we follow a method similar to TextTiling [8], as it was described in [14], using textual sliding windows and measuring the similarity of neighbor windows.

A sliding window (W_i) of N words moves across the entire text of a transcript with a certain step of $N/6$ words. On each step the similarity between two neighboring windows (W_i, W_{i+1}) is calculated. For each sliding window we follow the cue extraction process which is described above and each window is represented as a set of cues, C_i and C_{i+1} respectively. For each window a vector

$\mathbf{V}^C$ is calculated using one of the two approaches described in the cue representation subsection above. Finally, the cosine similarity is utilized to calculate the similarity between two neighbor windows.

Following the similarity calculation between adjacent windows across the entire transcript, an one-dimensional signal $y = f(x)$, where x represents time and the y represents two neighboring windows similarity score, is produced. Subsequently, the valleys and peaks (local minima and maxima) of the signal are detected. The deepest valleys are assigned as candidates for segment boundaries. The depth of a valley is calculated based on the distances from the peaks on both sides of the valley. Let val be the value of the signal in a local minimum, $peak_1$ the value of the signal in the closest peak on the left and $peak_2$ the value in the closest peak on the right. The depth of a valley $depth_{val}$ is calculated as: $depth_{val} = (peak_1 - val) + (peak_2 - val)$. $depth_{val}$ indicates how big the change in this particular time interval is. We make the assumption that when $depth_{val}$ is high, the semantic content of the windows on the two sides of the local minimum is highly dissimilar and therefore this time point is assigned as a fragment boundary.

Then, a fixed number of k valleys with the largest $depth_{val}$ can be selected as the boundaries of the fragments. As an alternative, valleys with $depth_{val}$ larger than a threshold,

$$Thr = m \cdot (\mu - \sigma) \tag{1}$$

where μ is the mean of the signal's values in all local minima, σ is the standard deviation and m a multiplier, are selected as the actual fragment boundaries.

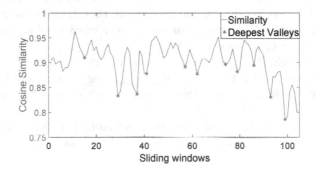

Fig. 3. An illustration of the similarities between neighboring windows of a synthetic video lecture, which is split in 12 fragments.

In Fig. 3 a sample of the fragmentation procedure results are presented. The curve represents the similarity between two neighboring windows, while the dots indicate the selected valleys with the largest depth value, which are the extracted fragment boundaries.

4   Experimental Results

4.1   Dataset

An important problem in the development and evaluation of video lecture fragmentation methods is the lack of annotated datasets, due to the difficultly and the time-consuming nature of manual annotation. Moreover, constructing such datasets is a difficult task due to the subjectiveness of defining fragment boundaries. In most of the cases it is not clear where exactly a fragment boundary exists, even to lecturer. Thus, in a 1–2 h lecture, where the transcripts of free continuous speech of a speaker are available, the fragmentation results will be quite arbitrary even if coming from a human expert.

To overcome this problem, we choose to follow an approach well-known in the document segmentation field. Following [3], in which document fragments of various lengths were concatenated and formed new documents, we have created a new dataset[1] of artificially-generated lectures. We used 1498 transcript files from the world's biggest academic online video repository, the VideoLectures.NET. These transcripts correspond to lectures from various fields of science, such as Computer science, Mathematics, Medicine, Politics etc. We split all transcripts in random fragments, the duration of which ranges between 4 and 8 min. A synthetic lecture is then created by combining exactly 20 randomly-selected parts. The first 300 such artificially-generated lectures were chosen for assembling our test dataset. Each such lecture file has a mean duration of about 120 min, and the overall dataset contains about 600 h of artificially-generated lectures. Every pair of consecutive fragments in these lectures originally comes from different videos, consequently the point in time where such two fragments are joined is a known ground-truth fragment boundary. All these boundaries form the dataset's ground truth. We should stress that we do not generate the corresponding video files for the artificially-generated lectures (only the transcripts) and we do not use in any way the visual modality for finding the fragments.

4.2   Evaluation Measures

To evaluate the performance of our video lecture fragmentation method, the Precision, Recall and F−Score measures were employed. In order to account for possible small differences between a ground truth fragment boundary F^{GT} and a predicted one F^{PR}, we assign a score to every $(F^{GT}, F^{PR})_q$ pair, $(q = 1, \ldots, Q)$, where Q is the total number of all pairs, which is calculated as follows:

$$S(F^{GT}, F^{PR})_q = \begin{cases} 1 & \text{if temporal distance between} (F^{GT}, F^{PR})_q < 30 sec \\ 0 & otherwise \end{cases}$$

In practice, this score introduces an error window to our calculations. We must mention that every F^{GT} can be associated with just one F^{PR}. Precision

---

[1] Large-scale video lecture dataset and ground truth fragmentation available at https://github.com/bmezaris/lecture_video_fragmentation.

(P) is defined as the fraction of the sum of all $(F^{GT}, F^{PR})_q$ pair scores over the number of the retrieved boundaries and Recall (R) is defined as the fraction of the sum of all $(F^{GT}, F^{PR})_q$ pair scores over the number of the ground-truth boundaries:

$$P = \frac{\sum_{q=1}^{Q} S(F^{GT}, F^{PR})_q}{L}, \quad R = \frac{\sum_{q=1}^{Q} S(F^{GT}, F^{PR})_q}{O}$$

where L is the total number of predicted boundaries F^{PR}, and O is the number of ground-truth boundaries F^{GT}. The F-Score is calculated by the standard formula: F-Score $= 2 \cdot P \cdot R / (P + R)$.

4.3 Results

In this subsection, our experimental results are presented. We evaluate the combination of the two cue extraction methods (i) NP and (ii) AVS, with the two different representations (i) BoW and (ii) Word2vec embeddings, as described in Sect. 3. First, we evaluate the performance of our method using a fixed number of 19 calculated fragment boundaries per video, which means we produce exactly 20 fragments for every artificially-generated video lecture. We also measure the performance of our system while the window size N changes.

We compare our methods with two competitive works. The first one is the transcript based lecture video fragmentation of [14], which is actually identical to the BoW-NP combination of our experiments setup, with a fixed window size of 120 words. Moreover, we compare with the supervised text segmentation method of [9].

Table 1 reports the evaluation results of the three variations of the proposed method and the performance of [14] for a set of different window sizes, in Precision, Recall and F-Score. In Table 2 the proposed methods, using the best-performing window size from Table 1, are compared with [9,14]. As shown in Table 2, the best overall performance was achieved by the combination of the text analysis using Noun Phrases and Word2Vec representation. More specifically, from Tables 1 and 2 we conclude the following:

- Using the Word2Vec model consistently leads to better performance in terms of F-Score, regardless of the cue extraction method being used.
- Sliding window size matters. In contrast to previous works [10,14], where a window was formed by a fixed number of 120 words, we show that performance can be significantly improved by varying the window size. When this is increased, the average number of the extracted cues that a window contains is also increased. Larger windows contain more semantically similar cues or multiple instances of the same cue, and are easier to distinguish from a neighboring window. However, there is an upper limit to the optimal window size, which possibly depends on the specifics of the lectures being fragmented (i.e., the size of the ground-truth fragments).
- The NP cue extraction method consistently outperforms the AVS approach.

Table 1. Experimental results (Precision, Recall and F-Score) of the three variations of the proposed approach, and comparison with [14] using different text window sizes.

	Window size (N)	120	240	360	480	600	720	840	960	1080
BoW NP [14]	Precision	0.287	0.228	0.204	0.262	0.349	0.415	**0.426**	0.408	0.391
	Recall	0.315	0.251	0.224	0.288	0.383	0.455	**0.459**	0.422	0.378
	F-Score	0.3	0.239	0.213	0.274	0.365	0.434	**0.442**	0.414	0.383
	Avg Num_of_Cues	20.78	42.03	63.15	84.28	105.30	126.18	146.98	167.68	188.25
	Fragment duration mean	330.5	330.5	330.5	330.5	330.7	332.0	338.6	354.0	380.1
	Fragment duration std	16.4	16.4	16.4	16.4	16.6	17.0	22.6	32.5	40.7
BoW AVS	Precision	0.27	0.281	0.287	0.315	0.365	0.398	**0.415**	0.386	0.377
	Recall	0.297	0.309	0.316	0.346	0.401	0.437	**0.455**	0.416	0.383
	F-Score	0.283	0.294	0.301	0.33	0.382	0.416	**0.434**	0.4	0.379
	Avg Num_of_Cues	17.31	34.93	52.49	70.13	87.54	104.95	122.22	139.42	156.57
	Fragment duration mean	330.5	330.5	330.5	330.5	330.5	330.6	332.1	338.6	361.0
	Fragment duration std	16.4	16.4	16.4	16.4	16.4	16.4	16.8	22.7	34.0
Word2Vec NP	Precision	0.335	0.248	0.252	0.29	0.373	0.427	**0.465**	0.448	0.427
	Recall	0.368	0.273	0.278	0.319	0.411	0.466	**0.491**	0.437	0.377
	F-Score	0.351	0.26	0.264	0.304	0.391	0.446	**0.477**	0.441	0.398
	Avg Num_of_Cues	20.77	42.07	63.20	84.28	105.30	126.18	146.98	167.68	188.25
	Fragment duration mean	330.5	330.5	330.5	330.5	330.6	333.0	345.3	375.3	417.1
	Fragment duration std	16.4	16.4	16.4	16.4	16.5	17.6	30.7	44.3	54.2
Word2Vec AVS	Precision	0.268	0.289	0.299	0.321	0.373	0.412	**0.425**	0.417	0.402
	Recall	0.295	0.318	0.329	0.353	0.41	0.453	**0.46**	0.423	0.377
	F-Score	0.281	0.303	0.313	0.336	0.391	0.431	**0.441**	0.419	0.388
	Avg Num_of_Cues	17.35	34.99	52.60	70.13	87.54	104.95	122.22	139.42	156.57
	Fragment duration mean	330.5	330.5	330.5	330.5	330.5	330.9	336.4	359.8	392.7
	Fragment duration std	16.4	16.4	16.4	16.4	16.4	17.0	22.1	36.8	52.2

- The proposed method outperforms both [9,14]. Compared to the supervised segmentation method [9], our method is significantly better despite the fact that [9] is based on training data. However, the training corpus does not have similar structure with an annotated dataset consisting of lecture video transcripts, so we assume that the lack of a proper large-scale training dataset may be the reason for the non-competitive performance of [9].

Figure 4 illustrates how the fragmentation performance is affected when we vary the number of fragments that are being generated. For this, in contrast to previous experiments, where the extracted number of fragments was fixed, in these experiments the number of fragments depends on a threshold Thr (Eq. (1)). By varying the multiplier m in (1) we can generate a variable number of fragments. The F-Score and corresponding number of fragments as a function of m are shown in Fig. 4, while the red x indicates the F-Score achieved in the corresponding Table 2 experiment with a fixed number of 20 fragments. We observe that the F-Score is relatively insensitive to small variations in the value of m and, correspondingly, in the number of fragments that are being generated.

Table 2. Experimental comparison of the three variations of the proposed approach, for the most appropriate window size (as shown in Table 1), with [14] and the supervised segmentation method of [9].

	BoW AVS	Word2Vec NP	Word2Vec AVS	BoW AVS [14]	Supervised segmentation [9]
Precision	0.415	**0.465**	0.425	0.426	0.237
Recall	0.455	**0.491**	0.46	0.459	0.393
F-Score	0.434	**0.477**	0.441	0.434	0.293

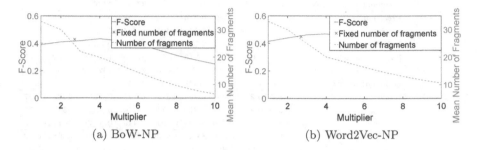

(a) BoW-NP   (b) Word2Vec-NP

Fig. 4. F-Score and mean number of generated fragments as a function of multiplier m for (a) the BoW-NP, (b) the Word2Vec-NP variations of our method.

5   Conclusions

In this work we proposed a new method to fragment lecture videos in meaningful parts. Our method takes advantage of the produced speech transcripts of a video, and analyzes them. We examined the performance of two different text analysis methods based on literature approaches in the video fragmentation and ad-hoc video search fields. A state-of-the-art word embedding was used for text representation, outperforming the classic N-gram approaches. Finally, we developed and provide online, a new large-scale dataset that consists of artificially-generated lectures and their corresponding ground truth fragmentation, which helps to overcome the lack of datasets for lecture video fragmentation evaluation.

Acknowledgements. This work was supported by the EUs Horizon 2020 research and innovation programme under grant agreement No. 693092 MOVING. We are grateful to JSI/VideoLectures.NET for providing the lectures transcripts.

References

1. Basu, S., Yu, Y., Singh, V.K., Zimmermann, R.: Videopedia: lecture video recommendation for educational blogs using topic modeling. In: Tian, Q., Sebe, N., Qi, G.-J., Huet, B., Hong, R., Liu, X. (eds.) MMM 2016. LNCS, vol. 9516, pp. 238–250. Springer, Cham (2016). https://doi.org/10.1007/978-3-319-27671-7_20
2. Bhatt, C.A., et al.: Multi-factor segmentation for topic visualization and recommendation: the MUST-VIS system. In: Proceedings of the 21st ACM International Conference on Multimedia, pp. 365–368. ACM (2013)

3. Brants, T., Chen, F., Tsochantaridis, I.: Topic-based document segmentation with probabilistic latent semantic analysis. In: Proceedings of the 11th International Conference on Information and Knowledge Management, CIKM 2002, pp. 211–218. ACM, New York (2002)
4. Che, X., Yang, H., Meinel, C.: Lecture video segmentation by automatically analyzing the synchronized slides. In: Proceedings of the 21st ACM International Conference on Multimedia, pp. 345–348. ACM (2013)
5. Chen, H., Cooper, M., Joshi, D., Girod, B.: Multi-modal language models for lecture video retrieval. In: Proceedings of the 22nd ACM International Conference on Multimedia, pp. 1081–1084. ACM (2014)
6. Finkel, J.R., Grenager, T., Manning, C.: Incorporating non-local information into information extraction systems by Gibbs sampling. In: Proceedings of the 43rd Annual Meeting on Association for Computational Linguistics, ACL 2005, pp. 363–370 (2005)
7. Glavaš, G., Nanni, F., Ponzetto, S.P.: Unsupervised text segmentation using semantic relatedness graphs. In: Association for Computational Linguistics (2016)
8. Hearst, M.A.: TextTiling: segmenting text into multi-paragraph subtopic passages. Comput. Linguist. **23**(1), 33–64 (1997)
9. Koshorek, O., Cohen, A., Mor, N., Rotman, M., Berant, J.: Text segmentation as a supervised learning task. In: Proceedings of the 2018 Conference of the North American Chapter of the Association for Computational Linguistics: Human Language Technologies, vol. 2 (Short Papers), pp. 469–473 (2018)
10. Lin, M., Chau, M., Cao, J., Nunamaker Jr., J.F.: Automated video segmentation for lecture videos: a linguistics-based approach. Int. J. Technol. Hum. Interact. (IJTHI) **1**(2), 27–45 (2005)
11. Ma, D., Zhang, X., Ouyang, X., Agam, G.: Lecture video indexing using boosted margin maximizing neural networks. In: 2017 16th IEEE International Conference on Machine Learning and Applications (ICMLA), pp. 221–227. IEEE (2017)
12. Markatopoulou, F., Galanopoulos, D., Mezaris, V., Patras, I.: Query and keyframe representations for ad-hoc video search. In: Proceedings of the 2017 ACM on International Conference on Multimedia Retrieval, ICMR 2017, pp. 407–411. ACM (2017)
13. Mikolov, T., Sutskever, I., Chen, K., Corrado, G.S., Dean, J.: Distributed representations of words and phrases and their compositionality. In: Advances in Neural Information Processing Systems 26, pp. 3111–3119. Curran Associates, Inc. (2013)
14. Shah, R.R., Yu, Y., Shaikh, A.D., Zimmermann, R.: TRACE: linguistic-based approach for automatic lecture video segmentation leveraging Wikipedia texts. In: 2015 IEEE International Symposium on Multimedia (ISM), pp. 217–220, December 2015
15. Shah, R.R., Yu, Y., Shaikh, A.D., Tang, S., Zimmermann, R.: ATLAS: automatic temporal segmentation and annotation of lecture videos based on modelling transition time. In: Proceedings of the 22nd ACM International Conference on Multimedia, pp. 209–212 (2014)
16. Toutanova, K., Klein, D., Manning, C.D., Singer, Y.: Feature-rich part-of-speech tagging with a cyclic dependency network. In: Proceedings of the 2003 Conference of the North American Chapter of the Association for Computational Linguistics on Human Language Technologies, NAACL 2003, vol. 1, pp. 173–180 (2003)
17. Yang, H., Siebert, M., Luhne, P., Sack, H., Meinel, C.: Automatic lecture video indexing using video OCR technology. In: 2011 IEEE International Symposium on Multimedia, pp. 111–116, December 2011
18. Yang, H., Meinel, C.: Content based lecture video retrieval using speech and video text information. IEEE Trans. Learn. Technol. **7**(2), 142–154 (2014)

Using Coarse Label Constraint
for Fine-Grained Visual Classification

Chaohao Lu[1] and Yuexian Zou[1,2(✉)]

[1] ADSPLAB, School of ECE, Peking University, Shenzhen, China
zouyx@pkusz.edu.cn
[2] Peng Cheng Laboratory, Shenzhen, China

Abstract. Recognizing fine-grained categories (e.g., dog species) relies on part localization and fine-grained feature learning. However, these classification methods use fine labels and ignore the structural information between different classes. In contrast, we take into account the structural information and use it to improve fine-grained visual classification performance. In this paper, we propose a novel coarse label representation and the corresponding cost function. The new coarse label representation idea comes from the category representation in the multi-label classification. This kind of coarse label representation can well express the structural information embedded in the class hierarchy, and the coarse labels are only obtained from suffix names of different category names, or given in advance like CIFAR100 dataset. A new cost function is proposed to guide the fine label convergence with the constraint of coarse labels, so we can make full use of this kind of coarse label supervised information to improve fine-grained visual classification. Our method can be generalized to any fine-tuning task; it does not increase the size of the original model; and adds no overhead to the training time. We conduct comprehensive experiments and show that using coarse label constraint improves major fine-grained classification datasets.

Keywords: Fine-grained classification · Multi-label learning
Coarse label constraint

1 Introduction

Fine-grained Visual categorization (FGVC) aims to distinguish very similar categories, such as species of birds [1, 2], dogs [3] and flowers [4], or models of vehicles [5]. These tasks are different from conventional image classification [6] in that they require expert level knowledge to find subtle differences. FGVC has a wide range of applications in many fields, such as image captioning, image generation, and machine teaching [7].

Most of the prior work in FGVC has focused on handling the variations in pose, lighting, viewpoint using part localization techniques [8, 9], attention mechanism [10–12], fine-grained feature extractors [7], and by adding training dataset with noisy data from web [13]. We observed that prior work in FGVC pays much attention to part localization or neural network architecture, and the supervised information used

© Springer Nature Switzerland AG 2019
I. Kompatsiaris et al. (Eds.): MMM 2019, LNCS 11296, pp. 266–277, 2019.
https://doi.org/10.1007/978-3-030-05716-9_22

includes fine labels, bounding box. We call them flat classification because they use fine label as supervised information and the fine labels do not take into account the structural information embedded in the class hierarchy.

The common taxonomy is hierarchical and structural. We take bird classification as an example, there are order, family, genus and species under the bird class, and the bird species are the specific bird label. In a fine-grained visual classification task, we need to distinguish different species of birds, not the corresponding family and genus. This makes me think about two questions. Firstly, can we use the biological taxonomy to promote fine-grained classification; secondly, how to realize it.

This paper answers the above two questions from a very basic point of view. We have created a new coarse label representation and the corresponding cost function to take advantage of this kind of coarse label supervised information. Coarse label representation method draws on multi-label classification [14, 15]. This coarse label can represent the structural relationship between categories, including the parent-child relationship between coarse label and fine label, parallel relationships between different fine labels that belongs to a same coarse label. The new cost function can make use of structural relationship between coarse labels and fine labels, using coarse label supervised information to constrain the error of fine label classification to a smaller interval and improving classification accuracy. Through our new label representation and cost function, we can improve any existing network and achieve 1%–7% improvement on the existing network. It does not change the size of original model and adds no overhead to the training time.

Our main contribution can be summarized as follows:

- We create a new coarse label representation that can well express the structural information embedded in the class hierarchy.
- We propose a new cost function to take advantage of this kind of coarse label supervised information.
- We conduct comprehensive experiments on four datasets (CUB Birds [1], Stanford Dogs [3], NABirds [2], CIFAR100), and achieve 1%–7% improvement on major fine-grained classification datasets.

The rest of the paper is organized as follows. Section 2 describes the related work. Section 3 introduces the proposed method. Section 4 introduces the datasets and networks. Section 5 provides the results and analysis, followed by the conclusion in Sect. 6.

2 Related Work

2.1 Fine-Grained Visual Classification

The research on fine-grained visual classification (FGVC) relies on part localization and discriminative feature learning. The most difference between FGVC task and conventional classification task is that there are subtle differences between fine-grained categories. For example, it may be the wings of birds are different in color. We use local information of the image to assist in classification, such as by extra processing of the bird's head and torso, to improve the overall classification performance [8–12, 16, 17].

Using discriminative feature extractors is also crucial for FGVC. Due to the success of convolutional neural network in conventional image classification, we can fine tune the model that pre-trained on conventional image datasets. Moreover, a bilinear structure [18, 19] is proposed to compute the pairwise feature interactions, and a boosted Deep Convolutional Neural Networks [20] is proposed to combine the merits of boosting and modern neural networks. These prior work can also be potentially combined with our method for future work.

2.2 Transfer Learning

Conventional Neural Networks trained on ImageNet [6] have been widely used for transfer learning [7]. The pre-trained network can be used as a feature extractor, or fine-tuned with the whole network. Compared with conventional image classification, the fine-grained classification datasets are much smaller. Additionally for fine-grained wildlife data collection, some species are harder to photograph, resulting in long-tails data distribution. Recently, some works using large noisy web data [13] to fine tune the network or use large fine-grained datasets [21] to fine tune the small dataset, and they have got incredible results.

2.3 Multi-label Learning

Multi-label learning [14] studies the problem where each example is represented by a single instance while associated with a set of labels simultaneously, whereas traditional multi-class learning studies the problem where each example is represented by a single instance while associated with a single labels. In a way, multi-class learning can be seen as a special case of multi-label learning. There are two main differences between our approach and multi-label learning. First, in multi-label classification, each dimension of the category vector represents whether the category appears. Assuming that there are N categories, a category representation of a multi-label category has 2^N possibilities. We use the representation rule of the multi-label category to represent the coarse label, but the amount of all coarse labels are smaller than N. Second, in multi-label learning, the output of a network is a multi-label vector; our method uses coarse labels as a kind of supervised information, and the final output is a single fine label.

3   Method

We create a novel coarse label representation that can well express the structural information embedded in the class hierarchy. Moreover, a new cost function is proposed to take advantage of this kind of coarse label supervised information.

3.1   Coarse Label Representation

The concept of coarse label is opposite to fine label. For an instance, a fine label represents the specific category it belongs to, and a coarse label is often an abstract label of several similar fine labels. We usually use extra label to describe the coarse label of an instance. This will bring extra overhead on the storage, and it is difficult to make the coarse and fine labels merge with each other during training.

CIFAR-100 dataset provides us with fine label and coarse label for each category. CIFAR100 has 100 classes containing 600 images each. The 100 classes in the CIFAR-100 are grouped into 20 super classes. Each image comes with a "fine" label (the class to which it belongs) and a "coarse" label (the superclass to which it belongs). For example, a super class called fish has 5 subcategories: aquarium fish, flatfish, ray, shark and trout. In this case, we use extra labels "fish" to represent coarse labels. Table 1 shows examples of CIFAR-100 fine labels and corresponding coarse labels.

Table 1. Example labels of CIFAR100 classes.

Super classes	Fine classes
Aquatic mammals	beaver, dolphin, otter, seal, whale
Fish	aquarium fish, flatfish, ray, shark, trout
Flowers	orchids, poppies, roses, sunflowers, tulips
Food containers	bottles, bowls, cans, cups, plates
Fruit and vegetables	apples, mushrooms, oranges, pears, sweet peppers

In multi-label learning, we use a category vector to represent an instance. Multi-label learning studies the problem where each example is represented by a single instance while associated with a set of labels simultaneously. Let's assume that there are a total of N categories, the position i of a multi-label vector is 1, indicating that the class i belongs to this instance. A N-dimensional multi-label vector that represent an instance looks like this:

$$[0, 0, 1, 0, 0 \ldots 1, 0, 0, 1, 0, 0] \tag{1}$$

In conventional fine-grained visual classification, an instance is associated with a single label. Let's assume that there are a total of N categories, the position i of a multi-class vector is 1, indicating that the class i belongs to this instance. A N-dimensional multi-class vector that represent an instance looks like this:

$$[0, 0, 0 \ldots 0, 1, 0, 0, 0, 0] \tag{2}$$

Each fine label has only one corresponding coarse label, while each coarse label has at least one fine label. We assume that there are a total of N fine labels. For a coarse label, we assume that there are n fine labels corresponding to the coarse label. The n fine labels are $a_1, a_2 \ldots a_n$, respectively. We use a multi-label vector to represent a fine-grained label while the position i of the vector is 1 indicating that it belongs to the class *i*. And the final coarse label can be a union of the label vectors of all corresponding fine labels. A *N*-dimensional coarse label vector that represent an instance looks like this:

$$[1, 1, 0, 0 \ldots 0, 0, 1, 0, 0] \tag{3}$$

All the *N*-dimensional fine label vectors corresponding to this coarse label are given as follows:

$$
\begin{aligned}
&[1, 0, 0, 0 \ldots 0, 0, 0, 0, 0] \\
&[0, 1, 0, 0 \ldots 0, 0, 0, 0, 0] \\
&\ldots \\
&[0, 0, 0, 0 \ldots 0, 0, 1, 0, 0]
\end{aligned} \tag{4}
$$

In taxonomy, the relationship of biological categories are often represented by parent-child nodes, which require a multi-layer tree structure for storage. The tree structure can represent many relationships such as parent-child relationship between categories. But this kind of category information is difficult to be effectively utilized in machine learning because of the tree structure. In machine learning, the supervised information is often a simple category tag rather than a complex data structure. Instead, our proposed coarse label representation approach is able to make use of the structural relationships between categories. Specifically, our proposed new coarse label representation contains the structural information between the fine labels. The structural information here includes not only the parent-child relationship of the fine labels corresponding to the coarse label, but also the parallel relationship between fine labels that belonging to the same coarse label.

3.2 Cost Function

A new cost function is proposed to take advantage of this kind of coarse label supervised information. This cost function combines sigmoid cross entropy with softmax cross entropy, which makes good use of coarse labels to improve fine label classification. The cost function is an important indicator for evaluating the training effect, and the adjustment of the network parameters minimizes the cost function. In the training of convolutional neural networks, commonly used cost functions include softmax cross entropy, sigmoid cross entropy and so on.

For a convolutional neural network with parameters θ that produces the conditional probability distribution $p_\theta(x)$ over *N* classes for input image *x*. For softmax cross entropy, the ground truth we use is fine label *y*, a multi-class vector representation, then we compute softmax cross entropy between conditional probability distribution $p_\theta(x)$ and ground truth y, where

$$L_{softmax}(x, y) = -\sum_{i=1}^{N} y_i * \log p_\theta(x)[i] \tag{5}$$

The sigmoid cross entropy measures the probability error in discrete classification tasks in which each class is independent and not mutually exclusive. For instance, one could perform multi-label classification where a picture can contain both a house and a tree at the same time. For sigmoid cross entropy, the ground truth we use is a coarse label z, the new proposed coarse label representation, then we compute sigmoid cross entropy between conditional probability distribution $p_\theta(x)$ and ground truth z, where

$$L_{sigmoid}(x, z) = \sum_{i=1}^{N} \max(p_\theta(x)[i], 0) - p_\theta(x)[i] * z_i + log(1 + exp(-abs(p_\theta(x)[i]))) \tag{6}$$

We formulate the final cost function for an input image x with fine label y and coarse label z as:

$$L_{final} = a * L_{softmax}(x, y) + b * L_{sigmoid}(x, z) \tag{7}$$

The final cost function in (7) consists of two parts, the first part is $L_{softmax}$ and the second part is $L_{sigmoid}$. Obviously, in conventional image classification, we usually use $L_{softmax}$ as the cost function. We minimize $L_{softmax}$ with fine labels and minimize $L_{sigmoid}$ with coarse labels. The coarse label contains the parallel relationships between different fine labels that belongs to the same coarse label. And in the process of minimizing the cost function, we use $L_{sigmoid}$ for making the errors constrained in similar categories and use $L_{softmax}$ for making the model learn how to correctly classify fine labels.

The parameters (a and b) in (7) are two super parameters which are the controlling parameter in measuring the effect of $L_{softmax}$ and $L_{sigmoid}$ on L_{final}. In this study, we usually set a to 1 and vary b.

4 Experimental Details

We use open-source TensorFlow [22] and Pytorch frameworks to implement and train all the models on Multiple NVIDIA TITAN X GPUs. We will have a brief introduction of three fine-grained classification datasets and one standard image classification dataset used in our paper, we will also briefly introduce the neural network used for fine tuning in this paper.

4.1 Datasets

Fine-Grained Visual Classification Datasets. We evaluate our method using three standard Fine-grained Visual Classification (FGVC) datasets.

The Caltech-UCSD Birds (CUB200) dataset has 5,994 training and 5,794 test images across 200 fine classes of birds. We only observe whether the suffixes of the category names are the same, and then divide them into 70 super classes. So for Caltech-UCSD Birds dataset, there are totally 200 fine labels and 70 coarse labels. The NABirds dataset contains 23,929 training and 24,633 test images across 555 bird categories, and we divide them into 156 super classes using the same method. The Stanford Dogs dataset has 12,000 training and 8,580 test images across 120 classes (dog breeds), and we divide them into 72 super classes using the same method. Labels of each dataset are in Table 2.

Table 2. Labels of each dataset.

Dataset	Fine labels	Coarse labels	Division method
CUB200 [1]	200	70	Same class name suffix
NABirds [2]	555	156	Same class name suffix
Stanford Dogs [3]	120	72	Same class name suffix
CIFAR100	100	20	Official division

Standard Image Classification Datasets. We also utilize a standard image classification dataset CIFAR-100 for study. The CIFAR-100 dataset has 100 classes containing 600 images each. There are 500 training images and 100 testing images per class. The 100 classes in the CIFAR-100 are grouped into 20 super classes. Each image comes with a "fine" label (the class to which it belongs) and a "coarse" label (the superclass to which it belongs). We use the official division as our division.

4.2   Network Architectures

We fine tune three types of network architecture for fine-grained visual classification datasets: VGG19 [23], Resnet50 [24] and Inception-V3 [25]. We fine tune VGG19 and Wide Residual Network [26] for the standard image classification dataset.

VGG. In fine-grained visual classification, VGG is a very common network, including Bilinear CNN, which uses VGG as feature extractor. VGG uses a deeper network structure than AlexNet [27], it won the first and second place respectively in the 2014 ILSVRC localization and classification. The VGG network is very deep, usually with 16–19 layers and a convolution kernel size of 3 × 3. We use a 19-layer VGG network.

Residual Network. Residual Network has residual connections that reduce the optimization difficulties and enable the network to be much deeper. We use the ResNet with 50 layers as representative for Residual Networks in our experiments.

Inception-V3. The Inception module was firstly proposed as GoogleNet that was designed to be very efficient. Inception module was then further optimized by using Batch Normalization, residual connections and so on. We use Inception-V3 as representative for Inception Networks in our experiments.

Wide Residual Network. Because ResNets is too deep, many residual blocks can only provide a small amount of information, or only a small number of blocks can learn important information. The author thinks that ResNet's main ability comes from the Residual block, and the depth increase is only an aid. He decreased depth and increased width of residual networks. The proposed 16-layer Wide Residual Network can be similar to the 1000-layer ResNet.

5 Results and Analysis

5.1 Experiments on Fine-Grained Visual Classification Datasets

We first describe our results on three fine-grained visual classification datasets. We fine tune three network models that pre-trained on the ImageNet. Our experiment is divided into two steps, the first step is to use only the fine label for fine-tuning, and the second step we use coarse label to constrain error. In the second step, we set the final loss parameters $a = 1$, $b = 1$, and training epochs is the same as the first step. We observe that our approach improves performance for any dataset, any pre-trained network. The results are in Tables 3, 4 and 5.

Table 3. CUB200 accuracies.

Network	Only fine labels	With coarse labels as supervision
VGG19	72.80%	79.67%
ResNet50	77.67%	79.31%
Inception-V3	80.64%	**81.72%**

Taking CUB200 dataset as an example, if VGG19 is used as the pre-trained model, the accuracy rate is increased by nearly 7 percentage points after using the coarse label constraint, and 2 percentage points is increased by using ResNet50 or Inception-V3. The result of VGG19 on the ImageNet is also worse than ResNet50 or Inception-V3, which indicates that VGG's feature extraction capability is not as strong as ResNet50 or Inception-V3, and we have greatly improved this by using the coarse label constraint. Through the improvement of our method, VGG19 can achieve the same effect as Resnet50.

In (7), the final loss is composed of $a * L_{softmax}$ and $b * L_{sigmoid}$, and parameters a, b affect the speed ratio of back propagation during training. We usually set a to 1, and change b. If b is greater than a, then the effect of the sigmoid cross entropy cost function is greater. In our experiment, we find that the value of b is usually larger than a, which makes the network get a better result. This will lead to a final increase of nearly one percentage point. For example, when we use Inception-V3 to fine tune the CUB200 dataset with coarse label constraint, we set $b = 2$ and the final result is 0.6% higher than $b = 1$. However, how to choose the values of parameters a, b still need to be manually adjusted. To get a better performance, the parameter values are not the same while we fine tune different datasets with different models, so we select $a = 1$, $b = 1$ in previous experiments.

5.2 Experiments on Standard Image Classification Dataset

We evaluate the performance of our approach on standard image classification dataset CIFAR-100 using two convolutional neural networks VGG19 and Wide Residual Network. CIFAR-100 has 100 fine classes and 20 super classes, with each super class containing five finer divisions. The results are in Table 6.

Table 4. NABirds accuracies.

Network	Only fine labels	With coarse labels as supervision
VGG19	73.54%	75.10%
ResNet50	77.20%	77.93%
Inception-V3	75.29%	**78.49%**

Table 5. Stanford Dogs accuracies.

Network	Only fine labels	With coarse labels as supervision
VGG19	76.90%	79.15%
ResNet50	79.61%	80.27%
Inception-V3	77.28%	**81.90%**

Table 6. CIFAR-100 accuracies.

Network	Only fine labels	With coarse labels
VGG19	71.95%	73.25%
Wide residual network	80.75%	81.82%

As shown in Fig. 1, after the introduction of the constraint mechanism, the test set accuracy of our network is steadily higher than original Wide Residual Network (WRN), which indicates that this constraint mechanism does improve performance of original WRN.

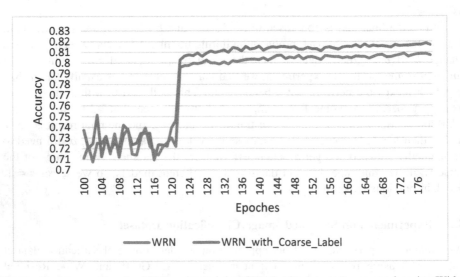

Fig. 1. Test accuracies after 100 epochs, training CIFAR-100 dataset from scratch, using Wide Residual Network (WRN) and WRN with coarse label constraint.

In our experiments, we set the same learning rate and total epoch for original networks and networks with coarse label constraint. We observe that the accuracy curve is very consistent. This shows that after the introduction of the constraint mechanism, there is no variability in the convergence of the network. Moreover, In the initial training phase, the network with coarse label constraint converges faster and the accuracy increases faster. We can see that the network with coarse label constraints can significantly accelerate convergence and promote the convergence of the entire network in the right direction. Comparison with existing methods in Table 7.

Table 7. CIFAR-100 comparison.

Methods	Test error
NIN [28]	35.67%
ResNet [24]	22.71%
WRN [26]	19.25%
WRN with coarse label	**18.18%**

6 Conclusion

In this work, we create a novel coarse label representation that can well express the structural information embedded in the class hierarchy. And we propose the corresponding cost function that take advantage of this kind of coarse label supervised information by guiding the fine label convergence with the constraint of coarse labels. We conduct comprehensive experiments in three fine-grained visual classification datasets and a standard image classification dataset, experimental results show that our method can accelerate network convergence and stably improve the original network performance.

Using coarse label constraint is easy to implement and can be generalized to any fine-tuning task; it does not increase the size of the original model and adds no overhead to training time. Therefore, our method should be beneficial to a wide range of pre-trained CNN models. In the future, we plan to combine our approach with existing methods to reduce the classification error.

Acknowledgment. This paper was partially supported by the Shenzhen Science & Technology Fundamental Research Program (No: JCYJ20160330095814461) & Shenzhen Key Laboratory for Intelligent Multimedia and Virtual Reality (ZDSYS201703031405467).

References

1. Wah, C., Branson, S., Welinder, P., Perona, P., Belongie, S.: The Caltech-UCSD Birds 200-2011 Dataset. California Institute of Technology (2011)
2. Horn, G.V., et al.: Building a bird recognition app and large scale dataset with citizen scientists: the fine print in fine-grained dataset collection. In: Computer Vision and Pattern Recognition, pp. 595–604 (2015)

3. Khosla, A., Jayadevaprakash, N., Yao, B., Li, F.: Novel dataset for fine-grained image categorization (2013)
4. Nilsback, M.E., Zisserman, A.: Automated flower classification over a large number of classes. In: Sixth Indian Conference on Computer Vision, Graphics and Image Processing, ICVGIP 2008, pp. 722–729 (2009)
5. Yang, L., Luo, P., Chen, C.L., Tang, X.: A large-scale car dataset for fine-grained categorization and verification. In: Computer Vision and Pattern Recognition, pp. 3973–3981 (2015)
6. Deng, J., Dong, W., Socher, R., Li, L.J., Li, K., Li, F.F.: ImageNet: a large-scale hierarchical image database. In: IEEE Conference on Computer Vision and Pattern Recognition, CVPR 2009, pp. 248–255 (2009)
7. Yin, C., Yang, S., Chen, S., Howard, A., Belongie, S.: Large scale fine-grained categorization and domain-specific transfer learning (2018)
8. Wei, X.S., Xie, C.W., Wu, J.: Mask-CNN: localizing parts and selecting descriptors for fine-grained image recognition (2016)
9. Huang, S., Xu, Z., Tao, D., Zhang, Y.: Part-stacked CNN for fine-grained visual categorization. In: Computer Vision and Pattern Recognition, pp. 1173–1182 (2016)
10. Sun, M., Yuan, Y., Zhou, F., Ding, E.: Multi-attention multi-class constraint for fine-grained image recognition (2018)
11. Zheng, H., Fu, J., Mei, T., Luo, J.: Learning multi-attention convolutional neural network for fine-grained image recognition. In: IEEE International Conference on Computer Vision, pp. 5219–5227 (2017)
12. Fu, J., Zheng, H., Mei, T.: Look closer to see better: recurrent attention convolutional neural network for fine-grained image recognition. In: Computer Vision and Pattern Recognition, pp. 4476–4484 (2017)
13. Krause, J., et al.: The unreasonable effectiveness of noisy data for fine-grained recognition. In: Leibe, B., Matas, J., Sebe, N., Welling, M. (eds.) ECCV 2016. LNCS, vol. 9907, pp. 301–320. Springer, Cham (2016). https://doi.org/10.1007/978-3-319-46487-9_19
14. Zhang, M.L., Zhou, Z.H.: A review on multi-label learning algorithms. IEEE Trans. Knowl. Data Eng. **26**, 1819–1837 (2014)
15. Gibaja, E., Ventura, S.: A tutorial on multilabel learning. ACM Comput. Surv. **47**, 1–38 (2015)
16. Zhang, N., Donahue, J., Girshick, R., Darrell, T.: Part-based R-CNNs for fine-grained category detection. In: Fleet, D., Pajdla, T., Schiele, B., Tuytelaars, T. (eds.) ECCV 2014. LNCS, vol. 8689, pp. 834–849. Springer, Cham (2014). https://doi.org/10.1007/978-3-319-10590-1_54
17. Xiao, T., Xu, Y., Yang, K., Zhang, J., Peng, Y., Zhang, Z.: The application of two-level attention models in deep convolutional neural network for fine-grained image classification. In: Computer Vision and Pattern Recognition, pp. 842–850 (2015)
18. Lin, T.Y., Roychowdhury, A., Maji, S.: Bilinear CNN models for fine-grained visual recognition, pp. 1449–1457 (2015)
19. Cui, Y., Zhou, F., Wang, J., Liu, X., Lin, Y., Belongie, S.: Kernel pooling for convolutional neural networks. In: IEEE Conference on Computer Vision and Pattern Recognition, pp. 3049–3058 (2017)
20. Moghimi, M., Belongie, S., Saberian, M., Yang, J., Vasconcelos, N., Li, L.J.: Boosted convolutional neural networks. In: British Machine Vision Conference, pp. 24.21–24.13 (2016)
21. Horn, G.V., et al.: The iNaturalist species classification and detection dataset (2018)
22. Abadi, M., et al.: TensorFlow: large-scale machine learning on heterogeneous distributed systems (2016)

23. Simonyan, K., Zisserman, A.: Very deep convolutional networks for large-scale image recognition. Computer Science (2014)
24. He, K., Zhang, X., Ren, S., Sun, J.: Deep residual learning for image recognition, pp. 770–778 (2015)
25. Szegedy, C., Vanhoucke, V., Ioffe, S., Shlens, J., Wojna, Z.: Rethinking the inception architecture for computer vision, pp. 2818–2826 (2015)
26. Zagoruyko, S., Komodakis, N.: Wide residual networks (2016)
27. Krizhevsky, A., Sutskever, I., Hinton, G.E.: ImageNet classification with deep convolutional neural networks. In: International Conference on Neural Information Processing Systems, pp. 1097–1105 (2012)
28. Lin, M., Chen, Q., Yan, S.: Network in Network. Computer Science (2014)

Gated Recurrent Capsules for Visual Word Embeddings

Danny Francis, Benoit Huet[(⊠)], and Bernard Merialdo

EURECOM, 450 route des Chappes, 06410 Biot, France
{danny.francis,benoit.huet,bernard.merialdo}@eurecom.fr

Abstract. The caption retrieval task can be defined as follows: given a set of images I and a set of describing sentences S, for each image i in I we ought to find the sentence in S that best describes i. The most commonly applied method to solve this problem is to build a multimodal space and to map each image and each sentence to that space, so that they can be compared easily. A non-conventional model called Word2VisualVec has been proposed recently: instead of mapping images and sentences to a multimodal space, they mapped sentences directly to a space of visual features. Advances in the computation of visual features let us infer that such an approach is promising. In this paper, we propose a new Recurrent Neural Network model following that unconventional approach based on Gated Recurrent Capsules (GRCs), designed as an extension of Gated Recurrent Units (GRUs). We show that GRCs outperform GRUs on the caption retrieval task. We also state that GRCs present a great potential for other applications.

Keywords: Multimodal embeddings · Deep learning
Capsule networks

1 Introduction

This paper proposes a novel deep network architecture for the caption retrieval task: given a set of images and a set of sentences, we build a model that ought to find the closest sentence to an input image. That task is important because retrieving captions in natural language using images implies getting closer to a human understanding of visual scenes. Numerous works have attempted to address that task; most of them are making use of a multimodal space where sentences and images are projected and compared [7,9,13,16]. Word2VisualVec [4,6] relies on another approach, the authors built a model to project sentences directly in a space of visual features: as the quality of visual features is constantly improving, the authors stated that learning visual sentence embeddings rather than projecting them in a more complicated multimodal space was a promising approach. In this paper, a model following this unconventional approach is proposed.

Projecting images and sentences in the same space, whether multimodal or simply visual, implies that representations of images and sentences as mathematical objects must be derived. Since the recent breakthrough of deep learning,

I. Kompatsiaris et al. (Eds.): MMM 2019, LNCS 11296, pp. 278–290, 2019.
https://doi.org/10.1007/978-3-030-05716-9_23

Convolutional Neural Networks (CNNs) have shown compellingly good performances in computer vision tasks. In particular, some of them [10,15] are able to learn visual features that they use to classify images from a big dataset such as ImageNet [3]. Some works have also shown that these visual features could be successfully used in other tasks with different datasets [24]. In particular, most recent works on caption retrieval have used features coming from a ResNet [10] which had been trained on ImageNet for a classification task [7,9]. In our work, we will extract features thanks to a ResNet that had been finetuned on MSCOCO [17] by the authors of [7]. Deriving visual sentence representations is the main part of our work. Recurrent Neural Networks (RNNs) such as Long Short-Term Memory units (LSTMs) [12] and Gated Recurrent Units (GRUs) [2] have proved to deliver state-of-the-art results on various language modeling tasks such as translation [21], automatic image captioning [23] or caption retrieval [7]. In the last version of Word2VisualVec [6], the authors showed that concatenating a representation derived by a GRU with a Word2Vec [18] representation and a bag-of-words representation to get a multi-scale sentence representation lead to better results in visual sentence embedding for caption retrieval. However, we argue that using these kinds of representations cannot be optimal: pooling all words together without putting attention on relevant parts of the sentence does not reflect the complexity of images; and the current state-of-the-art model for image and caption retrieval is based on object-detection and cross-attention [16], which corroborates our statement that sentences should be processed in a finer way. Our work aims at proposing a new architecture corresponding to and addressing that issue: how to analyze a sentence so that important visual elements are emphasized?

Our research has been inspired by recent works on capsule networks [11,20]. This new architecture shows promising results in computer vision. In capsule networks, neurons are replaced by so-called capsules, that take vectors as inputs and output vectors. These output vectors are routed towards subsequent capsules through a predefined routing procedure, that can be seen as an attention mechanism: relevant vectors are routed towards relevant capsules. We think that this principle can be successfully used in Recurrent Neural Networks, and the Gated Recurrent Capsule that we introduce in this paper is a novel architecture, and is to our best knowledge the very first occurrence of recurrent unit using capsules.

Our contributions in this paper are three-fold:

- we introduce Gated Recurrent Capsules (GRCs), a novel RNN architecture which extents conventional GRUs so that information flow focuses on critical data items;
- we propose to address the caption retrieval task using the newly proposed GRCs architecture;
- we demonstrate experimentally that GRC enable higher performance when compared to state of the art Word2VisualVec (employing GRUs) in the MSCOCO caption retrieval task.

Our paper is divided in five sections. Having introduced the extent of the paper in Sect. 1, we will describe related works in Sect. 2. In Sect. 3 we will describe our model for caption retrieval. Section 4 details results obtained by our model. We will conclude the paper in Sect. 5.

2   Related Work

Several works have been done on building visual-semantic embeddings. Most of them are based on the construction of a multimodal space where sentences and images are projected and compared. In [7], Faghri et al. used a GRU to map sentences to a multimodal space; images were simply mapped to that space through a linear transform. They obtained good results by finetuning the ResNet they used to produce visual features: that is the reason why we used one of their finetuned ResNets to produce visual features in our model. Another more complex model proposed by Gu et al. [9] showed that results could be boosted by the use of two generative models (one generating images and one generating sentences) in addition to a GRU and a ResNet. More recently, [16] has shown that even better performances could be reached by processing images with an object detection model combined with cross-attention instead of deriving global visual features.

Another approach has been proposed recently: instead of mapping images and sentences to a multimodal space, [4,6] proposed to derive visual features from images and to map directly sentences to the space of visual features. This approach is promising as the quality of visual features is constantly increasing. Moreover, it avoids mapping images to a more complex space. Our work follows that unconventional approach. It has been inspired by recent works on capsule networks [11,20]. Capsule networks have shown promising results in computer vision. However to our best knowledge they have not been used yet in a recurrent fashion for natural language processing apart from [8]; however, the architecture presented in [8] is using a complex GRUs setup to process and route the information, leading to much more learnable parameters, which is a drawback that our architecture does not have.

3   Visual Sentence Embeddings

Word2VisualVec is a non-conventional approach to caption retrieval, as it maps sentences directly to a visual features space. Our model follows that approach.

3.1   Word2VisualVec

In [4], a first version of Word2VisualVec was proposed. It consisted in applying a multilayer perceptron on vectorized sentences to project these sentences in a space of visual features. Three vectorization methods were discussed in that paper: bag-of-words, word hashing and averaging Word2Vec embeddings.

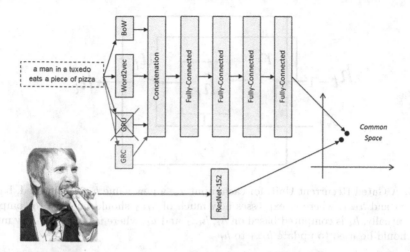

Fig. 1. Word2VisualVec and our variant with a GRC. In Word2VisualVec, three sentence representations (Word2Vec, BoW and GRU) are concatenated and then mapped to a visual features space. In our model, we replaced the final hidden state of the GRU by the average of all final hidden states of a GRC.

In [6], the authors of [4] improved Word2VisualVec by concatenating three sentence representations. In that paper, a sentence representation was produced by concatenating a bag-of-words, a Word2Vec and a GRU representation of the sentence. Then, it was projected in a space of visual features through a multilayer perceptron. Figure 1 shows how Word2VisualVec works in practice.

On top of good performances in caption retrieval, this visual representation of sentences showed an interest in multimodal query composition: the authors showed that visual words features could be added or subtracted to images features and form multimodal queries. Authors also stated that further gains could be expected by including locality in Word2VisualVec representations.

3.2 Gated Recurrent Capsules

Gated Recurrent Units were introduced by Cho et al. in [2]. They are similar to LSTMs: they have similar performances and are well adapted to NLP because they can handle long-term dependencies in sentences. We preferred GRUs to LSTMs because they have less parameters for similar performances. More formally, a GRU is composed of an update gate u_t and a reset gate r_t, and can be described with the following expressions:

$$u_t = \sigma(W_{xu}x_t + W_{hu}h_{t-1} + b_u), \tag{1}$$

$$r_t = \sigma(W_{xr}x_t + W_{hr}h_{t-1} + b_r), \tag{2}$$

$$\tilde{h}_t = \tanh(W_{xh}x_t + W_{hh}(r_t \circ h_{t-1}) + b_h), \tag{3}$$

$$h_t = (1 - u_t) \circ h_{t-1} + u_t \circ \tilde{h}_t, \tag{4}$$

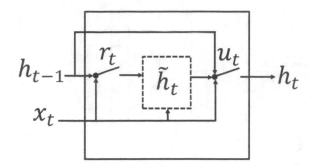

Fig. 2. A Gated Recurrent Unit: for each input x_t, a new value $\tilde{h}_t$ is computed, based on x_t, r_t and h_{t-1}, where r_t expresses how much of h_{t-1} should be reset to compute $\tilde{h}_t$. Eventually, h_t is computed based on $\tilde{h}_t$, h_{t-1} and u_t, where u_t expresses how much of $\tilde{h}_t$ should be used to update h_{t-1} to h_t

with x_t the t-th input and h_t the t-th output or hidden state of the GRU. Here and throughout the paper, $\circ$ denotes the Hadamard product and σ denotes the sigmoid function. The equations above can be explained as follows: for each input x_t, the GRU computes r_t and u_t based on the input and the previous state h_{t-1}. It computes a new value $\tilde{h}_t$ based on x_t, r_t and h_{t-1}, and r_t expresses how much of h_{t-1} should be reset to compute $\tilde{h}_t$. Eventually, h_t is computed based on $\tilde{h}_t$, h_{t-1} and u_t, and u_t expresses how much of $\tilde{h}_t$ should be used to update the hidden state h_t of the GRU. Learned parameters are $(W_{xu}, W_{hu}, b_u, W_{xr}, W_{hr}, b_r, W_{xh}, W_{hh}, b_h)$. In our case, the x_t correspond to word embeddings: if s is a sentence of length L, then it is first converted into a list $(w_1, ..., w_L)$ of one-hot vectors, and each one-hot vector is mapped to a word embedding using a lookup matrix W_e. Therefore, we have $(x_1, ..., x_L) = (W_e w_1, ..., W_e w_L)$. The coefficients of W_e are learned, but they are initialized to precomputed word embeddings to avoid overfitting problems (Fig. 2).

Capsules were designed by [20] for image processing. The idea behind capsules for computer vision consists in making complex computations and outputting a pose vector and an activation. This output is then routed towards subsequent capsules according to some predefined routing algorithm. The goal of that architecture is to have each capsule learning to recognize a visual feature based on what previous capsules have recognized before. For instance, some capsules could recognize eyes, a nose, a mouth and their respective positions. Then they would send their outputs to another capsule aiming at recognizing a whole face. It is architectured to avoid losing spatial information as common CNN do due to pooling operations. We think that capsules can also successfully perform other tasks such as NLP-related tasks, as our proposed model does.

In a nutshell, what we would like to do is to produce different embeddings that would attend to different semantic sides of the input sentence. A sentence would be divided into sub-sentences, and each of those sub-sentences would attend to a particular element of an image. These sub-sentences representations are then processed to build an embedding for the whole sentence.

In our model, all capsules share the same parameters and are similar to GRUs. In the following, we will explain the differences between them and actual GRUs. A recurrent capsule layer should process a sentence word-by-word and make updates in a way that would put attention on important words: the hidden state of each capsule should reflect one semantic side of the input sentence. Therefore, we need to define a routing procedure depending on current states and incoming words. For that purpose, we will use hidden states of capsules at time $t-1$ and the incoming word x_t to find how relevant a word is to a given capsule. More formally, if we consider the k-th capsule with $k \in \{1, ..., N_c\}$, update gates and reset gates will be the same as for a GRU:

$$u_t^{(k)} = \sigma(W_{xu}x_t + W_{hu}h_{t-1}^{(k)} + b_u), \tag{5}$$

$$r_t^{(k)} = \sigma(W_{xr}x_t + W_{hr}h_{t-1}^{(k)} + b_r), \tag{6}$$

We also compute $\tilde{h}_t^{(k)}$ as we do in a GRU:

$$\tilde{h}_t^{(k)} = \tanh(W_{xh}x_t + W_{hh}(r_t^{(k)} \circ h_{t-1}^{(k)}) + b_h), \tag{7}$$

We would like to make our routing procedure trainable via gradient descent, so we need to define differentiable operations. For that purpose, we will assume that for each capsule, for a given word w_t, we have a coefficient $p_t^{(k)} \in [0, 1]$ such that

$$h_t^{(k)} = (1 - p_t^{(k)})h_{t-1}^{(k)} + p_t^{(k)}\hat{h}_t^{(k)} \tag{8}$$

with

$$\hat{h}_t^{(k)} = u_t^{(k)} \circ \tilde{h}_t^{(k)} + (1 - u_t^{(k)}) \circ h_{t-1}^{(k)}, \tag{9}$$

which is the actual update computed in a GRU. The coefficient $p_t^{(k)}$ is a routing coefficient, describing to what extent a given capsule needs to be updated by the incoming word. As in [11], routing can be seen as an attention mechanism, putting attention on relevant words in our case. However, while the authors of [11] use Gaussians determined by EM-routing to compute this coefficient, we propose to compute it in a simpler manner. More details are provided in the next section. We can expand the last equation to get the following update:

$$h_t^{(k)} = (1 - p_t^{(k)}u_t^{(k)}) \circ h_{t-1}^{(k)} + p_t^{(k)}u_t^{(k)} \circ \tilde{h}_t^{(k)} \tag{10}$$

We can notice that it boils down to multiplying the update $u_t^{(k)}$ by a coefficient $p_t^{(k)}$. Then, how to compute $p_t^{(k)}$? For that purpose, we define an activation coefficient $a_t^{(k)}$ for each capsule:

$$a_t^{(k)} = |\alpha_k| + \log(P_t^{(k)}). \tag{11}$$

In the last equation, the α_k are random numbers drawn from a normal probability distribution (we found that 0.1 and 0.001 were good values for the mean and the standard deviation of the normal probability distribution). The α_k are important to our model because all capsules share the same parameters: if all activations are the same when they start processing a sentence, they will be all the same at the end. These random numbers break the symmetry between capsules; this is needed for our model to work properly. We assume $P_t^{(k)}$ ought to represent the semantic similarity between the current hidden state of the capsule $h_{t-1}^{(k)}$ and the incoming word x_t: if the incoming word is semantically similar to the previous hidden state, $P_t^{(k)}$ should be high, and if it is different, then it should be low. One can intuitively imagine that the cosine similarity $\cos(h_{t-1}^{(k)}, \hat{h}_t^{(k)}) = \frac{\left\langle h_{t-1}^{(k)} | \hat{h}_t^{(k)} \right\rangle}{\|h_{t-1}^{(k)}\|_2 \times \|\hat{h}_t^{(k)}\|_2}$ corresponds to a relevant definition of the semantic similarity between the current hidden state of the capsule and the incoming word: if the incoming word has a different meaning than previous words, then one can expect that $\hat{h}_t^{(k)}$ will reflect that different meaning. Therefore we define $P_t^{(k)}$ as:

$$P_t^{(k)} = \cos(h_{t-1}^{(k)}, \hat{h}_t^{(k)}). \tag{12}$$

Then we can compute $p_t^{(k)}$ according to the following formula:

$$p_t = \frac{\operatorname{softmax}(\frac{a_t^{(1)}}{T}, ..., \frac{a_t^{(N)}}{T})}{M} \tag{13}$$

where M is the maximal coordinate of the vector $\operatorname{softmax}(\frac{a_t^{(1)}}{T}, ..., \frac{a_t^{(N)}}{T})$ and T is a hyperparameter controlling the sharpness of the routing procedure (the higher T, the more we have one routing weight equal to 1 and all others equal to 0).

Our routing is different from those that were introduced in [11,20]: the outputs of capsules are not combinations of all previous capsules outputs. Only the weights of the routing procedure depend on these previous capsules outputs.

Please note that if $T \to +\infty$, then all capsules receive the same inputs and produce the same hidden states: it is strictly equivalent to a GRU. Therefore, GRCs are an extension of the GRUs. The interest of GRCs over GRUs is that they can provide different representations of the same sentence, with attention put on some relevant parts of it. This idea is shown on Fig. 3. Moreover, a GRC has the same number of trainable parameters as a GRU, but it has the ability to make more complex computations: for that reason we think that this architecture could be successfully used for other tasks than caption retrieval.

The model we propose for caption retrieval is similar to Word2VisualVec, but we replace the GRU by a GRC, as shown on Fig. 1. Instead of concatenating the last hidden state of a GRU to a Word2Vec and a bag-of-words representations, we concatenate the average of the last hidden states of a GRC. We also tried to derive a weighted average of the hidden states of a GRC based on a soft-attention mechanism described in [5] but results did not improve. We reported our results in Sect. 4.3 for information.

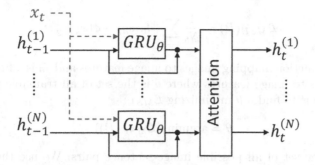

Fig. 3. Gated Recurrent Capsules: all capsules share the same learned parameters θ. The inputs of capsule i at time t are a word embedding x_t and its hidden state at time $t-1$ $h_{t-1}^{(i)}$. Its output is $h_t^{(i)}$, and it is computed through the routing procedure described in Sect. 3.2. This routing procedure can be seen as an attention model: each output depends on how semantically similar the incoming word is to previously processed words. It ensures that each capsule generates a sentence embedding corresponding to one important visual element of the sentence.

3.3   Improving Word2VisualVec with GRC

As we said in Sect. 3.1, Word2VisualVec relies on three representations of sentences: bag-of-words, average of Word2Vec embeddings and GRU. GRCs provide another representation that we can concatenate to the three previous ones. More precisely, let us assume that we processed a sentence of length L with a GRC containing N_c capsules. Then, if $h_L^{(1)}, ..., h_L^{(N_c)}$ are the final hidden states of its capsules, the corresponding representation v_{GRC} of the sentence is the average of all these hidden states:

$$v_{GRC} = \frac{1}{N_c} \sum_{k=1}^{N_c} h_L^{(k)}. \tag{14}$$

This representation is intermediate between the GRU and the Word2Vec representations: it is the sum of N_c different hidden states, each of them corresponding to a particular part of a whole sentence.

Our goal is to map sentences to corresponding images in a space of visual features. One way to measure the efficiency of that kind of mappings is to evaluate the model on caption retrieval. When the model projects both images and sentences in a common multimodal space, recent works have shown that triplet ranking losses were efficient [7]. However in our case, sentences are directly mapped to a space of visual features, no transformation is made on image feature vectors. We found, in accordance with [6], that using the mean squared error (MSE) gave better results than a triplet ranking loss. Therefore, considering a mini-batch $B = ((s_1, x_1), ..., (s_{N_b}, x_{N_b}))$ of sentence-image pairs (N_b is the size of the mini-batch), we defined the loss function $\mathcal{L}_{MSE}(B)$ as follows:

$$\mathcal{L}_{MSE}(B) = \frac{1}{N_b} \sum_{k=1}^{N_b} \|f_\theta(s_k) - \phi(x_k)\|_2^2, \tag{15}$$

where ϕ is a function mapping images to image features and f_θ is a function mapping sentences to image features where θ is the set of all trainable parameters. Our objective is to find a $\hat{\theta}$ minimizing $\mathcal{L}_{MSE}$:

$$\hat{\theta} = \text{argmin}_\theta(\mathcal{L}_{MSE}(\bar{B})) \tag{16}$$

where $\bar{B}$ is the set of all possible image-sentence pairs. We use the RMSProp method to optimize f_θ, following the procedure we describe in Sect. 4.2.

4   Comparison with Word2VisualVec

4.1   Dataset

We evaluated how our models performed on the caption retrieval task on the MSCOCO dataset [17]. This dataset contains 123000 images with 5 captions each, and we split it into a training set, a validation set and a test set according to [14]. The training set contains 113000 images, the validation set contains 5000 images and the test set contains 5000 images.

As for data preprocessing, we converted all sentences to lowercase and removed special characters (apart from spaces and hyphens). We limited the vocabulary to 5000 most used words, and replaced all other words by an "UNK" token. Regarding images, we projected them to a space of visual features. For that purpose, we used the penultimate layer of the ResNet-152 from [7] to get 2048-dimensional features vectors.

4.2   Parameters

Regarding the sentence embedding part of our model, we set its parameters as follows: we set the maximum sentence length to 24 (if longer the sentence is cut after the 24-th word). We initialized W_e using 500-dimensional Word2Vec embeddings trained on Flickr. We also used these embeddings to compute the Word2Vec part of sentences representations. These embeddings are the same as the ones that the authors of Word2VisualVec used in [6]. Regarding the GRC, we found that a model with 4 capsules and $T = 0.4$ performed well. The GRU in Word2VisualVec and the GRC capsules in our model have 1024-dimensional hidden states.

We trained our models using the RMSProp method [22] with mini-batches of 25 image-sentence pairs during 25 epochs. We followed the same learning rate decay procedure as in [6]: the learning rate was initially 0.0001 and we divided it by 2 when the performance of the model on the validation set did not increase during three consecutive epochs. We made all our implementations using the TensorFlow [1] library for Python and used the default parameters of the RMSProp optimizer: decay = 0.9, momentum = 0.0 and epsilon = 1e-10.

4.3   Results and Discussion

To prove the interest of our model, we compared it to Word2VisualVec. We compared the two versions we described in Sect. 3.2: the one with the average of final hidden states of capsules and the one with the soft-attention mechanism proposed in [5]. We reported our results in Table 1. They show that our model performs better than Word2VisualVec, and that the attention mechanism does not provide much improvement.

Table 1. Results of our experiments on MSCOCO. R@K denotes Recall at rank K (higher is better). Best results among all models are in bold.

MSCOCO			
Model	Caption Retrieval		
	R@1	R@5	R@10
Word2VisualVec	32.4	61.3	73.4
W2V + BoW + GRC	**33.4**	62.2	74.0
W2V + BoW + GRC + Attention	32.8	**62.3**	**74.2**

Moreover, we also wanted to see on which kind of sentences GRCs were more efficient than GRUs. For that purpose, we listed all the sentences that our model ranked in the top 9 sentences and that were ranked worse than rank 100 by Word2VisualVec. We also listed sentences ranked by Word2VisualVec in the top 9 that were ranked worse than rank 100 by our model. Our results are summarized in Table 2.

Table 2. For each model: number of sentences ranked in top 9 for the right image by one model and above rank 100 by the other model. Ten sentences are ranked in top 9 by Word2VisualVec while ranked above rank 100 by our model, and seventeen sentences are ranked in top 9 by our model while ranked above rank 100 by Word2VisualVec. We also reported these numbers of sentences without counting sentences containing "UNK" tokens. This table shows that GRCs are performing better than GRUs on much more sentences than GRUs compared to GRCs.

	Word2VisualVec	Our model
Total	10	17
Total without UNK tokens	3	11

We noticed that sentences on which GRCs were outperforming GRUs were more likely sentences containing multiple visual concepts. We provide some examples in Fig. 4. We think that this observation implies that GRCs could be used efficiently to derive finer visual sentence embeddings, taking into account

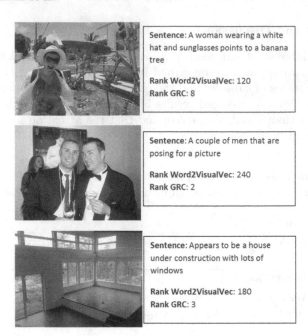

Fig. 4. Compared results of Word2VisualVec and our model on three images.

important local elements. A possible direction of research would be to find how to combine it with an object detection model such as Faster R-CNN [19] to take advantage of that interesting property of GRCs.

5 Conclusion

In this paper, we introduced a novel RNN architecture called Gated Recurrent Capsules (GRCs). We built a model to address the caption retrieval task by mapping images and sentences to a visual features space. We showed in our experimental work that the models obtained using the proposed GRCs are surpassing those from earlier works (employing GRUs). Moreover, we stated that GRCs could potentially be used in any typical RNN tasks, as they are an extension of GRUs. An interesting future research direction would be to map outputs of capsules to local visual features.

Acknowledgments. One of the Titan Xp used for this research was donated by the NVIDIA Corporation. This work was partially funded by ANR (the French National Research Agency) via the GAFES project and the European H2020 research and innovation programme via the project MeMAD (GA780069).

References

1. Abadi, M., et al.: TensorFlow: a system for large-scale machine learning. In: OSDI, vol. 16, pp. 265–283, November 2016
2. Cho, K., van Merrinboer, B., Bahdanau, D., Bengio, Y.: On the properties of neural machine translation: Encoder-Decoder approaches. Syntax Semant. Struct. Stat. Transl. **103** (2014)
3. Deng, J., Dong, W., Socher, R., Li, L. J., Li, K., Fei-Fei, L.: ImageNet: a large-scale hierarchical image database. In: IEEE Conference on Computer Vision and Pattern Recognition, CVPR 2009, pp. 248–255. IEEE, June 2009
4. Dong, J., Li, X., Snoek, C.G.: Word2VisualVec: image and video to sentence matching by visual feature prediction. arXiv preprint arXiv:1604.06838 (2016)
5. Dong, J., Huang, S., Xu, D., Tao, D.: DL-61-86 at TRECVID 2017: Video-to-Text Description (2017)
6. Dong, J., Li, X., Snoek, C.G.: Predicting visual features from text for image and video caption retrieval. IEEE Trans. Multimedia (2018)
7. Faghri, F., Fleet, D.J., Kiros, R., Fidler, S.: VSE++: improved visual-semantic embeddings. arXiv preprint arXiv:1707.05612 (2017)
8. Francis, D., Huet, B., Merialdo, B.: Embedding images and sentences in a common space with a recurrent capsule network. In Proceedings of the 16th International Workshop on Content-Based Multimedia Indexing. IEEE, September 2018
9. Gu, J., et al.: Look, imagine and match: improving textual-visual cross-modal retrieval with generative models. In: Proceedings of the IEEE Conference on Computer Vision and Pattern Recognition (2018)
10. He, K., Zhang, X., Ren, S., Sun, J.: Deep residual learning for image recognition. In: Proceedings of the IEEE Conference on Computer Vision and Pattern Recognition, pp. 770–778 (2016)
11. Hinton, G.E., Sabour, S., Frosst, N.: Matrix capsules with EM routing (2018)
12. Hochreiter, S., Schmidhuber, J.: Long short-term memory. Neural Comput. **9**(8), 1735–1780 (1997)
13. Karpathy, A., Joulin, A., Fei-Fei, L.: Deep fragment embeddings for bidirectional image sentence mapping. In: Proceedings of the 27th International Conference on Neural Information Processing Systems, vol. 2, pp. 1889–1897. MIT Press, December 2014
14. Karpathy, A., Fei-Fei, L.: Deep visual-semantic alignments for generating image descriptions. In: Proceedings of the IEEE Conference on Computer Vision and Pattern Recognition, pp. 3128–3137 (2015)
15. Krizhevsky, A., Sutskever, I., Hinton, G.E.: ImageNet classification with deep convolutional neural networks. In: Advances in Neural Information Processing Systems, pp. 1097–1105 (2012)
16. Lee, K. H., Chen, X., Hua, G., Hu, H., He, X.: Stacked cross attention for image-text matching. arXiv preprint arXiv:1803.08024 (2018)
17. Lin, T.-Y., et al.: Microsoft COCO: common objects in context. In: Fleet, D., Pajdla, T., Schiele, B., Tuytelaars, T. (eds.) ECCV 2014. LNCS, vol. 8693, pp. 740–755. Springer, Cham (2014). https://doi.org/10.1007/978-3-319-10602-1_48
18. Mikolov, T., Sutskever, I., Chen, K., Corrado, G.S., Dean, J.: Distributed representations of words and phrases and their compositionality. In: Advances in Neural Information Processing Systems, pp. 3111–3119 (2013)
19. Ren, S., He, K., Girshick, R., Sun, J.: Faster R-CNN: towards real-time object detection with region proposal networks. In: Advances in Neural Information Processing Systems, pp. 91–99 (2015)

20. Sabour, S., Frosst, N., Hinton, G.E.: Dynamic routing between capsules. In: Advances in Neural Information Processing Systems, pp. 3856–3866 (2017)
21. Sutskever, I., Vinyals, O., Le, Q.V.: Sequence to sequence learning with neural networks. In: Advances in Neural Information Processing Systems, pp. 3104–3112 (2014)
22. Tieleman, T., Hinton, G.: Lecture 6.5-rmsprop: divide the gradient by a running average of its recent magnitude. In: COURSERA: Neural Networks for Machine Learning (2012)
23. Vinyals, O., Toshev, A., Bengio, S., Erhan, D.: Show and tell: a neural image caption generator. In: Proceedings of the IEEE Conference on Computer Vision and Pattern Recognition, pp. 3156–3164 (2015)
24. Yosinski, J., Clune, J., Bengio, Y., Lipson, H.: How transferable are features in deep neural networks? In: Advances in Neural Information Processing Systems, pp. 3320–3328 (2014)

An Automatic System for Generating Artificial Fake Character Images

Yisheng Yue[1], Palaiahnakote Shivakumara[2], Yirui Wu[1,3],
Liping Zhu[4], Tong Lu[1(✉)], and Umapada Pal[5]

[1] National Key Lab for Novel Software Technology,
Nanjing University, Nanjing, China
abelyys@foxmail.com, wuyirui@hhu.edu.cn,
lutong@nju.edu.cn

[2] Faculty of Computer Science and Information Technology,
University of Malaya, Kuala Lumpur, Malaysia
shiva@um.edu.my

[3] College of Computer and Information, Hohai University, Nanjing, China

[4] School of Information Management, Nanjing University, Nanjing, China
chemzlp@163.com

[5] Computer Vision and Pattern Recognition Unit, Indian Statistical Institute,
Kolkata, India
umapada@isical.ac.in

Abstract. Due to the introduction of deep learning for text detection and recognition in natural scenes, and the increase in detecting fake images in crime applications, automatically generating fake character images has now received greater attentions. This paper presents a new system named Fake Character GAN (FCGAN). It has the ability to generate fake and artificial scene characters that have similar shapes and colors with the existing ones. The proposed method first extracts shapes and colors of character images. Then, it constructs the FCGAN, which consists of a series of convolution, residual and transposed convolution blocks. The extracted features are then fed to the FCGAN to generate fake characters and verify the quality of the generated characters simultaneously. The proposed system chooses characters from the benchmark ICDAR 2015 dataset for training, and further validated by conducting text detection and recognition experiments on input and generated fake images to show its effectiveness.

Keywords: Fake characters · Generative adversarial network
Shape information · Character editing

1 Introduction

It is noted that day by day crimes are increasing in all the departments including tampering texts in natural scene images. In order to find solutions to this problem, researchers have started developing systems and methods for forgery detection [1] recently. The main issue these methods met is dataset creation, which requires a large number of real images for experimentation. In addition, since such real data are often

© Springer Nature Switzerland AG 2019
I. Kompatsiaris et al. (Eds.): MMM 2019, LNCS 11296, pp. 291–301, 2019.
https://doi.org/10.1007/978-3-030-05716-9_24

sensitive, forensic teams do not share the information for experimentation and developing methods. In the same way, we notice that deep learning based methods [2, 3] use synthetic character images and artificially created images for feature extraction, classification and recognition in the recent days. For creating such a huge dataset for training, it always requires a large amount of time to create and label the samples. Therefore, in order to cope with the above-mentioned challenges, there is an urgent need for developing a novel system which can generate any number of fake character images such that an accurate and robust method can be developed and validated without involving much manpower and cumbersome tasks. At the same time, deep learning based methods can use the same system for generating any number of samples that match with input images. This is the main advantage of the proposed system.

Examples of fake character image generation are shown in Fig. 1, where the left image refers to the original image, while the right gives the result of the proposed system by replacing the characters in the red rectangular with the fake characters in the blue rectangular in each same image. It can be seen that the generated characters appear the same or very similar as the characters in the input images. The interesting point here is that the proposed system is faster than we creating a fake character similar to real character by hand. To achieve the above target, we propose to explore Generative Adversarial Network (GAN) [4], which is designed with a generator and a discriminator to provide a simple but powerful way to estimate target distributions based on the input distribution. Researchers thus utilize GAN to generate image samples based on the inputs [5, 6]. In fact, GAN has different types of architectures due to different designs of loss functions, such as WGAN [7] and Least-squares GAN [8]. Here we train our GAN network using least-square loss and adopt the L1 reconstruction loss as the reconstruct loss. The proposed system feeds shapes and background color features to GAN to guarantee the quality of generated fake characters.

(a)   (b)   (c)   (d)

Fig. 1. The results of automatically generated faked images, where (a), (c) are original images and (b), (d) are generated fake images. Note that several characters in (b) and (d) have been changed using our proposed system by an automatic way (red: the original characters; blue: fake characters). (Color figure online)

The main contribution of the proposed system is proposing an end-to-end generation system, Fake Character GAN (FCGAN) that supports automatic editing of characters inside natural scenes. Unlike style transfer methods that only involve transforms at pixel level, the proposed system considers shape information and translates characters on a higher level. Additionally, feeding shapes and background color information to GAN and using GAN for fake character image generation is new in the field of text detection and recognition in natural scene.

2 Related Work

As one of the most significant improvements on the research of deep generative models, GAN [4] has drawn a quantity of attentions from both deep learning and pattern recognition communities. It has been widely used in image generation [9], image editing [10], and representation learning [11]. The key idea of GAN stems from the two-player game designed by GAN, i.e., a generator and a discriminator that provide a powerful way to estimate target distributions and generate novel image samples. With this power for distribution modeling, GAN is suitable for unsupervised tasks. By combining traditional content loss and adversarial loss, super-resolution generative adversarial networks [12] achieve state-of-the-art performance for image super-resolution. In addition, for unsupervised learning tasks, GANs also show impressive potential for semi-supervised learning. For example, Salimans et al. [13] propose a GAN-based framework, where the discriminator not only outputs the probability to define whether an input image is extracted from real data, but also computes the probability of belonging to each class.

It is noted from Conotter et al. [14] and Abramova [15] that the methods used generated data to improve the performance of forgery detection. Inspired by this idea, relevant to the proposed system, we propose the GAN to perform image-to-image translation. For example, Isola et al. [16] use a conditional generative adversarial network to learn the mapping from input to output images. Reed et al. [17] propose a model to synthesize images given text descriptions based on conditional GANs. More recently, CoGAN [18] uses a weight-sharing strategy to learn a common representation across domains. Furthermore, Liu et al. [19] extend this framework with the combination of variational autoencoders and generative adversarial networks. These successful applications of GAN motivate us to develop a new fake character generation system based on GAN.

3 Proposed FCGAN

In this paper, we propose an end-to-end system FCGAN to automatically generate fake scene characters. We show the network architecture of the proposed system as in Fig. 2. The input of the generator consists of three kinds of images, which represent input characters, shapes of input characters, and styles of target characters, respectively. The proposed system can generate different types of characters with different shape information.

3.1 Network of FCGAN

The proposed FCGAN consists of a generator network and a discriminator network, as shown in Fig. 2. The generator uses the shape of an input character to make the generated character reality and use the style of a target character to show what kind of character is to be generated. Unlike common discriminator of GAN, which only need to judge whether the input is true or false, the discriminator of FCGAN has to discriminate whether the generated character is similar with the target real character. So we put two images into the discriminator together, one is the generated fake character while the other one is the real target character image, regarded as fake data or two same real

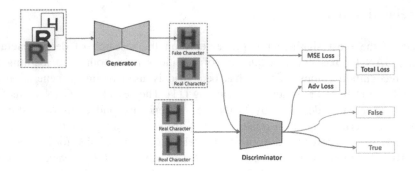

Fig. 2. Overview of the proposed FCGAN. The generator use an input character, the shape of the input character and the style of a target character to generate a forgery character image. The generator uses MSE loss to make sure the generated character reality. The discriminator uses two same real characters as real data and a generated fake character with a real character as fake data during training so that it can tell whether the generated character is like the target real character.

target character images regarded as real data. We also use the MSE loss to make sure that each generated character is similar to the real character.

The proposed generator network is composed of a series of convolutions, ResNet blocks [20] and transposed convolutions. The details of construction are shown in Table 1. The activation functions of the convolution and transposed convolution blocks are defined as a leaky-ReLu function, while the activation functions of the ResNet blocks refer to ReLu function. Specifically, we firstly concatenate the input character (3 channels), the shape image of the input character (1 channel), and the style image of the target character (1 channel) together, which are further involved into the Generator network. Then, we utilize a series of convolutions to produce 8x8x512 latent features, which describe the inherent information of the input data. After convolution operations, we encode the computation of the first layer with ResNet blocks. After encoding with 8 layers of ResNet blocks, we decode the latent feature with transposed convolution operations. Finally, we get a $64 \times 64 \times 3$ image, which is the result of the generated fake image.

The discriminator network takes a $64 \times 64 \times 6$ vector as the input, which comprises a pair of images. The discriminator network considers a target real image and a generated fake image as the input. The construction details of the discriminator network are shown in Table 2. During testing, we evaluate the reality of the input image, i.e., the generated fake image.

3.2   End-to-End Joint Training

In this subsection, we present the process of end-to-end joint training. We utilize the three types of images for training, namely, the input character image, the shape image of the input character shape, and the style image of the target character. Note that the input character and the target character are chosen from the same class, which means that these two types of images have the same background and foreground color but different character types. Our task is thus to generate a target character, i.e., a fake character, using the input character and the style of the target character.

Table 1. Construction details of the generator network.

	Type	Kernel	Stride	Padding	Out channel
Convolution blocks	Conv	7	1	3	64
	Conv	3	2	1	128
	Conv	3	2	1	256
	Conv	3	2	1	512
ResNet block x8	Conv	3	1	1	512
	InstanceNorm				
	Conv	3	1	1	512
	InstanceNorm				
ConvTranspose blocks	ConvTrans	3	2	1	256
	ConvTrans	3	2	1	128
	ConvTrans	3	2	1	64
	ConvTrans	1	1	0	3

Table 2. The Construction details of the discriminator network.

	Type	Kernel	Stride	Padding	Out channel
Convolution blocks	Conv	7	2	3	64
	Conv	3	2	1	128
	Conv	3	2	1	256
	Conv	3	2	1	512
	Conv	3	2	1	1024
	Conv	3	2	1	2048
	Conv	3	2	1	1

The proposed work explores the shape of the input character to improve the quality of the fake generated character. During the construction of generator, we adopt L1 loss to be the construction loss to improve our result, which is expressed as follows:

$$L_{construct} = E_{x \sim p_{source}, y \sim p_{target}, s, t}[|||G(x, s, t) - y|||] \tag{1}$$

where E represents the expectation value, function G(.) refers to the generator network, s refers to the shape image of the input character, t represents style image of target character, and p denotes data distribution. Note that we adopt L1 loss rather than L2 loss since training with L1 loss can be optimized by a faster way and produce harper and cleaner images.

To evaluate the overall performance, we adopt the least-square loss as the loss function of the GAN, which is defined as:

$$L_{adv} = E_{y \sim p_{target}}\left[(D(y, y) - 1)^2\right] + E_{x \sim p_{source}, y \sim p_{target}, s, t}\left[D(y, G(x, s, t))^2\right] \tag{2}$$

where D(.) is the discriminator network. Above all, the total loss of GAN can be computed as:

$$L_{total} = \arg min_G max_D L_{adv} + \lambda L_{construct} \qquad (3)$$

To solve Eq. 3, we use Adam [21] as our optimization method.

4   Experimental Results

4.1   Implementation Details

For experimentation, we use character images from ICDAR 2015 [22] as our training data. We adopt the label of text box information to extract single characters from the dataset. As these extracted characters have different sizes, hence we first resize them to standard size of 64 × 64.

Next, we generate our training dataset for FCGAN. Note that input characters have the same background and font style with real characters. The system thus requires a pair of characters for training, i.e., an input character and a real character which have similar background and font style. To make characters as pairs, we first classify character images into different classes based on background and font styles. Some example images belonging to the same class are shown in Fig. 3. It is noted that we classify characters into classes manually in this step. After classifying, we use character pairs to train the GAN network.

Fig. 3.   Some example images belonging to one class. Note that they have the same background and font style. When training the network, we randomly choose two images from one class of character images, which are regarded as the input character and the target character, respectively.

After pairing, we extract shape information from the image of the input character and the style of the target character. Note that we use the style image to define what type of a character to be generated, and use the shape to ensure the quality of generation. Specifically, we use Otsu method with an adaptive threshold to extract the shape information of the input character. We also augment the data by exchanging the RGB channel of one image. It is noted that all the character images are defined as 64 × 64. In total, we choose 52 styles of images as our target characters, which are used to show the detailed character types to be generated. The training data are shown in Fig. 4. After dataset processing, we totally get 12435 characters and 52 styles of target characters for training.

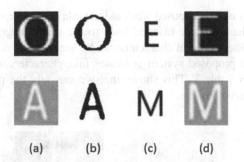

(a)   (b)   (c)   (d)

Fig. 4. The training data. From left to right: (a) are input character images, (b) are the shape of input characters, (c) are the style of target characters and (d) are the target character image.

During training, we randomly pairs of images, i.e., an input character and a real character belonging to the same class. The learning rate of the generator and the discriminator network are 0.0001 and 0.00001, respectively. We train the network with 32 batch size.

4.2 Performance Analysis

To test the quality of fake character images by the proposed system, we estimate the standard quality metrics, namely, SSIM and PSNR. SSIM is defined as:

$$SSIM(x, y) = \frac{(2\mu_x\mu_y + c_1)(2\sigma_{xy} + c_2)}{(\mu_x^2 + \mu_y^2 + c_1)(\sigma_x^2 + \sigma_y^2 + c_2)} \tag{4}$$

where μ refers to the average of data, σ means the variance of data, σ_{xy} means the covariance of x and y, and $c_1 = (k_1 L)^2, c_2 = (k_2 L)^2$, where L is the dynamic range of pixel-values, $k_1 = 0.01$ and $k_2 = 0.03$ by default.

PSNR is defined by

$$PSNR = 10 \cdot log_{10}\left(\frac{MAX_I^2}{MSE}\right) \tag{5}$$

$$MSE = \frac{1}{mn}\sum_{i=0}^{m-1}\sum_{j=0}^{n-1}[I(i,j) - K(i,j)]^2 \tag{6}$$

where MAX_I^2 is the maximum possible pixel value of the image.

For estimating the quality measures, fake generated and target character images are considered. It is noted that high PSNR and SSIM values indicate a fake character image has better quality.

Qualitative results of the proposed work at image level can be seen in Fig. 5, where the fake generated characters are inserted back to the same image. At the same time, individual fake characters for real characters can be seen in Fig. 6. It is observed from Figs. 5 and 6 that the proposed system generates fake characters well. The PSNR and SSIM are reported in Table 3. This shows that we can rely the proposed system for generating fake character images.

Fig. 5. The generated results, where the upper refers to the real source images, while the bottom represents images containing generated forgery characters. Note that we have changed several characters in these images.

To validate the effectiveness of the proposed system, we conduct experiments for text detection and recognition, respectively. For the text detection experiment, we use two state of the art text detection methods, namely, CTPN [23] and EAST [24] to detect the characters in real scene images and the images with generated characters. Note that generated fake images contain both fake generated characters and original ones. The results are reported in Table 4, where it can be seen that the measures of real images and the images containing fake character images score almost the same. We also expand the training dataset with the generated fake images to test the text detection result. The results can be seen in Table 5, which shows the detection result is improved after add images which contain generated characters. This means that most of the generated fake characters are treated as real ones.

We also conduct recognition experiments for real and generated fake characters to test whether the generated fake characters preserve the actual shapes or not. For this, we use CRNN algorithm [25], which explores deep learning for text recognition. The results of the recognition methods are reported in Table 6, where one can see that the recognition rate of the fake character is almost the same as the recognition rate of real characters.

Fig. 6. The examples of generated characters and its real target characters, where the upper shows real target character images, while the bottom gives generated forgery character images.

Table 3. Measurement results.

	SSIM	PSNR
The proposed	0.6719	17.457

Table 4. Comparison on performance of text detection.

Method	Real scene images			Generated fake images		
	Precision	Recall	F-Measure	Precision	Recall	F-Measure
CTPN [23]	0.66	0.535	0.59	0.65	0.519	0.577
EAST [24]	0.298	0.464	0.363	0.28	0.445	0.344

Table 5. Comparison on adding generated fake images as training data.

Method	900 real scene images			900 real scene images + 100 generated fake images		
	Precision	Recall	F-Measure	Precision	Recall	F-Measure
EAST [24]	0.315	0.481	0.381	0.336	0.51	0.405

Table 6. Comparison on performance of text recognition.

Category	CRNN
Real characters	0.523
Generated fake characters	0.541

5 Conclusion

In this paper, we propose an automatic system namely FCGAN to generate artificial fake characters. We use ICDAR 2015 dataset for experimentation. The experimental results on text detection and recognition shows that the proposed system preserve the quality of the images as real images, which is very useful and effective.

Acknowledgment. This work was supported by the Natural Science Foundation of China under Grant 61672273, Grant 61832008 and Grant 61702160, the Science Foundation for Distinguished Young Scholars of Jiangsu under Grant BK20160021, Scientific Foundation of State Grid Corporation of China (Research on Ice-wind Disaster Feature Recognition and Prediction by Few-shot Machine Learning in Transmission Lines), National Key R&D Program of China under Grant 2018YFC0407901, the Fundamental Research Funds for the Central Universities under Grant 2016B14114, the Science Foundation of JiangSu under Grant BK20170892, and the open Project of the National Key Lab for Novel Software Technology in NJU under Grant K-FKT2017B05.

References

1. Farid, H.: Image forgery detection. IEEE Signal Process. Mag. **26**(2), 16–25 (2009)
2. Jaderberg, M., et al.: Synthetic data and artificial neural networks for natural scene text recognition (2014). arXiv preprint: arXiv:1406.2227
3. Zheng, Z., Zheng, L., Yang, Y.: Unlabeled samples generated by GAN improve the person re-identification baseline in vitro (2017). arXiv preprint: arXiv:1701.07717
4. Goodfellow, I., et al.: Generative adversarial nets. In: Advances in Neural Information Processing Systems (2014)
5. Zhu, J.-Y., et al.: Unpaired image-to-image translation using cycle-consistent adversarial networks (2017). arXiv preprint: arXiv:1703.10593
6. Iizuka, S., Simo-Serra, E., Ishikawa, H.: Globally and locally consistent image completion. ACM Trans. Graph. (TOG) **36**(4), 107 (2017)
7. Arjovsky, M., Chintala, S., Bottou, L.: Wasserstein GAN (2017). arXiv preprint: arXiv: 1701.07875
8. Mao, X., et al.: Least squares generative adversarial networks. In: 2017 IEEE International Conference on Computer Vision (ICCV). IEEE (2017)
9. Denton, E.L., Chintala, S., Fergus, R.: Deep generative image models using a Laplacian pyramid of adversarial networks. In: Advances in Neural Information Processing Systems (2015)
10. Zhu, J.-Y., Krähenbühl, P., Shechtman, E., Efros, A.A.: Generative visual manipulation on the natural image manifold. In: Leibe, B., Matas, J., Sebe, N., Welling, M. (eds.) ECCV 2016, Part V. LNCS, vol. 9909, pp. 597–613. Springer, Cham (2016). https://doi.org/10.1007/978-3-319-46454-1_36
11. Radford, A., Metz, L., Chintala, S.: Unsupervised representation learning with deep convolutional generative adversarial networks (2015). arXiv preprint: arXiv:1511.06434
12. Ledig, C., et al.: Photo-realistic single image super-resolution using a generative adversarial network (2016). arXiv preprint: arXiv:1609.04802
13. Salimans, T., et al.: Improved techniques for training GANs. In: Advances in Neural Information Processing Systems (2016)
14. Conotter, V., Boato, G., Farid, H.: Detecting photo manipulation on signs and billboards. In: 2010 17th IEEE International Conference on Image Processing (ICIP). IEEE (2010)
15. Abramova, S.: Detecting copy-move forgeries in scanned text documents. Electron. Imaging **2016**(8), 1–9 (2016)
16. Isola, P., et al.: Image-to-image translation with conditional adversarial networks (2016). arXiv preprint: arXiv:1611.07004
17. Reed, S., et al.: Generative adversarial text to image synthesis (2016). arXiv preprint: arXiv: 1605.05396

18. Liu, M.-Y., Tuzel, O.: Coupled generative adversarial networks. In: Advances in Neural Information Processing Systems (2016)
19. Liu, M.-Y., Breuel, T., Kautz, J.: Unsupervised Image-to-Image Translation Networks (2017). arXiv preprint: arXiv:1703.00848
20. He, K., et al.: Deep residual learning for image recognition. In: Proceedings of the IEEE Conference on Computer Vision and Pattern Recognition (2016)
21. Kingma, D., Ba, J.: Adam: A method for stochastic optimization (2014). arXiv preprint: arXiv:1412.6980
22. Karatzas, D., et al.: ICDAR 2015 competition on robust reading. In: 2015 13th International Conference on Document Analysis and Recognition (ICDAR). IEEE (2015)
23. Tian, Z., Huang, W., He, T., He, P., Qiao, Y.: Detecting text in natural image with connectionist text proposal network. In: Leibe, B., Matas, J., Sebe, N., Welling, M. (eds.) ECCV 2016. LNCS, vol. 9912, pp. 56–72. Springer, Cham (2016). https://doi.org/10.1007/978-3-319-46484-8_4
24. Zhou, X., et al.: EAST: An Efficient and Accurate Scene Text Detector (2017). arXiv preprint: arXiv:1704.03155
25. Shi, B., Bai, X., Yao, C.: An end-to-end trainable neural network for image-based sequence recognition and its application to scene text recognition. IEEE Trans. Pattern Anal. Mach. Intell. **39**(11), 2298–2304 (2017)

Person Re-Identification Based on Pose-Aware Segmentation

Wenfeng Zhang[1], Zhiqiang Wei[1,2(✉)], Lei Huang[1,2,4], Jie Nie[1],
Lei Lv[3,4], and Guanqun Wei[1]

[1] Ocean University of China, Qingdao 266000, China
weizhiqiang@ouc.edu.cn
[2] Qingdao National Laboratory for Marine Science and Technology,
Qingdao 266000, China
[3] School of Information Science and Engineering, Shandong Normal University,
Ji'nan 250014, China
[4] Key Laboratory for Distributed Computer Software Novel Technology,
Ji'nan 250014, China

Abstract. Person re-identification (Re-ID) is a key technology for intelligent video analysis. However, it is still a challenging task due to various complex background, different poses of person, etc. In this paper we try to address this issue by proposing a novel method based on person segmentation. Contrary to the previous method, we segment the person region from the image first. A pose-aware segmentation method (PA) is proposed by introducing the human pose into segmentation scheme. Then the deep learning features are extracted based on the person region instead of the whole bounding box. Finally, the person Re-ID results are acquired through the rank of Euclidean distance. Comprehensive experiments on two public person Re-ID datasets show the effectiveness of our method and the comparison experiments demonstrate that our method can outperform the state-of-the-art method.

Keywords: Person re-identification · Complex background · Person region
Person segmentation · Deep learning

1 Introduction

Person Re-ID has important value in the field of intelligent monitoring. Given one single shot or multiple shots of a target pedestrian, person Re-ID aims at matching the same individuals among a large image gallery set from disjoint cameras. Due to the variability of person poses, person Re-ID is still a very challenging issue and deserves more research inputs under different light conditions and different camera shooting perspectives.

Background of the environment is a critical influencing factor in person Re-ID. This problem arises due to the variability and complexity of background. As shown in Fig. 1, the background for the same person is large different. The deep learning methods are popular in person Re-ID, due to its ability to learn features. The learned deep features can obtain local and global information, and good generalization for new

© Springer Nature Switzerland AG 2019
I. Kompatsiaris et al. (Eds.): MMM 2019, LNCS 11296, pp. 302–314, 2019.
https://doi.org/10.1007/978-3-030-05716-9_25

data. However, most existing deep learning methods for person Re-ID ignore the background noise of original image with person, and may get useless features by sending it to neural networks.

Fig. 1. Sample images for one person with different background. The two images in each black box represent the same identity.

In this paper, we propose a new method to reduce the influences of background noise on generating features. The details are as follows: firstly we segment the person region from the image. Pose estimation and DPM [1] detectors are used to segment pedestrian foreground. We have estimated person pose in the image with DPM detector, and use the pose estimation to segment people region. Secondly, the deep learning features are extracted based on the person region instead of the whole bounding box. Lastly, we get the person-identification results by ranking the Euclidean distance.

The remaining of the paper is organized as follows, In Sect. 2 an overview of existing person Re-ID methods is presented. In Sect. 3 the proposed method is presented. In Sect. 4, comprehensive experiments are done and comparative results are given. Finally, some conclusions are drawn in Sect. 5.

2 Related Works

There are already many jobs related to person Re-ID. The existing methods can be divided into three categories: the method based on feature extraction, the method based on distance measurement and the method based on deep learning.

The method based on feature extraction is mainly concerned with how to obtain features efficiently. Previous approaches have improved the differentiation of human visual features by incorporating multiple visual features. Zheng et al. [2] combined RGB, YCbCr and HSV color features, as well as Schmid and Garbor texture features. Li et al. [3] mainly focused on the visual attributes of clothing, including long-sleeved and short-sleeved. To address the problem of pedestrian misalignment, Zheng et al. [4] thought that person saliency is distinctive and reliable in pedestrian matching across disjoint camera views, and used pose estimation to generate a standard pose, and combined the original image to extract descriptor. Zhao et al. [5] proposed a novel perspective for person Re-ID based on learning person saliency and matching saliency distribution. Chen et al. [6] presented a new framework based on the camera correlation aware feature augmentation, which is capable of jointly learning both view-generic and view-specific discriminative information for person Re-ID.

The method based on distance measurement is mainly concerned with distance metric. Roth et al. [7] proposed method to obtain a Mahalanobis distance that can be used as a better image representation. Liao et al. [8] introduced Bayesian face and KISSME into distance metric learning. Chen et al. [9] clustered the samples by K-means, and constructed nine different distance metrics for different image according to the clustering results. Wang et al. [10] used the geodesic distance as the similarity measure. In order to further improve the accuracy of distance measurement, Wang et al. [11] proposed a reordering method based on user feedback to improve the results. Zhong et al. [12] thought re-ranking is a critical step to improve the accuracy of person Re-ID, and proposed a k-reciprocal encoding method to re-rank the Re-ID results. Yuan et al. [13] proposed a framework with updateable joint images re-ranking for Person Re-ID. Yu et al. [14] exploited the diverse information embedded in a high-dimensional feature, and proposed an unsupervised person re-ID re-ranking frame-work.

Methods based on deep learning introduce deep learning framework into the person Re-ID task. In recent years, deep learning has achieved excellent performance in many computer vision tasks [15, 16]. The researchers have introduced it into the person Re-ID. Li et al. [17] proposed a neural network model FPNN (Filter Pairing Neural Network) that are robust to viewpoints. Wang et al. [18] proposed a deep learning network that fuses the feature representation between images. Cheng et al. [19] proposed a multi-channel deep neural network structure that corresponds to the whole body and the four parts of the human body. Xiao et al. [20] proposed a deep learning network that unified detection and Re-ID processes. Zhao et al. [21] pro-posed a convolution neural network that fuses different body regions with a tree structure. Lin et al. [22] proposed a convolution neural network that learns a Re-ID embedding and predicts the pedestrian attributes simultaneously. Chen et al. [23] proposed a deep quadruplet network by designing a quadruplet loss.

3   The Proposed Method

The framework of the proposed method is illustrated in Fig. 2. Generally, our method can be divided into three steps: (1) pose-aware human body segmentation, (2) appearance features extraction based on deep learning, (3) similarity calculation. The details are discussed in the following.

Pose-Aware Human Body Segmentation. In this step, we firstly set person region and background region with pose estimation. According to characteristics of pedestrian images, we find that person must appear in some areas of image, and much possibly not appear in some regions. To apply this information into segmenting person region, we use DPM [1] to estimate the area where people appear. DPM as a target detection algorithm, the general process is as follows: firstly calculate the gradient direction histogram, then use SVM (Support Vector Machine) training to get the object's gradient model.

A complete DPM model generally includes several components. One component includes a root model and several part models. Figure 3 shows a DPM model with eight part models.

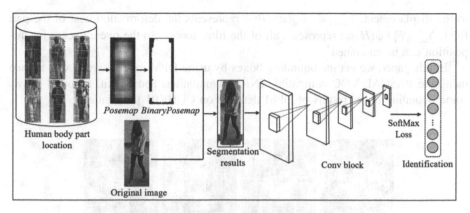

Fig. 2. Framework of the proposed method

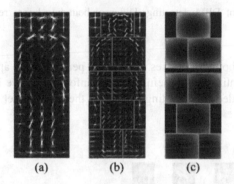

Fig. 3. Illustration of DPM model. It shows the result of visualization of a trained model. (a) is the root model. (b) is the part model and its position. (c) is deviation punishment of the part model on the root model. The farther the deviation is, the heavier the punishment is, and the lighter the area is, the heavier the punishment is.

The DPM model is represented by a filter. The filter can be defined as a two-dimensional array composed of n-dimensional weight vectors. The response of the filter can be obtained by performing an inner product operation with the corresponding n-dimensional feature vector extracted from a rectangular region of the image. Combine all filter responses to get the final score for this area. Its scoring formula is shown in formula:

$$score = \sum_{i=0}^{n} F_i' \cdot \phi(H, p_i) - \sum_{i=1}^{n} d_i \cdot \phi_d(dx_i, dy_i) + b \tag{1}$$

where F_i denotes the i-th filter, F_0 denotes the root filter. $\phi(H, p_i)$ denotes the HOG feature of the position. d_i denotes the coefficient of the deformation function of a certain part. $(dx_i, dy_i) = (x_i, y_i) - (2(x_0, y_0) + v_i)$ represents the offset displacement of the part relative to the root model, and ϕ_d represents the quadratic function with respect to the displacement. $\sum_{i=1}^{n} d_i \cdot \phi_d(dx_i, dy_i)$ represents the deformation cost of the part filter. $\sum_{i=0}^{n} F_i' \cdot \phi(H, p_i)$ represents all of the filter scores. So the overall score for this position can be combined.

In this paper, we get the bounding boxes by using DPM model, which was trained using the PASCAL VOC compatible INRIA annotations and devkit. Figure 4 shows some bounding boxes results of DPM detector on CUHK01 [24] dataset.

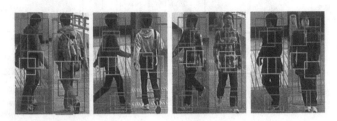

Fig. 4. Demonstration of DPM detecting. Different bounding boxes represent different body parts.

We can use these bounding boxes to estimate person would appear in certain areas of the image. To quantify these useful location information, we have count the pixel which has been included in bounding boxes on the training set. Figure 5 shows the counting process.

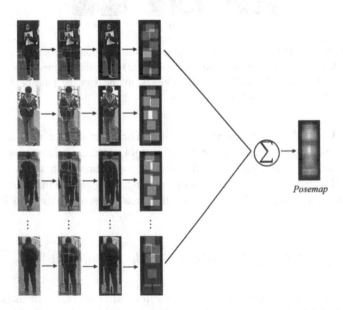

Fig. 5. The statistical process with bounding boxes. The first col is the original images. The second col is the DPM detecting results. The third col is the Segmentation results based on pose. The fourth col is the statistical pose map.

After we have obtained statistical matrix, we name it *Poserange* and range the matrix to $[0, 255]$ as *Posemap* matrix. Formula (2) shows the ranging process:

$$Posemap_{x,y} = round(V_{x,y})$$
$$V_{x,y} = (R_{max} - R_{min}) * (Poserange_{x,y} - M_{min})/(M_{max} - M_{min}) + R_{min} \quad (2)$$

where x denotes the horizontal coordinate and y denotes vertical coordinate. R_{max} equals 255, R_{min} equals 0, M_{max} represents the max value of *Poserange*, and M_{min} represents the min value of *Poserange*. The $round()$ function indicates that rounding to nearest integer. The *Posemap* result is shown in Fig. 5. The greater the brightness of the image is, the more the probability of the person appearing in the corresponding position is.

Next, we use binarization to extract the foreground. It can be written as follows:

$$BinaryPosemap_{x,y} = \begin{cases} 255 & if\ Posemap_{x,y} > T \\ 0 & else \end{cases} \quad (3)$$

To get more persons' foreground area while eliminating useless background areas, we set $T = 12$ in the experiment. Then we use the *BinaryPosemap* as a mask map to extract person foreground in the original image. This way of segmenting human areas from images is called pose-aware method (PA). Figure 2 shows the process of pose-aware method, and the deep learning training procedure.

Appearance Features Extraction Based on Deep Learning. In this step, we focus on extracting person deep features. Three popular methods, including ResNet-50 [25], [26], VGG-16 [27] and PAN [28] structure, are used to this process. VGG, ResNet and PAN methods have been proved to present promising results on person Re-ID in recent years.

For training ResNet-50 and VGG-16 on segmented images of person Re-ID dataset, we use pre-trained models, which have been previously trained on ImageNet dataset and contain the weights and biases that represent the features of whichever dataset it was trained on. After the training process, we extract the person features based on the last pool layer in ResNet-50 and the second to last full connection layer in VGG-16. Following [28], the fine-tuned PAN model is obtained by training segmented images and we get the person descriptor by weighting the fusion of the FC features of the base branch and the alignment branch.

Similarity Calculation. Before distance learning, the features are normalized to [0, 1]. Then the distance between every two images is calculated by Euclidean distance. The European distance formula is:

$$d_{12} = \sqrt{\sum_{k=1}^{n} (x_{1k} - x_{2k})^2} \quad (4)$$

Vectors $x_1 = (x_{11}, x_{12}, \ldots, x_{1n}), x_2 = (x_{21}, x_{22}, \ldots, x_{2n})$ represent the features of the two images, respectively.

4 Experiments and Discusses

In this section, we conduct comprehensive evaluations of our method. Firstly, baseline algorithms and evaluation metrics are described. Then, experiments on CUHK01 [24] and Market-1501 [29] datasets are performed to evaluate the proposed method.

4.1 Dataset, Baseline and Evaluation Metrics

Dataset. To evaluate the effectiveness of our method, we test it on two challenging public datasets: CUHK01 and Market-1501.
CUHK01 dataset: it consists of 971 identities from two surveillance cameras, and 3,884 pedestrian images manually cropped. Each person has 4 images. We divided this dataset into two partitions for training and testing. The first half images of dataset are used for training and the other half images are used for testing.

Market-1501 dataset: it contains 12,936 training images, 19,732 gallery images, and 3,368 query images from six cameras. It contains 751 identities in the training set and 750 identities in the testing set without overlapping. Each identity has 17.2 photos on average in the training set. All images are automatically cropped by DPM detector. By using all the 12,936 detected images to train the network, we follow the evaluation protocol in the original dataset. Samples of these two datasets are shown in Fig. 6.

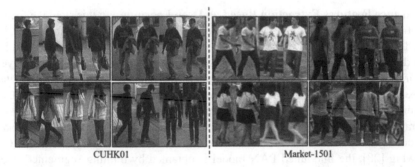

CUHK01   Market-1501

Fig. 6. Sample images from CUHK01 and Market-1501. For four images in each black bounding box, the first two images are obtained by one camera, the last two by another one.

Baseline. As a way to effectively remove background noise, our method is adaptive to previous models. We compare our method with PAN method, ResNet method and VGG method.

Evaluation Metrics. The widely used cumulative match curve (CMC) approach is adopted to quantify performance of person Re-ID. Rank-k matching rate is used to evaluate the performance of the methods. When the returned list contains an image of the same person as that in probe image, this probe is considered as rank k of true match. In our experiments, k = 1, 5, 10, 20. Also mean average precision (mAP) is reported.

All experiments use single query strategy, which is to put one image of one person as query.

4.2 Experiment Results

In our method, we firstly segment the person region from image. As mentioned in Sect. 3, we set the *BinaryPosemap* for person region segmentation. In the next experiment, we denote pose-aware method as PA, and add it to distinguish our method from baselines.

Performance on CUHK01. In Fig. 7, the CMC curves show that our method performs better than VGG, ResNet, and PAN on CUHK01 dataset. Table 1 lists the rank values of our method, VGG method, ResNet method, and PAN method. For VGG, our method can achieve 1.44% improvement on rank-1 accuracy and 1.34% on mAP. For ResNet, our method can achieve 2.68% improvement on rank-1 accuracy and 2.80% on mAP. For PAN, our method can achieve 2.71% improvement on rank-1 accuracy and 2.04% on mAP. From this table we can find that our method can get promising results.

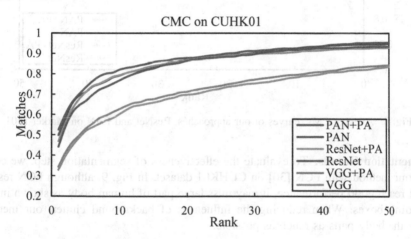

Fig. 7. Average CMC curves of our approaches, VGG, ResNet and PAN on CUHK01

Table 1. Comparisons with other methods on CUHK01

Method	Rank-1	Rank-5	Rank-10	Rank-20	mAP
VGG	0.3289	0.5196	0.6031	0.6979	0.3157
VGG+PA	0.3433	0.5309	0.6278	0.7134	0.3291
ResNet	0.4412	0.6670	0.7691	0.8649	0.4326
ResNet+PA	0.4680	0.7113	0.7948	0.8691	0.4606
PAN	0.4976	0.7113	0.7928	0.8701	0.4865
PAN+PA (Our method)	**0.5247**	**0.7340**	**0.8216**	**0.8784**	**0.5069**

Performance on Market-1501. In Fig. 8, the CMC curves show that our method performs better than ResNet and PAN on Market-1501 dataset. Table 2 lists the rank values of our method, ResNet method, and PAN method. For ResNet, our method can achieve 1.51% improvement on rank-1 accuracy and 0.47% on mAP. For PAN, our method can achieve 1.54% improvement on rank-1 accuracy and 1.23% on mAP. In this table, we can find that the improvement on Market-1501 performs worse than CUHK01, especially on mAP. The reason is that the images of CUHK01 dataset are manually cropped while the images of Market-1501 dataset are detected by DPM detector. The automatic detector suffers from excessive background error and part missing error.

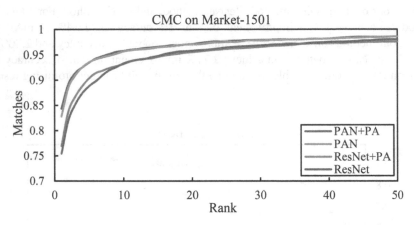

Fig. 8. Average CMC curves of our approaches, ResNet and PAN on Market-1501

Segmentation Results. To evaluate the effectiveness of segmentation step, we compare our method with FCN [30] on CUHK01 dataset. In Fig. 9, although FCN results could reach good performance, it may miss large part of human body as shown in red bounding boxes. When reducing the influences of background clutter, our method keeps the body parts as much as possible.

Table 2. Comparisons with other methods on Market-1501

Method	Rank-1	Rank-5	Rank-10	Rank-20	mAP
ResNet	0.7545	0.8881	0.9332	0.9581	0.5375
ResNet+PA	0.7696	0.9035	0.9320	0.9555	0.5422
PAN	0.8281	0.9353	0.9569	0.9706	0.6335
PAN+PA (Our method)	**0.8435**	**0.9347**	**0.9578**	**0.9712**	**0.6458**

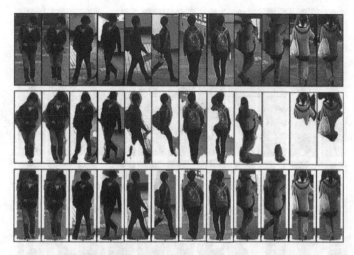

Fig. 9. Comparing results of segmentation between our method and FCN on CUHK01. The first row is the original images. The second row is the segmentation results of FCN, and the third row is ours.

In addition, more segmentation images are shown in Fig. 10.

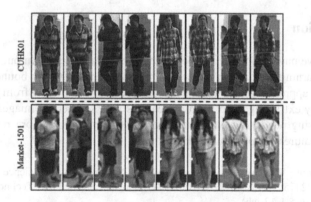

Fig. 10. Sample segmentation images on CUHK01 and Market-1501

In addition to the above quantified results, we highlight the performance in Fig. 11. It shows that our method is robust even when the background is complicated. For images with different light conditions and large differences of camera viewpoints, the Rank-1 matching rate is still need to be improved.

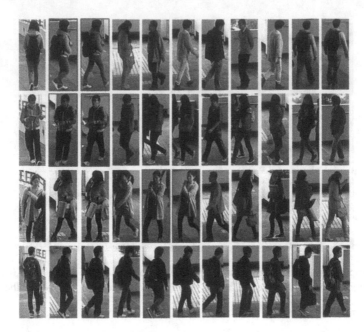

Fig. 11. Performance of our method. The first column is input images. The second column to the eleventh column is the Rank-10 results.

5   Conclusion

In this paper, we have proposed a novel method for person Re-ID. In our approach, we extract deep learning features on the person region instead of whole bounding box. We propose a new approach pose-aware that person region is extracted from the estimated pose region. By extracting deep learning features with segmented images, our method has got promising results. In our future work, we will explore more robust and distinguishable features for person Re-ID.

Acknowledgement. This work is supported by the National Natural Science Foundation of China (No. 61672475, No. 61402428, 61702471); Qingdao Science and Technology Development Plan (No. 16-5-1-13-jch).

References

1. Felzenszwalb, P.F., Girshick, R.B., McAllester, D., Ramanan, D.: Object detection with discriminatively trained part-based models. IEEE Trans. Pattern Anal. Mach. Intell. **32**, 1627–1645 (2010)
2. Zheng, W.S., Gong, S., Xiang, T.: Person re-identification by probabilistic relative distance comparison. In: Computer Vision and Pattern Recognition, pp. 649–656 (2011)

3. Li, A., Liu, L., Yan, S.: Person re-identification by attribute-assisted clothes appearance. In: Gong, S., Cristani, M., Yan, S., Loy, C.C. (eds.) Person Re-Identification. ACVPR, pp. 119–138. Springer, London (2014). https://doi.org/10.1007/978-1-4471-6296-4_6

4. Zheng, L., Huang, Y., Lu, H., Yang, Y.: Pose invariant embedding for deep person re-identification (2017)

5. Zhao, R., Ouyang, W., Wang, X.: Person re-identification by saliency learning. IEEE Trans. Pattern Anal. Mach. Intell. **39**, 356–370 (2016)

6. Chen, Y.C., Zhu, X., Zheng, W.S., Lai, J.H.: Person re-identification by camera correlation aware feature augmentation. IEEE Trans. Pattern Anal. Mach. Intell. **40**, 392–408 (2018)

7. Roth, P.M., Hirzer, M., Köstinger, M., Beleznai, C., Bischof, H.: Mahalanobis distance learning for person re-identification. In: Gong, S., Cristani, M., Yan, S., Loy, C.C. (eds.) Person Re-Identification. ACVPR, pp. 247–267. Springer, London (2014). https://doi.org/10.1007/978-1-4471-6296-4_12

8. Liao, S., Hu, Y., Zhu, X., Li, S.Z.: Person re-identification by local maximal occurrence representation and metric learning. In: 2015 IEEE Conference on Computer Vision and Pattern Recognition (CVPR), pp. 2197–2206 (2015)

9. Chen, Y., Zhao, C., Wang, X., Gao, C.: Robust color invariant model for person re-identification. In: You, Z., et al. (eds.) CCBR 2016. LNCS, vol. 9967, pp. 695–702. Springer, Cham (2016). https://doi.org/10.1007/978-3-319-46654-5_76

10. Wang, D., Yan, C., Shan, S., Chen, X.: Unsupervised person re-identification with locality-constrained Earth Mover's distance. In: IEEE International Conference on Image Processing, pp. 4289–4293 (2016)

11. Wang, Z., Hu, R., Liang, C., Leng, Q., Sun, K.: Region-based interactive ranking optimization for person re-identification. In: Ooi, W.T., Snoek, C.G.M., Tan, H.K., Ho, C.-K., Huet, B., Ngo, C.-W. (eds.) PCM 2014. LNCS, vol. 8879, pp. 1–10. Springer, Cham (2014). https://doi.org/10.1007/978-3-319-13168-9_1

12. Zhong, Z., Zheng, L., Cao, D., Li, S.: Re-ranking person re-identification with k-reciprocal encoding. In: IEEE Conference on Computer Vision and Pattern Recognition, pp. 3652–3661 (2017)

13. Yuan, M., et al.: A framework with updateable joint images re-ranking for Person Re-identification (2018)

14. Yu, R., Zhou, Z., Bai, S., Bai, X.: Divide and fuse: a re-ranking approach for person re-identification (2017)

15. Liu, X., Liu, W., Mei, T., Ma, H.: A deep learning-based approach to progressive vehicle re-identification for urban surveillance. In: Leibe, B., Matas, J., Sebe, N., Welling, M. (eds.) ECCV 2016. LNCS, vol. 9906, pp. 869–884. Springer, Cham (2016). https://doi.org/10.1007/978-3-319-46475-6_53

16. Liu, W., Mei, T., Zhang, Y., Che, C., Luo, J.: Multi-task deep visual-semantic embedding for video thumbnail selection. In: Computer Vision and Pattern Recognition, pp. 3707–3715 (2015)

17. Li, W., Zhao, R., Xiao, T., Wang, X.: DeepReID: deep filter pairing neural network for person re-identification. In: IEEE Conference on Computer Vision and Pattern Recognition, pp. 152–159 (2014)

18. Wang, F., Zuo, W., Lin, L., Zhang, D., Zhang, L.: Joint learning of single-image and cross-image representations for person re-identification. In: Computer Vision and Pattern Recognition, pp. 1288–1296 (2016)

19. Cheng, D., Gong, Y., Zhou, S., Wang, J., Zheng, N.: Person re-identification by multi-channel parts-based CNN with improved triplet loss function. In: 2016 IEEE Conference on Computer Vision and Pattern Recognition (CVPR), pp. 1335–1344 (2016)

20. Xiao, T., Li, S., Wang, B., Lin, L., Wang, X.: Joint detection and identification feature learning for person search (2016)
21. Zhao, H., et al.: Spindle net: person re-identification with human body region guided feature decomposition and fusion. In: Computer Vision and Pattern Recognition, pp. 907–915 (2017)
22. Lin, Y., Zheng, L., Zheng, Z., Wu, Y., Yang, Y.: Improving person re-identification by attribute and identity learning (2017)
23. Chen, W., Chen, X., Zhang, J., Huang, K.: Beyond triplet loss: a deep quadruplet network for person re-identification, pp. 1320–1329 (2017)
24. Li, W., Zhao, R., Wang, X.: Human reidentification with transferred metric learning. In: Lee, K.M., Matsushita, Y., Rehg, J.M., Hu, Z. (eds.) ACCV 2012. LNCS, vol. 7724, pp. 31–44. Springer, Heidelberg (2013). https://doi.org/10.1007/978-3-642-37331-2_3
25. Fan, H., Zheng, L., Yang, Y.: Unsupervised person re-identification: clustering and fine-tuning (2017)
26. He, K., Zhang, X., Ren, S., Sun, J.: Deep residual learning for image recognition. In: Computer Vision and Pattern Recognition, pp. 770–778 (2016)
27. Simonyan, K., Zisserman, A.: Very deep convolutional networks for large-scale image recognition. Comput. Sci. (2014)
28. Zheng, Z., Zheng, L., Yang, Y.: Pedestrian alignment network for large-scale person re-identification (2017)
29. Zheng, L., Shen, L., Tian, L., Wang, S., Wang, J., Tian, Q.: Scalable person re-identification: a benchmark. In: IEEE International Conference on Computer Vision, pp. 1116–1124 (2016)
30. Long, J., Shelhamer, E., Darrell, T.: Fully convolutional networks for semantic segmentation. In: IEEE Conference on Computer Vision and Pattern Recognition, pp. 3431–3440 (2015)

Neuropsychiatric Disorders Identification Using Convolutional Neural Network

Chih-Wei Lin[(⊠)] and Qilu Ding

College of Computer and Information Science,
Fujian Agriculture and Forestry University, Fuzhou, China
cwlin@fafu.edu.cn

Abstract. The neuropsychiatric disorders have become a high risk among the elderly group and their group of patients has the tendency of getting younger. However, an efficient computer-aided system with the computer vision technique to detect the neuropsychiatric disorders has not been developed yet. More specifically, there are two critical issues: (1) the postures between various neuropsychiatric disorders are similar, (2) lack of physiotherapists and expensive examinations. In this study, we design an innovative framework which associates a novel two-dimensional feature map with a convolutional neural network to identify the neuropsychiatric disorders. Firstly, we define the seven types of postures to generate the one-dimensional feature vectors (1D-FVs) which can efficiently describe the characteristics of neuropsychiatric disorders. To further consider the relationship between different features, we reshape the features from one-dimensional into two-dimensional to form the feature maps (2D-FMs) based on the periods of pace. Finally, we generate the identification model by associating the 2D-FMs with a convolutional neural network. To evaluate our work, we introduce a new dataset called Simulated Neuropsychiatric Disorders Dataset (SNDD) which contains three kinds of neuropsychiatric disorders and one healthy with 128 videos. In experiments, we evaluate the performance of 1D-FVs with classic classifiers and compare the performance with the gait anomaly feature vectors. In addition, extensive experiments conducting on the proposed novel framework which associates the 2D-FMs with a convolutional neural network is applied to identify the neuropsychiatric disorders.

Keywords: Neuropsychiatric disorder · Posture motion · Symptoms
Depth sensors · Convolutional neural network

1 Introduction

Aging population is a vital issue all over the world, it accompanies various diseases in which the neuropsychiatric disorders have the high incidence in the elderly people. Moreover, the group of patients who suffers from the neuropsychiatric disorders is getting younger in recent year. Neuropsychiatric disorders

© Springer Nature Switzerland AG 2019
I. Kompatsiaris et al. (Eds.): MMM 2019, LNCS 11296, pp. 315–327, 2019.
https://doi.org/10.1007/978-3-030-05716-9_26

identification is a difficult task because of the similarity of posture between different disorders. Therefore, it is an important issue to efficiently identify the neuropsychiatric disorders in the modern life.

In the medical study, the laboratorial inspection and medical images are widely used to detect and to distinguish the neuropsychiatric disorders. However, those inspections have the drawbacks of contact, intrusive, radioactivity, long inspection time or noisiness. Some studies consider to solve the problem of the neuropsychiatric disorders by analyzing the external behavior, because the external behavior between healthy and the people who suffer from neuropsychiatric disorders are different [5,14]. Those studies can be classified into marker-based system and markerless system. The marker-based system (MBS) sticks the marks on the different parts of the body and is firstly used to detect the 3D structure of the human body in the area of medicine. Although MBS can provide 3D structure information with high accuracy, it is an expensive equipment and needs the specific experimental environments. Recently, the markerless system, such as MS Kinect system, is used to extract the 3D skeleton with joints. MS Kinect system is a low-cost device for clinical and home-based rehabilitation, it is a useful assessment of disease symptoms. The markerless systems grab the physical characteristics of human to generate a model for the health status classification [7,13]. To verify the performance of markerless system (MS Kinect system) in the medical application, some researchers compare the MS Kinect system with various medical instruments, such as a Vicon motion system [3,15], and the marker-based system (MBS) [1], in different disorders. Moreover, researchers show that the markerless system is viable in 3D structure estimation because the accuracy and reliability of the marker-based and markerless systems are approximate [12]. Furthermore, some scholars utilize the data of 3D human motion, which is obtained from MS Kinect system to construct the rehabilitation or monitoring system for various neurological disorders [4,6,10]. Multiple sclerosis is also an important issue in medical, it can be treated by telerehabilitation with MS Kinect [9]. Although some studies consider neurological disorder with markerless system, only a few studies discuss the clinical diagnosis of neurological disorders [2,11]. The neuropsychiatric disorders can be identified from their posture, but they are imperceptible in their incipient stages and are difficult to distinguish from each other. Therefore, there has been much interest in providing the computer-aided system to assist the doctors.

The main contributions of this study are: (1) to design the discriminative feature vector in one-dimensional and two-dimensional (1D-FVs and 2D-FMs) which can efficiently describe the characteristics of different neuropsychiatric disorders and represent the relationship between various features; (2) to model the 2D-FMs with a convolutional neural network which can effectively identify the neuropsychiatric disorders.

2   Overview of the Proposed Framework

The proposed framework is designed to handle the problem of identifying the neuropsychiatric disorders as shown in Fig. 1. To identify various

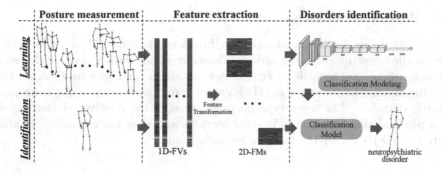

Fig. 1. The proposed framework for the neuropsychiatric disorders identification.

neuropsychiatric disorders, we firstly grab a number of posture patterns with various neuropsychiatric disorders which are observed by a depth sensor with multi-perspectives, and then we estimate the 3D skeletons of the body which include 25 joints as shown in Fig. 2 for each frame in the procedure of the posture measurement. Next, we consider the characteristics of various neuropsychiatric disorders and design the seven-type postures to generate the one-dimensional feature vectors (1D-FVs) for the representation of each disorder. After that, we further consider the relationship between different features and reshape the 1D-FVs from one-dimensional into two-dimensional to form the feature maps (2D-FMs) based on the periods of pace. Finally, to efficiently discriminate each neuropsychiatric disorder, we generate the identification model by associating 2D-FMs with a convolutional neural network.

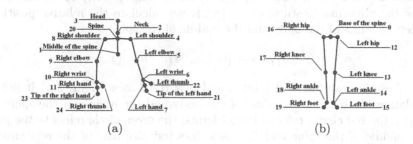

Fig. 2. Human skeleton and joints. (a) Upper part (b) Lower part.

3 Neuropsychiatric Disorders Identification

The proposed neuropsychiatric disorders identification method includes three parts: (1) posture feature extraction, (2) features transformation, (3) identification model generation.

3.1   Posture Features Extraction

We refer to the medical professional team, Stanford Medicine 25[1], which provides
the detailed description and wonderful demonstrations with videos, and design
the seven-type postures, $\Psi = \{\psi_1, ..., \psi_7\}$, as shown in Fig. 3 to generate the
one-dimensional feature vectors (1D-FVs) for the identification of the neuropsychiatric disorders. The seven-type postures consider the relative relationship of
each physical characteristic in posture motions and they are assembled to generate the 1D-FVs with 185 features for each frame.

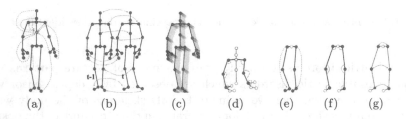

(a)   (b)   (c)   (d)   (e)   (f)   (g)

Fig. 3. Seven-type postures. (a) Type 1 (ψ_1), (b) Type 2 (ψ_2), (c) Type 3 (ψ_3), (d)
Type 4 (ψ_4), (e) Type 5 (ψ_5), (f) Type 6 (ψ_6), (g) Type 7 (ψ_7). (Color figure online)

Comparing the healthy groups with the people suffering from the studied
neuropsychiatric disorders, there are two obvious differences in motion: (1) the
walking speed, (2) the walking postures. Therefore, we design three types of postures according to the characteristics above: (1) the abnormal posture (ψ_1), (2)
the relative velocity of the object (ψ_2), (3) the average velocity of walking (ψ_3).
For the abnormal posture, $\psi_1 = \{\alpha_m^n\}$, we calculate the relative positions
between 24 joints of the body and the middle of the spine,

$$\alpha_i^n = J_i^n - J_1^n, \quad i = \{0, 2, .., 24\}, \quad n = \{x, y, z\} \tag{1}$$

where J_i is the coordinate at joint i, and n is the 3-axis. Figure 3(a) indicates
the relationship between 24 joints of the body and the middle of the spine. In
Fig. 3(a), the red circles refer to the 24 joints, the green circle refers to the joint
of the middle of the spine and the dash lines indicate part of the relationship
between the red and green circles. Using Eq. 1, we generate $24 \times 3 = 72$ features
for each frame. The relative velocity of each joint of the object, $\psi_2 = \{v_m^n\}$, is
generated by calculating the difference between current (t) and previous frames
($t-1$),

$$v_i^n = J_i^n(l) - J_i^n(l-1), \quad i = \{0, 1, .., 24\}, \quad n = \{x, y, z\} \tag{2}$$

where l is the frame number. Figure 3(b) shows the calculation of ψ_2. In Fig. 3(b),
the skeletons on the left and right sides are indicated as the current (t) and previous skeletons respectively, the red dash line indicates part of the relationship

---

[1]   http://stanfordmedicine25.stanford.edu/.

of each joint between previous and current frames. After using Eq. 2, we generate $25 \times 3 = 75$ features for each frame. The average velocity of walking (ψ_3) responses the level of speed of each object as shown in Fig. 3(c),

$$\psi_3 = D_z/N \tag{3}$$

where D_z is the walking distance of joint J_1 among z axis, and N is the total number of frames. The total number of features of those three types of symptoms is $72 + 75 + 1 = 148$.

The other types refer to the postures protrude from the upper body, such as the arm close to the body. We select the joints of the upper body to generate the 4th type of posture: (4) the angle and variance of the upper limb joints (ψ_4), as shown in Fig. 3(d). The 4th type of posture calculates the angles and variances of nine upper limb joints. The angle of each joint j is formulated as follows,

$$\cos\theta_j = \frac{\overrightarrow{J_{ij}}\overrightarrow{J_{jk}}}{|\overrightarrow{J_{ij}}||\overrightarrow{J_{jk}}|}, \quad j = \{4,5,6,8,9,10,20,21,23\} \tag{4}$$

$$\theta_j = \arccos(\cos\theta_j) \tag{5}$$

where $\overrightarrow{J_{ij}}$ and $\overrightarrow{J_{jk}}$ are the vectors between the joints i and j, and j and k, respectively. j is the current joint, and i and k are the former and after joints which are related to joint j. It can be calculated according to the following equation,

$$\overrightarrow{J_{ij}} = J_i - J_j \tag{6}$$

where J_i is the position of joint i. The variance is calculated according to the following equation,

$$\sigma_i = \frac{\sum_{i=1}^{N}(\theta_i - \overline{\theta_i})^2}{N} \tag{7}$$

where N is the number of frames, $\overline{\theta_i}$ is the average angle at joint i and θ_i is the angle of joint i. The joints which are considered to generate ψ_4 are indicated in Fig. 3(d) with the red dash line. The total number of features of the 4th type of posture is $6 + 6 = 12$.

The last three types focus on the lower body and consider the characteristics of the step width and the span of two legs. Those are (5) the average length of the lower limb (ψ_5), (6) the angles and variances of the lower limb on both sides (ψ_6), (7) the relative distance and relative position (ψ_7); the schematic are shown in Figs. 3(e), (f), and (g), respectively. The 5th type of posture, $\psi_5 = \gamma$, is calculated as follow,

$$\gamma = \frac{\sum_i \sum_n (J_i^n - J_{i+3}^n)^2}{2}, \quad i = \{12,16\}, \quad n = \{x,y,z\} \tag{8}$$

where J_i is the coordinate of the joints of the lower limb. In Fig. 3(e), the relationships are connected as red dash line. The total number of features of the 5th type of posture is 1. The 6th type of posture, ψ_6, is similar to the 4th type of posture and considers nine lower limb joints. Thus, we rewrite the Eqs. 4, 5, 6 and 7, with $j = \{0, 12, .., 15, 16, ..., 19\}$. Figure 3(f) shows the joints which are selected by red dash line to generate ψ_6. The total number of features of the 6th type of posture is $6 + 6 = 12$. In the 7th type of posture ($\psi_7 = \{\lambda_m^n, \chi_m\}$), we consider three combinations: (a) right hip and left hip, (b) right knee and left knee and, (c) right ankle and left ankle, and calculate the relative distance and relative position of each combination,

$$\lambda_i^n = J_i^n - J_{i+4}^n, \quad i = \{12, 13, 14\}, \quad n = \{x, y, z\} \tag{9}$$

$$\chi_i = \sum^n (J_i^n - J_{i+4}^n)^2, \{i = 12, 13, 14\}, n = \{x, y, z\} \tag{10}$$

where λ and χ are used to calculate the relative position and relative distance of each combination, respectively. Figure 3(g) indicates the corresponding joints between both legs. The total number of features of the 7th type of posture is $3 \times (3 + 1) = 12$. The total number of 1D-FVs is $72 + 75 + 1 + 12 + 1 + 12 + 12 = 185$ for each frame (skeleton).

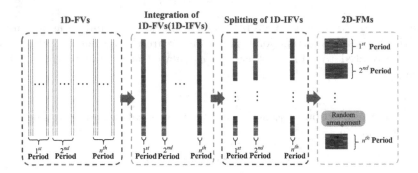

Fig. 4. The framework of generating the two-dimensional feature maps (2D-FMs). (Color figure online)

3.2 Feature Transformation (Two-dimensional Feature Maps, 2D-FMs)

Since the posture is an action of a series sequence, the relationships between frames along time have to be considered. Therefore, we consider the relationship between the features in the same frame and the relationship between the features in the sequence to generate the two-dimensional feature maps (2D-FMs).

Figure 4 demonstrates the procedure of the two-dimensional feature maps (2D-FMs) generation. First, we obtain the 1D-FVs with 185 features for each frame from Subsect. 3.1. Then, we take the 1D-FVs of each frame in a period of pace and arrange these features randomly to form the two-dimensional feature maps (2D-FMs), as shown in the middle of Fig. 4. In this phase, we consider the relationship of the extracted features in the timeline by taking the features in a period of pace. Moreover, we discuss the relationship of various features at different joints by randomly arranging the features to form the two-dimensional feature maps. In our study, we generate 185 features for each frame and take 10 frames for a period to create an initial two-dimensional feature map with the size of 185 × 10. The aspect ratio of the initial two-dimensional feature map is 18.5 which affects the generation of modeling. Therefore, we split the initial two-dimensional feature map with size of 185 × 10 into k parts along the vertical direction (the process marked with purple in the Fig. 4) and stitch each divided part along the horizontal direction to generate the two-dimensional feature maps (2D-FMs) (the process marked with yellow) in the Fig. 4.

3.3 Model Architecture

The convolutional neural network is a popular technique in machine learning and is widely used in image classification. There are numerous of frameworks of the deep neural network, such as AlexNet, VGGNet, GooLeNet, and ResNet, which are proposed for classification. In this paper, we aim at proving the feasibility of the proposed method which associated the 2D-FMs with the convolutional neural network. Therefore, we adopt the AlexNet, which is the classic convolutional neural network, as the deep neural network in this study.

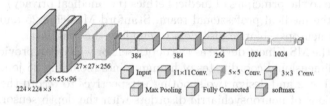

Fig. 5. Network architecture.

Figure 5 demonstrates the network architecture of AlexNet. There are eight layers including five convolutional layers and three full connection layers. We operate 96 convolutional kernels with 11 × 11 convolutional size and move with stride 4 for an input image to generate the feature maps of the first convolutional layer. The first convolution layer has 96 feature maps and each feature map has size 55 × 55. Then, we operate the max pooling operation to downsample and generate 96 feature maps with size 27 × 27. To generate the feature maps of the second convolutional layer, 256 convolutional kernels with size 5 × 5 are used and that move with stride 1. The second layer has 256 feature maps with 27 × 27, and be downsampled into the size of 13 × 13. The third and fourth layers have 384 feature maps with size 13 × 13 which are operated with 384 convolutional kernels with size 3 × 3 and move with stride 1. The fifth layer has 256 feature maps with the size of 13 × 13 which are generated by 256 convolutional kernels with the size of 3 × 3 and move with stride 1 on the feature maps of the fourth layer. The max pooling is operated on the feature maps of the fifth before the fully connected layer and generates 256 feature maps with size 6×6. The sixth and seventh layers are fully connected layers which have 4096 neurons, respectively. The eighth layer considers the softmax function to classify.

It should be noted that we abandon the process of the local response normalization (LRN) in this framework because LRN is not useful for classification and increase the computational cost.

4   Experimentals

In this section, we first describe the dataset which is used in this study. Then, we demonstrate the performance of the proposed 1D-FVs with popular classifiers. Finally, we represent the proposed framework which associates 2D-FMs with the convolutional neural network.

4.1   Experimental Dataset

In this study, three types of important neuropsychiatric disorders in the elderly are selected for analyzing including Parkinson, hemiplegia, and diplegia. The realistic data which is obtained from the people who suffering from the illness is the ideal resource for analyzing disorders; however, it is difficult to collect the real data due to the principles of medical ethics (i.e. medical privacy). Therefore, we refer to the medical professional team, Stanford Medicine 25 and construct the spurious neuropsychiatric disorders to emulate the real data.

We take the MS Kinect device as the depth sensor which can provide the real-time three-dimensional coordinates of human joints including 25 joint positions as shown in Fig. 2 and design two shooting perspectives to record the simulated posture motions of neuropsychiatric disorders with the depth sensor, as shown in Fig. 6. For the first shooting perspective, we set the depth sensor 1 m from the floor and the axis of the camera lens is perpendicular to the floor, as shown in Fig. 6(a). The other perspective of depth sensor is set 0.45 m from the floor and set the camera with 27° elevation angle, as shown in Fig. 6(b).

We select sixteen people including 8 males and 8 females, with an average height of 165 cm for females and 173 cm for males. Each person performs the studied postures including Parkinson, hemiplegia, diplegia, and normal posture,

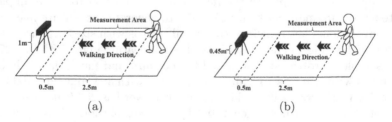

Fig. 6. Two shooting perspectives. (a) frontal view (b) upward view.

and generate four videos for studying disorders. In total, we collect $4 \times 16 \times 2 = 128$ videos for analyzing. To enhance readability, We sequentially numbered healthy, Parkinson, hemiplegia, and diplegia as 1, 2, 3, and 4 for the following experiments.

4.2 Experiments of 1D-FVs

In this section, we first demonstrate the feasibility of 1D-FVs by using the popular classifiers on the proposed datasets. Then, we present the performance of the 1D-FVs by comparing with the gait anomaly feature vectors (GFVs) [8]. There are $4 \times 16 = 64$ videos for each perspective view (front view and upward view) and they are used for the comparison based on 8-fold cross-validation. For each cross-validation, we randomly take two videos as testing videos and ensure each video is tested once.

We associate the 1D-FVs with two popular classifiers, support vector machine (SVM) and random forest (RF), to demonstrate the feasibility of the proposed features. In this experiment, the classifiers are trained and tested by using the same perspective view data. For example, if we want to evaluate the performance of 1D-FVs in frontal view, then we construct a classifier which is trained and tested by using the frontal view data of 1D-FVs.

Table 1 demonstrate the cross-validation results of 1D-FVs on frontal, upward and mixed view datasets with various classifiers, respectively. In Table 1, the average accuracy of 1D-FVs with both classifiers on frontal view datasets is more than 80%, in which the RF classifier has highest average accuracy and achieves 85.90%. In Table 1, the average accuracies of 1D-FVs by using RF and SVM classifiers on the upward view dataset are 79.78% and 75.52%, respectively. The average accuracies of 1D-FVs by using both classifiers on the upward view dataset are lower than those on the frontal view dataset. From Table 1, the perspective of capturing is an issue which affects the acquisition of joints information. When the height of the center of the camera is close to the center of gravity of the patient, it can obtain the most abundant joints information. In addition, the accuracy of Round-2 in Table 1 is the lowest on both classifiers, because it verifies the extreme instances in our experiments including people has overweight and overheight. Moreover, we analyze the performance of the 1D-FVs on the mixture dataset which mixes the frontal and upward view datasets. In

Table 1. The comparative results for identifying the neuropsychiatric disorders identification using 8-folds cross-validation test.

Dataset	Classifiers	Round-1	Round-2	Round-3	Round-4	Round-5	Round-6	Round-7	Round-8	Average
Frontal view	RF	95.61	73.10	94.32	89.30	98.41	79.73	78.78	77.98	85.90
	SVM	99.51	68.84	81.00	92.47	96.88	76.68	78.12	74.85	83.54
Upward view	RF	73.29	53.29	99.78	93.89	87.03	72.00	78.55	80.37	79.78
	SVM	87.97	53.49	85.61	86.14	81.22	72.99	62.30	74.46	75.52
Mixed view	RF	91.47	61.55	91.42	97.31	83.86	86.08	77.38	76.98	83.26
	SVM	90.76	52.02	88.05	89.86	89.55	79.17	70.22	72.76	79.05

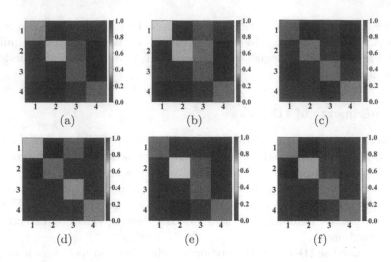

Fig. 7. Confusion matrix of neuropsychiatric disorders identification. (a) frontal view with RF, (b) frontal view with SVM, (c) upward view with RF, (d) upward view with SVM, (e) mixed view with RF, (f) mixed view with SVM

Table 1, the highest average accuracy on the mixture dataset is 83.26% which is higher than the average accuracy on the upward view dataset, but lower than the average accuracy on the frontal view dataset.

Figure 7, demonstrates the results of neuropsychiatric disorders identification in the form of confusion matrix. In Fig. 7, the performance of using the 1D-FVs to identify hemiplegia and diplegia on the frontal view dataset are better than on the upward view dataset in both classifiers, as shown in Figs. 7(a), (b), (c) and (d), respectively. The postures of hemiplegia and diplegia are similar but have obvious differences between the lower part of the body. However, the upward view focuses on the upper part of the body, the performance of using 1D-FVs to identify those disorders is low. To compare the results with using the frontal view dataset alone, the 1D-FVs performs well in identifying normal posture and Parkinson on mixed view dataset as shown in Figs. 7(e) and (f). However, the 1D-FVs performs well in identifying hemiplegia and diplegia on the frontal dataset. The differences are: (1) the characteristics of normal postures and Parkinson focus on the upper part of the body, (2) the characteristics of hemiplegia and diplegia focus on the lower part of the body.

Moreover, we present the performance of the 1D-FVs by comparing with the GFVs, as shown in Table 2. In Table 2, 1D-FVs and GFVs are associated with RF classifier, the accuracies of the 1D-FVs are the highest among all the datasets. Although GFVs considers the information of the relative position, the relative velocity, the angle of each joint, and the feature number of GFVs is five times that of 1D-FVs, the characteristics of the neuropsychiatric disorders are lost. The GFVs have a lot of features including the useless, and weak features, which reduce the classification accuracy.

Table 2. Quantitative comparison results

Features	Datasets		
	Frontal view	Upward view	Mixed view
GFVs	81.06	77.49	80.87
1D-FVs	85.90	79.78	83.26

Table 3. The results of two-dimensional feature map on mixed view dataset

Features	Round-1	Round-2	Round-3	Round-4	Round-5	Average
2D-GFVs	70.50	65.00	73.50	52.50	60.00	64.30
2D-FMs	94.00	96.00	94.00	93.00	92.50	93.90

In summary, the performance of the 1D-FVs associated with RF is better than SVM and the average accuracy remains more than 80%. Those perspectives focus on different part of the body and provide the various degree of strength of joints information. The frontal view provides the complete joints information of entire body, the upward view enhance the joints information of the upper part of the body but lose the joints information of the lower part of the body. The classification results by using the popular classifiers are affected by the quality of the data. Therefore, we alter the form of the extracted feature from one-dimensional into two dimensional and associate with the power machine learning approach to improve the performance of the neuropsychiatric disorders identification.

4.3   Experiments of 2D-FMs on Convolutional Neural Network

To train the convolutional neural network for neuropsychiatric disorders identification, there are several processes that need to be considered. Firstly, to reduce the overfitting during the training stage, we apply augmentation process to increase the dataset. The image augmentation includes affine transformation, simple image rotations, and image blur. Secondly, the images which include the original and augmented images are resized into 224 × 224 pixels in both training and testing processes. Thirdly, we randomly select four people with their videos as testing data and take the rest of videos as training data. And then, the parameters of AlexNet including batch, learning rate, epoch, and dropout are set as 64, 0.0001, 300, and 0.5, respectively.

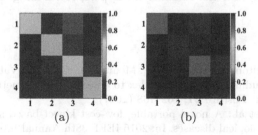

Fig. 8. Confusion matrix of neuropsychiatric disorders identification. (a) mixed view with 2D-GFVs, (b) mixed view with 2D-FMs

To discuss the spatial relationship between different features and to verify the stability of the proposed two-dimensional feature maps, we randomly arrange the features from 1D-FVs to from the two-dimensional feature maps (2D-FMs). Moreover, to demonstrate the performance of 2D-FMs, we compare 2D-FMs with two-dimensional gait anomaly feature vectors (2D-GFVs) on mixed view dataset by using the convolutional neural network (CNN). We produce five sets of experiments, each with a randomly arranged two-dimensional feature maps and the comparison results are shown in Table 3. In Table 3, 2D-FMs has the high and stable results and has the best results compared with 2D-GFVs at each set of experiment. In addition, Fig. 8 demonstrates the confusion matrix of 2D-GFVs and that of 2D-FMs with mixed view dataset, respectively. In Fig. 8, the identification accuracy of 2D-FMs by using CNN in different symptoms is higher than 2D-GFVs. Comparing the results of 2D-FMs with 1D-FVs, the performance of 2D-FMs with CNN is better than 1D-FVs with RF classifier. The 1D-FVs is designed by considering the obvious characteristics of neuropsychiatric disorders and the 2D-FMs further consider the spatial characteristics of different features.

5   Conclusion

In this paper, we propose a new framework to address the problem of identifying the neuropsychiatric disorders. To effectively describe the characteristics of the disorders, we design the seven-type postures which generate the discriminative 1D-FVs with 185 features for each frame. The 1D-FVs represents the posture motions of the full body by considering the relative relationship of each physical characteristic. To further consider the relationship between features, we transform the 1D-FVs into 2D-FMs. We associate the CNN to extract the relationships between various features from the 2D-FMs. To compare with the 1D-GFVs and 2D-GFVs, the effectiveness of the 1D-FVs and 2D-FMs is demonstrated in experiments. Although we take the emulated data for analysis, there are two main contributions of this study: (1) the features of each neuropsychiatric disorder are discussed and designed, (2) successfully combine the neuropsychiatric disorder identification with a convolutional neural network.

In the future, we attempt to test our framework on the real data of neuropsychiatric disorders and further consider the hyperspectral image for identification.

References

1. Auvinet, E., Multon, F., Manning, V., Meunier, J., Cobb, J.: Validity and sensitivity of the longitudinal asymmetry index to detect gait asymmetry using microsoft kinect data. Gait Posture **51**, 162–168 (2017)
2. Cunha, J.P.S., et al.: A novel portable, low-cost kinect-based system for motion analysis in neurological diseases. In: 2016 IEEE 38th Annual International Conference of the Engineering in Medicine and Biology Society (EMBC), pp. 2339–2342. IEEE (2016)

3. Galna, B., Barry, G., Jackson, D., Mhiripiri, D., Olivier, P., Rochester, L.: Accuracy of the microsoft kinect sensor for measuring movement in people with parkinson's disease. Gait Posture **39**(4), 1062–1068 (2014)

4. Galna, B., et al.: Retraining function in people with parkinsons disease using the microsoft kinect: game design and pilot testing. J. Neuroeng. Rehabi. **11**(1), 60 (2014)

5. Gehlsen, G., Beekman, K., Assmann, N., Winant, D., Seidle, M., Carter, A.: Gait characteristics in multiple sclerosis: progressive changes and effects of exercise on parameters. Arch. Phys. Med. Rehabil. **67**(8), 536–539 (1986)

6. González-Ortega, D., Díaz-Pernas, F., Martínez-Zarzuela, M., Antón-Rodríguez, M.: A kinect-based system for cognitive rehabilitation exercises monitoring. Comput. Methods Programs Biomed. **113**(2), 620–631 (2014)

7. Higashiguchi, T., Shimoyama, T., Ukita, N., Kanbara, M., Hagita, N.: Lesioned-part identification by classifying entire-body gait motions. In: Bräunl, T., McCane, B., Rivera, M., Yu, X. (eds.) PSIVT 2015. LNCS, vol. 9431, pp. 136–147. Springer, Cham (2016). https://doi.org/10.1007/978-3-319-29451-3_12

8. Higashiguchi, T., Shimoyama, T., Ukita, N., Kanbara, M., Hagita, N.: Classification of gait anomaly due to lesion using full-body gait motions. IEICE Trans. Inf. Syst. **100**(4), 874–881 (2017)

9. Ortiz-Gutiérrez, R., Cano-de-la Cuerda, R., Galán-del Río, F., Alguacil-Diego, I.M., Palacios-Ceña, D., Miangolarra-Page, J.C.: A telerehabilitation program improves postural control in multiple sclerosis patients: a spanish preliminary study. Int. J. Environ. Res. Publ. Health **10**(11), 5697–5710 (2013)

10. Pompeu, J., et al.: Feasibility, safety and outcomes of playing kinect adventures! for people with parkinson's disease: a pilot study. Physiotherapy **100**(2), 162–168 (2014)

11. Procházka, A., Schätz, M., Tupa, O., Yadollahi, M., Vysata, O., Walls, M.: The MS kinect image and depth sensors use for gait features detection. In: 2014 IEEE International Conference on Image Processing (ICIP), pp. 2271–2274. IEEE (2014)

12. Schmitz, A., Ye, M., Shapiro, R., Yang, R., Noehren, B.: Accuracy and repeatability of joint angles measured using a single camera markerless motion capture system. J. Biomech. **47**(2), 587–591 (2014)

13. Snijders, A.H., Van De Warrenburg, B.P., Giladi, N., Bloem, B.R.: Neurological gait disorders in elderly people: clinical approach and classification. Lancet Neurol. **6**(1), 63–74 (2007)

14. Stolze, H., et al.: Typical features of cerebellar ataxic gait. J. Neurol. Neurosurg. Psychiatry **73**(3), 310–312 (2002)

15. Yeung, L., Cheng, K.C., Fong, C., Lee, W.C., Tong, K.Y.: Evaluation of the microsoft kinect as a clinical assessment tool of body sway. Gait Posture **40**(4), 532–538 (2014)

Semantic Map Annotation Through UAV Video Analysis Using Deep Learning Models in ROS

Efstratios Kakaletsis, Maria Tzelepi, Pantelis I. Kaplanoglou,
Charalampos Symeonidis, Nikos Nikolaidis[(⊠)], Anastasios Tefas,
and Ioannis Pitas

Aristotle University of Thessaloniki, Thessaloniki, Greece
{nikolaid,tefas,pitas}@aiia.csd.auth.gr

Abstract. Enriching the map of the flight environment with semantic knowledge is a common need for several UAV applications. Safety legislations require no-fly zones near crowded areas that can be indicated by semantic annotations on a geometric map. This work proposes an automatic annotation of 3D maps with crowded areas, by projecting 2D annotations that are derived through visual analysis of UAV video frames. To this aim, a fully convolutional neural network is proposed, in order to comply with the computational restrictions of the application, that can effectively distinguish between crowded and non-crowded scenes based on a regularized multiple-loss training method, and provide semantic heatmaps that are projected on the 3D occupancy grid of Octomap. The projection is based on raycasting and leads to polygonal areas that are geo-localized on the map and could be exported in KML format. Initial qualitative evaluation using both synthetic and real world drone scenes, proves the applicability of the method.

Keywords: Drone imaging · Crowd detection · Deep learning
FCNN · Semantic mapping · Octomap · ROS

1 Introduction

A 3D map of the UAV flight environment with annotated regions that relate to safety, such as crowd gathering locations or no-fly zones in general, is crucial for drone path planning and navigation. Recently, imposed legislations for drones, forbid the flight in vicinity of crowds, for drone flight safety purposes.

The research leading to these results has received funding from the European Unions Horizon 2020 research and innovation programme under grant agreement number 731667 (MULTIDRONE). This publication reflects only the authors views. The European Union is not liable for any use that may be made of the information contained therein.

© Springer Nature Switzerland AG 2019
I. Kompatsiaris et al. (Eds.): MMM 2019, LNCS 11296, pp. 328–340, 2019.
https://doi.org/10.1007/978-3-030-05716-9_27

For example, the drone flight regulation rules for UK[1] define that drones should not be flown within 50 m of people and within 150 m of a crowd of over 1000 people, while in Italy[2] it is not allowed for the drone to operate at a distance less than 50 m of human crowds. Therefore, it is crucial for the drone to be capable of detecting crowds in order to define no-fly zones and proceed to re-planning during the flying operation. Towards this end, in this work we utilize deep Convolutional Neural Networks (CNN) [13]. In particular, we propose a fully convolutional architecture in order to comply with the computational limitations of the application.

During the recent years deep CNNs, have been established as one of the most efficient Deep Learning architectures in computer vision, accomplishing outstanding results in a plethora of computer vision tasks. More specifically, deep CNNs have been successfully applied in image classification [25], object detection [14], semantic segmentation [7], image retrieval [28], and pose estimation [26]. The main reasons behind their success are the availability of large annotated datasets, and the GPUs computational power and affordability.

Thus, in this paper we propose a fully convolutional neural model for crowd detection in drone-captured high-definition (HD) video frames. The fully convolutional nature of the model is crucial in handling input images with arbitrary dimension, and estimating pixel-level probability heatmaps, which in turn are projected on the 3D occupancy grid of Octomap [10]. The projection is based on raycasting and leads to polygonal areas that are geo-localized on the map and could be exported in Keyhole Markup Language (KML) format. Finally, a primary contribution of this paper is a reusable software architecture for Robotic Operating System (ROS) [20] and the implementation of a system that annotates maps with regions of crowd, that are recognized in video frames. That is, utilizing the generated heatmaps we describe the task of map projection that uses the heatmaps together with other sensor data that constitute the set of extrinsic and intrinsic camera parameters for the scene. The detection can be performed offline or during the flight depending on the architecture of the drone and the wireless network connectivity. The prototype implementation of our system demonstrates its applicability for annotating maps with regions of human crowds and exporting them in KML format, used by Google Earth API [9].

The main contributions of this work can be summarized as follows:

- We propose a lightweight fully convolutional model for crowd detection towards drone flight safety
- We propose a generic multiple-loss regularized training method in deep CNNs
- We propose a method that implements the projection of the crowded heatmaps, derived from the crowd detection convolutional model, onto the 3D occupancy grid of Octomap.
- We propose a software architecture for ROS and the implementation of a system that annotates maps with regions of semantic classes (i.e. crowded scene)

---

[1] http://publicapps.caa.co.uk/docs/33/CAP393_E5A3_MAR2018(p).pdf.

[2] https://www.enac.gov.it/repository/ContentManagement/information/
N1220929004/Regulation_RPAS_Issue_2_Rev2_eng.pdf.

The remainder of the manuscript is structured as follows. In Sect. 1.1, related work is described. In Sect. 2, we propose the crowd detection method for drone flight safety and in Sect. 3 we describe the proposed system architecture that implements the UAV mapping. In Sect. 4, we describe the acquisition of drone data and present results of our crowd detection scenario in both synthetic and real-world drone imagery. Conclusions follow.

1.1 Related Work

Although several works utilize deep CNNs for crowd analysis and understanding, e.g. [2, 3, 24], research in the topic of crowd detection is rather limited. Furthermore, to the best of our knowledge, crowd detection in drone-captured images, which bears additional challenges (e.g. small person size, occlusions etc.), is an uncharted territory. Since the crowd first needs to be detected, this emphasizes the demand for algorithms capable of efficiently distinguishing between crowded and non-crowded scenes in drone-captured images. A first attempt utilizing state-of-art deep CNNs is presented in [27], where a pretrained model is finetuned for the task of crowd detection.

As we negotiate about flying robots, namely UAVs, in the last years, several approaches have been followed to augment topological maps [21] with semantic information [29], [6], allowing robots to reason about more expressive concepts and to execute more sophisticated tasks. The goal of these techniques is to learn how to split the environment into regions that have a coherent semantic meaning to humans. The combination of semantics with topology is an important step towards closing the gap between the traditional robotic representation of the world and human cognitive maps, making it easier for robots and humans to communicate and cooperate. Recently, the focus of the robotics community has shifted towards semantic representations [15, 16, 19] and object relation modeling in semantic maps [1, 17, 18] to develop autonomous interactive robots that are capable of understanding the semantics and relationships between the objects in the environment, besides exploiting occupancy grid maps for navigation.

2   Proposed Crowd Detection Model

In this work, we propose a crowd detection method for drone flight safety, using deep CNNs. A main focus is to provide a lightweight CNN model, which, satisfying the computational and memory limitations of our application, can distinguish between crowded and non-crowded scenes, in drone-captured images. To achieve this goal, a fully convolutional model is proposed. The fully convolutional nature of the model is crucial in handling input images with arbitrary dimension, and estimating a heatmap of the probability of crowd existence in each location of the input image, that can be used to semantically augment the flying zones. Furthermore, this will allow for handling low computational and memory resources on-drone whenever other processes occur (*e.g.*, re-planning, SLAM, etc.), and only low-dimensional images can be processed on the fly for crowd avoidance.

We should also note that the fully convolutional architectures are accompanied by a series of benefits. For example, the convolutional neural layers preserve spatial information due to the spatial arrangement of the activations, as opposed to the fully connected layers that discard it since they are connected to all the input neurons. That is, the convolutional layers inherently produce feature maps with spatial information. Additionally, an architecture without fully connected layers drastically decreases the amount of the model parameters, and therefore the computational cost is restricted, since the fully connected layers of deep CNNs usually occupy the most of the model parameters. For example, in VGG the fully connected layers comprise 102M parameters out of a total of 138M parameters. Finally, we should note that state-of-the-art object detectors, like SSD, also use fully convolutional architectures.

2.1 CNN Architecture

The proposed CNN model contains six learned convolutional layers. The network accepts RGB images of size $128 \times 128 \times 3$. The output of the last convolutional layer is fed to a Softmax layer which produces a distribution over the 2 classes of *Crowd* and *Non-Crowd*. Each convolutional layer except for the last one is followed by a Parametric Rectified Linear Unit (PReLU) activation layer which learns the parameters of the rectifiers, since it has been proven to enhance the classification performance, while max-pooling layers follow the first and the fifth convolutional layers.

2.2 Multiple-Loss Training

In order to enhance the generalization ability of the proposed crowd detection model, we propose a multiple-loss training method. That is, motivated by the Linear Discriminant Analysis (LDA) method, which aims at best separating samples of different classes, by projecting them into a new low-dimensional space, which maximizes the between-class separability while minimizing their within-class variability, we also propose a new model architecture. The new model, apart from the softmax loss layer which preserves the between class separability, includes an additional loss layer that aims to bring the samples of the same class closer to each other.

That is, considering a labeled representation $\mathbf{z}_i$, we aim to minimize the squared distance between $\mathbf{z}_i$ and the mean representation of its class.

Let $\mathcal{I} = \{\mathbf{I}_i, i = 1, \ldots, N\}$ be the set of N images of the training set, $\mathcal{Z} = \{\mathbf{z}_i, i = 1, \ldots, N\}$ the set of N feature representations emerged in a certain layer of a deep neural model, and $\mathcal{C}^i = \{\mathbf{c}_k, k = 1, \ldots, K^i\}$ the set of K^i representations of the i-th image, belonging to the same class. We compute the mean vector of the K^i representations of $\mathcal{C}^i$ to the image representation $\mathbf{z}_i$, and we denote it by $\boldsymbol{\mu}_c^i$. That is, $\boldsymbol{\mu}_c^i = \frac{1}{K^i} \sum_k \mathbf{c}_k$.

Then our goal is defined by the following optimization problem:

$$\min_{\mathbf{z}_i \in \mathcal{Z}} \mathcal{J} = \min_{\mathbf{z}_i \in \mathcal{Z}} \sum_{i=1}^{N} \|\mathbf{z}_i - \boldsymbol{\mu}_c^i\|_2^2, \tag{1}$$

The Euclidean Loss (Sum of Squares) is utilized for implementing the additional formulated regression task in Eq. (1). We should note that the additional Euclidean Loss layer can be attached, either to a certain convolutional layer (e.g. last one) or to multiple layers. The proposed multiple-loss training method can be considered as an extra regularization layer that exploits information from the data samples that are relevant to the input image. Generally, multitask-learning [4] constitutes a way of improving the generalization performance of a model. Furthermore, the proposed regularization technique can be applied for generic classification purposes, and also in various deep architectures, which is of utmost importance since deep neural networks are prone to over-fitting due to their high capacity.

2.3   Crowd-Drone Dataset

Since there is no publicly available crowd dataset of drone-captured videos and images, we have constructed a *Crowd-Drone* dataset. The new dataset has been created by querying with specific keywords the Youtube video search engine. More specifically, we collected 57 drone videos using keywords that describe crowded events (*e.g.* marathon, festival, parade, political rally, protests, etc). We also selected non-crowded videos by searching for generic drone videos. Non-crowd images (e.g. cars, buildings, bikes, etc.) were also randomly gathered from the senseFly-Example-drone[3] and the UAV123[4] datasets. Subsequently, we manually annotated crowded regions from the extracted frames. A total number of 5,920 crowded regions and an equal number of non-crowded images formulated the *Crowd-Drone* dataset. Sample regions of crowded and non-crowded scenes are shown in Fig. 1.

Fig. 1. Sample regions of the *Crowd-Drone* dataset.

We have trained the proposed crowd detection model on the aforementioned dataset utilizing the proposed multiple-loss regularized training method on all the convolutional layers of the model.

---

[3] https://www.sensefly.com/drones/example-datasets.html.
[4] https://ivul.kaust.edu.sa/Pages/Dataset-UAV123.aspx.

3 Proposed System Architecture

3.1 Architecture Overview

The proposed ROS-based architecture (Fig. 2) that implements the UAV mapping is based on image analysis and consists of the Visual Semantics Analyser, Semantic Map Region Projector and the Semantic Map Manager that are described below.

For each drone a video stream from an on-board camera is published into ROS as a sequence of consecutive ROS image messages, each one corresponding to a grabbed video frame. During flight these messages are transmitted over a wireless network to the processing server which runs our software. Our system requires additional ROS messages for sensor data for the projection into the three-dimensional space of the flight environment. These include the position of the vehicle that is provided by the GPS sensor and pose of the gimbal on which the camera is mounted from the corresponding MCU and camera intrinsic parameters from the camera controller, e.g. the focal length of each input frame. In case of drones that are designed for ROS, these data are published as messages by specialized nodes that run on-board. In scenarios without ROS, sensor data can be received through other media and are published as ROS messages by our software.

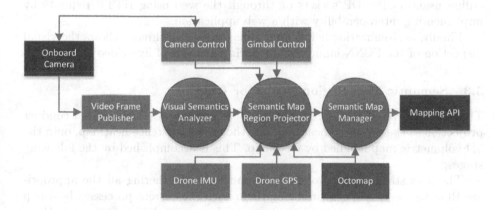

Fig. 2. Outline of the proposed system architecture.

3.2 Visual Semantics Analyzer (VSA)

The Visual Semantics Analyzer receives a single frame that belongs to a video sequence and provides an output in the form of numerical 2D annotations for each input pixel. The values can be either class identifiers (labels) or probabilities for occurrence of a specific class that can be subsequently thresholded for its discrimination. It subscribes to a multiple number of ROS topics and publishes an equal number of output topics. Each incoming ROS image message is tagged with an ID of its origin, e.g. 1 to indicate a frame from drone 1, and placed at a processing queue.

This part of the system uses the deep neural networks to analyze the incoming video frames and derive their visual semantics. Using an enlarged input size, compared to that of training, expands the single class prediction into a heatmap that contains a probability for each patch of the input image. The neural network expects input image with square dimensions and the source frame resolution is 1920×1080 pixels, thus the vertical dimension is padded with zeros and the input size is set to 1920×1920. The spatial dimensions of the FCNN's output activation tensor are significantly smaller due to down-sampling performed by max-pooling layers. It is resized to 1920×1920 using linear interpolation and then cropped to the original input size, providing pixel-level probabilities for the existence of crowds. The numerical annotations of the scene semantics are published as ROS image messages keeping the same timestamp with the source frame.

In addition, a compatibility layer was designed so that any UAV platform or synthetic data can be used with our system. Given a record of sensor data from the same moment in time it publishes messages in three topics that are required for 3D projection. The drone telemetry message contains the GPS coordinates provided by the onboard GPS. If the camera is mounted on a gimbal, a set of pitch, roll, yaw is published as gimbal status. The width and height of the camera sensor and the focal length in millimeters are published in ROS as the camera status. The data can be received offline in the form of a log or data file, online using TCP/UDP sockets or through the web using HTTP requests by implementing interoperability with a web application.

Finally, a visualization helper that runs on its own thread, allows the visual inspection of the FCNN input/output during analysis of live video streams.

3.3   Semantic Map Region Projector (SRP)

The Semantic Map Region Projector (SRP) comprises the processes that conduct projection of the produced heatmap, e.g. the crowd existence heatmap, onto the 3D volumetric map handled by Octomap. This is accomplished by the following stages:

The first stage of the process is responsible of gathering all the appropriate ROS messages and synchronizing them with the current processed heatmap based on their accompanying timestamps. The sensor data contained in these messages must be synchronized so that the camera extrinsic and intrinsic parameters match the moment that the frame was captured. These data include the drone position, gimbal orientation and camera intrinsic parameters that may vary like focal length. By applying thresholding on the heatmap in order to retain only image locations with high probabilities of crowd existence, we convert the image into a binary image where groups of adjacent pixels with value 1 (white) represent 2D regions occupied by crowd. Next we apply a contour following algorithm in order to find the contours of this image, resulting in a new binary image indicating the boundaries (white pixels) of the aforementioned crowd regions 2D polygons. If needed, the polylines are simplified maintaining their shape according to the Ramer-Douglas-Peucker algorithm [5], which takes a curve composed of line segments and finds a similar one with fewer points.

By traversing the points (pixels) of the regions' boundaries in a counter clockwise manner, we conduct ray casting [8,22]. More specifically, this contour image lies on the focal plane of the drone camera, for which we know the following parameters: (a) the location of the center of projection (COP) in the 3D world (derived from the drone location), (b) the camera orientation (derived from the gimbal state) (c) the distance of the focal plane from the COP (the camera focal length). Thus one can cast a ray from each of the boundary contour points towards the voxels of the Octomap. This results in finding the occupied voxel hit by each ray, leading to the evaluation of the X, Y, Z terrain coordinates where each of the contours' points is projected, as the Octomap is coordinates-referenced. Since the 2D boundary contour points are traversed sequentially, so are the points of the 3D boundary contour (polyline).

3.4 Semantic Map Manager (SMM)

The final stage of our pipeline is the Semantic Map Manager whose functionality can be summarized as follows: Firstly, the polygonal lines are fused and delineate crowd gathering locations (see Sect. 2) on the 3D map. As the drone moves, and its camera sees new areas of the terrain, the newly generated polygonal lines are merged with previous ones using the union operator.

Subsequently, the constantly updated geometric annotations are stored in an internal data layer as ROS messages that will be exported as KML files. These will be used for drone navigation and control purposes as well as for visual inspection by the flight/safety personnel. The KML is a file format used to display geographic data and to overlay annotations on a map such as Google Earth. KML uses a tag-based structure with nested elements and attributes and is based on the XML standard. In our case we use the polygon entity to store the coordinates of the earth surface locations that form the points of the polyline, delineating for example a crowd area.

4   Experiments and Qualitative Results

4.1   Data Creation and Acquisition

Synthetic Scenes. In order to test our system for the generation of automatic crowd annotations, we needed aerial footage of crowds at known positions on the 2D plane of the map. Setting up such data acquisition scenarios in the real world, would be very cumbersome. As an alternative, we have generated scenes that contain synthetic crowds in a virtual 3D world environment using Unreal Engine 4 (UE4) [12] and Microsoft AirSim [23].

UE4 is a game engine developed by Epic Games that can achieve high-quality photorealistic graphics, includes a physics engine to simulate real-world physics, supports development in C++ and provides flexible world and asset editors. The AirSim simulator includes a plugin for UE4 that can be used to navigate a virtual UAV inside any 3D world model. In our case various assets, such as crowd and landscape assets, were combined to produce crowd scenes and were programmed to interact and look as realistic as possible. The AirSim plugin was used for controlling the virtual drone and extracting high-definition (HD) images along with simulated sensor data, i.e. camera pose, camera intrinsic parameters, etc. Our setup allows the export of the synthetic crowd positions that are predefined in the 3D space as ground truth annotations for each rendered scene. We have used these annotations to verify the correctness of our system's output along with Full HD (1920 × 1080) synthetic frames.

Real-World Scenes. To test the applicability of our system in real-world environments we gathered video footage and sensor data using an off-the-shelf commercial quadrocopter. The DJI Phantom 4[5] can record video at various resolutions up to DCI 4K (4096 × 2160) [11], accompanied with a log file that contains values of several internal sensors and microcontrollers. The log file begins at the moment when the engines of the drone start, before take-off. To emulate a drone that operates with ROS we have paired the records from the DJI log file with the frames recorded from the video camera, giving them the same timestamp.

The events in the DJI log are recorded at a specific frequency of 10 Hz and the frequency of the published frames in ROS was adjusted accordingly from the 25FPS video stream. We have used the DJI drone to record video of a real crowd that has gathered to attend an open event inside the AUTH campus. The video footage was captured at DCI 4K resolution and has been resized to Full HD to reduce computational complexity of the deep neural network inference.

4.2 Results

Figure 3 shows a simulation depicting crowds that are gathered in front of a road presumably to watch an outdoor sports event, e.g. a bike race. In this simulation, a drone with a cinematographic camera flies above the 3D scene that contains the synthetic crowds and captures a video which is then fed to the VSA, thus producing crowd heatmaps. These are then projected on the 3D terrain and the obtained crowd polygons are exported in KML and visualized in Google Earth. The correctness of the crowd polylines created by the projection was verified by comparing them with ground truth boundaries of the synthetic crowd region on the terrain. A flat terrain was used in Octomap for the specific application of our system.

In the real world scenario, the DJI Phantom 4 drone flies and captures video footage of a crowd that was gathered in the AUTH chemistry square (Fig. 4a). The sequence of video frames was fed in the VSA module that had hosted the crowd detector FCNN which produced heatmaps (Fig. 4b). This crowd prediction was subsequently projected and led to the simplified polygon depicted as green in the Google Earth environment (Fig. 4c), used to visualize the results.

---

[5] https://www.dji.com/phantom-4/info.

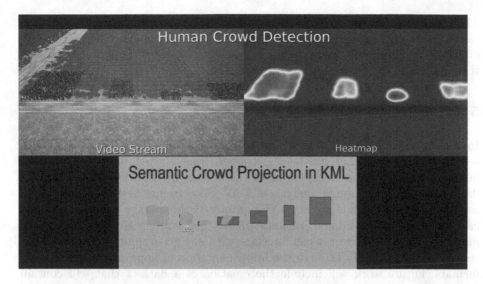

Fig. 3. Application of our system using synthetic crowd scenes and simulated drone sensor data in UE4 and AirSim. Left: Source video frame. Right: Respective heatmap at the output of the FCNN. Bottom: Visualization of the KML annotations (green) over ground truth locations of crowd (gray) (Color figure online)

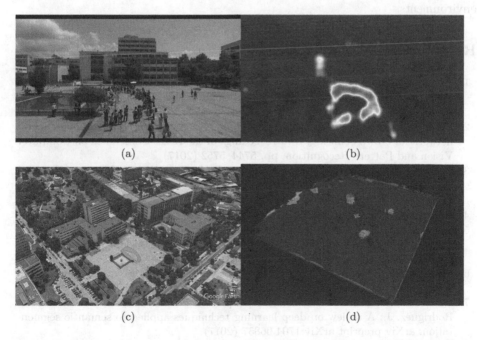

Fig. 4. Application of our system using real crowd scenes: (a) Source video frame, (b) Respective crowd heatmap, (c) 3D crowd region projection as depicted in Google Earth, (d) Respective 3D geometric map of the location in Octomap

The projection task used the Octomap terrain that is presented in Fig. 4d. The camera intrinsic and extrinsic parameters as well as the drone position are obtained by subscribing to ROS topics, which have been emulated to publish the contents of the DJI log file.

5   Conclusion and Future Work

In this paper we present a system that annotates maps automatically with semantic knowledge that has been extracted from video frames using a deep neural network. We have implemented the system in ROS for the scenario of discovering crowds through analysis of UAV video frames and projecting them as regions on its navigation map. Our proposed three stage software pipeline can be reused for additional semantic classes like landing zones, water, roads and tree ranges. Moreover it can interface with any geographic information system or web application through the implementation of appropriate interchange formats. Future work will include the creation of a dataset that will contain real crowd images and corresponding sensor data. The dataset will have ground truth annotations of the crowd regions defined by GPS coordinates. These will be used to evaluate the projection accuracy using common metrics like intersection-over-union (IoU). Furthermore we plan to use deep learning models for semantic image segmentation that can provide multiple heatmaps for a given scene, assisting the UAV navigation through semantic understanding of dynamic real-world environments.

References

1. Anand, A., Koppula, H.S., Joachims, T., Saxena, A.: Contextually guided semantic labeling and search for three-dimensional point clouds. Int. J. Robot. Res. **32**(1), 19–34 (2013)
2. Babu Sam, D., Surya, S., Venkatesh Babu, R.: Switching convolutional neural network for crowd counting. In: Proceedings of the IEEE Conference on Computer Vision and Pattern Recognition, pp. 5744–5752 (2017)
3. Boominathan, L., Kruthiventi, S.S., Babu, R.V.: CrowdNet: a deep convolutional network for dense crowd counting. In: Proceedings of the 2016 ACM on Multimedia Conference, pp. 640–644. ACM (2016)
4. Caruana, R.: Multitask learning. Mach. Learn. **28**(1), 41–75 (1997)
5. Douglas, D.H., Peucker, T.K.: Algorithms for the reduction of the number of points required to represent a digitized line or its caricature. Cartographica Int. J. Geogr. Inf. Geovisualization **10**(2), 112–122 (1973)
6. Friedman, S., Pasula, H., Fox, D.: Voronoi random fields: extracting topological structure of indoor environments via place labeling. IJCAI **7**, 2109–2114 (2007)
7. Garcia-Garcia, A., Orts-Escolano, S., Oprea, S., Villena-Martinez, V., Garcia-Rodriguez, J.: A review on deep learning techniques applied to semantic segmentation. arXiv preprint arXiv:1704.06857 (2017)
8. Glassner, A.S.: An Introduction to Ray Tracing. Elsevier, Amsterdam (1989)

9. Gorelick, N., Hancher, M., Dixon, M., Ilyushchenko, S., Thau, D., Moore, R.: Google earth engine: planetary-scale geospatial analysis for everyone. Remote Sens. Environ. **202**, 18–27 (2017)
10. Hornung, A., Wurm, K.M., Bennewitz, M., Stachniss, C., Burgard, W.: OctoMap: an efficient probabilistic 3D mapping framework based on octrees. Autonom. Robots **34**(3), 189–206 (2013)
11. Kaneko, K., Ohta, N.: 4K applications beyond digital cinema, pp. 133–136. IEEE (2010)
12. Karis, B., Games, E.: Real shading in unreal engine 4. In: Proceedings of Physically Based Shading Theory Practice, pp. 621–635 (2013)
13. Le Cun, B.B., Denker, J.S., Henderson, D., Howard, R.E., Hubbard, W., Jackel, L.D.: Handwritten digit recognition with a back-propagation network. Advances in Neural Information Processing Systems, vol. 2, pp. 396–404. Morgan Kaufmann Publishers Inc., San Mateo (1990)
14. Liu, W., et al.: SSD: single shot MultiBox detector. In: Leibe, B., Matas, J., Sebe, N., Welling, M. (eds.) ECCV 2016. LNCS, vol. 9905, pp. 21–37. Springer, Cham (2016). https://doi.org/10.1007/978-3-319-46448-0_2
15. Mitsou, N., et al.: Online semantic mapping of urban environments. In: Stachniss, C., Schill, K., Uttal, D. (eds.) Spatial Cognition 2012. LNCS (LNAI), vol. 7463, pp. 54–73. Springer, Heidelberg (2012). https://doi.org/10.1007/978-3-642-32732-2_4
16. de Nijs, R., Ramos, S., Roig, G., Boix, X., Van Gool, L., Kühnlenz, K.: On-line semantic perception using uncertainty. In: 2012 IEEE/RSJ International Conference on Intelligent Robots and Systems (IROS), pp. 4185–4191. IEEE (2012)
17. Pangercic, D., Pitzer, B., Tenorth, M., Beetz, M.: Semantic object maps for robotic housework-representation, acquisition and use, In: 2012 IEEE/RSJ International Conference on Intelligent Robots and Systems (IROS), pp. 4644–4651. IEEE (2012)
18. Polastro, R., Corrêa, F., Cozman, F., Okamoto, J.: Semantic mapping with a probabilistic description logic. In: da Rocha Costa, A.C., Vicari, R.M., Tonidandel, F. (eds.) SBIA 2010. LNCS (LNAI), vol. 6404, pp. 62–71. Springer, Heidelberg (2010). https://doi.org/10.1007/978-3-642-16138-4_7
19. Pronobis, A., Jensfelt, P.: Large-scale semantic mapping and reasoning with heterogeneous modalities. In: 2012 IEEE International Conference on Robotics and Automation (ICRA), pp. 3515–3522. IEEE (2012)
20. Quigley, M., et al.: ROS: an open-source robot operating system. In: ICRA Workshop on Open Source Software, vol. 3, p. 5. Kobe, Japan (2009)
21. Remolina, E., Kuipers, B.: Towards a general theory of topological maps. Artif. Intell. **152**(1), 47–104 (2004)
22. Roth, S.D.: Ray casting for modeling solids. Comput. Graph. Image Process. **18**(2), 109–144 (1982)
23. Shah, S., Dey, D., Lovett, C., Kapoor, A.: AirSim: high-fidelity visual and physical simulation for autonomous vehicles. In: Field and Service Robotics (2017). https://arxiv.org/abs/1705.05065
24. Shao, J., Kang, K., Change Loy, C., Wang, X.: Deeply learned attributes for crowded scene understanding. In: Proceedings of the IEEE Conference on Computer Vision and Pattern Recognition, pp. 4657–4666 (2015)
25. Szegedy, C., Ioffe, S., Vanhoucke, V., Alemi, A.A.: Inception-v4: inception-ResNet and the impact of residual connections on learning. In: AAAI, vol. 4, p. 12 (2017)
26. Toshev, A., Szegedy, C.: DeepPose: human pose estimation via deep neural networks. In: Proceedings of the IEEE Conference on Computer Vision and Pattern Recognition, pp. 1653–1660 (2014)

27. Tzelepi, M., Tefas, A.: Human crowd detection for drone flight safety using convolutional neural networks. In: 2017 25th European Signal Processing Conference (EUSIPCO), pp. 743–747. IEEE (2017)
28. Tzelepi, M., Tefas, A.: Deep convolutional learning for content based image retrieval. Neurocomputing **275**, 2467–2478 (2018)
29. Zender, H., Mozos, O.M., Jensfelt, P., Kruijff, G.J., Burgard, W.: Conceptual spatial representations for indoor mobile robots. Robot. Autonom. Syst. **56**(6), 493–502 (2008)

Temporal Action Localization Based on Temporal Evolution Model and Multiple Instance Learning

Minglei Yang, Yan Song[✉], Xiangbo Shu, and Jinhui Tang

Nanjing University of Science and Technology, Nanjing, China
songyan@njust.edu.cn

Abstract. Temporal action localization in untrimmed long videos is an important yet challenging problem. The temporal ambiguity and the intra-class variations of temporal structure of actions make existing methods far from being satisfactory. In this paper, we propose a novel framework which firstly models each action clip based on its temporal evolution, and then adopts a deep multiple instance learning (MIL) network for jointly classifying action clips and refining their temporal boundaries. The proposed network utilizes a MIL scheme to make clip-level decisions based on temporal-instance-level decisions. Besides, a temporal smoothness constraint is introduced into the multi-task loss. We evaluate our framework on THUMOS Challenge 2014 benchmark and the experimental results show that it achieves considerable improvements as compared to the state-of-the-art methods. The performance gain is especially remarkable under precise localization with high tIoU thresholds, e.g. mAP@tIoU=0.5 is improved from 31.0% to 35.0%.

Keywords: Temporal action localization · Temporal evolution model
Multiple instance learning

1 Introduction

Temporal action localization in untrimmed long videos is an important yet challenging problem, which has drawn increasing attention in the computer vision community recently due to its broad applications in video analysis, surveillance, and other areas. Given an untrimmed long video, the task of action localization is expected to output not only the action category, but also the precise start time and end time.

Current state-of-the-art methods [2,12,13,20,23] usually contain two steps. The first step performs a series of passes through the video to generate action proposals. The second step applies classifiers on each proposal to obtain detection result. However, such proposal-based methods suffer from imprecision of detected action boundaries which are restricted to the pre-determined boundaries of a fixed set of proposal segments. The temporal extents of actions are

© Springer Nature Switzerland AG 2019
I. Kompatsiaris et al. (Eds.): MMM 2019, LNCS 11296, pp. 341–351, 2019.
https://doi.org/10.1007/978-3-030-05716-9_28

usually ambiguous. Temporal contexts probably contain helpful information for the detection of actions. Thus recent existing methods adopt segments which contain both background and actions instead of pure action clips as positive training samples. Besides, proposals for testing also contain background frames. We argue that this issue can be formulated as a weakly-supervised learning problem. On the other hand, temporal structure modeling plays a crucial role in temporal action localization. Montes *et al.* [11] utilized recurrent neural network to model long-term temporal structure. Zhao *et al.* [23] took into account different stages in an activity when modeling temporal structure. The temporal model should not only capture discriminative information for different categories, but also be robust to intra-class variations.

In this paper, we propose a framework for temporal action localization based on several parts. Firstly, as mentioned above, we propose a simple yet effective method to model temporal information in action representation. Motivated by Structured Segment Network [23], which considers each activity as a composition of starting, course, and ending stages, we propose to model the evolution of an action with five parts. In addition to the three stages of the action itself, we also bring in the temporal context for modeling the whole temporal evolution of an action. Secondly, we resort to multiple instance learning (MIL) for modeling the temporal ambiguousness of actions. Specifically, we propose a deep MIL network, in which a MIL pooling layer [9] is adopted to generate a probability for an action clip based on the probabilities of several instances in it. In addition, a novel loss with smoothness constraint and boundary offset is used to jointly train classification and boundary refinement. During testing, proposal segments are fed into our framework in a cascade style [4] for accurate classification and precise localization.

The rest of this paper is organized as follows. Section 2 introduces the related works on temporal action localization. In Sect. 3, we detail our proposed framework. The experimental setup and results are reported in Sect. 4. Section 5 concludes this paper.

2   Related Work

2.1   Action Recognition

Action recognition in videos is an active research area for video content analysis. Just as image classification network can be used in image object detection, action recognition models can be used in temporal action localization for feature extraction. Earlier methods are generally concerned with hand-crafted visual features, such as iDT [17,18], which is currently the state-of-the-art among hand-crafted features. iDT feature is consisted of MBH, HOF and HOG features extracted along dense trajectories with camera motion influences eliminated. As in other areas of computer vision, recent works have concentrated on applying ConvNets to this task. Two-stream network [14] learns both spatial and temporal features by operating network on single frame and stacked optical flow field respectively.

C3D network [16] uses 3D convolution to capture spatio-temporal feature directly from video streams.

2.2 Temporal Action Localization

Temporal action localization is one of the most challenging and long standing problems in computer vision, and has received much attentions recently. Shou et al. [13] proposed a segment-based multi-stage 3D CNN framework which involves two stages. The first stage used proposal network to generate temporal action proposals and the second stage classified the proposal with localization network, which was trained using classification and localization loss. Zhao et al. [23] proposed a structured segment network framework, which split the proposal into three consecutive stages and applied two classifiers respectively for classifying actions and determining completeness to output only complete action instances. CDC [12] network performed temporal upsampling and spatial downsampling operations simultaneously to produce dense scores that were used to predict action instances with precise boundaries utilizing temporal boundary refinement. Gao et al. [4] proposed to use Cascaded Boundary Regression model to adjust temporal boundaries in a regression cascade, which outperformed other state-of-the-art temporal action localization methods.

2.3 Multiple Instance Learning

In the machine learning literature, multiple instance learning (MIL) is a variant of supervised learning, which was originally introduced for drug activity prediction [3] and has been widely used in computer vision problems where training data was often weakly supervised or incompletely labeled [1,9,10,15,19,22]. Kraus et al. [9] combined deep convolutional neural networks with multiple instance learning to classify and segment microscopy images, and proposed a novel MIL pooling function called Noisy-AND which was robust to outliers. Sultani et al. [15] proposed a deep MIL framework for anomaly detection by treating videos as bags and segments of each video as instances in a bag, in which a MIL ranking loss with sparsity and smoothness constraints was used to better localize anomaly during training.

3 Methods

The proposed framework is summarized in Fig. 1. Firstly, action clips are extracted from training videos, and each clip is modeled by the temporal evolution model. Secondly, C3D features are extracted for each clip based on the pre-trained C3D network and the temporal evolution model. Thirdly, features are fed into the deep MIL network which is trained using a multi-task loss for classifying clips and refining clip boundaries. For the testing phase, each proposal is fed into the temporal evolution model and the testing process in the MIL network is conducted in a cascade manner.

3.1   Temporal Evolution Model

Actions vary extremely in their appearance and motion characteristics over time. It has been proved in recent works [23] that simple temporal pyramid combined with efficient features could enhance action representation. To take advantage of the inherent temporal structure of actions, we model action clips based on the temporal evolution of actions. Here, we propose a simple yet effective method. As shown in Fig. 2, given an action clip X, we divide it into three parts uniformly, X_s, X_m and X_e, which represent the start part, the middle part and the end part respectively. We extract features of these three parts as internal features. Besides the internal parts, temporal context of X is also modeled. X_l and X_r are the previous and succeeding parts of X respectively, which have a fixed length, and features are extracted from these two parts. The final feature f_X for a clip is the concatenation of context features and internal features:

$$f_X = F(X_l)\|F(X_s)\|F(X_m)\|F(X_e)\|F(X_r) \tag{1}$$

where $\|$ represents vector concatenation, and F is the feature extractor. In this paper, we adopt C3D [16] as the feature extractor, which is widely used and has been proved efficient in video analysis area. In detail, for every 16-frame video clip, we extract visual features from the fully connected (FC) layer FC6 of the C3D network pre-trained by S-CNN [13] followed by $L2$ normalization and dimensionality reduction (from 4096 to 500) via pca [7]. Then we take the average of all the 16-frame clip features within each of the five parts.

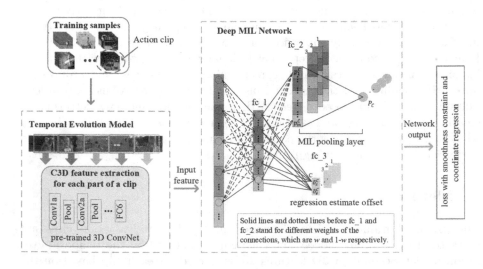

Fig. 1. The flow diagram of the proposed method.

3.2   Deep MIL Network

Our proposed network is mainly made up of three fully connected layers (fc_1, fc_2, fc_3) and one MIL pooling layer, whose architecture is shown in Fig. 1. fc_1 is the middle layer and fc_2 produces temporal instance scores for each action category, whose dimensionality is $C * m$ (C is the number of categories and m means the number of instances of each action category). fc_3 outputs boundary offsets of clips. Here, to retain the temporal information of the input space, we encourage the features from a specific part of the clip to connect more with the corresponding part of next layer. Specifically, we plug pre-defined weights into the connections before fc_1 and fc_2, which is w if the two parts are the counterparts in respective layers and $1 - w$ if they are not. w is set to 0.8 in the experiments.

We use a global pooling function for MIL called Noisy-and pooling function [9] to generate action scores of clips, which assumes that a bag is positive if the number of positive instances in that bag surpasses a certain threshold:

$$P_c = g_z(\{p_j^c\}) = \frac{\sigma(a(p_j^c - b_c)) - \sigma(-ab_c)}{\sigma(a(1 - b_c)) - \sigma(-ab_c)} \tag{2}$$

where $p_j^c = \frac{1}{|j|}\sum_j p_j^c$ and σ is the sigmoid function. The function is designed to activate a bag level score P_C once the mean of the instance level score p_j^c surpasses a certain threshold. The parameters a and b_c control the shape of the activation function. b_c is a set of parameters learned during training and is meant to represent an adaptable soft threshold for each category c. a is fixed parameter that controls the slope of the activation function.

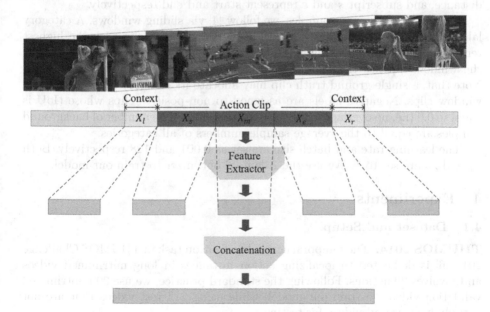

Fig. 2. Illustration of temporal evolution model.

3.3 Loss Function

Recently, as inspired by object detection in images, researchers tend to adopt multi-task learning in action detection [4,5] by combining classification and action boundary regression. Here, we follow this scheme and improve it by introducing a temporal smoothness constraint in the multi-task loss L to jointly train classification and coordinate regression:

$$L = L_{cls} + \lambda_1 L_{ts} + \lambda_2 L_{reg}, \tag{3}$$

where L_{cls} is a standard multi-class cross-entropy loss, L_{ts} enforces temporal smoothness constraint on the instance scores by minimizing the difference of scores for adjacent instances, and L_{reg} is for temporal coordinate regression. Both λ_1 and λ_2 are hyper-parameters, which are set empirically.

The smoothness constraint is defined as [15]:

$$L_{ts} = \frac{1}{N} \sum_{i=1}^{N} \sum_{c=1}^{C} l_i^c [\sum_{j}^{m-1} (p_{j,i}^c - p_{j+1,i}^c)^2], \tag{4}$$

where N is batch size, C is the total number of categories, l_i^c is the label. When the i-th sample is from category c, $l_i^c = 1$, otherwise, $l_i^c = 0$. p means the instance score.

The regression loss is defined as [4]:

$$L_{reg} = \frac{1}{N} \sum_{i=1}^{N} \sum_{c=1}^{C} l_i^z [R(\hat{o}_{s,i}^c - o_{s,i}^c) + R(\hat{o}_{e,i}^c - o_{e,i}^c)], \tag{5}$$

where $\hat{o}$ is the regression estimate offset, o is the ground truth offset, R is $L1$ distance, and subscript s and e represent start and end respectively.

For collecting training samples, we follow [4] via sliding windows. A category label is assigned to a sliding windows if: (1) the window clip with the highest temporal Intersection over Union(tIoU) overlaps with a ground truth clip; or (2) the window clip has tIoU larger than 0.5 with any of the ground truth clips. Note that, a single ground truth clip may allocate its category label to multiple window clips. Negative labels are assigned to non-positive clips whose tIoU is equal to 0.0 (i.e. no overlap) for all ground truth clips. The number of background samples are equal to the average sample numbers of all categories.

The learning rate and batch size are set as 0.001 and 128 respectively. Both λ_1 and λ_2 are set to 1. We use the Adam [8] optimizer to train our model.

4 Experiments

4.1 Dataset and Setup

THUMOS 2014. The temporal action localization task in THUMOS Challenge 2014 [6] is dedicated to localizing action instances in long untrimmed videos and involves 20 actions. Following the standard practice, we use 200 untrimmed validation videos to train our model, while using 213 test videos that are not entirely background videos for testing.

Experimental Setup. We perform the following experiments on THUMOS 2014: (1) evaluation of the impacts of the components used in the proposed model and (2) comparison with state-of-the-art approaches. Our approach is applicable to arbitrary segment proposal method, and we employ the publicly available proposals generated by the TURN [5], which achieve high recall on THUMOS 2014. Our model proceeds in a cascade framework following [4] to generate final boundaries and score for the predicted category. Finally, we follow [13,21] to perform standard post-processing steps such as non-maximum suppression.

Evaluation Metrics. We follow the conventional mean Average Precision (mAP) to measure localization performance. A prediction is marked as correct only when it has the correct category and its temporal overlap IoU with the ground truth is larger than the overlap threshold. The tIoU thresholds are {0.1, 0.2, 0.3, 0.4, 0.5, 0.6, 0.7}. The mAP at tIoU of 0.5 is used for comparing performance between different methods.

Parameters Setup. We explore two parameters of our model: (a) the cascade step which is used in the testing phase and (b) the number of instances in the MIL pooling layer (*i.e.* the m in Equation (4)). We present experimental results in Fig. 3. The results demonstrate that our model achieves the best performance when the cascade step and the number of instances are set to 3 and 10 respectively and thus we follow this setup for the further experiments.

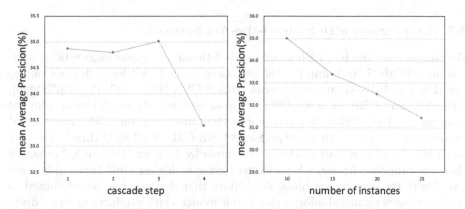

Fig. 3. Comparison of different cascade steps (left) and different numbers of instances in the MIL pooling layer (right) on temporal action localization when the tIoU threshold is set to 0.5.

4.2 Impacts of Different Components

We conduct a series of ablation studies to evaluate the impacts of different components used in our proposed model: (a) w/o TEM: use the entire clip to extract internal features instead of splitting a clip into three parts; (b) w/o TS: remove the temporal smoothness constraint in the loss function; (c) w/o MIL & TS: replace the mil pooling layer with a fully connected layer to output category scores. Note that when we remove the mil pooling layer, the temporal smoothness constraint is also removed because it makes no sense in this setting. We list the results in Table 1. The results show that each component makes contributions to the performance of our proposed framework. Specifically, the temporal evolution model improves the performance by about 3.2% at tIoU $= 0.5$, while the deep MIL network with smoothness constraint achieves about 11.7% improvement at tIoU $= 0.5$.

Table 1. Effects of three components of our proposed model

tIoU	0.1	0.2	0.3	0.4	0.5
w/o TEM	48.6	46.8	43.4	37.6	31.8
w/o TS	38.9	37.2	34.9	29.8	24.1
w/o MIL & TS	37.5	36.3	33.5	29.9	23.3
All	50.0	48.5	45.5	40.4	35.0

4.3 Comparison with State-of-the-Art Systems

We compare our method with other state-of-the-art temporal localization methods on THUMOS 2014, and list the results in Table 2. AP for each class can be found in Fig. 4. We compare our work with S-CNN [13], CDC [12], R-C3D [20], SSN [23], and CBR [4] with C3D features and two-stream features adopted respectively. Both CBR-C3D and our method are based on C3D features, and we observe that our method outperforms CBR-C3D at all tIoU thresholds. Our method outperforms state-of-the-art methods by 4.0% at tIoU $= 0.5$. We notice that the proposed framework performs better at higher tIoU thresholds compared with the existing methods. We believe that this gain can be attributed to the handling of temporal information in our model which produces more accurate boundaries.

Table 2. Temporal action localization performance (mAP %) comparison at different tIoU threshold on THUMOS 2014

tIoU	0.1	0.2	0.3	0.4	0.5	0.6	0.7
S-CNN [13]	47.7	43.5	36.3	28.7	19.0	10.3	5.3
CDC [12]	49.1	46.1	40.1	29.4	23.3	13.1	7.9
R-C3D [20]	54.5	51.5	44.8	35.6	28.9	-	-
SSN [23]	**60.3**	56.2	**50.6**	40.8	29.1	-	-
CBR-C3D [4]	48.2	44.3	37.7	30.1	22.7	13.8	7.9
CBR-TS [4]	60.1	**56.7**	50.1	**41.3**	31.0	19.1	9.9
Ours	50.0	48.5	45.5	40.4	**35.0**	**26.8**	**18.1**

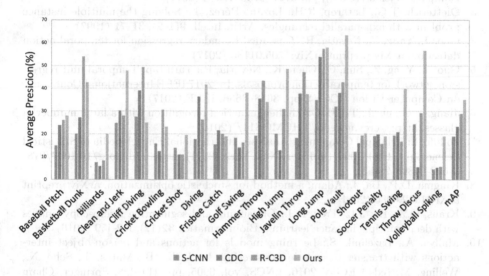

Fig. 4. Histogram of average precision (%) for each class on THUMOS 2014 when the overlap threshold is set to 0.5 during evaluation.

5   Conclusion

In this paper, we present an effective temporal action localization framework for untrimmed videos. We propose to model action clips based on the temporal evolution of actions which effectively leverages the temporal structure of actions and their surrounding temporal contexts. Furthermore, we propose a deep MIL network to recognize actions and refine boundaries simultaneously, which can address precise temporal action localization. The MIL layer in the network helps to make accurate decision for action classification by the ensemble of the decisions of several temporal instances. Experiments demonstrate that the proposed framework surpasses existing methods by a significant gain.

Acknowledgments. This work was supported in part by the National Nature Science Foundation of China under Grants 61672285; the work of Xiangbo Shu is supported by the National Natural Science Foundation of China (Grant No. 61702265), Natural Science Foundation of Jiangsu Province (Grant No. BK20170856), and CCF-Tencent Open Research Fund (PI: Xiangbo Shu).

References

1. Cinbis, R.G., Verbeek, J., Schmid, C.: Weakly supervised object localization with multi-fold multiple instance learning. IEEE transactions on pattern analysis and machine intelligence **39**(1), 189–203 (2017)
2. Dai, X., Singh, B., Zhang, G., Davis, L.S., Chen, Y.Q.: Temporal context network for activity localization in videos. In: 2017 IEEE International Conference on Computer Vision (ICCV), pp. 5727–5736. IEEE (2017)
3. Dietterich, T.G., Lathrop, R.H., Lozano-Pérez, T.: Solving the multiple instance problem with axis-parallel rectangles. Artif. Intell. **9**(1–2), 31–71 (1997)
4. Gao, J., Yang, Z., Nevatia, R.: Cascaded boundary regression for temporal action detection. arXiv preprint arXiv:1705.01180 (2017)
5. Gao, J., Yang, Z., Sun, C., Chen, K., Nevatia, R.: Turn tap: Temporal unit regression network for temporal action proposals. In: 2017 IEEE International Conference on Computer Vision (ICCV), pp. 3648–3656. IEEE (2017)
6. Jiang, Y.G., et al.: THUMOS challenge: action recognition with a large number of classes. http://crcv.ucf.edu/THUMOS14/ (2014)
7. Jolliffe, I.: Principal Component Analysis. International Encyclopedia of Statistical Science, pp. 1094–1096. Springer, New York (2011). https://doi.org/10.1007/978-3-642-04898-2_455
8. Kingma, D.P., Ba, J.: Adam: a method for stochastic optimization. arXiv preprint arXiv:1412.6980 (2014)
9. Kraus, O.Z., Ba, J.L., Frey, B.J.: Classifying and segmenting microscopy images with deep multiple instance learning. Bioinformatics **32**(12), i52–i59 (2016)
10. Mallya, A., Lazebnik, S.: Learning models for actions and person-object interactions with transfer to question answering. In: Leibe, B., Matas, J., Sebe, N., Welling, M. (eds.) ECCV 2016. LNCS, vol. 9905, pp. 414–428. Springer, Cham (2016). https://doi.org/10.1007/978-3-319-46448-0_25
11. Montes, A., Salvador, A., Pascual, S., Giro-i Nieto, X.: Temporal activity detection in untrimmed videos with recurrent neural networks. arXiv preprint arXiv:1608.08128 (2016)
12. Shou, Z., Chan, J., Zareian, A., Miyazawa, K., Chang, S.F.: CDC: convolutional-de-convolutional networks for precise temporal action localization in untrimmed videos. In: 2017 IEEE Conference on Computer Vision and Pattern Recognition (CVPR), pp. 1417–1426. IEEE (2017)
13. Shou, Z., Wang, D., Chang, S.F.: Temporal action localization in untrimmed videos via multi-stage CNNs. In: Proceedings of the IEEE Conference on Computer Vision and Pattern Recognition, pp. 1049–1058 (2016)
14. Simonyan, K., Zisserman, A.: Two-stream convolutional networks for action recognition in videos. In: Advances in Neural Information Processing Systems, pp. 568–576 (2014)
15. Sultani, W., Chen, C., Shah, M.: Real-world anomaly detection in surveillance videos. Center for Research in Computer Vision (CRCV), University of Central Florida (UCF) (2018)

16. Tran, D., Bourdev, L., Fergus, R., Torresani, L., Paluri, M.: Learning spatiotemporal features with 3D convolutional networks. In: Proceedings of the IEEE International Conference on Computer Vision, pp. 4489–4497 (2015)
17. Wang, H., Kläser, A., Schmid, C., Liu, C.L.: Action recognition by dense trajectories. In: 2011 IEEE Conference on Computer Vision and Pattern Recognition (CVPR), pp. 3169–3176. IEEE (2011)
18. Wang, H., Schmid, C.: Action recognition with improved trajectories. In: Proceedings of the IEEE International Conference on Computer Vision, pp. 3551–3558 (2013)
19. Wu, J., Yu, Y., Huang, C., Yu, K.: Deep multiple instance learning for image classification and auto-annotation. In: Proceedings of the IEEE Conference on Computer Vision and Pattern Recognition, pp. 3460–3469 (2015)
20. Xu, H., Das, A., Saenko, K.: R-c3d: region convolutional 3D network for temporal activity detection. In: IEEE International Conference on Computer Vision (ICCV), pp. 5794–5803 (2017)
21. Yeung, S., Russakovsky, O., Jin, N., Andriluka, M., Mori, G., Fei-Fei, L.: Every moment counts: dense detailed labeling of actions in complex videos. Int. J. Comput. Vis. **126**(2–4), 375–389 (2018)
22. Yun, K., Honorio, J., Chattopadhyay, D., Berg, T.L., Samaras, D.: Two-person interaction detection using body-pose features and multiple instance learning. In: 2012 IEEE Computer Society Conference on Computer Vision and Pattern Recognition Workshops (CVPRW), pp. 28–35. IEEE (2012)
23. Zhao, Y., Xiong, Y., Wang, L., Wu, Z., Tang, X., Lin, D.: Temporal action detection with structured segment networks. In: ICCV, October 2 (2017)

Near-Duplicate Video Retrieval Through Toeplitz Kernel Partial Least Squares

Jia-Li Tao[1], Jian-Ming Zhang[1], Liang-Jun Wang[1], Xiang-Jun Shen[1(✉)],
and Zheng-Jun Zha[2]

[1] School of Computer Science and Telecommunication Engineering,
Jiangsu University, Zhenjiang 212013, China
`xjshen@ujs.edu.cn`
[2] School of Information Science and Technology,
University of Science and Technology of China, Hefei, China

Abstract. The existence of huge volumes of near-duplicate videos shows a rising demand on effective near-duplicate video retrieval technique in copyright violation and search result re-ranking. In this paper, Kernel Partial Least Squares (KPLS) is used to find strong information correlation in near-duplicate videos. Furthermore, to solve the problem of "curse of kernelization" when querying a large-scale video database, we propose a Toeplitz Kernel Partial Least Squares method. The Toeplitz matrix multiplication can be implemented by the Fast Fourier Transform (FFT) to accelerate the computation. Extensive experiments on the widely used CC_WEB_VIDEO dataset demonstrate that the proposed approach exhibits superior performance of near-duplicate video retrieval (NDVR) over state-of-the-art methods, such as BCS, SE, SSBelt and CCA, achieving a mean average precision (MAP) score of 0.9665.

Keywords: Near-duplicate video · Correlation-based retrieval
KPLS · FFT · Toeplitz matrices

1 Introduction

With the rapid development of WEB 2.0 technology, videos can be published and shared in various applications such as social networking sites, blogs, Internet TV, mobile TV, and so on. It is indicated by [1] that in Google Video, YouTube, and Yahoo!, up to 27% of videos are duplicates or near-duplicates. According to the study of Wu et al. [2], near-duplicate videos (NDVs) are considered to be identical or close to exact duplicates of each other, but different in terms of file format, encoding parameters, photometric variations (color, lighting changes), editing operations (caption, logo and border insertion), lengths and other modifications.

Intensive studies have been conducted in near-duplicate video retrieval (NDVR) domain recently. Wu et al. [2] used exhaustive matching to measure the similarity by taking Scale Invariant Feature Transform (SIFT) as local features. Also, Liu et al. [3] demonstrated a reference-based histogram as a feature,

© Springer Nature Switzerland AG 2019
I. Kompatsiaris et al. (Eds.): MMM 2019, LNCS 11296, pp. 352–364, 2019.
https://doi.org/10.1007/978-3-030-05716-9_29

where each video is compared with a set of reference videos (seed videos) using 2-dimensional PCA features, and then the percentages of video frames which are closest to corresponding reference videos are recorded and combined as a histogram. Besides, Song et al. [4] presented an approach for Multiple Feature Hashing (MFH) based on multiple image features.

However, there are still a large number of near-duplicates in real Web videos and it is difficult to retrieve with similarity-based approaches using global color features, especially in terms of photometric variations, scene modification, video length changes, and so on. Furthermore, a recent study [5] has shown that users' judgement of near-duplicate videos is mainly based on the degree of information change they perceive, even when the features in the videos look very different. This brings great challenge to the tolerance of content changes in those conventional similarity-based NDVR methods.

In order to well adapt to the content changes in NDVs, a new direction which exploits video information correlation instead of content similarity was proposed by Liu et al. [6]. As one of correlation analysis methods, this Canonical Correlation Analysis (CCA) based approach makes two near-duplicate videos preserving strong information correlation even if their content has great differences. CCA is a technique of correlating linear relationships between two multidimensional variables, which can be seen in the field of recognition and classification problems [7–9].

Applying this idea of correlation analysis in NDVR, we employ Partial Least Square (PLS) to further discover video information correlation of video alignments. Compared with CCA, PLS has an advantage that it can define the information relationship more sufficiently between two near-duplicate videos sequences. To model the function of non-linear relationships among videos in NDVR, Kernel PLS (KPLS) is used, which can map the original video data into a Reproducing Kernel Hilbert Space (RKHS) [10], and therefore efficiently handle high-dimensional videos in NDVs.

However, kernel-based methods suffer from exceeding time and memory requirements when it is applied on large dataset. As the involved optimization problems typically scale polynomial in the number of data samples [11], it requires much time on querying large number of videos. To this end, Toeplitz circulant matrices are employed in our proposed method, which converts the kernelization operations into element-wise processing and the computation process is simplified by the Fast Fourier Transform (FFT). Therefore, it can provide a lower complexity, making KPLS that does not suffer from the "curse of kernelization" [12] in the Fourier domain.

To the best of our knowledge, no previous investigations have been conducted on the use of correlation analysis for the NDVR task in Fourier domain. The main contributions of our proposed method are summarized as follows:

1 To obtain a stronger adaptive ability to content changes in NDVs, Kernel Partial Least Square (KPLS) is used in our proposed method to map the original video data into a Reproducing Kernel Hilbert Space (RKHS) and learn the correlations between two near-duplicate videos.

2 To overcome the exceeding time and memory requirements of kernelization in our proposed method, Toeplitz matrix is used as a bridge to convert kernel operation into element-wise processing in Fast Fourier transform (FFT). This provides a general blueprint for creating fast algorithms that deal with translations, which provide a lower computing complexity.

3 Extensive experiments on CC_WEB_VIDEO dataset reveal that, compared with other near-duplicate video retrieval methods, such as BCS [13], SE [14], SSBelt [15] and CCA [6], our method TKPLS exhibits superior performance on mean average precision (MAP) and requires less computing time.

The rest of the paper is organized as follows: We present the formulation of the proposed correlation-based near-duplicate video retrieval (CNVR) framework TKPLS in Sect. 2. Section 3 evaluates the experiments and we conclude the paper in Sect. 4.

2 The Proposed Method

2.1 Kernel Partial Least Squares

Correlation analysis is a well-known family of statistical tools for analyzing associations between variables or sets of variables. Compared to direct calculating similarity on contents of signals, the correlation-based schemes can reveal deeper associations between data values. In this paper, Partial Least Squares (PLS) [16], as an efficient correlation analysis method, is adopted to solve near-duplicate video retrieval problem.

PLS is a multivariate technique that delivers an optimal basis in x-space for y onto x regression. Reduction to a certain subset of the basis introduces a bias but reduces the variance. In general, PLS is based on a maximization of the covariance between $\langle v, x \rangle$ and $\langle w, y \rangle$, which are successive linear combinations in x and y space respectively. Let coefficient vectors be normalized to unity and constrained to be orthogonal in x space, the optimization can be written as follows:

$$\max_{v,w} \mathrm{cov}\left(v^T x, w^T y\right) = v^T C_{xy} w$$
$$s.t. \ \|v\| = 1 = \|w\|, \ V^T V = I, \ W^T W = I \tag{1}$$

where v, w are the successive vectors in V and W respectively, $C_{xy} = X^T Y$ is the sample covariance matrix and I represents identity matrix. It also can be recast as a constrained least squared optimization:

$$J(v,w) = \sum_{i=1}^{D} \left\|x_i - v v^T x_i\right\|^2 + \left\|v^T x_i - w^T y_i\right\|^2 + \left\|y_i - w w^T y_i\right\|^2 \tag{2}$$

subject to the same constraints as above. This primal cost criterion aims at optimizing the coefficient vectors v and w, searching simultaneously the maximal projection of a data point in x and y space, and the maximal covariation with the corresponding projection of the point in y space [11].

After simplification, only the term $\langle v^T, x \rangle$ and $\langle w^T, y \rangle$ is preserved in $J(v, w)$, so it is equivalent to Eq. (1). Besides, in order to model the nonlinear relationship between data, the kernel trick can be applied to this problem. As such, we need modify term $v^T x$ and $w^T y$ to $v^T \varphi(x)$ and $w^T \varphi(y)$ for some mapping function $\varphi(\cdot)$. In addition, if a soft regularization is used to regularize the coefficient vectors v and w, one can get the following optimization:

$$\max_{v,w} J_{PLS}(v, w, e, r) = \gamma \sum_{i=1}^{D} e_i r_i - \frac{1}{2} v^T v - \frac{1}{2} w^T w \tag{3}$$

where $e_i = v^T \varphi(x_i)$ and $r_i = w^T \varphi(y_i)$ for $i = 1, \ldots, D$ with hyperparameter $\gamma \in \Re_0^+$.

By introducing a_i, b_i as Lagrange multiplier parameters, Eq. (3) can be rewritten into:

$$L(v, w, e, r; a, b) = \gamma \sum_{i=1}^{D} e_i r_i - \frac{1}{2} v^T v - \frac{1}{2} w^T w$$
$$- \sum_{i=1}^{D} a_i \left(e_i - v^T \varphi(x_i) \right) - \sum_{i=1}^{D} b_i \left(r_i - w^T \varphi(y_i) \right) \tag{4}$$

Taking the partial derivation of Lagrange function (4) with respect to each variable, then after some necessary processing to eliminate variables e, r, v, w and finally letting $\lambda = 1/\gamma$, one can convert the problem into the very system:

$$\begin{cases} K_{yy} b = \lambda a \\ K_{xx} a = \lambda b \end{cases} \tag{5}$$

where $[K_{xx}]_{ij} = \varphi(x_i)^T \varphi(x_j)$ and $[K_{yy}]_{ij} = \varphi(y_i)^T \varphi(y_j)$ are the kernel Gram matrices.

2.2   Toeplitz Kernel Partial Least Squares

The power of the kernel trick comes from the implicit use of a high-dimensional feature space, however, it is at the expense of the growing complexity with the number of samples. If the kernel matrix is with some special structure such as circular structure, the matrix operation can be done more efficiently than those regular ones.

Let us go back to see the Eq. (5), one can see that the computation amount of Eq. (5) mainly induced by the matrix-multiplication operations of the two kernel Gram matrices, K_{xx} and K_{yy}. It is unaffordable if one performs the matrix multiplication directly for video signals. Fortunately, using the cyclic shift model will allow us to efficiently exploit the redundancies in this expensive computation, and the efficiency arises from the following property of the cyclic matrix.

In particular, a circulant matrix X can be constructed by placing a generating vector $x = (x_1, x_2, \ldots, x_D)$ and its shifts in successive rows, as shown below:

$$X = Toep(x) = \begin{bmatrix} x_1 & x_2 & x_3 & \cdots & x_D \\ x_D & x_1 & x_2 & \cdots & x_{D-1} \\ x_{D-1} & x_D & x_1 & \cdots & x_{D-2} \\ \vdots & \vdots & \vdots & \ddots & \vdots \\ x_2 & x_3 & x_4 & \cdots & x_1 \end{bmatrix} \tag{6}$$

Then, X has an intriguing property: The matrix operation can be implemented by circular convolutions, that is $Toep(x)\, y = x * y$, hence calculated with the Fast Fourier Transform (FFT). Specifically, for any vector c:

$$Xc = F^{-1}(F(x) \odot F(c)) = F^{-1}(\hat{x} \odot \hat{c}) \tag{7}$$

where, F, F^{-1} denotes the FFT and Inverse FFT respectively, a hat $\hat{\ }$ denotes the FFT of a vector and $\odot$ is the element-wise multiplication of two vectors. Computation burden can be much alleviated since FFT has a computation complexity of $O(n \log n)$, especially in large-scale cases such as near-duplicate video retrieval.

It is proved in [12] that given any circulant data X, the kernel matrix K is also a circulant matrix as long as the kernel function satisfies the condition $\kappa(x, x') = \kappa(Mx, Mx')$, for any permutation matrix M. Fortunately, this condition holds for most common kernels such as Gaussian, linear and polynomial etc.

This theorem allows us to solve the Eq. (5) more efficiently. Especially, if a polynomial kernel $\kappa(x, x') = (x^T x' + a)^\beta$ is applied, one can get the generator vector $\mathrm{k}^{xx'}$ of the kernel matrix:

$$\mathrm{k}^{xx'} = \left(F^{-1}(\hat{x}^* \odot \hat{x}') + a\right)^\beta \tag{8}$$

Similarly,

$$\mathrm{k}^{yy'} = \left(F^{-1}(\hat{y}^* \odot \hat{y}') + a\right)^\beta \tag{9}$$

where $\hat{x}^*$, $\hat{y}^*$ are the complex-conjugate of $\hat{x}$ and $\hat{y}$ respectively.

By these transformations defined in Eqs. (8) and (9), the model defined in Eq. (5) finally can be rewritten as:

$$\begin{cases} \hat{\mathrm{k}}^{yy}\hat{b} = \lambda\hat{a} \\ \hat{\mathrm{k}}^{xx}\hat{a} = \lambda\hat{b} \end{cases} \tag{10}$$

where $\hat{\mathrm{k}}^{xx}$, $\hat{\mathrm{k}}^{yy}$ is the Fourier transform of k^{xx}, k^{yy}.

2.3   Application of TKPLS for NDVR

Given a video sequence that consists of a number of frames, one can model each frame as a variable that is represented as a high-dimensional feature vector.

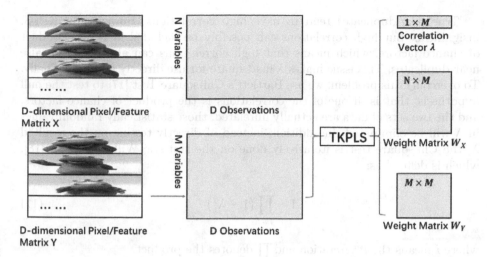

Fig. 1. TKPLS on two video matrices retrieval problem.

To explain the process more clearly, we follow the same notations in Sect. 2.1. Let X and Y are two video sequences with N and M frames each, and also assume each frame can be represented in a D-dimensional feature space, hence the signals can be described by $D \times N$ and $D \times M$ matrices, and denoted as $X = \{x_1, x_2, \ldots, x_D\}^T$ and as $Y = \{y_1, y_2, \ldots, y_D\}^T$ respectively. Each column in X and Y represents a frame as a variable, while each row, namely x_i and y_i, is i^{th} feature-value sequence of all frames. With such settings, there are M and N variables in the criteria and predictors respectively with the same number of observations (samples), that is, D. The objective now is to find two sets of weights of the frames, namely v_X and w_Y, in the correlation pattern such that the correlation between two videos is maximized. By solving the problem, one can obtain three outputs, the correlation λ, weights v_X for video X and w_Y for video Y. In order to make this clear, Fig. 1 is provided.

Without loss of generality, we assume $D > N \geq M$. Note that for a standard eigen-problem in the form $AX = \lambda X$, the number of solutions is less than or equal to $rank\,(X)$. With the implicit constraint that $\lambda X = \lambda Y$, and the notation of full-rank matrices $X\,(D \times N)$ and $Y\,(D \times M)$, it is clear that the number of solutions of λ is $\min\,(rank\,(X), rank\,(Y))$, which equals M in our case due to $D > N \geq M$. Now for each solution λ_i, there exists corresponding solutions to the weights of frames (projection basis vector) v_X and w_Y respectively. Grouping them together, we obtain $v_X\,(N \times M)$ and $w_Y\,(M \times M)$, in which each column contains the weights of frames (projection basis vector) for a particular correlation pattern.

By solving Eq. (10), we get an M-dimensional vector $\lambda = (\lambda_1, \ldots, \lambda_M)$ that contains their correlations, and two matrices $v_X = \{v_{X_1}, \ldots, v_{X_M}\}$ and $w_Y = \{w_{Y_1}, \ldots, w_{Y_M}\}$ that indicate the significances of frames in X and Y contributing to the corresponding correlation.

True near-duplicates tend to have high correlations. However, in KPLS, insignificant but high correlations can possibly be included in λ as a product of chance factors, which means that high correlations can also occur to false near-duplicates. This issue makes λ inadequate for use directly and individually. To overcome this problem, we use Bartlett's Chi-square Test [17] to test the null hypothesis, that is, if one of the correlations is the product of chance factors, and the two sets of data are actually unrelated, those statistically random values in λ will be eliminated. In addition, instead of directly testing on the resulted λ, the Chi-square test is iteratively done on the statistic Wilk's Lambda [18], which is defined as:

$$\Lambda = \prod_{j=i}^{M} \left(1 - \lambda_j^2\right) \tag{11}$$

where i means the ith iteration and $\prod$ denotes the product.

The null hypothesis is then tested against the ith value in λ, that is, λ_i, using the function below [19], which distributes approximately as Chi-square:

$$\chi^2 = -\left[(D-1) - 0.5\,(M+N+1)\right]\log_e \Lambda$$
$$s = \frac{\chi^2}{(M-i+1)\,(M-i+1)} \tag{12}$$

with $(M-i+1)\,(M-i+1)$ indicating the degree of freedom. s can be used to decide whether accept or reject the null hypothesis that two sets of variables are unrelated. Large s implies that there is a high possibility of the acceptance on null hypothesis. If the null hypothesis is rejected for some λ_i, two sets of variables are considered to be significantly related under λ_i. We iteratively execute this test from λ_1 to λ_M. For each λ_i, if corresponding s is greater than a predefined threshold ε, it is then considered as a random correlation value. After the Chi-square test, those random correlation values in λ can be wiped out. We will test the effect of ε in Sect. 3.3.

Finally, we use DoC values [6] that only involve all those significant correlations to determine whether two videos are near-duplicates. For any two videos X and Y, if the updated correlation vector $\bar{\lambda}$ is $\bar{M}$-dimensional after removing all insignificant correlation values, where $\bar{M} \leq M$, we have:

$$DoC\,(X,Y) = \frac{\sum_{i=1}^{\bar{M}} \bar{\lambda}_i}{N} \tag{13}$$

where N is the number of frames in X, and $\bar{\lambda}_i$ is the ith correlation value in $\bar{\lambda}$. Videos in the database can be ranked based on their DoC values with respect to a query video for retrieval purpose. The whole processing is shown in Algorithm 1.

Algorithm 1. Toeplitz Kernel Partial Least Squares on near-duplicate video retrieval

Input: Original video X, Query video Y, threshold ε
Output: The Degree of correlation (DoC)
1: Do TKPLS on X and Y then obtain $\hat{k}^{xx}$, $\hat{k}^{yy}$ by Eqs. (8) and (9)
2: Compute λ, $\hat{a}$ and $\hat{b}$ by Eq. (10)
3: Compute DoC by Eq. (13)

3 Experimental Results

3.1 Dataset

Experiments were performed on the CC_WEB_VIDEO dataset, which is made available by the research groups of City University of Hong Kong and Carnegie Mellon University. CC_WEB_VIDEO is a well-known NDVR benchmark which contains a total of 13,129 videos consisting of 397,965 keyframes. The collection consists of a sample of videos retrieved by submitting 24 popular text queries to popular video sharing websites (i.e. YouTube, Google Video, and Yahoo! Video). For every query, a set of video clips was collected and the most popular video was considered to be the query video. Subsequently, all videos in the video set retrieved by the query were manually annotated based on their near-duplicate relation to the query video.

3.2 Evaluation Metrics

Since the retrieved results may include both relevant and non-relevant videos, how to evaluate the effectiveness of the algorithm is an important topic. To measure detection accuracy, we employ the interpolated precision-recall (PR) curve. Precision is defined as the fraction of retrieved videos that are relevant to the query, while recall is the fraction of the total relevant videos that are retrieved. Furthermore, mean average precision (MAP) is adopted to examine the NDVR effectiveness.

With the returned results generated by the algorithm in the jth query Q_j, the average precision (AP) is calculated as:

$$AP(j) = \frac{1}{O} \sum_{i=1}^{O} \frac{i}{t_i} \tag{14}$$

where O is the number of relevant videos in this query and t_i is the position of the ith relevant video. MAP is the mean of AP and is then defined as:

$$MAP = \frac{\sum_{j=1}^{P} AP(j)}{P} \tag{15}$$

where P is the number of queries.

3.3 Determine the Parameter ε

In the proposed TKPLS system, s is used to present the level of significance between two videos as mentioned in Sect. 2.3, where a large value of s corresponds to a high level of significance, in turn, implies that there is a high acceptance probability in the null hypothesis. In the Chi-square significance test, ε, the threshold of s, is a critical parameter that has a great influence on the performance. Unfortunately, it is very hard to determine the value of it in advance due to lack of the knowledge. In order to address the problem, some experiments are conducted to analyze the influence of varying ε on the performance.

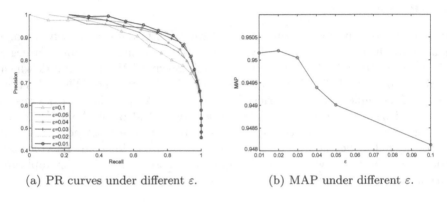

(a) PR curves under different ε.   (b) MAP under different ε.

Fig. 2. Influences of varying ε on PR and MAP.

Figure 2 demonstrates the effects of varying ε on NDVR accuracy for dataset CC_WEB_VIDEO. In Fig. 2(a), the trends of PR curves under different ε are quite similar, and lower ε can help to get a higher recall rate in the process. From Fig. 2(b), we can see MAP keeps stable in low values (i.e, 0.01 and 0.02) then drops as ε increases, which suggest us choose $\varepsilon = 0.02$ as our default setting in the following experiments.

3.4 Results Compared with State-of-the-Art Methods

Four methods are chosen to be compared, as listed in Table 1. All experiments for the five methods were conducted on Intel(R) Core(TM) i7-3770 CPU @ 3.40 GHz with 4 GB RAM in Windows 7 64-bit environment.

The first reference approach is the Bounded Coordinate System (BCS) [13] as a global feature-based SNVR approach. Particularly, to summarize a video, it computes a coordinate system, where each of its coordinate axes is identified by Principal Component Analysis (PCA) and bounded by the range of data projections along the axis. It basically summarizes feature distribution information. In our experiments, BCS features are processed offline and stored prior to the NDVR stage. Given a query video, its BCS feature is first generated. Then linear

Table 1. State-of-the-art methods to be compared

Method	Description
BCS	A global feature-based SNVR approach proposed by Huang et al. [13].
SE	An Edit-distance-based sequence matching method proposed by Yeh et al. [14].
SSBelt	A self-similarity belt based proposed by Wu et al. [15].
CCA	A Correlation-Based Retrieval approach proposed by Liu et al. [6].

search is performed in stored BCS features, where, for each candidate video, its signature similarity to the query video is computed. Candidate videos are finally ranked by their computed similarities.

Among the methods compared, the method SE proposed by Yeh et al. [14] is an Edit-distance-based method. In this method, they take color features as descriptors and utilize exhaustive search for retrieval. This color features are not suitable in dealing with spatial transformations (e.g., adding black boarder or text). In our experiment, we follow the parameter settings refer to [14].

Since SSBelt is a keyframe-based approach in NDVR, it can detect the boundary of the near-duplicate segments more accurately than SE. A frame-wise localization method IMark is utilized to localize the near-duplicate segments of the retrieved videos. We implement the SSBelt method with detecting the Interest Corners and quantizing the 64-dimensional descriptor as video features refer to [15].

The last method CCA employs Canonical Correlation Analysis (CCA) for video information correlation discovery [6]. It is obviously that CCA's MAP is much similar to our proposed method TKPLS's.

Table 2 provides the performance comparison results on CC_WEB_VIDEO dataset in terms of both MAP and mean processing time. As shown in the table, BCS shows a good performance in real time re-traveling of 0.6 s in this dataset, though the lowest MAP compared to other methods of 0.8175. SE improves MAP performance compared to BCS, but at the cost of multiple magnitudes of search time to other comparisons. SSBelt achieves a remarkable performance of 0.9218, it shows better than the above two methods in re-traveling with none-temporal transformation, such as frame dropping and slow motion in this dataset. However, the lower MAP of SSBelt reveals its insufficient scalability for lacking the temporal transformation tolerance with IMark. SSBelt shows about 4–5% lower in MAP compared to the correlation-based methods, CCA and our proposed method. The proposed method displays a better performance in MAP, and defeats all other competitor without any exception. Meanwhile, the processing time is much less than others due to the use of FFT technique. The time of our method (0.12 s) is about 1.4% of that of the CCA's (8.3 s), although it is close to ours on MAP performance.

Figure 3 illustrates the PR curves of the compared approaches. TKPLS outperforms all other methods up to 90% of recall. Additionally, CCA is at the same level with TKPLS for small recall values, however, it drops more heavily as the recall value increases. The performances of SE and SSBelt are close to

Table 2. Performance comparison in terms of MAP and mean processing time on CC_WEB_VIDEO

Method	BCS	SE	SSBelt	CCA	TKPLS
MAP	0.8175	0.8849	0.9218	0.9603	0.9665
Time (s)	0.6	1425.4	6.36	8.3	0.12

each other, and both are better than the worst one BCS. The figure, together with Table 2, proves that the proposed is more efficient than others in terms of MAP under various recall cases.

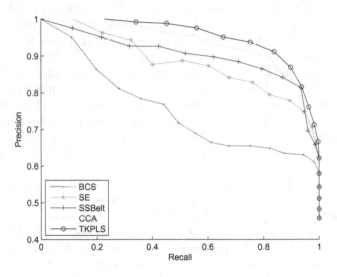

Fig. 3. Precision-Recall curve comparison of the proposed approach with four state-of-the-art methods.

4   Conclusion

There are diverse changes in NDVs currently, including multiple categories or intensive changes, and some of them, especially uploaded by users, could be even partial NDVs. These facts have made it much more difficult for existing similarity-based near-duplicate video retrieval (SNVR) approaches to achieve high accuracy while maintaining reasonable efficiency. Unlike conventional SNVR approaches, we proposed a novel CNVR framework that facilitates NDVR by assessing video near-duplicate relationships more accurately with correlation analysis. We defined the formulation and solutions of TKPLS in an NDVR perspective and described major components in the CNVR framework. We also explained the TKPLS's capability in detecting near-duplicates of intensive content changes from information theory perspective. In the experimental section, we verified our CNVR framework on real video dataset CC_WEB_VIDEO with comprehensive and comparative experiments, where the results showed its great effectiveness and reasonable efficiency. This work also could be extended to deep learning domain with convolutional neural networks (CNNs) at next step.

Acknowledgments. This work was funded in part by the National Natural Science Foundation of China (No. 61572240, 61601202), Natural Science Foundation of Jiangsu Province (Grant No. BK20140571).

References

1. Wu, X., Ngo, C.W., Hauptmann, A.G., Tan, H.K.: Real-time near-duplicate elimination for web video search with content and context. IEEE Trans. Multimed. **11**(2), 196–207 (2009)
2. Wu, X., Hauptmann, A.G., Ngo, C.W.: Practical elimination of near-duplicates from web video search. In: ACM International Conference on Multimedia, pp. 218–227 (2007)
3. Liu, L., Lai, W., Hua, X.-S., Yang, S.-Q.: Video histogram: a novel video signature for efficient web video duplicate detection. In: Cham, T.-J., Cai, J., Dorai, C., Rajan, D., Chua, T.-S., Chia, L.-T. (eds.) MMM 2007. LNCS, vol. 4352, pp. 94–103. Springer, Heidelberg (2006). https://doi.org/10.1007/978-3-540-69429-8_10
4. Song, J., Yang, Y., Huang, Z., Shen, H.T., Luo, J.: Effective multiple feature hashing for large-scale near-duplicate video retrieval. IEEE Trans. Multimed. **15**(8), 1997–2008 (2013)
5. Cherubini, M., De Oliveira, R., Oliver, N.: Understanding near-duplicate videos: a user-centric approach. In: International Conference on Multimedia 2009, Vancouver, British Columbia, Canada, October, pp. 35–44 (2009)
6. Liu, J., Huang, Z., Shen, H.T., Cui, B.: Correlation-based retrieval for heavily changed near-duplicate videos. ACM Trans. Inf. Syst. **29**(4), 21 (2011)
7. Hardoon, D.R., Szedmak, S.R., Shawe-Taylor, J.R.: Canonical Correlation Analysis: An Overview with Application to Learning Methods. MIT Press, Cambridge (2004)
8. Kim, T.K., Kittler, J., Cipolla, R.: Discriminative learning and recognition of image set classes using canonical correlations. IEEE Trans. Pattern Anal. Mach. Intell. **29**(6), 1005 (2007)
9. Kim, T.K., Cipolla, R.: Canonical correlation analysis of video volume tensors for action categorization and detection. IEEE Trans. Pattern Anal. Mach. Intell. **31**(8), 1415–1428 (2009)
10. Wahba, G.: Spline models for observational data, CBMS-NSF regional conference series in applied mathematics. Watson Research Center, no. 59 (1990)
11. Hoegaerts, L., Suykens, J.A.K., Vandewalle, J., De Moor, B.: Primal space sparse kernel partial least squares regression for large scale problems, vol. 1, p. 563 (2004)
12. Henriques, J.F., Rui, C., Martins, P., Batista, J.: High-speed tracking with kernelized correlation filters. IEEE Trans. Pattern Anal. Mach. Intell. **37**(3), 583–596 (2014)
13. Huang, Z., Shen, H.T., Shao, J., Zhou, X., Cui, B.: Bounded coordinate system indexing for real-time video clip search. ACM Trans. Inf. Syst. **27**(3), 1–33 (2009)
14. Yeh, M.C., Cheng, K.T.: Video copy detection by fast sequence matching. In: ACM International Conference on Image and Video Retrieval, CIVR 2009, Santorini Island, Greece, July, pp. 1–7 (2009)

15. Wu, Z., Aizawa, K.: Self-similarity-based partial near-duplicate video retrieval and alignment. Int. J. Multimed. Inf. Retr. **3**(1), 1–14 (2014)
16. Wold, H.: Estimation of principal components and related models by iterative least squares. Multivar. Anal. **1**, 391–420 (1966)
17. Snedecor, G.W., Cochran, W.G.: Statistical Methods, 8th edn. Iowa State University Press, Ames (1989)
18. Mardia, K.V., Kent, J.T., Bibby, J.M.: Multivariate analysis. Math. Gaz. **37**(1), 123–131 (1979)
19. Clark, D.: Understanding canonical correlation analysis. Geo Abstracts (1990)

Action Recognition Using Visual Attention with Reinforcement Learning

Hongyang Li[1,3](✉), Jun Chen[1,2], Ruimin Hu[1,2], Mei Yu[3], Huafeng Chen[4], and Zengmin Xu[1]

[1] National Engineering Research Center for Multimedia Software,
School of Computer Science, Wuhan University, Wuhan, China
{lihy,chenj,hrm,xzm1981}@whu.edu.cn

[2] Hubei Key Laboratory of Multimedia and Network Communication Engineering,
Wuhan University, Wuhan, China

[3] College of Computer and Information Technology, China Three Gorges University,
Yichang, China
yumei_sim@whu.edu.cn

[4] Jingchu University of Technology, Jingmen, China
chenhuafeng@whu.edu.cn

Abstract. Human action recognition in videos is a challenging and significant task with a broad range of applications. The advantage of the visual attention mechanism is that it can effectively reduce noise interference by focusing on the relevant parts of the image and ignoring the irrelevant part. We propose a deep visual attention model with reinforcement learning for this task. We use Recurrent Neural Network (RNN) with Long Short-Term Memory (LSTM) units as a learning agent. The agent interact with video and decides both where to look next frame and where to locate the most relevant region of the selected video frame. REINFORCE method is used to learn the agent's decision policy and backpropagation method is used to train the action classifier. The experimental results demonstrate that this glimpse window can focus on important clues. Our model achieves significant performance improvement on the action recognition datasets: UCF101 and HMDB51.

Keywords: Human action recognition · Reinforcement learning Visual attention

1 Introduction

Action recognition is a prominent research area in video understanding, which can be applied to many applications such as video surveillance, human-computer interaction, human behavior understanding, etc. Though significant progresses have been made [2,17,20,23], action recognition still remains a challenging task due to intra-class variations, background complexity, high-dimensional feature description, and other difficulties.

© Springer Nature Switzerland AG 2019
I. Kompatsiaris et al. (Eds.): MMM 2019, LNCS 11296, pp. 365–376, 2019.
https://doi.org/10.1007/978-3-030-05716-9_30

Previous research in action recognition focus on Bag of Words (BoW) model based on shallow high-dimensional encodings of local features. Local feature vector of the video is commonly expressed by Motion Boundary Histogram (MBH), Histogram of Oriented Gradient (HOG), and Histogram of Optical Flow (HOF), etc. Improved Dense trajectories (IDT) feature [20] is a new local visual feature by combining trajectory shape descriptor, HOG, HOF and MBH, which is superior to other local feature in the most challenging video datasets.

Recently, Convolutional Neural Network (CNN) have show a great ability to produce a rich representation of the image and have highly successful in image understanding, such as image classification, object detection, image segmentation. Classifying videos instead of images adds a temporal information to the model of image classification. Wang et al. [21] extend convolutional kernel to multiple video frames to extract temporal information. Although they achieve great performance, much temporal information is still missing. LSTM have also been used to learn an effective representation of videos [15,19], which has been proven to be effective for action recognition task from video sequences. There are many approaches also tend to have CNN underlying the LSTM and classify sequences directly or do temporal pooling of features prior to classification [3]. For the target object is not in a fixed position, the policy of sampling in a fixed area is difficult to adapt to video frame sequences with large time span. Xu et al. [26] try to solve the problem by visual salient region boundary based dense sampling strategy. These salient regions model are not obtained for action recognition task and do not take full advantage of supervise information.

Attention mechanisms have become an integral part of compelling sequence modeling in mangy tasks. The most important function of selective visual attention is to quickly turn our attention to objects of interest in the visual environment. This ability to focus on regions in cluttered visual scenes is of evolutionary significance. The key instinct is that humans do not immediately focus on the whole scene, but rather focus on the sequential parts of the scene to extract relevant information. The process of action recognition is continuous and iterative observation and refinement. This paper draws inspiration from works that have used REINFORCE to learn spatial glimpse policy for image classification [1,14], and to learn temporal glimpse policy for action detection [27].

Main contributions of this work are: (1) We directly estimate the next video frame location and next retina region based on current and historical information by reinforcement learning method. (2) The next glimpse location is relative to the current position instead of the whole image.

2   Related Work

Two-stream convolutional network model combines the predictions of two convolutional neural networks: one trained on single video frames and the other trained on short sequences of dense optical flow images [17]. This deep architecture is competitive with the classical shallow representations in spite of being trained on relatively small datasets. On this basis, researchers have proposed more improved models [5,7,22,24]. Karpathy et al. [9] used a multi-resolution

CNN architecture to perform action recognition in videos. ARTNet architecture to are constructed by stacking multiple generic building blocks, whose goal is to simultaneously model appearance and relation from RGB input in a separate and explicit manner [23]. Using reinforcement learning, Ji et al. [8] separate human action to several patterns and learn temporal transition expected values in activity sequences.

Attention networks were originally proposed on the basis of the REINFORCE algorithm, that is called hard attention. Soft attention mechanisms were proposed by using weighted averages instead of hard selections. Long et al. [13] propose a local feature integration framework based on multimodal soft-attention clusters, and introduce a shifting operation to capture more diverse signals. VideoLSTM based on soft attention LSTM is an end-to-end sequence learning model [12]. Girdhar et al. [6] introduce soft-attention pooling model to action recognition and human object interaction tasks. Soft-attention model is also used in action recognition. Sharma et al. [16] propose a soft attention based model for the task of action recognition in videos, which learns which parts in the frames are relevant for the task at hand and attaches higher importance to them and classifies videos after taking a few glimpses. Zhang et al. [28] propose a novel attention mechanism that leverages the gate system of LSTM to compute the attention weights, which is embedded in a recurrent attention network that can explore the spatial-temporal relations between different local regions to concentrate important ones.

RAM model based on a recurrent neural network is capable of extracting information from an image or video by adaptively selecting a sequence of regions or locations and only processing the selected regions at high resolution; While the model is non-differentiable, it can be trained using reinforcement learning methods to learn task-specific policies [14]. DRAM extends attention based model for recognizing multiple objects in images [1]. Xu et al. [25] use both soft attention and hard attention mechanisms to describe the content of images. Yeung et al. [27] formulate the hard attention model as a recurrent neural network based agent that interacts with a video over time and decides both where to look next and when to emit a prediction for action detection task.

3   The Method

Our task is to take a long sequence of video as input and predict any class labels of a given human action. Figure 1 shows the model structure. At each time step, the RNN as an agent processes the glimpse from one video frame, integrates information over time, and chooses how to act and how to locate next frame and get glimpse at each time step.

3.1   Architecture

The architecture is built around a RNN, which consists of four main components: an observation network, a convolutional neural network, a recurrent network and a prediction network. The observation network is used to select video frame and choose focusing image patch. The image patch is then sent to the CNN, which is responsible for transforming this two-dimensional images patch into one-dimensional feature vector. RNN is the core component and used to process feature vector sequences from CNN. The prediction network takes the current state of RNN as input and makes a prediction on when and where to extract the next video frame patch for the observation network. We explain how we use a combination of back-propagation and REINFORCE method to train the model in end-to-end fashion.

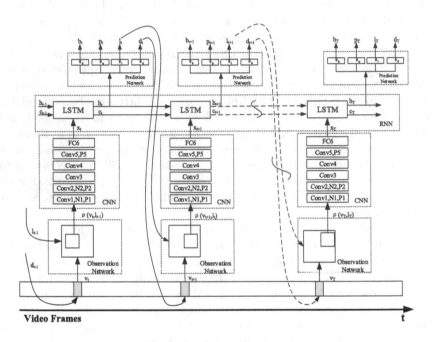

Fig. 1. Model architecture.

Observation Network. At each step t the agent receives a image patch from one video frame. The agent does not have full access to the video frame but rather can extract information by focusing on particular region. The location of this region is determined by two parameters: l_t and d_t. At training time, the location d_t' of observation next frame is sampled from Gaussian distribution with a mean of d_t and a fixed variance; at test time, the maximum a posteriori estimate is used. When the value of d_t' goes beyond the range $[0, 1]$, we clip it by 0 or 1. We define D as maximum span which is the number of frames that observation network can be skipped. Given next frame location of d_t', we get $d = d_t' \cdot D$, this means we can skip $d + 1$ frames to get the next frame. Similarly, the location l_t' of observation region center is sampled from Gaussian distribution with a mean of l_t and a fixed variance. The difference between the two parameters is that d_t' is a scalar and l_t' is a two-dimensional vector. The l_t' represent horizontal and vertical position relative to the previous retina region. The range of value of l_t' is $\{[-1, 1], [-1, 1]\}$. We set the L as maximum pixel distance from reference position. Given next glimpse location of l_t' and the coordinates c_{t-1} in the image of previous image patch, we get $l = l_t' \cdot L$. This means that the center position of the next glimpse region location is $l + c_{t-1}'$.

Convolutional Network. In our implementation, we choose the configurations similar to two-stream CNN [17] due to their good performance on the challenging datasets. The CNN structure from the first to the fifth layer is similar to spatial stream ConvNet [17], except the first layer's stride equal 1. Using shorthand notation, the CNN configuration is $C1(96, 7, 1) - N1 - P1(2, 2) - C2(256, 5, 2) - N2 - P2(2, 2) - C3(512, 3, 1) - C4(512, 3, 1) - C5(512, 3, 1) - P5(2, 2) - FC6(1024)$. where $C\#(c, k, s)$ indicates a convolutional layer with c filters of spatial size $k \times k$, applied to the input with stride s. $P\#(k, s)$ is max pooling layer with spatial size $k \times k$ and stride s. $FC\#(n)$ is a fully connected layer with n nodes. $N\#$ is local response normalization layer described in Krizhevsky et al. [10] and use the same parameters: $k = 2, n = 5, \alpha = 10^{-4}, \beta = 0.5$. The Rectified Linear Units (ReLU) activation function is applied to the output of every convolutional and fully-connected layer. The final layer is connected to LSTM cell as frame presentation feature vector. Except the $FC6$ layer, the parameter values of the other layers using the existing values from the model of [17].

Recurrent Network. The video can be taken as a sequence frames, We use the LSTM implementation in [25], which is given as follows;

$$i_t = \sigma \left(W_i \cdot [h_{t-1}, x_t] + b_i \right)$$
$$f_t = \sigma \left(W_f \cdot [h_{t-1}, x_t] + b_f \right)$$
$$o_t = \sigma \left(W_o \cdot [h_{t-1}, x_t] + b_o \right)$$
$$g_t = \tanh \left(W_g \cdot [h_{t-1}, x_t] + b_g \right)$$
$$c_t = f_t \odot c_{t-1} + i_t \odot g_t$$
$$h_t = o_t \odot \tanh \left(c_t \right)$$

where i_t is the input gate, f_t is the forget gate, o_t is the output gate, band c_t is the cell state, h_t is the hidden state, and the vector x_t is the input to the LSTM at time-step t. The x_t is the CNN feature representation vector, capturing the visual information associated with a particular input glimpse. σ and $\odot$ be the logistic sigmoid activation and element-wise multiplication respectively. The trainable parameters are weight matrices W and biases vectors b.

Prediction Network. This network acts as a controller that directs attention based on the current internal states from the RNN. As the agent reasons on a video, four outputs are produced at each timestep: temporal location d_t indicating the frame to observe next. spatial location l_t indicating the glimpse region. p_t represents the classification results of the prediction; Whether in the training or testing stage, only the last unit output p_t is used. b_t is just an auxiliary output.

Loaction of Next Frame: The temporal location $d_t \in [0, 1]$ indicate the video frame location that the agent chooses to observe. The next video frame location d_t is relative to current frame location l_{t-1}. The difference from [27] is that our agent only skip forwards a video, which is more consistent with human's cognitive habits and more easier to handle online. The d_t is computed as $d_t = f_d(h_t, \theta_d)$, where the f_d is a fully connected layer, such that the agent's decision is a function of its past observations and current observation.

Location of Next Observation Region: The spatial location $l_t \in [-1, 1]$ is a two-tuples, which is computed as $l_t = f_l(h_t, \theta_l)$, where the f_l is a fully connected layer with parameters θ_l. The elements of the two tuples correspond to the coordinates of the focusing region center relative to the previous location. The parameters of θ_l are a two-dimensional matrix and a biases vector.

Classifier of Video: Our task is to recognize the human action category in videos, So we need a classifier for this task. $p_t = f_p(h_t, \theta_p)$, where f_p is a fully connected hidden layer with parameters θ_p followed by a softmax output layer. In course of training, we use softmax loss as its loss function and back-propagation method to update parameters θ_p. Whether in the course training or testing, his component outputs the result only at the final timestep.

Baseline of State Value: In reinforcement learning, it is generalized to include a comparison of the action value to an arbitrary baseline $b(s)$. The choice of the baseline does not affect the expected update of the algorithm, but it does affect the variance of the update and thus the rate of convergence. $b_t = f_b(h_t, \theta_b)$, where f_b is a fully connected layer with parameters θ_b. Taken the cumulative reward R as reference value, we use back-propagation method to update parameters θ_b, but gradient is not transferred to the RNN layer. In course of testing, this component is not used.

3.2 Training

The observation location outputs $\{l_t, d_t\}$ are non-differentiable components of our model that cannot be trained with standard back-propagation. The parameters of our agent are given by the $\{\theta_l, \theta_d\}$ parameters of the prediction network. After executing an action the agent receives a new visual observation of the video frame v_t and obtains a reward r_t. The goal of the agent is to maximize the cumulative reward which is usually very sparse and delayed: $R = \sum_{t=1}^{T} r_t$. In this paper, our goal is to make a correct classification of the videos. So we set $r_T = 1$ if the action is classified correctly after T steps and 0 otherwise.

The above setup is a special instance of what is known in the RL community as a Partially Observable Markov Decision Process (POMDP). The true state of the environment is unobserved. In this view, the agent needs to learn a policy $\pi((l_t, d_t)|s_{1:t}; \theta)$ with parameters θ that, at each step t, maps the history of past interactions with the environment $s_{1:t} = x_1, l_1, d_1, ..., x_{t-1}, l_{t-1}, d_{t-1}, x_t$ to a distribution over actions for the current time step, subject to the constraint of the observation network. In this paper, the policy π_θ is defined by the prediction

---

Algorithm 1. Prediction Network Parameters Algorithm

Input: differentiable policy $\pi(l_t|h_t,\theta_l), \pi(d_t|h_t,\theta_d)$,step size λ

    Initialize policy parameters θ

1: $\delta_l \leftarrow 0, \delta_d \leftarrow 0$
2: **for** $m = 1 \rightarrow M$ **do**
3:     **if** $(argmax(p_T) == y)$ **then**
4:         $R^m \leftarrow 1$
5:     **else**
6:         $R^m \leftarrow 0$
7:     **end if**
8:     **for** $t = 1 \rightarrow T$ **do**
9:         $\delta_R^m \leftarrow R^m - b_t^m$
10:        $\delta_l \leftarrow \delta_R^m \nabla_{\theta_l} \ln\pi\left(l_t^m|h_t^m,\theta_l\right)$
11:        $\delta_d \leftarrow \delta_R^m \nabla_{\theta_d} \ln\pi\left(d_t^m|h_t^m,\theta_d\right)$
12:     **end for**
13: **end for**
14: $\theta_l \leftarrow \theta_l + \lambda\delta_l, \ \theta_d \leftarrow \theta_d + \lambda\delta_d$

---

network outlined above, and the history s_t is summarized in the state of the hidden units h_t. Give an agent interacting with a video, π_θ is the agent's policy. The objective function of learning distribution over actions conditioned on the interaction sequences is defined as:

$$J(\theta) = \mathrm{E}\left(\left(\sum_{t=1}^{T} r_t\right); \pi_\theta\right) = \sum_{s} \pi(s,\theta)R$$

where s is interaction sequence obtained by running the current agent π_θ, R is the sum of rewards, $\pi(s,\theta)$ is the agent's policy, $\sum_{s} \pi(s,\theta)$ represents averaging multiple sequences. The aim of reinforcement learning is to find the best parameter θ to maximize the objective function $J(\theta)$. The process of finding the optimal parameter θ is to find the optimal policy or the optimal path. The above problem is essentially an optimization problem. The simplest and most commonly used method is the gradient descent method. That is:

$$\theta_{new} = \theta_{old} + \lambda\nabla J(\theta)$$

The gradient of the object function is:

$$\nabla_\theta J(\theta) = \nabla_\theta \sum_{s} \pi(s,\theta)R$$
$$= \sum_{s} \nabla_\theta \pi(s,\theta)R$$
$$= \sum_{s} \pi(s,\theta) \frac{\nabla_\theta \pi(s,\theta)R}{\pi(s,\theta)}$$
$$= \sum_{s} \pi(s,\theta)R\nabla_\theta \log \pi(s,\theta)$$

The upper formula is equivalent to the $R\nabla_\theta \log \pi (s, \theta)$ expectation. This expression can be estimated by Monte Carlo sampling, that is, we get multiple episodes according to the current policy. So, the approximation is:

$$\nabla_\theta J (\theta) \approx \frac{1}{M} \sum_{m=1}^M R^m \nabla_\theta \log \pi (s^m, \theta)$$

The $\pi (s, \theta)$ is probability of T timesteps episode, which is represents as:

$$\pi (s, \theta) = \prod_{t=1}^T \pi (s_t, \theta)$$

Then, the gradient of object function is:

$$\nabla_\theta J (\theta) \approx \frac{1}{M} \sum_{m=1}^M \sum_{t=1}^T R^m \nabla_\theta \log \pi \left(s_t^m, \theta\right)$$

To reduce the variance of the gradient estimate, a baseline reward b_t^m is often estimated, e.g. via $b = f_b (h_t, \theta_b)$ in prediction network, and subtracted so that the gradient equation becomes:

$$\nabla_\theta J (\theta) \approx \frac{1}{M} \sum_{m=1}^M \sum_{t=1}^T \left(R_t^m - b_t^m\right) \nabla_\theta \log \pi \left(s_t^m, \theta\right)$$

where $R_t^m = \sum_{n=t}^T r_n^m$ is the cumulative reward obtained from t step to T step. In this paper $R_t^m = R^m$. And b_t^m is the estimated value at the h_t state of the mth episode. Due to $\pi (\theta) = \pi (\theta_d) \pi (\theta_l)$, we get:

$$\nabla_\theta \log \pi (s, \theta) = \nabla_{\theta_d} \log \pi (s, \theta_d) + \nabla_{\theta_l} \log \pi (s, \theta_l)$$

Since $\pi (s, \theta_d)$ is Gaussian distribution, we get:

$$\nabla_{\theta_d} \log \pi (s, \theta_d) = \frac{\left(l_d' - l_d\right)}{\sigma^2}$$

Here l_d is prediction output, that is taken as mean of this Gaussian distribution. l_d' is the sampled value. As a hyper-parameter, σ is the fixed variance of this Gaussian distribution. In the same way, we can calculate the $\nabla_{\theta_l} \log \pi (s, \theta_l)$.

The resulting algorithm increases the log-probability of an action that was followed by a larger than expected cumulative reward, and decreases the log-probability if the cumulative reward was smaller. After update $\{\theta_l, \theta_d\}$ parameters, other parameters under the prediction network, e.g. (W, b) of RNN and $FC6$ of CNN, are updated using back-propagation, because they are differentiable. Besides the policy optimization, we also need to optimize the classifier, whose loss function of classifier is defined as softmax loss. To update baseline parameter θ_b, we define its loss function as Euclidean loss. The baseline gradient does not propagate backward to the next layer. Algorithm 1 shows the basic process of gradient descent method. In experiments, we actually use stochastic gradient descent algorithm.

Fig. 2. Sample frames from different actions datasets. (a) UCF101 (b) HMDB51

4   Experiments

In this section, we evaluate performance of the proposed method for action recognition on two action data sets, and compare it with previous methods in literature. The experiments were doing in two datasets that are the most challenging datasets in recently. The performance of the action recognition is evaluated by the average precise. Some example frames are illustrated in Fig. 2.

4.1   Datasets

The **UCF101** dataset [18] has 101 action categories and contains 13,320 videos, consisting of realistic videos taken from YouTube ranging from general sports to daily life exercises, with each category containing at least 100 clips. The dataset is particularly interesting because it gives the largest diversity in terms of actions and with the presence of large variations in camera motion, object appearance and pose, object scale, viewpoint, cluttered background, illumination conditions, etc. There are three splits for training and testing (70% training and 30% testing).

The **HMDB51** dataset [11] collects video clips in abundant source, both from movies and Internet, there are 6,766 videos and 51 action categories in total. We follow the original protocol using three train-test splits. For every class and split, there are 70 videos for training and 30 videos for testing. We report average accuracy over the three splits as performance measure on the original videos.

4.2   Implementation Detail

All the videos in the datasets, the observation image patch is 76×76. For the RNN, the LSTM cell has 512 hidden units. The agent is given a fixed number of observations for each episode, typically $T = 10$ in our experiments. We train model by using stochastic gradient descent optimization algorithm with mini-batches of size 128 episodes and momentum of 0.9, weight decay of 0.0005, initial learning rate of 0.001. Other hyper-parameters were selected using random search. In this paper, we set the $D = 10$, the $L = 70$, the Gaussian distribution variance fixed 0.1.

4.3   Comparison to Baseline

We train our model only using RGB video frames, not using optical flow data. The CNN model [17] and CNN+LSTM model [3] are taken as baseline. As can be seen from Table 1, our model obtains robust improvements over the baseline on UCF101 and HMDB51. The result of the experiment demonstrates that the hard attention approach can decrease the irrelative visual information influence and increase the correctness of classifier.

Table 1. Comparison to baseline on the UCF101 and HMDB51 data sets.

Model	UCF101		HMDB51	
	RGB	RGB+Flow	RGB	RGB+Flow
CNN (Two Stream Network) [17]	73.0	88.0	40.5	59.4
CNN+LSTM [3]	68.2	82.7	-	-
Our Hard-attention Model	93.2	-	66.8	-

4.4   Comparison to State-of-the-Art

Finally, we compare our method against the state-of-the art models. As shown in Table 2, our model can achieve competitive results in comparison with existing published methods. Our results are closed to the [2,13,23] which used much larger pre-train data sets. It is also interesting to observe that in some cases, the model is able to attend to important objects in the video frames and attempts to track them to some extent in order to correctly identify the performed activity.

Table 2. Action Recognition mAP (%) on the UCF101 and HMDB51 data sets.

Model	UFC101	HMDB51	Year	Pre-train dataset
IDT [20]	72.4	40.2	2013	None
Two Stream Network [17]	88.0	59.4	2014	ImageNet
CNN+LSTM [3]	82.7	-	2015	ImageNet
Spatial TDD [22]	82.8	50.0	2015	ImageNet
CNN+LSTM fusion [5]	92.5	65.4	2016	ImageNet
Spatial Stream ResNet [4]	82.3	43.4	2016	ImageNet
TSN Spatial Network [24]	86.4	53.7	2016	ImageNet
RGB-I3D [2]	95.6	74.8	2017	ImageNet+Kinetics
ARTNet with TSN [23]	94.3	70.9	2018	Kinetics
Attention Cluster RGB+Flow [13]	94.6	69.2	2018	Kinetics
Our Hard-attention Model	93.2	66.8	2018	ImageNet

5   Conclusion

In this paper, we have proposed reinforcement learning method for action recognition in videos, which aims to select the most informative frames and the retina region of the input sequences. because of the stochasticity in the glimpse policy during training, The hard-attention based model is less prone to over-fitting than common deep model. Our architecture should be applicable to related tasks such as action localization and detection in video. In terms of future work, we hope to add optical information for prediction of next frame location.

Acknowledgement. The research was supported by the National Nature Science Foundation of China (61671336, U1611461, U1736206), Technology Research Program of Ministry of Public Security (2016JSYJA12), Hubei Province Technological Innovation Major Project (2016AAA015, 2017AAA123), Hubei Provincial Education Department Project (16Q070), Nature Science Foundation of Jiangsu Province (BK20160386).

References

1. Ba, J., Mnih, V., Kavukcuoglu, K.: Multiple object recognition with visual attention. In: ICLR (2015)
2. Carreira, J., Zisserman, A.: Quo vadis, action recognition? A new model and the kinetics dataset. In: CVPR (2017)
3. Donahue, J., et al.: Long-term recurrent convolutional networks for visual recognition and description. In: CVPR (2015)
4. Feichtenhofer, C., Pinz, A., Wildes, R.: Spatiotemporal residual networks for video action recognition. In: NIPS (2016)
5. Feichtenhofer, C., Pinz, A., Zisserman, A.: Convolutional two-stream network fusion for video action recognition. In: CVPR (2016)
6. Girdhar, R., Ramanan, D.: Attentional pooling for action recognition. In: NIPS (2017)
7. Girdhar, R., Ramanan, D., Gupta, A., Sivic, J., Russell, B.: ActionVLAD: learning spatio-temporal aggregation for action classification. In: CVPR (2017)
8. Ji, Y., Yang, Y., Xu, X., Shen, H.T.: One-shot learning based pattern transition map for action early recognition. Signal Process. **143**, 364–370 (2018)
9. Karpathy, A., Toderici, G., Shetty, S., Leung, T., Sukthankar, R., Fei-Fei, L.: Large-scale video classification with convolutional neural networks. In: CVPR (2014)
10. Krizhevsky, A., Sutskever, I., Hinton, G.E.: Imagenet classification with deep convolutional neural networks. In: NIPS (2012)
11. Kuehne, H., Jhuang, H., Garrote, E., Poggio, T., Serre, T.: HMDB: a large video database for human motion recognition. In: ICCV (2011)
12. Li, Z., Gavrilyuk, K., Gavves, E., Jain, M., Snoek, C.G.: VideoLSTM convolves, attends and flows for action recognition. Comput. Vis. Image Underst. **166**, 41–50 (2018)
13. Long, X., Gan, C., de Melo, G., Wu, J., Liu, X., Wen, S.: Attention clusters: purely attention based local feature integration for video classification. In: CVPR (2018)
14. Mnih, V., Heess, N., Graves, A., Kavukcuoglu, K.: Recurrent models of visual attention. In: NIPS (2014)

15. Ng, J.Y.H., Hausknecht, M., Vijayanarasimhan, S., Vinyals, O., Monga, R., Toderici, G.: Beyond short snippets: deep networks for video classification. In: CVPR (2015)
16. Sharma, S., Kiros, R., Salakhutdinov, R.: Action recognition using visual attention. In: ICLR (2016)
17. Simonyan, K., Zisserman, A.: Two-stream convolutional networks for action recognition in videos. In: NIPS (2014)
18. Soomro, K., Zamir, A.R., Shah, M.: UCF101: a dataset of 101 human actions classes from videos in the wild. arXiv preprint arXiv:1212.0402 (2012)
19. Srivastava, N., Mansimov, E., Salakhudinov, R.: Unsupervised learning of video representations using LSTMs. In: ICML (2015)
20. Wang, H., Schmid, C.: Action recognition with improved trajectories. In: ICCV (2013)
21. Wang, K., Wang, X., Lin, L., Wang, M., Zuo, W.: 3D human activity recognition with reconfigurable convolutional neural networks (2014)
22. Wang, L., Qiao, Y., Tang, X.: Action recognition with trajectory-pooled deep convolutional descriptors. In: CVPR (2015)
23. Wang, L., Li, W., Li, W., Van Gool, L.: Appearance-and-relation networks for video classification. In: The IEEE Conference on Computer Vision and Pattern Recognition (CVPR) (2018)
24. Wang, L., et al.: Temporal segment networks: towards good practices for deep action recognition. In: Leibe, B., Matas, J., Sebe, N., Welling, M. (eds.) ECCV 2016. LNCS, vol. 9912, pp. 20–36. Springer, Cham (2016). https://doi.org/10.1007/978-3-319-46484-8_2
25. Xu, K., et al.: Show, attend and tell: neural image caption generation with visual attention. In: ICML (2015)
26. Xu, Z., Hu, R., Chen, J., Chen, H., Li, H.: Global contrast based salient region boundary sampling for action recognition. In: Tian, Q., Sebe, N., Qi, G.-J., Huet, B., Hong, R., Liu, X. (eds.) MMM 2016. LNCS, vol. 9516, pp. 187–198. Springer, Cham (2016). https://doi.org/10.1007/978-3-319-27671-7_16
27. Yeung, S., Russakovsky, O., Mori, G., Fei-Fei, L.: End-to-end learning of action detection from frame glimpses in videos. In: CVPR (2016)
28. Zhang, M., Yang, Y., Ji, Y., Xie, N., Shen, F.: Recurrent attention network using spatial-temporal relations for action recognition. Signal Process. **145**, 137–145 (2018)

Soccer Video Event Detection
Based on Deep Learning

Junqing Yu[1,2(⊠)], Aiping Lei[1], and Yangliu Hu[1]

[1] School of Computer Science and Technology,
Huazhong University of Science and Technology, Wuhan 430074, China
yjqing@hust.edu.cn
[2] Center of Network and Computation,
Huazhong University of Science and Technology, Wuhan 430074, China

Abstract. Automatically identifying the most interesting content in a long video remains a challenging task. Event detection is an important aspect of soccer game research. In this paper, we propose a model that is able to detect events in long soccer games with a single pass through the video. Combined with replay detection, we generate story clips, which contain more complete temporal context, meeting audiences' needs. We also introduce a soccer game dataset that contains 222 broadcast soccer videos, totaling 170 video hours. The dataset covers three annotation types: (1) shot annotations (type and boundary), (2) event annotations (with 11 event labels), and (3) story annotations (with 15 story labels). Finally, we report the performance of the proposed model for soccer events and story analysis.

Keywords: Soccer video · Event detection · Deep learning · Video analysis

1 Introduction

With the growth of online media, the development of techniques through which users can efficiently locate specific clips from videos has become an active research topic. As a motivating example, the many soccer games broadcast across the Internet increase the need for automatic video analysis, especially event detection, which is the fundamental component of video summarization, providing interesting highlights and quick browsing [1]. Research about soccer event detection based on traditional machine learning methods has made some achievements in the last decade. However, these detection results have coarse granularity, and only a few event types can be detected. Besides, traditional methods often need the help of audio commentary or text information related to the game, which are not stable for a soccer game video. Recently, event recognition and detection has benefited from the development of deep learning and large-scale datasets [2–5]. However, most of those studies are limited to single-person action detection, so there is a lack of research about multi-person activity analysis.

Owing to the large number of players in various movements and the complex game rules, soccer is the one of the most difficult ball games to analyze. Most existing datasets of sports consist of video clips with different kinds of sports or action labels,

© Springer Nature Switzerland AG 2019
I. Kompatsiaris et al. (Eds.): MMM 2019, LNCS 11296, pp. 377–389, 2019.
https://doi.org/10.1007/978-3-030-05716-9_31

Fig. 1. Three kinds of annotation in our dataset.

instead of temporal annotations of events in full games. Event analysis for ball games is different from other general event analysis. A complete clip contains necessary interesting context other than the key action clip. For example, in soccer games, the wonderful delivery before shooting, the celebration after the goal, and the clear replay for the highlight are also important components of a complete soccer event. Therefore the context of events and relationships among different components also matters in soccer games.

Therefore we collected a new soccer dataset consisting of three kinds of annotations, as shown in Fig. 1: events, stories, and shots. We propose a soccer event detection model using 11 annotations to identify 15 different types of stories that combine events and replay analysis. The third kind of annotation, i.e., shots, which represent a continuous action or event, are series of frames that are continuously captured by the same camera. we hope that the shot annotations of the dataset could additionally help researchers detect events—we using the replay annotation for story generation in the proposed method.

The contributions of this work can be summarized as follows:

(1) We introduce a method for detecting events across multiple temporal scales that span the video in a single pass.
(2) We analyze the context of events and generate story clips through replay location and replay event recognition.
(3) We provide a new soccer video dataset including event and shot annotations across 222 soccer videos. There are 71936 shots, 6850 events, and 6294 story instances.

2   Related Work

Dataset. Datasets for action or event analysis comprise two types: recognition and detection. The datasets for action or event recognition, such as HMDB [6], TRECVID-MED [7], UCF101 [4], and Sports-1 M [2], consist of trimmed videos, and each video has only one class label. Those datasets are mostly about single-person actions or activities in different scenes. Some recent datasets provide temporal annotations of untrimmed videos about complex multi-person activities. THUMOS 2014 [3] provides temporal annotations for 20 action classes in the test set, yet the training set and validation set are trimmed videos. ActivityNet [5] provides temporal annotations for each video, covering 203 activity classes. The NCAA basketball dataset [8] contains 257 basketball games with 14000 event annotations corresponding to 11 event classes. In addition, it provides bounding boxes of all players in a subset of 9000 frames from training videos for the detailed analysis of players.

Action Recognition in Videos. Some researchers have achieved good results in action recognition based on convolutional neural network (CNN) features, and they improved the model with some other processing methods such as optical flow images, improved dense trajectory (IDT) features, and feature fusion from multiple CNN layers [9–11]. Other researchers have inserted the temporal fusion strategies in the middle of the basic CNN structure to extract spatiotemporal information from video clips [12–14]. More recently, three-dimensional (3D) convolution in the convolution stages of CNNs has been explored to compute features from both the spatial and temporal dimensions, especially for C3D, which is a flexible program applied in some CNNs [15–17]. Some studies have simultaneously used 2D CNN and 3D CNN to extract features from RGB images and optical flow images, respectively, and represent the final video through the fusion of the two kinds of features [17, 18]. Finally, researchers have achieved state-of-the-art results by combining CNN with recurrent neural network (RNN) [19–22]. We follow this line of work to achieve multiple temporal scales for soccer event and story detection.

Event Detection in Untrimmed Videos. In sports games, event detection covers single-person action detection, multi-person activity detection, and highlight detection. Traditionally, multimodal information, such as visual features, text from the Internet related to the game, and audio, are jointly used to detect events in sports games [23–26]. Ramanathan et al. [8] applied multiple RNNs representing the frame, player, and event state to detect basketball events. Ibrahim et al. [27] analyzed each player's state with long short-term memory (LSTM) to deduce the entire game state according to the players' states in a volleyball game. Some methods have used models based on a fixed-length sliding window to obtain the temporal boundaries of events [28–31]. However, those methods can only identify events on multiple temporal scales by running multiple sliding windows with different lengths. Yeung et al. [32] explored the idea of a visual attention model with reinforcement learning for action detection, which gave the action temporal boundaries from the RNN hidden state. Shou et al. [28] detected actions via multi-stage CNNs by improving C3D to include proposal, classification, and location networks. Detection model have been constructed by combining C3D and RNN to directly propose multiple temporal boundaries of actions [33, 34]. Krishna et al. [35] used data analysis protocols (DAPs) and a language model with an attention model to identify all events of a video in a single pass while simultaneously describing the detected events with natural language. Yao et al. [36] used a 2D CNN and a 3D CNN for spatial and temporal feature extraction, respectively, and obtained highlights from first-person video through a ranking method. One aspect of this work is the construction of a model that produces multi-length soccer event clips in a single pass.

This literature review reveals that there are many excellent works about action or event detection. However, the characteristics of soccer games, such as small players and ball in frame, which are difficult to track, and the audience's need for the complete content of each event, differs from general activity analysis. Thus, it is necessary to explore effective methods about soccer event detection.

3   Soccer Video Dataset

This dataset aims to provide multi-type annotations to meet various needs. We use 222 soccer games available from the Internet, spanning several recent soccer competitions including the FIFA World Cup 2014, the AFC Asian Cup 2015, the UEFA EURO 2016, and the 2016/2017 Premier League. Each video comprises half of a game, which is approximately 45 min long. The dataset consists of videos in both high-definition (1080p) and low-definition (360p) resolutions; all videos have a frame rate of 25 fps. To ensure the accuracy of annotations, each video or sequence was annotated by a person (an annotator), and the results were cross-checked.

3.1   Shot

The video shot annotations consist of two parts: shot boundary and shot type. Each shot is annotated with the first and last frame number and the shot transition type: either cut or gradual transition. The shots in videos are manually grouped into five semantic classes [6]: far-view shot, medium-view shot, close-view shot, off-field shot, playback shot. Sometimes, a single shot may contain more than one shot type. We have marked the boundaries of these shots as "other", and annotated all shot types included during these shots, in order.

3.2   Event

Event detection in soccer games plays an important role in soccer video analysis. We define two types of event boundaries: events and stories. Events are fine-grained clips with action-driven definitions. The boundaries of events are defined according to the key player's action and the position of the ball. In contrast, stories have coarser granularity when compared with the boundaries of events, and they include the complete temporal context of an event.

4   Proposed Method

Our goal is to design an architecture that jointly locates the events and then proposes the temporal boundaries of stories, which contain the event clip and additional interesting temporal context. The sequence of work is to (1) detect replay clips throughout a full soccer game and recognize the event type of the replay clip, (2) detect matching event clips for the segments, and (3) generate story clips. Figure 2 shows the processing pipeline for a full soccer game. The main challenges we face are developing methods that can detect and recognize multi-length multi-type events and replay clips.

4.1   Replay Detection

>Replay is an important video editing method for soccer videos, by which audiences may view important and interesting segments. A replay shot in soccer videos is usually sandwiched between two logo-transitions, which usually contain approximately

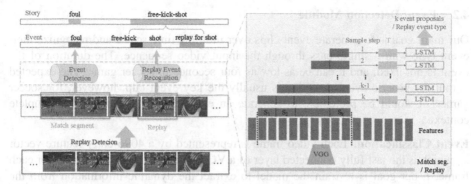

Fig. 2. Complete pipeline for soccer story detection in videos. We first detect the replay clips in the input video; then, we detect events in the match segments before the replay clips and identify the event type of the replay clips using the same event detection model. We separately extract VGG features from match segments and replay clips. The event detection model locates the event and evaluates the event type in the event detection part, whereas it only evaluates the replay event type of an input replay clip in the replay event recognition part. Finally, we concatenate relevant event clips and replay clips into a story.

30 frames. The shape of the logo varies drastically over different competitions, yet they are consistently highlighted and located at the center of the frame. Many methods exist to approach this problem. We use the CNN model to evaluate whether there is a logo in an input frame every five frames. If the model detects a logo for more than three sequential frames, the frame sequence that contains these detected logos is designated as a logo-transition. Overall, N logo-transitions will be detected from an input video; then, the logo-transitions are matched with their corresponding replay clips. The duration of a replay clip is usually less than one minute (1500 frames), so the distance between two logo-transitions belonging to one replay is much less than the distance between two replay clips. The total number of successfully matched logo-transition pairs decreases if there are incorrect pairings. According to these features of replay clips, we use dynamic programming to match logo-transitions to maximize the total number of logo-transition pairs, and the transfer equation is as follows:

$$
\begin{cases}
dp[i][1] = \begin{cases} dp[i-1][0] + 1, & \textit{if } \log o[i] - \log o[i-1] \leq 1500, \\ -1, & \textit{if } \log o[i] - \log o[i-1] > 1500, \end{cases} \\
dp[i][0] = \max(dp[i-1][0], dp[i-1][1]),
\end{cases}
\tag{1}
$$

where $dp[i][j]$ is the maximum number of logo-transition pairs for the first i logo-transitions, and j is set to 0 when the i-th logo-transition is not paired with the last logo-transition and 1 otherwise. For an input video, $\max(dp[N][0], dp[N][1])$ is the maximum number of logo-transition pairs. Therefore, we can obtain the logo-transition pairs according to the array dp. The segment between each logo pair is a replay clip.

4.2   Event Detection Module

Our main goal is to generate event clips over multiple time scales and recognize their event type with a single pass through the input video sequence. The duration of the event is not fixed, and it can be as low as four seconds in soccer game. The expected output for generic event detection is usually the key event clip; however, for soccer games, it would be preferable to generate an event clip that presents the complete context.

Event Classification. Each video frame is represented by a 4096-entry feature vector x_i, which is the last fully connected layer of a VGG-16 network [37]. Given x_t for each frame, t, our goal is to train the model to extract the dynamic information from the feature sequences and then recognize the event type for the input clip. We use an LSTM to represent the state of the event at time t:

$$h_t = \mathrm{LSTM}(x_t, h_{t-1}).$$

The output confidence scores, $s_{t,j}$, are given by a fully connected layer with sigmoid nonlinearity. Namely, $\{s_{t,j}\}_{j=1}^{C}$ corresponds to C event types at time step t. During training, we penalize the network for errors for an input clip, X, according to the softmax loss:

$$L(t, p, X, y) = -\sum_{c} y_c log(p_{t,c}),$$

where y_c is 1 if the clip belongs to class c or -1 otherwise. The model back-propagates at every time step t, so the total loss for all training examples χ is

$$L_{train} = \sum_{(X,y)\in\chi} \sum_{t=1}^{T} L(t, p, X, y).$$

Feature Fusion Among Multiple Frames. In the standard LSTM, a feature from a single frame is input to a timestamp cell. The cell can indirectly get information of other frames from the hidden state and memory cell. When the context information is complicated and the recognition task is multi-label, it is difficult to extract enough required information from one single frame feature. Therefore, we employ multi-feature fusion to extract additional features from adjacent frames available to each LSTM timestamp. Given a video feature sequence, $(x_1, x_2, \ldots, x_T)$, the input, v_t, to the LSTM at time step t is a weighted feature fusion, $v_t = \sum_{l} \alpha_{tl} x_l$, where l spans a fixed-size window of frames preceding i (i.e., five in this work) and α_{tl} is the contribution of frame x_l to input v_t as computed by the method by Yeung et al. [38].

Multi-length Event Detection. Many exists studies generate the temporal boundary of an event through sliding window methods [8, 28, 29, 32]. The event length is fixed to the length of the sliding window. With these methods, multi-length events are generated through several passes with multiple sliding windows of different lengths. We improve the processing method of an essential sliding window to generate multiple time scales with a single pass. As illustrated in Fig. 2, the sliding window, which begins with L_s and ends with L_e, contains L frame features. We equally partition the sliding window into k parts $s_1, s_2, ..., s_k$. There are k clips $[s_1, s_k], [s_2, s_k], ..., [s_{k-1}, s_k]$ and $[s_k, s_k]$ that have the same end-point, L_e, and different start-points. These k clips are different training samples, whereas they are multi-length event proposals during testing. The length of the LSTM is T, so k clips are sampled with k sample steps. For instance, the sample step for the clips $[s_1, s_k]$ and $[s_k, s_k]$ are k and 1, respectively. The length of the sliding window is $k \times T$. We can obtain k event proposals for each event class in a sliding window. We run the sliding window with stride δ, which is kept small to allow for dense generation of training data and proposals.

Replays occur after many events, especially for shots, goals, fouls, and penalty kicks. Therefore, it is likely that there is event in the temporal region just before a replay clip. We use the temporal relationship between events and replays to update the scores of event proposals. Finally we merge the event clips that overlap and belong to the same event type into one event.

4.3 Story Generation

A story segment contains event clips and replay clips about the same event. We recognize the event type of a replay using the event detection module, where the input is the trimmed replay clip and the output is the replay event. Next, we group the event clip and the replay that belongs to an event. We set a region of L frames just before a replay as the possible region for where the story begins. If there is an event clip that has the same event type as the replay and is close to the replay compared to other event clips with the same event type, we group the event clip and the replay into a story that begins with event clip and ends with the replay. As for unions, two contiguous event clips should be detected: e.g., corner and shot event clips should be detected for a corner-shot story. Other event clips that are not grouped with the replay are transformed into a story.

5 Experimental Evaluation

We evaluate the effectiveness of each module in the proposed method. In this section, we present our experimental settings and results.

Dataset. To train and evaluate the proposed method, we use three parts of the soccer dataset for each module: (1) the dataset that contains frames that do or do not contain logos for replay detection, (2) the dataset for event detection, and (3) the dataset for replay event type recognition. The 222 soccer videos were randomly split into 133 training, 43 validation, and 46 test videos, and each dataset for different modules was constructed from this split. The dataset for replay detection contains two classes (i.e., with logo or without logo) of four different logos from different soccer competitions. This resulted in 20890 training frames and 5222 validation frames. The training and validation sets for event detection consist of some trimmed clips containing 256 frames of at least one event, and the test set consists of 46 untrimmed soccer games. We treat all windows that do not overlap with any annotated event by more than 50% as negative. The dataset for replay event recognition consists of trimmed replay clips.

Implementation Details. We employ a pre-trained VGG-16 for the feature extractor and logo recognition model. We generate $k = 8$ proposals for each sliding window. We use two layers and a hidden state dimension of 512 for the LSTM and the length of the LSTM is $T = 16$. The stride, δ, is 16. We use a batch size of 128, and a learning rate of 0.005, which is reduced by a factor of 0.1 every 4 epochs with RMSProp. We implement the model and training/validation pipeline using PyTorch and Caffe.

5.1 Replay Detection

Replay detection includes logo-transition detection and logo pairing. The results of each step in this task are presented in Table 1. We achieve great performance both in logo detection and logo pairing. There are some incorrect detections because the features of close-up shots can sometimes be quite similar to the logo frame. Additionally, the use of dynamic programming improved the performance of logo pairing.

Table 1. Results for replay detection

Evaluation metrics	Logo detection	Logo pairing	
		non-DP	DP
Precision	0.997	0.986	0.996
Recall	1	0.963	0.996

5.2 Event Detection

In this section we evaluate the ability of the proposed methods to temporally locate events in untrimmed soccer videos. We compare the ability of each pipeline of the proposed method and compare against different baseline models explained below:

- Devnet [39]: We use the pre-trained VGG-16 for feature extraction with an SVM classifier.
- LRCN [22]: We use an LRCN model with fc7 features of VGG-16.
- SST [33]: We use VGG-16 features with SST temporal location and multi-scale event proposal generation.

The detection results are shown in Table 2. The method using both multi-features fusion ("Multi-Fea") and detection updates from replays ("Replay+") outperforms the methods without those optimization methods. The performance varies by class—the best performance was for "corner" events. In particular, the performance is much poorer (for all methods) for classes such as "offside" and "foul." This occurred because a large number of negative instances were introduced in the detection setting. Soccer videos are usually shown in the far-view, where the players are small, and whether an event happens is judged according to the relationship among multiple players' movements.

Table 2. Precision and recall for event detection

Method		Goal	Shot	Corner	Free-Kick	Yellow-card	Foul	Offside	Mean
Devnet [38]	Precision	0.013	0.070	0.086	0.028	0.025	0.049	0.005	0.039
	Recall	0.243	0.377	0.460	0.153	0.508	0.211	0.193	0.306
LRCN [21]	Precision	0.0	0.261	0.104	0.063	0.138	0.076	0.0	0.092
	Recall	0.0	0.244	0.709	0.659	0.618	0.724	0.0	0.422
SST [32]	Precision	0.032	0.371	0.739	0.561	–	–	–	–
	Recall	0.023	0.472	0.883	0.376	–	–	–	–
VGG-16	Precision	0.154	0. 226	0. 528	0. 181	0. 229	0. 140	0. 100	0. 223
	Recall	0.364	0. 818	0. 883	0. 582	0. 746	0. 371	0. 189	0. 565
VGG-16 Replay+	Precision	0.229	0. 251	0. 528	0. 181	0. 285	0. 184	0. 127	0. 253
	Recall	0.432	0. 836	0. 883	0. 582	0. 718	0. 399	0. 216	0. 581
VGG-16 Multi-Fea	Precision	0.309	0. 311	0. 710	0. 054	0. 146	0. 169	0. 047	0. 250
	Recall	0.383	0. 740	0. 854	0. 729	0. 831	0. 334	0. 297	0. 596
VGG-16 Multi-Fea Replay+	Precision	0.340	0. 335	0. 710	0. 054	0. 179	0. 211	0. 075	0. 272
	Recall	0.409	0. 756	0. 854	0. 729	0. 830	0. 392	0. 378	0. 621

5.3   Story Generation

Table 3 shows the results of replay event recognition. The performance of "shot" and "foul" are much better than the other event types. This occurs for two reasons: the number of instances is insufficient for model training or there is noise due to the replay clip because we give a complete replay clip one event label.

Table 3. Precision and recall for replay event recognition

Method		Goal	Shot	Corner	Free-kick	Yellow-card	Foul	Offside	Mean
SingleFea.	Precision	0.506	0.844	0.778	1.000	1.000	0.896	0.677	0.814
	Recall	0.782	0.787	0.500	0.556	0.529	0.919	0.724	0.685
Multi-Fea.	Precision	0.512	0.835	0.778	1.000	0.769	0.929	0.667	0.784
	Recall	0.8	0.826	0.500	0.611	0.588	0.879	0.758	0.709

Table 4. Result for story generation

Story	Position	Recall	True positive + False negative	True positive + False positive	True positive
goal	0.429	0.343	35	28	12
shot	0.382	0.642	338	568	217
corner	0.698	0.651	192	179	125
free-kick	0.052	0.611	149	1746	91
yellow-card	0.313	0.729	70	163	51
foul	0.404	0.442	362	396	160
offside	0.108	0.237	38	83	9
corner-goal	1.000	0.500	4	2	2
corner-shot	0.667	0.182	11	3	2
free-kick-goal	0.000	0.000	3	2	0
free-kick-shot	0.273	0.194	31	22	6
Mean	0.393	0.412	–	–	–

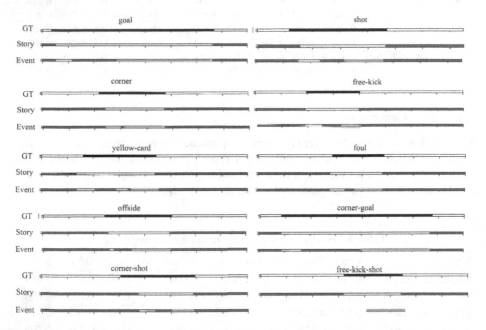

Fig. 3. Some instances of story generation. For each class, the first line is the ground truth (GT) annotated story; the yellow clips in the second line are story segments generated; in third line, the yellow clips are event clip detected while different shades of yellow in a continuous clip represent different event clips, and the red clip is replay. (Color figure online)

The story generation results are presented in Table 4. We list not only the precision and recall for the story generation but also the number of instances of each story class. The detection performance varies with the number of instances of each story class. The performance of story generation is a little poorer than the performance of event detection. This occurs because at least two independent clips, i.e., event and replay, comprise one story. Incorrect detection for either component results in failure for story generation, especially for union stories, which are generated when two contiguous events are detected and the replay event is recognized correctly. We visualize some successful story generation results for each class in Fig. 3. We also give the event detection results contained by the story.

6   Conclusion

We have introduced a new soccer video dataset that contains shot annotation and event annotation. In addition, we have introduced a model for soccer event detection across multiple temporal scales and story generation using the relationship between events and replays in soccer videos. We will add more valuable labels in the dataset, such as player annotation, and deeply analyze key players' actions in future work.

Acknowledgments. We gratefully acknowledge the granted financial support from the National Natural Science Foundation of China (No. 61572211, 61173114, 61202300).

References

1. D'Orazio, T., Leo, M.: A review of vision-based systems for soccer video analysis. Pattern Recognition (2010)
2. Karpathy, A., Toderici, S. Shetty, T. Leung, R. Sukthankar, Fei-Fei, L.: Large-scale video classification with convolutional neural networks. In: The IEEE Conference on Computer Vision and Pattern Recognition (CVPR) (2014)
3. Jiang, Y.-G., Liu, J., Roshan Zamir, A., Toderici, G., Laptev, I., Shah, M., Sukthankar, R.: THUMOS Challenge: Action Recognition with a Large Number of Classes (2014). http://crcv.ucf.edu/THUMOS14/
4. Soomro, K., Zamir, A.R., Shah, M.: UCF101: a dataset of 101 human actions classes from videos in the wild. arXiv preprint arXiv:1212.0402 (2012)
5. Caba Heilbron, F., Escorcia, V., Ghanem, B., Carlos Niebles. J.: Activitynet: a large-scale video benchmark for human activity understanding. In: The IEEE Conference on Computer Vision and Pattern Recognition (CVPR) (2015)
6. Kuehne, H., Jhuang, H., Garrote, E., Poggio, T., Serre, T.: HMDB: a large video database for human motion recognition. In: The IEEE International Conference on Computer Vision (ICCV) (2011)
7. Over, P., Fiscus, J., Sanders, G., Joy, D., Michel, M., Awad, G., Smeaton, A., Kraaij, W., Quénot, G.: Trecvid 2014–an overview of the goals, tasks, data, evaluation mechanisms and metrics. In: Proceedings of TRECVID (2014)
8. Ramanathan, V., Huang, J., Abu-El-Haija, S., Gorban, A., Murphy, K., Fei-Fei, L.: Detecting events and key actors in multi-person videos. In: The IEEE Conference on Computer Vision and Pattern Recognition (CVPR) (2016)

9. Chéron, G., Laptev, I., Schmid, C.: P-CNN: pose-based CNN features for action recognition. In: The IEEE International Conference on Computer Vision (ICCV) (2015)
10. Xu, Z., Yang, Y., Hauptmann, A.G.: A discriminative CNN video representation for event detection. In: The IEEE Conference on Computer Vision and Pattern Recognition (CVPR) (2015)
11. Yang, X., Molchanov, P., Kautz, J.: Multilayer and multimodal fusion of deep neural networks for video classification. In: Proceedings of the 2016 ACM on Multimedia Conference (2016)
12. Sun, L., Jia, K., Yeung, D.-Y., Shi, B.E.: Human action recognition using factorized spatio-temporal convolutional networks. In: The IEEE International Conference on Computer Vision (ICCV) (2015)
13. Feichtenhofer, C., Pinz, A., Wildes, R.P.: Spatiotemporal multiplier networks for video action recognition. In: The IEEE Conference on Computer Vision and Pattern Recognition (CVPR) (2017)
14. Wang, Y., Long, M., Wang, J., Yu, P.S.: Spatiotemporal pyramid network for video action recognition. In: The IEEE Conference on Computer Vision and Pattern Recognition (CVPR) (2017)
15. Ji, S., Xu, W., Yang, M., Yu, K.: 3D convolutional neural networks for human action recognition. IEEE Trans. Pattern Anal. Mach. Intell. 35(1), 221–231 (2013)
16. Tran, D., Bourdev, L., Fergus, R., Torresani, L., Paluri, M.: Learning spatiotemporal features with 3D convolutional networks. In: The IEEE International Conference on Computer Vision (ICCV) (2015)
17. Tran, D., Bourdev, L.D., Fergus, R., Torresani, L., Paluri, M.: C3D: generic features for video analysis. CoRR, abs/1412.0767 (2014)
18. Feichtenhofer, C., Pinz, A., Zisserman, A.: Convolutional two-stream network fusion for video action recognition. In: The IEEE Conference on Computer Vision and Pattern Recognition (CVPR) (2016)
19. Li, Q., Qiu, Z., Yao, T., Mei, T., Rui, Y., Luo, J.: Action recognition by learning deep multi-granular spatio-temporal video representation. In: Proceedings of the 2016 ACM on International Conference on Multimedia Retrieval (2016)
20. Yue-Hei Ng, J., Hausknecht, M., Vijayanarasimhan, S., Vinyals, O., Monga, R., Toderici, G.: Beyond short snippets: deep networks for video classification. In: The IEEE Conference on Computer Vision and Pattern Recognition (CVPR) (2015)
21. Srivastava, N., Mansimov, E., Salakhutdinov, R.: Unsupervised learning of video representations using lstms. CoRR, abs/1502.04681 (2015)
22. Donahue, J., Anne Hendricks, L., Guadarrama, S., Rohrbach, M., Venugopalan, S., Saenko, K., Darrell, T.: Long-term recurrent convolutional networks for visual recognition and description. In: The IEEE Conference on Computer Vision and Pattern Recognition (CVPR) (2015)
23. Doman, K., Tomita, T., Ide, I., Deguchi, D., Murase, H.: Event detection based on twitter enthusiasm degree for generating a sports highlight video. In: Proceedings of the 22nd ACM International Conference on Multimedia (2014)
24. Tavassolipour, M., Karimian, M., Kasaei, S.: Event detection and summarization in soccer videos using bayesian network and copula. IEEE Trans. Circuits Syst. Video Technol. 24(2), 291–304 (2014)
25. Kolekar, M.H., Sengupta, S.: Bayesian network-based customized highlight generation for broadcast soccer videos. IEEE Trans. Broadcast. 61(2), 195–209 (2015)
26. Arbat, S., Sinha, S.K., Shikha, B.K.: Event detection in broadcast soccer video by detecting replays. Int. J. Sci. Technol. Res. 3(5), 282–285 (2014)

27. Ibrahim, M.S., Muralidharan, S., Deng, Z., Vahdat, A., Mori: A hierarchical deep temporal model for group activity recognition. In: The IEEE Conference on Computer Vision and Pattern Recognition (CVPR) (2016)

28. Shou, Z., Wang, D., Chang: Temporal action localization in untrimmed videos via multi-stage CNNs. In: The IEEE Conference on Computer Vision and Pattern Recognition (CVPR) (2016)

29. Wang, L., Qiao, Y., Tang, X.: Action recognition and detection by combining motion and appearance features. THUMOS14 Action Recogn. Challenge 1(2), 2 (2014)

30. Lea, C., Flynn, M.D., Vidal, R., Reiter, A., Hager, G.D.: Temporal convolutional networks for action segmentation and detection. In: The IEEE Conference on Computer Vision and Pattern Recognition (CVPR) (2017)

31. Shou, Z., Chan, J., Zareian, A., Miyazawa, K., Chang, S.-F.: CDC: convolutional-de-convolutional networks for precise temporal action localization in untrimmed videos. In: The IEEE Conference on Computer Vision and Pattern Recognition (CVPR) (2017)

32. Yeung, S., Russakovsky, O., Mori, G., Fei-Fei, L.: End-to-end learning of action detection from frame glimpses in videos. In: The IEEE Conference on Computer Vision and Pattern Recognition (CVPR) (2016)

33. Buch, S., Escorcia, V., Shen, C., Ghanem, B., Niebles, J.C.: SST: single-stream temporal action proposals. In: The IEEE Conference on Computer Vision and Pattern Recognition (CVPR) (2017)

34. Escorcia, Victor, Caba Heilbron, Fabian, Niebles, J.C., Ghanem, Bernard: DAPs: deep action proposals for action understanding. In: Leibe, Bastian, Matas, Jiri, Sebe, Nicu, Welling, Max (eds.) ECCV 2016. LNCS, vol. 9907, pp. 768–784. Springer, Cham (2016). https://doi.org/10.1007/978-3-319-46487-9_47

35. Krishna, R., Hata, K., Ren, F., Fei-Fei, L., Niebles, J.C.: Dense-captioning events in videos. In: The IEEE International Conference on Computer Vision (ICCV) (2017)

36. Yao, T., Mei, T., Rui, Y.: Highlight detection with pairwise deep ranking for first-person video summarization. In: The IEEE Conference on Computer Vision and Pattern Recognition (CVPR) (2016)

37. Simonyan, K., Zisserman, A.: Very deep convolutional networks for large-scale image recognition. arXiv preprint arXiv:1409.1556 (2014)

38. Yeung, S., Russakovsky, O., Jin, N., Andriluka, M., Mori, G., Li, F.-F.: Every Moment Counts: Dense Detailed Labeling of Actions in Complex Videos. CoRR (2015)

39. Gan, C., Wang, N., Yang, Y., Yeung, D.-Y., Hauptmann, A.G.: Devnet: a deep event network for multimedia event detection and evidence recounting. In: The IEEE Conference on Computer Vision and Pattern Recognition (CVPR) (2015)

Spatio-Temporal Attention Model Based on Multi-view for Social Relation Understanding

Jinna Lv$^{(\boxtimes)}$ and Bin Wu$^{(\boxtimes)}$

Beijing Key Laboratory of Intelligent Telecommunications Software and Multimedia, Beijing University of Posts and Telecommunications, Beijing 100876, China
{lvjinna,wubin}@bupt.edu.cn

Abstract. Social relation understanding is an increasingly popular research area. Great progress has been achieved by exploiting sentiment or social relation from image data, however, it is also difficult to attain satisfactory performance for social relation analysis from video data. In this paper, we propose a novel Spatio-Temporal attention model based on Multi-View (STMV) for understanding social relations from video. First, in order to obtain rich representation for social relation traits, we introduce different ConvNets to extract multi-view features including RGB, optical flow, and face. Second, we exploit temporal features of multi-view through time using Long Short-Term Memory (LSTM) for social relation understanding. Specially, we propose multiple attention units in our attention module. Through this manner, we can generate an appropriate feature representation focusing on multiple aspects of social relation traits from video, thus excellent mapping function from low-level video pixels to high-level social relation space can be built. Third, we introduce a tensor fusion layer, which learns interactions among multi-view features. Extensive experiments show that our STMV model achieves the state-of-the-art performance on the SRIV video dataset for social relation classification.

Keywords: Social relation understanding · Video analysis
Deep learning · Attention mechanism

1 Introduction

Social relation understanding is an increasingly popular area of affective computing research [1,2]. Given a video clip, social relation understanding is to automatically recognize the types of social relations among persons appearing in the video. A precise social relation analysis model will promote in-depth understanding video content and benefit a broad range of applications such as relation extraction [3,4], and video summarization [5,6].

Human can easily understand social relations between two persons, however, comprehending this form of communication remains a significant challenge for

© Springer Nature Switzerland AG 2019
I. Kompatsiaris et al. (Eds.): MMM 2019, LNCS 11296, pp. 390–401, 2019.
https://doi.org/10.1007/978-3-030-05716-9_32

artificial intelligence. There are still some challenges for this problem: (1) it is hard to learn a satisfactory mapping function from low-level video pixels to high-level social relation space; (2) how to efficiently select the relevant information for the task of recognizing social relation from noisy and unsegmented video; (3) how to efficiently fuse the latent features from multi-view.

Existing methods for social relation analysis can be divided into two categories according to the input data. The first class is image-based. They learn social relation traits from static images including facial, distance of persons, and object features [7,8]. Different from image data, the second class is video-based [9,10]. For example, Bojanowski et al. used script and movie to find actors and actions in video [9]. However, most of these methods extract limited and rough video features, which ignore the special characteristics of social relations. Therefore, it is generally hard to learn a satisfactory mapping function from low-level video pixels to high-level social relation space.

For the second challenge, there are many attention mechanisms to solve this problem. They can be divided in two aspects: CNN-based [7,11,12] and LSTM-based [13,14]. For example, Zhu et al. [11] used attention unit to capture spatial regularization between labels, which learned an attention map for each label. However, these attention models always use a single attention unit or layer to learn one attention weight vector, which can be viewed as focusing on just one aspect of the data. Thus, more efficient attention models need to be proposed for social relation understanding.

The third challenge in social relation understanding is efficiently exploring intra-view dynamics of a specific modality. Sun et al. [7] used concatenate method to fuse age, head appearance, clothing, and proximity information to recognize the people's social relations. Lv et al. [10] employed RGB, optical flow, and audio using late fusion method. A shortcoming of these early fusion methods is lacking detailed modeling for view-specific dynamics. In addition, late fusion methods have no access to whether its predict labels due to which visual features.

In this paper, we propose a novel Spatio-Temporal attention network based on Multi-View, named STMV, which learns spatial and temporal information using multiple attention units. Specially, a tensor fusion layer is introduced, which can learn the intra and inter views dynamics. Our network models three views embeddings including RGB, optical flow, and faces images.

In summary, our proposed STMV model has the following advantages:

- In order to obtain a rich representation from low-level pixels to high level social relation space, we propose a novel spatio-temporal attention model based on multi-view (STMV) including RGB, optical flow, and face images of the video.
- Multiple attention units module is proposed in the STMV, which can focus on multiple aspects of each feature. Thus, more robust feature representation for social relations can be obtained.
- In order to learn both the intra-view and inter-view dynamics end-to-end, A tensor fusion layer is introduced. It can explicitly aggregate multi-view feature for social relation space.

The structure of this paper is as follows. We first discuss the related work in Sect. 2. Our proposed method is detailed introduced in Sect. 3. The experimental results are provided and discussed in Sect. 4. Finally, Sect. 5 concludes the paper.

2   Related Work

Social Relation Analysis. Social relation is an important element in our daily lives. Early method, Yang et al. [15] analyzed social relation from structured data. Later, several studies have investigated face features of people from image data to recognize social relations. For example, Zhang et al. [8] introduced a Siamese-like deep convolutional network to learn face feature from pairs of face images. Sun et al. [7] used an end to end deep network, which fuse age, head appearance, clothing, and proximity information to recognize the people's social relations. However, its fusion method is simply concatenating these feature vectors. Recently, social relation analysis from video data has also emerged. For example, Bojanowski et al. used script and movie to find actors and actions in video [9]. Lv et al. [10] introduced multi-view features, RGB, optical flow, and audio using late fusion method. For artificial intelligence, it is difficult to understand the gap between the low level pixels and the high level social relation space with single view. Therefore, new method for social relation recognition needs to be proposed.

Attention Mechanism. Attention mechanism was demonstrated to be beneficial in many tasks in computer vision field, such as image or video caption [12,13], machine translation [16], and video classification [17,18]. These approaches used attention mechanism on top of the ConvNets or LSTM model to introduce extra information, which can be categorized into spatial and temporal attention mechanisms. For example, the spatial attention mechanism adaptively focuses on related regions of the image when the deep network is trained with spatially related labels [11]. In the temporal attention mechanism, the attention-gated units accumulated the summative hidden states, and represent the sequence as the last state [19]. However, in those methods, the most common way is to add a max pooling or averaging step across all time steps. In our model, we introduce multiple attention units to learn different hidden features.

Multi-view Feature Fusion. Multiple views may be obtained from multiple sources or different feature subsets [20]. First, some studies have used multi-view features concatenation instead of modeling view-specific, which concatenation technique is known as early fusion. For example, Poria et al. [21] employed multiple kernel learning to organize multi-view features into groups. Second, late fusion methods were introduced by researchers to combine the multi-view features. For example, in order to combine learned unimodal predictions into a final prediction, Nojavanasghari et al. [22] used averaging and deep fusion method. Lv et al. [10] introduced late fusion method logistic regression to fuse the prediction results of multi-view. While aforementioned works are specifically designed for view-specific dynamics, they can not cope well with cross-view dynamics.

3   STMV Model

In this section, we discuss our STMV model for social relation understanding, which is designed to automatically recognize social relations between people from video. Figure 1 shows the overall architecture of our STMV network, which mainly consists of spatio-temporal feature extraction, multiple attention units, and a tensor fusion layer.

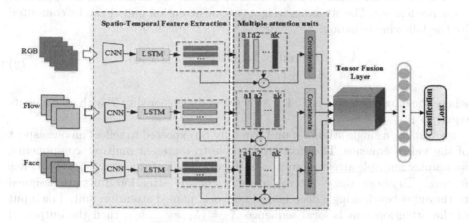

Fig. 1. Overview of the STMV model for social relation classification.

3.1   Spatio-Temporal Feature Extraction

In order to build excellent mapping function from low-level pixels to high level social relation space, we extract multi-view features from video using different ConvNets. For a video V, we can obtain three-view features for RGB, optical flow, and face images, which denoted as V_r, V_w, V_f, respectively.

The goal of the recurrent attention subnetwork LSTM is to learn a hidden sequence representation for each view. Given an input feature sequence $V_F = (x_1, x_2, ..., x_t, ..., x_T)$ of length T in which $x_t \in R^D$ denotes the observation at the t-th time step.

A basic LSTM unit consists of three gates: input gate $\mathbf{i}_t$, forget $\mathbf{f}_t$ and output $\mathbf{o}_t$. LSTM cell is calculated as follows:

$$\begin{aligned}
\mathbf{i}_t &= \sigma(W_i y_t + U_i h_{t-1} + b_i) \\
\mathbf{f}_t &= \sigma(W_f y_t + U_f h_{t-1} + b_f) \\
\mathbf{o}_t &= \sigma(W_o y_t + U_o h_{t-1} + b_o) \\
g_t &= \sigma(W_g y_t + U_g h_{t-1} + b_g) \\
m_t &= \mathbf{f}_t \odot m_{t-1} + \mathbf{i}_t \odot g_t \\
h_t &= \mathbf{o}_t \odot \phi(m_t)
\end{aligned} \tag{1}$$

Through the LSTM subnetwork, a sequence of features with temporal social relationships is generated. We denote this feature sequence of a video as $X = (h_1, h_2, ..., h_t)$ for each view.

3.2 Multiple Attention Units

At each timestamp t, various cross-view dynamics can occur simultaneously, therefore, a single attention unit may discard a considerable amount of information. In our STMV model, multiple attention units module is proposed, which can help the STMV model to capture multiple different aspect features of social relations.

We rely on an attention mechanism to obtain the importance of each local sequence feature. The attention weights of one attention unit A can be computed by the following equation:

$$A = softmax(w_2^T \tanh(w_1^T X + b_1) + b_2),$$
$$and \quad A = \tfrac{1}{T}\mathbf{1}, \tag{2}$$

where the dimension of A is T, $\mathbf{1}$ is a vector of dimensionality T with all elements equal to 1.

Normally, a single attention unit can only be expected to reflect on one aspect of the video sequence. Therefore, to be able to represent multiple components, we employ multiple attention units that focus on different parts of local sequence features. To obtain the K attention coefficients, K attention units are assigned to the subnetwork using a deep neural network, named attention unit. The input of the attention unit is local sequence $X = (h_1, h_2, ..., h_t)$, then the output of the k-th attention unit can be denoted as

$$F_k = A \odot X, \tag{3}$$

where $\odot$ represents the element-wise multiplication operation. Assuming there are K attention units, the final output for each view ban be denoted as

$$F = \oplus_{k=1}^K F_k, \tag{4}$$

where $\oplus$ represents the concatenate operation.

3.3 Tensor Fusion Layer

Existing works have introduced concatenation as an approach for multi-view fusion, which discounted the interactions among different views. Inspired by canonical correlation analysis, we employ a tensor fusion layer to fuse the latent features from video of multiple views.

Multi-view embeddings of the video from the previous stage denote as F^r, F^w, and F^f, respectively. The tensor fusion layer is defined as the following equation using Cartesian product:

$$F^m = (\begin{bmatrix} F^r \\ 1 \end{bmatrix} \otimes \begin{bmatrix} F^w \\ 1 \end{bmatrix}) \oplus (\begin{bmatrix} F^w \\ 1 \end{bmatrix} \otimes \begin{bmatrix} F^f \\ 1 \end{bmatrix}) \oplus (\begin{bmatrix} F^r \\ 1 \end{bmatrix} \otimes \begin{bmatrix} F^f \\ 1 \end{bmatrix}), \tag{5}$$

where $\otimes$ indicates the outer product between vectors, and $\oplus$ represents the concatenate operation. The definition is mathematically equivalent to a differentiable outer product between two of the F^r, F^w, and F^f. This layer has no learnable parameters.

The output space can represent all multi-view embeddings. Although each neural coordinate (F^r, F^w, and F^f) can be seen as a 3D point by the three-fold Cartesian product, this method will product very high dimensional output resulting in memory overflow. Therefore, we introduce $F^r \otimes F^w, F^r \otimes F^f$, and $F^w \otimes F^f$ to capture two views interactions in tensor fusion. Finally, concatenate operation obtains the three views interactions.

3.4 Social Relation Classification

The final feature of the video can be obtained after the tensor fusion layer, which is denoted as F_T^m. Then, we employ a fully connected layers and a sigmoid activation units instead of softmax connected to the decision layer.

$$p_i = \frac{1}{1 + \exp\{-(W_i^T F_T^m + b_i)\}}, \tag{6}$$

where i represents the i-class. We employ the cross-entropy loss in Eq. 7 to obtain the target social relation label.

$$loss = -\frac{1}{N} \sum_{n=1}^{N} \sum_{i=1}^{I} [label_i \log(p_i) + (1 - label_i) \log(1 - p_i)], \tag{7}$$

where $label_i$ is the ground truth of the i-th class, and p_i is the probability of predicted class computed by sigmoid function.

4 Experiments

4.1 Dataset and Comparison Methods

Dataset. The dataset used in this paper is collected from movies and TV dramas, named SRIV [10]. SRIV is the first video dataset for social relation recognition from videos, to our best knowledge. It contains 3,124 videos with multi-label, about 25 h, which is collected from 69 TV dramas and movies. Table 1 shows the basic statistics of the SRIV dataset. The top of the table shows the overall statistics, and the followings are the statistics of the number of different classes of social relations.

Comparison Methods. In the experiments, we compare the STMV model with a few state-of-the-art baselines by conducting extensive experiments on the SRIV dataset.

C3D: A network structure based on 3D convolution was proposed, which has excellent performance in video feature extraction [23].

Table 1. The basic statistics of the SRIV dataset.

Number of videos		Total length		Length range		Number of classes	
3124		25 h		5 s–220 s		16	
Sub-relation							
Dominant	Competitive	Trusting	Warm	Friendly	Attached	Inhibited	Assured
770	840	1614	1482	2221	600	594	810
Obj-relation							
Supervisor	Peer	Service	Parent	Mating	Sibling	Friendly	Hostile
627	469	238	321	600	141	1073	434

LSTM: The basic LSTM model [24], which is a popular technique for sequence modeling with various improved.

TSN: TSN [25] is a typical two-stream CNN network which has achieved the state-of-the-art performance on many video classification datasets. It not only employed spatial and temporal features, but also introduced a sparse temporal sampling strategy to enable efficient and effective learning.

Multi-stream: Multiple features representing social relations of people were used to improve the recognition performance [10]. Besides visual features, the author considered that audio characteristic generated when two people interacting contained useful relationship information.

STMV: Our model fusion of multi-view (i.e. RGB, optical flow, and face) using multiple attention units to learn spatio-temporal information for social relation understanding.

4.2   Evaluation Metrics

We adopt accuracy as the main evaluation metric, which is typically for social relation analysis [8]. The accuracy is computed by

$$accuracy = \frac{1}{2}(TP/N_p + TN/N_n),\tag{8}$$

where N_p and N_n are the number of positive and negative samples. In addition, we introduce other evaluation metrics, such as F_1 value, and the $sub_{accuracy}$. The F_1 value is computed by the following equation

$$F_1(i) = 2 \times TP(i)/(2 \times TP(i) + FP(i) + FN(i)),\tag{9}$$

where $TP(i)$, $FP(i)$, $TN(i)$ and $FN(i)$ denote the number of correct positive, false positive, true negative, and false negative of the i-th class respectively.

$$sub_{accuracy}(h) = \frac{1}{n}\sum_{k=1}^{n} I(h(x_k) = Y_k),\tag{10}$$

where $I(true) = 1$, $I(false) = 0$.

4.3 Feature Extraction

ConvNets have shown their powerful representation learning abilities in various image classification tasks. For multi-views features, we employ different ConvNets to extract high level features - RGB, optical flow and face images of video - to represent the social relation traits. For RGB feature, we use Resnet101 (trained on the Imagenet dataset) to extract RGB frame feature, with results in feature vector of 2,048 dimensions. For optical flow feature, we use the TSN network [25] (trained on the SRIV dataset). We set a fixed length feature vector every 5 pair optical flow frames, which encodes motion features computed around the middle of the window. For face feature, we use Deepid [26] (trained on the Youtube face dataset) to extract deep face feature of person, with results in feature vector of 4,096 dimensions.

4.4 Results of Social Relation Classification

Evaluation of Classification Performance. We first compare our STMV model with other video classification baselines on SRIV dataset. Table 2 presents the comparison results between the STMV and other baselines. We can see that the STMV outperforms all other baselines under investigation by 1.3% to 35.4% on accuracy. The performance of C3D and LSTM is pretty poor, which indicates that it is difficult to extract the feature representation of the social relations, although these methods can better describe the characteristics of the entire video. Our STMV achieves the best performance, which is because the multiple attention model can focus on more important information and could provide more hints for social relation analysis.

Table 2. Performance of different methods on SRIV.

Classifications	Methods	$accuracy$	$sub_{accuracy}$	F_1
Sub-relation	C3D [23]	0.5565	0.0347	0.3886
	LSTM [24]	0.6667	0.2797	0.5776
	TSN [25]	0.7089	0.3482	0.6142
	Multi-Stream [10]	0.7436	0.5213	0.6683
	STMV	**0.7535**	**0.5249**	**0.6795**
Obj-relation	C3D [23]	0.5568	0.1451	0.3018
	LSTM [24]	0.6147	0.3792	0.4193
	TSN [25]	0.5412	0.3045	0.4894
	Multi-Stream [10]	0.6136	0.5291	0.6383
	STMV	**0.6322**	**0.5311**	**0.6492**

Comparison with the Varying Size of Attention Units. Next, we consider the effect of different number of the attention units K. A single attention unit can be viewed as focusing on just one aspect of the video. Therefore, different hint information for social relations should be attended to by different units. In order to verify our idea, for fairness of comparison, we ensure that the numbers of other network parameters are completely identical, except for parameters of the units. As shown in Fig. 2, we find that with an increase in the number of attention units K, the accuracy performance significantly increases too. More importantly, the iteration also increases for increasing attention units. However, more computation are required with larger attention units. In our experiment, we set the number of attention units 64 to obtain the final results.

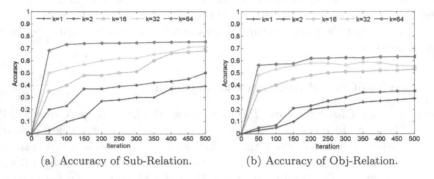

(a) Accuracy of Sub-Relation.   (b) Accuracy of Obj-Relation.

Fig. 2. The performance of accuracy in each epoch, learned with different number of attention units.

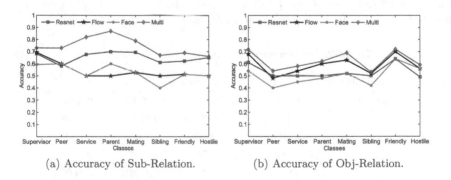

(a) Accuracy of Sub-Relation.   (b) Accuracy of Obj-Relation.

Fig. 3. The performance of accuracy curves of single view and multi-view fusion.

Comparison with Single View and Multi-view. In order to verify our multi-view fusion module, we compare the results of single view and multi-view, which are shown in Fig. 3. Form the comparison, we can find that STMV model can significantly improve the accuracy of social relation classification. Which suggests that the fusion of different views information of social relation traits is definitely various useful. As an example, the accuracy performance of face view is very poor on the class "Sibling", conversely very high on the class "Parent".

It suggest that different features may express the relationship between persons from different perspectives. Therefore, multi-view fusion module in the STMV can better describe the characteristics of social relations.

The Results of Different Classes. Figure 4 shows the classification performance of the sixteenth relations. We can see our STMV model has the best performance on almost all classes, which shows that STMV has well generalization ability to classify relations more accurately. However, there are a few classes that are not the best performance with STMV model. For example, the

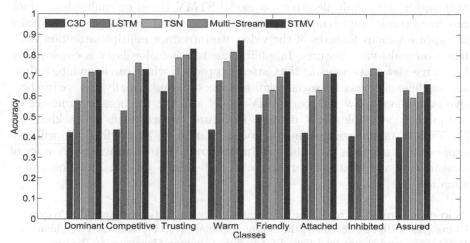

(a) Performance of different methods on the Sub-Relation.

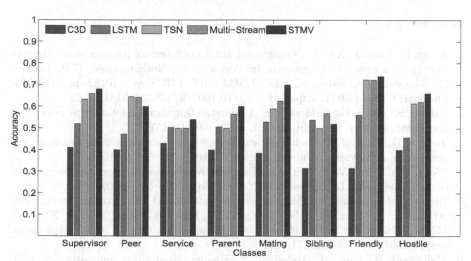

(b) Performance of different methods on the Obj-Relation.

Fig. 4. Social relation prediction performance of each class.

performance in term of accuracy on classes of "Inhibited" and "Sibling" are lower than Multi-stream method. This explains that the social relation traits of these classes are visually subtle compared to other relations. Specially, the predictions of "Friendly" class are significantly better than other classes. The reason is that "Friendly" class has more training samples than others.

5   Conclusion

In this paper, we study social relation understanding from video. Specially, we proposed a novel multiple attention model STMV based on multi-view, which can learn spatial and temporal information for social relation traits. In order to capture various features of the video, we introduce multiple attention units based on multi-view features. In addition, a tensor fusion layer is employed to fuse three-view features using the Cartesian product, which can learn interactions among different views for social relation understanding. Finally, the comprehensive evaluations show that our STMV model achieves the best performance on the publicly available SRIV dataset. In future, we will focus on tackling the challenge of multi-task learning for social relation understanding. We will also explore other methods to combine multiple knowledge to improve the accuracy of classification and weakly-supervised label embeddings for social relation understanding.

Acknowledgment. This research is supported by the National Key R&D Program of China (No. 2018YFC0831500), the National Social Science Foundation of China (No. 16ZDA055), and the Special Found for Beijing Common Construction Project.

References

1. Xiang, L., Sang, J., Xu, C.: Demographic attribute inference from social multimedia behaviors: a cross-OSN approach. In: Amsaleg, L., Guðmundsson, G.Þ., Gurrin, C., Jónsson, B.Þ., Satoh, S. (eds.) MMM 2017. LNCS, vol. 10132, pp. 515–526. Springer, Cham (2017). https://doi.org/10.1007/978-3-319-51811-4_42
2. Alletto, S., Serra, G., Calderara, S.: Understanding social relationships in egocentric vision. Pattern Recognit. **48**(12), 4082–4096 (2015)
3. Tran, Q.D., Jung, J.E.: Cocharnet: extracting social networks using character co-occurrence in movies. J. Univers. Comput. **21**(6), 796–815 (2015)
4. Weng, C.Y., Chu, W.T., Wu, J.L.: RoleNet: movie analysis from the perspective of social networks. IEEE Trans. Multimed. **11**(2), 256–271 (2009)
5. Hirai, T., Morishima, S.: Frame-wise continuity-based video summarization and stretching. In: Tian, Q., Sebe, N., Qi, G.-J., Huet, B., Hong, R., Liu, X. (eds.) MMM 2016. LNCS, vol. 9516, pp. 806–817. Springer, Cham (2016). https://doi.org/10.1007/978-3-319-27671-7_67
6. Mahasseni, B., Lam, M., Todorovic, S.: Unsupervised video summarization with adversarial LSTM networks. In: CVPR, pp. 2982–2991 (2017)
7. Sun, Q., Schiele, B., Fritz, M.: A domain based approach to social relation recognition. In: CVPR, pp. 435–444 (2017)

8. Zhang, Z., Luo, P., Loy, C.C., Tang, X.: Learning social relation traits from face images. In: ICCV, pp. 3631–3639 (2015)
9. Bojanowski, P., Bach, F., Laptev, I., Ponce, J., Schmid, C., Sivic, J., Finding actors and actions in movies. In: ICCV, pp. 2280–2287 (2013)
10. Lv, J., Liu, W., Zhou, L., Wu, B., Ma, H.: Multi-stream fusion model for social relation recognition from videos. In: Schoeffmann, K., et al. (eds.) MMM 2018. LNCS, vol. 10704, pp. 355–368. Springer, Cham (2018). https://doi.org/10.1007/978-3-319-73603-7_29
11. Zhu, F., Li, H., Ouyang, W., Yu, N., Wang, X.: Learning spatial regularization with image-level supervisions for multi-label image classification. In: CVPR, pp. 2027–2036 (2017)
12. You, Q., Jin, H., Wang, Z., Fang, C., Luo, J.: Image captioning with semantic attention. In: CVPR, pp. 4651–4659 (2016)
13. Pan, Y., Yao, T., Li, H., Mei, T.: Video captioning with transferred semantic attributes. In: CVPR, pp. 984–992 (2017)
14. Yu, H., Gui, L., Madaio, M., Ogan, A., Cassell, J., Morency, L.P.: Temporally selective attention model for social and affective state recognition in multimedia content. In: MM, pp. 1743–1751 (2017)
15. Yang, Y., et al.: Mining competitive relationships by learning across heterogeneous networks. In: CIKM, pp. 1432–1441 (2012)
16. Luong, T., Pham, H., Manning, C.D.: Effective approaches to attention-based neural machine translation. In: EMNLP, pp. 1412–1421 (2015)
17. Long, X., Gan, C., de Melo, G., Wu, J., Liu, X., Wen, S.: Attention clusters: Purely attention based local feature integration for video classification. CoRR, abs/1711.09550 (2017)
18. Zadeh, A., Liang, P.P., Poria, S., Vij, P., Cambria, E., Morency, L.: Multi-attention recurrent network for human communication comprehension. arXiv:1802.00923 (2018)
19. Pei, W., Baltrusaitis, T., Tax, D.M.J., Morency, L.: Temporal attention-gated model for robust sequence classification. In: CVPR, pp. 820–829 (2017)
20. Xu, C., Tao, D., Xu, C.: A survey on multi-view learning. CoRR, abs/1304.5634 (2013)
21. Poria, S., Chaturvedi, I., Cambria, E., Hussain, A.: Convolutional MKL based multimodal emotion recognition and sentiment analysis. In: ICDM, pp. 439–448 (2016)
22. Nojavanasghari, B., Gopinath, D., Koushik, J., Baltrusaitis, T., Morency, L.: Deep multimodal fusion for persuasiveness prediction. In: ICMI, pp. 284–288 (2016)
23. Du, T., Bourdev, L., Fergus, R., Torresani, L., Paluri, M.: Learning spatiotemporal features with 3D convolutional networks. In: CVPR, pp. 4489–4497 (2015)
24. Findler, N.V.: Short note on a heuristic search strategy in long-term memory networks. Inf. Process. Lett. 1(5), 191–196 (1972)
25. Wang, L., et al.: Temporal segment networks: towards good practices for deep action recognition. In: Leibe, B., Matas, J., Sebe, N., Welling, M. (eds.) ECCV 2016. LNCS, vol. 9912, pp. 20–36. Springer, Cham (2016). https://doi.org/10.1007/978-3-319-46484-8_2
26. Sun, Y., Wang, X., Tang, X.: Deep learning face representation from predicting 10,000 classes. In: CVPR, pp. 1891–1898 (2014)

Detail-Preserving Trajectory Summarization Based on Segmentation and Group-Based Filtering

Ting Wu[1], Qing Xu[1(✉)], Yunhe Li[1], Yuejun Guo[1,2(✉)],
and Klaus Schoeffmann[3]

[1] School of Computer Science and Technology, Tianjin University, Tianjin, China
qingxu@tju.edu.cn, guoyuejun13@gmail.com
[2] Graphics and Imaging Lab, University of Girona, Girona, Spain
[3] Klagenfurt University, Universitaetsstr. 65-67, 9020 Klagenfurt, Austria

Abstract. In this paper, aiming at preserving more details of the original trajectory data, we propose a novel trajectory summarization approach based on trajectory segmentation. The proposed approach consists of five stages. First, the proposed relative distance ratio based abnormality detection is performed to remove outliers. Second, the remaining trajectories are segmented into sub-trajectories using the minimum description length (MDL) principle. Third, the sub-trajectories are combined into groups by considering both spatial proximity, through the use of searching window, and shape restriction. And the sub-trajectories within the same group are resampled to have the same number of sample points. Fourth, a non-local filtering method based on wavelet transformation is performed on each group. Fifth, the filtered sub-trajectories which derived from the same trajectory are linked together to present the summarization result. Experiments show that our algorithm can obtain satisfactory results.

Keywords: Trajectory summarization · Trajectory segmentation
Non-local filtering · Detail-preserving

1 Introduction

The rapid growth of the deployment of the position acquisition devices such as Global Positioning System (GPS) has generated massive trajectory data, which contains lots of valuable information and has already been used in many practical applications including urban computing [20] and intelligent transportation systems [19]. To discover the knowledge and to reveal the common trends behind the large amount of trajectory data, clustering is by far one of the most widely used techniques [15]. Classical clustering algorithms include k-means [17], DBSCAN [10] and OPTICS [6], but these methods are mainly focus on point data. Because trajectory has complex properties and usually has varying number of sample points, the feature vector of a trajectory and the distance measure

© Springer Nature Switzerland AG 2019
I. Kompatsiaris et al. (Eds.): MMM 2019, LNCS 11296, pp. 402–413, 2019.
https://doi.org/10.1007/978-3-030-05716-9_33

between the feature vectors of two trajectories are pretty hard to establish [19]. Even so, many clustering methods dedicated for trajectories have been proposed to tackle aforementioned difficulties. By utilizing a regression mixture model to represent the trajectories and EM algorithm to deal with the cluster memberships, Gaffney et al. [11,12] proposed a method to cluster trajectory as a whole. However, as argued in [16], clustering based on the unit of entire trajectory could miss the common trends embedded in their sub-portions. To mine more knowledge from the trajectory data, Lee et al. in [16] proposed a partition-and-group framework for trajectory clustering. They first use the minimum description length (MDL) principle to partition each trajectory into a set of line segments, and then cluster all these line segments through a density-based clustering method. Although their method generally produces satisfactory results for finding common patterns among sub-trajectories, the approximation by using a line segment to represent the sub-trajectory and the density-based clustering method may lost a lot of information and can either not preserve details of the original trajectories.

Due to the intrinsic complexity of trajectory data, the performance of the clustering algorithms is not so satisfactory. Inspired by the Block-Matching and 3D Filtering (BM3D) [8] image denoising algorithm, in [13,18], Guo et al. proposed a new method to summarize the information contained in the trajectory data by viewing the trajectory as signal that changes over time and space and taking advantage of the non-local information from the trajectories within its similarity group. Specifically, they first resampled the trajectories to make all the trajectories have the same number of sample points, then for each resampled trajectory, they found its similar trajectories and put them into one group based on their respective Euclidean distance (Note that for a particular trajectory, it can belong to many groups), finally, group-based filtering was performed on each group of trajectories and the final result for each trajectory was obtained by taking average of the corresponding trajectory from the groups it belongs to. By iteratively applying the group-based filtering approach on the trajectory data, their algorithm can produce multi-granularity abstractions of the input data. However, this method has two major drawbacks. First, resampling all the trajectories to have equal number of sample points may introduce significant error. Second, the entire trajectory based summarizing framework fail to preserve details of the original trajectory data.

In this paper, aiming at addressing the aforementioned disadvantages, we propose a novel trajectory summarization approach based on trajectory segmentation, which is different from all the previous studies. The key idea is that trajectory segmentation can effectively preserve the details of the trajectories, so we incorporated it into existing summarization procedures. The proposed approach consists of five stages, abnormality detection, trajectory segmentation, grouping, wavelet transformation based non-local filtering and linking. These five stages are performed iteratively to achieve detail-preserving trajectory summarization. The remainder of the paper is organized as follows. Section 2 shows the details of the novel trajectory summarization approach. Experimental results are given in Sect. 3. Finally, Sect. 4 concludes paper.

2   Proposed Method

The proposed detail-preserving trajectory summarization approach consists of five stages. By iteratively performing these five stages, our proposed method can produce multi-granularity summarizations of trajectories without sacrificing details. This section shows the details of each stage.

2.1   Abnormality Detection

For ease of explanation, we define the jth trajectory in the kth iterative output as

$$T_{k,j} = \left\{ p_1^{k,j}, p_2^{k,j}, ..., p_n^{k,j} \right\}, k \geq 0, \tag{1}$$

where $p_i^{k,j} = (x_i^{k,j}, y_i^{k,j})$ is the coordinate of ith sample points and $T_{0,j}$ is the input jth trajectory for the first iteration.

Inspired by non-local means algorithm [7], we can construct a searching window for each trajectory $T_{k,j}$, which is defined as

$$\Omega_{k,j} = \{(x, y)|x_{min} \leq x \leq x_{max}, y_{min} \leq y \leq y_{max}\}, \tag{2}$$

where x_{min} is the x-coordinate of the leftmost point of $T_{k,j}$, and x_{max}, y_{min}, y_{max} are all defined similarly. Then, we define two trajectories $T_{k,j}$ and $T_{k,m}$ as neighbors if their corresponding searching windows satisfy

$$\Omega_{k,j} \cap \Omega_{k,m} \neq \emptyset. \tag{3}$$

Finally, for a particular trajectory $T_{k,j}$, its neighbor set $\mathbf{N}(T_{k,j})$ is given by

$$\mathbf{N}(T_{k,j}) = \{T_{k,m}|\Omega_{k,j} \cap \Omega_{k,m} \neq \emptyset\}, \tag{4}$$

and we also define $\mathbf{N}^0(T_{k,j}) = \mathbf{N}(T_{k,j}) \backslash T_{k,j}$. For a better illustration, Fig. 1 shows three trajectories, $T_{0,1}$, $T_{0,2}$ and $T_{0,3}$. $T_{0,1}$ is the trajectory under consideration. Since the searching windows of $T_{0,1}$ and $T_{0,2}$ are overlapped, so $T_{0,2}$ is a neighbor of $T_{0,1}$ and will be put into the neighbor set of $T_{0,1}$. Conversely, $T_{0,3}$ will not be put into that set.

The searching window scheme is reasonable and intuitive. First, it can guarantee that the distance between two neighbor trajectories will not large. Second, the construction of the searching window is very straightforward. We only need to consider the four boundary points of that sub-trajectory. Third, the problem of judging neighborhood relationship between two sub-trajectories can be directly converted to judging the corresponding searching windows whether overlapped or not.

Abnormality detection is performed as follows. For a given trajectory $T_{k,j}$, we first calculate its neighbor set $\mathbf{N}(T_{k,j})$. Then for each trajectory $T_{k,m} \in \mathbf{N}(T_{k,j})$,

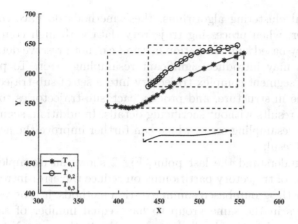

Fig. 1. Diagram of the searching window scheme, $T_{0,1}$ is the trajectory under consideration, $T_{0,2}$ is a neighbor of $T_{0,1}$ while $T_{0,3}$ is not.

we calculate the Euclidean distance $d_{m,n}^k$ between it and every trajectory $T_{k,n}$ that also satisfies $T_{k,n} \in \mathbf{N}(T_{k,j})$. If $T_{k,m}$ and $T_{k,n}$ have different number of sample points, we pad the smaller one with its last sample points to align with the longer one. The average Euclidean distance of $\mathbf{N}(T_{k,j})$ can be calculated by

$$d_j^k = \frac{\sum\limits_m \sum\limits_n d_{m,n}^k}{|\mathbf{N}(T_{k,j})|^2}, \tag{5}$$

where $|\mathbf{N}(T_{k,j})|$ is the number of trajectories in $\mathbf{N}(T_{k,j})$. Similarly, the average Euclidean distance D_j^k of $\mathbf{N}^0(T_{k,j})$ can also be calculated. We define the relative distance ratio of $T_{k,j}$ as

$$\eta_j^k = \frac{d_j^k}{D_j^k + \epsilon}, \tag{6}$$

where ϵ is a small positive number included to avoid dividing zero. η_j^k provides a way to measure how closeness the particular trajectory is related to its neighbors. If η_j^k is small, it means that the distances between $T_{k,j}$ and all its neighbors are relatively small, and $T_{k,j}$ is less likely to be an outlier. In contrast, outlier should have larger relative distance ratio value. We use the Box plot outlier identification [14] to determine the upper threshold γ. For any trajectory $T_{k,j}$ that satisfies $\eta_j^k > \gamma$, it is considered as outlier and removed without further processing.

2.2   Trajectory Segmentation

Existing group-based trajectory summarization methods process trajectory as a whole, to abstract the common patterns shared by entire trajectories. Compared

with traditional clustering algorithms, these methods do have some improvements. However, when processing trajectory data with high complexity, these
entire-trajectory based summarization method can not preserve details very well,
and sometimes may introduce significant resampling error. To preserve more
details, we can segment complex trajectory into a set of sub-trajectories, which
are more simple in structure, and process each sub-trajectories to get a better
summarization results without sacrificing details. In addition, segmentation can
also reduce the resampling error, which can further improve the accuracy of the
summarization results.

To better understand the last point, Fig. 2 shows an example to illustrate
the effectiveness of trajectory partitioning on reduce the error introduced during
resampling. For the group-based summarization methods, it is necessary to make
all the members in the same group to have equal number of sample points.
In [13, 18], Guo et al. resample all the trajectories to the same N sample points,
and N is chosen to make all the trajectories in the dataset achieve minimum
average Jensen-Shannon divergence (JSD) before and after being resampled.
However, since trajectories even in the same dataset usually have varying number
of sample points and the differences can not be overlooked, the error introduced
in the resampling procedure is significant. Plot (a) shows the original trajectory.
Plot (b) is the directly resampled trajectory, and the number of sample points is
chosen to minimize the JSD before and after resampling. And plot (c) gives the
result of first partitioning the trajectory, then resampling all its sub-portions. As
can be clearly seen from Fig. 2, trajectory segmentation can effectively reduce
the resampling error.

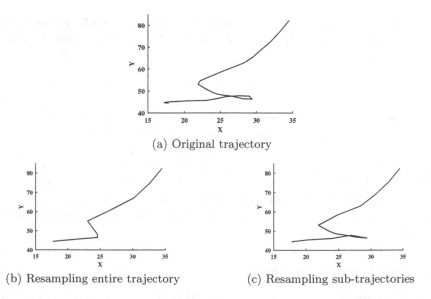

(a) Original trajectory

(b) Resampling entire trajectory   (c) Resampling sub-trajectories

Fig. 2. An example of showing the effectiveness of trajectory partitioning on reducing
resampling error.

For different applications, there are many trajectory segmentation methods, such as those in [5, 9]. In this paper, for our purpose, we use the method proposed by Lee et al. [16], but with a crucial difference. Specifically, in their original paper, each trajectory is segmented into sub-trajectories by using the MDL principle, and the segmented sub-trajectories are approximated by a line segment. The MDL principle consists of two terms, $L(H)$ and $L(D|H)$. In [16], $L(H)$ is the sum of the total length of segmented line segments, and $L(D|H)$ is the sum of differences between the original trajectory and its partitioned line segments. By minimizing the sum of $L(H) + L(D|H)$, each trajectory is partitioned into a set of line segments. They also proposed an approximation algorithm to speed up the segmentation process. However, in our algorithm, to preserve more details, the segmented sub-trajectory is keep intact and is not approximated by a simple line segment.

2.3   Grouping

The segmented sub-trajectories are treated as independent trajectories and are combined into groups, by considering both the spatial proximity and shape restriction. In concrete, for each trajectory $T_{k,j}$, it is considered as a "center trajectory", and any trajectory $T_{k,i}$ which is similar to $T_{k,j}$ is put into $\mathbf{G}(T_{k,j})$, the similarity group of $T_{k,j}$. Here the similarity is three fold. First, the spatial distance between $T_{k,j}$ and $T_{k,i}$ should be small, to emphasize the spatial similarity between two trajectories. This is done by using the searching window scheme mentioned in Subsect. 2.1. More specifically, if $T_{k,i}$ belongs to $\mathbf{N}(T_{k,j})$, the spatial distance between $T_{k,i}$ and the center trajectory $T_{k,j}$ is small, and $T_{k,i}$ has high spatial similarity to $T_{k,j}$. Second, the length difference between $T_{k,i}$ and $T_{k,j}$ should be small, so that they can be aligned properly. In our paper, the length of a trajectory is approximated by the length of a line segment which connects the starting point to the ending point of the trajectory. Through extensive experiments, we found the length difference smaller than half of the length of the center trajectory is enough. Third, the shape between these two trajectories should be as similar as possible. The shape of a trajectory is determined by its sampling points, as a result, the shape difference between two trajectories is modeled by the sum of the Euclidean distances between the corresponding sample points of these two trajectories. The problem of trajectories having different number of sample points is addressed by padding the smaller one with its last sample points, as we describe in Subsect. 2.1. So, the shape difference is limited by

$$Diff(T_{k,j}, T_{k,i}) < \mu, \tag{7}$$

where $Diff()$ is the sum of the Euclidean distances, and μ is an adaptively selected threshold. The above three similarities can be classified into two categories, the first belongs to spatial proximity, and the rest two belong to shape restriction. For each trajectory, we search for its similar trajectories and form its similarity group, according to the spatial proximity and shape restriction.

It is necessary to make all the trajectories within the same group align properly, for the subsequent group-based filtering phase. To do so, we need to resample each group of trajectories. One important parameter to determine is the number of resampling points. In our approach, after grouping, the shape and the length of the trajectories within the same group are close, so for each group, the number of resampling points is set equal to the average sample points of all the trajectories belonging to the group, and equal-distance resampling was applied on each trajectory.

2.4 Wavelet Transformation Based Non-local Filtering

To effectively summarize the common patterns shared by the trajectories, non-local filtering based on wavelet transformation is performed on each group. To be more specific, in the $k+1$th iteration, suppose $T_{k,j}$ is the input center trajectory, which has t similar trajectories, the similarity group of $T_{k,j}$ can be denoted by

$$\mathbf{G}(T_{k,j}) = \left[T_{k,j}^0, T_{k,j}^1, T_{k,j}^2, \ldots, T_{k,j}^t \right]^{\mathbf{T}}. \tag{8}$$

where $T_{k,j}^0$ is $T_{k,j}$ itself. Let $\mathbf{s}_i$ be a column vector that contains the ith points of all the trajectories in $\mathbf{G}(T_{k,j})$. In our framework, first, as in [18], non-local filtering based on wavelet transformation is performed. Each $\mathbf{s}_i$ was filtered by using

$$\widehat{\mathbf{s}_i} = \Psi^{-1} \left(\tau \left(\Psi \left(\mathbf{s}_i \right) \right) \right), \tag{9}$$

where $\tau(.)$, $\Psi(.)$ and $\Psi^{-1}(.)$ denote the wavelet thresholding of high frequency components, Haar wavelet transform and inverse Haar wavelet transform, respectively. Note that for wavelet thresholding, only the high frequency coefficients that smaller than the given threshold β are completely compressed. After filtering, $\mathbf{G}(T_{k,j})$ is given by

$$\mathbf{G}(\widehat{T_{k,j}}) = \left[\widehat{T_{k,j}^0}, \widehat{T_{k,j}^1}, \widehat{T_{k,j}^2}, \ldots, \widehat{T_{k,j}^t} \right]^{\mathbf{T}}. \tag{10}$$

And $T_{k,j}$ after the group-based filtering is set equal to $\widehat{T_{k,j}^0}$.

2.5 Linking

After the non-local filtering phase, the sub-trajectories derived from the same trajectory may shift to different directions, resulting in unsatisfactory summarization results. To address this disadvantage, we need to find a way to link the sub-trajectories.

Suppose now we are given two sub-trajectories $T_{k,j} = \left\{ p_1^{k,j}, p_2^{k,j}, \ldots, p_n^{k,j} \right\}$ and $T_{k,m} = \left\{ p_1^{k,m}, p_2^{k,m}, \ldots, p_l^{k,m} \right\}$, which are derived from the same trajectory, and $T_{k,j}$ is the previous adjacent neighbor of $T_{k,m}$. We want to connect these two sub-trajectories with two required properties. First, the connection should preserve their original shapes as much as possible. Second, the connecting point should be smoothed, so that in the subsequent iterations it will not likely to be a segmented point.

In our approach, we first translate $T_{k,m}$ to a different position, so that the first point of $T_{k,m}$ after translation has the same coordinate as the last point of $T_{k,j}$. Specifically, we define $\mathbf{a} = p_n^{k,j} - p_1^{k,m}$, and the translated $T_{k,m}$ is defined as

$$\widetilde{T_{k,m}} = \left\{ \widetilde{p_1^{k,m}}, \widetilde{p_2^{k,m}}, ..., \widetilde{p_l^{k,m}} \right\} \tag{11}$$

where $\widetilde{p_i^{k,m}}$ is the translated ith point of $T_{k,m}$, it is defined as

$$\widetilde{p_i^{k,m}} = p_i^{k,m} + \mathbf{a}. \tag{12}$$

Note that after translation $p_n^{k,j} = \widetilde{p_1^{k,m}}$. Next, we set the coordinate of the connection point $c_{j,m}^k$ as

$$c_{j,m}^k = \frac{p_{n-1}^{k,j} + \lambda \cdot \widetilde{p_2^{k,m}}}{1 + \lambda}, \tag{13}$$

to smooth the connection, where λ is defined as

$$\lambda = \frac{len(p_{n-1}^{k,j} p_n^{k,j})}{len(\widetilde{p_1^{k,m}} \widetilde{p_2^{k,m}})}, \tag{14}$$

the ratio between the length of $p_{n-1}^{k,j} p_n^{k,j}$ over the length of $\widetilde{p_1^{k,m}} \widetilde{p_2^{k,m}}$.

After linking, $T_{k,j}$ and $T_{k,m}$ now is defined as $T_{k,j}' = \left\{ p_1^{k,j}, p_2^{k,j}, ..., c_{j,m}^k \right\}$ and $T_{k,m}' = \left\{ c_{j,m}^k, \widetilde{p_2^{k,m}}, ..., \widetilde{p_l^{k,m}} \right\}$, respectively.

3   Experiments

In order to evaluate the proposed segmentation based trajectory summarization approach, we compare its performance with that of the non-segmented method proposed in [18]. All the parameters are set as they reported in [18]. We have conducted extensive experiments on many trajectory datasets. Due to the space limit, only the results of four very complex real trajectory datasets are shown in the paper. These four trajectory datasets include the hurricane track dataset [2], the Edinburgh dataset [3], the animal movements dataset [1] and the school bus dataset [4]. The hurricane track dataset is named Best Track, and we choose 44 trajectories with varying number of sampling points from it. The Edinburgh dataset we used has 277 trajectories and 83710 points. We select two animal movements datasets Elk1993, which consists of 33 trajectories and 47204 sample points, and Deer1995, which consists of 32 trajectories and 20065 points, from the animal movements datasets. And the Bus dataset we used has 30 trajectories and 16165 points.

3.1   Parameters Selection

There are two parameters should be predetermined before we can conduct the simulation, the Euclidean distances threshold μ for the grouping phase and the parameter β used in the wavelet transformation based non-local filtering phase.

We first consider the selection of μ. Since trajectories in different datasets usually have various properties, even trajectories within the same dataset can differ greatly in their shapes and lengths. It is hard to give a fixed threshold value for μ that is applicable for all the datasets. However, as we illustrated above, the searching window scheme can effectively encode the local relationships among the center trajectory and its neighbors, so we can adaptively select a value for μ based on it. More specifically, we first calculate the Euclidean distance between each neighbor trajectory and the center trajectory, and then set μ equal to the median Euclidean distance, to avoid potential fluctuation.

Another important question is how to set the parameter β. Through extensive experiments, we have observed that the parameter β has close relationship with μ, which can be approximated by a linear function. The linear function is denoted as

$$\beta = b \cdot \mu, \tag{15}$$

where b is the slope, and $b = 5.7$ is used in our experiments.

As for the stopping criterion, we choose to terminate the iterative summarization approach when the outputs of two successive iterations do not change or the maximum number of iterations K_{max} is reached. In our paper, $K_{max} = 5$ is enough.

3.2   Visual Comparison of Summarization Results

Figure 3 shows the original trajectories and the summarization results of the Best Track by different methods. Figure 3(b)–(e) show the 1st to 4th iteration results by our method, respectively. Figure 3(f) is the result of the method proposed in [18]. Overall, our proposed approach can not only greatly abstract complex trajectories, but also effectively preserve the details of the trajectories. This makes the compression result more practical.

3.3   Objective Evaluation

To objectively evaluate the performance of the proposed method, Table 1 lists the best Fidelity (FID) [18] scores of five tested datasets. A high FID value indicates the summarization results can preserve more information of the original dataset. As can be clearly seen from the table, our approach performs significantly better than previous methods.

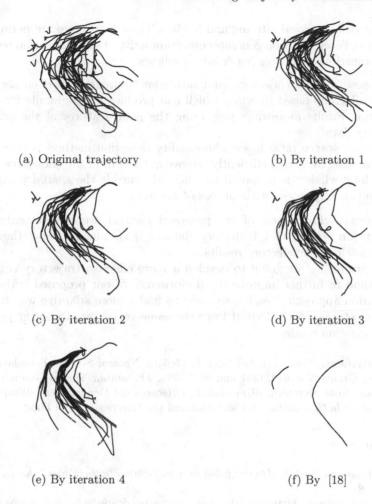

(a) Original trajectory

(b) By iteration 1

(c) By iteration 2

(d) By iteration 3

(e) By iteration 4

(f) By [18]

Fig. 3. Comparison of summarization results on best track.

Table 1. FID scores of summarization results

	Best track	Edinburgh	Elk1993	Deer1995	Bus
[18]	0.456	0.771	0.400	0.478	0.153
Ours	0.756	0.934	0.833	0.993	0.548

4   Conclusion

In this paper, from the perspective of signal processing, we propose a novel approach for trajectory summarization. The proposed approach consists of five stages, Abnormality detection, trajectory segmentation, grouping, wavelet transformation based non-local filtering and linking. These five stages are performed iteratively, and each iteration generates one granularity of summarization results. The main contribution of this paper are as follows:

- We propose a novel trajectory summarization approach based on segmentation and group-based filtering, which can produce multi-granularity summarization results meanwhile preserving the main features of the original trajectory data.
- A relative distance ratio based abnormality detection method is proposed, which can effectively and efficiently remove outliers from the trajectory data.
- A searching window is proposed to efficiently encode the spatial proximity between two trajectories without loss of accuracy.

To evaluate the effectiveness of our proposed method, we conduct extensive experiments on several real trajectory dataset. Experiments show that our method can achieve satisfactory results.

In the future, we are going to develop a more effective trajectory segmentation method to further improve the performance of our proposed trajectory summarization approach. Besides, we need to find a more adaptive way to link the sub-trajectories which derived from the same trajectory, to better present the summarization results.

Acknowledgment. This work has been funded by Natural Science Foundation of China under Grants Nos. 61471261 and 61771335. The author Yuejun Guo acknowledges support from Secretaria dUniversitats i Recerca del Departament dEmpresa i Coneixement de la Generalitat de Catalunya and the European Social Fund.

References

1. Animal movements. http://www.fs.fed.us/pnw/starkey/data/tables/. Accessed 13 Apr 2018
2. Best track dataset. http://weather.unisys.com/hurricane/atlantic/. Accessed 13 Apr 2018
3. Edinburgh dataset. http://homepages.inf.ed.ac.uk/rbf/FORUMTRACKING/. Accessed 13 Apr 2018
4. School bus dataset. http://chorochronos.datastories.org/?q=node/6. Accessed 13 Apr 2018
5. Alewijnse, S., Buchin, K., Buchin, M., Kölzsch, A., Kruckenberg, H., Westenberg, M.A.: A framework for trajectory segmentation by stable criteria. In: Proceedings of the 22nd ACM SIGSPATIAL International Conference on Advances in Geographic Information Systems, pp. 351–360. ACM (2014)
6. Ankerst, M., Breunig, M.M., Kriegel, H.P., Sander, J.: OPTICS: ordering points to identify the clustering structure. ACM SIGMOD Rec. **28**, 49–60 (1999)
7. Buades, A., Coll, B., Morel, J.M.: A non-local algorithm for image denoising. In: 2005 IEEE Computer Society Conference on Computer Vision and Pattern Recognition, CVPR 2005, vol. 2, pp. 60–65. IEEE (2005)
8. Dabov, K., Foi, A., Katkovnik, V., Egiazarian, K.: Image denoising by sparse 3-D transform-domain collaborative filtering. IEEE Trans. Image Process. **16**(8), 2080–2095 (2007)

9. Das, R.D., Winter, S.: Automated urban travel interpretation: a bottom-up approach for trajectory segmentation. Sensors **16**(11), 1962 (2016)
10. Ester, M., Kriegel, H.P., Sander, J., Xu, X., et al.: A density-based algorithm for discovering clusters in large spatial databases with noise. In: Kdd, vol. 96, pp. 226–231 (1996)
11. Gaffney, S., Smyth, P.: Trajectory clustering with mixtures of regression models. In: Proceedings of the Fifth ACM SIGKDD International Conference on Knowledge Discovery and Data Mining, pp. 63–72. ACM (1999)
12. Gaffney, S.J., Robertson, A.W., Smyth, P., Camargo, S.J., Ghil, M.: Probabilistic clustering of extratropical cyclones using regression mixture models. Clim. Dyn. **29**(4), 423–440 (2007)
13. Guo, Y., Xu, Q., Luo, X., Wei, H., Bu, H., Sbert, M.: A group-based signal filtering approach for trajectory abstraction and restoration. Neural Comput. Appl. **29**, 1–17 (2018)
14. Laurikkala, J., Juhola, M., Kentala, E., Lavrac, N., Miksch, S., Kavsek, B.: Informal identification of outliers in medical data. In: Fifth International Workshop on Intelligent Data Analysis in Medicine and Pharmacology, vol. 1, pp. 20–24 (2000)
15. Laxhammar, R., Falkman, G.: Online learning and sequential anomaly detection in trajectories. IEEE Trans. Pattern Anal. Mach. Intell. **36**(6), 1158–1173 (2014)
16. Lee, J.G., Han, J., Whang, K.Y.: Trajectory clustering: a partition-and-group framework. In: Proceedings of the 2007 ACM SIGMOD International Conference on Management of Data, pp. 593–604. ACM (2007)
17. Lloyd, S.: Least squares quantization in PCM. IEEE Trans. Inf. theory **28**(2), 129–137 (1982)
18. Luo, X., Xu, Q., Guo, Y., Wei, H., Lv, Y.: Trajectory abstracting with group-based signal denoising. In: Arik, S., Huang, T., Lai, W.K., Liu, Q. (eds.) ICONIP 2015, Part III. LNCS, vol. 9491, pp. 452–461. Springer, Cham (2015). https://doi.org/10.1007/978-3-319-26555-1_51
19. Zheng, Y.: Trajectory data mining: an overview. ACM Trans. Intell. Syst. Technol. **6**(3), 29 (2015)
20. Zheng, Y., Capra, L., Wolfson, O., Yang, H.: Urban computing: concepts, methodologies, and applications. ACM Trans. Intell. Syst. Technol. **5**(3), 38 (2014)

Single-Stage Detector with Semantic Attention for Occluded Pedestrian Detection

Fang Wen[1], Zehang Lin[2], Zhenguo Yang[2,3(✉)], and Wenyin Liu[2(✉)]

[1] Department of Automation, Guangdong University of Technology,
Guangzhou, China
120107030056w@gmail.com
[2] School of Computer Science and Technology,
Guangdong University of Technology, Guangzhou, China
gdutlin@outlook.com, liuwy@gdut.cn
[3] Department of Computer Science, City University of Hong Kong,
Hong Kong, China
zhengyang5-c@my.cityu.edu.hk

Abstract. In this paper, we propose a pedestrian detection method with semantic attention based on the single-stage detector architecture (i.e., Retina-Net) for occluded pedestrian detection, denoted as PDSA. PDSA contains a semantic segmentation component and a detector component. Specifically, the first component uses visible bounding boxes for semantic segmentation, aiming to obtain an attention map for pedestrians and the inter-class (non-pedestrian) occlusion. The second component utilizes the single-stage detector to locate the pedestrian from the features obtained previously. The single-stage detector adopts over-sampling of possible object locations, which is faster than two-stage detectors that train classifier to identify candidate object locations. In particular, we introduce the repulsion loss to deal with the intra-class occlusion. Extensive experiments conducted on the public CityPersons dataset demonstrate the effectiveness of PDSA for occluded pedestrian detection, which outperforms the state-of-the-art approaches.

Keywords: Occluded pedestrian detection · Single-stage detector
Repulsion loss · Semantic segmentation network

1 Introduction

Pedestrian detection is a significant research topic in object detection, which benefits many applications, e.g., driverless cars, intelligent robotics and intelligent transportation. It is quite common to utilize the methods proposed in object detection [1–3] to detect pedestrians directly. However, these methods can hardly obtain the optimal performance. The main reason is that pedestrians always gather together and are easily obscured by other objects in reality. Therefore, it is challenging and meaningful to deal with occlusion problems in pedestrian detection.

Quite a few researchers focus on the inter-class occlusion, i.e., pedestrians are occluded by non-pedestrian objects, e.g., buildings, trees and cars. It is difficult to locate the pedestrians based on parts of the bodies since there are rich categories of

I. Kompatsiaris et al. (Eds.): MMM 2019, LNCS 11296, pp. 414–425, 2019.
https://doi.org/10.1007/978-3-030-05716-9_34

obstruction, e.g., right-left and bottom-up occlusions. Intuitively, it is easy for detectors to learn features from the exposed parts compared with the heavily occluded pedestrians. In previous work, constructing pedestrian templates is the mainstream for pedestrian detection, which divides a pedestrian into different parts as templates, and then utilizes these templates to train different classifiers for various occlusions. However, it suffers from high computational cost. Recently, Zhang et al. [4] apply attention mechanism to handle different occlusion patterns, which achieves the state-of-the-art performance on heavy occlusion. However, their method only works on the two-stage models, i.e., Faster-RCNN [3], which consists of proposing regions and computing the confidences of object classes.

Recently, the advanced models are based on the single-stage models, e.g., YOLOv2 [5], DSSD [6] and RetinaNet [2], which directly calculate both bounding boxes and confidences of object classes. In this paper, we aim to use the single-stage detection model to handle different occlusion patterns on pedestrian detection, by designing a novel network named as pedestrian detection with semantic attention (PDSA). More specially, PDSA contains two components, i.e., a semantic segmentation component and a detector component. The semantic segmentation component is used to reduce the influence of the heavily occluded parts with the visible bounding boxes of pedestrians. It takes low-level features as input and try to learn a feature map supervised by the visible bounding boxes. Furthermore, the feature map will guide as attention to the input features. The detector component uses a single-stage detection model, i.e., RetinaNet [2], which combines feature pyramids [1] to predict the bounding boxes and the confidences of object classes. The input of the detector component is obtained from the semantic segmentation component, which helps the detection model to detect the heavily occluded pedestrians. In particular, we also consider the intra-class occlusion, which occurs when a pedestrian is occluded by other pedestrians, and introduce the repulsion loss [7] to improve the performance of our model.

The main contributions of our work in this paper are summarized as follows:

- We propose the PDSA model that exploits semantic segmentation to address the inter-class occlusion, and introduce the repulsion loss to deal with intra-class occlusion.
- PDSA utilizes semantic segmentation information to reduce the influence of the heavily occluded parts. To the best of our knowledge, it is the first attempt to utilize visible bounding boxes with semantic segmentation component to obtain the semantic attention for pedestrian detection.
- We conduct extensive experiments on the CityPersons dataset containing heavily occluded pedestrians, and outperforming the state-of-the-art approaches.

The rest of the paper is organized as follows. In Sect. 2, related work is reviewed. In Sect. 3, the motivation is introduced. In Sect. 4, the proposed PDSA model is presented. In Sect. 5, extensive experiments are conducted and analyzed. Finally, Sect. 6 offers some concluding remarks.

2 Related Work

In this section, we review some existing research works on the pedestrian detection and occlusion handling, respectively.

2.1 Pedestrian Detection

Recently, the convolutional neural network (CNN) has achieved great progress on pedestrian detection. In the early time, quite a few works [8–10] tried to apply CNN directly for pedestrian detection. Li et al. [11] proposed SA-Fast RCNN to detect pedestrians in different scales, and Cai et al. [12] used MS-CNN to obtain competitive performance on pedestrian detection. Meantime, Zhang et al. [13] refined the Faster R-CNN network by combining region proposal networks with Boosted Forest, which improves the performance on small objects and hard negative samples. However, these methods are based on the two-stage detectors (i.e., Faster R-CNN [3]), which suffer from high computational cost.

2.2 Occlusion Handling

In term of occlusion handling, part-based methods are one of the mainstream approaches. Ouyang et al. [14] designed a framework that models the part visibility as latent variables to predict the scores of part detectors. Mathias et al. [15] proposed the Franken-classifiers method, which utilized multiple classifiers to learn a specific type of occlusion for different occluded pedestrians. Tian et al. [16] proposed a DeepParts model to obtain competitive performance on occlusion handling. The authors constructed an extensive part pool and integrated these parts scores to the final score of the predicted results. However, the part-based methods usually require the part classifiers to learn corresponding occlusion pattern independently, which results in a lot of computations. Zhang et al. [4] applied channel-wise attention mechanism to handle the occlusion. However, their methods are only suitable for the two-stage detectors, while the single-stage detectors are faster with high performance.

3 Motivation

In the context of occluded pedestrian detection, detectors usually fail to detect the pedestrians due to that detectors learn features from the whole bounding boxes in the training stage. However, the bounding boxes not only contain pedestrians but also may include parts of other pedestrians (i.e., intra-class occlusion) or non-pedestrian objects (i.e., inter-class occlusion).

(a) For the intra-class occlusion, it happens commonly in the crowd, which results in high overlap rate between bounding boxes. The detectors are easy to predict only a single pedestrian. Inspired by Wang et al. [7], we introduce the repulsion loss to narrow down the gap between a proposal and its designated target, and keep it away from other ground-truth objects.

(b) For the inter-class occlusion, non-pedestrian objects occupy part of the bounding boxes. The features obtained by detectors may result in false detection when similar non-pedestrian objects appear, and fail to detect the pedestrians that the occlusion is heavy. Intuitively, if we reduce the weight of the non-pedestrian objects and emphasize the parts of pedestrians, the detectors will learn positive knowledge. Therefore, we introduce the semantic segmentation component to obtain the semantic attention map, which uses the information of the visible bounding boxes. Through the semantic attention map, the detectors tend to focus more on the parts of pedestrians. The details are presented in the next section.

4 Methodology

4.1 Overview

As shown in Fig. 1, our PDSA consists of two parts: a detector component and a sematic segmentation component. The first part adopts a single-stage detector (i.e., RetinaNet [2]) to predict the bounding boxes and the probability of pedestrians. The sematic segmentation component utilizes the visible bounding boxes as the input to train a sematic attention map for reducing the influence of the heavily occluded parts. We will introduce these components in more details subsequently.

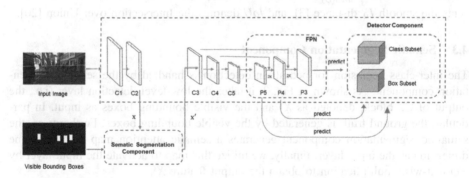

Fig. 1. Overview of our PDSA. FPN denotes the feature pyramid network.

4.2 Detector Component

Our detector component is a single-stage detector (i.e., RetinaNet). We replace the basic model ResNet [17] with VGG16 [18]. Therefore, our detector contains five blocks of convolution layers (i.e., C1, C2, C3, C4 and C5). In addition, RetinaNet utilizes the feature pyramid networks (FPN) [1] to adapt multi-scale pedestrians, which contains additional three convolution layers (i.e., P5, P4 and P3) that combine with the previous convolution layers (i.e., C5, C4 and C3). More specifically, P5, P4 and P3 utilize 1×1 convolutional layer with ReLU function [19], and the input of P5 comes from C5 directly. The input of P4 is the combination of P5 with upsampling method [1] and C4, and the input of P3 is same combination of P4 and C3. In addition, we utilize the focal loss [2] to train the classification loss, which is defined as follows:

$$L_{Classification} = \begin{cases} -(1-p)^\gamma \log(p) & \text{if } y = 1 \\ -p^\gamma \log(1-p) & \text{otherwise} \end{cases} \tag{1}$$

where $y \in \{0, 1\}$ is a ground truth class, $p \in [0, 1]$ is the probability for the class with label $y = 1$.

In addition, in order to handle the intra-class occlusion, we introduce the repulsion loss [7] to optimize the detector. In particular, we only add the repulsion term loss, which repels the proposal from its neighboring ground truth objects. Here, we assume that P is the positive proposals set ($IoU \geq 0.5$), and B is the predicted bounding box regressed from proposal P, and G is the ground truth bounding box. The repulsion loss can be defined as:

$$L_{Rep} = \frac{\sum_{p \in P} Smooth_{L1}\left(IoG\left(B^p, G^p_{Rep}\right)\right)}{|P|} \tag{2}$$

$$G^P_{Rep} = max_{G \backslash max_G IoU(G,P)} IoU(G, P) \tag{3}$$

where $IoG(B, G) = \frac{area(B \cap G)}{area(G)}$ denotes the overlap between B and G, $Smooth_{L1}$ represents the smooth L_1 distance [3], and IoU denotes the Intersection over Union [20].

4.3　Sematic Segmentation Component

The inter-class occlusion for pedestrian detection is handled by the sematic segmentation component. As shown in Fig. 2, it takes the low-level detection layer (i.e., the output of C2 block, denoted as X) and the visible bounding boxes as input. In particular, the ground truth is generated by the visible bounding boxes. Furthermore, the semantic segmentation component generates a semantic attention map with the same dimension as the input layer. Finally, we utilize this map to activate the input layer by element-wise multiplication to obtain the output feature X'.

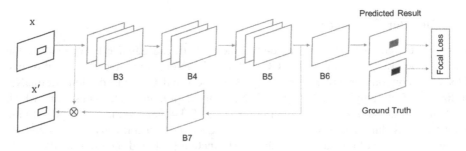

Fig. 2. The structure of sematic segmentation component.

For the segmentation network, we use the same structure with VGG16 but remove the pooling layers, and replace the subsequent two convolution blocks with the dilated convolution blocks (i.e., B4 and B5) [21]. Furthermore, we utilize two 1×1 convolutional layers with sigmoid function (i.e., B6 and B7) to generate the segmentation prediction and the sematic attention map, respectively. However, the ground truth is the visible bounding boxes, which are only four coordinate points and cannot be input directly. Here, we scale the visible bounding boxes into 1/4, which is the same size as the result of segmentation prediction. Furthermore, we set the whole pixels in the visible bounding boxes as 1 and the others as 0, which obtains the segmentation ground truth.

In addition, the visible part occupies a small area which leads to the imbalance between the positive and negative samples. To make the sematic segmentation task converged, we introduce the focal loss for optimization as follows:

$$L_{Segmentation} = \begin{cases} -(1-p)^\gamma \log(p) \; if \; y = 1 \\ -p^\gamma \log(1-p) \; otherwise \end{cases} \tag{4}$$

where $y \in \{0, 1\}$ is ground truth class for each pixel, $p \in [0, 1]$ is the probability for the class with label $y = 1$.

By adding the aforementioned loss function, the final objective function of PDSA is given follows:

$$L = L_{Regression} + L_{Classification} + \alpha L_{Rep} + \beta L_{Segmentation} \tag{5}$$

where $L_{Regression}$ is the original bounding box regression loss. The parameters α and β balance different tasks. The convergence of the segmentation loss is shown in Sect. 5.6.

5 Experiments

In this section, we introduce the dataset used for pedestrian detection, and evaluate the performance of the proposed approaches and baselines.

5.1 Dataset

The CityPersons dataset [22] consists of cityscape images containing persons, with backgrounds including Germany and some other surrounding countries. The ground truth of the images contains bounding box annotation, visible bounding box annotation, and five class labels (i.e., ignore regions, pedestrians, riders, sitting persons, other persons with unusual postures, and group of people). As show in Table 1, the dataset contains 3,475 images in total with rich annotations including 23k pedestrians and 9k ignored regions. The training set contains nearly 3,000 images, with an average of seven pedestrians per image. Only 30% of the pedestrians are visible completely, which shows that the CityPersons dataset have rich types of occlusion.

Table 1. Statistics of the CityPersons dataset

	Train	Val	Total
#Images	2,975	500	3,475
#Persons	19,654	3,938	23,592

5.2 Evaluation Metrics

We use a commonly used metric on the CityPersons dataset [22] for evaluations, i.e., the average value of miss rate for the false positive per image (MR), ranging from 10^{-2} to 10^0 (the smaller the better). In this paper, we care more about the occlusion and only consider pedestrians with height $\in [50, inf]$. We show the results across three different occlusion levels. In addition, we visualize the distribution of pedestrian at different occlusion level on CityPersons, as shown in Fig. 3.

(1) Reasonable (R): visibility $\in [0.65, inf]$;
(2) Heavy occlusion (HO): visibility $\in [0.2, 0.65]$;
(3) Reasonable + Heavy occlusion (R + HO): visibility $\in [0.2, inf]$.

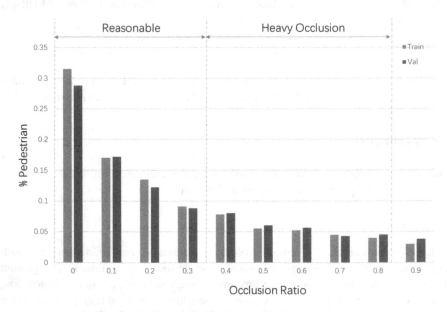

Fig. 3. Occlusion distribution on CityPersons dataset.

5.3 Implementation Details

In our experiment, we adopt VGG16 [18] as the fundamental network structure, and the other convolution layers in detector component are same as [2]. For the semantic segmentation component, the previous three convolution layers (i.e., B3, B4 and B5) are the same with VGG16 [18], but we remove the pooling layers and utilize the dilated convolution in the last two layers (i.e., B4 and B5). In particular, the dilation rates of dilated convolution are set as 2 and 4, respectively. B6 is a 1×1 convolution with sigmoid function and the channel number is 1, while B7 is also a 1×1 convolution with sigmoid function and the channel number is same as the channel number of the input X.

For the optimizations, we use the parameters of the pre-trained VGG16 to initialize our model, and initialize the dilated convolution parameters in the segmentation component by Xavier initialization [23]. We adopt the Adam solver [24] with the learning rate of 10^{-4} for 14,000 iterations, and take the image in original size as the input. In addition, the balance parameter for repulsion loss α set as 0.5 following [7], and the balance parameter for the semantic segmentation loss β set as 0.5 since our main task is not semantic segmentation.

5.4 Comparing with the State-of-the-Art Methods

The baselines include a number of state-of-the-art methods on pedestrian detection, such as FasterRCNN [13], FasterRCNN + ATT-part [4], FasterRCNN + RepLoss [7], Somatic Topology Line Localization (TLL) [25] and RetinaNet [2]. The performances of the approaches are shown in Table 2. From the table, we can observe that the proposed PDSA achieves competitive performance for HO and R + HO, which out-performs the previous state-of-the-art detectors. The proposed PDSA benefits from the semantic attention map and the repulsion loss, which can detect heavily occluded pedestrians effectively. Note that our PDSA cannot outperform the best baselines for R. The reason is that we use the single-stage detector (i.e., RetinaNet), which is not fully optimized for the small-scale pedestrian detection, while the baselines use the two-stage detector (i.e., Faster RCNN).

Table 2. MR performance of the approaches on the CityPersons dataset.

Method	R	HO	R + HO
FasterRCNN	15.52%	64.83%	41.45%
FasterRCNN + ATT-part	15.96%	56.66%	38.23%
FasterRCNN + RepLoss	**13.20%**	56.90%	-
TLL	14.40%	52.00%	-
RetinaNet	17.92%	56.22%	36.61%
PDSA	16.51%	**48.24%**	**31.88%**

5.5 Evaluation on Different Strategies

PDSA utilizes the single-stage detector (i.e., RetinaNet). We adopt the repulsion loss to deal with the intra-class occlusion. Besides, we introduce a semantic segmentation component to deal with the inter-class occlusion. To evaluate the two components, we denote PDSA with repulsion loss as PDSA-r and PDSA with semantic segmentation component as PDSA-s, respectively. The results are shown in Table 3. We notice that

PDSA-r performs well for R since it is robust to the influence of intra-class occlusion. In addition, PDSA-s outperforms the RetinaNet on different occlusions, which demonstrates that the semantic segmentation component is effective for addressing occlusion. Furthermore, we combine repulsion loss with the semantic segmentation component and finally obtain the best performance, taking into account both intra-class and inter-class occlusions.

Table 3. Comparison of different strategies on the CityPersons dataset (lower is better).

Method	+Repulsion Loss	+Segmentation	R	HO	R + HO
RetinaNet	-	-	17.92%	56.22%	36.61%
PDSA-r	✓	-	16.73%	56.51%	35.80%
PDSA-s	-	✓	16.86%	48.77%	32.46%
PDSA	✓	✓	**16.51%**	**48.24%**	**31.88%**

5.6   Convergence of PDSA

PDSA consists of four loss terms, i.e., regression loss, classification loss, semantic segmentation loss, and repulsion loss. As shown in Fig. 4, we can see that all the losses are converged after 10,000 iterations. The experimental results demonstrate the effectiveness of our training procedures.

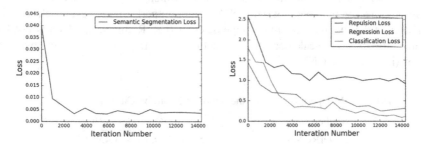

Fig. 4.   Convergence of PDSA

5.7   Visualizations

As shown in Fig. 5, we visualize the semantic attention map trained by the semantic segmentation component. We can see that the full bodies and the visible parts of occluded persons result in obvious response on the heatmap. For instance, two pedestrians are occluded heavily by cars while their upper bodies still show obvious response. The heatmap demonstrates that our sematic segmentation component can extract features from heavily occluded pedestrians.

Furthermore, we visualize the bounding boxes predicted by RetinaNet and the proposed PDSA model in Fig. 6. The RetinaNet fails to detect pedestrians that are occluded by other non-pedestrian objects, while our pedestrian detector obviously

Fig. 5. Visualization of the visible parts of persons on the heatmap.

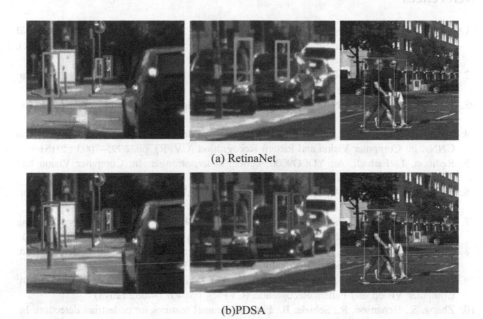

(a) RetinaNet

(b)PDSA

Fig. 6. Detected results of RetinaNet and PDSA. The red bounding boxes represent the detected results, and the green ones represent the ground truth. (Color figure online)

reduces the samples of false positives and missed detections. In addition, we find that our PDSA can locate the different pedestrians in the crowd, which demonstrates that our method is effective for both inter-class and intra-class occlusions.

6 Conclusion

In this paper, we propose a novel method PDSA for occluded pedestrian detection. In order to handle the inter-class pedestrian occlusion, we introduce a semantic segmentation component, which utilizes the visible bounding boxes to obtain the semantic attention map. This component helps the subsequent detector component to focus on the pedestrians when the occlusion happened. In particular, we introduce the repulsion loss to deal with the intra-class occlusion, which helps to improve the performance of our PDSA. The experiment results have demonstrated the effectiveness of our proposed approach, which achieves the state-of-the-art performance on heavy occlusion.

Acknowledgments. This work is supported by the National Natural Science Foundation of China (No. 61703109, No. 91748107), China Postdoctoral Science Foundation (No. 2018M643026), and the Guangdong Innovative Research Team Program (No. 2014ZT05G157).

References

1. Lin, T., Dollár, P., Girshick, R., He, K., Hariharan, B., Belongie, S.: Feature pyramid networks for object detection. In: Computer Vision and Pattern Recognition (CVPR), pp. 2117–2125 (2017)
2. Lin, T., Goyal, P., Girshick, R., He, K., Dollár, P.: Focal loss for dense object detection. In: International Conference on Computer Vision (ICCV), pp. 2999–3007 (2017)
3. Girshick, R.: Fast R-CNN. In: Computer Vision and Pattern Recognition (CVPR), pp. 1440–1448 (2015)
4. Zhang, S., Yang, J., Schiele, B.: Occluded pedestrian detection through guided attention in CNNs. In: Computer Vision and Pattern Recognition (CVPR), pp. 6995–7003 (2018)
5. Redmon, J., Farhadi, A.: YOLO9000: better, faster, stronger. In: Computer Vision and Pattern Recognition (CVPR) (2017)
6. Fu, C., Liu, W., Ranga, A., Tyagi, A., Berg, A.: DSSD: deconvolutional single shot detector. arXiv preprint arXiv:1701.06659 (2017)
7. Wang, X., Xiao, T., Jiang, Y., Shao, S., Sun, J., Shen, C.: Repulsion loss: detecting pedestrians in a crowd. In: International Conference on Computer Vision (CVPR) (2018)
8. Luo, P., Tian, Y., Wang, X., Tang, X.: Switchable deep network for pedestrian detection. In: Computer Vision and Pattern Recognition (CVPR) (2014)
9. Hosang, J., Omran, M., Benenson, R., Schiele, B.: Taking a deeper look at pedestrians. In: Computer Vision and Pattern Recognition (CVPR), pp. 4073–4082 (2015)
10. Zhang, S., Benenson, R., Schiele, B.: Filtered channel features for pedestrian detection. In: Computer Vision and Pattern Recognition (CVPR) (2015)
11. Li, J., Liang, X., Shen, S., Xu, T., Yan, S.: Scale-aware fast R-CNN for pedestrian detection. IEEE Trans. Multimedia **20**(4), 985–996 (2017)
12. Cai, Z., Fan, Q., Feris, Rogerio S., Vasconcelos, N.: A unified multi-scale deep convolutional neural network for fast object detection. In: Leibe, B., Matas, J., Sebe, N., Welling, M. (eds.) ECCV 2016. LNCS, vol. 9908, pp. 354–370. Springer, Cham (2016). https://doi.org/10.1007/978-3-319-46493-0_22
13. Zhang, L., Lin, L., Liang, X., He, K.: Is faster R-CNN doing well for pedestrian detection? In: Leibe, B., Matas, J., Sebe, N., Welling, M. (eds.) ECCV 2016. LNCS, vol. 9906, pp. 443–457. Springer, Cham (2016). https://doi.org/10.1007/978-3-319-46475-6_28
14. Ouyang, W., Wang, X.: A discriminative deep model for pedestrian detection with occlusion handling. In: Computer Vision and Pattern Recognition (CVPR) (2012)
15. Mathias, M., Benenson, R., Timofte, R., Van, L.: Handling occlusions with Franken-classifiers. In: International Conference on Computer Vision (ICCV) (2013)
16. Tian, Y., Luo, P., Wang, X., Tang, X.: Deep learning strong parts for pedestrian detection. In Proceedings of the IEEE International Conference on Computer Vision (ICCV), pp. 1904–1912 (2015)

17. He, K., Zhang, X., Ren, S., Sun, J.: Deep residual learning for image recognition. In Proceedings of the IEEE conference on computer vision and pattern recognition, pp. 770–778 (2016)
18. Simonyan, K., Zisserman, A.: Very deep convolutional networks for large-scale image recognition. In: International Conference on Learning Representations (ICLR) (2014)
19. Krizhevsky, A., Sutskever, I., Hinton, G.E.: ImageNet classification with deep convolutional neural networks. In: International Conference on Neural Information Processing Systems, vol. 60, pp. 1097–1105 (2012)
20. Jiang, Y., Jiang, Y., Cao, Z., Cao, Z., Huang, T.: UnitBox: an advanced object detection network. In: ACM on Multimedia Conference, pp. 516–520 (2016)
21. Chen, L.C., Papandreou, G., Kokkinos, I., Murphy, K., Yuille, A.: DeepLab: semantic image segmentation with deep convolutional nets, atrous convolution, and fully connected CRFs. IEEE Trans. Pattern Anal. Mach. Intell. 40(4), 834–848 (2018)
22. Zhang, S., Benenson, R., Schiele, B.: CityPersons: a diverse dataset for pedestrian detection. In: Computer Vision and Pattern Recognition (CVPR) (2017)
23. Glorot, X., Bengio, Y.: Understanding the difficulty of training deep feedforward neural networks. In: Proceedings of the Thirteenth International Conference on Artificial Intelligence and Statistics (ICAI), pp. 249–256 (2010)
24. Kingma, D.P., Ba, J.: Adam: a method for stochastic optimization. arXiv preprint arXiv:1412.6980 (2014)
25. Song, T., Sun, L., Xie, D., Sun, H., Pu, S.: Small-scale pedestrian detection based on somatic topology localization and temporal feature aggregation. arXiv preprint arXiv:1807.01438 (2018)

Poses Guide Spatiotemporal Model for Vehicle Re-identification

Xian Zhong[1], Meng Feng[1], Wenxin Huang[1,2(✉)], Zheng Wang[3], and Shin'ichi Satoh[3]

[1] Wuhan University of Technology, Wuhan, China
[2] Wuhan University, Wuhan, China
wenxin.huang@whu.edu.cn
[3] National Institute of Informatics, Tokyo, Japan

Abstract. In this paper, we tackle the vehicle Re-identification (Re-ID) problem, which is important in the urban surveillance. Utilizing visual appearance information is limited on performance due to occlusions, illumination variations, etc. To make the best of our knowledge, the recent few methods consider the spatiotemporal information to solve vehicle Re-ID problem, and neglect the influence of driving direction. In this paper, we explore that the spatiotemporal distribution of vehicle movements follows certain rules, moreover the vehicles' poses on camera view indicate their directions are closely related to the spatiotemporal cues. Inspired by these two observations, we propose a vehicles' Poses Guide Spatiotemporal model (PGST) for assisting vehicle Re-ID. Firstly, a Gaussian distribution based spatiotemporal probability model is exploited to predict the vehicle's spatiotemporal movement. Then a CNN embedding poses classifier is exploited to estimate driving direction by evaluating vehicle's pose. Finally, PGST model is integrated into the framework which fuses the results of visual appearance model and spatiotemporal model together. Due to the lack of vehicle dataset with spatiotemporal information and topology of cameras, experiments are conducted on a public vehicle Re-ID dataset which is the only one meeting the experiments requirements. The proposed approach achieves competitive performances.

Keywords: Vehicle re-identification · Spatiotemporal model
Vehicle poses classifier

1 Introduction

Vehicle Re-identification (Re-ID) is a task of matching vehicles with same identities from different cameras distributed over non-overlapping scenes. It has drawn significant attentions. However, compared to person Re-ID [1–4], vehicle Re-ID is still a frontier topic. Generally, previous researches [5–8, 10, 13] on vehicle Re-ID can be divided into three categories, i.e., appearance based, license based and spatiotemporal based.

© Springer Nature Switzerland AG 2019
I. Kompatsiaris et al. (Eds.): MMM 2019, LNCS 11296, pp. 426–439, 2019.
https://doi.org/10.1007/978-3-030-05716-9_35

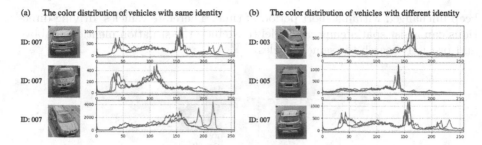

Fig. 1. (a) Illustration of the RGB color histogram distributions of same vehicle. (b) Illustration of the RGB color histogram distributions of different vehicles.

In recent years, massive vehicle Re-ID methods based on appearance are proposed. For example, Liu et al. [6,7] utilized convolutional neural network to explore appearance features such as texture, color and semantic properties. Liu et al. [8] proposed a Region-Aware Deep Model extracting features from a series of local regions. Liu et al. [9] proposed the Repression Network to learn discriminative features for each vehicle image from both coarse-grained and detailed level simultaneously. Wang et al. [10] exploited orientation invariant features and local region features of different orientations based on 20 key point locations. As Fig. 1 shows, different vehicles may have similar appearance features, while the same vehicle in different environments expresses various appearance features. Methods mentioned above only focused on vehicles' visual appearance features, which can not solve the vehicle Re-ID problem well due to occlusions, illumination variations. Besides vehicle's visual appearance, vehicle's license plate is another concern for vehicle Re-ID research. Parks and highways have adopted license plate recognition system to identify vehicles [11,12]. Recently, Liu et al. [13] proposed a plate-SNN method to solve plate recognition problem in the unconstrained situations. However, existing vehicle license based methods do not achieve good performance in open traffic environment, where high-quality license plate images are hard to obtain.

In person Re-ID, some recent researches [14–17] exploited the spatiotemporal information in camera networks to improve the Re-ID performance. Compared with person Re-ID, vehicle spatiotemporal information is more effective for vehicle Re-ID, since driving behaviors are constrained by traffic rules and vehicle's movement follows in certain directions in different driving roads. In recent vehicle Re-ID works, Kettnaker et al. [18] adopted a Bayesian estimation model to assemble likely paths of objects over different cameras. Liu et al. [13] considered spatiotemporal information as contextual data to assist progressive vehicle Re-ID framework. Wang et al. [10] modeled a conditional spatiotemporal distribution to regularize the vehicle Re-ID. However these spatiotemporal models [10,13,18] neglect the problem that different vehicles in the same section probably have similar spatiotemporal information, as Fig. 2 illustrates. Inspired by this, we observe that vehicles' driving directions can be estimated by vehicles' poses captured under camera's fixed shooting directions and vehicles' driving directions keep unchanged within a short period of time. Therefore vehicles' driving directions can assist spatiotemporal model to exclude the situation mentioned above and precisely search the same vehicles.

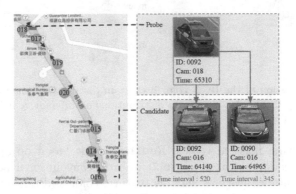

Fig. 2. Illustration of the problem that the spatiotemporal model can't correctly distinguish vehicle's identity. The correct match is denoted by the red box and the time interval between it is 520 s. The non-corresponding match is denoted by green box and the time interval between it is 345 s. (Color figure online)

For vehicle Re-ID, similar vehicles are difficult to be distinguished in the real traffic environments, because their spatiotemporal information is not fully exploited. In this paper, firstly a spatiotemporal based on Gaussian distribution in each pair of cameras is proposed. The parameters of model are related to the topology of cameras and historical traffic conditions. Secondly, a CNN embedding poses classifier is utilized to judge vehicles' poses, and driving directions can be estimated by vehicles' poses and camera shooting directions. Candidate vehicles with the same driving direction as the query vehicles are selected out from the gallery and calculate their spatiotemporal probability. The role of this process is to guide our spatiotemporal model and precisely identify vehicles. Finally, compared with those only appearance based algorithms, we attempt to incorporate the Poses Guide Spatiotemporal model (PGST) and appearance based model together to implement a better vehicle Re-ID framework. Considering difference between the data structures of vehicle visual appearance features and spatiotemporal features, this framework based on Bayesian conditional probability method to integrate the results of appearance based model and PGST model.

This paper includes the following contributions: (1) We construct a spatiotemporal model (ST) based on Gaussian distribution in each pair of cameras. The parameters of model are generated from the topology of cameras and historical traffic conditions. (2) The PGST model is proposed to estimate the vehicles driving directions based on the vehicles poses, and then optimize the spatiotemporal model by utilizing driving directions. (3) We propose a framework that contains the PGST model collaborating with visual features to improve vehicle Re-ID performance. In this section, we introduce two observations based on experiments and analyze the data in real surveillance system.

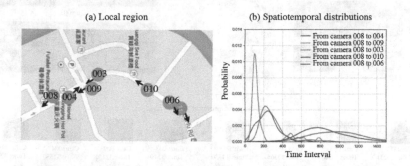

Fig. 3. Illustration of spatiotemporal distributions of five pairs of cameras. (a) The orange circles on the map represents the cameras in local region. (b) The curves represent respectively the time interval distribution between camera 008 and other cameras (004, 009, 003, 010, 006). The time interval distribution between any pair of cameras represents the probability of that vehicles passed through the pairs of cameras.

2 Motivation

Vehicles' movements are constrained by spatiotemporal cues. The time interval that a vehicle drives through a pair of cameras must be in a normal range. For example, a vehicle can not drive exceed 10 km within one second in urban surveillance environment. We analyze spatiotemporal information on VeRi dataset [7], which contains vehicle images and spatiotemporal data collected in real surveillance environment, and the results are illustrated in Fig. 3(a). With consideration of the topology of cameras, the experiment indicates that the movement pattern of vehicles is represented as a spatiotemporal distribution. The spatiotemporal distribution of same vehicle from different pairs of cameras follows Gaussian distribution with different parameters. Therefore, we construct a spatiotemporal model based on Gaussian distribution to describe how the time interval changes while the vehicles transfer between different pairs of cameras. It can be exploited to calculate the spatiotemporal probability of the same vehicle captured by any pairs of cameras.

As Fig. 2 illustrates, the spatiotemporal model overlooks the problem that the time intervals that different vehicles drive through the same pair of cameras from different directions are probably the same or close. We observe that vehicles' driving directions can assist to distinguish whether the vehicles are the same or not and it can be utilized to optimize our spatiotemporal model. As Fig. 4 illustrates, the fixed shooting directions of cameras in the camera network

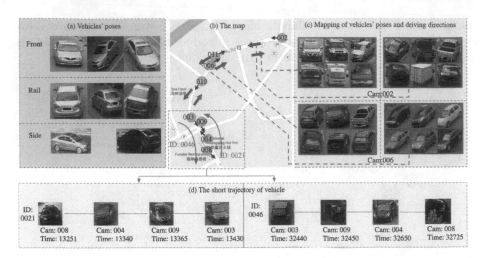

Fig. 4. Illustration of observations about the relationship of vehicles' poses and spatiotemporal information. (a) shows vehicles' poses captured by cameras are sorted to four categories, eg. front, rail, left side, right side. (b) shows a local region on map. The orange circle on the map represents cameras. The black arrow on circle denotes camera's shooting direction. The purple arrow and red arrow denote the relative movement direction of vehicle under camera. (c) shows that mapping of vehicles' poses under fixed shooting directions and the relative movements direction of vehicles. (d) are examples of short trajectories of vehicle 0021 and 0046 within green region on map. The arrows on green region denote vehicles' driving directions (eg. clockwise, anti-clockwise). The movement of vehicle 0021 is from camera 008 to camera 003 based on spatiotemporal information, while vehicle 0046 on the opposite side. We also can infer it's driving direction from the vehicle's pose captured by fixed shooting direction. (Color figure online)

are different, a vehicle's poses captured by cameras are different. With consideration of collaborating of the vehicles' poses and camera shooting directions, the relative movement directions of vehicles can be estimated. For example, when vehicle's pose captured by camera is front, we can infer the vehicle is approaching the camera, vice versa. The driving direction of the vehicle in the region can be estimated by the location of cameras and the relative direction. Due to the fact of vehicles' driving directions are generally stable in real traffic environment, the vehicles which have same driving directions captured by each camera are most likely to be the same. Consequently, the Poses Guide Spatiotemporal model (PGST) is proposed, which introduces estimation of driving directions to optimize spatiotemporal model.

3   Our Approach

The task of vehicle Re-ID is to retrieve all vehicles which have the same identity with query vehicle in the camera network. For the clarity of the problem

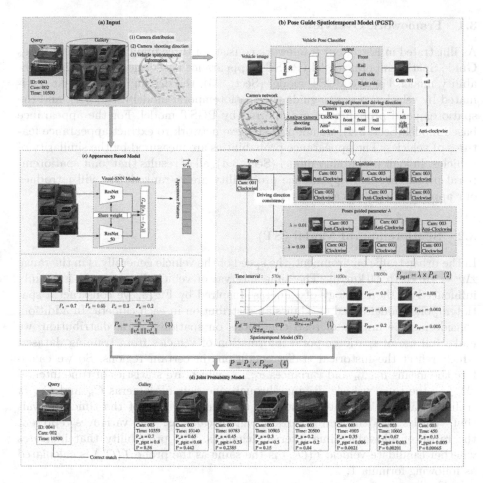

Fig. 5. Illustration of an overview of our framework for vehicle Re-ID. The framework includes (b) Pose Guide Spatiotemporal model (PGST), (c) appearance based model, and (d) joint probability model.

definition, some notations describing vehicle Re-ID are introduced as followings. In the urban surveillance system, we define a camera network C, which is composed of $M + 1$ cameras with non-overlapping field of views, and it can be represented as $C = \{C_0, C_1, C_2, \ldots, C_M\}$. The ith vehicle at C_n is represented by O_n^i. The t_n^i denotes the moment that vehicle O_i^n captured by C_n. The time interval $\Delta t_{n \to m}^{i,j} = t_n^i - t_m^j$ when vehicles pass through a pair of camera can be calculated out. For vehicle Re-ID, we expect to find the vehicles which have same identity as query vehicle in different camera views and it can be described as $\Pr(\Upsilon(O_n^i) = \Upsilon(O_m^j), n \neq m)$.

3.1   Framework Overview

As illustrated in Fig. 5, our framework consists of three main components, Poses Guide Spatiotemporal model (PGST), appearance based model and joint probability model. For the PGST model (Sect. 3.3), the driving directions are estimated by vehicles' poses to guide the spatiotemporal model (Sect. 3.2), and the spatiotemporal probabilities are inferred by PGST model. For the appearance based model (Sect. 3.4), we adopt a siamese network to extract appearance features of vehicles. The appearance probabilities are measured by the similarity of vehicles. In joint probability model (Sect. 3.4), all of results that joint spatiotemporal probability and appearance probability are re-ranked. We will introduce our approach in details as follows.

3.2   Spatiotemporal Model (ST)

In the urban traffic environment, the speed of the vehicle generally is in the range $\Delta v = [10\,\text{km/h}\;90\,\text{km/h}]$. The time interval of vehicles' movement is mainly influenced by the topology of cameras. Inspired by Fig. 3, we construct a spatiotemporal model based on Gaussian distribution in each camera. In addition, considering the impact of road conditions on spatiotemporal distribution, we make full use of spatiotemporal information of vehicles from training dataset, which reflect the historical traffic conditions in certain regions. So we calculate the means $\mu_{n\to m}$ and variances $\sigma_{n\to m}$, which are statistics of time interval $\Delta t_{n\to m}^{i,j}$ the same vehicle driving through one pair of cameras C_n and C_m in training dataset. The means indicate the general range of the time intervals that vehicles pass through a certain pair of cameras. The variances represent the range of allowable time intervals changes. The probability that indicates whether candidate vehicle $\Upsilon(O_m^j)$ is the same as the probe $\Upsilon(O_n^i)$ is calculated as following formula 1.

$$P_{st}(\Upsilon(O_n^i) = \Upsilon(O_m^j) \mid \Delta t_{n\to m}^{i,j}) = \frac{1}{\sqrt{2\pi}\sigma_{n\to m}} \exp^{-\frac{(\Delta t_{n\to m}^{i,j} - \mu_{n\to m})^2}{2(\sigma_{n\to m})^2}} \tag{1}$$

3.3   Poses Guide Spatiotemporal Model (PGST)

As it is shown in Fig. 5(b), We adopt a CNN embedding model as vehicles' poses classifier to acquire the vehicles' poses. The model consists of a ResNet_50 [19] embedding module, which contains a hierarchy of residual blocks to improve the capacity of the network. We replace the original output layer with a dropout layer and a softmax layer with four outputs (eg. front, rail, left side, right side), as Fig. 7(a) shows. Since it is a classification task, we adopt a classic cross entropy loss for the model. We manually label vehicles' poses on certain part of VeRi dataset. The poses classifier is pre-trained on CompCars dataset [23] which includes vehicle's viewpoint labels, then it is trained on a part of VeRi dataset, finally we adopt incremental optimization based on user feedback mechanism to optimize the classifier.

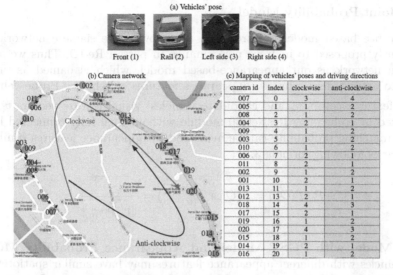

Fig. 6. Illustration of mapping poses and driving directions on VeRi dataset. (a) shows four vehicles' poses categories. Front, rail, left side, and right side are labeled respectively $1, 2, 3, 4$. (b) The orange circle on the map represents the cameras. Camera's ID is tagged beside. The black arrow on circle denotes camera's shooting direction. Driving directions are sorted to clockwise and anti-clockwise. (c) It shows a mapping of vehicles' poses and driving directions.

In the urban surveillance system, camera shooting directions are fixed and easily obtained. We exploit shooting directions of each camera in the camera network and establish a mapping of vehicles' poses and driving directions. For instance of VeRi dataset, Fig. 7 shows a mapping of vehicles' poses and driving directions. The driving directions of vehicles O_n^i in camera C_n is denoted as $\Phi(O_n^i) \in \{clockwise, anti\text{-}clockwise\}$. On the base of the hypothesis that a vehicle's driving direction generally maintains stable within a small region, we introduce λ as poses guided parameter to guide ST model. Thus λ can be regarded as a penalty term. The probability of spatiotemporal between the probe vehicles O_n^i and the candidate vehicles O_m^j is very low when their driving directions are different. Combined with the formula 1, Poses Guide Spatiotemporal model (PGST) is established by formula 2.

$$P_{pgst}(\Upsilon(O_n^i) = \Upsilon(O_m^j) \mid \Delta t_{n \to m}^{i,j}, \Phi(O_n^i), \Phi(O_m^j))$$
$$= \begin{cases} \lambda \times P_{st}, & if \ \Phi(O_n^i) \neq \Phi(O_m^j) \\ (1-\lambda) \times P_{st}, & if \ \Phi(O_n^i) = \Phi(O_m^j) \end{cases} \tag{2}$$

where λ is set to 0.01 on VeRi dataset.

3.4 Joint Probability Model

Appearance based model is introduced as follows. The siamese network [20] is recently proposed to improve performance in person Re-ID. Thus we adopt siamese network as our appearance-based model, which is named as visual-SNN, to extract discriminative appearance features of vehicles. Probe vehicles' visual feature vectors $\vec{v_n^i}$ and candidate vehicles' visual feature vectors $\vec{v_m^j}$ are extracted by embedding ResNet_50 module without final fully-connected layer. Visual matching probability can be measured by appearance features similarity distance as following formula 3.

$$P_a(\Upsilon(O_n^i) = \Upsilon(O_m^j) \mid \vec{v_n^i}, \vec{v_m^j}) = \frac{\vec{v_n^i} \cdot \vec{v_m^j}}{\|\vec{v_n^i}\|\|\vec{v_m^j}\|} \tag{3}$$

Joint Model with PGST Model and Appearance Probability Model. The vehicles with different appearance features may have similar spatiotemporal distribution. In contrast, the vehicles with similar appearance features may have different spatiotemporal distribution. Therefore, vehicle appearance features probability distribution and spatiotemporal probability distribution are independent of each other. We consider that appearance features probability distribution and spatiotemporal probability distribution obey the Bayesian conditional probability, which is shown as 4.

$$P(\Upsilon(O_n^i) = \Upsilon(O_m^j) \mid \vec{v_n^i}, \vec{v_n^i}, t_m^j, t_m^j, \Phi(O_n^i), \Phi(O_m^j)) = P_{pgst} \times P_a \tag{4}$$

4 Experiments

In this section, we implement the proposed approach on the VeRi [7] dataset which offers the spatiotemporal information of vehicles' movements and camera topology. Based on VeRi dataset, the experiments show the approach effectively improves the performance of vehicles re-identification without license plate.

4.1 Dataset

CompCars dataset [23] is a public relatively large vehicle database consisting of data obtained from surveillance videos and network. CompCars includes stratification, properties, viewpoints and partial images of vehicles. The viewpoints of vehicles are labeled into five categories, front, rear, side, front-side, and rear-side.

VeRi dataset [7] For vehicle public Re-ID dataset, there are VeRi [7] and VehicleID [9]. However, VeRi dataset is the only one containing spatiotemporal information and topology of cameras. VeRi is collected with 20 cameras in real traffic surveillance environment. The cameras are installed in arbitrary positions and directions. It contains approximately 50000 images and 9000 tracks of 776 vehicles. The dataset is split into a training set containing 37,781 images of 576 vehicles and a testing set with 11579 images of 200 vehicles. The query set consists of 1678 images of each vehicle ID from each camera. Due to VeRi dataset laking poses labels of vehicles, we utilize images of CompCars which are labeled the vehicle viewpoints to train the poses classifier. We manually label four categories (eg. front, rail, left side, right side) on 1500 images of VeRi training dataset. Finally, these images are utilized to fine-tune the poses classifier for estimating the vehicles' poses.

4.2   Experimental Settings

In this paper, We use 1678 query vehicles and 2021 testing tracks in the VeRi dataset for evaluation. We introduce evaluation method [13] that conducts the vehicle Re-ID in an image-to-track (HIT) metric, in which the image is used as the query, while the gallery consists of tracks of the same vehicle captured by other cameras. A track is a trajectory of a vehicle recorded by one camera at a time, which means the images in a track are organized together. The similarity between an image and a track is computed by max-pooling over images in the test track. Cumulative match curves (CMC), HIT@1 (precision at rank 1), HIT@5 (precision at rank 5) and mean average precision (mAP) are also adopted to evaluate the accuracy of the methods.

Experimental environment includes Ubuntu 14.04 LTS OS, 256 GB Memory, CPU Intel(R)@ 2.40 GHz, GPU NVIDIA Tesla P100-PCIE-16GB.

4.3   Evaluation of Vehicle Poses Classifier

We train the poses classifier on 16016 images of CompCars [23] which are labeled the vehicle viewpoints, and fine-tunning the poses classifier on 1500 manual labeling images of VeRi training dataset. We evaluate the vehicle poses classifier on thousands of images of VeRi verification dataset. The results of the vehicle poses classifier show that the accuracy of front side, rail side, left side and right side are respectively 97.71%, 95.93%, 93.51%, 94.79%.

4.4   Evaluation of Vehicle Re-ID Methods

In this section, we compare our approach with the state-of-art methods on the VeRi dataset, and the results show that our approach achieves an good performance. NuFACT [13], LOMO [22], FACT [6], BOW-CN [21] are the appearance based methods, and they only measure the similarity of vehicle appearance features to solve vehicle Re-ID. Orientation Invariant Feature Embedding [10] (shorted by OIFE) proposes that local region features of different orientations can be extracted based on 20 key point locations to problem of viewpoint variations. Orientation Invariant Feature Embedding and Spatial Temporal Regularization (shorted by OIFE+ST) [10] combine orientation invariant feature embedding and spatiotemporal regularization to handle vehicle Re-ID. PROVID [13] proposes a deep learning-based approach to progressive vehicle re-identification and makes full use of appearance features, plate license and spatiotemporal information.

Table 1 illustrates results of models above in the mAP, HIT@1, and HIT@5. The CMC curves of different methods are shown in Fig. 7(a), and we discuss the results as follows:

Our basic ST model and PGST model based on spatiotemporal information both achieve good performances on mAP and HIT@1, which proves the proposed spatiotemporal methods are effective. Since we consider vehicle's driving directions are estimated by vehicles' poses and camera shooting directions, the PGST model achieve 23.94% improvement in mAP and 12.54% improvement in the HIT@1 compared with ST model. All of the PROVID [13], OTFE+ST [10], our ST+visual-SNN, and our PGST+visual-SNN take advantage of multi-source information. As Fig. 7(b), (c) show, both OTFE+ST [10] and our PGST+visual-SNN concern on the role of vehicle's pose captured by cameras. OTFE+ST [10] exploit the vehicle's view to extract orientation invariant feature of vehicle appearance, while we use vehicles' poses to guide spatiotemporal model. Specifically, in our PGST+visual-SNN, driving directions which are estimated by vehicles' poses and camera shooting directions are utilized to optimize spatiotemporal model. Though OTFE+ST are higher performance on the HIT@1, our PGST+visual-SNN is 35.6% higher performance on mAP. Compared with PROVID which considers plate information, spatiotemporal information and appearance features, our framework also achieves 30.0% and 9.5% separately improvements on mAP and HIT@1.

Table 1. Comparison of the performance on spatiotemporal model

Data source	Methods	mAP	HIT@1	HIT@5
Appearance based	BOW-CN [21]	12.20	33.91	53.69
	FACT [6]	18.75	52.21	72.17
	LOMO [22]	9.64	25.33	46.48
	NuFACT [13]	48.47	76.76	91.42
	OIFE [10]	48.00	89.43	-
	visual-SNN [20]	58.75	75.21	91.29
Spatiotemporal based	our ST model	43.69	64.35	88.89
	our PGST model	54.15	72.42	91.29
Mulit-source information	baseline [7]	27.77	61.44	78.78
	OIFE + ST [10]	51.42	92.35	-
	PROVID [13]	53.42	81.56	95.11
	our ST + visual-SNN	64.33	86.41	94.40
	our PGST + visual-SNN	**69.47**	**89.36**	94.40

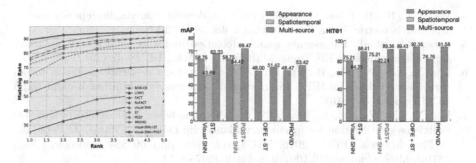

Fig. 7. The CMC curves, mAP and HIT of comparison with the proposed framework and state-of-art vehicle Re-ID on VeRi. Owing to OIFE+ST and PROVID methods laking spatiotemporal-based experiment, the spatiotemporal results of them are vacant on mAP and HIT.

5   Conclusion

This paper puts forward a new framework for vehicle Re-ID. To solve the vehicle Re-ID problem, two observations of vehicles' movements in real traffic environment are explored by analyzing spatiotemporal information and topology of cameras in urban surveillance system. On this basis, a spatiotemporal model based on Gaussian distribution in each pair of cameras is constructed. The parameters of model are related to camera's topology and historical traffic conditions. Vehicle's Poses Guide Spatiotemporal model (PGST) is proposed. Driving directions which are estimated by vehicles' poses and camera shooting directions optimize the spatiotemporal model. Finally, our framework in which PGST model collaborates with vehicle visual features achieves improvements in vehicle Re-ID. The experiments are conducted on VeRi datasets which are the only existing dataset that provides spatiotemporal information. The results show improvement in efficiency and accuracy compared with the existing state-of-art methods.

Acknowledgement. The research was supported by National Nature Science Foundation of China (61572012, 61801335), Hubei Provincial Natural Science Foundation of China (2015CFB52, 2017CFA012).

References

1. Zheng, L., Yang, Y., Hauptmann, A.G.: Person re-identification: past, present and future. arXiv preprint arXiv:1610.02984 (2016)
2. Wang, Z., Hu, R., et al.: Statistical inference of gaussian-laplace distribution for person verification. In: ACM Proceedings of the 2017 ACM on Multimedia Conference (ACMMM), vol. 9, pp. 1609–1617 (2017)
3. Wang, Z., Ye, M., Yang, F., et al.: Cascaded SR-GAN for scale-adaptive low resolution person re-identification. In: Proceedings of the Twenty-Seventh International Joint Conference on Artificial Intelligence (IJCAI), vol. 18, pp. 3891–3897 (2018)

4. Wang, Z., Hu, R., Chen, C., et al.: Person re-identification via discrepancy matrix and matrix metric. IEEE Trans. Cybern. **48**, 3006 (2017)
5. Feris, R.S., et al.: Large-scale vehicle detection, indexing, and search in urban surveillance videos. IEEE Trans. Multimedia (TMM) **14**, 28–42 (2012)
6. Liu, X., Liu, W., Ma, H., Fu, H.: Large-scale vehicle re-identification in urban surveillance videos. In: IEEE International Conference on Multimedia and Expo (ICME), pp. 1–6 (2016)
7. Liu, X., Liu, W., Mei, T., Ma, H.: A deep learning-based approach to progressive vehicle re-identification for urban surveillance. In: Leibe, B., Matas, J., Sebe, N., Welling, M. (eds.) ECCV 2016. LNCS, vol. 9906, pp. 869–884. Springer, Cham (2016). https://doi.org/10.1007/978-3-319-46475-6_53
8. Liu, X., et al.: RAM: a region-aware deep model for vehicle re-identification. In: IEEE International Conference on Multimedia and Expo (ICME), arXiv preprint arXiv:1806.09283 (2018)
9. Liu, H., Tian, Y., Wang, Y., Pang, L., Huang, T.: Deep relative distance learning: tell the difference between similar vehicles. In: IEEE Conference on Computer Vision and Pattern Recognition (CVPR), pp. 2167–2175 (2016)
10. Wang, Z., et al.: Orientation invariant feature embedding and spatial temporal regularization for vehicle re-identification. In: IEEE International Conference on Computer Vision (ICCV), pp. 379–387 (2017)
11. Du, S., Ibrahim, M., Shehata, M., Badawy, W.: Automatic license plate recognition (ALPR): a state-of-the-art review. IEEE Trans. Circ. Syst. Video Technol. (TCSVT) **23**, 311–325 (2013)
12. Wen, Y., Lu, Y., Yan, J., Zhou, Z., von Deneen, K.M., Shi, P.: An algorithm for license plate recognition applied to intelligent transportation system. IEEE Trans. Intell. Transp. Syst. (TITS) **12**, 830–845 (2011)
13. Liu, X., Liu, W., Mei, T., Ma, H.: PROVID: progressive and multimodal vehicle re-identification for large-scale urban surveillance. IEEE Trans. Multimedia (TMM) **20**, 645–658 (2018)
14. Huang, W., Hu, R., Liang, C., Yu, Y., Wang, Z., Zhong, X., Zhang, C.: Camera network based person re-identification by leveraging spatial-temporal constraint and multiple cameras relations. In: Tian, Q., Sebe, N., Qi, G.-J., Huet, B., Hong, R., Liu, X. (eds.) MMM 2016. LNCS, vol. 9516, pp. 174–186. Springer, Cham (2016). https://doi.org/10.1007/978-3-319-27671-7_15
15. Martinel, N., Foresti, G.L., Micheloni, C.: Person re-identification in a distributed camera network framework. IEEE Trans. Cybern. **47**, 3530–3541 (2017)
16. Javed, O., Shaque, K., Rasheed, Z., Shah, M.: Modeling inter-camera space-time and appearance relationships for tracking across non-overlapping views. Comput. Vis. Image Underst. (CVIU) **109**, 146–162 (2008)
17. Lv, J., Chen, W., Li, Q., Yang, C.: Unsupervised cross-dataset person re-identification by transfer learning of spatial-temporal patterns. In: IEEE Conference on Computer Vision and Pattern Recognition (CVPR), pp. 7948–7956 (2018)
18. Kettnaker, V., Zabih, R.: Bayesian multi-camera surveillance. In: IEEE Computer Society Conference on Computer Vision and Pattern Recognition (CVPRW) vol. 2, p. 259 (1999)
19. He, K., Zhang, X., Ren, S., Sun, J.: Deep residual learning for image recognition. In: IEEE Conference on Computer Vision and Pattern Recognition (CVPR), pp. 770–778 (2016)
20. Zheng, Z., Zheng, L., Yang, Y.: A discriminatively learned CNN embedding for person re-identification. In: ACM Transactions on Multimedia Computing, Communications, and Applications (TOMM), vol. 14, p. 13 (2017)

21. Zheng, L., Shen, L., Tian, L., Wang, S., Wang, J., Tian, Q.: Scalable person re-identification. a benchmark. In: IEEE International Conference on Computer Vision (ICCV), pp. 1116–1124 (2015)
22. Liao, S., Hu, Y., Zhu, X., Li, S.: Person re-identification by local maximal occurrence representation and metric learning. In: IEEE Conference on Computer Vision and Pattern Recognition (CVPR), pp. 2197–2206 (2015)
23. Yang, L., Luo, P., Loy, C.C., Tang, X.: A large-scale car dataset for fine-grained categorization and verification. In: IEEE Conference on Computer Vision and Pattern Recognition (CVPR), pp. 3973–3981 (2015)

Alignment of Deep Features in 3D Models for Camera Pose Estimation

Jui-Yuan Su[1,2(✉)], Shyi-Chyi Cheng[2], Chin-Chun Chang[2], and Jun-Wei Hsieh[2]

[1] Department of New Media and Communications Administration, Ming Chuan University, Taipei, Taiwan
rysu@mail.mcu.edu.tw
[2] Department of Computer Science and Information Engineering, National Taiwan Ocean University, Keelung, Taiwan
{rysu,csc,cvml,shieh}@mail.ntou.edu.tw

Abstract. Using a set of semantically annotated RGB-D images with known camera poses, many existing 3D reconstruction algorithms can integrate these images into a single 3D model of the scene. The semantically annotated scene model facilitates the construction of a video surveillance system using a moving camera if we can efficiently compute the depth maps of the captured images and estimate the poses of the camera. The proposed model-based video surveillance consists of two phases, i.e. the modeling phase and the inspection phase. In the modeling phase, we carefully calibrate the parameters of the camera that captures the multi-view video for modeling the target 3D scene. However, in the inspection phase, the camera pose parameters and the depth maps of the captured RGB images are often unknown or noisy when we use a moving camera to inspect the completeness of the object. In this paper, the 3D model is first transformed into a colored point cloud, which is then indexed by clustering—with each cluster representing a surface fragment of the scene. The clustering results are then used to train a model-specific convolution neural network (CNN) that annotates each pixel of an input RGB image with a correct fragment class. The prestored camera parameters and depth information of fragment classes are then fused together to estimate the depth map and the camera pose of the current input RGB image. The experimental results show that the proposed approach outperforms the compared methods in terms of the accuracy of camera pose estimation.

Keywords: Unsupervised fragment classification · 3D model · Deep learning Camera pose estimation · 3D point cloud clustering

1 Introduction

The per-pixel depth map sequence in multi-view RGB-D video enhances the quality of the reconstructed 3D models when the parameters of the camera that captures the video have been accurately calibrated. The usage of 3D models is central in many research areas including robotics, virtual reality (VR), augmented reality (AR), 3D scene surveillance, geodesy, remote sensing, and 3D printing. Previous remote sensing

© Springer Nature Switzerland AG 2019
I. Kompatsiaris et al. (Eds.): MMM 2019, LNCS 11296, pp. 440–452, 2019.
https://doi.org/10.1007/978-3-030-05716-9_36

research shows two promising approaches including airborne image photogrammetry [1] and light detection and ranging (LiDAR) [2] to capture accurate depth maps from a real-world scene. However, the acquisition cost of these approaches is essentially high and hard to implement on a moving camera. Instead, many low-cost depth acquiring techniques using a set of multi-view images have been presented [3–7]. To construct high-quality 3D models, the key to success for these approaches is the estimation of accurate parameters of the camera pose.

A publicly available implementation of 3D reconstruction [8] takes an RGB-D video as input and conducts the following three-step procedure: (1) construct local surface fragments from short frame segments of the input RGB-D video; (2) align fragments in the global space; (3) integrate all RGB-D images into a single truncated signed distance field (TSDF) volume [9] and extract a mesh as the result. The key to success in reconstructing a high-quality 3D model from an RGB-D video is to include point cloud registration for fragment construction and fragment alignment [10]. However, these two problems can often be solved by graph optimization algorithms [11], which are recognized to be very time consuming. In this paper, we use deep learning approaches to extract robust deep features for integrating color into geometric registration algorithms that establish accurate correspondences in a higher-dimensional space rather than the physical three-dimensional space [12–14]. This facilitates the updating of the 3D model of the scene by integrating current RGB-D images into corresponding fragments in the inspecting phase.

Template-based 3D scene reconstruction uses a set of image templates to represent individual view structures of a scene, where the RGB information in each template describes the visual appearance and the depth map while the camera parameters offer the geometric structure [15, 16]. Given a pre-learned template-based 3D scene model, in the inspecting phase, we can perform a pre-learned fragment classifier to locate the fragments in which the 3D points are projected to render the current test RGB (or RGB-D) frame. In this paper, using the stored depth maps and the camera pose parameters and by corresponding the deep features of pixels between the test frame and the view templates, the scheme to estimate the missing depth map of camera pose parameters is also presented. Using the depth map and the estimated camera parameters of the test frame as input data, we can compute a set of 3D points covering a specific view of the target 3D scene. To perform a 3D point cloud registration algorithm, the correspondences between the test point cloud and the fragment point cloud constitute a fine-grained way to inspect a scene using a moving camera.

The performance of 3D modeling using RGB-D templates is extremely good, however it still has some critical issues to be solved [15, 16]. First, the selection of optimal templates to cover all the fragments of a scene model is not a trivial task. Second, the appearance of samples from different views are quite inconsistent [17]. Third, the view-invariant visual feature is difficult to extract. Lastly, the depth map and the camera pose parameters estimated by corresponding the test frame with the representative template are only approximately correct when the number of templates to describe a 3D object is small. The emerging deep learning methods [18–21] can be exploited to deal with these difficulties because they have been proved to perform well in many computer vision applications.

In this work, we propose a deep learning approach to train a fragment classifier that learns the feature representation of a 3D model. The algorithm starts by performing the 3D reconstruction algorithm [8] to represent the scene as a 3D point cloud using the training depth maps and the given camera pose parameters. Next, a 3D point clustering algorithm is performed on the 3D model to group 3D points into clusters. With each cluster representing a surface fragment, the clustering results of the 3D points in the model automatically generate the fragment label maps for all the training RGB-D images that cover all viewpoints of the scene. The training RGB-D images plus their fragment labels are then collected as the training dataset for learning the fragment classifier using the convolutional neural network (CNN) based deep architecture [22, 23]. The optimal set of template images are also determined by the clustering results. Thus, the proposed image-based 3D scene modeling uses the fusion of the fragment classifier and the template images to represent the contents of the 3D scene.

In the inspecting phase, the fragment class of each pixel in a test RGB image is first recognized by the fragment classifier. Next, we accurately match the input frame against the corresponding fragment template to estimate the depth map and the camera pose parameters of the input frame. The estimation results can then be transformed into a set of 3D point clouds for further scene inspection or recognition. We evaluated our system on an open RGB-D benchmark provided by the Technical University of Munich [24]. Experimental results show that our approach outperforms the compared methods in terms of the accuracy of view classification and camera pose estimation.

2   Image-Based 3D Scene Modeling Using RGB-D Multi-view Video

Given the parameters of a moving camera to capture a multi-view RGB-D video, Fig. 1 shows the basic concept to build up the image-based 3D object model. In this simple example, the shape of the cube object can be approximate by eight 3D planes, each defines a view. For the sake of illustration, we refer to these planes as the principal planes of the object. To project every point in the cube along the normal vector of a principal plane, we can capture an RGB-D template image using a Kinect-like camera. One can reconstruct the 3D object by integrating each depth map with its camera pose parameters into a TSDF volume.

TSDFs are 3D image structures that implicitly represent geometry by sampling on a uniform lattice (voxel) with a signed distance to the nearest surface. A negative sign implies that the distance is sampled from within a solid shape. On the contrary, a positive sign means the voxel is sampled in free space. The approximate location of surfaces can be extracted as the zero-level set. Let p be a voxel in 3D space. The distance between p and its nearest point q in the closed surface Q in that models the shape of a scene can be defined as the distance value of p: $d(\mathrm{p}) = \arg\min_{\mathrm{q} \in Q} \|\mathrm{p} - \mathrm{q}\|_2$.

If there is no hole in the surface Q, one can assume every surface point has an associative outward-oriented normal vector n(q). This defines the sign of the distance value of p to be: $s(\mathrm{p}) = sign(\mathrm{n}(\mathrm{q})^T \cdot (\mathrm{p} - \mathrm{q}))$, where $s(\mathrm{p})$ indicates on which side of the surface p is located on. Finally, truncating the value of the distance field in an interval

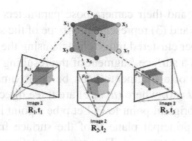

Fig. 1. The depth maps and camera pose parameters of frames in multi-view video can be used to reconstruct the shape of a 3D object.

$[d_{\min}, d_{\max}]$ produces the TSDF defined, for any closed surface, as $d(p) = \min(d_{\max}, \max(d_{\min}, s(p) \arg\min_{q \in Q} \|p - q\|_2))$. In the reconstruction of a TSDF volume from a multi-view RGB-D video, the detection of the zero-level set in terms of the signed distance field is not a trivial task. In this paper, we propose the MPP analysis as a method of dealing with this difficulty.

The first step of integrating depth maps into a TSDF is to transform the pixel coordinates into 3D points in the real-world coordinate system. Let $p_c = [x_c, y_c, z_c, 1]^T$ be the homogeneous coordinates of a 3D point in the camera coordinate system. The pinhole camera model projects the 3D point into the pixel $x = [x, y, 1]^T$ in an image plane using the following equation:

$$x = \pi(p_c) = \left(\frac{f_x x_c + c_x}{z(x)}, \frac{f_y y_c + c_x}{z(x)}, 1\right)^T \tag{1}$$

where f_x and f_y are the x and y direction focal length, respectively; c_x and c_y are the principal point offsets; $z(x)$ is the depth value of the 2D point x. Obviously, given the depth value $z(x)$, the inverse projection function $\pi^{-1}(\cdot)$ projects a 2D point x back to the 3D point p_c:

$$p_c = \pi^{-1}(x, z(x)) = z(x) \left(\frac{x - c_x}{f_x}, \frac{y - c_y}{f_y}, 1\right)^T \tag{2}$$

Based on the theory of the three-dimensional special orthogonal group (SO (3)) Lie group, the pose of the classical rigid body can be described by the six-degree-of-freedom (6DOF), the camera motion model that constitutes an orthogonal rotation matrix $R_{3\times3}$ and a translation vector $t_{3\times1} \in R^3$. Thus, a 3D point p_c in the camera coordinate system can be transformed into a 3D point $p_g = (x_g, y_g, z_g, 1)^T$ by the following equation:

$$[x_g, y_g, z_g, 1]^T = \begin{bmatrix} R_{3\times3} & t_{3\times1} \\ 0_{1\times3} & 1 \end{bmatrix} [x_c, y_c, z_c, 1]^T \tag{3}$$

Using the depth maps and their camera pose parameters associated with a given multi-view video, Eqs. (2) and (3) represents the shape of the scene as a 3D point cloud $\{p_i \in X\}_{i=1}^n$ which is further clustered into k clusters using the proposed MPP analysis, where each cluster defines a surface fragment of the resulting 3D model. In this work, we assume that the shape of a fragment F can be approximated by a parameterized plane P: $ax + by + cz - d = 0$, where (a, b, c) are three directional numbers of P and d is the distance from the original point to P. Let p be a point in F. The signed distance from p $= (x, y, z)$ to the principal plane P of the surface fragment F is easy to be computed as $sd(p) = ax + by + cz - d$. This equation defines the distance field of the TSDF of the scene as $d(p) = \min(d_{max}, \max(d_{min}, sd(p)))$.

The MPP clustering iteratively applies a point separation process which consists of three steps: (1) translate the origin point to the center of the point cloud, i.e., $p_i = p_i - \bar{p}, i = 1, \ldots, n$, where $\bar{p}$ is the center of the cloud X; (2) compute the maximal symmetry plane (principal plane) P of X; (3) using P, divide the points into two sub-clouds, i.e. X_1 and X_2. To translate the original point to the center of a point cloud, we can parameterize P as $ax + by + cz = 0$. We define the sum of inertial moments of points in X to P: $I(a, b, c) = \sum_{p \in X} (ax + by + cz)^2$.

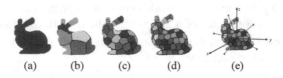

(a)	(b)	(c)	(d)	(e)

Fig. 2. Model simplification results for Stanford 'bunny' using the proposed MPP analysis with different numbers of surfaces: (a) the original model; (b)–(d) are the vertex clustering results with 10, 50, and 100 surfaces, respectively; (e) outer red vertices are the viewpoints which represent the virtual camera centers of the selected templates. (Color figure online)

If P is the maximal symmetry plane of X, the value of I should be minimized. This implies the values of (a, b, c) by taking the following partial derivations $(\partial I/\partial a, \partial I/\partial I, \partial I/\partial c)$ and setting them to zero. This generates the following results:

$$\mathbf{M} \begin{bmatrix} a \\ b \\ c \end{bmatrix} = 0, \mathbf{M} = \begin{bmatrix} m_{2,0,0} & m_{1,1,0} & m_{1,0,1} \\ m_{1,1,0} & m_{0,2,0} & m_{0,1,1} \\ m_{1,1,0} & m_{1,0,1} & m_{0,0,2} \end{bmatrix} \tag{4}$$

where $m_{s,t,u} = \sum\sum\sum_{(x,y,z)\in X} x^s y^t z^u$ are 3D moments. It is easy to compute the three eigenvalues $\lambda_1 \geq \lambda_2 \geq \lambda_3$ and the associated eigenvectors (v_1, v_2, v_3) from M. The values of (a, b, c) are then equal to v_3 which is the eigenvector corresponding to the smallest eigenvalue of M. That means that the principal plane P is spanned by the two bases: v_1 and v_2. If the value of λ_3 is too large, the plane P is used to divide X into two sub-clouds. On the contrary, if the value of λ_3 is very small, the shape of the point cloud X nears a 3D plane and thus P is a good approximation of X in 3D space. Notice that $n(\bar{p}) = v_3$ is the associative outward-oriented normal vector of P. Figure 2 shows an example where the MPP clustering has been applied to separate the input point cloud into multiple principal planes.

3 Visual Feature Representation of a 3D Scene

As mentioned above, one can reconstruct the 3D model of a scene from a multi-view video if its depth maps and camera pose parameters are given. However, the rich information given by the RGB channels is skipped in the reconstruction process. With the aid of the visual features, the accuracy of establishing reliable correspondences between 3D points transformed from different images is improved. We may assume that each fragment of a 3D model has a unique visual feature vector. In this paper, we propose to use a deep learning approach to learn the robust feature representation and use that to model a 3D scene.

Let $\Phi = \{X_i\}_{i=1}^k$ be the set of point clouds obtained by performing the MPP analysis on a 3D model which is reconstructed by the depth frames of a training multi-view video $V = \{I_j\}_{j=1}^m$. For each training image I_j, we generate a label image L_j by setting the pixel value at $x = (x, y)$ to be i if $p_g(x) \in X_i$, where $p_g(x)$ is the corresponding global 3D point of x. This process automatically constructs a new training dataset $DS = \{[I_j, L_j]\}_{j=1}^m$ for training the deep pixel-wise fragment classifier (DPFC), shown in Fig. 3. Inspired by the work of Xie et al. [25], the proposed fragment classification algorithm (DPVC) has two phases: (1) parameter initialization with a deep autoencoder [23] and (2) parameter optimization (i.e. pixel-wise view prediction) by minimizing the Kullback-Leibler (KL) divergence to the target distributions which are determined by the MPP clustering results.

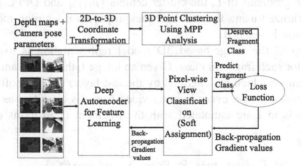

Fig. 3. The proposed pixel-wise deep fragment classification (DPFC) for grouping pixels in RGB images of the same fragment label into a cluster. A post processing exercise is conducted to generate the fragment segmentation of the input RGB image.

The SegNet [23] is trained using the dataset $DS = \{[I_j, L_j]\}_{j=1}^{m}$ to provide the initial parameters for the network that generates the visual feature map for each training RGB image. To combine the deep visual features and the MPP clustering results, we generate the initial fragment feature centroids $\{\bar{\mu}_i\}_{i=1}^{k}$ which are improved in the second phase of the DPFC algorithm. The fragment centroids, i.e. $\{\bar{\mu}_i\}_{i=1}^{k}$ and $\{\bar{p}_i\}_{i=1}^{k}$, can be used to softly label the fragment class of a pixel in the training image:

$$[p_{ij}, f_{ij}] = [\frac{(1 + ||p_j - \bar{p}_i||^2)^{-1}}{\sum_{j'}(1 + ||p_{j'} - \bar{p}_i||^2)^{-1}}, \frac{(1 + ||\vec{f}_j - \bar{\mu}_i||^2)^{-1}}{\sum_{j'}(1 + ||\vec{f}_{j'} - \bar{\mu}_i||^2)^{-1}}] \tag{5}$$

where p_{ij} and f_{ij} are the probabilities to assign the j-th pixel to the i-th fragment class in terms of depth and RGB features, respectively. We propose to iteratively refine the visual centroid to minimize the KL divergence loss L between the target distribution P and Q:

$$L = \mathrm{KL}(P||VF) = \sum_i \sum_j p_{ij} \log \frac{p_{ij}}{f_{ij}} \tag{6}$$

Next, the gradients of L with respect to visual feature $\vec{f}_j$ and fragment feature centroid $\bar{\mu}_i$ are computed as:

$$\frac{\partial L}{\partial \vec{f}_j} = 2 \sum_i (1 + ||\vec{f}_j - \bar{\mu}_i||^2)^{-1}(p_{ij} - q_{ij})(\vec{f}_j - \bar{\mu}_i), \tag{7}$$

$$\frac{\partial L}{\partial \bar{\mu}_i} = -2 \sum_j (1 + ||\vec{f}_j - \bar{\mu}_i||^2)^{-1}(p_{ij} - q_{ij})(\vec{f}_j - \bar{\mu}_i). \tag{8}$$

Based on the gradients of L, the cluster centers $\{\bar{\mu}_i\}_{i=1}^{k}$ and DPFC parameters are interactively optimized using the standard backpropagation learning method until the converge condition is reached.

The last step of the image-based 3D model representation is to determine the template image for each fragment class. Given an image I, the DFVC annotates I with a fragment label image which is generated by the last layer, i.e., the softmax classifier. Based on the labeled image, every training video frame is classified as fragment $i*$ if most of the pixels in I are annotated with the fragment $i*$ in terms of deep visual features:

$$i^* = \arg \max_{i=1,...,k} \Pr_i, \Pr_i = \sum_{\vec{f}_j \in I} \mathrm{softmax}(\vec{f}_j). \tag{9}$$

We select a training RGB-D image as the representative template of the fragment class i according to the following equation:

$$T_i = \arg \max_{I_j \in Fragment\ i} \Pr(I_j) \tag{10}$$

Notice that the pixels in a template image may belong to several surface fragments in the resulting TSDF volume.

Figure 4 shows the proposed scheme to estimate the depth map and camera pose parameters which are often unknown when we use a moving camera to conduct 3D object inspection. To deal with this issue, the proposed image-based object modeling can be used to accurately estimate the depth map as well as the camera pose parameters of the input frame. The first step of the proposed video surveillance scheme is to detect the target objects in the input frame I_j using the well-proved CNN object recognition system [22]. Next, the detected object O as the input data, the DPFC algorithm returns a set of discriminative visual features and the fragment class i. This implies that the i-th RGB-D template T_i would be retrieved from the image-based 3D model. We set the depth map and the camera pose parameters of T_i as the initial parameters for the test image I_j. Obviously, the depth map and the camera pose parameters should be modified because the positions of the cameras to capture the test image and the template are not possible to be the same. In this work, we use a corresponding algorithm to align the set of discriminative visual features of T_i with that of I_j. This provides a rotation matrix R_i^j and the scaling factor s (the ratio of object size in I_j to that in T_i) to modify the camera pose parameters: $[\tilde{D}_j, \tilde{R}_j, \tilde{t}_j] = [sD_i, R_i^j R_i, st_i]$, where $\tilde{D}_j$ and $[\tilde{R}_j, \tilde{t}_j]$ are the estimated depth map and camera pose of the test RGB image based on the depth map and camera pose of the template i. Obviously, the estimated parameters can be further optimized to improve their accuracy.

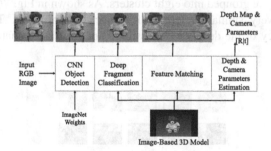

Fig. 4. Model-based estimation of the depth map and the camera pose parameters of an RGB image.

4 Experimental Results

The system is implemented on a PC with Intel Core i7 3.4 GHz CPU and Nvidia GTX 1060 GPU. In this work, all the deep learning algorithms are implemented under the Google Tensorflow Environment. The RGB-D benchmark provided by the Technical University of Munich [24] is used to verify the effectiveness of our approach in terms of the pose estimation accuracy. In this benchmark, several datasets including color and depth sequences captured with a single RGB-D camera are provided. The accurate ground-truth of the camera pose in each frame is also provided, which is measured by an external motion capture system. The frames of each dataset are separated into two disjoint sets—a training dataset and a test dataset. Figure 5 shows example frames of several test datasets.

'freiburg1_desk' 'freiburg1_desk2' 'freiburg2_desk' 'freiburg3_teddy' 'freiburg1_plant' 'freiburg1_teddy'

Fig. 5. Example frames of test datasets.

The number of clusters k specified in our MPP clustering plays an import role in ensuring the performance of the proposed deep-view classifier. The larger the value of k, the less cross-view distortion can be found. However, finding the optimal value of k remains an open issue in the research area of data clustering. In this work, we use the elbow method to determine the number of clusters (views) for reconstructing our 3D object models. Figure 7 shows an example of the MPP clustering results using the model built by the 'freiburg3_teddy' dataset, as shown in Fig. 6. In this case, $k = 8$ and the training images are grouped into eight clusters. As shown in Fig. 7(e), images in the same cluster are very similar in terms of subjective evaluation. This ensures the recognition accuracy of the deep-view classifiers and the discriminative power of the

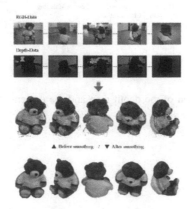

Fig. 6. An example of 3D object reconstruction using the 'freiburg3_teddy' dataset.

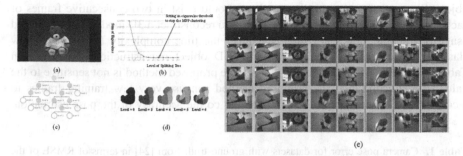

Fig. 7. An example of MPP clustering: (a) the reconstructed 3D Model; (b) setting the threshold on sum-of-eigenvalues to stop the growing of the splitting tree; (c) the splitting tree result, each leaf node corresponding to a cluster; (d) the points belonging to the same cluster are plotted with the same color; (e) each column lists the example training images grouped into the same cluster.

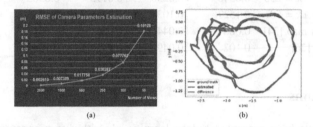

Fig. 8. The root mean square error (RMSE) on the estimation of camera parameters using the 'freiburg3_teddy' dataset: (a) the results of using different numbers of views to construct the view classifier; (b) the trajectories of the ground-truth, estimated, and error camera parameters for all frames in the dataset by setting the number of clusters (views) to be 115.

extracted deep features, which are used to estimate the camera parameters of the test frames in the testing phase. Experimental results show that the accuracy of the view classification can reach up to 97.76% for the 'freiburg3_teddy' dataset and 98.96% in average for all datasets. In practice, as shown in Fig. 8, we prefer to using larger values of k because this brings us less error in the succeeding camera parameter estimation though we just need a few clusters (cf. Fig. 7) to construct a high-quality object model.

To compare the performance of our approach with other state-of-the-art methods in pose estimation [24, 26], six typical datasets are selected as the test samples. In [24], the compared approach is a model-based method, which is similar to our approach. In [26], the authors proposed an RGB-D SLAM system. Some post-processing methods like global optimization are used to modify the global camera trajectory in these methods. Table 1 summarizes the experiment results. The first column is the dataset name. The other columns are the results for the root mean square error (RMSE) of the relative errors. The relative error is the translational drift in m/s between the estimated pose and the ground-truth. The parameter k is the number of clusters required to select the training frames from the datasets. For each cluster, we just use the template images as the training samples. The larger value of k implies that more frames are selected in the training sequences to build up the 3D model for reconstructing the target scene or object. Since a large amount of redundancy could exist in two consecutive frames of each sequence, we could use very few frames to reconstruct a 3D model. The decreased usage of training frames also highly reduces the time complexity to learn the view classifier to achieve the goal of real-time 3D object reconstruction. As shown in Table 1, compared with the state-of-the-art, the proposed method is not sensitive to the value of k. Accordingly, the proposed method can use very few training frames to reconstruct a 3D scene without compromising co the accuracy of the pose estimation.

Table 1. Camera pose error for datasets with ground-truth from [24] in terms of RMSE of the relative error. The value of k is the number of training images selected from the test datasets.

Sequences		Frei.1 desk2	Frei.1 desk	Frei.1 plant	Frei.3 teddy	Frei.2 desk
Our Approach	k = 2000	**0.0030**	**0.0031**	**0.0019**	**0.0026**	**0.0029**
	k = 1000	0.0071	0.0041	0.0035	0.0074	0.0075
	k = 250	0.0340	0.0258	0.0193	0.0363	0.0399
	k = 50	0.1527	0.1034	0.0968	0.1813	0.3097
Multi-resolution map [24]		0.060	0.044	0.036	0.061	0.091
RGB-D SLAM [26]		0.102	0.049	0.142	0.138	0.143

5   Conclusions

In this paper, we have presented a deep learning algorithm to reconstruct an image-based 3D object model using multi-view RGB-D video. The 3D model can be used to monitor the status of the object using a moving camera. The contributions of the proposed method are as follows: To start from a 3D model, the MPP analysis automatically annotates the fragment classes of training images for learning the deep fragment classifier. The usage of a CNN-based fragment classifier speeds up the searches of model templates to estimate the camera parameters of a test frame. The high discriminative deep features for object matching are obtained using the proposed fragment classifier. In our experiments on publicly available datasets, we show that our approach outperforms the state-of-the-art methods in terms of the estimation of camera parameters.

In the next step we plan to explore a fully deep learning architecture that automatically reconstruct the 3D scene or object using a training video. Furthermore, based on the reconstruction models, we want to extend our approach to 3D object detection, segmentation, reconstruction, and printing.

Acknowledgement. This work was supported in part by Ministry of Science and Technology, Taiwan under Grant Numbers MOST 107-2221-E-019 -033 -MY2 and 107-2634-F-019 -001.

References

1. Wolf, P.R., Dewitt, B.A.: Elements of Photogrammetry: With Applications in GIS. McGraw-Hill, New York (2000)
2. Ackermann, F.: Airborne laser scanning – present status and further expectations. ISPRS J. Photogram. Remote Sens. **54**, 64–67 (1999)
3. Davison, A., Reid, I., Molton, N., Stasse, O.: MonoSLAM: real-time single camera SLAM. IEEE Trans. Pattern Anal. Mach. Intell. **29**(6), 1052–1067 (2007)
4. Furukawa, Y., Curless, B., Seitz, S.M., Szeliski, R.: Towards internet-scale multi-view stereo. In: Proceedings of IEEE Computer Society Conference on Computer Vision and Pattern Recognition (2010)
5. Furukawa, Y., Ponce, J.: Accurate, dense, and robust multi-view stereopsis. IEEE Trans. Pattern Anal. Mach. Intell. **32**(8), 1362–1376 (2010)
6. Goldlucke, B., Aubry, M., Kolev, K., Cremers, D.: A super-resolution framework for high-accuracy multiview reconstruction. Int. J. Comput. Vision **106**(2), 172–191 (2014)
7. Maier, R., Kim, K., Cremers, D., Kautz, J., Nießner, M.: Intrinsic3d: high-quality 3D reconstruction by joint appearance and geometry optimization with spatially-varying lighting. In: Proceedings of the IEEE International Conference on Computer Vision (2017)
8. Zhou, Q., Park, J., Koltun, V.: Open3D: A modern library for 3D data processing. arXiv: 1801.09847 (2018)
9. Curless, B., Levoy, M.: A volumetric method for building complex models from range images. In: Proceedings of the 23rd Annual Conference on Computer Graphics and Interactive Techniques, pp. 303–312 (1996)
10. Park, J., Zhou, Q.-Y., Koltun, V.: Colored point cloud registration revisited. In: Proceedings of ICCV (2017)
11. Choi, S., Zhou, Q.-Y., Koltun, V.: Robust reconstruction of indoor scenes. In: Proceedings of CVPR (2015)
12. Johnson, A.E., Kang, S.B.: Registration and integration of textured 3D data. Image Vis. Comput. **17**, 135–147 (1999)
13. Korn, M., Holzkothen, M., Pauli, J.: Color supported generalized-ICP. In: Proceedings of VISAPP (2014)
14. Men, H., Gebre, B., Pochiraju, K.: Color point cloud registration with 4D ICP algorithm. In: Proceedings of ICRA (2011)
15. Li, J.N., Wang, L.H., Li, Y., Zhang, J.F., Li, D.X., Zhang, M.: Local optimized and scalable frame-to-model SLAM. Multimedia Tools Appl. **75**, 8675–8694 (2016)
16. Hinterstoisser, S., et al.: Model based training, detection and pose estimation of texture-less 3D objects in heavily cluttered scenes. In: Lee, K.M., Matsushita, Y., Rehg, James M., Hu, Z. (eds.) ACCV 2012. LNCS, vol. 7724, pp. 548–562. Springer, Heidelberg (2013). https://doi.org/10.1007/978-3-642-37331-2_42
17. Kan, M., Shan, S., Chen, X.: Multi-view deep network for cross-view classification. In: Proceedings of IEEE ICCVPR (2016)
18. Cheng, S.-C., Su, J.-Y., Chen, J.-M., Hsieh, J.-W.: Model-based 3D scene reconstruction using a moving RGB-D camera. In: Amsaleg, L., Guðmundsson, G.Þ., Gurrin, C., Jónsson, B.Þ., Satoh, S. (eds.) MMM 2017. LNCS, vol. 10132, pp. 214–225. Springer, Cham (2017). https://doi.org/10.1007/978-3-319-51811-4_18
19. Eigen, D., Fergus, R.: Predicting depth, surface normals and semantic labels with a common multi-scale convolutional architecture. In: Proceedings of ICCV (2015)
20. Žbontar, J., LeCun, Y.: Stereo matching by training a convolutional neural network to compare image patches. J. Mach. Learn. Res. **17**, 1–32 (2016)

21. Qi, C.R., Su, H., Nießner, M., Dai, A., Yan, M., Guibas, L. J.: Volumetric and multi-view CNNs for object classification on 3D data. arXiv:1604.03265v2 [cs.CV] 29 (2016)
22. Simonyan, K., Zisserman, A.: Very deep convolutional networks for large-scale image recognition. arXiv:1409.1556 (2015)
23. Badrinarayanan, V., Kendall, A., Cipolla, R.: SegNet: a deep convolutional encoder-decoder architecture for image segmentation. IEEE Trans. PAMI **39**(12), 2481–2495 (2017)
24. Endres, F., Hess, J., Engelhard, N., Sturm, J., Cremers, D., Burgard, W.: An evaluation of the RGB-D SLAM system. In: Proceedings of the IEEE International Conference on Robotics and Automation (ICRA) (2012)
25. Xie, J., Girshick, R., Farhadi, A.: Unsupervised deep embedding for clustering analysis. In: Proceedings of ICML (2016)
26. Stückler, J., Behnke, S.: Multi-resolution surfel maps for efficient dense 3D modeling and tracking. J. Vis. Commun. Image Represent. **25**(1), 137–147 (2014)

Regular and Small Target Detection

Wenzhe Wang[✉], Bin Wu[✉], Jinna Lv, and Pilin Dai

Beijing Key Laboratory of Intelligent Telecommunication Software and Multimedia,
Beijing University of Posts and Telecommunications, Beijing 100876, China
{wangwenzhe,wubin,lvjinna,daipilin}@bupt.edu.cn

Abstract. Although remarkable results have been achieved in the areas
of object detection, the detection of small objects is still a challenging
task now. The low resolution and noisy representation make small objects
difficult to detect, and further recognition will be much harder. Aiming
at the small objects that have regular positions, shapes, colors or other
features, this paper proposes an approach of Regular and Small Target
Detection based on Faster R-CNN (RSTD) for the detection and recognition of regular and small targets such as traffic signs. In this approach, a
regular and small target feature extraction layer is designed to automatically extract the surrounding background and internal key information
of the proposal objects, which benefits the detection and recognition.
Extensive evaluations on Tsinghua-Tencent 100K and GTSDB datasets
demonstrate the superiority of our approach in detecting traffic signs over
well-established state-of-the-arts. The source code and model introduced
in this paper are publicly available at: https://github.com/zhezheey/
RSTD/.

Keywords: Regular and small target · Traffic sign detection
Traffic sign recognition · Faster R-CNN

1 Introduction

As one of the main tasks of computer version, object detection is widely used in
automatic driving, image retrieval, the field of security and so on. Recently, deep
learning methods have shown superior performance on object detection. Among
them, Faster R-CNN [21] is one of the most popular approaches, and many of the
state-of-the-art detectors are built on it [1,5,10,15,22]. Two benchmarks widely
used to evaluate detection performance are PASCAL VOC [6] and Microsoft
COCO [18], in which the target objects always occupy a large proportion of
an image. However, some objects of interest may have low resolution and only
occupy a small fraction of an image, such as traffic signs in the wild, logos and
trademarks in large natural images, pedestrians and car signs in monitoring
videos, or objects in aerial photos. While the difficulty of feature extraction
is significantly increased, the computational complexity is also increased. The
accuracy of detecting and recognizing these small objects using these algorithms
is not satisfactory.

© Springer Nature Switzerland AG 2019
I. Kompatsiaris et al. (Eds.): MMM 2019, LNCS 11296, pp. 453–464, 2019.
https://doi.org/10.1007/978-3-030-05716-9_37

Many efforts have been presented to addressing small object detection problems [1,3,16,17,19,24]. Existing small object detection algorithms can be divided into the following two categories. Some of them [3,17,19] try to increase image size or generate super-resolved representations for small objects to produce high-resolution feature maps. Others [1,16,24] focus on generating multi-scale representation to get richer features. However, all of those approaches detect small objects in a general way, while the small objects to be detected, such as traffic signs and trademarks, which are common in practical applications, mostly have regular positions, shapes, colors or other features. Some of them are shown in Fig. 1. Making full use of the characteristics of these regular and small targets will provide high detection and recognition accuracy.

(a) Traffic signs in the wild   (b) Trademarks in natural images [14]

Fig. 1. Some examples of regular and small objects in large images, where the orange rectangles mark the objects to be detected.

In this paper, we propose an approach of regular and small target detection and recognition, where the term "regular" means objects that generally appear in similar contexts and have structures with low variability. Taking traffic sign targets as an example, they always occupy a small fraction of a traffic image. Besides, the location, shape and color of common traffic signs are regular. When driving, people mainly find the traffic signs through their locations and determine the specific categories of them by their internal information. Similarly, in our approach, we extract the surrounding background information of the targets to help detect them and focus on the internal key information to classify them better. In order to prove the effectiveness of our approach, we compare its detection and recognition results with the state-of-the-art approaches Faster R-CNN and LOCO on two real-world traffic sign datasets, which demonstrates its superiority.

The contributions of this paper are as follows.

- A Regular and Small Target Detection approach based on Faster R-CNN (RSTD) is designed and proposed, which focus on the detection and recognition of the regular and small objects such as traffic signs.
- In this framework, we design a regular and small target feature extraction layer to extract the surrounding background and internal key information of the proposal objects.
- Successful applications on two traffic sign detection datasets Tsinghua-Tencent 100K and GTSDB have been achieved with the state-of-the-art performance.

The rest of this paper is organized as follows. Section 2 briefly reviews the related work. In Sect. 3, our proposed approach of Regular and Small Target Detection are illustrated. Section 4 presents and analyzes the experimental results. Finally, Sect. 5 concludes this paper.

2 Related Work

2.1 Object Detection

Recently, the CNN based object detection algorithms [2,5,8–11,21,25] have shown remarkable performance in object detection competitions. Among them, the Region-based CNN (R-CNN) approach is one of the most widely used. These approaches first calculate some general object proposals, then perform classification and bounding box regression. R-CNN [9] was the first to use this strategy, while each candidate object proposal needed to be input into the CNN independently, which was very inefficient. The Spatial Pyramid Pooling Network (SPP-Net) [11] calculated a convolutional feature map for the entire image, which increased the speed by a factor of 100. Based on SPP-Net, Fast R-CNN [8] replaced the SVM classifier with a softmax layer, which greatly improved its accuracy. In Faster R-CNN [21], Ren et al. proposed the Region Proposal Network (RPN) and achieved a frame rate of 5 fps on a GPU. Based on Faster R-CNN, Dai et al. [5] presented fully convolutional networks that can achieve a competitive result to Faster R-CNN at a higher speed.

2.2 Small Object Detection

Due to the poor performance of the general object detection algorithms on small objects and the importance to detect and recognize them, various studies have been devoted to the small object detection task [1,3,7,16,17,20,24]. Among them, the detection of small traffic signs in the wild is one of the most popular tasks because of its significance to automatic driving.

Recently, CNN approaches have been widely adopted in the task because of their high accuracy. In particular, IJCNN conference competitions in 2013 published the Traffic Sign Detection Benchmark (GTSDB) [12], which greatly promoted the research in the field of traffic sign and small object detection. Fang et al. [7] proposed a novel object detection framework in extreme Low-Resolution images via sparse representation. Bell et al. [1] presented the Inside-Outside Net (ION), an object detector that exploits information both inside and outside the region of interest, which further enhanced the detection accuracy of small objects. Besides, Zhu et al. [26] created a more realistic traffic sign benchmark (Tsinghua-Tencent 100 K), in which each traffic sign was annotated with its bounding box, pixel mask and class. They also trained a CNN for detecting and classifying traffic signs. Li et al. [17] proposed a new Perceptual Generative Adversarial Network (Perceptual GAN) model that improved small object detection through narrowing representation difference of small objects from the large ones.

In particular, Cheng et al. [4] introduced a local context layer into the Faster R-CNN framework to capture the vertical and horizontal context information surrounding the traffic signs, they treated all traffic signs as one category, and achieved the state-of-the-art on the traffic sign detection problem.

3 Our Approach: RSTD

3.1 Overview

For the state-of-the-art detectors such as Faster R-CNN [21], they use features from the top layer of the convolutional neural networks to detect objects. The existed RoI-pooling layers will gradually reduce the feature maps and resolution of the input images, which makes them easily ignore the small targets. Especially, owing to the 4 times downsamplings in Faster R-CNN, the final region of interest of a traffic sign which has a scale of 16×16 pixels will be less than 1 pixel, it's impossible to recognize it even if the region proposal is correct.

Aiming at the limitations of Faster R-CNN, we need to extract more information from the RoI-pooling layer. The LOCO model [4] proposed by Cheng et al. added a new local context layer in the original Faster R-CNN framework to extract the vertical and horizontal context information surrounding the traffic signs to help localize them. However, LOCO also has its limitations. On the one hand, the local context layer introduced by LOCO is only suitable for traffic sign targets due to its particularity, whose scalability is poor; On the other hand, in the experiment, they treat all traffic signs as one category during training and testing, while in real-world tasks, it will be more practical to detect and recognize them instead of only detecting them.

In order to solve the above problems, we design and propose the RSTD, which targets at the small objects which have regular location, shape, color and so on. By paying more attention to their surrounding background and internal key information, RSTD performs better on the tasks of regular and small object detection and recognition.

3.2 Architecture

As shown in Fig. 2, RSTD uses the Faster R-CNN as the basic framework, which consists of two stages as follows.

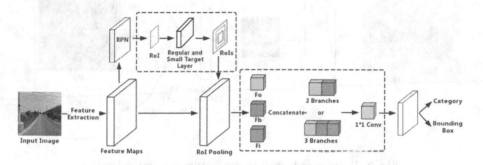

Fig. 2. Architecture of RSTD: The model is divided into 2 branches and 3 branches structure. The dotted lines mark its difference between Faster R-CNN.

Stage 1. We first extract the feature maps of the input image $I(w, h)$ using the basic CNN such as VGG or ResNet, and use the RPN to generate the region proposal R_o, then we expand the RoI through the newly introduced regular and small target feature extraction layer, and output RoIs: R_o, R_b, R_i (see Sect. 3.3 for details).

Stage 2. Next, similar to LOCO, the expanded regions are sent to the RoI-pooling part, then we get the feature maps F_o, F_b, F_i. In order to make use of the surrounding background information and internal key information provided by F_b and F_i, we simply concatenate F_o, F_b, F_i on the channel and compress the channel size to the original one by a convolution layer. Finally, the new feature maps are sent to the next convolution layer for classification.

In addition, in order to prove the effectiveness of surrounding background and internal key information separately, our model is divided into 2 branches and 3 branches structure. The 2 branches structure only focus on the surrounding background information (by F_o and F_b), while the 3 branches structure pays another attention to the internal key information (by F_o, F_b and F_i).

3.3   Regular and Small Target Feature Extraction Layer

Aiming at extracting the characteristics of the regular and small objects, we design and introduce a regular and small target feature extraction layer to extract the surrounding background and internal key information. From Fig. 3, we can find that the layer successfully extracts the background and internal information of the objects, which will benefit the detection and recognition.

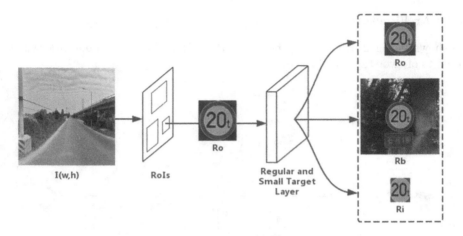

Fig. 3. Regular and small target feature extraction layer.

In detail, for each input image $I(w, h)$, it will be processed by the CNN networks and sent to the Region Proposal Network (RPN) to generate RoIs. For each $R_o = (x_s, y_s, x_e, y_e)$, where (x_s, y_s) and (x_e, y_e) are the upper left corner and lower right corner points of the rectangle, we input it into the regular and small target feature extraction layer. Through expansion of the new layer, we get the original R_o, the RoI which focus on the surrounding background information R_b and the RoI which focus on the internal key information R_i. R_b and R_i are defined as follows. For different target objects, Equation (2) could be adjusted.

$$R_b = (\max(0, x_s - w_b(x_e - x_s)), \max(0, y_s - w_b(y_e - y_s)), \\ \min(w, x_e + w_b(x_e - x_s)), \min(h, y_e + w_b(y_e - y_s))). \tag{1}$$

$$R_i = (x_s + w_i(x_e - x_s), y_s + w_i(y_e - y_s), \\ x_s - w_i(x_e - x_s), y_s - w_i(y_e - y_s)). \tag{2}$$

Where w and h represent the width and height of the input image. Respectively, w_b and w_i represent the parameters for extracting surrounding background and internal key information. After training and comparison, we find that for traffic sign targets, when the value of w_b is about 1 and the value of w_i is about 0.15, RSTD performs best.

4   Experiments

4.1   The Tsinghua-Tencent 100 K Dataset

The Tsinghua-Tencent 100 K dataset[1] is a traffic sign detection benchmark created by Zhu et al. [26] in 2016. It contains 100,000 images of street view in China under different illuminance and weather conditions. Of these, 10,000 images contain 30,000 traffic signs in total. Most (more than 90%) traffic signs in the dataset have a resolution below 96 × 96 pixels, accounting for only 0.2% of the entire image. Nearly half of the traffic signs have a resolution below 32 × 32 pixels.

In the experiment, we choose the same methods to preprocess the dataset as Zhu. In detail, there are 6,105 images for training and verification, 3,065 images for testing. Differently from Zhu et al., no data augmentation has been applied. We choose the different pixel images as input. As shown in Table 1, with tuning parameters and taking 2048 × 2048 pixel images as input, our RSTD (3 branches) performs the best, which achieves 84.64% mAP value.

Table 1. Comparison of results for different methods on Tsinghua-Tencent 100K.

Approach	Image scale	mAP
Faster R-CNN	1820 × 1820	76.11%
Faster R-CNN	2048 × 2048	79.65%
LOCO	2048 × 2048	83.58%
RSTD (2 branches)	2048 × 2048	84.29%
RSTD (3 branches)	2048 × 2048	**84.64%**

4.2   The German Traffic Sign Detection Benchmark

The German Traffic Sign Detection Benchmark[2] is a single-image detection assessment introduced on the IEEE International Joint Conference on Neural Networks 2013 [12]. The dataset contains a total of 900 images with natural traffic scenes, the signs may appear in every perspective and under every lighting condition. It contains 1,213 traffic signs in total. The resolutions of images are 1360 × 800 pixels, and the sizes of traffic signs in the images vary from 16 × 16 to 128 × 128 pixels.

In the experiment, we don't choose the 43 refined categories to recognize because the number of traffic signs is too small. Instead, we choose the 3 categories (prohibitive, danger and mandatory) of traffic signs to recognize. Similarly, no data augmentation has been applied in this experiment. We choose the original pixel images as input. As a result, RSTD (3 branches) achieves better performance than Faster R-CNN and LOCO at a mAP value of 93.59%. The detailed results are shown in Table 2.

[1] http://cg.cs.tsinghua.edu.cn/traffic-sign/.
[2] http://benchmark.ini.rub.de/?section=gtsdb&subsection=dataset.

Table 2. Comparison of results for different methods on GTSDB.

Approach	Image scale	mAP
Faster R-CNN	1360 × 800	90.29%
LOCO	1360 × 800	90.50%
RSTD (2 branches)	1360 × 800	93.31%
RSTD (3 branches)	1360 × 800	**93.59%**

4.3   Implementation Details

Our experimental evaluation in this section of both training and testing are all performed on a Linux PC with a single NVIDIA GeForce GTX 1080Ti (11GB). The implementations of RSTD (2 branches, 3 branches), LOCO and Faster R-CNN are based on the publicly available Faster R-CNN framework [21] built on the Caffe learning framework [13]. VGG16 [23] is used as the feature extraction network. Besides, we also train the networks on the same datasets for same epochs. In particular, we change the LOCO networks to not only detect the objects but also recognize them.

In order to improve the detection performance of these networks better, we set RPN_{min} to 5 instead of the default 16 to avoid them ignoring the small objects, and the other parameters keep the default configuration in LOCO. In the experiment, we set the values of w_v and w_h in LOCO to 1 and the values of w_b and w_i in RSTD to 1 and about 0.15 according to Sect. 3.3. We choose the Intersection over Union (IoU) to 0.5 as the threshold for detection and use mean Average Precision (mAP, the mean value of APs for all object classes on all images) to evaluate the performance of detection and recognition. More details about the network and training methods in the experiment can be found in the source code.

4.4   Performance Comparison

The experimental results on Tsinghua-Tencent 100 K and GTSDB show that RSTD performs better than Faster R-CNN and LOCO, it can get higher mAP value. Besides, due to the relatively low complexity of the newly added part in RSTD, RSTD can process one image of 2048 × 2048 pixels within 0.7 s for testing, which is comparable with Faster R-CNN and LOCO. Some examples of the results are shown in Fig. 4. We can find that compared to LOCO and Faster R-CNN, RSTD can detect the boundaries of targets more accurately and have a higher recall rate, especially for the small objects. In addition, the surrounding background and internal key information extracted by the regular and small target layer can both improve the mAP value of the detection and recognition.

Especially, LOCO networks can utilize the vertical and horizontal local context information to extract more effective information. When the region proposal has insufficient information, context information can improve the networks'

(a) Images   (b)   (c)   (d)   (e)

Fig. 4. Some detection and recognition results of different approaches on same images. (b) Faster R-CNN; (c) LOCO; (d) RSTD (2 branches); (e) RSTD (3 branches).

capacity to locate and classify traffic signs. For the RSTD networks in the paper, RSTD (2 branches) expands the context information based on LOCO, which further enhances the ability to detect small objects. RSTD (3 branches) pays another attention to the internal key information of the regular objects, which enhances the accuracy in detecting and recognizing the target objects.

For convenience, we have uploaded our trained RSTD (3 branches) model on Tsinghua-Tencent 100K and developed a simple web demo to show its performance on detection and recognition in the source code.

5   Conclusion

In this paper, we propose a new approach of Regular and Small Target Detection based on Faster R-CNN (RSTD) to detect and recognize the regular and small targets. In this approach, we introduce a regular and small target feature extraction layer and make use of the objects' characteristics by extracting the surrounding background and internal key information of them. Experimental results show that our approach achieves higher mAP on the two public traffic sign detection benchmarks compared with the well-established state-of-the-arts Faster R-CNN and LOCO.

In the future, we plan to further optimize the network structure to improve the accuracy of detection. What's more, try other regular and small object detection datasets to verify the robustness of RSTD.

Acknowledgement. This work is partially supported by the National Key R&D Program of China (No. 2018YFC0831500), the National Social Science Foundation of China (No. 16ZDA055), the National Natural Science Foundation of China (No. 61772082), and the Special Found for Beijing Common Construction Project.

References

1. Bell, S., Zitnick, C.L., Bala, K., Girshick, R.: Inside-outside net: detecting objects in context with skip pooling and recurrent neural networks. In: IEEE Conference on Computer Vision and Pattern Recognition (CVPR), pp. 2874–2883 (2016)
2. Cai, Z., Vasconcelos, N.: Cascade R-CNN: delving into high quality object detection. In: IEEE Conference on Computer Vision and Pattern Recognition (CVPR), pp. 6154–6162 (2018)
3. Chen, X., et al.: 3D object proposals for accurate object class detection. In: Annual Conference on Neural Information Processing Systems (NIPS), pp. 424–432 (2015)
4. Cheng, P., Liu, W., Zhang, Y., Ma, H.: LOCO: local context based faster R-CNN for small traffic sign detection. In: Schoeffmann, K., et al. (eds.) MMM 2018. LNCS, vol. 10704, pp. 329–341. Springer, Cham (2018). https://doi.org/10.1007/978-3-319-73603-7_27
5. Dai, J., Li, Y., He, K., Sun, J.: R-FCN: object detection via region-based fully convolutional networks. In: Annual Conference on Neural Information Processing Systems (NIPS), pp. 379–387 (2016)
6. Everingham, M., Van Gool, L., Williams, C.K.I., Winn, J., Zisserman, A.: The PASCAL visual object classes (VOC) challenge. Int. J. Comput. Vis. **88**(2), 303–338 (2010)
7. Fang, W., Chen, J., Liang, C., Wang, X., Nan, Y., Hu, R.: Object detection in low-resolution image via sparse representation. In: International Conference on Multimedia Modeling (MMM), pp. 234–245 (2015)

8. Girshick, R.: Fast R-CNN. In: IEEE Conference on Computer Vision and Pattern Recognition (CVPR), pp. 1440–1448 (2015)
9. Girshick, R., Donahue, J., Darrell, T., Malik, J.: Rich feature hierarchies for accurate object detection and semantic segmentation. In: IEEE Conference on Computer Vision and Pattern Recognition (CVPR), pp. 580–587 (2014)
10. He, K., Gkioxari, G., Dollár, P., Girshick, R.: Mask R-CNN. In: International Conference on Computer Vision (ICCV), pp. 2980–2988 (2017)
11. He, K., Zhang, X., Ren, S., Sun, J.: Spatial pyramid pooling in deep convolutional networks for visual recognition. In: Fleet, D., Pajdla, T., Schiele, B., Tuytelaars, T. (eds.) ECCV 2014. LNCS, vol. 8691, pp. 346–361. Springer, Cham (2014). https://doi.org/10.1007/978-3-319-10578-9_23
12. Houben, S., Stallkamp, J., Salmen, J., Schlipsing, M. Igel, C.: Detection of traffic signs in real-world images: The German traffic sign detection benchmark. In: International Joint Conference on Neural Networks (IJCNN), pp. 1–8 (2013)
13. Jia, Y., et al.: Caffe: convolutional architecture for fast feature embedding. In: ACM International Conference on Multimedia (MM), pp. 675–678 (2014)
14. Joly, A., Buisson, O.: Logo retrieval with a contrario visual query expansion. In: ACM International Conference on Multimedia (MM), pp. 581–584 (2009)
15. Kong, T., Sun, F., Yao, A., Liu, H., Lu, M., Chen, Y.: RON: reverse connection with objectness prior networks for object detection. In: IEEE Conference on Computer Vision and Pattern Recognition (CVPR), pp. 5244–5252 (2017)
16. Li, H., Lin, Z., Shen, X., Brandt, J., Hua, G.: A convolutional neural network cascade for face detection. In: IEEE Conference on Computer Vision and Pattern Recognition (CVPR), pp. 5325–5334 (2015)
17. Li, J., Liang, X., Wei, Y., Xu, T., Feng, J., Yan, S.: Perceptual generative adversarial networks for small object detection. In: IEEE Conference on Computer Vision and Pattern Recognition (CVPR), pp. 1951–1959 (2017)
18. Lin, T.-Y., et al.: Microsoft COCO: common objects in context. In: Fleet, D., Pajdla, T., Schiele, B., Tuytelaars, T. (eds.) ECCV 2014. LNCS, vol. 8693, pp. 740–755. Springer, Cham (2014). https://doi.org/10.1007/978-3-319-10602-1_48
19. Liu, W., et al.: SSD: single shot MultiBox detector. In: Leibe, B., Matas, J., Sebe, N., Welling, M. (eds.) ECCV 2016. LNCS, vol. 9905, pp. 21–37. Springer, Cham (2016). https://doi.org/10.1007/978-3-319-46448-0_2
20. Meng, Z., Fan, X., Chen, X., Chen, M., Tong Y.: Detecting small signs from large images. In: International Conference on Information Reuse & Integration for Data Science (IRI), pp. 217–224 (2017)
21. Ren, S., He, K., Girshick, R., Sun, J.: Faster R-CNN: towards real-time object detection with region proposal networks. In: Annual Conference on Neural Information Processing Systems (NIPS), pp. 91–99 (2015)
22. Shrivastava, A., Gupta, A.: Contextual priming and feedback for faster R-CNN. In: Leibe, B., Matas, J., Sebe, N., Welling, M. (eds.) ECCV 2016. LNCS, vol. 9905, pp. 330–348. Springer, Cham (2016). https://doi.org/10.1007/978-3-319-46448-0_20
23. Simonyan, K., Zisserman, A.: Very deep convolutional networks for large-scale image recognition. arXiv preprint arXiv: 1409.1556 (2014)
24. Yang, F., Choi, W., Lin, Y.: Exploit all the layers: fast and accurate CNN object detector with scale dependent pooling and cascaded rejection classifiers. In: IEEE Conference on Computer Vision and Pattern Recognition (CVPR), pp. 2129–2137 (2016)

25. Zhou, P., Ni, B., Geng, C., Hu, J., Xu, Y.: Scale-transferrable object detection. In: IEEE Conference on Computer Vision and Pattern Recognition (CVPR), pp. 528–537 (2018)
26. Zhu, Z., Liang, D., Zhang, S., Huang, X., Li, B., Hu, S.: Traffic-sign detection and classification in the wild. In: IEEE Conference on Computer Vision and Pattern Recognition (CVPR), pp. 2110–2118 (2016)

From Classical to Generalized Zero-Shot Learning: A Simple Adaptation Process

Yannick Le Cacheux[1]([✉]), Hervé Le Borgne[1], and Michel Crucianu[2]

[1] CEA LIST, Gif-sur-Yvette, France
{yannick.lecacheux,herve.le-borgne}@cea.fr
[2] CEDRIC – CNAM, Paris, France
michel.crucianu@cnam.fr

Abstract. Zero-shot learning (ZSL) is concerned with the recognition of previously *unseen* classes. It relies on additional semantic knowledge for which a mapping can be learned with training examples of *seen* classes. While classical ZSL considers the recognition performance on unseen classes only, generalized zero-shot learning (GZSL) aims at maximizing performance on both seen and unseen classes. In this paper, we propose a new process for training and evaluation in the GZSL setting; this process addresses the gap in performance between samples from unseen and seen classes by penalizing the latter, and enables to select hyper-parameters well-suited to the GZSL task. It can be applied to any existing ZSL approach and leads to a significant performance boost: the experimental evaluation shows that GZSL performance, averaged over eight state-of-the-art methods, is improved from 28.5 to 42.2 on CUB and from 28.2 to 57.1 on AwA2.

Keywords: Zero-shot learning · Multimodal classification

1 Introduction

Zero-shot learning (ZSL) [14,16,17] aims to recognize classes for which no training example is available. This is often achieved by relying on additional semantic knowledge, consisting for example in vectors of attributes. During training, a relation between visual features and semantic attributes is learned from training examples belonging to the *seen* classes, for which both modalities (visual and semantic) are available. This model is then applied in the testing phase on examples from *unseen* classes, for which no visual instance was available during training. Predictions on these classes can thus be made on the basis of the inferred relation between visual and semantic features.

In classical ZSL, the test set only contains examples from the novel, unseen classes, and these classes alone can be predicted. Although this setting has enabled significant progress in methods linking visual content to semantic information in the last few years [27], it is hardly realistic. It seems much more reasonable to assume that objects which are to be classified can belong to either

The supplementary material is available at https://arxiv.org/pdf/1809.10120.pdf

© Springer Nature Switzerland AG 2019
I. Kompatsiaris et al. (Eds.): MMM 2019, LNCS 11296, pp. 465–477, 2019.
https://doi.org/10.1007/978-3-030-05716-9_38

a seen class or an unseen class, since in real-life use-cases one could legitimately want to recognize both former and novel classes. This setting is usually referred to as generalized zero-shot learning (GZSL).

However, recent work shows that a direct use of a ZSL model in a GZSL setting usually leads to unsatisfactory results. Indeed, in addition to the number of candidate classes being higher due to the presence of the seen classes among them, most samples from unseen classes are incorrectly classified as belonging to one of the seen classes [6]. Different methods have been proposed to measure this discrepancy, such as the area under the curve representing all the possible trade-offs between the accuracies on samples from seen classes versus samples from unseen classes [6], or their harmonic mean [27] to penalize models with strong imbalance between the two. While these proposals only measure the extent of the problem, we aim to explicitly address this issue in addition to quantifying its impact.

The main contribution of this paper is a new process for training and evaluating models in a GZSL setting. In accordance with recent studies, we show that the application of a ZSL model "out of the box" gives results that are far from optimal in the GZSL context. We demonstrate how two simple techniques – the calibration of similarities and the use of appropriately balanced regularization – can dramatically improve the performance of most models. The final score for the GZSL task can thus be increased up to a factor of two, with no change regarding the underlying hypotheses of the GZSL task or the data available at any given time, which means that our process is applicable to any ZSL model. We also provide new insights on the reasons why these two techniques are relevant and on the fundamental differences between samples from seen and unseen classes.

We extensively evaluate these techniques on several recent ZSL methods. For sanity-check, we independently reproduce results obtained in the literature before applying our process. We find that some models show a variability in performance with respect to their random initialization, so measures averaged over several runs should be preferred. We eventually find that, with fair comparison under unbiased conditions as enabled by our process, a regularized linear model can give results close to or even better than the state-of-the-art.

2   Related Work

An early rigorous definition and evaluation of GZSL was put forward in [6]. The authors argue that this setting is more realistic than ZSL and highlight the gap between accuracies on seen and unseen classes when labels from *all* classes can be predicted (denoted respectively $A_{\mathcal{U} \to \mathcal{C}}$ and $A_{\mathcal{S} \to \mathcal{C}}$, and formally defined in Sect. 3.1). They also introduce the idea of calibration to address this issue and suggest a new metric for GZSL, *Accuracy Under Seen-Unseen Curve (AUSUC)*, which measures the trade-off between the two accuracies but does not directly provide the expected performance in real use-cases.

An extensive evaluation of recent ZSL methods with a common protocol is provided in [27], both in ZSL and GZSL settings. The authors use a different

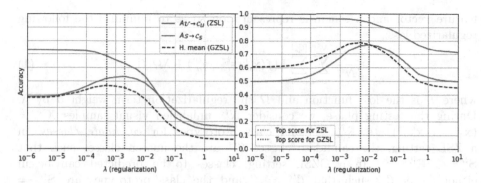

Fig. 1. Illustration of how the regularization parameter λ affects the accuracies on samples from seen and unseen classes $A_{\mathcal{U} \to \mathcal{C}_u}$ and $A_{\mathcal{S} \to \mathcal{C}_s}$ (see Sect. 3.1) as measured on CUB [23] (left) and AwA2 [25] (right). Optimal regularization is not the same in a ZSL setting, where performance is measured by $A_{\mathcal{U} \to \mathcal{C}_u}$ (red dotted line), and in a GZSL setting, where it is measured by the harmonic mean of $A_{\mathcal{U} \to \mathcal{C}}$ and $A_{\mathcal{S} \to \mathcal{C}}$ (black dotted line). (Color figure online)

metric for GZSL, the harmonic mean between $A_{\mathcal{U} \to \mathcal{C}}$ and $A_{\mathcal{S} \to \mathcal{C}}$, which does not directly quantify the trade-off between accuracies but better estimates the practical performance of a given model. However, they do not explicitly address the gap between similarities evaluated on seen and unseen classes [6], which has a significant impact on the final performance as we show in Sect. 4.3.

Further GZSL results based on the harmonic mean metric are provided in [4, 13,26]. All three methods rely on generators of artificial training examples from unseen classes. However, these methods assume that a semantic description of all unseen classes is available during training. This assumption is not necessarily met in practice and makes the inclusion of additional unseen classes more difficult.

Transductive ZSL methods [9,11,19] also assume that additional information, taking the form of unlabeled samples from unseen classes, is available during training. This can naturally lead to improved performance. In this article, we make none of these assumptions and consider that *no* information regarding unseen classes is available at training time.

3   Proposed Approach

3.1   Problem Statement

We denote by $\mathcal{C}_s$ the set of classes *seen* during training and by $\mathcal{C}_u$ the set of *unseen* classes. We define $\mathcal{C} = \mathcal{C}_s \cup \mathcal{C}_u$, with $\mathcal{C}_s \cap \mathcal{C}_u = \emptyset$. During the training phase, we consider N^{tr} training samples consisting of D-dimensional visual features $\mathbf{X}^{tr} = (\mathbf{x}_1^{tr}, \ldots, \mathbf{x}_{N^{tr}}^{tr})^\top \in \mathbb{R}^{N^{tr} \times D}$ and corresponding labels $\mathbf{y}^{tr} = (y_1^{tr}, \ldots, y_{N^{tr}}^{tr})^\top \in \mathcal{C}_s^{N^{tr}}$, as well as K-dimensional semantic *class prototypes* noted by $\mathbf{S}^{tr} = (\mathbf{s}_1^{tr}, \ldots, \mathbf{s}_{|\mathcal{C}_s|}^{tr})^\top \in \mathbb{R}^{|\mathcal{C}_s| \times K}$. We seek to learn a function $f : \mathbb{R}^D \times \mathbb{R}^K \to \mathbb{R}$ assigning a similarity score to each pair composed of a visual feature vector and a semantic representation so as to minimize the following regularized loss:

$$\frac{1}{N^{tr}} \sum_{n=1}^{N^{tr}} \sum_{c=1}^{|\mathcal{C}_s|} L(f(\mathbf{x}_n^{tr}; \mathbf{s}_c^{tr}), y_n^{tr}) + \lambda \Omega[f] \tag{1}$$

where L is the loss function and Ω the regularization term weighted by λ. During the testing phase, we consider N^{te} unlabeled visual samples $\mathbf{X}^{te} = (\mathbf{x}_1^{te}, \ldots, \mathbf{x}_{N^{te}}^{te})^\top \in \mathbb{R}^{N^{te} \times D}$ and class prototypes for *candidate classes*. In a ZSL setting, the candidate classes $\mathcal{C}^{te}$ are the unseen classes such that $\mathbf{S}^{te} \in \mathbb{R}^{|\mathcal{C}_u| \times K}$. In a GZSL setting, classes to be predicted can be in either $\mathcal{C}_u$ or $\mathcal{C}_s$, such that $\mathcal{C}^{te} = \mathcal{C}$ and the class prototypes are $\mathbf{S}^{te} = (\mathbf{s}_1^{te}, \ldots, \mathbf{s}_{|\mathcal{C}_s|}^{te}, \mathbf{s}_{|\mathcal{C}_s|+1}^{te}, \ldots, \mathbf{s}_{|\mathcal{C}_s|+|\mathcal{C}_u|}^{te})^\top \in \mathbb{R}^{|\mathcal{C}| \times K}$. In both cases, given a function $\hat{f}$ learned in the training phase, we want to estimate a prediction $\hat{y}$ for a visual testing sample $\mathbf{x}$ such that:

$$\hat{y} = \underset{c \in \mathcal{C}^{te}}{\operatorname{argmax}} \hat{f}(\mathbf{x}; \mathbf{s}_c^{te}) \tag{2}$$

In classical ZSL, performance is measured by the *accuracy of unseen classes among unseen classes*, noted $A_{\mathcal{U} \to \mathcal{C}_u}$, while in GZSL we are interested in the *accuracy of unseen classes among all classes* and the *accuracy of seen classes among all classes*, noted respectively $A_{\mathcal{U} \to \mathcal{C}}$ and $A_{\mathcal{S} \to \mathcal{C}}$ as in [6]. $A_{\mathcal{S} \to \mathcal{C}_s}$ is similarly defined.

3.2 Calibration and GZSL Split

As evidenced by [6], when a ZSL model is applied in a GZSL setting, $A_{\mathcal{S} \to \mathcal{C}}$ is usually significantly higher than $A_{\mathcal{U} \to \mathcal{C}}$. This is because most samples from unseen classes are incorrectly classified into one of the seen classes. To address this, a *calibration factor* γ is added in [6] to penalize seen classes. Equation (2) then becomes:

$$\hat{y} = \underset{c \in \mathcal{C}^{te}}{\operatorname{argmax}} \left(\hat{f}(\mathbf{x}; \mathbf{s}_c^{te}) - \gamma \mathbb{1}[c \in \mathcal{C}_s] \right) \tag{3}$$

where $\mathbb{1}[\cdot]$ is an indicator function.

The *Accuracy Under Seen-Unseen Curve (AUSUC)* metric also proposed in [6] is defined as the area under the curve representing $A_{\mathcal{S} \to \mathcal{C}}$ versus $A_{\mathcal{U} \to \mathcal{C}}$ when γ varies from $-\infty$ to $+\infty$, which shows the trade-off between the two.

Instead of computing a metric involving all possible trade-offs between $A_{\mathcal{U} \to \mathcal{C}}$ and $A_{\mathcal{S} \to \mathcal{C}}$, we look for a single specific value of γ, corresponding to the best compromise between the two as measured by the harmonic mean of $A_{\mathcal{U} \to \mathcal{C}}$ and $A_{\mathcal{S} \to \mathcal{C}}$ [27]. We propose to determine the optimal value of γ with a cross-validation specific to GZSL. Usually in machine learning a dataset is divided at random into three parts: a training, a validation and a testing set. In classical ZSL, this splitting process is done with respect to the classes as opposed to the samples: a set of classes is used for training, a disjoint set for validation and a final mutually disjoint set for testing. In GZSL, a fraction (usually 20%) of the samples from the validation and training sets are kept for testing time to be used as test samples from seen classes. We refer to this set as the *seen test set*. Note that here *seen* only indicates that these samples belong to seen classes, not that they have been used during training. To be able to cross-validate parameters for GZSL, we further keep an additional 20% of the remaining training set to be used as samples from seen classes when cross-validating parameters; we refer to this set as the *seen validation set*. Figure 2 illustrates this partitioning.

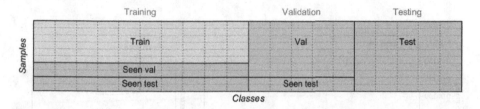

Fig. 2. Illustration of the different splits. Each column is a class and each cell is a sample. In this example there are 20 different classes with 10 samples per class. Five classes are used for testing, five other for validation and the remaining ten for training. Among the samples from the validation and training classes, 20% are kept for testing (*seen test set*) and 20% more samples from training classes are kept for validation (*seen validation set*).

To determine the optimal value of γ we first train a model on the GZSL training set. We then use the (GZSL) validation set and the seen validation set to compute the GZSL metric (the harmonic mean) and keep the value γ^* that maximizes this metric. The ZSL model is subsequently re-trained on the training, validation and seen validation sets, then class similarities are computed for the test set. The value γ^* is subtracted from the similarities of seen classes and the resulting similarities are used to compute the final GZSL score.

3.3 Regularization for GZSL

The usual approach to optimize the regularized loss (Eq. (1)) in GZSL consists in using the value of λ determined on the ZSL task. We argue here that this is unlikely to be optimal and provide some insight to justify our position. Then, we propose a simple method to determine a better value of λ to improve performance in GZSL.

Figure 1 shows $A_{\mathcal{U} \to \mathcal{C}_u}$ and $A_{\mathcal{S} \to \mathcal{C}_s}$ as a function of λ for a regularized linear model (ridge regression [3,24]), measured on the first validation splits of the *proposed splits* of [27] on CUB [23] and AwA2 [25].

In each case, there is a value of λ that maximizes the ZSL score $A_{\mathcal{U} \to \mathcal{C}_u}$, indicated by the red dotted vertical line, that we note λ^*_{ZSL}. The overall tendency for $A_{\mathcal{S} \to \mathcal{C}_s}$ is to decrease as λ increases. This is not a concern for the ZSL task, since it only considers samples from unseen classes. However, for the GZSL task, we want the best trade-off between $A_{\mathcal{U}\to\mathcal{C}}$ and $A_{\mathcal{S}\to\mathcal{C}}$. Note that $A_{\mathcal{U}\to\mathcal{C}} \leq A_{\mathcal{U}\to\mathcal{C}_u}$ and $A_{\mathcal{S}\to\mathcal{C}} \leq A_{\mathcal{S}\to\mathcal{C}_s}$, with equality only if we are able to perfectly distinguish samples from seen and unseen classes. It follows that λ^*_{GZSL}, the value of λ that maximizes the GZSL score, is not necessarily the same as λ^*_{ZSL}: a small decrease from λ^*_{ZSL} can significantly increase $A_{\mathcal{S}\to\mathcal{C}_s}$ while only slightly penalizing $A_{\mathcal{U}\to\mathcal{C}_u}$. This has a similar impact on the maximum values obtainable by $A_{\mathcal{S}\to\mathcal{C}}$ and $A_{\mathcal{U}\to\mathcal{C}}$, and can ultimately improve the GZSL score. We quantify in Sect. 4.3 the gains attributed to the use of λ^*_{GZSL}.

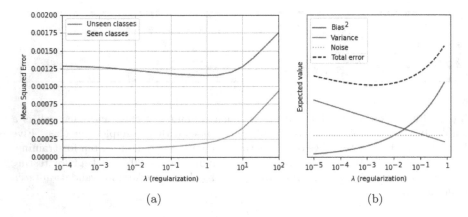

(a)   (b)

Fig. 3. (a) MSE of predicted attributes (averaged over attributes and samples) as a function of the regularization parameter λ; (b) Illustration of the bias-variance decomposition. (Color figure online)

The reason why λ affects $A_{\mathcal{U}\to\mathcal{C}_u}$ and $A_{\mathcal{S}\to\mathcal{C}_s}$ in this way can be explained with the bias-variance decomposition. For regression, we generally assume that we are given a dataset $\mathcal{D} = (\mathbf{X}, \mathbf{t})$, with samples $(\mathbf{x}_n, t_n)$ independently drawn from a joint distribution $p(\mathbf{x}, t)$, such that $p(t|\mathbf{x}) = \mathcal{N}(t|h(\mathbf{x}), \sigma^2)$, where h is the true dependence. For a prediction function $\hat{h}$ estimated from $\mathcal{D}$ we can then write the expected loss on a new pair $(\mathbf{x}, t)$ as:

$$\mathbb{E}_{\mathcal{D},\mathbf{x},t}[(t - \hat{h}(\mathbf{x}))^2] = \sigma^2 + \mathbb{E}_{\mathcal{D},\mathbf{x}}[(h(\mathbf{x}) - \hat{h}(\mathbf{x}))^2] + \text{var}_{\mathcal{D},\mathbf{x}}[\hat{h}(\mathbf{x})] \qquad (4)$$

where the first term is the intrinsic noise of the dataset, the second is the (squared) bias of the predictor and the third is the variance in the estimation of the predictor. It can be shown [3,24] that for ridge regression the bias increases and the variance decreases with the regularization parameter λ, as illustrated in Fig. 3(b).

In the case of ZSL, $\mathbf{x}$ corresponds to visual samples and t to attribute(s) to be estimated from $\mathbf{x}$. The variance comes from both the differences between samples from the same class (intra-class variance) and from the differences between classes (inter-class variance). Intra-class variance is usually significantly smaller than inter-class variance in ZSL; therefore, most of the variance in Eq. (4) can be attributed to the choice of training classes $\mathcal{C}_s$. For samples from unseen classes, the bias-variance decomposition applies and there exists a λ corresponding to the best trade-off between the two. This is evidenced in Fig. 3(a), where the red curve shows the Mean Squared Error (MSE) in the predictions of attributes from unseen classes as a function of λ, for a regularized linear model on the first validation split of AwA2 [25].

For a sample from a seen class, the variance attributable to the choice of the training classes is much smaller since, by definition, the seen class is present in the training dataset. This allows to better estimate attributes from seen classes and most of the expected error therefore comes from the intrinsic noise and the bias. Thus, the expected error mostly increases with λ, as evidenced by the blue curve in Fig. 3(a). If we plausibly assume that the accuracy of predictions for samples from a given class depends on how well we estimate their attributes, this explains both why predictions are better for samples from seen classes than from unseen classes and why their behavior with respect to λ is different.

We then suggest the following procedure to select the optimal value of λ: we repeat the protocol described in Sect. 3.2 for selecting γ^* and we take the value of λ which gives the best result for the harmonic mean between $A_{\mathcal{U} \to \mathcal{C}}$ and $A_{\mathcal{S} \to \mathcal{C}}$ on the validation set *after* having subtracted γ^* from the similarities of seen classes. The rest of the process is identical: we retrain the ZSL model on the training, validation and seen validation sets with the hyperparameter λ^*_{GZSL} that we just determined, we compute similarities for the test set, subtract γ^* from the similarities of seen classes and compute the resulting GZSL score.

4 Experimental Evaluation

4.1 Methods

We independently reimplemented six methods frequently cited in the literature to evaluate them with our protocol: ALE [1], DeViSE [8], SJE [2], Sync [5], ESZSL [20] and SAE [12].

In addition, we also evaluate two simple linear models. Linear$_{\mathcal{V} \to \mathcal{S}}$ applies a linear mapping $\mathbf{W} \in \mathbb{R}^{K \times D}$ from the visual space $\mathcal{V}$ to the semantic space $\mathcal{S}$ to minimize standard MSE. With $\mathbf{T}^{tr} = (\mathbf{s}^{tr}_{y^{tr}_1}, ..., \mathbf{s}^{tr}_{y^{tr}_N})^\top \in \mathbb{R}^{N^{tr} \times K}$ the matrix whose rows correspond to the class prototypes associated to each training sample based on its label, the loss function can be formulated as:

$$\frac{1}{N^{tr}} \|\mathbf{X}^{tr}\mathbf{W}^\top - \mathbf{T}^{tr}\|^2_F + \lambda \|\mathbf{W}\|^2_F \tag{5}$$

Linear$_{\mathcal{S} \to \mathcal{V}}$ is based on [21] where the authors argue that using the semantic space as the embedding space reduces the variance of the projected points and thus aggravates the hubness problem [18]. They suggest instead to project semantic class prototypes onto the visual space and to compute similarities in this space. Keeping $\mathbf{W} \in \mathbb{R}^{K \times D}$ as our linear mapping, we formulate the loss function as:

$$\frac{1}{N^{tr}} \|\mathbf{X}^{tr} - \mathbf{T}^{tr}\mathbf{W}\|^2_F + \lambda \|\mathbf{W}\|^2_F \tag{6}$$

We can easily obtain closed-form solutions for the two models from the objective functions (5) and (6). For the Linear$_{\mathcal{V} \to \mathcal{S}}$ model we have

$$\mathbf{W} = \mathbf{T}^{tr \top} \mathbf{X}^{tr} (\mathbf{X}^{tr \top} \mathbf{X}^{tr} + \lambda N^{tr} \mathbf{I}_D)^{-1} \tag{7}$$

and for the Linear$_{\mathcal{S} \to \mathcal{V}}$ model

$$\mathbf{W} = (\mathbf{T}^{tr \top} \mathbf{T}^{tr} + \lambda N^{tr} \mathbf{I}_K)^{-1} \mathbf{T}^{tr \top} \mathbf{X}^{tr}. \tag{8}$$

4.2 Experimental Setting

Datasets. We perform our experiments on two standard datasets for ZSL: Caltech-UCSD-Birds 200–2011 (CUB) [23] and Animals with Attributes2[1] (AwA2) [25]. CUB is a fine-grained dataset composed of 11788 pictures of birds from 200 species (*black footed albatross, . . . , common yellowthroat*). It comes with 312-dimensional binary attributes for each picture, that are averaged by class to obtain semantic class prototypes. AwA2 is a coarse-grained dataset comprising 37322 pictures of 50 animal species (*antelope, . . . , zebra*). For each class, 85-dimensional attributes are provided.

Splits. The best performing ZSL methods usually rely on visual features obtained with deep neural networks pre-trained on ImageNet [7], such as GoogLeNet [22] or ResNet [10]. As evidenced by [27], this induces a huge bias for ZSL datasets whose classes are not disjoint from categories of ImageNet, as is the case with AwA2, since test classes cannot be considered truly unseen. We therefore adopt the approach of [27] and use their terms *Standard Split* (S.S.) for the split widely used in the literature and *Proposed Split* (P.S.) for the split they introduce. The training and validation splits are further divided for GZSL as described in Sect. 3.2.

Settings. Attributes are normalized such that each class prototype has unit $\ell 2$ norm. We use the 101-layered ResNet [10] pre-trained on ImageNet [7] as visual features extractor, keeping the $D = 2048$ activations of the last pooling units.

Metrics. For ZSL, we evaluate the accuracy of samples from unseen classes among unseen classes $A_{\mathcal{U} \to \mathcal{C}_u}$. There are two possible ways to define accuracy: most of the literature uses *per sample* accuracy, defined as $100 \cdot \frac{1}{N^{te}} \sum_{n=1}^{N^{te}} \mathbb{1}[\hat{y}(\mathbf{x}_n^{te}) = y_n^{te}]$, while in [27] it is argued that *per class* accuracy, defined as $100 \cdot \frac{1}{|\mathcal{C}^{te}|} \sum_{c \in \mathcal{C}^{te}} \frac{1}{|\{n|y_n=c\}|} \sum_{y_n=c}^{n} \mathbb{1}[\hat{y}(\mathbf{x}_n^{te}) = y_n^{te}]$, better takes class imbalance into account.

We report per class accuracy for fair comparison with the extensive results of [27]. Nonetheless, to enable comparison with the rest of the literature, we

---

[1] AwA2 was recently proposed in [25] as a replacement for the Animals with Attributes (AwA) dataset [15] whose images are not publicly available.

also provide per sample accuracy results in Table 3. For GZSL we compute the harmonic mean between $A_{\mathcal{U} \to \mathcal{C}}$ and $A_{\mathcal{S} \to \mathcal{C}}$, defined as $\frac{2 \cdot A_{\mathcal{U} \to \mathcal{C}} \cdot A_{\mathcal{S} \to \mathcal{C}}}{A_{\mathcal{U} \to \mathcal{C}} + A_{\mathcal{S} \to \mathcal{C}}}$. Accuracy is again assumed to be per class unless otherwise stated.

4.3   Results

We first evaluate the performances of the different methods in a classical ZSL setting. Table 1 shows the average per class accuracy measured on testing sets of the Standard Splits (S.S.) and the Proposed Splits (P.S.) [27] of CUB [23] and AwA2 [25]. We report the average score and the standard deviation over 5 runs with different random initializations. We also report the results from [27]. We see that some methods such as SJE [2] have high variability with respect to the initialization; for such methods, it is good practice to report average results since a single test run may not be representative of the true performance of the model. On the other hand, methods with closed-form or deterministic solutions such as the Linear$_{\mathcal{V} \to \mathcal{S}}$, Linear$_{\mathcal{S} \to \mathcal{V}}$, ESZSL [20] or SAE [12] are not dependent on the initialization and thus have a standard deviation of 0.

Table 1. ZSL score: per-class accuracy $A_{\mathcal{U} \to \mathcal{C}_u}$, as reported in [27] and independently reproduced. S.S.: Standard Split, P.S.: Proposed Split [27]. Averaged over 5 runs.

| Method | CUB [23] | | | | AwA2 [25] | | | |
| | Reported in [27] | | Reproduced | | Reported in [27] | | Reproduced | |
	S.S.	P.S.	S.S.	P.S.	S.S.	P.S.	S.S.	P.S.
Linear$_{\mathcal{V} \to \mathcal{S}}$	n/a	n/a	41.0 ± 0.0	41.8 ± 0.0	n/a	n/a	68.2 ± 0.0	49.7 ± 0.0
Linear$_{\mathcal{S} \to \mathcal{V}}$	n/a	n/a	56.0 ± 0.0	53.5 ± 0.0	n/a	n/a	**85.5 + 0.0**	**68.9** ± 0.0
ALE [1]	53.2	54.9	54.8 ± 0.8	54.0 ± 1.2	80.3	**62.5**	80.3 ± 2.2	62.9 ± 2.3
DeViSE [8]	53.2	52.0	52.5 ± 0.9	52.6 ± 1.3	68.6	59.7	76.6 ± 1.6	62.1 ± 1.6
SJE [2]	**55.3**	53.9	53.8 ± 2.3	49.2 ± 1.4	69.5	61.9	80.4 ± 2.9	62.2 ± 1.2
ESZSL [20]	55.1	53.9	34.9 ± 0.0	34.9 ± 0.0	75.6	58.6	70.5 ± 0.0	50.8 ± 0.0
Sync [5]	54.1	**55.6**	**56.4** ± 0.9	**54.8** ± 0.6	71.2	46.6	65.6 ± 0.8	58.1 ± 0.8
SAE [12]	33.4	33.3	56.2 ± 0.0	53.3 ± 0.0	**80.7**	54.1	81.1 ± 0.0	62.8 ± 0.0

Most of the reproduced scores are consistent with [27], with two notable exceptions: first, a significant increase in performance is observed with SAE [12] and can be explained by the fact that similarities are computed in the visual space, with results close to those of the Linear$_{\mathcal{S} \to \mathcal{V}}$ model (results are close to those of Linear$_{\mathcal{V} \to \mathcal{S}}$ when similarities are computed in the semantic space). Second, the score for ESZSL [20] is significantly lower than reported in [27]. We found that the use of non-normalized attributes enables to reach performances comparable with [27], but we could not reproduce the reported results for ESZSL [20] with normalized attributes. For the sake of consistency, we chose to report results obtained with normalized attributes.

Table 2 shows results for GZSL. We measure the harmonic mean between per class accuracies $A_{\mathcal{U} \to \mathcal{C}}$ and $A_{\mathcal{S} \to \mathcal{C}}$ on the testing set of the Proposed Split [27].

Table 2. GZSL score (harmonic mean of $A_{\mathcal{U} \to \mathcal{C}}$ and $A_{\mathcal{S} \to \mathcal{C}}$, per class accuracy) with and without calibration and GZSL regularization. On Proposed Split [27], averaged over 5 runs.

Method	CUB [23]				AwA2 [25]			
	Reported in [27]	Ours			Reported in [27]	Ours		
with **calibration**	-	-	✓	✓	-	-	✓	✓
with $\lambda^*_{\mathbf{GZSL}}$	-	-	-	✓	-	-	-	✓
Linear$_{\mathcal{V} \to \mathcal{S}}$	n/a	18.2	34.3	35.5	n/a	8.3	47.3	48.1
Linear$_{\mathcal{S} \to \mathcal{V}}$	n/a	32.5	41.9	43.5	n/a	44.3	62.7	64.0
ALE [1]	34.4	35.6	45.1	46.2	23.9	26.9	55.8	55.8
DeViSE [8]	32.8	35.1	43.6	43.4	27.8	17.4	54.6	54.6
SJE [2]	33.6	29.7	41.2	44.2	14.4	28.9	58.2	59.0
ESZSL [20]	21.0	17.9	33.7	33.9	11.0	39.9	53.6	53.7
Sync [5]	19.8	33.2	46.2	47.6	18.0	30.6	61.0	61.0
SAE [12]	13.6	25.7	43.1	43.1	2.2	29.5	60.2	60.2
Average	25.9	28.5	41.1	**42.2**	16.2	28.2	56.7	**57.1**

Table 3. ZSL and GZSL scores with 10-crop features, evaluated with per class (p.c.) and per sample (p.s.) accuracies. With calibration and λ^*_{GZSL}. On P.S. [27], averaged over 5 runs.

Method	CUB [23]				AwA2 [25]			
	ZSL		GZSL		ZSL		GZSL	
	Acc. p.c.	Acc. p.s.	H. p.c.	H. p.s.	Acc. p.c.	Acc. p.s.	H. p.c.	H. p.s.
Linear$_{\mathcal{V} \to \mathcal{S}}$	45.6	45.6	39.8	39.8	51.0	43.6	49.0	45.6
Linear$_{\mathcal{S} \to \mathcal{V}}$	57.1	57.2	47.7	48.0	**70.4**	**69.3**	**65.1**	**68.7**
ALE [1]	57.4	57.5	**49.2**	**49.3**	63.0	61.1	56.9	55.5
DeViSE [8]	52.9	52.9	42.4	42.5	63.1	62.2	55.0	50.6
SJE [2]	51.9	52.1	46.7	46.9	63.8	61.6	59.4	57.6
ESZSL [20]	39.0	38.8	38.7	38.6	52.6	51.9	54.4	57.9
Sync [5]	**57.5**	**57.6**	48.9	49.1	59.3	56.1	62.6	63.2
SAE [12]	56.1	56.2	46.3	46.6	63.5	65.4	62.3	63.6

We evaluate three settings: a ZSL model applied directly in a GZSL setting, i.e. with no calibration and a regularization specific to ZSL (λ^*_{ZSL}) as opposed to GZSL (λ^*_{GZSL}); a ZSL model with calibration and ZSL regularization λ^*_{ZSL}; and a ZSL model with calibration and regularization λ^*_{GZSL} specific to the GZSL problem. We report the average score over 5 runs; standard deviations are available in the supplementary material. We also report the results from [27], which correspond to the setting with no calibration and no λ^*_{GZSL}. We can see that the calibration process significantly improves GZSL performance: in our experiments, the average score for all models improves from 28.5 with no calibration to 41.1 with calibration on CUB, and from 28.2 to 56.7 on AwA2. It is worth noting that the lowest score with calibration is close to or higher than the highest score without. The use of a regularization parameter specific to the GZSL task can lead to an additional improvement in performance. In some cases, the optimal λ is the same for the ZSL task and the GZSL task on the validation set, leading to no additional improvement over the score with calibration. However, every time they are different, λ^*_{GZSL} is smaller than λ^*_{ZSL}, as expected from the results in Sect. 3.3. The only exception is with DeViSE [8] on CUB: a λ^*_{GZSL} higher than λ^*_{ZSL} was selected during cross-validation, probably due to random noise, resulting in a slightly lower final GZSL score.

Table 3 shows results with improved visual features; each original 256×256 image is cropped into ten 224×224 images: one in each corner and one in the center for both the original image and its horizontal symmetry. The ResNet features of the resulting images are averaged to obtain a 2048-dimensional vector. We report results for ZSL ($A_{\mathcal{C} \to \mathcal{C}_u}$, abbreviated *Acc.*) and GZSL (using the harmonic mean metric, abbreviated *H.*) on the testing set of the Proposed Split [27]. In order to facilitate fair comparison with the rest of the literature, both per class *(p.c.)* and per sample *(p.s.)* metrics are reported. Results with 10-cropped visual features are almost always better than the results with standard visual features in Table 2. The per sample metrics are on average not very different from the per class metrics. This is not surprising since classes in both CUB and AwA2 are fairly balanced.

5 Conclusion

We proposed a simple process for applying ZSL methods in a GZSL setting. This process is based on the empirical observation that ZSL models perform differently on samples from seen and unseen classes. We provided insights about why this should be expected and suggested steps to overcome these problems. Through extensive experiments, we showed that this process enables significant improvements in performance for many existing ZSL methods. Finally, we provided results under optimal conditions for these methods with different metrics to support fair comparison with the rest of the state-of-the-art.

References

1. Akata, Z., Perronnin, F., Harchaoui, Z., Schmid, C.: Label-embedding for image classification. IEEE Trans. Pattern Anal. Mach. Intell. **38**(7), 1425–1438 (2016)
2. Akata, Z., Reed, S., Walter, D., Lee, H., Schiele, B.: Evaluation of output embeddings for fine-grained image classification. In: Proceedings of the CVPR 2015, pp. 2927–2936. IEEE (2015)
3. Bishop, C.M.: Pattern Recognition and Machine Learning. Springer, New York (2006)
4. Bucher, M., Herbin, S., Jurie, F.: Generating visual representations for zero-shot classification. In: ICCV Workshops: TASK-CV. IEEE (2017)
5. Changpinyo, S., Chao, W.L., Gong, B., Sha, F.: Synthesized classifiers for zero-shot learning. In: Proceedings of the CVPR 2016, pp. 5327–5336. IEEE (2016)

6. Chao, W.-L., Changpinyo, S., Gong, B., Sha, F.: An empirical study and analysis of generalized zero-shot learning for object recognition in the wild. In: Leibe, B., Matas, J., Sebe, N., Welling, M. (eds.) ECCV 2016. LNCS, vol. 9906, pp. 52–68. Springer, Cham (2016). https://doi.org/10.1007/978-3-319-46475-6_4

7. Deng, J., Dong, W., Socher, R., Li, L.J., Li, K., Fei-Fei, L.: ImageNet: a large-scale hierarchical image database. In: Proceedings of the CVPR 2009, pp. 248–255. IEEE (2009)

8. Frome, A., et al.: Devise: a deep visual-semantic embedding model. In: Proceedings of the NIPS 2013, pp. 2121–2129 (2013)

9. Fu, Y., Hospedales, T.M., Xiang, T., Gong, S.: Transductive multi-view zero-shot learning. IEEE Trans. Pattern Anal. Mach. Intell. **37**(11), 2332–2345 (2015)

10. He, K., Zhang, X., Ren, S., Sun, J.: Deep residual learning for image recognition. In: Proceedings of the CVPR 2016, pp. 770–778. IEEE (2016)

11. Kodirov, E., Xiang, T., Fu, Z., Gong, S.: Unsupervised domain adaptation for zero-shot learning. In: Proceedings of the CVPR 2015, pp. 2452–2460. IEEE (2015)

12. Kodirov, E., Xiang, T., Gong, S.: Semantic autoencoder for zero-shot learning. In: Proceedings of the CVPR 2017, pp. 4447–4456. IEEE (2017)

13. Kumar Verma, V., Arora, G., Mishra, A., Rai, P.: Generalized zero-shot learning via synthesized examples. In: Proceedings of the CVPR 2010, pp. 4281–4289. IEEE (2018)

14. Lampert, C.H., Nickisch, H., Harmeling, S.: Learning to detect unseen object classes by between-class attribute transfer. In: Proceedings of the CVPR 2009, pp. 951–958. IEEE (2009)

15. Lampert, C.H., Nickisch, H., Harmeling, S.: Attribute-based classification for zero-shot visual object categorization. IEEE Trans. Pattern Anal. Mach. Intell. **36**(3), 453–465 (2014)

16. Larochelle, H., Erhan, D., Bengio, Y.: Zero-data learning of new tasks. In: AAAI, vol. 1, p. 3 (2008)

17. Palatucci, M., Pomerleau, D., Hinton, G.E., Mitchell, T.M.: Zero-shot learning with semantic output codes. In: Proceedings of the NIPS 2009, pp. 1410–1418 (2009)

18. Radovanović, M., Nanopoulos, A., Ivanović, M.: Hubs in space: popular nearest neighbors in high-dimensional data. J. Mach. Learn. Res. **11**, 2487–2531 (2010)

19. Rohrbach, M., Ebert, S., Schiele, B.: Transfer learning in a transductive setting. In: Proceedings of the NIPS 2013, pp. 46–54 (2013)

20. Romera-Paredes, B., Torr, P.: An embarrassingly simple approach to zero-shot learning. In: Proceedings of the ICML 2015, pp. 2152–2161 (2015)

21. Shigeto, Y., Suzuki, I., Hara, K., Shimbo, M., Matsumoto, Y.: Ridge regression, hubness, and zero-shot learning. In: Appice, A., Rodrigues, P.P., Santos Costa, V., Soares, C., Gama, J., Jorge, A. (eds.) ECML PKDD 2015. LNCS (LNAI), vol. 9284, pp. 135–151. Springer, Cham (2015). https://doi.org/10.1007/978-3-319-23528-8_9

22. Szegedy, C., et al.: Going deeper with convolutions. In: Proceedings of the CVPR 2015, pp. 1–9. IEEE (2015)

23. Wah, C., Branson, S., Welinder, P., Perona, P., Belongie, S.: The Caltech-UCSD Birds-200-2011 dataset (2011)

24. van Wieringen, W.N.: Lecture notes on ridge regression. arXiv preprint arXiv:1509.09169 (2015)

25. Xian, Y., Lampert, C.H., Schiele, B., Akata, Z.: Zero-shot learning - a comprehensive evaluation of the good, the bad and the ugly. arXiv preprint arXiv:1707.00600 (2017)
26. Xian, Y., Lorenz, T., Schiele, B., Akata, Z.: Feature generating networks for zero-shot learning. In: Proceedings of the CVPR 2018. IEEE (2018)
27. Xian, Y., Schiele, B., Akata, Z.: Zero-shot learning - the good, the bad and the ugly. In: Proceedings of the CVPR 2017, pp. 3077–3086. IEEE (2017)

Industry Papers

Bag of Deep Features for Instructor Activity Recognition in Lecture Room

Nudrat Nida[1][iD], Muhammad Haroon Yousaf[1]([✉])[iD], Aun Irtaza[2],
and Sergio A. Velastin[3,4,5][iD]

[1] Department of Computer Engineering,
University of Engineering and Technology, Taxila, Pakistan
{16F-PHD-CP-53,haroon.yousaf}@uettaxila.edu.pk
[2] Department of Computer Science,
University of Engineering and Technology, Taxila, Pakistan
aun.irtaza@uettaxila.edu.pk
[3] Department of Computer Science, Applied Artificial Intelligence Research Group,
University Carlos III de Madrid, 28270 Madrid, Spain
[4] Cortexica Vision Systems Ltd., London SE1 9LQ, UK
[5] School of Electronic Engineering and Computer Science,
Queen Mary University of London, London E1 4NS, UK
sergio.velastin@ieee.org

Abstract. This research aims to explore contextual visual information in the lecture room, to assist an instructor to articulate the effectiveness of the delivered lecture. The objective is to enable a self-evaluation mechanism for the instructor to improve lecture productivity by understanding their activities. Teacher's effectiveness has a remarkable impact on uplifting students performance to make them succeed academically and professionally. Therefore, the process of lecture evaluation can significantly contribute to improve academic quality and governance. In this paper, we propose a vision-based framework to recognize the activities of the instructor for self-evaluation of the delivered lectures. The proposed approach uses motion templates of instructor activities and describes them through a Bag-of-Deep features (BoDF) representation. Deep spatio-temporal features extracted from motion templates are utilized to compile a visual vocabulary. The visual vocabulary for instructor activity recognition is quantized to optimize the learning model. A Support Vector Machine classifier is used to generate the model and predict the instructor activities. We evaluated the proposed scheme on a self-captured lecture room dataset, IAVID-1. Eight instructor activities: pointing towards the student, pointing towards board or screen, idle, interacting, sitting, walking, using a mobile phone and using a laptop, are recognized with an 85.41% accuracy. As a result, the proposed framework enables instructor activity recognition without human intervention.

Keywords: Human activity recognition
Instructor activity recognition · Motion templates
Academic quality assurance

© Springer Nature Switzerland AG 2019
I. Kompatsiaris et al. (Eds.): MMM 2019, LNCS 11296, pp. 481–492, 2019.
https://doi.org/10.1007/978-3-030-05716-9_39

1   Introduction

An effective teacher is a source of inspiration and responsible for students achievement. The students' academic performance is highly dependent upon the teacher's effectiveness and their behavioral traits. In educational institutes, students are surveyed for the evaluation of instructor effectiveness and quality of the delivered lecture. In this regard, institutes are evaluating the effectiveness of teachers and lectures mainly through student feedback. This feedback is based on the standard survey mechanism "Student's Evaluating Teaching (SET)". The prime motive to examine feedback is to improve the quality of the lecture. Unfortunately, in SET a teacher's instructional and behavioral skills are evaluated on a smaller scale. Moreover, SET feedback are usually collected at the end of the semester which is not beneficial for students enrolled in a current semester. These performance evaluation statistics have being collected for a long time and empirically have been fount to have no significant impact on ratings of teaching [5]. The root cause of inaccurate instructor's performance insight is due to poorly designed questionnaires, personal biases, and non-serious student's response. Hence, an alternative system is required to support the evaluation process that can provide a consistent view of the quality of lecture and effectiveness of the teachers.

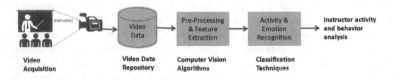

Fig. 1. The visual classroom information for the development of intelligent application using actions and emotion recognition techniques.

Everyday numerous hours of video data are recorded in academic institutes across the world. However, the majority of institutes rarely analyze the recorded or live stream videos for instructor performance evaluation or estimation of the lecture effectiveness, as illustrated in Fig. 1. Such real-time classroom data has an enormous potential to explore various problem domains within a classroom and to provide a solution to academicians to understand visual semantics using computer vision and pattern recognition techniques as shown in Fig. 1. Recently, some computer vision findings have been reported to automatically estimate instructor performance using pose, gesture and activity recognition [15,19,20]. In [15], vision-based instructor activity recognition uses silhouette representation to train a Hidden Markov Model (HMM). The system was able to identify five activities: walking, writing, pointing towards the board, standing and pointing towards presentations with a recognition accuracy of 90%. Similarly, in [19] face recognition and pose estimation techniques were applied to analyze academic performance within a lecture room. Structure and texture features were used to localize objects and the instructor within the classroom. A Bayesian classifier was used to model five activities: standing, walking, pointing, writing and addressing. The achieved accuracy was reported to be 96%. In [20], instructor activities were used to record a lecture automatically through localization of classroom objects and instructor. Then morphological features were used to generate fuzzy rules for instructor activities recognition. Such techniques [15,19,20] use spatial data for activity recognition but have ignored temporal information and have had to resort to their own datasets because of the unavailability of standard activity datasets for instructor evaluation. Consequently, there is a need to develop standard datasets for researchers to compare and improve results.

Especially during the last decade, understanding visual information using computer vision techniques and systems has been useful to recognize human activities and behaviors in real-time in applications such as in surveillance, robot navigation, elderly home care, etc. The literature on human action recognition can be grouped into two broad categories: handcrafted and deep learning techniques. Activity recognition based on handcrafted features can be further categorized into spatio-temporal [10], motion template [14] and action trajectory information [18]. Spatio-temporal features tend to be sparse and not of fixed length, which affects accuracy [10,21]. The varying length of spatio-temporal features may be overcome through time evolution of actor silhouettes [14,21]. However, accurate segmentation of actor silhouettes is a challenging problem. Action trajectory information [18] is very effective but it is computationally expensive to capture temporal movement information of actor which is also sensitive to occlusion and noise. Handcrafted action representations target specific applications and thus fail to provide generic solutions [21]. Recently, deep learning based techniques have been shown to outperform traditional methods in most recognition tasks and that has motivated researchers to explore its capabilities for action recognition especially using spatio-temporal data. In the action recognition domain, deep learning solutions can be categorized as frame learning [2,12], transformed frame learning [1], handcrafted features with deep representation [4], 3D convolutional neural network [3] and hybrid models [7,16]. Deep learning based solutions can find generalized models for real-time application but suffer from the scarcity of standard video datasets [21]. Frame learning tries to predict action recognition without learning temporal information [2,12] optimizes the models by tuning the weights. A limitation of the frame learning technique is that resolution and number of frames are fixed for all action sequences, yet realistic action videos are not of fixed length. Transformed frame learning overcomes limitations of frame learning by incorporating temporal information from adjacent frames. However, it works best on smaller resolution video frames that makes it inadequate for high resolution action prediction. Recurrent neural networks are used to learn the sequential action information and predict activities [7]. Deep models for action representation using handcrafted features as input data may be appropriate for human action recognition, assuming that adequate features can be found [4]. 3D CNN [3] techniques use modified 2D CNN to embed temporal information. However, prediction results are not much better than 2D frame learning techniques [21]. Deep learning techniques are data hungry methods that require large-scale data representation and powerful computational resources. Among these techniques, a fusion of handcrafted and deep learning features might offer promising recognition results, as compared to state of the art techniques, due to higher dimensional action representation [21].

This research work proposes a technique for action recognition that uses a fusion of handcrafted and deep learning features to generate Bag-of-Deep-Features (BoDF) for instructor activity recognition. Such holds a high dimensional discriminative power to recognize different objects [21], and performs promisingly to recognize instructor activities. We evaluated this technique on a newly created video dataset: "Instructor Activity Video-I (IAVID-I)". Our contributions are: (i) To utilize a computer vision technique for understanding the visual semantics of classroom for academic quality assurance, (ii) Proposing a novel Bag-of-Deep-Features technique for instructor activity recognition, (iii) The proposed technique has the potential to solvic action recognition irrespective of the application domain, as the motion template generated from human silhouette captures the spatio-temporal representation of an actor that is benefical for accurate prediction of activities, (iv) To make available to other researchers a new dataset and a baseline set of results.

2   Proposed Methodology

Bag of Feature (BoF) is one of the most effective frameworks for various image and video classification applications [11]. The BoF for action recognition follows a generic pipeline: (i) extraction of 3D feature detector and descriptor, (ii) Construction of visual vocabulary, (iii) Quantization of visual vocabulary, (iv) Generation of a training model for action prediction, (v) Testing. Boradly, our technique is based on the fusion of handcrafted features (i.e. MT) and deep features for construction of a BoDF representation. We believe that the fusion of handcrafted motion templates of instructor and deep representation is capable

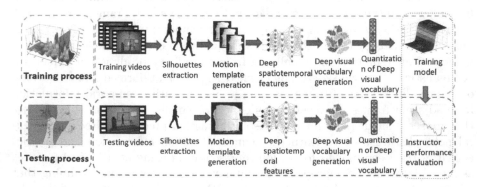

Fig. 2. The visual classroom information for the development of intelligent application using actions and emotion recognition techniques.

to predict the instructor's activities. To validate this hypothesis, handcrafted motion templates of instructor's activities and deep features from different layers of a CNN network [6] are fused together and each video sequence is represented by a feature vector of fixed size. The proposed technique is based on a generic BoF [13] representation with some modifications at the feature computation step. Since deep learning techniques have improved image classification performance [6], therefore it is amenable to utilize deep features for action representation using BoF paradigm. In BoDF, the deep features are computed as $Z = z_i, i \epsilon (1, \ldots, N)$, where $z_i \epsilon DSTF^D$ is deep spatio-temporal action descriptor computed from action video sequences and N is the length of DSTF of fixed size D. Where D is 4096 or 1000 depending upon the fully connected layer used for feature extraction. Then, encoding these DSTF to obtain an optimal representation of action videos through function, $f: DSTF^D \Rightarrow DSTF^K$. The coding function f maps the deep spatio-temporal $DSTF$ into deep visual dictionary representation into K clusters. Then, the histogram h is used to quantize the deep visual vocabulary to train a SVM model for instructor action prediction. The vocabulary size is varied to examine the behavior of the model. The experiential results are discussed in the results and findings section. The following subsection will explain the methodology in detail.

2.1 Preprocessing

Initially, RGB video action sequences of classroom lectures are presented to the framework as input. Then, instructor silhouettes are extracted using graph cut segmentation. In minimum graph cut segmentation, each pixel of the instructor activity video frame is represented by a graph node. Each node is connected to each other through a vertex. In our technique, Gaussian distribution is used to assign probability weights to each vertex and segment the instructor silhouetted $s(x, y, t)$ from the classroom static background based on associated probability weights. The minimum probability at the vertex is responsible to segment the instructor silhouettes from the static background. We extract instructor silhouettes to encode instructor motion information of the entire video sequence through motion templates. On application of graph cut segmentation, instructor silhouettes $s(x, y, t)$ are obtained for each video frame, i.e. the spatial location of the instructor as a binary representation.

2.2 Motion Template (MT) Generation

The instructor binary silhouettes generated from the video sequence are processed further to form motion templates, as shown in Fig. 2. These templates hold the spatio-temporal representation of action sequences and computed for all the training and testing video sequences. The motion template (MT) is a function of intensity for holding information on the most recent spatial location of motion [8]. A brighter pixel indicates recent motion location of instructor within the classroom. MT is computed using Eq. 1, where MT is spatio-temporal template generated from a silhouette frame $s(x, y, t)$ represents the object of interest, i.e. instructor at time t at location (x, y) as shown in expression (1).

$$MT = \begin{cases} \tau & if s(x, y, t) = 1 \\ max(0, s_{t-1}(x, y) - 1) & otherwise \end{cases} \quad (1)$$

Here, τ is total number of frames used for generation of MT for every action sequence in a similar way. The benefit of using MT is to reduce the spatial and computational complexity of action recognition. The resultant MT is cumulative greyscale motion representation of the instructor in an action video sequence, as 3D instructor spatial and temporal information are mapped into 2D greyscale MT. All the videos MT are normalized, wrapped to 227×227 or 224×224 dimension and centered to reduce redundant information. The wrapping and centering processes are applied to overcome constraints of spatial location, viewpoint variation, and scale, as motion templates are sensitive to spatial location and viewpoint.

2.3 Deep Spatiotemporal Features (DSTF)

Then, these spatio-temporal MTs are described through deep features from a pre-trained AlexNet CNN network [6] and VGG19 [17] to form deep visual words (DVW). The aim is to obtain higher dimensional spatio-temporal instructor action representation of MT using deep visual words at different network depth. Visual patches of motion templates are represented as deep numerical vectors to represent each type of instructor activities. The input layer in the CNN receives the MT and passes it to the convolutional layer. The convolutional layer performs convolution of MT at the smaller region with weights to generate a y feature map of neurons. Assume that we have spatio-temporal template MT of dimension MxM and present into CNN to extract $DSTF$, ultimately forming the DVW for instructor activity recognition. The receptive field or kernel of size is $r \times r$ and w is the number of the kernel, the convolutional layer will generate an output neuron volume of $(M - r + 1) \times (M - r + 1)$ in Eq. 2.

$$DSTF_{mn} = \sum_{\alpha=0}^{r-1} \sum_{\beta=0}^{r-1} w y_{x+i, y+i}^{r-1} \quad (2)$$

We have computed the DVW from a 25 layered Alexnet [6] at different network depths, such as deep features are extracted from fully connected layer $17(DVW_{17})$, $20(DVW_{20})$ and $23(DVW_{23})$ respectively. There are 196,608 deep visual words generated when DVW_{17} and DVW_{20} are used for feature extraction and 43,000 deep visual words are generated when DVW_{23} is used for feature computation. Similarly, we have computed the DVW from 47 layered VGG19 [17] at different network depths, and in this case deep features are extracted from fully connected layer $39(DVW_{39})$, $42(DVW_{42})$ and $45(DVW_{45})$ respectively.

There are 196,608 deep visual words generated when DVW_{39} and DVW_{42} are used for feature extraction and 43,000 deep visual words generated when DVW_{45} is used for feature computation. We have explored the deep features capability to represent actions through BoDF representation, as it was not yet explored for action representation. We argue that the deep representation of motion templates is a major factor for precise action recognition, due to higher dimensional feature representation.

2.4 Deep Visual Vocabulary Generation and Quantization

Then, as illustrated in Fig. 2, the next step includes generation of visual vocabulary through unsupervised clustering of deep visual words (DVW) by K-means clustering algorithm. Suppose there are N activities of the instructor that are divided into K clusters, such that all the DVW are assigned to centroids of the cluster through minimizing the distance between the cluster centroid and $DSTF$. The K or vocabulary size is varied from 100 to 500 and the performance of the proposed technique was analyzed. The deep visual vocabulary represents the DVW of each instructor activities as the frequency of occurrence of DVW. The visual vocabulary is beneficial for estimating the instructor activities through DVW histogram to quantize the deep visual vocabulary. We have selected the 40% strongest DVW for quantization of deep visual vocabulary. These DVW are divided into 4,800 bins of final histogram.

2.5 The Training and Testing Video for Instructor Action Recognition

A Support Vector Machine (SVM) classifier is used to train the instructor activity recognition model from the quantized deep visual vocabulary representation of instructor activities. The SVM classifier defines decision boundaries separating the set of instructor actions having different class memberships. SVM performs classification through the generation of hyperplanes across multidimensional space that discriminate video samples of different instructor action classes. Later on, the test video is represented by a histogram of DVW and an SVM used to predict the instructor's activity.

3   Results and Findings

In this section, we describe a series of experiments performed on the Instructor Activity Video (IAVID-I) dataset, for evaluation of our system at various deep CNN depth for feature learning and computational cost is also estimated. Hardware and software specification of our system is an NVIDIA GTX-950 GPU card, Windows 10, an Intel i7-7700K processor with 4.5 GHz and 12 GB memory. The framework was implemented using MATLAB's Deep Learning Toolbox.

3.1   IAVID-I Dataset

We have recorded video dataset, Instructor Activity Video (IAVID-I), to recognize the activities of the instructor using real-time classroom video data. The environmental condition remains the same during recording, 12 actors participated in the acquisition phase focusing on stage. There are 100 videos having 854 × 480 high-resolution RGB 24 bit videos. There are eight actions in this dataset, i.e. interacting or idle, pointing towards the board, pointing towards the screen, using a mobile phone, using a laptop, sitting, walking and writing on the board, as illustrated in Fig. 3.

Table 1. Evaluation of deep BoDF for instructor activity recognition at various network depth and vocabulary size.

sr.no	DVW	DSTF	DVW dimension	Accuracy
1	DVW_{17} [6]	4096	196608	84.32%
2	DVW_{20} [6]	4096	196608	85.41%
3	DVW_{23} [6]	1000	48000	83.33%
4	DVW_{39} [17]	4096	196608	70.00%
5	DVW_{42} [17]	4096	196608	75.56%
6	DVW_{45} [17]	1000	48000	66.67%

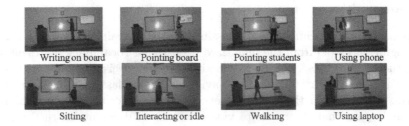

Fig. 3. The visual classroom information for the development of intelligent application using actions and emotion recognition techniques.

3.2   Evaluation of Deep BoDF at Various Network Depth

We followed a cross validation scheme on the IAVID-I dataset by randomly holding half of the video sequences for testing, while the other half was used for training the model. The hyper-parameters were set as per the pre-trained network Alexnet [6] and VGG19 [17]. Deep features are extracted from fully connected layers at network depth of 17, 20, 23, 39, 42, and 45. The prediction accuracy is the most reliable measure to estimate the robustness of the learned model. Therefore, Table 1 summarizes the performance of the deep BoDF model in terms of prediction accuracy. It is notable that DVW_{20} performed better than DVW_{17} and DVW_{23} at visual vocabulary size of 100, due to higher dimensional feature representation as compared to DVW_{23}. DVW_{17}, computed from shallower fully connected layer reduces performance by 1.09% compared with DVW_{20}, due to the fact that some features at shallower layers correlate with each other, and resulted in slight variation in prediction accuracy. From Table 1, it is observed that the greater the number of visual words, the better will be the representation of action classes. The DVW extracted from Alexnet performed better than VGG19, as hyper-parameter and network architecture varies. However, this adoption needs a lot of experimentation i.e. architecture configuration and extension to make it able to be used as an real time system giving a performance comparable to humans in an efficient way. Thus, experimental results portray that the optimal choice of DVW computation is from 20 layers of Alexnet pretrained network [6]. We have computed the confusion matrix, as shown in Fig. 4, using a visual vocabulary size of 100 generated from DVW_{20}, achieving 85.41% accuracy. From the confusion matrix it can be observed that the lowest prediction accuracy occurs for writing on board, due to the fact that in some sequences actors were walking while writing on board, therefore the writing action class is confused with walking. Similarly, instructor action pointing towards the student is also confused with pointing towards the board because of the visual similarity of motion templates of two action classes. To further examine the performance of the proposed method, we have plotted a box and whisker plot to analyze the spread of prediction accuracy, as shown in Fig. 5. The box and whisker plot presents the distribution of accuracy across the number line and divides it into four quartiles, and median accuracy. From the spread of plot, it is notable that visual words DVW_{20} perform better than DVW_{17} and DVW_{23} at all vocabulary size and the accuracy spectrum is position at upper half of the box and whisker plot, representing higher prediction score. The deep features hold higher discrimination representation among the classes, therefore at minimum vocabulary size, DVW performed well to fitting data into suitable class boundaries for precise prediction of instructor activities. Moreover, shallower fully connected layers of CNN networks holds higher dimensional deep features to generate discriminative DVW for BoDF representation. Table 2 describes the computational cost of the proposed method. In the preprocessing step, instructor silhouette extraction and MT generation required 1 min per sequence on average for 30 fps. The computational cost is averaged for all the task. It is concluded that deep BoDF requires a smaller vocabulary size to learn prediction model at a lower computational time. On average, the minimum time required for prediction of action is 0.43 s. In the IAVID-I dataset, there is a total of 8 action classes having 100 videos sequences and each frame is 854 × 480 resolution. Using the cross-validation scheme, training and testing of 100 video sequences takes 30 s, i.e. on average it takes 0.43 s per sequence at a frame rate of 139.53 frames/second (FPS). It is concluded that BoDF requires a small vocabulary size to learn prediction model at the lower computational time.

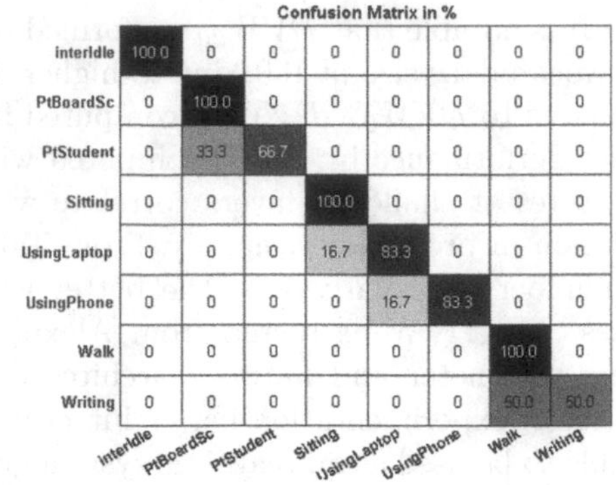

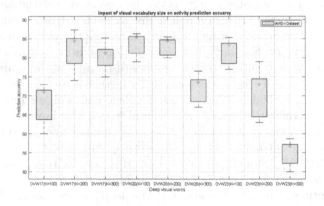

Confusion Matrix in %

	InterIdle	PtBoardSc	PtStudent	Sitting	UsingLaptop	UsingPhone	Walk	Writing
InterIdle	100.0	0	0	0	0	0	0	0
PtBoardSc	0	100.0	0	0	0	0	0	0
PtStudent	0	33.3	66.7	0	0	0	0	0
Sitting	0	0	0	100.0	0	0	0	0
UsingLaptop	0	0	0	16.7	83.3	0	0	0
UsingPhone	0	0	0	0	16.7	83.3	0	0
Walk	0	0	0	0	0	0	100.0	0
Writing	0	0	0	0	0	0	50.0	50.0

Fig. 4. Confusion matrix achieved from the deep BoDF representation of DVW_{20} [6] at vocabulary size of 100.

Fig. 5. Impact of visual vocabulary size on prediction accuracy.

Table 2. Evaluation of deep BoDF for instructor activity recognition at various network depth and vocabulary size.

	Propose technique	Time (hh:mm:ss)
1	Preprocessing and motion template generation	2:00:00
2	BoDF (training)	0:05:00
3	BoDF (testing)	0.43 s

4   Conclusion

In this paper, we have presented a BoDF method for instructor activity recognition. The deep model learns instructor activities through spatio-temporal deep features to form deep visual words. These deep visual words enable an SVM classifier to recognize the activities of the instructor. Such application is significant to understand the classroom contextual information and helpful for instructor self-evaluation. Through empirical analysis on network depth and different type of CNN model, reveals that AlexNet performs better than VGG19. The goal of our work is improved academic performance for societal gain rather than solely profit gain. As future work, we are focusing on instructor activities for self-evaluation of the instructor, and later on, we will analyze the behaviors, emotions of the instructor along with audience engagement for a more comprehensive evaluation of lecture effectiveness. For real time action recognition we will explore temporal action segmentation method [9], as instructors perform multiple activities sequentially. In conclusion, the availability of a commercial lecture effectiveness tool will enhance teachers' effectiveness and lifelong learning of instructors to overcome many classroom challenges.

Acknowledgements. Sergio A Velastin has received funding from the Universidad Carlos III de Madrid, the European Union's Seventh Framework Programme for research, technological development and demonstration under grant agreement no 600371, el Ministerio de Economía, Industria y Competitividad (COFUND2014-51509) el Ministerio de Educación, cultura y Deporte (CEI-15-17) and Banco Santander.

References

1. Hinton, G.E., Osindero, S., Teh, Y.W.: A fast learning algorithm for deep belief nets. Neural Comput. **18**(7), 1527–1554 (2006)
2. Ijjina, E.P., Chalavadi, K.M.: Human action recognition using genetic algorithms and convolutional neural networks. Pattern Recognit. **59**, 199–212 (2016)
3. Ji, S., Xu, W., Yang, M., Yu, K.: 3D convolutional neural networks for human action recognition. IEEE Trans. Pattern Anal. Mach. Intell. **35**(1), 221–231 (2013)
4. Kim, H.-J., Lee, J.S., Yang, H.-S.: Human action recognition using a modified convolutional neural network. In: Liu, D., Fei, S., Hou, Z., Zhang, H., Sun, C. (eds.) ISNN 2007. LNCS, vol. 4492, pp. 715–723. Springer, Heidelberg (2007). https://doi.org/10.1007/978-3-540-72393-6_85
5. Knol, M.H., Dolan, C.V., Mellenbergh, G.J., van der Maas, H.L.: Measuring the quality of university lectures: development and validation of the instructional skills questionnaire (ISQ). PloS One **11**(2), e0149163 (2016)
6. Krizhevsky, A., Sutskever, I., Hinton, G.E.: Imagenet classification with deep convolutional neural networks. In: Advances in Neural Information Processing Systems, pp. 1097–1105 (2012)
7. Li, W., Wen, L., Chang, M.C., Lim, S.N., Lyu, S.: Adaptive RNN tree for large-scale human action recognition. In: ICCV, pp. 1453–1461 (2017)
8. Murtaza, F., Yousaf, M.H., Velastin, S.A.: Multi-view human action recognition using 2D motion templates based on MHIS and their hog description. IET Comput. Vis. **10**(7), 758–767 (2016)
9. Murtaza, F., Yousaf, M.H., Velastin, S.A.: PMHI: proposals from motion history images for temporal segmentation of long uncut videos. IEEE Signal Process. Lett. **25**(2), 179–183 (2018)
10. Nazir, S., Yousaf, M.H., Nebel, J.C., Velastin, S.A.: A bag of expression framework for improved human action recognition. Pattern Recognit. Lett. **103**, 39–45 (2018)

11. Nazir, S., Yousaf, M.H., Velastin, S.A.: Evaluating a bag-of-visual features approach using spatio-temporal features for action recognition. Computers & Electrical Engineering (2018)

12. Ning, F., Delhomme, D., LeCun, Y., Piano, F., Bottou, L., Barbano, P.E.: Toward automatic phenotyping of developing embryos from videos. IEEE Trans. Image Process. **14**(9), 1360–1371 (2005)

13. O'Hara, S., Draper, B.A.: Introduction to the bag of features paradigm for image classification and retrieval. arXiv preprint arXiv:1101.3354 (2011)

14. Orrite, C., Rodriguez, M., Herrero, E., Rogez, G., Velastin, S.A.: Automatic segmentation and recognition of human actions in monocular sequences. In: 2014 22nd International Conference on Pattern Recognition (ICPR), pp. 4218–4223. IEEE (2014)

15. Raza, A., Yousaf, M.H., Sial, H.A., Raja, G.: HMM-based scheme for smart instructor activity recognition in a lecture room environment. SmartCR **5**(6), 578–590 (2015)

16. Simonyan, K., Zisserman, A.: Two-stream convolutional networks for action recognition in videos. In: Advances in Neural Information Processing Systems, pp. 568–576 (2014)

17. Simonyan, K., Zisserman, A.: Very deep convolutional networks for large-scale image recognition. arXiv preprint arXiv:1409.1556 (2014)

18. Wang, Y., Mori, G.: Human action recognition by semilatent topic models. IEEE Trans. Pattern Anal. Mach. Intell. **31**(10), 1762–1774 (2009)

19. Yousaf, M.H., Azhar, K., Sial, H.A.: A novel vision based approach for instructor's performance and behavior analysis. In: 2015 International Conference on Communications, Signal Processing, and Their Applications (ICCSPA), pp. 1–6. IEEE (2015)

20. Yousaf, M.H., Habib, H.A., Azhar, K.: Fuzzy classification of instructor morphological features for autonomous lecture recording system. Inf. J. **16**(8), 6367 (2013)

21. Zhu, F., Shao, L., Xie, J., Fang, Y.: From handcrafted to learned representations for human action recognition: a survey. Image Vis. Comput. **55**, 42–52 (2016)

A New Hybrid Architecture for Human Activity Recognition from RGB-D Videos

Srijan Das[1(✉)], Monique Thonnat[1], Kaustubh Sakhalkar[1], Michal Koperski[1], Francois Bremond[1], and Gianpiero Francesca[2]

[1] Inria, Sophia Antipolis, 2004 Rte des Lucioles, 06902 Valbonne, France
{srijan.das,monique.thonnat,kaustubh.sakhalkar,michal.koperski,
francois.bremond}@inria.fr
[2] Toyota Motor Europe, Hoge Wei 33, 1930 Zaventem, Belgium
gianpiero.francesca@toyota-europe.com

Abstract. Activity Recognition from RGB-D videos is still an open problem due to the presence of large varieties of actions. In this work, we propose a new architecture by mixing a high level handcrafted strategy and machine learning techniques. We propose a novel two level fusion strategy to combine features from different cues to address the problem of large variety of actions. As similar actions are common in daily living activities, we also propose a mechanism for similar action discrimination. We validate our approach on four public datasets, CAD-60, CAD-120, MSRDailyActivity3D, and NTU-RGB+D improving the state-of-the-art results on them.

Keywords: Activity recognition · RGB-D videos · Data fusion

1 Introduction

Action Recognition has been a popular problem statement in the vision community because of its large scale applications. In this paper, we focus on Activities of Daily Living (ADL) which can be used for monitoring hospital patients, smarthome applications and so on. We propose a new architecture aiming to be effective and efficient for ADL recognition from RGB-D videos. ADL recognition includes challenges such as viewpoint changes, occlusions, same environment and similar actions. Over time, with the development of technology, features used for action recognition have taken new strides from computing simple SIFT features to deep CNN features. The emergence of deep learning, inspired the authors in [10,13] to use CNN features for modeling the appearance of actions in video sequences. The introduction of cheap kinect sensors motivated the researchers to use 3 dimensional information of human poses to exploit the human skeleton geometry [16,23]. Our approach leverages the advantages of using handcrafted features along with features from deep networks. Compared to object detection, action recognition involves encoding object information involved in the action, pose information of the subject performing the action and their motion.

I. Kompatsiaris et al. (Eds.): MMM 2019, LNCS 11296, pp. 493–505, 2019.
https://doi.org/10.1007/978-3-030-05716-9_40

Time is also an important factor in this problem domain. Spatio-temporal contextual association is an important challenge to be explored. The diversity of actions in ADL makes the problem of action recognition complex. This problem can be solved by using different visual cues as in [17,24] where each cue is responsible for modeling actions of specific categories. Current approaches using multiple visual cues fail to achieve high performance rate and consistency in modeling the actions.

In this work, we propose an answer to the following questions:

1. Which visual cue is effective for which action?
2. How these visual cues should be combined in order to mitigate the disadvantages of each cue?
3. How to disambiguate similar actions?

In the following we will focus on three types of visual cues: appearance, pose and short-term motion. We propose a **novel two-level fusion strategy** to combine the features in a common feature space to appropriately model the actions. We also address the challenge of recognizing similar actions in daily living activities by proposing a mechanism for **similar action discrimination**.

2   Related Work on Action Recognition

Handcrafted Approaches - Earlier approaches on action recognition are based on extracting handcrafted features frame by frame and aggregating them to form a global representation of the video. Wang et al. in [19] propose to compute local descriptors around the dense trajectories to recognize actions and further improve the technique in [20] by subtracting the camera motion. These local descriptors are used with fisher vector encoding so as to have fixed size video descriptors. Handcrafted approaches demand resources in terms of time and expertise but at the same time they successfully capture the local temporal structure of the actions in the videos.

CNN Based Approaches - Following the breakthrough of convolutional neural networks (CNN) on object recognition [13], it is natural to extend them for videos. Early models extract CNN features from video frames and aggregates them with pooling for classifying by SVM. The authors in [5,8] use different body part patches to extract features from a convolutional network in order to recognize actions. The requirement to introduce spatio-temporal relationship in videos motivated the authors in [4] to use 3D convolutions. They use convolutional inflation in 2D networks expanding it to 3D. Such deep architectures successfully model the appearance but fail to model long-term motion. This motivates us to use such architectures to encode the color statistics.

RNN Based Approaches - RNNs being sequential models capture temporal information. In [9] temporal information is encoded using input from fc6 layer of convolutional network. With the advancement in camera technologies now, it is possible to get more accurate information from the scene including depth of the scene with the help of cameras like RGB-D sensors along with skeleton joints information. This motivates the authors in [7,16,23] to utilize 3D human geometry of the subject performing action using RNNs. LSTMs (special kind of RNN) being capable of understanding the human dynamics can model the pose based motion in a video. Such sequence models including variants like [7,16] have shown to successfully encode long-term temporal information which is an important aspect for recognizing ADL.

Multi-stream Fusion Based Approaches - It can be concluded from the aforementioned approaches that we need pose based motion, short term motion as well as appearance information for robust action recognition. The strategy of combining appearance and motion features in an early stage before classification as in [5,17,24] has been popular. This is because appearance and motion are complementary and their early fusion utilizes the correlation between features from different modalities. Thus making them more discriminative in common feature space rather than their individual feature space. The use of different modalities via a Markov chaining is proposed in [24]. The authors in [24] use pose, appearance and motion, fusing them in order to have a sequential refinement of action labels. But the drawback of such chaining models includes mutual dependence of the visual cues used for action classification. The existing studies on action recognition show the diversity of approaches and information used. This gives us a hint of different visual cues for modeling the actions along with eliminating the mutual dependence among them. Understanding the pose, appearance and motion of the subject performing the action in a video is important for action recognition. Thus, we focus on combining the pros of different visual cues with a learning strategy optimized for modeling ADL.

3   Feature Relevance Depending on Action Types

ADL consists of high variation of actions categories ranging from actions with similar poses like *stacking and unstacking objects, rubbing two hands and clapping,* actions with low motion like *typing keyboard, relaxing on couch,* and actions having temporal evolution of body dynamics like *walking, falling down* and so on. For optimizing action recognition it is important to establish a proper relationship between the nature of features and action categories to be modeled. For ADL, features corresponding to mainly three types of visual cues are widely used in the literature, say

- **appearance** modeling the spatial layout of the action videos from convolutional neural networks.
- **short-term motion** which is often computed through optical flow for instantaneous motion or based on short-term tracklets as in dense trajectories [19,20].
- **pose based motion** obtained from recurrent neural networks modeling the temporal evolution of 3D human body dynamics.

In Table 1, we show the importance of appearance based features for action recognition. We use the average number of local features of some actions from [11] to describe the motion of the actions. The 3rd column in Table 1 shows the difference in classification accuracy using appearance and short-term motion features (where $D = Accuracy$(Appearance)-$Accuracy$(Motion)). In Fig. 1, we show a comparison of action recognition accuracy for some actions using short-term and pose based motion. For dense trajectories, we do not use the HOG features (for this figure only) in order to neglect appearance and have a fair comparison with pose based motion features from LSTM. In spite of both features modeling the motion, the statistics in Fig. 1 shows the complementary nature of both the features and their relevance with temporal dynamics of the subject performing action.

Now, the remaining question is how to combine the features to take advantages from each visual cue? Early fusion is preferred when all the features characterize the actions because the correlation between them materialize in a precise level. If not, it is better to compute late fusion in order to balance the feature weights at the latest stage. So, in the next section we propose a two level fusion strategy to combine features at the most appropriate level depending on action categories.

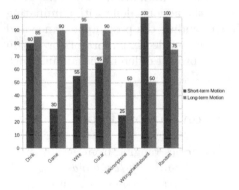

Fig. 1. Comparison of action recognition accuracy using short-term and pose based motion. Short-term motion is modeled by dense trajectories [19] and pose based motion is modeled by LSTM [7].

Table 1. Comparison of action recognition based on appearance and motion. The table shows average number of detected features using Dense Trajectories [19] taken from [11]. Third Column shows clear importance of appearance with little motion.

Action	Number of features	D
Relaxing on couch	1346	+100 %
Working on computer	1356	+50%
Still	1510	+75%
Talking on couch	2060	+50%
Drinking water	3079	−50%
Cooking (chopping)	4448	0%
Cooking (Stirring)	4961	0%
Brushing teeth	5527	−25%

4   Proposed Architecture for Action Recognition

In the following first, we describe the two level fusion strategy then we explain how to disambiguate similar actions. Figure 2 shows the overall architecture for the testing phase.

4.1 Two-Level Fusion Strategy

The first level of fusion (early) is intended to combine features in a balanced way to address actions which are characterized by most of the features. The second level of fusion (late) puts more emphasize on selection of features which are characterizing specific actions in a prominent manner.

For early fusion, we concatenate appearance (F_1) and short-term motion (F_2) leading to $F_x = [F_1, F_2]$ because they are often highly correlated. For late fusion, we put more importance on pose based motion because this feature is very complementary to the previous ones. Temporal information from poses is not discriminative for all the actions, so fusing temporal information at an early stage adds noise to the classifier. For actions like *relaxing on couch, talking on phone, writing on whiteboard* and so on temporal information may not be important. Thus encoding the vector which is representative of time in a video to a common feature space along with appearance and motion leads to common feature space where the actions are not discriminative. Thus we propose to fuse the pose based motion (F_3) features using a late fusion strategy where the fusion focuses on the individual strength of modalities.

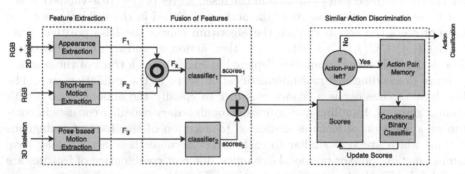

Fig. 2. Big picture of the architecture proposed to combine the features with two-level fusion strategy for the testing phase. The action-pair memory module keeps track of action pairs with high similarities. Such action pairs are forwarded to binary classifier to disambiguate the similar actions.

In the two-level fusion strategy, the fused representation of appearance and motion of a video F_x and the pose based motion representation of a video F_3 is input to two linear SVM classifiers. Classifiers clf_1 and clf_2 learn the mapping $\mathbb{X} \rightarrow \mathbb{Y}$, where $F_x \in \mathbb{X}$ for clf_1, $F_3 \in \mathbb{X}$ for clf_2 and $y \in \mathbb{Y}$ is a class label. For a given SVM parameter θ, the algorithm performs a parameter search on a large number of SVM parameter combinations to obtain the optimal value θ^*. So, θ_1^* and θ_2^* are the optimal SVM parameter of clf_1 and clf_2 respectively. The second level of fusion is performed on the test set by fusing the classification scores of the respective classifiers. For this, we introduce a fusion parameter α to balance the visual cues; α ranging between $[0, 1]$. Let $scores_1 = P(y|F_x, \theta_1^*)$ and $scores_2 = P(y|F_3, \theta_2^*)$ be the classification scores computed by clf_1 and

clf_2 respectively (see Fig. 2). Then the second level of fusion is performed by computing the action classification score s.

$$s = \alpha P(y|F_x, \theta_1^*) + (1 - \alpha)P(y|F_3, \theta_2^*) \tag{1}$$

A small value of α means that the temporal information is the dominant visual cue. Thanks to the fusion strategy, an optimized pool of features is extracted to feed the classifiers dedicated to the different action categories. See Sect. 6.2 for hyper-parameter α setting.

4.2   Similar Action Discrimination

Daily living action datasets contain similar actions like *stacking, unstacking objects; cleaning objects, taking food* and so on. Thus the classifier misclassifies similar action types and degrades its performance. So, we propose a mechanism for similar action discrimination consisting of a memory module and a binary classifier. The objective is to disambiguate similar actions by exploiting their predicted scores from the fusion phase. In the training stage, the algorithm checks the confused pair of actions in the fused scores of the cross-validation set. Let C be the confusion matrix of the actions classified in the validation set and a_r represents the action r, then the algorithm checks the false positives from C. If $C(i, j) + C(j, i) \geq \epsilon$ with $i \neq j$, then action a_i and a_j are misclassified. The action pair memory module depicted in Fig. 2 keeps a track of these action pairs in descending order of misclassification score in the validation step. The last level of classifier is a binary classifier to classify the actions (a_i, a_j) with similar gestures. Handling ambiguities through binary classifier consists in combining a selection of features dedicated to selection of small set of ambiguous actions which are very similar to each other. Because these actions may have similar motion, pose or temporal dynamics, different combination of features are used to classify the two ambiguous actions. Thus the action-pair memory module keeps track of which features to use or fuse for disambiguating the similar actions in the validation set. The feature or combination of features with maximum classification accuracy in the validation set is recorded in the action pair memory module. In the training phase, the action-pair memory module learns to record the similar action pairs along with the entity of features required to disambiguate them by a greedy approach from the cross-validation. See Sect. 6.2 for hyper-parameter ϵ setting.

In the testing phase, the classification scores are generated from the fusion phase (scores from the late fusion). The video samples with predicted labels from the scores obtained if present in the action pair module, are classified by a conditional binary classifier using the features mentioned in the action-pair memory module. The final classification score is updated from the classification score of the binary classifier and the same process is repeated unless all the confused action pairs undergo binary classification. This finite looping of discriminating similar actions in a binary classifier is bounded by the number of action-pairs recorded in the action-pair memory module in terms of time complexity. This strategy of employing conditional binary classifier is capable of discriminating similar actions which is a challenge in daily living applications.

5   Implementation Details

Feature Extraction - For *appearance extraction*, we use 2D convolutional features (from ResNet-152 pre-trained on ImageNet) from different body regions (cropped using pose information from Depth) of the subject as in [5]. In the case of availability of large training database, we also use 3D convolutional features from I3D [4] network. We use the strategy of selecting the most salient body part based features by employing a feature selection mechanism as in [7]. For *short-term motion extraction*, we use improved dense trajectories toolbox provided in [20]. Fisher vector representation of a video is obtained from its frame-level features using standard Mixture of Gaussians (MoG) model as described in [12]. For *pose based motion extraction*, we build a 3 layered stacked LSTM framework on the platform of keras toolbox [6] with TensorFlow [1]. Adam optimizer initialized with learning rate 0.005 is used to train the network. Parameters like Dropout, gradient clipping, number of neurons in each LSTM layer for each dataset are used as in [7]. The latent temporal representation of the skeleton sequence is extracted from the trained LSTM which is a concatenated feature vector of the output hidden states of the LSTM from each time step.

Fusion of Features - For $classfier_1$ and $classifier_2$, we use scikit-learn [15] implementation of SVM.

Similar Action Discrimination - This stage of disambiguating similar actions is implemented in *Python* with a scikit-learn [15] implementation of SVM for the binary classifier.

6   Experimental Analysis

6.1   Dataset Description

As discussed in the introduction, we are interested in daily living action recognition due to their application in health care and robotics. So, we have selected 4 public datasets which contain daily living actions to evaluate our architecture.

CAD-60 [18] - contains 60 RGB-D videos with 4 subjects performing 14 actions each. These actions are performed in 5 different environments: office, kitchen, bedroom, bathroom and living room.

CAD-120 [18] - contains 120 RGB-D videos with 4 different subjects performing 10 high level activities. Each action is repeated thrice with different objects. Actions with similar motion in this dataset make it more challenging.

MSRDailyActivity3D [21] - contains 320 RGB-D videos with 10 subjects performing 16 actions.

NTURGB+D [16] - contains 56880 RGB-D videos with 40 subjects performing 60 different actions. Samples are captured from 17 camera setups.

The standard evaluations on these datasets include Cross-Subject evaluation where the training and testing split is made either by leave-one-person out schema or split mentioned in the dataset (as in NTURGB+D). We are not focusing on Cross-View problem. Hence, we have not evaluated cross-view accuracy on NTURGB+D dataset.

6.2   Hyper-parameter Setting

Parameter α responsible for score fusion of classifiers clf_1 and clf_2 is trained in the Fusion of Features phase. This is done by globally searching the best value of α ranging between $[0, 1]$ for which the cross-validation data yields maximum action classification accuracy in the training phase. This trained α is used for testing. Parameter ϵ used for selecting confused action-pairs is handcrafted. Its value depends on the action categories present in the training samples. The value of ϵ is set manually in function of the confusion matrix during training of the second level fusion stage. The value of ϵ ranges from 0.1 for NTU-RGB+D to 0.44 for CAD-120.

6.3   Qualitative Results

In this section, we perform a qualitative evaluation of our two-level fusion strategy by visualizing the high dimensional data using t-SNE tool [14]. For instance in Fig. 3, we visualize the actions *drink* and *sitdown* using short-term motion, appearance, and their combination. From the figure, it is clear that the action groups are visually more discriminative using their combination. This depicts the effectiveness of using common feature space for appearance and short-term motion.

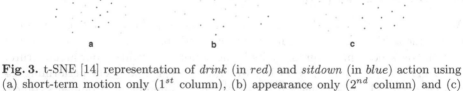

a   b   c

Fig. 3. t-SNE [14] representation of *drink* (in *red*) and *sitdown* (in *blue*) action using (a) short-term motion only (1st column), (b) appearance only (2nd column) and (c) both appearance and short-term motion (3rd column) where the actions are more discriminative as compared to their individual feature space. (Color figure online)

6.4   Quantitative Results

In this section, we report the action classification scores of the individual features along with their combination. Table 2 reports the action classification accuracy on three datasets CAD-60, CAD-120 and MSRDailyActivity3D using appearance, short-term and pose based motion. The performance obtained using different features are very data-dependent. For example, we get better results on MSR-DailyActivity3D using pose based motion, CAD-120 using short-term motion and CAD-60 using appearance features. Table 2 shows the importance of using the two-level fusion scheme which takes into account the advantages of all features by performing a late fusion of appearance, short-term motion with pose based motion. This is shown by comparing our fusion strategy with naive early fusion of all features. Our proposed fusion outperforms the former as depicted in Table 2.

Table 2. Ablation study on how each feature performs individually and with different combination techniques for action classification on CAD-60, CAD-120 and MSRDaily-Activity3D. In early fusion, we fused all the features with $l2-$ normalization and proposed fusion is our two-level fusion strategy. $MSR3D$ signifies MSRDailyActivity3D, F_1 is appearance, F_2 is short-term motion and F_3 is pose based motion.

Dataset	F_1 (2D-CNN)	F_2 (IDT)	F_3 (LSTM)	$F_1 + F_2$	$F_1 + F_2 + F_3$ Early fusion	Proposed fusion
CAD-60	**89.70**	72.05	67.64	95.58	70.58	**98.53**
CAD-120	72.58	**79.84**	63.70	83.06	63.70	**87.90**
MSR3D	80.93	81.87	**91.56**	90	91.56	**97.81**

6.5   Effect of Using the Mechanism of Similar Action Discrimination

This section presents an ablation study on the similar action discrimination mechanism and how the action-pair module works. In Table 3, we show the confused actions with their corresponding misclassification rate in CAD-120 for every subject based splits. The action-pair module keeps a track of the confusing actions which are classified separately in a binary classifier which is also a linear SVM. For CAD-120, IDT+FV (short-term motion along with appearance because of presence of the HOG) discriminates the confused action pairs with 100% accuracy. The drawback of this module includes its thorough dependency on cross-validation set. This drawback is depicted in Table 3 where the cross-validation fails to capture confused action pairs like *cleaning objects and taking food* (in 3rd row, left). Table 3 reports the action classification accuracy on all the datasets used before and after applying the action-pair module. This module does not have any effect on CAD-60 and MSRDailyActivity3D on which the actions are already classified with remarkable accuracy.

Table 3. Action-pair memory content for different splits in CAD-120 (on *left*). Each split signifies cross-actor setup for classification evaluation. The second column represents the action pairs confused among each other with their summation of misclassification accuracy in third column (in validation set). Improvement in action classification accuracy on using conditional binary classifier for all the datasets used (on *right*). *MSR3D* signifies MSRDailyActivity3D.

split	Action Pairs	$C(i,j)+$ $C(j,i)$
1	*cleaning object* and *taking food*	0.44
1	*stacking* and *unstacking objects*	0.67
2	*cleaning object* and *taking food*	0.66
2	*stacking* and *unstacking objects*	0.66
3	*stacking* and *unstacking objects*	0.55
4	*cleaning object* and *taking food*	0.55
4	*stacking* and *unstacking objects*	0.44

Dataset	Acc. before binary classifier	Acc. after binary classifier
CAD-60	98.52 %	98.52 %
CAD-120	87.90%	94.40 %
MSR3D	97.81%	97.81 %
NTU-RGB+D	84.95 %	87.09 %

6.6   State-of-the-Art Comparison

In this section, we compare our action classification performance with the state-of-the-art. Our proposed two-level fusion along with action-pair module outperforms the existing methods on all the datasets as described in Table 4.

NTU-RGB+D is a relatively large dataset and is suitable for using deeper models. In order to show the robustness of our framework, we use I3D [4] to model the appearance instead of using 2D CNN [7] and report **92.2%** accuracy (illustrated by *ProposedMethod + I3D*). This performance boosting is because I3D can model better appearance information (90.4%) for large available data than 2D CNN architecture.

6.7   Runtime Analysis

The fully automated architecture has been trained on two GTX 1080 Ti GPUs (each for extracting RGB based video descriptors from CNN network and training LSTM on skeleton sequences) and a single CPU (for extracting IDT features with fisher vector encoding) in parallel. IDT being computationally expensive (with a processing speed of less than 4 fps) decides the computational time involved in the feature extraction process. The proposed architecture including the fusion strategy along with the action-pair module only takes as additional cost 10 ms time delay for a forward pass of an image frame on a single CPU.

Table 4. Recognition Accuracy comparison for CAD-60 , CAD-120, MSRDailyActivity3D (Performance of baseline is taken from [7,8,12] respectively) and NTU-RGB+D dataset.

Method	Accuracy [%]	Method	Accuracy [%]
CAD-60		*MSRDailyActivity3D*	
Object Affordance	71.40	Actionlet Ensemble	85.80
HON4D	72.70	RGGP + fusion	85.60
Actionlet Ensemble	74.70	MSLF	85.95
MSLF	80.36	DCSF + joint	88.20
JOULE-SVM	84.10	JOULE-SVM	95.00
P-CNN + kinect + Pose machines	95.58	Range Sample	95.60
Proposed Method	**98.52**	DSSCA-SSLM	97.50
		Proposed Method	**97.81**
CAD-120		*NTU-RGB+D*	
Salient Proto-Objects	78.20	Geometric features [23]	70.26
TDD	80.38	VA-LSTM [22]	79.4
SVM + CNN	78.30	CMN [24]	80.8
STS	84.20	STA-hands [2]	82.5
Object Affordance	84.70	Glimpse Clouds [3]	86.6
MSLF	85.48	**Proposed Method**	**87.09**
R-HCRF	89.80	**Proposed Method (with I3D)**	**92.20**
RSVM + LCNN	90.10		
Proposed Method	**94.40**		

7   Conclusion

In this paper, we have proposed a new architecture for action recognition mixing a high level fusion strategy and machine learning techniques. The proposed hybrid architecture is fully automated enabling the hyper-parameters except ϵ to learn themselves. We justify the use of this two-level fusion mechanism by qualitative and quantitative analysis. We also propose an action-pair memory module to disambiguate similar actions. Our proposed effective and efficient action recognition architecture improves the state-of-the-art on four publicly available datasets.

We emphasize the fact that the existing features are quite capable of distinguishing the daily living activities if combined in a strategic way. The quality of recognition rate achieved in this work ranging from 87% to 98% is satisfactory. A future direction of this work can be to eliminate the handcrafted use of ϵ to record the confused action pairs. This can be done by a technique of regression on the confusion matrix in the training phase.

References

1. Abadi, M., et al.: TensorFlow: large-scale machine learning on heterogeneous systems (2015). Software available from tensorflow.org. https://www.tensorflow.org/
2. Baradel, F., Wolf, C., Mille, J.: Human action recognition: pose-based attention draws focus to hands. In: 2017 IEEE International Conference on Computer Vision Workshops (ICCVW), pp. 604–613, October 2017
3. Baradel, F., Wolf, C., Mille, J., Taylor, G.W.: Glimpse clouds: human activity recognition from unstructured feature points. In: The IEEE Conference on Computer Vision and Pattern Recognition (CVPR), June 2018
4. Carreira, J., Zisserman, A.: Quo vadis, action recognition? A new model and the kinetics dataset. In: 2017 IEEE Conference on Computer Vision and Pattern Recognition (CVPR), pp. 4724–4733. IEEE (2017)
5. Cheron, G., Laptev, I., Schmid, C.: P-CNN: pose-based CNN features for action recognition. In: ICCV (2015)
6. Chollet, F., et al.: Keras (2015). https://github.com/fchollet/keras
7. Das, S., Koperski, M., Bremond, F., Francesca, G.: A fusion of appearance based CNNs and temporal evolution of skeleton with LSTM for daily living action recognition. ArXiv e-prints, February 2018
8. Das, S., Koperski, M., Bremond, F., Francesca, G.: Action recognition based on a mixture of RGB and depth based skeleton. In: AVSS (2017)
9. Donahue, J., et al.: Long-term recurrent convolutional networks for visual recognition and description. In: The IEEE Conference on Computer Vision and Pattern Recognition (CVPR), June 2015
10. Karpathy, A., Toderici, G., Shetty, S., Leung, T., Sukthankar, R., Fei-Fei, L.: Large-scale video classification with convolutional neural networks. In: CVPR (2014)
11. Koperski, M.: Human action recognition in videos with local representation. Ph.D. thesis, University COTE D'AZUR (2017)
12. Koperski, M., Bremond, F.: Modeling spatial layout of features for real world scenario RGB-D action recognition. In: AVSS (2016)
13. Krizhevsky, A., Sutskever, I., Hinton, G.E.: Imagenet classification with deep convolutional neural networks. In: NIPS (2012)
14. van der Maaten, L., Hinton, G.E.: Visualizing data using t-SNE (2008). https://lvdmaaten.github.io/tsne/
15. Pedregosa, F., et al.: Scikit-learn: machine learning in Python. J. Mach. Learn. Res. **12**, 2825–2830 (2011)
16. Shahroudy, A., Liu, J., Ng, T.T., Wang, G.: NTU RGB+D: a large scale dataset for 3D human activity analysis. In: The IEEE Conference on Computer Vision and Pattern Recognition (CVPR), June 2016
17. Simonyan, K., Zisserman, A.: Two-stream convolutional networks for action recognition in videos. In: Advances in Neural Information Processing Systems, pp. 568–576 (2014)
18. Sung, J., Ponce, C., Selman, B., Saxena, A.: Unstructured human activity detection from RGBD images. In: ICRA (2012)
19. Wang, H., Kläser, A., Schmid, C., Liu, C.L.: Action recognition by dense trajectories. In: IEEE Conference on Computer Vision & Pattern Recognition, Colorado Springs, United States, pp. 3169–3176, June 2011
20. Wang, H., Schmid, C.: Action recognition with improved trajectories. In: IEEE International Conference on Computer Vision, Australia, Sydney (2013)

21. Wu, Y.: Mining actionlet ensemble for action recognition with depth cameras. In: CVPR (2012)
22. Zhang, P., Lan, C., Xing, J., Zeng, W., Xue, J., Zheng, N.: View adaptive recurrent neural networks for high performance human action recognition from skeleton data. In: The IEEE International Conference on Computer Vision (ICCV), October 2017
23. Zhang, S., Liu, X., Xiao, J.: On geometric features for skeleton-based action recognition using multilayer LSTM networks. In: 2017 IEEE Winter Conference on Applications of Computer Vision (WACV), pp. 148–157, March 2017
24. Zolfaghari, M., Oliveira, G.L., Sedaghat, N., Brox, T.: Chained multi-stream networks exploiting pose, motion, and appearance for action classification and detection. In: 2017 IEEE International Conference on Computer Vision (ICCV), pp. 2923–2932. IEEE (2017)

Utilizing Deep Object Detector for Video Surveillance Indexing and Retrieval

Tom Durand[1,2], Xiyan He[1], Ionel Pop[1(✉)], and Lionel Robinault[1]

[1] Foxstream, 69120 Vaulx-en-Velin, France
{x.he,i.pop,l.robinault}@foxstream.fr
[2] INSA-Lyon, 69621 Villeurbanne cedex, France
tom.durand@insa-lyon.fr

Abstract. Intelligent video surveillance is one of the most challenging tasks in computer vision due to high requirements for reliability, real-time processing and robustness on low resolution videos. In this paper we propose solutions to those challenges through a unified system for indexing and retrieval based on recent discoveries in deep learning. We show that a single stage object detector such as YOLOv2 can be used as a very efficient tool for event detection, key frame selection and scene recognition. The motivation behind our approach is that the feature maps computed by the deep detector encode not only the category of objects present in the image, but also their locations, eliminating automatically background information. We also provide a solution to the low video quality problem with the introduction of a light convolutional network for object description and retrieval. Preliminary experimental results on different video surveillance datasets demonstrate the effectiveness of the proposed system.

Keywords: Video surveillance · Event detection
Key frame selection · Video indexing · Video retrieval

1 Introduction

Video surveillance systems aim to find a reliable way to identify and recognize particular events in real time, such as the detection of an intrusive person near an industrial area or retrieval tasks as queries for a specific vehicle on a car park. Those cases can be easily recognized by human (though laborious) but it is harder to make the camera be able to interpret them. The efficiency of such systems relies on trade-offs between accuracy, speed, video quality and the overall price of the installation. These special characteristics, coupled with the massive amount of data to treat, make video indexing and retrieval quite difficult in the domain of video surveillance.

Supported by Foxstream: http://www.foxstream.fr.

I. Kompatsiaris et al. (Eds.): MMM 2019, LNCS 11296, pp. 506–518, 2019.
https://doi.org/10.1007/978-3-030-05716-9_41

In traditional video surveillance industry, methods based on motion detection and foreground objects extraction are preferred mainly due to their low computational cost. Background modeling [23] and/or motion analysis [9] are often considered as a prerequisite step of a video analysis system. The scene characterization usually comes after by various components like structure analysis (event detection, film segmentation, key frame selection, etc.), features extraction (key frame features, object features, etc. [22]) and classification to build the indexing and retrieval system [8]. This can be really efficient in terms of speed and precision, especially for high resolution videos without sudden changes. However, they struggle in the cases where differences between foreground objects are not clear.

Recent advances in machine learning have led to the widespread use of deep learning methods in various domains [12]. The philosophy behind is to directly go after the interpretation through quite greedy architectures [24] in order to recognize patterns targeted by the system. However, the power needed to run the best existing deep models hinders their development in real world applications such as video surveillance. One of the pioneer work on video indexing and retrieval based on deep learning was proposed by Podlesnaya and Podlesnyy for cinema applications [17]. The authors showed the possibility to use features extracted by a simple deep CNN as a basis for a video indexing and retrieval system. In [26], an object detection oriented feature pooling method is proposed for video semantic indexing. First, multiple feature vectors, each corresponding to a bounding box are extracted by Faster R-CNN [21]. These feature vectors are pooled together according to their position, the size or the aspect ratio of their bounding boxes. Multiple SVM classifiers are then trained, each with the classical CNN features and one type of the pooled features. The final indexing is obtained by a weighted combination of the scores from all the individual SVM. Using only deep features within the proposed bounding boxes can remove some background information. However, the pooling of all the feature vectors disregards information with respect to each object, resulting in less semantic features for indexing. Moreover, these raw deep features do not always fit with the quality offered by video surveillance cameras, as shown in [27].

In this paper, we develop a unified deep detector based video indexing and retrieval framework for applications in the video surveillance field. We bring the possibility to use a single stage object detector like YOLOv2 [19] as a very efficient tool for motion detection, scene interpretation, video indexing and retrieval while maintaining a very low computational cost. We also introduce the possibility to use a tiny convolutional neural network (CNN) on top of an object detector predictions in order to make object retrieval tasks doable, dealing with the low resolution issues. The remainder of this paper is organized as follows. Section 2 presents the proposed framework for video indexing and retrieval. Section 3 focuses on efficient event detection based on deep object detectors. Sections 4 and 5 describe the efficient video indexing and retrieval system, with details of the proposed tiny CNN. Section 6 presents some comparative experiments on different video surveillance datasets. We draw conclusion and future work in Sect. 7.

2   A Simple, Unified Framework

Figure 1 presents the global architecture of the framework proposed in this paper. Considering a video file as input we first subsample the images it contains and then apply a single stage object detector, as the well-known YOLOv2 in our case, to extract a feature map for each of them. These feature maps represent the real basis needed for an efficient system since they can serve for both the indexing and the retrieval tasks with very promising results. The indexing relies on a classic shots extraction followed by key frames selection and description. For this purpose we first measure the similarities between frames using the obtained feature maps to achieve the events detection segmentation and determine shots boundaries. Then, we select key frames to summarize each shot based on the object predictions coming from the feature maps. The objects present in those key frames are also extracted and their feature map is computed thanks to the tiny CNN we introduced, dealing with the low resolution issue faced in video surveillance systems. In the end the information stored per shot are the prediction results for each frames in the shot, the features maps of the key frames and the features maps of the objects in them.

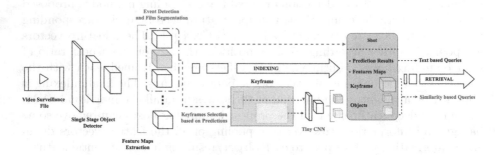

Fig. 1. The proposed deep object detector based video indexing and retrieval framework.

The retrieval step can then easily be done either for scene recognition by comparing feature maps obtained with the deep detector, or for object recognition through the features extracted from our light network. Note that the proposed system can also accomplish text based retrieval for object or scene queries relying on the detector predictions, which will not be detailed in this paper. The following parts will focus on our main contributions, going through video indexing and retrieval to make the best of the features maps obtained from a deep detector and to work efficiently with low resolution videos with the help of a tiny CNN.

3   A Smart and Robust Event Detector

In video surveillance context we are particularly interested in the event detection efficiency because it is the first step of every algorithm. An event is defined as the apparition of a new object or at least of an interesting movement in the scene. Deep object detectors [3,5,6,13,14,18–21] could be a good solution to this problem by directly detecting special events. However, the prediction results of a deep detector may be unreliable because of possible omissions or false predictions. Methods combining deep detectors with temporal dimension [16,28] are powerful tools for video analysis. A main disadvantage of these methods is that they are too expensive to train and run on real systems because of the computing power and the amount of data required.

In the proposed system, we tried to use the feature maps computed by an object detector as the basis of a motion detector. The YOLOv2 [19], which is one of the fastest and the most accurate algorithm, is employed as the deep detector. The motivation behind our approach is that the features of an object detector should be very sensitive to the apparition of a new object or to a movement. Indeed, even if the final prediction will filter weak predictions, they will still be responsible for some variations in the image feature map.

We choose this feature map to be the output of the last YOLOv2 layer, the one right before the interpretation of the results. By doing this we assure a relatively high resistance to the noise but also a high sensibility to the present objects, their category and their position. This is also a way to keep a relatively low feature map dimension ($13 \times 13 \times 425$ with YOLOv2) compared to previous convolutional layers. The cosine distance is used as the similarity metric as it shows better performances compared to other distances (like the euclidean one) in our experiments. Consecutive frames producing distances higher than the threshold are interpreted as frames containing events and are grouped into shots.

4   Efficient Indexing

4.1   Key Frame Selection

The objective of the proposed key frame selection is to have each object in the shot to appear at least once on the selected key frame in order to make the object retrieval task possible, keeping as fewest redundancy as possible. As presented in Sect. 3, in the proposed system shot boundaries are determined by grouping consecutive frames where events occurred. The process of key frame selection is as follows. We select key frame by comparing frames one by one in a recursive procedure. If the total number of objects present in a frame A is greater than that in frame B, then frame A is considered as the main frame. Furthermore, if all the objects present in frame B are also recognized as present in the main frame A, then the frame B will be deleted from the candidate key frame set. Letting (x_A, y_A) and (x_B, y_B) be the center coordinates of the bounding box of an object in each frame, with C_A and C_B the predicted class of the object, the criterion to determine whether an object in frame B is also present in frame A can be written as follows:

$$P_{objA=objB} = \begin{cases} 1, & \text{if} \quad \sqrt{(x_A - x_B)^2 + (y_A - y_B)^2} < T \quad \text{and} \quad C_A = C_B \\ 0, & otherwise \end{cases} \quad (1)$$

where T is a predefined threshold. Note that by using this selection procedure, one or more key frames may be selected for a single shot.

4.2   A Tiny CNN for Low Resolution Videos

One of the biggest limitation in the development of intelligent video surveillance is the ability to exploit very low quality images, especially for the case of object retrieval in a scene. It can be hard, even for human, to recognize a particular car model or to confirm that a person already appeared in the video. The results in the MIO-TCD (MIOvision Traffic Camera Dataset) competition [15] demonstrate that classic object detectors such as YOLOv2 or SSD [14] provide really good results but deeper models are the solution to detect and differentiate vehicle types, even from quite low quality images. The actual best accuracy is obtained by the method of Jung *et al.* [11], in which an ensemble of several ResNet architectures are combined to state about the class of the vehicles. However, the idea of an ensemble of ResNet results in a long execution time which is not applicable in practice for a video surveillance system. Besides, as shown in [27], very deep models aren't always the best solution to deal with low resolution problems. The work realized in [27] showed that low resolution recognition can benefit from higher resolution image training. The combination of layers obtained from both low and high resolution based trainings leads to very impressive performances for different low resolution recognition tasks. However it is supposed that images of high quality are available for training, which is not the case in the context of video surveillance.

We introduce a new light CNN based on the GoogleNet architecture [24], avoiding any super resolution tricks [2] and requiring only very few parameters to train. The objective is to extract relevant features for recognizing similar objects through different key frames in the video, in which objects may appear with very low resolution. In our case, we want to be able to work with different resolutions, not for a classification purpose but for an effective feature extraction. We solve this situation by proposing a light model that is able to catch discriminative features for images from both low and high resolution origin. The idea is to take advantage of different filter sizes for more flexibility in the input resolution and compress the information about the objects to a very low dimension: (1×96), as shown in Fig. 2. The proposed light convolutional neural network is composed of two inception modules in cascade. In the context of video surveillance, very few data is usually available for training. With batch normalization [10] between each convolution layers, we avoid any overfitting and improve the generalization ability of the network. We use exclusively convolutional and pooling layers

directly before the classification layer in order to force the network to learn efficient filters, keeping the number of parameters low compared to the use of fully
connected layers. The resulting low inference time is a huge asset considering the
massive amount of data in video surveillance databases. More precision about
the training and the retrieval results can be found in the experiments section.

4.3   Indexing

One advantage of the use of an object detector in our system is that it provides
the categories and the confidence scores for the objects present in the shot as
well as their absolute and relative positions. The proposed indexing system is a
combination of:

- semantic indexing, that is all the prediction results of the deep detector for
  all the frames in a shot,
- high dimensional indexing, that is the feature maps obtained by the deep
  detector of the key frames and the feature maps obtained by the tiny CNN of
  each object (by considering only the region in the bounding box) in the key
  frames.

Keeping this list of key frame characteristics per shot simplifies and increases
substantially the relevance in indexing with a deep detector.

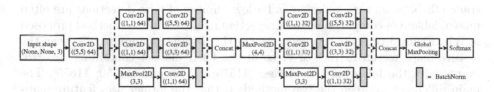

Fig. 2. The architecture of our tiny CNN.

5   A Retrieval System Based on Features Similarities

Image content based retrieval has become more desirable compared to text based
retrieval due to the fact that the latter relies solely on the annotation of each
image, which may be incomplete and subjective.

Feature maps extracted by a deep detector present a high discriminant power
chiefly due to their strong ability to extract precise information about all the
objects in the scene. This ability to catch the global content of the scene in terms
of objects is a very strong asset to perform the scene recognition. Considering an
input image of a scene, we compute its feature map with the deep detector and
use the key frames' feature maps from the database to retrieve similar situations.
We use the cosine distance to measure the similarity between feature maps.

Even if all feature maps of the key frames are already computed, this can be quite expensive to retrieve a scene if we need to compute the distance from each of them for a huge database. Predictions results can then help to filter out some shots and key frames before the comparison. For the query of an object image, we simply compare the object feature maps obtained by the tiny CNN of the input image with those of the same category of each key frame in the database.

6   Experiments

For the sake of space limitation, in this section we present only experimental results obtained for the main parts of our framework on two color video surveillance datasets, including the dataset provided by the PUT (Poznan University of Technology) [4] and a dataset captured on a parking entrance (named CPD (Car Park Database)). Both datasets contain video sequences captured by fixed cameras during daytime and exhibit natural lighting variations. Details of each dataset will be described in the related experiments. Note that the ground truths of each task are all annotated manually. All experiments were conducted on a PC with a single NVIDIA Titan Xp GPU.

6.1   Event Detection

A good event detection algorithm should be able to detect all interesting movements in a sequence and filter out the undesired ones. In real-world applications, trade-offs between zero omission and a low number of false detections are often unavoidable. We compare our event detection method with the method proposed in [17]. Figure 3 presents a general case of the distances computed between the feature maps for an extract of video of the CPD dataset containing two real events with the following boundaries: [11575; 11730] and [11750; 11855]. The main difference between the two methods is that the former uses feature maps generated by a deep detector YOLOv2 whereas the latter employs feature vectors obtained from the last global pooling layer of the Inception network (here we use the latest version Inceptionv3 [25], which gives feature vectors of size (1×2048)). We note thus in the figure the results of the two methods by YOLOv2 and Inceptionv3 respectively to illustrate this difference. No fine tuning was done, we used the weights obtained on a COCO training for YOLOv2 [19] and an ImageNet training for Inceptionv3. We set the threshold for both methods as the value which ensures the detection of each event as soon as it appears in the scene. Note that the value of the threshold depends on the camera and the extracted features. In practice, we find that the value 0.001 works well for all scenes for YOLOv2 and the value 0.0015 works well for InceptionV3. From the figure, we can see that for both of the approaches we can easily get zero omission. We can also observe three small peaks on the figure due to camera shaking or quick illumination changes and YOLOv2 is far less sensible to those variations. Visually InceptionV3 has the drawback to lead to more false detections that are hardly filtered with a simple threshold approach as opposed to YOLOv2. This illustrates well that an single stage object detector gives more importance about the global context with the objects' positions and consequently detect better the apparitions of new elements.

6.2   Key Frame Selection

In order to evaluate our key frame selection method we first used the publicly available PUT database. This dataset is composed of 3 sequences captured in traffic surveillance context with a lot of movements and objects, making the key frame selection challenging. The ground truth key frames are selected manually according to the following criteria:

- Every object present in the shot needs to be on at least one key frame.
- The number of key frames per shot is minimised by keeping only the ones with the most number of objects.

Figure 4 presents the obtained results on the 3 sequences. For each sequence, ground truth key frames are on the first line and key frames selected by our algorithm are on the second one. We can see that for Sequence 1 (Fig. 4a) the last key frame containing a new person on the right is missed. This is due to the fact that the recursive selection procedure recognizes one person has already been present at this location on a selected key frame which contains a bigger number of objects. All ground truth key frames for the other two sequences are selected successfully by our method. An additional frame is selected for the sequence 3 because a person (highlighted in the pink square in Fig. 4c) was omitted by YOLOv2 predictions on the third key frame.

With the same process we evaluate the overall precision of our algorithm on a 1.5 h long video containing 100 events of the CPD dataset. Suppose that a ground truth key frame has the time index t, we use a time margin of 1 s to define true positive selection. That is, if a selected key frame has a time index belonging to the interval $[t-1, t+1]$, then it is considered as true positive.

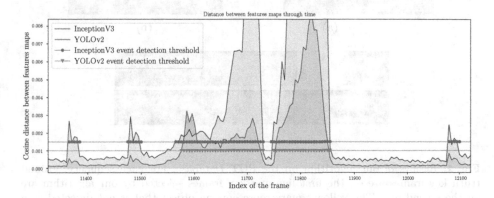

Fig. 3. Distance between feature maps computed for YOLOv2 and Inceptionv3.

We obtained 89.7% of the 117 ground truth key frames. On a total of 194 objects present on the targeted key frames only 3 were missing, proving the relevance of our approach.

6.3   Retrieval

We evaluate the object retrieval task in the context of a video surveillance system for vehicle and pedestrian recognition. In order to demonstrate the effectiveness of feature maps obtained by the proposed tiny CNN for low resolution object recognition, we compare our method with features extracted by two methods.

– Fisher Vector [22], which has shown significant performances in video indexing and retrieval tasks [1]. In contrast to deep learning based method, FV is an attractive choice when only limited training samples are available.
– ResNet50 [7], which has demonstrated record breaking performances on a variety of tasks, especially on the MIO-TCD challenge, as mentioned in Sect. 4.2.

Both tiny CNN and ResNet50 were pre-trained on the MIO-TCD Dataset [15] and fine-tuned on the CPD training dataset. The MIO-TCD dataset is considered as the largest traffic dataset which is composed of images of 11 categories acquired at different times by traffic surveillance cameras. The CPD dataset consists of videos, up to a duration of about 15 min, captured continuously during one month on a car park entrance. The CPD training set is composed of 930 images split in 6 categories (car, person, truck, bicycle, motorbike, rest) with

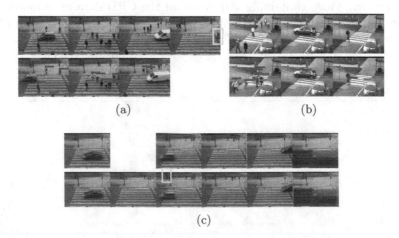

(a)   (b)

(c)

Fig. 4. Results of our algorithm on the PUT Database. For each sequence, ground truth key frames are on the first line and key frames selected by our algorithm are on the second one. The yellow square represents an object that is not detected as a new one by our algorithm and the pink square corresponds to a YOLOv2 omission. (a) Sequence 1; (b) Sequence 2; (c) Sequence 3. (Color figure online)

the following corresponding percentages: (39.14, 32.04, 13.66, 3.12, 1.72, 10.32).
Note that the category "rest", contains only negative examples, has been added
with the purpose of improving the recognition performance. Various data aug-
mentations have been performed to the data, such as rotation, shift, zoom and
horizontal flip, after a simple normalization preprocessing. The Fisher Vector
method was trained only on CPD training dataset due to the expensive memory
access in Fisher Vector computing. Objects sizes (bounding box sizes obtained by
the deep detector) vary from around (10×30) to (100×200). For our tiny CNN
and Fisher Vector we resize the ROI corresponding to each object to (64×64)
and for ResNet50 to (200×200) in order to have a size big enough to go through
all layers. The feature vectors extracted have a size of (1×96) for our light CNN
and (1×2048) for ResNet50, taking for both the output of the last global pooling layer. Around 7 h of videos of the CPD dataset have been selected as the
retrieval database.

The object retrieval results of each method are presented in Table 1. The precision measure is computed as the percentage of objects from the same category
as the queried one within the top 5 results. The relevance measure is defined
as the percentage of pertinent results among the top 5 results based on human
interpretation. Taking a query of a red car for example, a blue car in the retrieval
results would be counted in the precision measure (the same category) whereas
it would not be considered as relevant (not red) for the relevance measure. The
test query images are either selected from video files of the CPD dataset different from the 7 h retrieval database or downloaded via google image research. It
can be observed that ResNet50 performs the best in terms of precision, showing
its strong ability to extract category related features. Our proposed tiny CNN

Table 1. Results on the object retrieval task of different methods.

Methods	Fisher Vector	ResNet50	Tiny-CNN
Precision	21.3	**57.5**	46.3
Relevance	10	32.5	**36.3**
Inference Time (ms)	38	28	**6**
Number of Parameters	/	25M	**48K**

Table 2. Retrieval relevance per category of different methods.

Methods	Fisher vector	ResNet50	Tiny-CNN
Car	10	40	**60**
Truck	13.3	26.7	**40**
Bicycle	6.7	6.7	6.7
Motorcycle	0	**13.3**	6.7
People	20	**73.3**	60

has the best performance in terms of relevance. This demonstrates well that our proposed method is able to recognize the most relevant features for object retrieval. In addition, the tiny CNN is about 4.67 times faster than ResNet50, which is a crucial advantage in real time applications. Table 2 shows the details of the retrieval relevance per category of different methods. We can see that the imbalanced proportion of examples of different categories in the training set plays an important role in the performance of the retrieval task. Both tiny CNN and ResNet50 outperform significantly the standard Fisher Vector method for almost all the categories except for the class of bicycle, for which all the three methods perform equally. This may be due to the fact that the class bicycle has a limited amount of training samples. For the class motorbike which has an extremely small training set, Fisher vector failed to find relevant results whereas both deep learning methods benefit from pre-training on a larger dataset and perform better.

7   Future Work

In this paper we have presented a unified deep learning based video indexing and retrieval framework in the context of video surveillance. We show that the feature maps and the predictions obtained from a single stage object detector can be very efficient for video segmentation, indexing and retrieval tasks. A tiny convolutional neural network has also been proposed in order to improve the performance of the system for low-resolution videos. Several preliminary tests have been executed on the PUT and the CPD color video surveillance datasets. It is an important part of our future work to conduct detailed experimental analysis of each part of the proposed general video indexing and retrieval system. In our method we only tested the behavior of the YOLOv2 object detector but new architectures [13,20] may lead to better results. Moreover, we use one light CNN that shows good trade-offs between speed and accuracy for object retrieval. Further improvements may be obtained by using an ensemble strategy as in [11].

References

1. Awad, G., Snoek, C.G.M., Smeaton, A.F., Quénot, G.: Trecvid semantic indexing of video: a 6-year retrospective. ITE Trans. Media Technol. Appl. **4**(3), 187–208 (2016)
2. Dong, C., Loy, C.C., He, K., Tang, X.: Image super-resolution using deep convolutional networks. IEEE Trans. Pattern Anal. Mach. Intell. **38**(2), 295–307 (2016)
3. Fu, C.Y., Liu, W., Ranga, A., Tyagi, A., Berg, A.C.: DSSD : deconvolutional single shot detector. arXiv preprint arXiv:1701.06659 (2017)
4. Fularz, M., Kraft, M., Schmidt, A., Niechciał, J.: The PUT surveillance database. In: Choraś, R.S. (ed.) Image Processing and Communications Challenges 7. AISC, vol. 389, pp. 73–79. Springer, Cham (2016). https://doi.org/10.1007/978-3-319-23814-2_9
5. Girshick, R.B.: Fast r-cnn. In: ICCV, pp. 1440–1448. IEEE Press, Santiago (2015)

6. He, K., Gkioxari, G., Dollár, P., Girshick, R.B.: Mask R-CNN. In: ICCV, pp. 2980–2988. IEEE Press, Venise (2017)
7. He, K., Zhang, X., Ren, S., Sun, J.: Deep residual learning for image recognition. In: CVPR, pp. 770–778. IEEE Press, Las Vegas (2016)
8. Hu, W., Xie, N., Li, L., Zeng, X., Maybank, S.: A survey on visual content-based video indexing and retrieval. IEEE Trans. Syst. Man Cybern. Part C (Appl. Rev.) 41(6), 797–819 (2011)
9. Hu, W., Tan, T., Wang, L., Maybank, S.: A survey on visual surveillance of object motion and behaviors. IEEE Trans. Syst. Man Cybern. Part C (Appl. Rev.) 34(3), 334–352 (2004)
10. Ioffe, S., Szegedy, C.: Batch normalization: accelerating deep network training by reducing internal covariate shift. In: ICML, pp. 448–456. JMLR.org (2015)
11. Jung, H., Choi, M.K., Jung, J., Lee, J.H., Kwon, S., Jung, W.Y.: Resnet-based vehicle classification and localization in traffic surveillance systems. In: CVPRW, pp. 934–940. IEEE Press, Honolulu (2017)
12. Krizhevsky, A., Sutskever, I., Hinton, G.E.: Imagenet classification with deep convolutional neural networks. In: Advances in Neural Information Processing Systems, vol. 25, pp. 1097–1105. Curran Associates Inc., Lake Tahoe (2012)
13. Lin, T.Y., Goyal, P., Girshick, R.B., He, K., Dollár, P.: Focal loss for dense object detection. In: ICCV, pp. 2999–3007. IEEE Press, Venise (2017)
14. Liu, W., et al.: SSD: single shot multibox detector. In: Leibe, B., Matas, J., Sebe, N., Welling, M. (eds.) ECCV 2016. LNCS, vol. 9905, pp. 21–37. Springer, Cham (2016). https://doi.org/10.1007/978-3-319-46448-0_2
15. Luo, Z., et al.: MIO-TCD: a new benchmark dataset for vehicle classification and localization. IEEE Trans. Image Process. 27, 5129–5141 (2018)
16. Ning, G., et al.: Spatially supervised recurrent convolutional neural networks for visual object tracking. In: ISCAS, pp. 1–4. IEEE Press, Baltimore (2017)
17. Podlesnaya, A., Podlesnyy, S.: Deep learning based semantic video indexing and retrieval. In: Bi, Y., Kapoor, S., Bhatia, R. (eds.) IntelliSys 2016. LNNS, vol. 16, pp. 359–372. Springer, Cham (2018). https://doi.org/10.1007/978-3-319-56991-8_27
18. Redmon, J., Divvala, S.K., Girshick, R.B., Farhadi, A.: You only look once: unified, real-time object detection. In: CVPR, pp. 779–788. IEEE Press, Las Vegas (2016)
19. Redmon, J., Farhadi, A.: Yolo9000: better, faster, stronger. In: CVPR, pp. 6517–6525. IEEE Press, Honolulu (2017)
20. Redmon, J., Farhadi, A.: Yolov3: an incremental improvement. arXiv preprint arXiv:1804.02767 (2018)
21. Ren, S., He, K., Girshick, R.B., Sun, J.B.: Faster r-cnn: towards real-time object detection with region proposal networks. IEEE Trans. Pattern Anal. Mach. Intell. 39(6), 1137–1149 (2015)
22. Sánchez, J., Perronnin, F., Mensink, T., Verbeek, J.J.: Image classification with the fisher vector: theory and practice. Int. J. Comput. Vis. 105(3), 222–245 (2013)
23. Stauffer, C., Grimson, W.E.L.: Adaptive background mixture models for real-time tracking. In: CVPR, pp. 2246–2252. IEEE Press, Ft. Collins (1999)
24. Szegedy, C., et al.: Going deeper with convolutions. In: CVPR, pp. 1–9. IEEE Press, Boston (2015)
25. Szegedy, C., Vanhoucke, V., Ioffe, S., Shlens, J., Wojna, Z.: Rethinking the inception architecture for computer vision. In: CVPR, pp. 2818–2826. IEEE Press, Las Vegas (2016)
26. Ueki, K., Kobayashi, T.: Object detection oriented feature pooling for video semantic indexing. In: VISIGRAPP, pp. 44–51. SciTePress (2017)

27. Wang, Z., Chang, S., Yang, Y., Liu, D., Huang, T.S.: Studying very low resolution recognition using deep networks. In: CVPR, pp. 4792–4800. IEEE Press, Las Vegas (2016)
28. Xu, Z., Hu, J., Deng, W.: Recurrent convolutional neural network for video classification. In: ICME, pp. 1–6. IEEE Press, Seattle (2016)

Deep Recurrent Neural Network
for Multi-target Filtering

Mehryar Emambakhsh$^{(\boxtimes)}$, Alessandro Bay, and Eduard Vazquez

Cortexica Vision Systems, London, UK
{mehryar.emambakhsh,alessandro.bay,eduard.vazquez}@cortexica.com

Abstract. This paper addresses the problem of fixed motion and measurement models for multi-target filtering using an adaptive learning framework. This is performed by defining target tuples with random finite set terminology and utilisation of recurrent neural networks with a long short-term memory architecture. A novel data association algorithm compatible with the predicted tracklet tuples is proposed, enabling the update of occluded targets, in addition to assigning birth, survival and death of targets. The algorithm is evaluated over a commonly used filtering simulation scenario, with highly promising results (https://github. com/mehryaragha/MTF).

Keywords: Multi-target filtering · Recurrent neural network
Random finite sets · Long short-term memory

1 Introduction

Multi-target filtering consists of automatically excluding clutter from (usually unlabelled) input data sequences. It has numerous applications in denoising spatio-temporal data, object detection and recognition, tracking, and data-, object- and track-level sensor fusion [4,14,16]. It is also frequently used as part of various military applications (target recognition), automation pipelines, autonomous vehicles, and localisation and occupancy-grid mapping (using optical, e.g. stereo camera or LiDAR, or radar sensors) for robotics. Particularly for a tracking problem, the performance of a multi-target tracking algorithm heavily relies on its filtering step. A robust filtering algorithm is capable of considering occlusions, probability of detection, possibility of birth and spawn of targets, and incorporating clutter densities. An accurate filtering algorithm can improve the lifespan of the generated tracklets and the localisation of targets. Target state estimation by a filtering algorithm can be achieved by considering prior motion and measurement models. In a Bayesian filtering framework, motion models are used to predict the location of the target at the next time step, while measurement models are used to map predictions to the measurement space to perform correction (the update step). Due to the high complexity of a target motion, the use of fixed models, however, may not result in satisfactory outputs and therefore, can deteriorate the filtering performance.

© Springer Nature Switzerland AG 2019
I. Kompatsiaris et al. (Eds.): MMM 2019, LNCS 11296, pp. 519–531, 2019.
https://doi.org/10.1007/978-3-030-05716-9_42

Considering this challenge and inspired by the recurrent neural network tracker proposed in [9] and random finite sets (RFS) multi-target filtering paradigm [7,8,13], in this work, we propose a novel algorithm to perform multi-target filtering while simultaneously learning the motion model. To this end, a long short-term memory (LSTM, [5]) recurrent neural network (RNN) architecture is defined over sets of target tuples and trained online using the incoming data sequences. The prediction step is performed by applying the trained LSTM network to data patch generated from targets. This LSTM network (which is then trained using the new updated states) gradually learns a global transferable motion model of the detected targets. After obtaining the measurements, we use a novel data association algorithm, which is compatible with the generated tracklet tuples to assign survivals, deaths and births of new targets. The updated patches for each target are then used to train the LSTM model in the next time steps. To evaluate our algorithm we have designed a multi-target simulation scenario. During the simulation, by increasing the clutter (false positive rate) intensity, we evaluate the filtering robustness. This work which is one of the first papers addressing the multi-target filtering task with recurrent neural networks shows remarkable potential, while outperforming well-known multi-target filtering approaches.

This paper is organised as follows: First, related work in the literature is explained in Sect. 2 and the overall pipeline is briefly explained in Sect. 3. Incorporation of recurrent neural networks for motion modelling is explained in Sect. 4. Tracklet tuples and data association is explained in Sect. 5. Section 6 is dedicated to the experimental results. We conclude the paper in Sect. 7, giving future working directions.

1.1   Scientific Contribution

The proposed algorithm is capable of filtering multiple targets, with non-linear motion and non-Gaussian error models. Unlike [11,16], no prior motion modelling is performed and mapping from state to observation space is learned from the incoming data sequence. Moreover, unlike [9] the proposed algorithm is being trained online and does not rely on a separate training phase. Since the predicted targets are being concatenated over time within the target tuples, higher Markov order is preserved, enabling longer term target state memorisation. Compared with RFS multi-target filtering algorithms [11,16], there are significantly fewer number of hyper parameters for the proposed algorithm. For example, [13] requires hyper parameters to perform pruning, merge and truncation of the output density function, in addition to clutter distribution, survival and detection probabilities. To the best of our knowledge, this is one of the first papers addressing the multi-target filtering task with recurrent neural networks, particularly without the need of pre-training the network.

2   Related Work

Model-Based Approaches: In a Bayesian formulation of a multi-target filtering, the goal is to estimate the (hidden) target state x_k at the kth time step, from a set of observations in the previous time steps $z_{1:k}$, i.e.,

$$p_k(x_k|z_{1:k}) = \frac{g_k(z_k|x_k)p_{k|k-1}(x_k|z_{1:k-1})}{\int g_k(z_k|x)p_{k|k-1}(x|z_{1:k-1})dx}, \tag{1}$$

where $g_k(z_k|x_k)$ and $p_{k|k-1}(x_k|z_{1:k-1})$ are the likelihood and transition densities, respectively. From (1), it is clear that this is an recursive problem. The state estimation at the kth iteration is usually obtained by Maximum A Posteriori (MAP) criterion. Kalman filter is arguably the most popular online filtering approach. It assumes linear motion models with Gaussian distributions for both of the prediction and update steps. Using the Taylor series expansion and deterministic approximation of non-Gaussian distributions, non-linearity and non-Gaussian behaviour are addressed by Extended and Unscented Kalman Filters (EKF, UKF), respectively. Using the importance sampling principle, particle filters are also used to estimate the likelihood and posterior densities. Particle filters are one of the most widely used multi-target filtering algorithms capable of addressing non-linearity and non-Gaussian motions [14,17].

Mahler proposed random finite sets (RFS) formulation for multi-target filtering [8]. RFS provides an encapsulated formulation for multi-target filtering, incorporating clutter density, probabilities of detection, survival and birth of targets [7,8,14]. To this end, targets and measurements assume to form sets with variable random cardinalities. Using Finite Set Statistics [8], the posterior distribution in (1) can be extended from vectors to RFS as follows,

$$p_k(X_k|Z_{1:k}) = \frac{g_k(Z_k|X_k)p_{k|k-1}(X_k|Z_{1:k-1})}{\int g_k(Z_k|X)p_{k|k-1}(X|z_{1:k-1})\mu_s(dX)}, \tag{2}$$

where Z_k and X_k are measurement (containing both clutter and true positives) and target RFS, respectively, and μ_s an appropriate reference measure [13]. One approach to represent targets is to use Probability Hypothesis Density (PHD) maps [13,14]. These maps have two basic features: (1) Their peaks correspond to the location of targets; (2) Their integration gives the expected number of targets at each time step. Vo and Ma proposed Gaussian Mixture PHD (GM-PHD), which propagates the first-order statistical moments to estimate the posterior in (2) as a mixture of Gaussians [13].

Non-model Based Approaches: While GM-PHD is based on Gaussian distributions, a particle filter-based solution is proposed by Sequential Monte Carlo PHD (SMC-PHD) to address non-Gaussian distributions [17]. Since a large number of particles needs to be propagated during SMC-PHD, the computational complexity can be high and hence gating might be necessary.

Cardinalised PHD (CPHD) is proposed by Mahler to also propagate the cardinality of the targets over time in [7], while its intractability is addressed in [10]. The Labelled Multi-Bernoulli Filter (LMB) is introduced in [11] which performs track-to-track association and outperforms previous algorithms in the sense of not relying on high signal to noise ratio (SNR). Vo *et al.* proposed Generalized Labelled Multi-Bernoulli (GLMB) as a labelled multi-target filtering [16].

RNNs and LSTM Networks: RNNs are neural networks with feedback loops, through which past information can be stored and exploited. They offer promising solutions to difficult tasks such as system identification, prediction, pattern classification, and stochastic sequence modelling [2]. Unfortunately, RNNs are known to be particularly hard to train, especially when long temporal dependencies are involved, due to the so-called vanishing gradient phenomenon. Many attempts were carried on in order to address this problem from choosing an appropriate initial configuration of the weights to exploiting orthogonality in the hidden-to-hidden weight matrix [18]. Also modifications in the architecture [5] were proposed to sidestep this problem through gating mechanism, which enhance the memory of the network.

The latter case includes LSTMs (which is the architecture we consider in this paper as well). Formally, an LSTM is defined by four gates (input, candidate, forget and output, respectively), i.e. [5]

$$i_k = \phi_i\left(A_i x_k + B_i h_{k-1} + b_i\right), \qquad j_k = \phi_j\left(A_j x_k + B_j h_{k-1} + b_j\right) \quad (3)$$

$$f_k = \phi_f\left(A_f x_k + B_f h_{k-1} + b_f\right), \qquad o_k = \phi_o\left(A_o x_k + B_o h_{k-1} + b_o\right), \quad (4)$$

for each time step k, where $\phi_\bullet$ represent element-wise non-linear activation functions (with $\bullet = i, j, f, o$), $A_\bullet, B_\bullet, b_\bullet$ are the learning weights matrices and bias, x_k is the input, and h_{k-1} is the hidden state at the previous time step. These gates are then combined to update the memory cell unit and compute the new hidden state as follows [5],

$$c_k = c_{k-1} \odot f_k + i_k \odot j_k, \qquad h_k = \tanh(c_k) \odot o_k, \quad (5)$$

where $\odot$ represent the element-wise product.

Finally, the hidden state is mapped through a fully-connected layer to estimate the predicted output y_k [5],

$$y_k = \phi_y(C h_k + b_y), \quad (6)$$

where similarly to the RNN equation, ϕ_y is the element-wise output function and C and b_y are learning weight matrix and bias vector, respectively.

3   Overall Pipeline

The overall pipeline is shown in Fig. 1 in a block diagram. First, the predicted locations of the target tuples from the previous time step are computed. Then given the current measurements, a set of "residuals" are calculated for each target. These residuals are then used to perform filtering (rejecting the false positives and obtain survivals) and birth assignments. The union of the resulting birth and survival tuple sets are finally used as the targets for the kth iteration. In the following sections each of these steps are detailed.

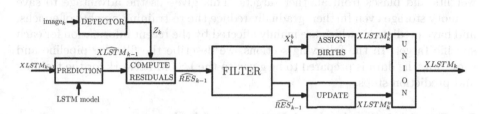

Fig. 1. Overall pipeline of the proposed multi-target filtering algorithm: target tuples set $XLSTM_{k-1}$ is given to the predictor, which loads the LSTM model for each target, trains it over the target's latest data patch and predicts the target state set $X\hat{LST}M_{k-1}$. The measurement set Z_k is obtained from the detector, which is used to compute the residual set. The filtering, data association and update (correction) steps are then performed over the residual set to remove clutter from the data and assign births, which eventually, form the target tuple set $XLSTM_k$.

4   Online Motion Modelling via LSTM

The target state variations over video frames can be seen as a sequential learning problem. The target tuples are predicted using an LSTM network. After being updated with their associated measurement, training patches are updated for each target which are used to re-train the very same LSTM model. As a result of this recursive process, motion modelling of the incoming data is performed. Using this approach, a non-linear/non-Gaussian input is learned without incorporating any prior knowledge about the motion. In our work, we investigated assigning an LSTM network to each target, which is separately trained over the predicted data from the previous time steps in order to predict for the following target position. The main issue with this approach is the (GPU) memory management and its re-usability. When the number of targets increases, it becomes infeasible to release the (GPU) memory part related to the absent targets and re-allocate the memory to the new targets.

One solution to this is to define a single LSTM network as a graph, whose nodes are simply "placeholders" [1] pointer variables. Every time a target is present in the scene, the placeholder nodes are updated with those weights and biases corresponding to this target. Once the prediction is performed, the memory is released. Such memory allocation enables learning a *global target motion* over the video sequence, which can be useful in crowd behaviour detection, but will provide poor results analysing the targets separately.

Thus, as a solution we propose an online LSTM training, where each target shares the same LSTM weights (i.e. $A_\bullet, B_\bullet, b_\bullet, C, b_y$) with the other targets. During the online training step, these weights and biases are shared from other targets and fine-tuned based on the past measurements. In other words, we fine-tune the LSTM weights and biases for each target by transferring the learned weights and biases from another targets. This gives us the advantage to save memory storage even further, gradually reduce the re-training number of epochs, and have predictions which are mainly affected by the recent information for each specific target. In the following sections, we describe the filtering pipeline and show how the data is prepared to be given to the LSTM network for the training and prediction steps.

5   Tracklet Tuples and Data Association

We define a tracklet tuple $xlstm$ as a subset of $xlstm \subset XLSTM_k$ at time k, containing the following four components,

$$xlstm = \left(x \in X_k, m_k \in \mathbb{Z}, g_k \in \mathbb{R}^+, f_k \in \{0, 1\}\right). \tag{7}$$

x is an $M \times d$ target state matrix over a d-dimensional space. M is the number of previous prediction appended for this target, which are used as the training patch for the LSTM network. m_k is an integer indicating the target *maturity* until the kth iteration. g_k is a real positive number containing the target *genuinity* error. f_k is a binary *freeze* state variable, which is either 1 when an observed measurement is used to update the state of the target, or is 0 when the update is performed without any measurement but with the target's past states. $XLSTM_k$ and X_k are random finite sets with M_k cardinalities, containing all the target tuples at k, i.e. $xlstm \in XLSTM_k$ and $x \in X_k$.

5.1   Filtering and Birth Assignment

The LSTM architecture explained in Sect. 4 is used to predict target state $x_{k|k-1}$. This is performed by first sequentially training the LSTM network with its M samples from the $xlstm$ tuple. Then the sample in the last (the Mth) row of x is given to the trained network to predict $\hat{x}$, which is then appended to the input tuple $xlstm$ to create the predicted tuple $xlstm \in XLSTM_{k|k-1}$. The resulting $XLSTM_{k|k-1}$ is hence an RFS with M_{k-1} cardinality, similar to $XLSTM_{k-1}$. At the kth time step, a set of residuals are calculated using the obtained measurement RFS Z_k. If Z_k has N_k cardinality, assuming no gating is performed, there will be $N_k \times M_{k-1}$ residuals which are stored as $RES_{k|k-1}$, where $r\hat{e}s \in RES_{k|k-1}$ has the following structure,

$$r\hat{e}s = \left(x\hat{l}stm \in XLSTM_{k|k-1}, T \in \mathbb{R}^+, z \in Z_k\right), \tag{8}$$

in which T is the *targetness* error parameter, which is computed from $T = \|\hat{x} - z\|_2$. The value of T shows how close the predicted target is to the current measurement.

$RES_{k|k-1}$ is used to perform the filtering step, at which survival of targets are determined, new births are assigned and false positive targets and measurements are removed. To do this, first an $N_k \times M_{k-1}$ targetness matrix $T_{k|k-1}$ is constructed, whose element at the n_k^{th} row and $\hat{m}_k^{th}$ column shows the second norm between the n_k^{th} measurement and $\hat{m}_k^{th}$ predicted target ($n_k = 1, 2, \ldots N_k$ and $\hat{m}_k = 1, 2, \ldots M_{k-1}$). In the next section, we detail how $T_{k|k-1}$ is used to perform data association.

Data Association: For each column and row of $T_{k|k-1}$ the measurement and target indexes are computed, respectively, as follows,

$$C^I_{k|k-1} = \underset{\hat{m}_k}{\arg\min} \left(T_{k|k-1} \right), \qquad R^I_{k|k-1} = \underset{n_k}{\arg\min} \left(T_{k|k-1} \right), \qquad (9)$$

where $C^I_{k|k-1}$ and $R^I_{k|k-1}$ are $N_k \times 1$ and $1 \times M_{k-1}$ vectors, containing the minimum target and measurement indexes, respectively. In addition, the minimum of each column of $T_{k|k-1}$ is also computed,

$$mg_{k|k-1} = \underset{\hat{m}_k}{\min} \left(T_{k|k-1} \right), \qquad g_{k|k-1} = \underset{n_k}{\min} \left(T_{k|k-1} \right), \qquad (10)$$

where $mg_{k|k-1}$ and $g_{k|k-1}$ are $N_k \times 1$ and $1 \times M_{k-1}$ vectors containing the measurement and target genuinity errors, respectively. In other words, $mg_{k|k-1}(n_k)$ and $g_{k|k-1}(\hat{m}_k)$ are the measurement and target genuinity errors for the n_k^{th} and $\hat{m}_k^{th}$ measurement and target, respectively. During the next step, the histogram bin of both $C^I_{k|k-1}$ and $R^I_{k|k-1}$ are computed as $H^{C^I}_{k|k-1}$ and $H^{R^I}_{k|k-1}$, respectively as follows,

$$H^{C^I}_{k|k-1} = \text{hist}(C^I_{k|k-1}), \qquad H^{R^I}_{k|k-1} = \text{hist}(R^I_{k|k-1}). \qquad (11)$$

Each element of $H^{C^I}_{k|k-1}(\hat{m}_k)$ shows how many associations exist for the $\hat{m}_k$ predicted target. On the other hand, each element of $H^{R^I}_{k|k-1}(n_k)$ indicates the number of association to the n_k^{th} measurement. The states of the targets are then updated using the data association approach explained as a pseudo code in Algorithm 1.

5.2 Update Survivals and Assign Births

The survived targets form an RFS $RES^f_{k|k-1}$. A set member $res^f \in RES^f_{k|k-1}$ has the same structure as $r\hat{e}s$ in (8), with the only difference that its m, g, f and z are being updated according to the cases explained in Algorithm 1. During the update stage (shown in the block diagram of Fig. 1), if the freeze state of a target is zero, meaning that a measurement z_k has successfully been associated with the target, its x_k is being updated by appending the associated measurement z_k, i.e., $x_k = \begin{bmatrix} x_{k-1} \\ \hline z_k \end{bmatrix}$. On the other hand, if the freeze state is

Input: $m_{min}, g_{min}, g_{max}, H_{k|k-1}^{C^I}, H_{k|k-1}^{R^I}, g_{k|k-1}, mg_{k|k-1},$
$XLSTM_{k|k-1}, Z_k$
Output: Survived targets and births: $RES_{k|k-1}^f$ and X_k^b
% Iterate over M_{k-1} targets in $XLSTM_{k|k-1}$:
for $\hat{m}_k = 1, 2, \ldots, M_{k-1}$ do

    if $(H_{k|k-1}^{C^I}(\hat{m}_k) == 0$ AND $\hat{m}_k^{th}$'s target maturity $\geq m_{min})$ OR

    $(H_{k|k-1}^{C^I}(\hat{m}_k) \geq 1$ AND $g_{min} \leq g_{k|k-1}(\hat{m}_k) \leq g_{max})$ then
        Possible occluded target or association with clutter: Freeze and
        decrement maturity;
    end

    if $H_{k|k-1}^{C^I}(\hat{m}_k) \geq 1$ AND $g_{k|k-1}(\hat{m}_k) < g_{min}$ then
        Possible target survival: Unfreeze, increment maturity and associate the
        target with the $R_{k|k-1}^I(\hat{m}_k)^{th}$ measurement in Z_k;
    end

end
% Iterate over N_k measurements in Z_k:
for $n_k = 1, 2, \ldots, N_k$ do

    if $H_{k|k-1}^{R^I}(n_k) == 0$ OR $mg_{k|k-1}(n_k) > g_{max}$ then
        Possible birth of a target: Initialise a new $xlstm$ tuple with m_{min}
        maturity;
    end

end

Algorithm 1: Data association algorithm.

one, meaning that the association step failed to find a measurement for the current target (possibly due to occlusion, measurement failure or the target itself is a false positive), the predicted target state $\hat{x}_k$ is appended to x_{k-1} to create the new state matrix $x_k = \begin{bmatrix} x_{k-1} \\ \overline{\hat{x}_k} \end{bmatrix}$. For both cases, to optimise memory allocation we define a maximum batch size. If the number of rows in x_k was greater than the batch size, the first row of x_k which corresponds to the oldest saved prediction or measurement is being removed. Using the updated target states, an RFS $XLSTM_k^u$ is generated for the survived targets. Each of its members $(xlstm^u \in XLSTM_k^u)$ is a tuple, having the same structure as (7), with updated states computed according to the data association.

In parallel with the above procedure, for each $1 \times d$ birth vector x^b, a target tuple is assigned as, $xlstm^b \in XLSTM_k^b = (x^b, m_{init}, g = 0, f = 0)$. The target tuple at the kth time step is calculated as the union of births and survivals, i.e. $XLSTM_k = XLSTM_k^b \cup XLSTM_k^u$, which has M_k cardinality.

6   Experimental Results

In this section we present the experimental results of our method in a controlled simulation on synthetic multi-target data. We compute the Optimal Sub-Pattern Assignment (OSPA, [12]) distance, an improved version of the Optimal Mass

Transfer (OMAT) metric to quantitatively evaluate the proposed algorithm. Assuming two sets $A = \{a_1, a_2, \ldots, a_\alpha\}$ and $B = \{b_1, b_2, \ldots, b_\beta\}$, the OSPA distance of order p and cut-off c is defined as [12],

$$\text{OSPA}(A, B) = \frac{1}{\max\{\alpha, \beta\}} \left(c^p |\alpha - \beta| + cost \right)^{1/p}, \tag{12}$$

where α and β are the number of elements in A and B, respectively. It essentially consists of two terms: one is related to the difference in the number of elements in the sets X and Y (cardinality error); and the other related to the localisation *cost* (Loc), which is the smallest pair-wise distance among all the elements in the two sets (the best-worst objective function [3]). In our work, we have used the Hungarian assignment to compute this minimal distance. As in [12], we choose $p = 1$ and $c = 100$. OSPA has been widely used for evaluating the accuracy of the filtering and tracking algorithms [4,15]. The overall pipeline is implemented (end-to-end) in Python 2.7, and all the experiments are tested using an NVIDIA GeForce GTX 1080 GPU and an $i5 - 8400$ CPU. We have used a 3-layer LSTM network, each having 20 hidden units, outputting a fully-connected layer (6), with ϕ_y as an identity function. The network is trained online at each time step for 50 epochs over the currently updated patch for each target, minimising the mean square error as the loss function and using Adam optimisation method [6].

Table 1. OSPA error for different methods: we compared our approach to PHD, CPHD [7,10], LMB [11], and GLMB [15,16] algorithm, when EKF, SMC, and UKF are used for prediction and update steps. The best performer method is highlighted in bold.

Algorithm	OSPA Card	OSPA Loc	OSPA
PHD-EKF	9.25 ± 15.44	20.86 ± 9.83	30.11 ± 14.82
PHD-SMC	12.76 ± 15.67	46.08 ± 17.36	58.84 ± 15.85
PHD-UKF	10.33 ± 18.17	19.73 ± 8.14	30.06 ± 16.21
CPHD-EKF	7.10 ± 14.91	23.00 ± 11.06	30.10 ± 16.16
CPHD-SMC	11.18 ± 13.72	46.08 ± 18.59	57.25 ± 17.72
CPHD-UKF	5.50 ± 14.79	22.39 ± 11.21	27.89 ± 15.43
LMB-EKF	4.59 ± 14.60	22.59 ± 8.60	27.18 ± 13.96
LMB-SMC	12.07 ± 19.75	23.47 ± 13.49	35.54 ± 17.95
LMB-UKF	$\mathbf{3.77 \pm 13.82}$	21.94 ± 10.22	25.72 ± 14.39
GLMB-EKF	6.37 ± 17.66	20.13 ± 8.02	26.50 ± 15.20
GLMB-SMC	6.11 ± 11.91	21.07 ± 6.78	27.19 ± 11.49
GLMB-UKF	11.79 ± 16.34	19.84 ± 9.75	31.63 ± 15.12
OURS	10.36 ± 13.25	$\mathbf{8.77 \pm 7.50}$	$\mathbf{19.12 \pm 14.39}$

In order to evaluate our algorithm over different filtering problems, such as occlusions, birth and death of the targets, non-linear motion and spawn, we have used the multi-target simulation introduced by Vo and Ma [11,16]. In this scenario, there are 10 targets appearing in the scene having various birth times and lifespans. The measurements is performed by computing the range and bearing (azimuth) of a target from the origin. It also contains clutter with uniform distribution along range and azimuth, with a random intensity sampled from a Poisson distribution with λ_c mean. The obtained measurements are degraded by a Gaussian noise with zero mean and $\sigma_r = 10$ (unit distance) and $\sigma_\theta = \pi/90$ (rad) standard deviation, respectively. The problem is to perform online multi-target filtering to recover true positives from clutter. In our first experiment we compute the OSPA error, assuming $\lambda_c = 20$ clutter intensity.

In Table 1, we report the average and standard deviation for the overall OSPA (see (12)) and its two terms related to cardinality error (OSPA Card) and optimal Hungarian distance (OSPA Loc - the *cost* term in (12)). We compare our method with PHD, CPHD, LMB, and GLMB algorithm, when EKF, SMC, and UKF used as basis for the prediction and update steps (The following Matlab implementation of these algorithms is used: http://ba-tuong.vo-au.com/codes.html). Our method outperform all the other algorithms in terms of overall OSPA. In particular, this is due to a significant drop of the Loc error, while cardinality error is comparable with most of the others. For example, despite our algorithm has ≈ 7 (samples) higher average OSPA cardinality error than LMB-UKF, our Loc and overall OSPA distances are about ≈ 13 and 6 (unit distances) lower, respectively. The resulting trajectories of this experiment for our method are illustrated in Fig. 2. The red dots represent the predicted location of the targets at every time step, filtered out from the measurements clutters (black dots). They almost overlap with the ground truth (green dots), except very few (only three) false positives (predicted but no ground truth) and false negatives (ground truth but no prediction).

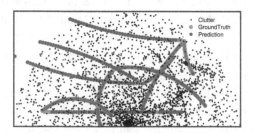

Fig. 2. Results of trajectories for the ten simulated points. (Color figure online)

Moreover, in Fig. 3, we show the overall OSPA at every time steps. During the initial time steps (frame number < 6), our OSPA error is higher. This is mostly due to the under-fitting of the LSTM model because of lack of data. However, after $\approx 7^{th}$ iteration our OSPA error becomes significantly lower than other approaches, having an overall average of ≈ 18, while the average OSPA error for other algorithms are >25. In order to show the robustness of our algorithm for higher clutter densities, in the second experiment, we increase the clutter intensity λ_c and find the average OSPA over all time steps. Figure 4 shows the results of this experiment, for $\lambda_c = 10, 20, \ldots, 50$. Our filtering algorithm provides a relatively constant and comparably lower overall OSPA error even when the clutter is increased to 50. Both of the SMC-based algorithms (GLMB-SMC and LMB-SMC) generate highest OSPA error, which can be due to the particle filter algorithm divergence. On the other hand, lower OSPA errors generated by the LMB with an EKF model shows how successfully this particular simulated scenario can be modelled using such non-linear filter. It should be mentioned, however, that our method does not rely on any prior motion model capable of learning the non-linearity within the data sequence.

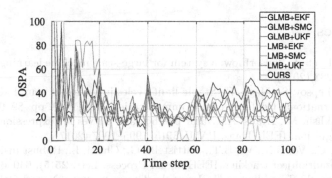

Fig. 3. Comparison of overall OSPA error for different methods for $\lambda_c = 20$. Except the very early time steps when the LSTM have not yet learned the motion, our method has a remarkable better performance than the other filters.

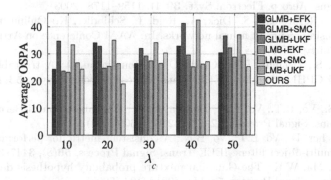

Fig. 4. Overall OSPA for different methods, using different clutter intensity λ_c.

7   Conclusions

This paper addressed the problem of fixed motion and measurement models for the multi-target filtering using an adaptive deep learning framework. This is performed by defining target tuples with random finite set terminology and utilisation of LSTM networks, learning to model the target motion while simultaneously filtering the clutter. We defined a novel data association algorithm compatible with the predicted tracklet tuples, enabling the update of occluded targets, in addition to assigning birth, survival and death of targets. Finally, the algorithm is evaluated over a commonly used filtering scenario via OSPA metric computation.

Our algorithm can be extended by investigating an end-to-end solution for tracking, encapsulating the data association step within the recurrent neural network architecture.

References

1. Abadi, M., et al.: TensorFlow: a system for large-scale machine learning. In: OSDI, pp. 265–283 (2016)
2. Bay, A., Lepsoy, S., Magli, E.: Stable limit cycles in recurrent neural networks. In: 2016 International Conference on Communications (COMM), pp. 89–92 (2016)
3. Emambakhsh, M., Evans, A.: Nasal patches and curves for expression-robust 3D face recognition. IEEE Trans. PAMI **39**(5), 995–1007 (2017)
4. Fantacci, C., Vo, B.N., Vo, B.T., Battistelli, G., Chisci, L.: Robust fusion for multisensor multiobject tracking. IEEE Signal Process. Lett. **25**(5), 640–644 (2018)
5. Hochreiter, S., Schmidhuber, J.: Long short-term memory. Neural Comput. **9**(8), 1735–1780 (1997)
6. Kingma, D.P., Ba, J.: Adam: a method for stochastic optimization. arXiv preprint arXiv:1412.6980 (2014)
7. Mahler, R.: PHD filters of higher order in target number. IEEE Trans. Aerosp. Electron. Syst. **43**(4), 1523–1543 (2007)
8. Mahler, R.P.S.: Multitarget Bayes filtering via first-order multitarget moments. IEEE Trans. Aerosp. Electron. Syst. **39**(4), 1152–1178 (2003)
9. Milan, A., Rezatofighi, S., Dick, A., Reid, I., Schindler, K.: Online multi-target tracking using recurrent neural networks. In: AAAI Conference on Artificial Intelligence Thirty (2017)
10. Nagappa, S., Delande, E.D., Clark, D.E., Houssineau, J.: A tractable forward-backward CPHD smoother. IEEE Trans. Aerosp. Electron. Syst. **53**(1), 201–217 (2017)
11. Reuter, S., Vo, B.T., Vo, B.N., Dietmayer, K.: The labeled multi-Bernoulli filter. IEEE Trans. Signal Process. **62**(12), 3246–3260 (2014)
12. Schuhmacher, D., Vo, B.T., Vo, B.N.: A consistent metric for performance evaluation of multi-object filters. IEEE Trans. Signal Process. **56**(8), 3447–3457 (2008)
13. Vo, B.N., Ma, W.K.: The Gaussian mixture probability hypothesis density filter. IEEE Trans. Signal Process. **54**(11), 4091–4104 (2006)
14. Vo, B.N., Singh, S., Doucet, A.: Sequential Monte Carlo methods for multitarget filtering with random finite sets. IEEE Trans. Aerosp. Electron. Syst. **41**(4), 1224–1245 (2005)

15. Vo, B.N., Vo, B.T., Hoang, H.G.: An efficient implementation of the generalized labeled multi-Bernoulli filter. IEEE Trans. Signal Process. **65**(8), 1975–1987 (2017)
16. Vo, B.N., Vo, B.T., Phung, D.: Labeled random finite sets and the Bayes multi-target tracking filter. IEEE Trans. Signal Process. **62**(24), 6554–6567 (2014)
17. Vo, B.N., Singh, S., Doucet, A.: Sequential Monte Carlo implementation of the PHD filter for multi-target tracking. In: Proceedings of the Sixth International Conference of Information Fusion, vol. 2, pp. 792–799 (2003)
18. Vorontsov, E., Trabelsi, C., Kadoury, S., Pal, C.: On orthogonality and learning recurrent networks with long term dependencies. arXiv preprint arXiv:1702.00071 (2017)

Adversarial Training for Video Disentangled Representation

Renjie Xie[1], Yuancheng Wang[1], Tian Xie[1], Yuhao Zhang[1], Li Xu[2], Jian Lu[1], and Qiao Wang[1(✉)]

[1] School of Information Science and Engineering and Shing-Tung Yau Center, Southeast University, Nanjing 210096, China
{renjie_xie,wangyuancheng,xietian,yuhao_zhang,lujian1980, qiaowang}@seu.edu.cn
[2] Intel(China) Corporation, Shanghai 200241, China
beryl.xu@intel.com

Abstract. The strong demand for video analytics is largely due to the widespread application of CCTV. Perfectly encoding moving objects and scenes with different sizes and complexity in an unsupervised manner is still a challenge and seriously affects the quality of video prediction and subsequent analysis. In this paper, we introduce adversarial training to improve DrNet which disentangles a video with stationary scene and moving object representations, while taking the tiny objects and complex scene into account. These representations can be used for subsequent industrial applications such as vehicle density estimation, video retrieval, etc. Our experiment on LASIESTA database confirms the validity of this method in both reconstruction and prediction performance. Meanwhile, we propose an experiment that vanishes one of the codes and reconstructs the images by concatenating these zero and non-zero codes. This experiment separately evaluates the moving object and scene coding quality and shows that the adversarial training achieves a significant reconstruction quality in visual effect, despite of complex scene and tiny object.

Keywords: Disentangled representation · Video reconstruction Adversarial training · Video analysis

1 Introduction

With the increasing needs in public security and traffic control, the use of surveillance cameras, as well as the generated video data, has rapidly grown over the past few years. Effective analysis of the massive surveillance without much labels becomes more and more important. The scarcity of video labels and the importance of representation to video scenarios have made unsupervised learning and weakly supervised learning the ideal paradigms. With the emergence of deep generative models, particularly Generative Adversarial Networks (GANs) in recent years, there has been remarkable progress in this direction.

© Springer Nature Switzerland AG 2019
I. Kompatsiaris et al. (Eds.): MMM 2019, LNCS 11296, pp. 532–543, 2019.
https://doi.org/10.1007/978-3-030-05716-9_43

As surveillance video is usually captured by fixedly mounted cameras, the content consists of static parts (backgrounds) and dynamic parts (moving objects or pedestrians). Disentangling factors in video will greatly facilitate the storage and analysis in industry. For example, the static part can be used to detect the scenes and action recognition, while traffic flow estimation and video prediction can be performed by the dynamic representations. Thanks to the low dimension, we can even use this representations for video retrieval.

By carefully examining the video pieces generated by the code of a state-of-the-art DrNet [8] on the other datasets, we found small dynamic objects and complex backgrounds in generated videos pieces were partially reconstructed, even unidentifiable by human eyes. These shortcomings are fatal for several tasks, particularly camera surveillance task.

To address this issues, [9, 15, 17] indicate traditional losses like L_2 loss only works well on simple and smooth images and provide a possible solution called adversarial training. The main idea is that to view the discriminator in GAN as a learned metric, this solution has been proven to achieve a better reconstruction to the fine and complex textures in images.

In this paper, we employ [8] as the baseline and introduce the adversarial training into these models. Rather than the action recognition dataset KTH [25] in baseline article, we work on the outdoor part of moving object detection dataset LASIESTA [7] which contains more complex background and small objects.

Finally, we have conducted extensive experiments to validate the effectiveness of the added adversarial techniques. Visualization of the pose code-only generated image shows that the adversarial training significantly improves the representation quality of small objects in images.

2   Related Work

Unsupervised learning and weakly supervised learning have recently exhibited a great potential in computer vision tasks. Auto-Encoder [11], Siamese network [5], generative adversarial network (GAN) [10] have also become the state-of-the-arts in this domain. Auto-encoder network is the most popular self-supervised structures that creates an information bottleneck for a purpose of learning the efficient data coding [16]. The variants with different regularizations [2, 23, 29], its generative model (Variational Auto-Encoder (VAE) [14]) and semi-supervised version [22] improve its robustness and broadly extend the use of this models, such as video feature alignments [33], video hashing [26], event detection [4] in video tasks. In another hand, auto-encoder is also used to pre-train the network as an embedding method [29]; Siamese network provides another embedding approach for differentiating classes of data using similarity measures which gathers the intra-class samples and separates inter-class samples. The variants with 0–1 output and different networks in branches [32] have also spawned a large number of applications for frame comparison in video, such as person re-identification, scene comparison [1, 19]; Generative Adversarial Networks [10] have made a great success at producing realistic natural images [21]. The generator tries to generate a realistic image with random value drawn from a pre-defined distribution and the discriminator aims to identify whether the input images is generated or not. Therefore, these two networks compete with each other until the Nash Equilibrium is reached [35]. The convolutional GAN, conditional GAN, semi-supervised GAN and the versions with different loss functions emerged later [6].

Modeling natural invariance with above three models or their hybrid models have become efficient in recent years which permits to characterize the objects in images by encoding their position, orientation, size, etc, furthermore it's also essential to create robust video representation and realistic video. [34] proposes to add the spatial coding on pooling layers to improve the generation quality in Convolutional Auto-encoder; [3] indicates the fact that GAN trained without constraint always has highly entangled representation and introduce a low-dimensional latent code by regarding the generator and discriminator respectively as a decoder and an encoder, this latent code is evaluated to well represent the salient features through experiments on several scenarios; [18] proposes to disentangle the image factors with 'specified' and 'unspecified' variability with a VAE-GAN framework; More specifically, DR-GAN [27] employs personal identity and pose diversity as two facial factors and made a good result in face alignment. [24] tries to learn a set of latent invariant features with a supervised model.

For video generation, most of the works divides the contents in video into static and dynamic parts. To obtain a finer generation of the videos, [31] pre-defines several isolated categories for moving objects and predicts the future frames directly using sequential auto-encoder. Combining the Siamese network with GAN, [8] represents images by concatenating time-independent code and time-varying pose code, this method predicts the pose coding from current concatenated code with LSTM by fixing the pre-trained networks; MC-GAN [28] predicts the pose code by consecutive frames with convolutional LSTM; [30] combines the spatial-temporal convolutional encoder with foreground mask generator to more explicitly disentangle two factors. [12] addresses the same task by converting the pose code as inverse spatial transformer and introduces a transition variable to predict future pose code.

3   Model

DrNet [8], the previous method, is the unsupervised video disentangle framework using two encoders to produce scene and motion embedding representations from each video frame respectively, and the representations are reconstructed by an encoder with regularization of mean squared error (MSE). Due to the smoothness of MSE loss, such framework seems to ignore the small moving objects. Especially in the surveillance videos analysis, the tiny moving objects are actually very common. In this section, we propose a new kind of video disentangle framework, so-called Improved-DrNet, also including two encoders for scene and motion object, while the additional reconstruction discriminator with adversarial training can effectively force the decoder to recover the small moving objects, so that the motion encoder can well capture the small objects.

3.1 Problem Formulation

Given a set of surveillance video $T = \{V_1, V_2, ..., V_N\}$, and the sequence of n_i images $V_i = \{x_i^{(1)}, x_i^{(2)}, ..., x_i^{(n_i)}\}$ from video i, where N is the number of videos, and n_i is the number of frames, our goal is to learn E_S, E_M and D_e with some constraint. More concretely, the scene encoder E_S should obtain the time-invariant representations, and the Decoder D_e should reconstruct the $(t + k)$ th frame by t th frame's scene information and $(t+k)$ th frame's motion information, we can formulate the problem as follows:

For the scene encoder E_S:

$$
\min_{E_S} \quad Dist_{represent}(E_S(x_i^{(t)}), E_S(x_i^{(t+k)}))
$$
$$
s.t. \quad x_i^{(t)}, x_i^{(t+k)} \in V_i \quad \forall i = 1, 2, ...N
$$
(1)

For the Decoder D_e and the motion encoder E_M:

$$
\min_{D_e, E_M} \quad Dist_{recons}(D_e(E_S(x_i^{(t)}), E_M(x_i^{(t+k)}), x_i^{(t+k)}))
$$
$$
s.t. \quad x_i^{(t)}, x_i^{(t+k)} \in V_i \quad \forall i = 1, 2, ...N
$$
(2)

Where $Dist_{represent}$ and $Dist_{recons}$ are certain kinds of distance metric in the representation space and the input space respectively.

3.2 DrNet

To solve the above problems, the distance metric of representation space and the input space are set as L_2 distance by DrNet, and the objective function of DrNet contains three parts, which are illustrated as follows.

Let $\hat{x}_i^{(t)}$ denote the prediction of tth frame in the video i. For all $V_i \in T$ and $x_i^{(t)}, x_i^{(t+k)} \in V_i$:

MSE Scene Similarity Loss: By minimizing the L_2 distance of the embedding representations between the future frame $x_i^{(t+k)}$ and the current frame $x_i^{(t)}$, the scene encoder E_s is able to extract the time-invariant features, in other word, scene information.

$$
\min_{E_S} \quad L_{Scene-Simi} = \| E_S(x_i^{(t)}) - E_S(x_i^{(t+k)}) \|_2
$$
(3)

MSE Reconstruction Loss: Optimizing the mse reconstruction loss confirms that the representations from E_S and E_M are carrying sufficient information for decoder D to recover the future frame.

$$
\min_{E_S, E_M, D} \quad L_{Rec-MSE} = \| \hat{x}_i^{(t+k)} - x_i^{(t+k)} \|_2
$$
$$
s.t. \quad \hat{x}_i^{(t+k)} = D_e(E_S(x_i^{(t)}), E_M(x_i^{(t+k)}))
$$
(4)

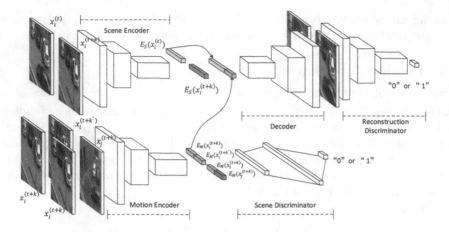

Fig. 1. Schematic diagram of Improved-DrNet.

Adversarial Scene Loss: The Scene discriminator D_{scene} (2-layers net) is used for distinguishing different scenes in the representations from E_m, and E_m tries to confuse the discriminator by discarding the information from different scenes. With the help of D_{scene} and the Reconstruction loss, the motion encoder could well preserve the motion information in the videos.

$$\min_{D_{scene}} \quad L_{adv-D_{scene}}$$

$$= -\log(D_{scene}(E_M(x_i^{(t)}), E_M(x_i^{(t+k)}))) \tag{5}$$
$$- \log(1 - D_{scene}(E_M(x_i^{(t)}), E_M(x_j^{(t+k)})))$$

$$\min_{E_M} \quad L_{adv-E_M}$$

$$= -\frac{1}{2}\log(D_{scene}(E_M(x_i^{(t)}), E_M(x_i^{(t+k)}))) \tag{6}$$
$$- \frac{1}{2}\log(1 - D_{scene}(E_M(x_i^{(t)}), E_M(x_i^{(t+k)})))$$

3.3   Improved-DrNet

Because the small objects would be ignored by MSE loss function, we use the additional nerual network – Reconstruction Discriminator D_{recons} to replace the distance metric in the input space for guiding reconstruction processes. As is shown in Fig. 1, Improved-DrNet totally consists of five neural networks: Scene Encoder E_S, Motion Encoder E_M, Decoder D_e, Scene Discriminator D_{scene} and proposed reconstruction Discriminator D_{recons}.

Adversarial Reconstruction Loss: D_{recons} is mainly used to distinguish differences even slight differences between the input real frame and the reconstructed frame. D_e and E_M need to spoof the D_{recons} as much as possible, so that the discriminator can not distinguish the difference between the real frame and the reconstructed frame. This process will better provide gradients for the decoder and motion encoder, allowing the motion encoder to more accurately capture tiny objects moving in the video.

$$\min_{D_{recons}} L_{adv-D_{recons}}$$

$$= -\log(D_{recons}(E_M(\hat{x}_i^{(t+k)}), E_M(x_i^{(t+k)}))) \tag{7}$$

$$- \log(1 - D_{recons}(E_M(x_i^{(t+k)}), E_M(x_i^{(t+k)})))$$

$$\min_{E_M, E_S, D_e} L_{adv-E_M, E_S, D_e}$$

$$= -\log(D_{recons}(E_M(x_i^{(t+k)}), E_M(x_i^{(t+k)}))) \tag{8}$$

$$- \log(1 - D_{recons}(E_M(\hat{x}_i^{(t+k)}), E_M(x_i^{(t+k)})))$$

The Final Loss: The final loss function of Improved-DrNet is as followed:

$$L_{final} = L_{Scene-Simi} + L_{Rec-MSE}$$

$$+ \beta(L_{adv-Dscene} + L_{adv-E_M}) \tag{9}$$

$$+ \gamma(L_{adv-D_{recons}} + L_{adv-E_M, E_S, D_e})$$

Where β and γ are the hyper-parameters Controlling the adversarial training strength. In Algorithm 1, we summarize the training details in Improved-DrNet.

4   Experiments

The necessary experiment setting details are given in Sect. 4.1. Then we visualize the video decomposition results of the proposed approach and compare it with the results of DrNet to verify the effectiveness in Sect. 4.2. Finally, the video prediction experiment is conducted in Sect. 4.3.

4.1   Experiment Setting

Data Set: As is shown in Table 1, the experiment in this paper uses the outdoor surveillance video in eight scenes of the four weather conditions in the LASIESTA data set [7] as the training set. Among them, moving objects include pedestrians and vehicles, and most of them account for a small proportion of video frames. All the video frames are resized to 64*64, as the input of Improved-DrNet.

Architectures, Hyper-parameters and Training: The scene encoder E_S, the motion encoder E_M, the decoder D_e, and the reconstruction discriminator D_{recons} are all built with the same architectures with DCGAN [20]. D_{scene} is a 2-layers neural network with 100 hidden units. The Scene embedding has 64 dimensions, and the dimension of motion embedding is 5. We use 2-layers LSTM model with 256 cells in motion prediction and we set $\beta = 0.001$ and $\gamma = 1.0$.

All the models trained by Adam optimizer [13] with initialize learning rate 0.002, $\beta_1 = 0.9, \beta_2 = 0.999$. The training batch size is 100, totally 200 epochs.

Algorithm 1. Improved-DrNet Training

    Input: A Set of Surveillance Video T
    Output: all parameter of Improved-DrNet

1 Initialize all parameter of Improved-DrNet **while** *not converge* **do**
2 | **Train** D_{scene}:
3 | Sample two pairs of images:
4 | $x_{p1} = \{x_i^{(t+k)}, x_i^{(t+k')}\}$,
5 | $x_{p2} = \{x_i^{(t+k)}, x_j^{(t+k)}\}$
6 | where $\forall q \neq j, k \neq k'$;
7 | Compute $L_{adv-D_{scene}}$
8 | Update parameter of D_{scene}
9 | **Train** E_M, E_s, D_e:
10 | Sample $\{x_i^{(t)}, x_i^{(t+k)}, x_i^{(t+k')}\}$
11 | $\hat{x}_i^{(t+k)} \leftarrow D_e(E_s(x_i^{(t)}), E_M(x_i^{(t+k)}))$
12 | **for** $p = 1$ *to* P **do**
13 | | **Train** D_{recons}:
14 | | Input $\{\hat{x}_i^{(t+k)}, x_i^{(t+k)}\}$
15 | | Compute $L_{adv-D_{recons}}$
16 | | Update parameters of D_{recons}
17 | Compute $L_{Scene-simi}, L_{Rec-MSE}$,
18 | $L_{adv-E_M}, L_{adv-E_M, E_s, D_e}$
19 | Update parameter of E_M, E_s, D_e

Table 1. Outdoor sequences of LASIESTA data set

Video Id	Num. of frames	Num. of objs.
CL-01	225	1
CL-02	425	2
RA-01	1400	2
RA-02	375	2
SN-01	500	1
SN-02	850	1
SU-01	250	2
SU-02	400	2

4.2 Video Reconstruction and Disentangle Analysis

In this part, we evaluate Improved-DrNet by visualizing the reconstructed video frames.

We use the $0th$ frame of videos to obtain the scene representations $E_S(x_i^{(0)})$, then vary t to get the motion representations $E_M(x_i^{(t)})$. The video is recon-

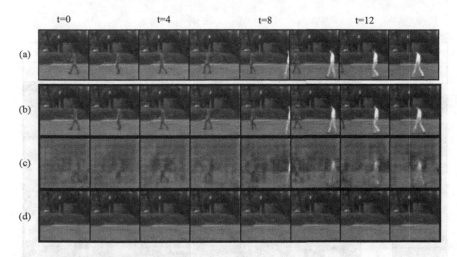

Fig. 2. Sample video reconstructed by Improved-DrNet: Using the scene embedding from the first frame, and the motion embedding by varying t to reconstruct video (a) Ground True; (b) Reconstructed frames; (c) Reconstructed frames that only contain motion information $(E_S(x_i^{(0)}) = 0)$; (d) Reconstructed frames that only contain scene information $(E_M(x_i^{(t)}) = 0)$.

structed by $E_S(x_i^{(0)})$, $E_M(x_i^{(t)})$, and D_e. Reconstructed frames visualizing in Fig. 2(b) shows that Improved-DrNet can perfectly reconstruct origin video shown in Fig. 2(a).

Furthermore, we artificially zeroed the scene coding and motion coding to reconstruct a video containing only scene information or motion information $(E_S(x_i^{(0)}) = 0$ or $E_M(x_i^{(t)}) = 0)$, which indicates the effectiveness of the video disentangling. Figure 2(c) shows that the motion representations can well capture the small moving objects without the scenes information, and the scene reconstruction in Fig. 2(d) reveals that the scene representations successfully get rid of the motion information.

The comparison between DrNet and Improved-DrNet is shown in Fig. 3 that Improved-DrNet overcomes the drawback of DrNet [8] in previous study which ignore the small dynamic objects in the complex scene. Thanks to the significant separated representations, the proposed method can reconstruct video frames with high quality and accurately preserve more details of the moving object in the original video. In contrast, DrNet has missing or blurred moving objects during the reconstruction process.

This explains from the side that reconstruction discriminator not only enhances the reconstructed image, but also makes the motion encoder and scene encoder excellent during the training process through gradient transfer.

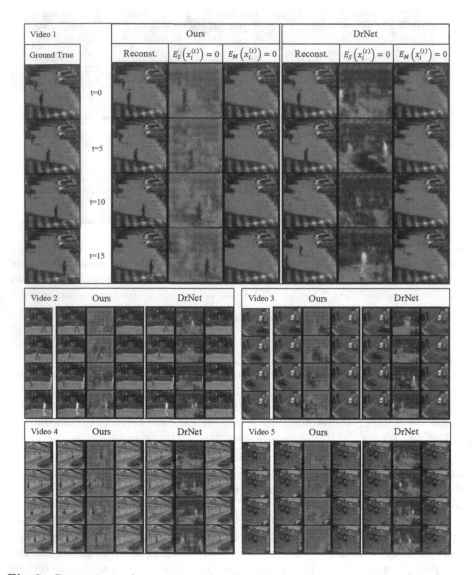

Fig. 3. Comparison of reconstructed videos between Improved-DrNet (Ours) and DrNet. Each of these boxes represents a comparison experiment of a video. In the box, the first column is Ground True, and the second to fourth columns are the reconstructed frames corresponding to the proposed method, and the fifth to seventh columns are the reconstructed videos of DrNet. Due to the limitation of the layout, the remaining four small size videos are consistent with video 1. Motion reconstruction frames of DrNet do not clearly capture moving objects. Frames are rich in textures that are not related to moving objects, and scene reconstruction frames of DrNet are also not pure enough at all.

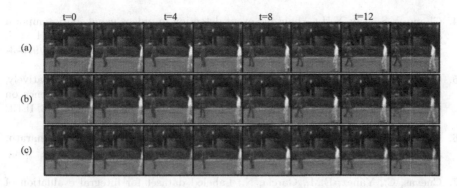

Fig. 4. Comparison of LSTM video predictions between Improved-DrNet (Ours) and DrNet. (a) Ground True; (b) Improved-DrNet; (c) DrNet.

4.3 LSTM Video Prediction

Given the trained motion encoder, scene encoder and decoder, and the first 10 frames of video, we try to predict the motion of the next 15 frames by 10 frames of motion representations through LSTM. The experimental results are shown in Fig. 4. Compared with Ground True, pedestrians in DrNet gradually become faint over time and cannot estimate their pose well; as a comparison, the method proposed in this paper is more consistent with the Ground True. Obviously, the proposed method is more robust than DrNet.

5 Conclusions

In this paper, we have proposed a new kind of video disentangled framework based on DrNet, the so-called Improved-DrNet, which introduces adversarial training for video reconstruction and boosts the disentangling performance of the framework with small moving objects in complex scene. Experimental reconstruction visualization shows that the proposed method can significantly improve video disentangled and reconstruction performance. In the follow-up study, we will apply the method proposed in this paper to the analysis of industrial videos, such as traffic flow estimation, video retrieval, etc.

References

1. Baraldi, L., Grana, C., Cucchiara, R.: A deep siamese network for scene detection in broadcast videos. In: Proceedings of the 23rd ACM International Conference on Multimedia, pp. 1199–1202. ACM (2015)
2. Boureau, Y.l., Cun, Y.L.: Sparse feature learning for deep belief networks. In: Advances in Neural Information Processing Systems, pp. 1185–1192 (2008)
3. Chen, X., Duan, Y., Houthooft, R., Schulman, J., Sutskever, I., Abbeel, P.: Info-Gan: interpretable representation learning by information maximizing generative adversarial nets. In: Advances in Neural Information Processing Systems, pp. 2172–2180 (2016)

4. Chong, Y.S., Tay, Y.H.: Abnormal event detection in videos using spatiotemporal autoencoder. In: Cong, F., Leung, A., Wei, Q. (eds.) ISNN 2017, Part II. LNCS, vol. 10262, pp. 189–196. Springer, Cham (2017). https://doi.org/10.1007/978-3-319-59081-3_23

5. Chopra, S., Hadsell, R., LeCun, Y.: Learning a similarity metric discriminatively, with application to face verification. In: IEEE Computer Society Conference on Computer Vision and Pattern Recognition, CVPR 2005, vol. 1, pp. 539–546. IEEE (2005)

6. Creswell, A., White, T., Dumoulin, V., Arulkumaran, K., Sengupta, B., Bharath, A.A.: Generative adversarial networks: an overview. IEEE Signal Process. Mag. 35(1), 53–65 (2018)

7. Cuevas, C., Yáñez, E.M., García, N.: Labeled dataset for integral evaluation of moving object detection algorithms: LASIESTA. Comput. Vis. Image Underst. 152, 103–117 (2016)

8. Denton, E.L.: Unsupervised learning of disentangled representations from video. In: Advances in Neural Information Processing Systems, pp. 4414–4423 (2017)

9. Dumoulin, V., et al.: Adversarially learned inference. arXiv preprint arXiv:1606.00704 (2016)

10. Goodfellow, I., et al.: Generative adversarial nets. In: Advances in Neural Information Processing Systems, pp. 2672–2680 (2014)

11. Hinton, G.E., Salakhutdinov, R.R.: Reducing the dimensionality of data with neural networks. Science 313(5786), 504–507 (2006)

12. Hsieh, J.T., Liu, B., Huang, D.A., Fei-Fei, L., Niebles, J.C.: Learning to Decompose and Disentangle Representations for Video Prediction. arXiv preprint arXiv:1806.04166 (2018)

13. Kingma, D.P., Ba, J.: Adam: A method for stochastic optimization. arXiv preprint arXiv:1412.6980 (2014)

14. Kingma, D.P., Welling, M.: Auto-encoding variational bayes. arXiv preprint arXiv:1312.6114 (2013)

15. Larsen, A.B.L., Sønderby, S.K., Larochelle, H., Winther, O.: Autoencoding beyond pixels using a learned similarity metric. arXiv preprint arXiv:1512.09300 (2015)

16. Liou, C.Y., Cheng, W.C., Liou, J.W., Liou, D.R.: Autoencoder for words. Neurocomputing 139, 84–96 (2014)

17. Makhzani, A., Shlens, J., Jaitly, N., Goodfellow, I., Frey, B.: Adversarial autoencoders. arXiv preprint arXiv:1511.05644 (2015)

18. Mathieu, M.F., Zhao, J.J., Zhao, J., Ramesh, A., Sprechmann, P., LeCun, Y.: Disentangling factors of variation in deep representation using adversarial training. In: Advances in Neural Information Processing Systems, pp. 5040–5048 (2016)

19. McLaughlin, N., Martinez del Rincon, J., Miller, P.: Recurrent convolutional network for video-based person re-identification. In: Proceedings of the IEEE Conference on Computer Vision and Pattern Recognition, pp. 1325–1334(2016)

20. Radford, A., Metz, L., Chintala, S.: Unsupervised representation learning with deep convolutional generative adversarial networks. arXiv preprint arXiv:1511.06434 (2015)

21. Ranzato, M., Szlam, A., Bruna, J., Mathieu, M., Collobert, R., Chopra, S.: Video (language) modeling: a baseline for generative models of natural videos. arXiv preprint arXiv:1412.6604 (2014)

22. Rasmus, A., Berglund, M., Honkala, M., Valpola, H., Raiko, T.: Semi-supervised learning with ladder networks. In: Advances in Neural Information Processing Systems, pp. 3546–3554 (2015)

23. Rifai, S., Vincent, P., Muller, X., Glorot, X., Bengio, Y.: Contractive auto-encoders: Explicit invariance during feature extraction. In: Proceedings of the 28th International Conference on International Conference on Machine Learning, pp. 833–840. Omnipress (2011)
24. Sabour, S., Frosst, N., Hinton, G.E.: Dynamic routing between capsules. In: Advances in Neural Information Processing Systems. pp. 3856–3866 (2017)
25. Schuldt, C., Laptev, I., Caputo, B.: Recognizing human actions: a local SVM approach. In: 2004 Proceedings of the 17th International Conference on Pattern Recognition, ICPR 2004, vol. 3, pp. 32–36. IEEE (2004)
26. Song, J., Zhang, H., Li, X., Gao, L., Wang, M., Hong, R.: Self-supervised video hashing with hierarchical binary auto-encoder. IEEE Trans. Image Process. **27**(7), 3210–3221 (2018)
27. Tran, L., Yin, X., Liu, : X.: Disentangled representation learning GAN for pose-invariant face recognition. In: CVPR, vol. 3, p. 7 (2017)
28. Villegas, R., Yang, J., Hong, S., Lin, X., Lee, H.: Decomposing motion and content for natural video sequence prediction. arXiv preprint arXiv:1706.08033 (2017)
29. Vincent, P., Larochelle, H., Bengio, Y., Manzagol, P.A.: Extracting and composing robust features with denoising autoencoders. In: Proceedings of the 25th International Conference on Machine Learning, pp. 1096–1103. ACM(2008)
30. Vondrick, C., Pirsiavash, H., Torralba, A.: Generating videos with scene dynamics. In: Advances in Neural Information Processing Systems, pp. 613–621 (2016)
31. Yingzhen, L., Mandt, S.: Disentangled sequential autoencoder. In: International Conference on Machine Learning, pp. 5656–5665 (2018)
32. Zagoruyko, S., Komodakis, N.: Learning to compare image patches via convolutional neural networks. In: Proceedings of the IEEE Conference on Computer Vision and Pattern Recognition, pp. 4353–4361 (2015)
33. Zhang, J., Shan, S., Kan, M., Chen, X.: Coarse-to-fine auto-encoder networks (CFAN) for real-time face alignment. In: Fleet, D., Pajdla, T., Schiele, B., Tuytelaars, T. (eds.) ECCV 2014, Part II. LNCS, vol. 8690, pp. 1–16. Springer, Cham (2014). https://doi.org/10.1007/978-3-319-10605-2_1
34. Zhao, J., Mathieu, M., Goroshin, R., LeCun, Y.: Stacked What-Where Auto-encoders. arXiv:1506.02351 [cs, stat], June 2015
35. Zhao, J., Mathieu, M., LeCun, Y.: Energy-based generative adversarial network. arXiv preprint arXiv:1609.03126 (2016)

Demonstrations

A Method for Enriching Video-Watching Experience with Applied Effects Based on Eye Movements

Masayuki Tamura[✉] and Satoshi Nakamura

Meiji University, 4-21-1 Nakano-ku, Tokyo, Japan
mogamusa3l@gmail.com

Abstract. We propose a method to enrich the experience of watching videos by applying effects to video clips which are shared on the Web on the basis of eye movements. We implemented a prototype system as a Web browser extension and created several effects that are applied depending on the point of a viewer's gaze. In addition, we conducted an experimental test, and clarified the usefulness of our effects, and investigated how adding the effects affected viewer experience.

Keywords: Eye movements · Effect · Video · Watching experience

1 Introduction

There are various services and studies that have tried to make video content more enjoyable by adding special effects. For example, on the video-sharing Web site *Nico Nico Douga*[1], comments are superimposed onto videos, which makes the content more enjoyable by enabling viewers to share their feelings with others. Yamaura et al. [1] presented a method that extends the experience of digital content by simply super-imposing blurring effects that follow the gaze point of the user, and due to this method, almost all psychological impression items (immersion, stereoscopic effect and so on) to the video became higher.

For content such as animation and comics, effects such as emphasis lines and solid flashes are often used. These effects are used to add impact and to make it easier to grasp the situation being depicted. For example, emphasis lines can be superimposed towards the periphery of an object, thereby emphasizing the object's movement. A solid flash can surround a certain object and express changes in circumstances, among other things. In other words, it is possible to make content more enjoyable and easier to understand by applying effects onto content with moving images.

It is now possible to acquire a gaze-detection device even at home because eye tracking devices have become inexpensive. In addition, in the near future, laptop cameras are expected to come with a built-in gaze-detection function. DELL have already launched a laptop named Alienware 17 that is equipped with an eye-tracking device. Line of sight expresses the interest of a viewer well, so there are studies that

---

[1] http://www.nicovideo.jp.

I. Kompatsiaris et al. (Eds.): MMM 2019, LNCS 11296, pp. 547–553, 2019.
https://doi.org/10.1007/978-3-030-05716-9_44

propose methods for using Web sites to determine where the user was looking at [2]. In addition, there are studies that use blurring to guide the human gaze [6]. In the previous work, rather than using line of sight to analyze the user or operate the GUI, we used it to change the position of an effect being applied to on-screen content.

The objective of our work is to enrich the video-watching experience. In order to enrich the experience, we propose a method which overlays the effect on a video clip on the Web along the viewer's line of sight. We believe that the method makes the content more enjoyable by shifting the position of the effect each time the center is shifted. We also implement the prototype system as a browser extension, allowing effects to be applied to any video clips on the Web, with the goal of making content more enjoyable. Further, by conducting an evaluation experiment, we determined the usefulness of the proposed method and used viewers' gaze logs to analyze the effects the proposed method had on their behavior.

2 Related Work

There are various studies on enriching viewing experiences. *VRMixer* [3] enables a new viewing experience by letting viewers appear in the video they are watching. By displaying avatars that imitate others in accordance with their degree of excitement, they implemented a system that allows viewers to watch videos while feeling the presence of others through the avatars, thus enriching the viewing experience.

In contrast to these studies, our research is to enrich the viewing experience by applying effects onto videos on the basis of gaze information.

There are various studies on conducting gaze guidance using effects. For example, Kadaba et al. [4] proposed a method using somatic depth of field for enabling users to intuitively understand necessary items when there are multiple gaze point candidates. With this method, the researchers realized that intelligent acquisition of necessary information could be facilitated by blurring the information that is unnecessary for the viewer to the extent that the viewer notices the blur. Hata et al. [5], in contrast, focused on the fact that a person's line of sight is naturally guided from a blurred portion to a clear portion of an image. Hagiwara et al. [6] induced gaze by changing the image so that the salience of the area that the gaze was guided to be the highest in the image. They proposed and implemented a method of dynamically guiding the viewer's line of sight without the viewer noticing by partially blurring or clearing the resolution of the image. This technique uses the characteristics of the line of sight successfully. Differing from this, our research simply enriches the viewing experience by applying gaze.

The objective of our research is to enrich the experience of watching videos with only an individual's own gaze information.

3 Proposed Method

The proposed method enriches the video-viewing experience by adding effects to original content with moving pictures. There are various effects that could be applied depending on the line of sight, but in this paper, we prepared only the effects listed below. They were chosen because these effects are actually used in comics, animation, games, and similar media. The effects are as follows.

- **Emphasis line:** An effect to amplify a sense of momentum. This effect is often expressed with emphasis lines around an object in animation and comics. This is mainly used to amplify the sense of the object's momentum by directing the object with emphasis lines. By superimposing the emphasis line effect centered on the viewer's gaze point, a sense of momentum is amplified.
- **Flashlight:** An effect for amplifying fear. To amplify the element of fear in horror games, there are times when the player is directed to illuminate the dark with a flashlight. This is intended to amplify the viewer's sense of tension by limiting the field of vision to only that area lit by the flashlight, darkening other areas. By superimposing effects that darken everything other than what the viewer is looking at, fear is amplified.
- **Spotlight:** An effect that emphasizes an object or amplifies a feeling of searching for something. The spotlight is used when you want someone to look at a specific scene in an animation or on a stage. The spotlight is a dimly lit effect that emphasizes only the range you want to see. To emphasize and amplify the feeling of searching for something, we superimposed the effect of the spotlight onto a moving element of the video.
- **Fog:** An effect to amplify anxiety. People become uneasy if visibility is impaired in reality. Therefore, anxiety is amplified by making fog appear thin in some places and darker in others.
- **Pixelization:** An effect to amplify impression of violence or sex. Pixelization is applied to censor violent and sensual depictions in television dramas, animation, comics, and other media. Therefore, by using this effect and displaying a pixelated visual at the end of the viewer's line of sight, we amplify the sense of violence or sensuality of the scene because viewers cannot see what is pixelated even if they want to.

We implemented the prototype system as a browser extension for *Google Chrome* using JavaScript. For this study, the averaged gaze coordinates of both eyes were used. It is not possible to directly obtain the information from *Tobii EyeX* with JavaScript, so a mechanism was implemented with C# to send the gaze information obtained by *Tobii EyeX* to the *Chrome* extension via WebSocket. The Chrome extension superimposed the effects onto the videos with the center set to the coordinates of the gaze. The proposed system supports *Nico Nico Douga* and *YouTube*. Figure 1 shows examples in which each of the effects proposed is added to the video. When the user accesses a corresponding Web page after installing the proposed system, the effect assigned to that Web page is superimposed on the screen[2].

---

[2] https://www.youtube.com/watch?v=J152z3NN00Q.

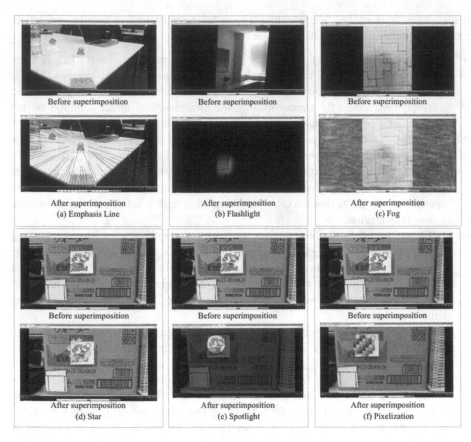

Fig. 1. Examples of adding effects to video clips

4 Experiment

We performed an experiment to evaluate how the video-viewing experience was enriched by applying effects following the line of sight. In the experiment, we examined the impressions of viewers when the effects were and were not superimposed on the videos to clarify the extent to which the viewing experience was enriched. In this experiment, we explained to the experiment participants the content of the experiment and how to proceed in advance, calibrated the gaze-measuring instrument, and then started the experiment.

In this experiment, we chose five effects (emphasis line, spotlight, flashlight, fog, and pixelization) that we felt were particularly compatible with gaze. For the video used in the experiment, we selected two videos that match each effect to ensure no bias due to the video, and prepared ten videos in total. The criteria for selecting the animation in each effect is as follows: a race animation from the racing driver viewpoint for the emphasis line, a reasoning video for the spotlight, a live video of a horror game for the flashlight, a video that induces insecurity in viewers similar to high altitude for the fog, and a video showing a person wearing a swimsuit for the pixelization. We divided the experiment participants (eight male university students in their twenties) into two groups, A and B. One of the two videos selected in advance for each effect was set to α, and the other was set to β. Then, the participants of group A watched α with the effect applied and β with no effect applied. Likewise, the participants of group B watched α without the effect and β with the effect. This was done so as to circumvent the order effect.

We acquired line-of-sight logs while the experiment participants were watching the videos. The time to conduct the experiment per person was about 1 h. In a questionnaire conducted after the experiment, we investigated how the viewers' impressions of the videos changed with the application of the effects. Using Plutchik's wheel of emotions as a reference, we selected "surprise," "terror," "impressiveness," "interest," "frustration," "sadness," "disgust," and "enjoyment" as questionnaire items. Each participant was asked to respond to each item using the five-point Likert scale. Also, in all the experiments, we asked for opinions and comments on the videos.

Table 1. Results of the questionnaire in each effect and impression.

		Surprise	Terror	Impressiveness	Interest	Frustration	Sadness	Disgust	Enjoyment
Emphasis line	Using	-0.13	-0.88	0.50	1.00	0.00	-1.50	0.00	1.00
	None	-0.13	-1.13	0.00	0.88	-0.75	-1.63	-1.38	0.13
Flashlight	Using	1.38	1.38	0.63	1.63	0.63	-1.50	0.38	0.38
	None	0.63	0.50	-0.13	0.88	0.88	-1.50	0.50	0.00
Spotlight	Using	-0.25	-1.50	0.50	1.50	-0.38	-1.75	-1.25	0.88
	None	-0.75	-1.63	0.50	1.00	0.00	-1.75	-0.38	0.63
Fog	Using	0.13	0.38	0.50	0.25	-0.38	-1.63	-0.88	-0.25
	None	1.25	0.63	0.75	1.13	-1.63	-1.75	-1.13	0.00
Pixelization	Using	0.13	-1.88	1.13	1.50	0.75	-0.38	0.25	0.25
	None	0.00	-1.88	1.00	1.00	-1.13	-1.38	-1.50	0.25

Table 1 lists the average evaluation values given by the experiment participants for each pair of videos (for a total of ten videos) for each effect. As shown in Table 1, for the emphasis line effect, impressiveness, enjoyment, frustration, and disgust were amplified. For the flashlight effect, surprise, fear, impressiveness, and interest were amplified. For the spotlight effect, interest increased, and surprise decreased. For the fog effect, however, frustration was amplified while surprise and interest decreased. Interest, frustration, sadness, and disgust were all amplified with the pixelization effect.

5 Discussion

The questionnaire results indicate that negative evaluations such as frustration and disgust increased for the emphasis line effect, but because the values were not high, it is safe to assume that the evaluators were not particularly frustrated and did not feel a strong sense of disgust. Moreover, enjoyment and impressiveness increased, which suggests that by applying the effect, the impact and presence of the video were amplified, viewers felt more of a sense of momentum, and their enjoyment increased.

For the flashlight effect, evaluations of surprise, fear, impressiveness, and interest increased. This effect was expected to enrich the viewing experience with a component of fear by amplifying the viewer's interest in the invisible part. Because part of the screen was made dark, the viewer's surprise and interest increased. For the spotlight effect, interest and surprise increased, and irritation decreased. We presume that irritation decreased because this effect was able to emphasize central vision without obstructing peripheral vision. Contrary to our expectations for the fog effect, evaluations for surprise and interest decreased. One possible reason for this is that the ease of viewing may have been reduced; however, the evaluations of frustration were low. For the pixelization effect, negative evaluations such as frustration, sadness, and disgust all increased. However, evaluations of interest also increased, which suggests that there was a sense of morbid curiosity, and viewers were interested in the part of the video that they could not see in their central view.

6 Conclusion

In this paper, we proposed a method to enrich the experience of viewing videos by displaying effects on the basis of the viewer's gaze, evaluated the development and usefulness of the system, and determined the effect on user behavior of applying the proposed effects. We found that the viewer's impression of the video changed in the way we expected for many of the effects. However, we did find that the fog effect had the opposite effect of what we intended.

In this study, there was an effect that did not produce the expected effect like the fog effect because we chose the effects subjectively. Therefore, in the future work, we will analyze a detailed feature of effects with good and poor results in this study and upgrade the effects.

Acknowledgments. This work was supported in part by JST ACCEL Grant Number JPMJAC1602, Japan.

References

1. Yamaura, H., Tamura, M., Nakamura, S.: Image blurring method for enriching digital content viewing experience. In: Proceedings of HCII 2018, pp. 355–370 (2018)
2. Umemoto, K., Ymamoto, T., Nakamura, S., Tanaka, K.: Search intent estimation from user's eye movements for supporting information seeking. In: Proceedings of AVI 2012, pp. 349–356 (2012)
3. Hirai, T., Nakamura, S., Yumura, T., Morishima, S.: VRMixer: mixing video and real world with video segmentation. In: Proceedings of ACE 2014, pp. 1–7 (2014)
4. Kadaba, N.R., Yang, X.-D., Irani, P.P.: Facilitating multiple target tracking using Semantic Depth of Field (SODF). In: CHI EA 2009, pp. 4375–4380 (2009)
5. Hata, H., Koide, H., Sato, Y.: Visual guidance with unnoticed blur effect. In: Advanced Visual Interfaces (AVI 2016), pp. 28–35 (2016)
6. Hagiwara, A., Sugimoto, A., Kawamoto, K.: Saliency-based image editing for guiding visual attention. In: PETMEI 2011, pp. 43–48 (2011)

Fontender: Interactive Japanese Text Design with Dynamic Font Fusion Method for Comics

Junki Saito[(⊠)] and Satoshi Nakamura

Meiji University, 4-21-1 Nakano, Nakano-Ku, Tokyo, Japan
jonki.fms@gmail.com

Abstract. Comics consist of frames, drawn images, speech balloons, text, and so on. In this work, we focus on the difficulty of designing the text used for the narration and quotes of characters. In order to support creators in their text design, we propose a method to design text by a font fusion algorithm with arbitrary existing fonts. In this method, users can change the font type freely by indicating a point on the font map. We implement a prototype system and discuss its effectiveness.

Keywords: Font · Text design · Font fusion · Comic

1 Introduction

Since the emergence of tablet PCs that can be used with a stylus, the creation and transmission of comics by individuals have become popular. In Japan, the number of services that can easily distribute comics created by individuals, such as MediBang [1] and LINE Manga [2], are increasing. The key elements of comic creation include drawing characters and backgrounds and designing text balloons and banners. Another element is the text design, which greatly influences the greatness of comics.

When a comic creator designs texts with the atmosphere of the scene or the characters' personality in mind, great care is taken to select a font from a list of available ones that fits the desired image. However, there are fewer types of Japanese fonts compared to European and American ones because Japanese fonts require over 7000 characters. This fact significantly narrows the choices of Japanese comic creators and makes it difficult for them to come up with text design that suits the situation.

There have been several studies on transforming existing fonts and acquiring new glyph shapes. Suveeranont et al. [3] proposed a system that creates a new font by fusing an arbitrary font with a character handwritten by the user. However, when this system merges the handwritten character and the font, the users have to adjust the corresponding stroke. Campbell et al. [4] proposed a method that detects corresponding strokes by placing fonts on two-dimensional flat surface so that fonts with similar shapes are placed close to each other. The problem with this method is that the combination of fusible fonts is limited.

We propose three methods in this work. The first is a dynamic font fusion method featuring an averaging technique. The second is a method of generating Japanese fonts interactively by indicating a point in two-dimensional space, thus enabling users to

I. Kompatsiaris et al. (Eds.): MMM 2019, LNCS 11296, pp. 554–559, 2019.
https://doi.org/10.1007/978-3-030-05716-9_45

design texts that match any scene in the comic. The third is a method to acquire new fonts by arbitrarily combining multiple fonts. We also implement a prototype system to determine how well the proposed methods can be used to design the texts used in comics.

2 Fontender

We propose a method called "Fontender", a new font generation method that uses arbitrary existing fonts and freely changes the shape of the fonts. This method sets existing fonts on a two-dimensional surface with the impression words input by the user as its axis, and it fuses multiple fonts according to the position on the space selected by the user with our font fusion algorithm.

2.1 Algorithm for Blending Fonts

We grasp information on the core and thickness of the font as a mathematical expression and blend the font by fusing the mathematical expressions. In this work, we assume that letters can be formed with a locus of a circle whose radius changes, and express a font by drawing a locus of the circle so that the point on the core line is the center coordinates.

The procedure for formulating a font is shown in Fig. 1. First, our method locates the locus of the circle expressing the font. Next, in order to express the font smoothly, cubic spline interpolation connects sets of the circles as much as possible and circles occupying the space are generated. Next, our method locates circle sets of the closed curves by folding back sets of the circles to which spline interpolation is applied. The reason for making it a closed curve is that if the starting point and the ending point of mathematical expression are separated by Fourier series expansion, the curve will be wavy near both ends trying to connect both ends. We denote the parametric representation of plane curve passing through this circle sets as $(x, y, z) = (f(t), g(t), h(t))(-\pi \leq t \leq \pi)$. $(f(t), g(t))$ at t is the point on the core line of the font, and $h(t)$ is the largest radius of inscribed circle at t in the font. Although $f(t)$, $g(t)$, and $h(t)$ are not a periodic function, we define them as periodic function by defining them like the formula shown in (1).

$$f(t) = f(t + 2n\pi) \qquad n = 0, 1, 2 \ldots \tag{1}$$

Furthermore, $f(t)$, $g(t)$, and $h(t)$ can be expressed by a Fourier series by considering the corner of the character as a curved line approximating steeply bent. Therefore, $f(t)$ can be expressed by an equation as shown in (2).

$$f(t) = \frac{a_0}{2} + \sum_{n=1}^{\infty} (a_n \cos nt + b_n \sin nt) \tag{2}$$

a_n and b_n are obtained by the formulas as shown in (3).

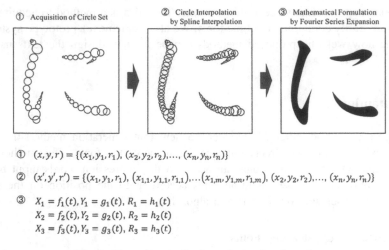

① Acquisition of Circle Set   ② Circle Interpolation by Spline Interpolation   ③ Mathematical Formulation by Fourier Series Expansion

① $(x, y, r) = \{(x_1, y_1, r_1), (x_2, y_2, r_2), \ldots, (x_n, y_n, r_n)\}$

② $(x', y', r') = \{(x_1, y_1, r_1), (x_{1,1}, y_{1,1}, r_{1,1}), \ldots (x_{1,m}, y_{1,m}, r_{1,m}), (x_2, y_2, r_2), \ldots, (x_n, y_n, r_n)\}$

③ $X_1 = f_1(t), Y_1 = g_1(t), R_1 = h_1(t)$
$X_2 = f_2(t), Y_2 = g_2(t), R_2 = h_2(t)$
$X_3 = f_3(t), Y_3 = g_3(t), R_3 = h_3(t)$

Fig. 1. Procedure to display a font using formulas.

$$\begin{cases} a_n = \frac{1}{\pi} \int_{-\pi}^{\pi} f(t) \cos ntdt \\ b_n = \frac{1}{\pi} \int_{-\pi}^{\pi} f(t) \sin ntdt \end{cases} \tag{3}$$

Finally, using these formula, n kinds of fonts are blended at arbitrary ratios. When we denote the formula of each font's stroke as $(x, y, z) = (f_i(t), g_i(t), h_i(t))$ and the blend ratios of each font as $\alpha_1 \sim \alpha_n$, the formula of the stroke of the blended font can be expressed as in (4). Changing this blending ratio makes it possible to create arbitrary fonts.

$$\begin{cases} x = \sum_{i=1}^{n} \alpha_i f_i(t) \\ y = \sum_{i=1}^{n} \alpha_i g_i(t) \\ r = \sum_{i=1}^{n} \alpha_i h_i(t) \end{cases} \tag{4}$$

2.2   Impression Estimation for Font

In Fontender, in order to make the impression word of the font usable as input, it is necessary to obtain the impression value of the existing font and the factor structure of the impression people receive.

In order to obtain the impression value and the impression factor structure, we asked 17 experimental participants (university students aged 20 to 23 years old) to make an impression evaluation of the font. A total of 18 types of fonts were evaluated (see Fig. 2). We selected 35 adjective pairs used in an earlier impression study [5, 6] of Japanese fonts and asked the participants to perform a seven-step evaluation by the semantic differential method.

In order to confirm what type of impression structure is formed from the obtained data, we performed a factor analysis by the main factor method and Promax rotation for all 18 types of fonts. After excluding an adjective pair whose commonality was less

Fig. 2. Font list to be evaluated.

than 0.35 and an adjective pair belonging to a plurality of factors, 18 pairs of adjectives (hard-soft, square-round, dopey-clear, loose-tense, formal-casual, sharp-dull, harsh-mild, imitative-creative, unstable-stable, mature-childish, bad-good, uncomfortable-comfortable, dislike-like, ugly-beautiful, painful-pleasant, gloomy-happy, feeble-powerful, sober-flashy) and four factors (mild, attractive, optimistic, active) were extracted. In the prototype system described in Sect. 3, it is possible to designate the four factors extracted by factor analysis along with the 18 adjective pairs.

3 Prototype System

We implemented a prototype system[1] for character design support in comics (see Fig. 3). This system consists of two parts: one for generating a font and one for previewing the generated font. This system was implemented by Processing.

The proposed system arranges existing fonts on a two-dimensional surface based on two impression words input by the user after viewing the image. Since we used factor names and adjective pairs (obtained by factor analysis in Sect. 2) as input words, we use a value obtained by normalizing the value obtained by averaging the evaluation values of experimental collaborators to –1 to +1 as an impression values of the font. In addition, we normalized the impression values of each factor was –1 to +1.

The user can set impression words using the factor name or the adjective selection interface at the bottom of the font generating part. In addition, we installed a toggle button so that the user can switch between the mode in which factor names can be selected and the mode in which adjectives can be selected. The impression word selected first by the user is the horizontal axis of the two-dimensional plane, and the second impression word is the vertical axis of the two-dimensional plane so that further selection is not accepted. When the user selects impression words, 18 kinds of fonts are arranged according to the impression value with the two impression words selected by the user as the axis.

When 18 kinds of fonts are arranged, the user can generate blended fonts. Specifically, by changing the position of the mouse pointer on the two-dimensional

---

[1] https://www.youtube.com/watch?v=6tLaz4dCfTE.

Fig. 3. A screen shot of the prototype system. In this screen shot, the user designs the text "うめえ (delicious in Japanese)" in the speech balloon. The user generates a new font by pointing in the right area of this window.

surface, this system blends the four adjacent fonts by changing the fusion ratio according to the distance to each mouse pointer. The fusion ratio is the ratio of the inverse of the distance to the mouse pointer, and the closest font has the highest fusion ratio. Blending results are displayed in real time.

Figure 4 shows how to design the expression "しあわせだ (happy in Japanese)" using the prototype system. Figure 4 left is a text design in which the degree of "like" and "warm" is high. This text design is rounded and has a shape that expresses femininity. In another example, Fig. 4 right is a text design in which the degree of "like" and "warm" is low. This text design is thick and has a shape that makes you feel powerful. In the implementation at this point, since smoothing cannot be performed to change the thickness, some noise remains partly in the character.

To verify the usefulness of our system, we conducted experiments comparing the proposed method with two baseline systems. One is a pull down interface and the other

Fig. 4. Left: Font creation example with high "like" and "warm" degrees. Right: Font creation example with low "like" and "warm" degrees low. This image uses the excerpts from "Aosugiru Haru" written by Momoko Okuda in Manga 109 [7].

is a map interface without font fusion. We asked 15 subjects (aged from 21 to 23) to design five times with three systems, and asked them to evaluate the degree of satisfaction after each design task by the five level Likert scale. As a result of two variance analysis of them, the main effect of the design task was not significant in either question, but the main effect of the method is the map arrangement form ($F [1, 4] = 4.95$, $p < 0.05$) and list format ($F [1, 4] = 6.54$, $p < 0.05$).

4   Conclusion and Future Work

To solve the inherent problems in text design, we proposed a method of blending existing fonts to match the impression of users' intended impression and generating a new font. We also implemented a prototype system for character design support using the proposed method and showed through examples under various conditions that this method is effective.

In the future work, we will improve the system so that it can support the design of letters used in comics in general. Specifically, we plan to implement a function that allows users to easily compare previous and next characters, creating a log of the font blend results, and an adjust function by outlining the blending results of multiple fonts or the blending results of fonts and handwriting.

Our method is not only for comics but also for every content design. For example, we can apply our system for poster design and digital publishing such as a name card, a handout, a presentation slide, a web page, a Christmas card, and so on. In the future, we will realize such system.

Acknowledgments. This work was supported in part by JST ACCEL Grant Number JPMJAC1602, Japan.

References

1. MediBang. https://medibang.com/creators. Accessed 15 Sep 2018
2. LINE Manga. https://manga.line.me/indies/debut. Accessed 15 Sep 2018
3. Suveeranont, R., Igarashi, T.: Example-based automatic font generation. In: Taylor, R., Boulanger, P., Krüger, A., Olivier, P. (eds.) SG 2010. LNCS, vol. 6133, pp. 127–138. Springer, Heidelberg (2010). https://doi.org/10.1007/978-3-642-13544-6_12
4. Campbell, N., Kautz, J.: Learning a manifold of fonts. ACM Trans. Graph. (SIGGRAPH) **33**(4) (2014)
5. Inoue, M., Yoroizawa, I.: Impression received from letter form and examination of quality evaluation factor. IEICE Trans. **J67-B**(3), 328–335 (1984)
6. Inoue, M., Kobayashi, T.: The research domain and scale construction of adjective-pairs in a semantic differential method in Japan. Jpn. J. Educ. Psychol. **33**(3), 253–260 (1985)
7. Matsui, Y., et al.: Sketch-based Manga Retrieval using Manga109 Dataset. Multimedia Tools Appl. **76**, 21811–21838 (2017)

Training Researchers with the MOVING Platform

Iacopo Vagliano[1]([✉]), Angela Fessl[2], Franziska Günther[3]
Thomas Köhler[3], Vasileios Mezaris[4], Ahmed Saleh[1], Ansgar Scherp[5],
and Ilija Šimić[2]

[1] ZBW – Leibniz Information Centre for Economics, Kiel, Germany
{i.vagliano,a.saleh}@zbw.eu
[2] Know Center, Graz, Austria
{afessl,isimic}@know-center.at
[3] Technische Universität Dresden, Dresden, Germany
{franziska.guenther1,thomas.koehler}@tu-dresden.de
[4] Centre for Research and Technology Hellas, Thessaloniki, Greece
bmezaris@iti.gr
[5] University of Stirling, Stirling, Scotland, UK
ansgar.scherp@stir.ac.uk

Abstract. The MOVING platform enables its users to improve their information literacy by training how to exploit data and text mining methods in their daily research tasks. In this paper, we show how it can support researchers in various tasks, and we introduce its main features, such as text and video retrieval and processing, advanced visualizations, and the technologies to assist the learning process.

Keywords: Technology enhanced learning · Information retrieval
Text and video analysis · Recommender systems

1 Introduction

Researchers in academia and industry struggle in being aware of publications, patents, products, and also funding opportunities to properly address a new research topic because of the fast-growing amount of relevant content. Similarly, students need to learn to exploit a large and steadily increasing number of previous publications and other online educational resources (video lectures, tutorials, blogs, etc.). While nowadays information is often freely available in various formats, such as text and media, extracting useful knowledge from all the accessible educational resources requires a lot of time, and often researchers lack strategies and tools to effectively do so.

The MOVING platform[1] aims to address these issues. It integrates various kinds of educational resources such as documents, videos, and social media data.

---

[1] http://platform.moving-project.eu.

© Springer Nature Switzerland AG 2019
I. Kompatsiaris et al. (Eds.): MMM 2019, LNCS 11296, pp. 560–565, 2019.
https://doi.org/10.1007/978-3-030-05716-9_46

Through the platform, users can search these resources and display the search results in different ways thanks to the advanced visualizations available. Users can improve their skills in information literacy through a curriculum designed by experts in learning, and the platform can track their progress in using its features and support their learning in various ways.

The paper is organized as follows. In Sect. 2, we briefly describe how young researchers can be trained through the MOVING platform. In Sect. 3, we introduce the platform, while in Sect. 4 its main features. We conclude the paper in Sect. 5.

2 Training Young Researchers

The MOVING platform can assist researchers in various ways. Firstly, it can support them in reviewing the state of the art on a research topic. Through its advanced search features, users can search for relevant topics, as well as refine their search. They can filter the results by authors, subject area, content type (videos, books, articles, website, social media posts), etc., and select the open-access publications. The advanced search allows users to search specific fields such as author, title, abstract and define boolean queries.

As the list of results can be very long, users can exploit a graph visualization to start progressively exploring the content, identify key authors and topics, as well as discover relations among topics, authors and documents. Users can personalize the ranking of the results based on their interest. By selecting keywords, they can focus on the topics more relevant to them, and they can assign different weights to the various keywords to give more or less importance to each topic. Tag clouds are available to obtain an overview of the results and charts can show the most frequent topics and sources.

Additionally, the platform helps researchers in finding funding opportunities and suitable partners for research projects. Users can search funding opportunities similarly to other documents. Using the community functionality, they can connect with other users and search them by their research area and skills. Finally, the learning environment enables users to access learning material on information literacy and data mining, such as tutorials and MOOCs.

3 The MOVING Platform at a Glance

The MOVING platform integrates various kinds of educational resources such as documents, videos, and social media data. Some of these resources are automatically harvested from the Web and social networks, while some datasets are manually integrated from Videolectures.net[2], EconBiz[3], and the Social Science Open Access Repository (SSOAR)[4]. Through the platform, users can search

---

[2] http://videolectures.net/.
[3] https://www.econbiz.de/.
[4] https://www.gesis.org/ssoar/home/.

these resources and display the search results in different ways thanks to the advanced visualizations available. They are also assisted in progressing with the information literacy curriculum and in more effectively using the platform.

The architecture of the platform is depicted in Fig. 1. The crawlers automatically ingest data from the Web and store them into the index. Then, data processing techniques, including entity extraction, author disambiguation, data deduplication, and automatic concepts annotation, are applied to the data indexed. The data in the index can then be retrieved through the search engine. WevQuery [1] tracks the users behavior on the platform by capturing UI events which are saved in the user database (User data), while the Adaptive Training Support (ATS) [3] analyses these data to help users to better use the platform and progress in the selected curriculum, depending on their usage patterns. The recommender system builds users' profiles based on their search history and suggests documents according to such profiles. In Sect. 4, we describe the search engine, the ATS, the video processing techniques used, the advanced visualizations and the recommender system.

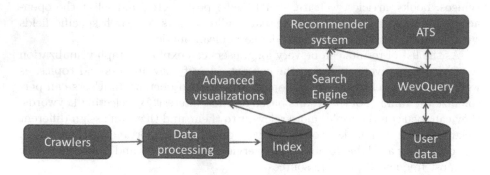

Fig. 1. The MOVING platform's architecture.

4   Main Features of the MOVING Platform

The MOVING Search Engine. The MOVING search page (Fig. 2) provides multimodal and faceted search and handles multiple document types. To retrieve relevant results, the search engine exploits various metadata such as title, abstract and also the concepts with which documents are annotated. For videos, these concepts are automatically assigned to video fragments. Specific fragments of video can be searched through an ad-hoc facet. In addition to more traditional filters such as author, date, subject area, and document type, users can also filter the open access publications. The search engine exploits HCF-IDF [8], a novel ranking and document profile method, which ranks the search results based on their relevance to the user query relying only on titles. This is key because in the MOVING platform document's titles and other metadata are usually available, but the platform stores a limited number of full texts due to copyright issues.

Fig. 2. The search page. On the left, the facets allow users to refine the search; in the middle results are shown; on the right the ATS summarizes the use of the various platform features and provides reflective prompts.

Adaptive Training Support. The ATS [3] supports users to improve their use of the MOVING platform by mirroring back the user behavior in combination with reflective prompts. These prompts stimulate users to reflect on their experience in using some features and to try new features. Specifically, it tracks the use of the various features through WevQuery. The ATS also assists users in completing the selected curriculum, summarizing their progress in a progress bar, providing reflective questions related to their progress and suggesting activities to do next.

Video Processing. We distinguish between two genres of video in the platform: lecture videos, and non-lecture videos. For both, we use suitable fragmentation and annotation approaches for enabling fragment-level access to the video content. Lecture video fragmentation is performed using a method previously developed [5]. This involves first processing the textual transcripts of the video (generated by an off-the-shelve automatic speech recognition component) to extract *noun phrases*; and then using Word2Vec, a neural network based on word embeddings, to represent every word of every noun phrase in a semantic vector space. Sliding temporal windows in the transcripts define larger parts of the text, which are represented in the same semantic space by averaging the aforementioned vector representations of the corresponding words; and the similarity of such windows is assessed using the cosine similarity. Doing so for all pairs of successive sliding windows in a transcript results in a 1D signal. Its local minima (if they also satisfy certain other criteria) are selected as lecture fragment boundaries. Finally, the annotation of each fragment is performed by selecting the most prominent words from the transcripts of each fragment, based on TF-IDF. Alternatively, we can associate each fragment with high-level concepts from a pre-specified concept pool with an adaptation of a previous work [4]. Non-lecture videos are fragmented to video shots using the method of Apostolidis and Mezaris [2], which detects both abrupt and gradual transitions by appropriately assessing the visual similarity of neighboring frames of the video. Then, a representative keyframe is extracted from each shot and is annotated with concepts from a pre-specified concept pool [7]. This method is based on a deep learning architecture that exploits concept relations at two different levels to learn to more accurately detect the concepts in the video.

Advanced Visualizations. In addition to the classical result lists, users can browse the results through alternative and more advanced interfaces. With the concept graph (Fig. 3) users can explore relations between documents, authors, institutions, and topics. Alternatively, uRank (Fig. 4) enables users to personalize the results list by selecting the keywords more relevant to them and assigning to these keywords different weights. Every time a keyword is added or removed as well a weight changed, the results are re-ranked and an information on the positions gained or lost by each result is provided.

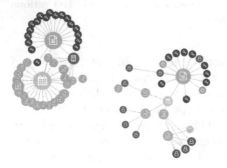 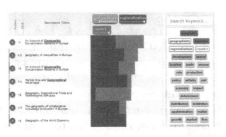

Fig. 3. An example of a concept graph   **Fig. 4.** Results displayed in uRank

Recommender System. HCF-IDF [8] is also used to provide recommendations by matching documents with a user profile. The MOVING recommender system builds users' profiles based on users' search history. It obtains the latter from the user data previously logged through WevQuery, and then it suggests documents based on such users profiles. In our case, the user profile refers to the terms users have previously searched for. It is a set of pairs term-weight, $\langle k_i, w_i \rangle$, where k_i is a term and w_i a weight. The weight of a term depends on how often and how recently the term has been searched for. More formally, the weight w_i of a term k_i is defined by $w_i = \alpha_t \cdot \frac{t}{T} + \alpha_h \cdot \frac{h}{H}$, where α_t is the time coefficient and α_h is the hits coefficient. The h term is the number of times a term has been searched by the user and H the total number of searches made by the user; the timestamp (t) of the last search for the term is normalized by the current time (T). We are also considering to integrate more advanced recommendation techniques based on autoencoders [6] and Linked Data [9].

5   Conclusions

We showed how the MOVING platform may support researchers and its main features. The platform is still being improved and soon new features will be released, such as a more complete learning environment and additional community functionalities.

Acknowledgments. This work was supported by the EU's Horizon 2020 programme under grant agreement H2020-693092 MOVING. The Know-Center is funded within the Austrian COMET Program under the auspices of the Austrian Federal Ministry of Transport, Innovation and Technology, the Austrian Federal Ministry of Economy, Family and Youth and by the State of Styria. COMET is managed by the Austrian Research Promotion Agency FFG.

References

1. Apaolaza, A., Vigo, M.: WevQuery: testing hypotheses about web interaction patterns. Proc. ACM Hum. Comput. Interact. 1(EICS), 4:1–4:17 (2017)
2. Apostolidis, E., Mezaris, V.: Fast shot segmentation combining global and local visual descriptors. In: Proceedings of the IEEE International Conference on Acoustics, Speech and Signal Processing (ICASSP), May 2014
3. Fessl, A., Wertner, A., Pammer-Schindler, V.: Digging for gold: motivating users to explore alternative search interfaces. In: Pammer-Schindler, V., Pérez-Sanagustín, M., Drachsler, H., Elferink, R., Scheffel, M. (eds.) EC-TEL 2018. LNCS, vol. 11082, pp. 636–639. Springer, Cham (2018). https://doi.org/10.1007/978-3-319-98572-5_62
4. Galanopoulos, D., Markatopoulou, F., Mezaris, V., Patras, I.: Concept language models and event-based concept number selection for zero-example event detection. In: Proceedings of ACM ICMR (2017)
5. Galanopoulos, D., Mezaris, V.: Temporal lecture video fragmentation using word embeddings. In: Kompatsiaris, I., et al. (eds.) MMM 2019. LNCS, vol. 11296, pp. 254–265. Springer International Publishing (2019)
6. Galke, L., Mai, F., Vagliano, I., Scherp, A.: Multi-modal adversarial autoencoders for recommendations of citations and subject labels. In: Proceedings of the 26th Conference on User Modeling, Adaptation and Personalization, UMAP 2018, pp. 197–205. ACM (2018)
7. Markatopoulou, F., Mezaris, V., Patras, I.: Implicit and explicit concept relations in deep neural networks for multi-label video/image annotation. IEEE Trans. Circ. Syst. Video Technol., 1 (2018, in press)
8. Nishioka, C., Scherp, A.: Profiling vs. time vs. content: what does matter for top-k publication recommendation based on twitter profiles? In: Proceedings of the 16th ACM/IEEE-CS on Joint Conference on Digital Libraries, JCDL 2016, pp. 171–180. ACM (2016)
9. Vagliano, I., Monti, D., Scherp, A., Morisio, M.: Content recommendation through semantic annotation of user reviews and linked data. In: Proceedings of the Knowledge Capture Conference, K-CAP 2017, pp. 32:1–32:4. ACM (2017)

Space Wars: An AugmentedVR Game

Kyriaki Christaki$^{(\boxtimes)}$, Konstantinos C. Apostolakis, Alexandros Doumanoglou, Nikolaos Zioulis, Dimitrios Zarpalas, and Petros Daras

Visual Computing Lab, Information Technologies Institute,
Centre for Research and Technology Hellas, Thessaloniki, Greece
{kchristaki,kapostol,aldoum,nzioulis,zarpalas,daras}@iti.gr
http://vcl.iti.gr

Abstract. Over the past couple of years, Virtual and Augmented Reality have been at the forefront of the Mixed Reality development scene, whereas Augmented Virtuality has significantly lacked behind. Widespread adoption however requires efficient low-cost platforms and minimalistic interference design. In this work we present *Space Wars*, an end-to-end proof of concept for an elegant and rapid-deployment Augmented VR platform. Through the engaging experience of *Space Wars*, we aim to demonstrate how digital games, as forerunners of innovative technology, are perfectly suited as an application area to embrace the underlying low-cost technology, and thus pave the way for other adopters (such as healthcare, education, tourism and e-commerce) to follow suit.

Keywords: Augmented Virtuality · Virtual Reality (VR)
Mixed Reality (MR) · 3D Capture

1 Introduction

Augmented Virtuality (Augmented VR), is defined as an intermediate state of the reality-virtuality continuum, which refers predominantly to the blending of real world physical elements (such as objects or people) into virtual worlds [3]. In the context of Augmented VR [2], technological advances over the past several years have allowed the development of interactive, immersive applications where user representation utilizes 3-dimensional digitalization of their physical appearance, which is then embedded into the virtual 3D world and offers enhanced and engaging experiences. The development of such systems remains a challenging task however, at it requires an end-to-end pipeline of multiple modules tapping into different technological fields, such as computer vision, data compression and transmission, networking and computer graphics.

We have realized a portable and easy-to-deploy (indoor) platform that can be operated as a local user digitalization node for Augmented VR applications. The platform uses 4 RGB-D sensors, and utilizes an easy-to-use, multi-sensor calibration scheme, which allows for coarse sensor positioning around a pre-defined capturing space without restrictions. By integrating technologies from

© Springer Nature Switzerland AG 2019
I. Kompatsiaris et al. (Eds.): MMM 2019, LNCS 11296, pp. 566–570, 2019.
https://doi.org/10.1007/978-3-030-05716-9_47

multiple fields, the user's full-body 3D appearance, as well as real-time motion are captured and transmitted, to be used as assets in remote virtual and game environments, where interaction between the remote participants is facilitated. In this work, we demonstrate the concept and low-cost Augmented VR platform in the form of *Space Wars*, an immersive one-vs-one networked game where the physical appearance of the two players is dynamically integrated into the game world, cementing a direct, real-time link between the real world and the digital game arena. A motion-control, gesture-based interface allows exploring intuitive aspects of user movement to interact with the game world, while simultaneously maintaining seamless, real-time visual communication and consistency with the other player.

The remainder of this paper is organized as follows: An overview of the underlying platform to achieve Augmented VR experiences is presented in Sect. 2. Section 3 presents the *Space Wars* demonstrator. Finally. Section 4 discusses the Augmented VR experience and concludes with insight on future work.

2 Augmented VR Platform

Our end-to-end Augmented VR pipeline comprises three modules, each respectively responsible for (i) Capturing and Reconstruction, (ii) Compression and Transmission, (iii) Rendering and Interaction. The overall architecture showcasing placement of these modules is shown in Fig. 1. An overview of the three distinctive modules, that reflect the multidisciplinary nature of the presented platform, is presented in the following paragraphs.

Capturing and Reconstruction. Each capturing station comprises 4 low-cost RGB-D sensors placed in a circular setup around the capturing area and 5 computing units. The central unit is responsible for the configuration of the setup, and acts as a hub where the sensor data are collected and processed. The 4 remaining units are assigned to operate one sensor each. At this stage, geometry and appearance reconstruction of users inside the capturing area is implemented by processing a stream of spatially and temporally aligned color and depth frames acquired by the 4 sensor units. The user mesh geometry is complemented by a multi-texturing approach which is used to embed appearance to the generated geometry [5]. To emphasize on the platform's portability and ease of use, the 4 sensors are calibrated using an automated method requiring a stack of standard packing boxes be placed at the center of the capturing area prior to the platform use [1,5]. The output of this module is a stream of timestamped mesh data incorporating attributes such as mesh vertices, triangles, normals and texture blend weights, along with 4 RGB frame viewports to be used as texture maps [5].

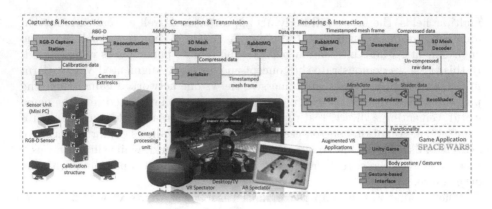

Fig. 1. Augmented VR Platform Architecture.

Compression and Transmission. AugmentedVR applications need to minimize end-to-end latency as it has a huge impact on the perceived Quality of Experience (QoE). Depending on the network conditions different compression schemes perform optimal. On fast network lines low compression is preferable as it often means that the compression time will be minimum. For slow network links higher compression rates are required to minimize end-to-end delay. The current AugmentedVR platform employs various mesh codecs that can be chosen to be used such as OpenCTM, Draco, Corto and O3DGC. For texture compression, standard JPEG compressor is used due to the processing latency requirements.

Rendering and Interaction. The Rendering and Interaction module was developed to embed user representation in the Unity3D game engine[1]. The module is based on a number of Unity3D component scripts, which transform raw data streamed over a RabbitMQ network into a Unity3D renderable asset. Its main components include:

- A **Network Stream Reconstruction Provider (NSRP)**, which handles communication with the RabbitMQ server and notifies module whenever new data arrives. Each update cycle, the component re-builds a 3D mesh into a custom *MeshData* structure using the list of attributes defined in the Capturing and Reconstruction module.
- A **Reconstruction Renderer (RecoRenderer)**: The component "translates" the custom *MeshData* data structure of the NSRP into standard Unity3D Mesh Renderer component data, embedding appearance through a custom RecoRenderer shader. During each update cycle, the component re-builds a standard Unity3D Mesh asset, and updates values of the Shader Material toward blending texture information and retrieving the mesh color

---

[1] https://unity3d.com.

appearance characteristics. Additional effects can be added through the shader to manipulate the resulting mesh in meaningful ways to the game logic, such as adding a highlight to indicate team affiliation (Red or Blue) and exploding/restructuring the mesh geometry as a result of collision with projectiles.

3   Demonstrator

Space Wars is built in Unity3D and utilizes a centralized multi-player game architecture, in which a game server is responsible for game state synchronization. A client-side prediction approach is utilized in order to overcome transfer latency on the game clients that would result to an undesirable "lag" effect. An extensive event messaging system is responsible for the executing the game logic, and for synchronization and communication both locally and over the network through a server-client paradigm.

Game Setting and Goal. *Space Wars* is a sci-fi, 1-vs-1 Capture the Flag (CTF) experience [4] in which two players maneuver a futuristic arena on hoverboards trying to locate and recover the opposing player's flag before theirs is captured. The first player to successfully capture the other player's flag and carry it back to his/her base wins the Round. Players can fire projectiles at one another to force their opponent back to his/her spawning ground and potentially restore their flag back to their base. The game ends when one side wins three Rounds. Example in game screenshots are illustrated in Fig. 2.

Augmented VR Interface. Apart from integrating 3D photorealistic representations of the players on top of each hoverboard, *Space Wars* also utilizes sensor information to control movement in the virtual environment. Using an in-house developed gesture-based interface, users navigate the 3D world and play the game using their body posture. Hoverboard acceleration is controlled by bending the knees, while torso leaning left or right turns the hoverboard towards that direction. Additionally, projectiles can be fired by performing a throwing gesture using their hands.

Live Spectators. The system offers the possibility to non-participating users to connect to the platform as VR spectators. In this "spectator mode", viewers, using VR headsets and controllers, can enter the virtual world of the game and view the CTF match in progress. This immersive experience adds on the attractiveness of the game.

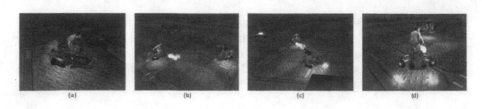

Fig. 2. Space Wars screenshots depicting two players in action. The 3D reconstructed representations of the players appear in the game world and interact with the game and the opponent player in real-time.

4   Conclusion

Augmented VR technology carries a significant potential for ground-breaking innovations delivered to the currently booming Mixed Reality market. The support for photo-realistic user representation opens up opportunities for vastly broadening the MR application spectrum (e.g. immersive collaborative games, tele-presence applications, etc.), while delivering a significant breakthrough in social-minded VR scenarios. Our *Space Wars* demonstrator paves the way for talented people and studios in the VR industry to experiment with the platform, resulting in a significant number of high quality products that people will be able to enjoy both with those around them as well as distant friends and family.

Acknowledgement. This work was supported and received funding from the European Union Horizon 2020 Framework Programme for Research and Innovation Action under Grant Agreement no 762111 VRTogether.

References

1. Alexiadis, D.S., et al.: An integrated platform for live 3D human reconstruction and motion capturing. IEEE Trans. Circuits Syst. Video Technol. **27**(4), 798–813 (2017). https://doi.org/10.1109/TCSVT.2016.2576922
2. Karakottas, A., Papachristou, A., Doumanoglou, A., Zioulis, N., Zarpalas, D., Daras, P.: Augmented VR, IEEE Virtual Reality, 18–22 March 2018. https://www.youtube.com/watch?v=7O_TrhtmP5Q
3. Milgram, P., Kishino, F.: A taxonomy of mixed reality visual displays. IEICE Trans. Inf. Syst. **77**(12), 1321–1329 (1994)
4. Rocha, J.B., Mascarenhas, S., Prada, R.: Game mechanics for cooperative games. ZON Digital Games **2008**, 72–80 (2008)
5. Zioulis, N., et al.: 3D tele-immersion platform for interactive immersive experiences between remote users. In: 2016 IEEE International Conference on Image Processing (ICIP), pp. 365–369, September 2016. https://doi.org/10.1109/ICIP.2016.7532380

ECAT - Endoscopic Concept Annotation Tool

Bernd Münzer[✉], Andreas Leibetseder, Sabrina Kletz, and Klaus Schoeffmann

Institute of Information Technology, Klagenfurt University, Klagenfurt, Austria
{bernd,aleibets,sabrina,ks}@itec.aau.at

Abstract. The trend to video documentation in minimally invasive surgery demands for effective and expressive semantic content understanding in order to automatically organize huge and rapidly growing endoscopic video archives. To provide such assistance, deep learning proved to be the means of choice, but requires large amounts of high quality training data labeled by domain experts to produce adequate results. We present a web-based annotation system that provides a very efficient workflow for medical domain experts to conveniently create such video training data with minimum effort.

Keywords: Medical multimedia · Video interaction · Deep learning

1 Introduction

Performing a body internal surgery in a minimally invasive manner typically involves inserting surgical equipment through natural orifices or small incisions created on a patient's body. As a very popular practice of MIS, *endoscopy* revolves around administering such a surgery via an external monitor, displaying the feed of a high-tech camera (*endoscope*), which captures the surgeon applying patient treatments by utilizing several highly specialized instruments. With this technology in place, it stands to reason to record corresponding live-streams in order to allow for revisiting specific surgeries at any point in time. Apart from legal safeguarding, this custom offers a great variety of advantages ranging from more effective treatment planning up to greatly improving educational training [1,5]. On the downside, however, this practice quickly results in huge video archives, especially when considering that hours-long surgeries are performed on a daily basis. This of course entails several unpleasant side effects such as the requirement of safe long-term data storage and finding a way to efficiently search those archived videos. The latter is not merely about optimizing retrieval of recorded surgeries but more importantly about intelligently searching within such videos, since their manual perusal is a tedious and time-consuming task rather representing a burden than a benefit for physicians, who typically are working on tight schedules. Therefore, more sophisticated ways for computer-aided surgery analysis in order to support medical practitioners are in high demand.

© Springer Nature Switzerland AG 2019
I. Kompatsiaris et al. (Eds.): MMM 2019, LNCS 11296, pp. 571–576, 2019.
https://doi.org/10.1007/978-3-030-05716-9_48

Much effort is already spent on optimizing and analyzing endoscopic video [6] and the successful appliance of deep learning within the multimedia community naturally triggers similar applications in the medical domain, e.g. for classifying diseases. A crucial step when taking such an approach is gathering a large and representative amount of training data needed in order to train well-performing prediction models [7]. Since in this specialized medical domain most of the content cannot be interpreted by laymen, domain expert knowledge is essential for preventing the creation of inaccurate training data. As mentioned before, the time of medical practitioners is limited, so the ground truth creation process has to be as efficient and convenient as possible.

When collecting training data from endoscopic video, usually single frames or frame sequences are annotated, i.e., assigned one or more specific *concepts*. A simple example would be converting all video frames into images and moving selected ones into distinct folders associated with some concept. Of course such a naive approach would be very effortful and could as well prove error prone. In order to facilitate this process, scientific communities are working on creating more sophisticated tools, e.g. [2] or [4], that optimally enable a quick and comfortable annotation workflow.

In this demo paper, we propose an interactive annotation tool specifically designed to meet aforementioned requirements. Nevertheless, the tool is generic enough to be also applicable to any other domain. Moreover, it can easily be extended for specific requirements and therefore might be of big interest for the entire multimedia research community.

2   Endoscopic Concept Annotation Tool

ECAT is essentially a rich web application that mainly builds on PHP, MySQL, Javascript and ffmpeg. The lack of critical dependencies makes it easily applicable on any major platform. The data source is simply a directory containing a (potentially very large) collection of web-compatible video files (e.g., mp4) and can be extended at any time without affecting previous annotations.

An annotation item consists of a list of *concepts* and a *segment*, which is defined by a video name, a start and end timecode as well as a keyframe timecode. ECAT also supports annotation of single images, but internally they are nevertheless treated as segments (with start timecode equals end timecode as well as keyframe timecode). Each annotated concept can additionally contain one or multiple *sketches* that define a spatial area in the image that the corresponding concept is associated with.

2.1   User Interface

The main user interface (depicted in Fig. 1) is organized as follows:

- The left part contains a hierarchical *concept tree* that represents the taxonomy of semantic concepts that can be annotated. It can easily be edited and extended by the user. It is also possible to assign hotkeys to any concept for an even smoother workflow.

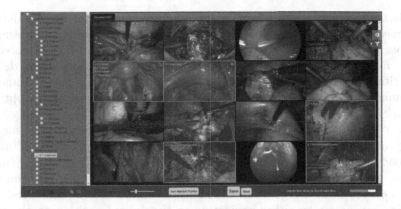

Fig. 1. Screenshot of the main user interface.

- The main content area on the right contains tabs with different functionality. We can mainly distinguish between two types of tabs: *grid tabs* and others with various secondary features. Grid tabs always show a two-dimensional grid of images, each representing an annotation item. The different types of Grid tabs and other tabs are described in the following sections.
- The bottom area provides a status and navigation area that on the one hand displays relevant information about the current system state (e.g., zoom level, dataset size, and random buffer fill level) and on the other hand provides links to the various special features of the tool.
- The two icons on the right can be clicked to optionally open a settings and filter pane that allow to modify various system parameters.

2.2   Annotation Features

The default tab that is displayed upon start is the so-called *random tab*. It shows $m \times n$ images (depending on the current zoom level) taken from random positions within the entire data set. The underlying idea of the random selection strategy is to maximize the variability of annotated images in order to provide a high generality, which is much harder to reach with a traditional linear navigation through individual videos. The random images are extracted at client-side by a pool of background HTML5 video elements. The random positions are determined with respect to the entire dataset, i.e., each frame has the same chance to be selected, regardless of the duration of the video it belongs to. For a smooth transition to new random frames, a buffer with random images is continuously filled. Thus, new images can be displayed immediately without delay.

To create a basic annotation, the user just needs to click on one of the images. The currently selected concept from the Concept Tree is then associated with the respective image. Each image can have multiple assigned concepts. A user can basically pursue two annotation strategies, depending on their annotation goal:

(1) selecting a concept and browsing the random selection for images showing this concept or (2) selecting interesting images and exhaustively annotating all concepts that apply. Beyond that, the random selection can be influenced by various filters, which restrict the random selection to frames that fulfill defined filter criteria. Currently supported criteria are (1) video name patterns and (2) minimum prediction confidences for pre-defined classes based on an optional a-priori classification step.

For concepts that incorporate a certain temporal context (e.g. surgical errors), annotation of single images is not sufficient. Therefore, ECAT allows to extend an annotation to a segment. The *editing window* (see Fig. 2a) can be used to define such a segment. It is opened by clicking a playback icon that appears on top of an image when the mouse is moved over it. Start, end, and keyframe can be set by either navigating to the desired position on the time-line and clicking a button, or by dragging the according handles. The visible range of the video timeline can be modified with the mousewheel to enable different degrees of navigation granularity. The temporal context is visualized by a small additional timeline on top. In order to avoid duplicate or overlapping annotations, previously existing annotations are also visualized on the timeline.

The editing window additionally enables the user to add one or more spatial annotations (sketches) to each associated concept (inspired by [2]). Sketches are always created on the keyframe. Currently, three different sketching modalities are supported: rectangles, polygons and freehand drawings. Sketches can be edited and complemented with a textual comment.

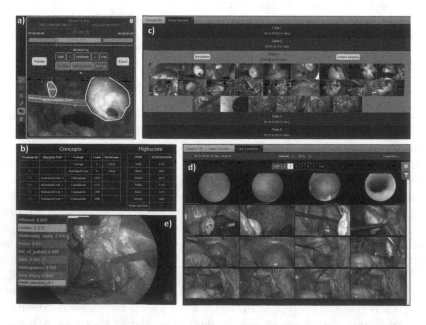

Fig. 2. Screenshots of further interface elements: (a) editing window, (b) statistics tab, (c) case overview, (d) uniform sampled grid tab, (e) classification feedback visualization. (Color figure online)

2.3   Inspection of Annotated Data

Annotations have to be explicitly saved by the user. The server additionally stores a JPG file for each keyframe, so it does not have to be extracted from the video again. The context menu in the concept tree provides a link to an overview tab showing all existing annotation items with the according concept (including sub-concepts, if desired) in a Grid Tab with an efficient paging mechanism. Existing annotations can also be displayed per video or case. Additional information like annotation time, annotator username, or comments can optionally be displayed. Annotations can be modified in the same way as in the Random Tab, i.e. concepts and sketches can be added or removed, and the segment boundaries as well as the keyframe can be changed. Annotation might also be performed by non-experts (e.g. for "simple" concepts that do not need the highest level of domain expertise). In this case, an expert can still go over the list of annotations and explicitly confirm them using a special *confirmation mode*.

The stored images can be exported in the form of an archive file containing directory structure that corresponds to the concept hierarchy, and thus can easily be used to train a classifier. A planned extension of the system will directly integrate a training as well as an evaluation component into the system, providing an all-in-one solution for creating deep learning models.

A further tab (see Fig. 2b) shows statistics about the annotation database (number of annotations, distribution across concepts etc.). Furthermore, it contains a "highscore" of annotations per user, which transforms the annotation task to a kind of competition between users. This rudimental gamification turned out to be a nice additional incentive in practice.

2.4   Uniform Sampling and Classification Feedback

While the default random image selection provides high data variability, some annotation scenarios require a more structured navigation ability. An example is the annotation of disease patterns like endometriosis, which mainly are visible in the early stage of a procedure. Such an alternative presentation is realized with uniformly sampled Grid Tabs, which split a selected video clip into ranges with equal duration (e.g., 10 s), each represented by one grid item. The relative position of the range within the clip is visualized by a green bar below the image. Existing annotations within a range are visualized as well and can be selected and modified (see Fig. 2d). Additionally to uniform tabs containing a single video clip, ECAT supports uniform tabs containing multiple clips that belong to the same surgical *case* (this information must be provided in a text file in the video directory). Also a summary of all cases in the dataset is available (see Fig. 2d), including a thumbnail image for each clip for better overview.

Once a classification model has been trained based on the annotated images, it is interesting to see how it performs on previously unseen data. ECAT defines a simple request format to send one of more images of annotation items to an external classification service in order to obtain classification confidences for a set of predefined classes. The returned confidence values are displayed in an additional overlay that also visualizes the distribution of confidences across the classes (see Fig. 2e). This feature can on the one hand be used to qualitatively spot-check the classification performance, but also for improvement of the classification model. In the latter scenario, users can either confirm the prediction by clicking on the class with the highest confidence, or correct it by clicking on the actually correct class. This feedback information is stored in the database and can be used to refine the classification model. We are currently evaluating different strategies how this can be successfully achieved.

3   Conclusions and Further Work

We have presented an interactive video tool for efficient video concept annotation. It allows to annotate video segments with multiple classes very quickly, to sketch/define relevant objects in video frames, as well as to visualize classification results (i.e., confidences) of a given model for a set of predefined classes. The tool can be easily used via the web, which makes it perfectly suited for external video annotation – such as in a medical multimedia setting, where the experts/clinicians work in different hospitals and do not have much time for video annotation. We have already successfully used the tool for several studies and for creating the laparoscopic gynecology dataset LapGyn4[1] [3]. As one of the next steps we intend to release it to the public as an open source tool.

References

1. Gambadauro, P., Magos, A.: Surgical videos for accident analysis, performance improvement, and complication prevention: time for a surgical black box? Surg. Innov. **19**(1), 76–80 (2012)
2. Leibetseder, A., Münzer, B., Schoeffmann, K., Keckstein, J.: Endometriosis annotation in endoscopic videos. In: 2017 IEEE International Symposium on Multimedia (ISM), pp. 364–365, December 2017
3. Leibetseder, A., et al.: LapGyn4: a dataset for 4 Automatic content analysis problems in the domain of laparoscopic gynecology. In: Proceedings of the 9th ACM Multimedia Systems Conference. MMSys 2018, pp. 357–362. ACM, New York (2018)
4. Lux, M., Riegler, M.: Annotation of endoscopic videos on mobile devices: a bottom-up approach. In: Proceedings of the 4th ACM Multimedia Systems Conference, pp. 141–145. ACM (2013)
5. Makary, M.A.: The power of video recording: taking quality to the next level. JAMA **309**(15), 1591 (2013)
6. Münzer, B., Schoeffmann, K., Böszörmenyi, L.: Content-based processing and analysis of endoscopic images and videos: a survey. Multimedia Tools Appl. **77**(1), 1323–1362 (2018)
7. Petscharnig, S., Schöffmann, K.: Learning laparoscopic video shot classification for gynecological surgery. Multimedia Tools Appl. **77**(7), 8061–8079 (2018)

---

[1] http://www.itec.aau.at/ftp/datasets/LapGyn4.

Automatic Classification and Linguistic Analysis of Extremist Online Material

Juan Soler-Company[1]([⊠]) [iD] and Leo Wanner[1,2] [iD]

[1] TALN Group, Pompeu Fabra University, Roc Boronat 138, 08018 Barcelona, Spain
{juan.soler,leo.wanner}@upf.edu
[2] ICREA, Barcelona, Spain
https://www.upf.edu/
https://www.icrea.cat/

Abstract. The growth of the Internet in the last decade has created great opportunities for sharing content and opinions at a global scale. While this may look like a completely positive feature, it also facilitates the dissemination of discriminative material, propaganda calling for violence, etc. We present a system for recognition, classification and inspection of this kind of material in terms of different characteristics and identification of its authors. The system is illustrated using different sources – including Jihadist magazines and White Supremacist forum posts. We show experiments on the detection of offensive content, on its classification and provide a visualization and enrichment of extremist data.

Keywords: Extremist material · Abusive content · Hate speech
Classification

1 Introduction

The Internet is the source of an immense variety of knowledge repositories (Wikipedia, Wordnet, etc.) and applications (YouTube, Reddit, Twitter, etc.) that everybody can access and take advantage of; it is also **the** communication forum of our time and the most important instrument to ensure freedom of speech. It allows us to freely state and disseminate our view on any private or public matter to vast audiences. An undesired effect of this free flow of communication that the Internet provides is that it can be easily used to disseminate racist or any other discriminative material, encourage violence, defame, etc. – often under fake identities or pseudonyms. Due to the devastating impact that this kind of content can cause on our society and the impossibility of manually analyzing user-generated web content, the automatic analysis and classification of web material from pertinent sources has become an active research topic. For instance, de Smedt et al. [6] automatically detect online Jihadist hate speech with over 80% accuracy using character trigrams as features and 45K Twitter messages as training corpus. Xu et al. [8] use content and network-based features

© Springer Nature Switzerland AG 2019
I. Kompatsiaris et al. (Eds.): MMM 2019, LNCS 11296, pp. 577–582, 2019.
https://doi.org/10.1007/978-3-030-05716-9_49

to automatically classify Twitter accounts between normal and ISIS propaganda accounts. In [1], the authors perform affect analysis to measure the presence of hate and violence in U.S. and Middle Eastern extremist group forum postings. For this purpose, they draw upon an affect lexicon, applying probabilistic disambiguation techniques. Rudinac et al. [5] present a multimodal approach to the categorization of posts in accordance with the topic they address. They analyze text, visual content and user interactions of extremist data. To perform text classification, graph convolutional networks are used. Offensive content is also analysed in several works; see e.g., [3] for the analysis, classification, and detection of offensive content in the web.

The problem of the overwhelming majority of the implementations of the analysis and classification of textual extremist data is that they use only distributional, lexical and morpho-syntactic (such as part of speech) features. As a result, they tend to capture content similarities. This is useful for a coarse-grained distinction between, e.g., extremist vs. non-extremist material. However, this is not sufficient for a fine-grained distinction of different types of extremist material, such as, e.g., different publication fora of IS propaganda. Such a fine-grained distinction requires the consideration of stylistic features captured, first of all, via syntactic dependency and discourse features.

We present a system for automatic classification and analysis of extremist online material that takes into account both content-oriented and stylistic features. The system is able to perform the following three tasks: (i) recognize extremist material; (ii) classify the recognized extremist material in terms of more fine-grained categories; and (iii) analyze the extremist material with respect to its linguistic characteristics, material relevance, and author prominence. Given that the first two tasks are carried out offline, the system video at https://youtu.be/6QQacgqy5xw focuses on the demonstration of the third task.

2   System Setup

The system consists of two different modules. The first module deals with the first two tasks introduced above, while the second module offers via an interactive interface different aspects of the third task.

2.1   Recognition and Classification of Extremist Material

The recognition of extremist material and its further more fine-grained categorization is done using supervised machine learning. We explored several machine learning techniques. For demonstration, we use a standard SVM with a linear kernel, which showed to be one of the most stable and highest performing techniques. The SVM is trained with mainly generic linguistic features, which cover character-, word-, sentence-, dictionary-, syntactic-, lexical and discourse-based characteristics of written material; see [7] for a detailed description. For some experiments, embedded word features in terms of Google word embeddings have been used [4].

2.2   Analysis of Extremist Material

As already mentioned above, the system offers an analysis of given extremist material with respect to its linguistic characteristics, its relevance in a larger context and the prominence of the author in the scene.

The linguistic characteristics offered for analysis are of semantic, syntactic and distributional nature. The semantic characteristics consist of the entities (or concepts) in the material and of the DBpedia entities these entities are linked to as well as of the entities that co-refer to each other. All three semantic characteristics are obtained using the *Pikes* toolkit [2]. The syntactic characteristics concern, first of all, the dependency structures of the sentences in the material and cover, e.g., the syntactic depth per sentence, i.e., the maximum distance between root and leaf, which is an important author-specific stylistic feature. The distributional characteristics consist of such information as the number of characters, number of subtrees per sentence, number of words and sentences, number of nouns/adjective/verb/adverbs, ratio of nouns/adjective/verb/adverbs, the frequency of each punctuation mark, and references to other material.

3   Demonstration

The capacity of our system is demonstrated for all three of the above tasks.

3.1   Datasets Used for Demonstration

For demonstration, we use the following corpora: **1.** our own heterogeneous "offensive material" corpus[1], which contains 1,744 texts from different sources, including, on the one hand, clearly offensive material of different categories from forums such as `stormfront`, `chimpmania`), blogs (as, e.g., `returnofkings`, `rooshv` and `godhatesfags`) or the comment sections of a web page (as, e.g., `breitbart`), and, on the other hand, "non-offensive" material about politics, history and society – topics that are also often discussed in offensive forums; **2.** a publicly available corpus of 2,685 quotes from two English Jihadist propaganda magazines[2], with the following distribution of the number of quotes across different original sources: 62: Bible, 729: Hadith, 77: politician or analyst statements, 998: Quran, 136: Jihadist authorities, 261: classical Islam scholar; **3.** a corpus consisting of 2,356 complete threads from the White Supremacist forum *stormfront*.

3.2   Recognition of Extremist Material

The task of the recognition of extremist material is demonstrated on the three corpora introduced above. More precisely, it consists of the binary classification of the three corpora in terms of "offensive" (O) vs. "non-offensive" (NO), Jihadist (J) vs. "non-Jihadist (NJ), and White Supremacist (WS) vs. "non-White Supremacist" (NWS). Table 1 shows the results for 10-fold cross-validation.

---

[1] Available at https://github.com/joanSolCom/Datasets/blob/master/OffSet.tar.gz.

[2] Available at https://www.kaggle.com/fifthtribe/isis-religious-texts.

Table 1. Results of the binary classification task ('ling.f'= linguistic features introduced in [7], 'w.e.' = Google word embeddings, 'b.of.w.' = bag of the 700 most common words)

Features	O vs. NO (accuracy)	J vs. NJ (accuracy)	WS vs. NWS (accuracy)
ling.f.	73.58%	85.62%	85.32%
w.e.	84.93%	73.45%	92.14%
b.of.w	70.35%	65.25%	82.33%

The "bag of words" features, which are often drawn upon in the state of the art serve as baseline. We can observe that the linguistic (stylistic) features are better than the baseline, while embedded lexical features capture best the distinction between all types of extremist material and non-extremist material.

3.3 Material Categorization

The task of fine-grained categorization of extremist material is demonstrated on the Jihadist data. Two experiments have been performed: magazine (*Dabiq* vs. *Rumiyah*) and quote type classification in which we distinguish between quotes from Bible, Quran, Hadith, Classical Islam Scholar writings, Tafsir, Jihadist, and Politician or Political Analyst articles in media. Table 2 summarizes their outcome in terms of accuracy. In contrast to the recognition of extremist material, the categorization of extremist material works better with linguistic (stylistic) features. This is plausible given that some of the material sources may use very similar words, but the way they are written are likely to be different. The confusion matrix in Fig. 1 gives us more details in this respect. Quran quotes are recognized best because they are the most numerous in our corpus. Some of the Jihadist and Tafsir quotes are mistaken for Quran, Hadith or Classic Islam Scholar quotes, but hardly ever for Bible or Media quotes. Note that even though not many quotes from the Media are present in the corpus, they are fairly well recognized due to their stylistic differences to the other types of quotes.

Table 2. Results of the categorization of extremist material

Features	Magazine class. (accuracy)	Quote origin (accuracy)
ling.f.	79,65%	73.02%
w.e.	78.54%	66.56%
b.of.w	67.21%	61.33%

```
  a   b   c   d   e   f   g    <-- classified as
 17   7   1  35   1   0   1 |   a = Bible
  7 552   4  91  11  13  51 |   b = Hadith
  2   6  46  10   8   0   5 |   c = MediaPoliticianorAnalyst
  5  57   6 916   7   2   5 |   d = Quran
  0  22   7  32  58   1  16 |   e = Jihadist
  0  42   0  14   4  16  29 |   f = Tafsir
  1  82   2  23   8  21 124 |   g = ClassicalScholar
```

Fig. 1. Confusion matrix for the categorization of extremist material

3.4 Analysis of Extremist Material

The task of the analysis of extremist material, for which an interactive interface is available (cf. Fig. 2 and https://youtu.be/6QQacgqy5xw for a video), is demonstrated on posts of the White Supremacist forum *stormfront*. Each post has a button grid with 'Entities', 'Coreferences', 'Linked Entities', 'Sentences', 'Post Features' and 'Clear' to inspect the corresponding characteristics (see Sect. 2.2). 'Sentences' shows the sentences that compose the post. 'Post Features' displays the lexical, syntactic, and distributional features of a post. At the level of a thread, relevance scores for each post and user and the relevant entities that appear in a thread are offered. Any relevance metrics can be used; we used a simple metric that takes into account the number of entities in the post, the "hub" status of the post, i.e., the (relative) number of references to other posts in this post, and the "authority" status of its author, i.e., the (relative) frequency of the mention of this author by other authors. This information can be very useful to discard irrelevant comments, off-topic posts, jokes and other content that does not contribute to the general discussion. The "Show User Relevance" button opens an info box that displays the ranking of the most relevant authors in the analyzed thread (i.e., the authors ordered by author relevance score). The relevance score of the author is computed taking into account: (i) the number of

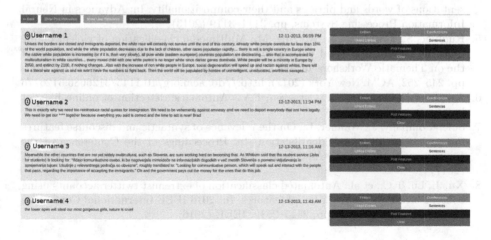

Fig. 2. Interactive interface for analysis of extremist forums

times an author is mentioned in a thread, (ii) the number of entities per post of the author, (iii) the percentage of the posts of the author that contain referenced entities, (iv) the percentage of posts quoting other posts, (v) the percentage of the posts of the thread that the author has written, (vi) the number of times the author mentions other users in the thread. Finally, the "Show Relevant Concepts" button opens an info box in which relevant concepts detected by Pikes in a thread are displayed. All concepts of a thread that are among the most frequent 30% in the corpus are considered relevant.

4 Conclusions and Future Work

We presented an operational system setup for state-of-the-art recognition, categorization and analysis via an interactive interface of extremist material in the web. We have illustrated the performance of this setup on several datasets, including generic extremist material, Jihadist magazines and White Supremacist forums. In the future, we plan to extend the functionality and interactiveness of our implementation.

References

1. Abbasi, A.: Affect intensity analysis of dark web forums. In: 2007 IEEE Intelligence and Security Informatics, pp. 282–288. IEEE (2007)
2. Corcoglioniti, F., Rospocher, M., Palmero Aprosio, A.: Frame-based ontology population with pikes. IEEE Trans. Knowl. Data Eng. 28(12), 3261–3275 (2016)
3. Djuric, N., Zhou, J., Morris, R., Grbovic, M., Radosavljevic, V., Bhamidipati, N.: Hate speech detection with comment embeddings. In: Proceedings of the 24th International Conference on World Wide Web, WWW 2015 Companion, pp. 29–30. ACM, New York (2015). http://doi.acm.org/10.1145/2740908.2742760
4. Mikolov, T., Sutskever, I., Chen, K., Corrado, G.S., Dean, J.: Distributed representations of words and phrases and their compositionality. In: Advances in Neural Information Processing Systems, pp. 3111–3119 (2013)
5. Rudinac, S., Gornishka, I., Worring, M.: Multimodal classification of violent online political extremism content with graph convolutional networks. In: Proceedings of the on Thematic Workshops of ACM Multimedia 2017, Thematic Workshops 2017, pp. 245–252. ACM, New York (2017). http://doi.acm.org/10.1145/3126686.3126776
6. Smedt, T.D., Pauw, G.D., Ostaeyen, P.V.: Automatic detection of online jihadist hate speech. CoRR (2018)
7. Soler-Company, J., Wanner, L.: On the relevance of syntactic and discourse features for author profiling and identification. In: Proceedings of the Conference of the European Chapter of the Association for Computational Linguistics, pp. 681–687 (2017)
8. Xu, J., Lu, T.C., et al.: Automated classification of extremist twitter accounts using content-based and network-based features. In: 2016 IEEE International Conference on Big Data (Big Data), pp. 2545–2549. IEEE (2016)

Video Browser Showdown

Autopiloting Feature Maps: The Deep Interactive Video Exploration (diveXplore) System at VBS2019

Klaus Schoeffmann[✉], Bernd Münzer, Andreas Leibetseder, Jürgen Primus, and Sabrina Kletz

Institute of Information Technology, Klagenfurt University, Klagenfurt, Austria
{ks,bernd,aleibets,mprimus,sabrina}@itec.aau.at

Abstract. We present the most recent version of our *Deep Interactive Video Exploration (diveXplore)* system, which has been successfully used for the latest two Video Browser Showdown competitions (VBS2017 and VBS2018) as well as for the first Lifelog Search Challenge (LSC2018). diveXplore is based on a plethora of video content analysis and processing methods, such as simple color, texture, and motion analysis, self-organizing feature maps, and semantic concept extraction with different deep convolutional neural networks. The biggest strength of the system, however, is that it provides a variety of video search and rich interaction features. One of the novelties in the most recent version is a *Feature Map Autopilot*, which ensures time-efficient inspection of feature maps without gaps and unnecessary visits.

Keywords: Video retrieval · Interactive video search · Video analysis

1 Deep Interactive Video Exploration

The *diveXplore* (Deep Interactive Video Exploration) system has been used for the Video Browser Showdown [3] two times in a row with quite decent success. It achieved the 2nd place at VBS2017 [6] and at VBS2018 it was even used by two teams in two different variants: one mainly focusing on *Feature Map Browsing* [5], and another one with a main focus on *Interactive Sketching* [2]. The two teams performed almost equally well and scored 2nd and 3rd, respectively. In addition to that, we also used a customized variation of diveXplore, called *lifeXplore* [4], for the first Lifelog Search Challenge (LSC2018) [1], where we could secure the 2nd place as well. Most notably, the performance of novice users (in comparison to other novice users on competing tools) constantly exceeded the performance of expert users, proving the high usability and efficacy of diveXplore. We argue that the main reason of the consistently strong performance of our tool is the fact that it provides a powerful toolbox with many different possibilities for interactive content-based search in a video archive, as well as interactive browsing in single video sequences. This enables users to choose the right search feature for the

© Springer Nature Switzerland AG 2019
I. Kompatsiaris et al. (Eds.): MMM 2019, LNCS 11296, pp. 585–590, 2019.
https://doi.org/10.1007/978-3-030-05716-9_50

current needs and use alternative search paths in case the first trial resulted in a dead end.

As in previous versions, the tool is built around feature maps that cluster similar shots and allow the user to interactively browse and look around. These maps are created with the help of self-organizing maps, utilizing color information and neural codes extracted with deep convolutional neural networks (see Fig. 1). Additionally to global maps containing all shots of the data set, users can now search in a large set of semantic sub-maps that cluster the according content by a specific semantic feature (such as cars, streets, faces, etc.). Furthermore, the tool allows to (i) search for shots by keywords, based on concepts detected with several neural networks, (ii) filter shots by color, and (iii) search for shots by a color sketch, as well as (iv) search for other shots that are similar to the currently selected one. All the different interaction features are linked to feature maps (i.e., provide entry points for browsing the feature map at the position the currently selected shot is located).

For this year's iteration of the Video Browser Showdown (VBS2019), we combine both systems used last year into one single system and improve several search features, including the feature map browsing. More specifically, we introduce a novel *Browsing Auto Pilot* that automatically navigates the feature map by following the *shortest path* (i.e., one that maximizes the number of keyframes to be presented in a specific time) without any re-visitations (i.e., it avoids visiting several parts of the feature map twice). With this new feature we address former usability issues that hampered efficient usage of the feature maps. Furthermore, the current version of diveXplore contains numerous other incremental optimizations and improvements. One of them is the sketch-based search that has been optimized with a pivot-table index. Another improvement is a more powerful color filter that allows to combine color and concept search.

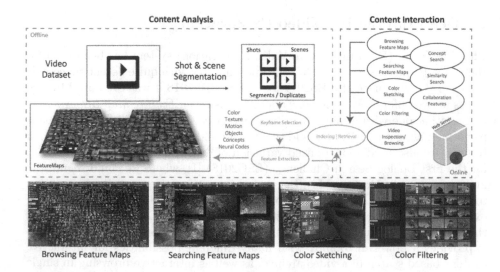

Fig. 1. Features of the *diveXplore* system

2   Browsing Auto Pilot

The most prominent novelty of the latest version of diveXplore is the *Browsing Auto Pilot* feature. It addresses usability issues of the central feature maps that became apparent during the last competitions. More specifically, we noticed that users often end up searching around in the feature map without finding the right shot but with the feeling that something might have been overlooked (because of the browsing/dragging interaction), or that many positions in the map have redundantly been visited several times (which wastes time, of course). As a consequence, users rather concentrated on the plain linear result lists of concept search or other search modalities, which were originally intended to be entry points to the feature map.

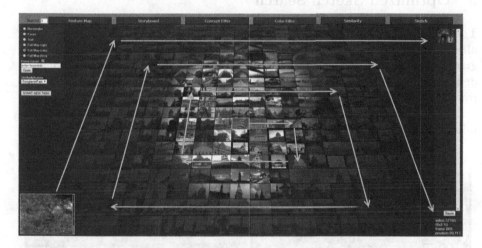

Fig. 2. The new Auto Pilot feature. The yellow arrows denote the navigation path that is automatically followed with configurable speed. Keyframes distant to the center are smoothly hidden. (Color figure online)

To overcome these problems and make the feature maps more user-friendly, we propose an *Auto Pilot* that automatically follows an optimized path on the feature map, thus obviating the need for manual navigation (by mouse or keyboard) and ensuring that every keyframe in the target area is "visited" exactly once, but no keyframe is redundantly visited again. Moreover, keyframes in far distance are smoothly hidden, so that the user can fully concentrate on the current presentation focus and does not get overwhelmed by too many images (which was another issue of our previous versions). The Auto Pilot supports different types of paths (spiral, row-wise, zig-zag) and enables the user to easily control parameters like direction and speed. Basically, we consider two different usage scenarios:

1. The user defines a starting point on the feature map (e.g., based on a result item of concept search or color filter) and wants to inspect the surrounding area on the map. In this case, a spiral path (as visualized in Fig. 2) is very well suited to present the most similar items with increasing distance to the starting point in the self-organizing map.
2. The user selects a specific region by dragging a rectangle on the minimap and wants to inspect this part of the map. In this scenario, a row-wise or zig-zag path might be more appropriate, depending on the users preferences. In case of custom maps that only contain a smaller number of keyframes sharing a specific property (like a detected concept), it might also make sense to scan the entire map instead of selecting a sub-area.

3   Optimized Sketch Search

The sketch search component [2], introduced in the VBS2018 challenge as an alternative use case and extension to the diveXplore system, is now fully integrated as well as improved for speeding up the sketching workflow, which is demonstrated in Fig. 3. Using this functionality, users are able to hand-draw rough sketches of desired scenes, which the system retrieves by utilizing *HistMap* – a colorpatch-based descriptor pre-calculated for all shot keyframes and optimized for fast pivot table lookup.

(a) Sketching functionality on a pen-enabled tablet.

(b) Retrieved results using *HistMap* as basis for sketch search.

Fig. 3. Sketch Search enables users to roughly draw a desired scene for retrieval using the custom developed color-based *HistMap* descriptor.

Among adapting sketch search for operating with the new dataset, a few interface changes are made in order to facilitate using this feature. Instead of drawing in a much larger separate overlay only to show results after finishing a sketch, in this version sketching is performed in a smaller window right next to the result display. This way results can continuously be updated with every stroke added to the sketch and thereby give the user a much better estimation if the currently taken approach in drawing a scene might be successful or not. Thus, changing strategy becomes much simpler than with the approach utilized in VBS2018. Furthermore, an additional sketch history enables quickly loading past sketches into the drawing canvas for continuing previous strategies, therefore, even further speeding up changing approaches.

4   System Evolution

Besides the aforementioned major novelties, we refined our system by numerous incremental usability and performance improvements. The latter mainly concern tweaks for smoother loading and rendering of the feature map and optimizations of the retrieval component for faster delivery of results. Due to space limitations, only a few selected new features improving the general usability of the system can be shortly described in the following.

Result List Visualization. We performed a major refactoring of the result list container, which is shared among the various search modalities (like concept, color, sketch). Result list items can now be zoomed, enabling the user to choose between better overview and more detailed inspection. Moreover, the found shots can now optionally be grouped by video, which is especially useful for AVS (ad-hoc video search) tasks where the goal is to find matching shots from as many distinct videos as possible. The alternative is to show a plain grid list of all results, ordered by relevance. In that case, shots belonging to the same video can be highlighted by pressing a hotkey when hovering over an item. Finally, the peek-preview feature that shows a preview image based on the mouse position over a keyframe has been extended to also show preview images of the preceding and succeeding shot at the boundary. This can be very useful to quickly obtain information about the temporal context of a shot. Such context is often very important to successfully complete a challenging KIS (known-item search) task that is characterized by a specific sequence of shots.

Submission History. The adoption of AVS tasks in VBS2017 introduced new challenges that have to be mastered by a successful retrieval tool, as compared to the previous editions that solely included KIS tasks. One of these challenges is to keep track of shots that have already been submitted, in order to avoid duplicate submissions. The latest version of diveXplore takes account of these aspects with a submission history that marks all shots that already have been submitted during the current task (either by the active user, or by another collaborating user). The indication of submitted shots is implemented for result lists, feature maps as well as the video player timeline, which visualizes the shot segmentation. In this context, we also have to consider the divergence between our custom shot segmentation (which is the basis of all keyframes in our system) and the master shot reference (which forms the reference for assessment of submissions) by using different highlighting colors for (i) shots that are completely included in a respective master shot and (ii) shots with only partial overlap.

Similarity Search. Also the similarity search has undergone a refactoring and now enables the user to select the image descriptor that is used to determine the similarity between two shots, depending on the current needs. The currently supported descriptors are HistMap (for purely visual similarity) and neural codes (for semantic similarity). Moreover, the history of previous similarity searches is buffered in the background and visualized with thumbnails of the respective query images, which serve as link to easily recall the respective result list. Similar history features are also planned for other result lists in future versions, in order to make it easier to go back in the search path.

5   Conclusions

We present an improved version of our diveXplore system to participate in VBS2019. Our system integrates many different interactive video search features, resulting in a very flexible tool that supports different search needs. While performing a lot of small improvements (and also discarding less promising features, such as the Storyboard that is not appropriate for the new, larger dataset), our system introduces a novel and powerful feature – the Auto Pilot – for feature map inspection. It allows to quickly inspect a set of shots (in forward or reverse mode) with varying speed, as configured by the user. In combination with the rich set of additional search features and efficient interaction mechanisms, we are confident to remain competitive for the new increased dataset of VBS2019.

References

1. Dang-Nguyen, D.-T., Schoeffmann, K., Hurst, W.: LSE 2018 panel - challenges of lifelog search and access. In: Proceedings of the 2018 ACM Workshop on the Lifelog Search Challenge, LSC 2018, pp. 1–2. ACM, New York (2018)
2. Leibetseder, A., Kletz, S., Schoeffmann, K.: Sketch-based similarity search for collaborative feature maps. In: Schoeffmann, K., et al. (eds.) MMM 2018. LNCS, vol. 10705, pp. 425–430. Springer, Cham (2018). https://doi.org/10.1007/978-3-319-73600-6_45
3. Lokoc, J., Bailer, W., Schoeffmann, K., Muenzer, B., Awad, G.: On influential trends in interactive video retrieval: video browser showdown 2015–2017. IEEE Trans. Multimedia **20**(12), 3361–3376 (2018). https://ieeexplore.ieee.org/abstract/document/8352047
4. Münzer, B., Leibetseder, A., Kletz, S., Primus, M.J., Schoeffmann, K.: lifeXplore at the lifelong search challenge 2018. In: Proceedings of the 2018 ACM Workshop on the Lifelong Search Challenge, LSC 2018, pp. 3–8. ACM, New York (2018)
5. Primus, M.J., Münzer, B., Leibetseder, A., Schoeffmann, K.: The ITEC collaborative video search system at the video browser showdown 2018. In: Schoeffmann, K., et al. (eds.) MMM 2018. LNCS, vol. 10705, pp. 438–443. Springer, Cham (2018). https://doi.org/10.1007/978-3-319-73600-6_47
6. Schoeffmann, K., et al.: Collaborative feature maps for interactive video search. In: Amsaleg, L., Guðmundsson, G.Þ., Gurrin, C., Jónsson, B.Þ., Satoh, S. (eds.) MMM 2017. LNCS, vol. 10133, pp. 457–462. Springer, Cham (2017). https://doi.org/10.1007/978-3-319-51814-5_41

VISIONE at VBS2019

Giuseppe Amato, Paolo Bolettieri, Fabio Carrara, Franca Debole,
Fabrizio Falchi, Claudio Gennaro, Lucia Vadicamo$^{(\boxtimes)}$, and Claudio Vairo

Institute of Information Science and Technologies (ISTI), Italian National Research
Council (CNR), Via G. Moruzzi 1, 56124 Pisa, Italy
{giuseppe.amato,paolo.bolettieri,fabio.carrara,franca.debole,
fabrizio.falchi,claudio.gennaro,lucia.vadicamo,claudio.vairo}@isti.cnr.it

Abstract. This paper presents VISIONE, a tool for large–scale video
search. The tool can be used for both known-item and ad-hoc video
search tasks since it integrates several content-based analysis and
retrieval modules, including a keyword search, a spatial object-based
search, and a visual similarity search. Our implementation is based on
state-of-the-art deep learning approaches for the content analysis and
leverages highly efficient indexing techniques to ensure scalability. Specifically, we encode all the visual and textual descriptors extracted from the
videos into (surrogate) textual representations that are then efficiently
indexed and searched using an off-the-shelf text search engine.

Keywords: Content-based video retrieval · Video search
Known item search · Convolutional neural networks

1 Introduction

The Video Browser Showdown (VBS) [4,10] is an international video search
competition that evaluates the performance of interactive video retrievals systems. It is performed annually since 2012; however, it is becoming increasingly
challenging as the used video archive grows and new query tasks are introduced
in the competition. The VBS 2019 uses the V3C1 dataset that consists of 7,475
video files (amounting for 1000 h of video content) and encompasses three content
search tasks: *Known-Item-Search (KIS), textual KIS* and *Ad-hoc Video Search
(AVS)*. The KIS task models the situation in which someone wants to find a
particular video clip that he has already seen, assuming that it is contained in a
specific collection of data. The textual KIS is a variation of the KIS task, where
the target video clip is no longer visually presented to the participants of the
challenge but it is rather described in details by text. This task simulates situations in which a user wants to find a particular video clip, without having seen
it before, but knowing the content of the target video exactly. For the AVS task,
instead, a general textual description is provided (e.g. "A person playing guitar
outdoors") and participants need to find as many correct examples as possible,
i.e. video shots that fit the given description.

© Springer Nature Switzerland AG 2019
I. Kompatsiaris et al. (Eds.): MMM 2019, LNCS 11296, pp. 591–596, 2019.
https://doi.org/10.1007/978-3-030-05716-9_51

In this paper, we present the first version of VISIONE, a system which integrates several search capabilities for efficient video retrieval (Fig. 1). Specifically, it supports:

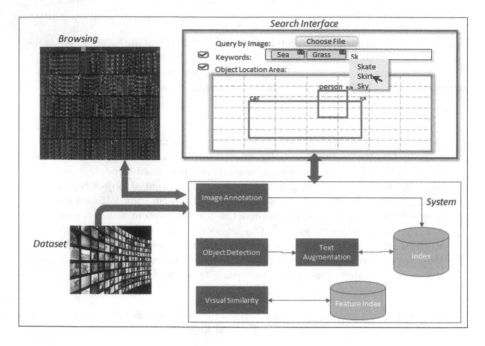

Fig. 1. A sketch of VISIONE's architecture.

– query by keywords, i.e. the user can specify some textual keywords/tags related to the target video segment(s) to be retrieved;
– query by object location, i.e. the user can draw simple object-based diagrams specifying the spatial location of the objects appearing in the target scene;
– query by example, i.e. the user can upload an image or select a keyframe of a video to search for videos with similar visual content.

State-of-the-art deep learning approaches are used to analyze and annotate about 1.1M of representative keyframes selected from V3C1 dataset. We encode all the features extracted from the videos (visual features, tags, object locations, and metadata) into textual representations that are then indexed using inverted files. We use a text surrogate representation [6], which has been appositely extended to support efficient spatial object queries on large scale dataset. It will be possible to build queries by placing wanted objects in the scene and to efficiently search for compatible images in an interactive way. This choice allows us to exploit efficient and scalable search technologies and platform used nowadays for text retrieval. In particular, VISIONE relies on the Elasticsearch[1].

---

[1] https://github.com/elastic/elasticsearch.

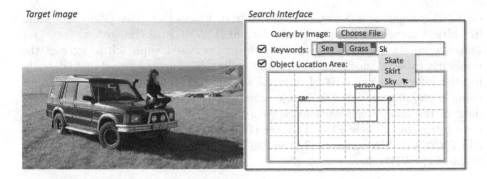

Fig. 2. VISIONE user interface for: keyword-based, object spatial position and the query by image search.

2   VISIONE: Content Based Video Retrieval System

VISIONE relies heavily on deep learning techniques, trying to bridge the semantic gap between text and image. In our system, we focus on bridging these two descriptions using the following approaches:

- keyword search: we use keywords including scenes, places or concepts (e.g. outdoor, building, sport) to query video shots. Our image annotation system is based on different Convolutional Neural Networks to extract scene attributes.
- object location search: we use the location of the objects in a scene to query video shots. We exploit the efficiency of YOLO[2] as a state of the art real-time object detection system to retrieve the video shot containing the objects sketched by the user.
- visual similarity search: we use an image as query to retrieve the most similar video shots. The similarity search is performed by calculating the cosine similarity of the visual features on the entire visual data set, represented using the R-MAC [16] visual descriptor.

2.1   Keyword-Based Search

Since, the categories with which Hybrid-CNN was trained are insufficient to associate relevant tags to the images, VISIONE exploits our automatic annotation system to annotate untagged images [1]. This system is based on YFCC100M-HNfc6, a set of deep features we extracted from the YFCC100M dataset [15]. The YFCC100M-HNfc6 feature dataset was created using the Caffe framework [8]. In particular, we use the neural network Hybrid-CNN whose model and weights are publicly available in the Caffe Model Zoo. The Hybrid-CNN[3] was trained

---

[2] https://pjreddie.com/darknet/yolo/.
[3] http://github.com/BVLC/caffe/wiki/Model-Zoo.

on 1,183 categories: 205 scene categories from Places Database (Places205) and 978 object categories from the train data of ILSVRC2012 (ImageNet) [14]. Our image annotation system is based on an unsupervised approach to extract the implicitly existing knowledge in the huge collection of unstructured texts describing the images of YFCC100M dataset, allowing us to label the images without using a training model. The image annotation system also exploits the metadata of the images validated using WordNet [5]. For the competition the idea is to integrate the new Place Dataset (Places365-CNN [18]), other concepts as 345 TRECVID SIN concepts [3], the 239 categories from Fudan-Columbia Video Dataset (FCVID) [9].

2.2   Object Location Search

Following the idea that the human eye is able to identify objects in the image very quickly, we decide to take advantage of the new technologies available to search for object instances in order to retrieve the exact video shot.

For this purpose, we use YOLOv3 [13] as object detector, both because it is extremely fast and because of its accuracy. Our image query interface is subdivided into a $N \times N$ grid in the same way that YOLO segments images to detect objects. Each object detected in the single image I by YOLO is indexed using a specific encoding ENC conceived to put together the location and the class corresponding to the object ($cod_{pos}cod_{text}$). The idea of using YOLO to detect objects within video has already been exploited in VBS, e.g. by Truong et al. [17], but our approach is distinguished by being able to encode the class and the location of the objects in a single textual description of the image, allowing us to search by similarity using a standard text search engine. Basically for each I entry on the index, we have a space-separated concatenation of ENCs, one for all the possible cells (cod_{pos}) in the grid that contains the object (cod_{text}). For example, for the image in Fig. 2 the object car is indexed with the sequence $c_1 car$ $c_2 car$ ... $c_n car$, where c_i is the code of the i-th cell containing the car.

In order to approach the KIS task, the user can take advantage of our UI to sketch the objects appearing in the target video by specifying the desired location for each object (as shown in the "Object Location Area" of Fig. 2).

2.3   Visual Similarity Search

VISIONE also supports content-based visual search functionalities, i.e., it allows users to retrieve scenes containing keyframes visually similar to a query image given by example. To start the search the user can select any keyframe of a video as query (e.g. any one presented in the results-set of a previous search) or he can directly upload an image (e.g. selected using an external image search engine, like Bing or Google). In order to represent and compare the visual content of the images, we use the Regional Maximum Activations of Convolutions (R-MAC) [16], which is a state-of-art descriptor for image retrieval. The R-MAC descriptor effectively aggregates several local convolutional features (extracted at multiple position and scales) into a dense and compact global image representation.

We use the ResNet-101 trained model provided by Gordo et al. [7] as an R-MAC feature extractor since it achieved the best performance on standard benchmarks. To efficiently index the R-MAC descriptor we transform the deep features into a textual encoding suitable for being indexed by a standard full-text search engine, such as Elasticsearch. The process to transform the deep features into a textual representation is done as follows. We first use the Deep Permutation technique [2] to encode the deep features into a permutation vector, which is then transformed into a Surrogate Text Representation (STR) as described in [6]. The main rationale of this approach is that if two features are very close one to the other, they will have similar Deep Permutations and thus the corresponding text representations will be close as well. The advantage of using the textual encodings is that we can efficiently exploit off-the-shelf text search engines for performing image searches on large scale.

3   Conclusion

We present the first version of VISIONE, a system that will be used in the Video Browser Showdown 2019 challenge. The system can be used for both the Known Item Search or Ad-hoc Video Search tasks. It supports three types of queries: query by keyword, query by object location, and query by visual similarity. All the features used to represent the video keyframes are extracted using state-of-the-art deep learning approaches. VISIONE also exploits ad-hoc surrogate text encodings of the extracted features in order to use efficient technologies and platforms for text retrieval, without the need for the definition of dedicated access methods. Inspired by the SIRET system [11,12] that won the VBS2018, we plan to integrate other useful search capabilities (such as query-by-color sketches) in a future version of our system.

Acknowledgements. This work was partially funded by "Smart News: Social sensing for breaking news", CUP CIPE D58C15000270008, by VISECH ARCO-CNR, CUP B56J17001330004, and by "Automatic Data and documents Analysis to enhance human-based processes" (ADA), CUP CIPE D55F17000290009. We gratefully acknowledge the support of NVIDIA Corporation with the donation of the Tesla K40 GPU used for this research.

References

1. Amato, G., Falchi, F., Gennaro, C., Rabitti, F.: Searching and annotating 100M images with YFCC100M-HNfc6 and MI-file. In: Proceedings of the 15th International Workshop on Content-Based Multimedia Indexing, CBMI 2017, Florence, Italy, 19–21 June 2017, pp. 26:1–26:4 (2017). https://doi.org/10.1145/3095713.3095740
2. Amato, G., Falchi, F., Gennaro, C., Vadicamo, L.: Deep permutations: deep convolutional neural networks and permutation-based indexing. In: Amsaleg, L., Houle, M.E., Schubert, E. (eds.) SISAP 2016. LNCS, vol. 9939, pp. 93–106. Springer, Cham (2016). https://doi.org/10.1007/978-3-319-46759-7_7

3. Awad, G., Snoek, C.G.M., Smeaton, A.F., Quénot, G.: TRECVid semantic indexing of video: a 6-year retrospective (2016)
4. Cobârzan, C., et al.: Interactive video search tools: a detailed analysis of the video browser showdown 2015. Multimedia Tools Appl. **76**(4), 5539–5571 (2017). https://doi.org/10.1007/s11042-016-3661-2
5. Fellbaum, C. (ed.): WordNet: An Electronic Lexical Database. MIT Press, Cambridge (1998)
6. Gennaro, C., Amato, G., Bolettieri, P., Savino, P.: An approach to content-based image retrieval based on the lucene search engine library. In: Lalmas, M., Jose, J., Rauber, A., Sebastiani, F., Frommholz, I. (eds.) ECDL 2010. LNCS, vol. 6273, pp. 55–66. Springer, Heidelberg (2010). https://doi.org/10.1007/978-3-642-15464-5_8
7. Gordo, A., Almazán, J., Revaud, J., Larlus, D.: End-to-end learning of deep visual representations for image retrieval. Int. J. Comput. Vis. **124**(2), 237–254 (2017)
8. Jia, Y., et al.: Caffe: Convolutional architecture for fast feature embedding. arXiv preprint arXiv:1408.5093 (2014)
9. Jiang, Y.G., Wu, Z., Wang, J., Xue, X., Chang, S.F.: Exploiting feature and class relationships in video categorization with regularized deep neural networks. IEEE Trans. Patt. Anal. Mach. Intell. **40**(2), 352–364 (2018). https://doi.org/10.1109/TPAMI.2017.2670560
10. Lokoc, J., Bailer, W., Schoeffmann, K., Muenzer, B., Awad, G.: On influential trends in interactive video retrieval: video browser showdown 2015–2017. IEEE Trans. Multimedia **20**(12), 3361–3376 (2018). https://doi.org/10.1109/TMM.2018.2830110
11. Lokoč, J., Kovalčík, G., Souček, T.: Revisiting SIRET video retrieval tool. In: Schoeffmann, K., et al. (eds.) MMM 2018. LNCS, vol. 10705, pp. 419–424. Springer, Cham (2018). https://doi.org/10.1007/978-3-319-73600-6_44
12. Lokoč, J., Souček, T., Kovalčik, G.: Using an interactive video retrieval tool for lifelog data. In: Proceedings of the 2018 ACM Workshop on the Lifelog Search Challenge, LSC 2018, pp. 15–19. ACM, New York (2018). https://doi.org/10.1145/3210539.3210543
13. Redmon, J., Farhadi, A.: YOLOv3: an incremental improvement. arXiv (2018)
14. Russakovsky, O., et al.: ImageNet large scale visual recognition challenge. Int. J. Comput. Vis. (IJCV) **115**(3), 211–252 (2015). https://doi.org/10.1007/s11263-015-0816-y
15. Thomee, B., et al.: YFCC100M: the new data in multimedia research. Commun. ACM **59**(2), 64–73 (2016). https://doi.org/10.1145/2812802
16. Tolias, G., Sicre, R., Jégou, H.: Particular object retrieval with integral max-pooling of CNN activations. arXiv preprint arXiv:1511.05879 (2015)
17. Truong, T.D., et al.: Video search based on semantic extraction and locally regional object proposal. In: Schoeffmann, K., et al. (eds.) MMM 2018. LNCS, vol. 10705, pp. 451–456. Springer, Cham (2018). https://doi.org/10.1007/978-3-319-73600-6_49
18. Zhou, B., Lapedriza, A., Khosla, A., Oliva, A., Torralba, A.: Places: a 10 million image database for scene recognition. IEEE Trans. Patt. Anal. Mach. Intell. **40**, 1452–1464 (2017)

VIRET Tool Meets NasNet

Jakub Lokoč, Gregor Kovalčík, Tomáš Souček, Jaroslav Moravec, Jan Bodnár,
and Přemysl Čech[(⊠)]

SIRET Research Group, Department of Software Engineering,
Faculty of Mathematics and Physics, Charles University, Prague, Czech Republic
{lokoc,cech}@ksi.mff.cuni.cz, gregor.kovalcik@gmail.com,
tomas.soucek1@gmail.com, jaroslav.moravec@centrum.cz,
jan.bodnar@seznam.cz

Abstract. The results of the last Video Browser Showdown in Bangkok 2018 show that multimodal search with interactive query reformulation represents a competitive search strategy for all the evaluated task categories. Therefore, we plan to target the effectiveness of involved retrieval models by making use of the most recent deep network architectures in the new version of our interactive video retrieval VIRET tool. Specifically, we apply the NasNet deep convolutional neural network architecture for automatic annotation and similarity search in the set of selected frames from the provided video collection. In addition, we implement temporal sequence queries and subimage similarity search to provide higher query formulation flexibility for users.

Keywords: Known-item search · Deep learning · NasNet
Interactive video retrieval

1 Introduction

Known-item search (KIS) in video represents a challenging task, where users search for one particular previously observed scene (visual KIS) or described scene (textual KIS) in a large video archive. Methods for known-item search are fostered by the Video Browser Showdown [4,6], where participating teams use their tools to solve selected KIS tasks on a shared dataset in a highly competitive way. Since 2017, the competition focuses also on Ad-Hoc search, where users try to find all scenes corresponding to a given textual description. Due to time constraints of the competition, the time to solve each task is limited (5–7 min) and thus highly efficient methods are required. The competition consists also of novice sessions, addressing the complexity of interfaces for non-expert users.

The most successful tools participating the last year relied on several components. During video preprocessing, the tools employed deep neural networks (e.g., GoogleNet [13]) to automatically annotate selected frames and extract features for similarity models. For visual KIS tasks, color-based descriptors were successfully utilized as well [8,10]. In several tasks, VITRIVR team [12] successfully employed OCR and ASR data.

© Springer Nature Switzerland AG 2019
I. Kompatsiaris et al. (Eds.): MMM 2019, LNCS 11296, pp. 597–601, 2019.
https://doi.org/10.1007/978-3-030-05716-9_52

The tool interfaces usually consisted of simple querying panels for each retrieval model (focus on a usability gap) and visualization grids presenting either top matching frames or an organized view of selected frames. The overall winner, the VIRET tool [8,9] created by our team, relied mostly on querying and combinations of 2–3 query modalities. The intersection of results of different models was sorted by a selected model and presented to the user. The visualization consisted of two simple grids. The top grid presented the found frames (sorted by relevance), while the bottom grid presented contextual frames from a video corresponding to the selected frame in the top grid. This contrasts to more complex interactive browsing interfaces presented by ITEC [11] and HTW [1] tools/teams (2nd and 4th place). Both tools used hierarchical image maps organized by various similarity models, where users can browse like in classical maps by zooming and panning. However, this interactive visualization of frames did not result in an overall superior performance. Surprisingly, the novice users operating the ITEC tool (often using keyword search) performed better than expert users (often using image maps). Therefore, in our new version we investigate and proceed with potentially more effective retrieval models instead of implementing more complex interactive browsing interfaces.

2   New Features of the VIRET Tool

The most significant change of our tool is in the data preprocessing phase where we apply the state-of-the-art NasNet deep neural network architecture [15] (GoogLeNet was used previously [13]). Since the new video dataset has a higher resolution, we also consider subimage similarity search. The subimages are defined in advance by a fixed grid. Since the interface is very similar to the previous version of the VIRET tool [9] (see Fig. 1) used at the Lifelog Search Challenge and the same ranking approaches are employed for frame-based retrieval (temporal sequence queries use the ranking approaches), we focus our description on data preprocessing for the utilized retrieval models.

2.1   Data Model and Frame Selection

The V3C1 video collection is provided with already identified segments. The segmentation used a color histogram for every frame divided to 3×3 partitions. A threshold between two successive histograms was used to identify segment boundaries. However, the segmentation was not designed to identify shots and thus we consider our own approach relying on 3D deep convolutional neural networks. As a result, the tool considers the set of automatically identified shots for each video. The shot duration can be used for filtering of non-relevant shots.

Since our tool is designed for frame-based retrieval, a frame selection method is necessary to further identify representative frames from each shot. A naive approach is to take the middle frame. However, longer shots could contain more semantically interesting frames and thus we assume that each shot can contain more than one selected frame. For this task, selection heuristics can be employed

Fig. 1. On the left, the tool with the keyword query "juice OR cup" to filter 50% of all the frames and three selected example frames to filter 70% of all the frames. The intersection of the unfiltered frames is sorted by the relevance to the frame examples and color sketch. Multiple frames from the searched collection are presented in the upper grid. Single frame is selected at position [0, 2], showing a yellow cup being held in hand. The summary of the video for inspection is presented in the bottom grid. An example of the timeline display is presented on the right figure (for fast examination of temporal context of found frames). Middle vertical column shows relevant frames from distinct videos. Each row shows temporal context of the frame in the middle column with an adjustable level of details.

relying either on traditional descriptors (e.g., position color signatures) or deep convolutional neural networks. Our tool supports both options, however, the option has to be decided in the preprocessing phase.

Detection of more representative frames is convenient for the presentation of temporal context and also for localization of concepts by querying. On the other hand, a higher number of ranked frames is returned by querying, with more potentially non-relevant results in the first positions. Therefore, we consider grouping of visually similar frames in each video such that the result lists could contain only the best ranked frame from each group.

2.2 Automatic Annotation

Similar as the last year [9], we again rely on our own set of distinct keywords selected from the set of available ImageNet categories. However, to prevent using two or more visually similar categories for training, we have first clustered category representatives[1] from ImageNet and then selected the unique ones. The selected categories are used to define the last layer of a preferred deep network architecture. This year, we consider the state-of-the-art NasNet architecture [15] to automatically annotate selected frames. We also use specialized networks for face [5] and text [14] detection. Since the specialized networks provide also bounding boxes, our tool enables localization of searched faces and texts in the color-sketch canvas.

---

[1] The representative was selected as a mean descriptor of images in one category. The original GoogLeNet was used to extract descriptors.

2.3 Similarity Search by Semantic Features

Features from the last pooling layer of the original GoogLeNet proved to be useful in several tasks for filtering and ranking. However, since the network was trained for classification, similarity search using extracted features suffers from many false hits. Apart from using the NasNet network to extract the features, we also consider to employ NasNet in a siamese network configuration for training embeddings suitable for the considered cosine distance. Based on the experience with various supported extracted features for a given dataset, users can decide which features to use (features can be replaced easily on demand).

For subimage search, the number of extracted features grows significantly. Memory and computation requirements would require a persistent similarity index. To simplify the tool, we employ our MapReduce based implementation of approximate k-NN similarity joins [3] and store top k nearest frames for each subimage.

2.4 Temporal Sequence Queries

Whereas our tool from VBS 2018 focused on the retrieval of one particular frame from the searched sequence, in the new version we re-introduce temporal sequence queries enabling users to describe and target more than one frame in a video sequence. This approach was already used in the previous versions of our tool [2,7] to target distributions of various features in consecutive distinct selected frames. In the new version, we consider temporal sequences of keywords, color-sketches and example images. The user interface supports to insert an additional query initialization block of the three query modalities. The vertical ordering of the blocks in the tool represents the expected temporal ordering of the searched frames.

Acknowledgments. This paper has been supported in part by Czech Science Foundation (GAČR) project Nr. 17-22224S and by Charles University grant SVV-260451.

References

1. Barthel, K.U., Hezel, N., Mackowiak, R.: Navigating a graph of scenes for exploring large video collections. In: Tian, Q., Sebe, N., Qi, G.-J., Huet, B., Hong, R., Liu, X. (eds.) MMM 2016. LNCS, vol. 9517, pp. 418–423. Springer, Cham (2016). https://doi.org/10.1007/978-3-319-27674-8_43
2. Blazek, A., Lokoc, J., Kubon, D.: Video hunter at VBS 2017. In: MultiMedia Modeling - 23rd International Conference, MMM 2017, Proceedings, Part II, Reykjavik, Iceland, 4–6 January 2017, pp. 493–498 (2017)
3. Čech, P., Maroušek, J., Lokoč, J., Silva, Y.N., Starks, J.: Comparing MapReduce-based k-NN similarity joins on hadoop for high-dimensional data. In: Cong, G., Peng, W.-C., Zhang, W.E., Li, C., Sun, A. (eds.) ADMA 2017. LNCS (LNAI), vol. 10604, pp. 63–75. Springer, Cham (2017). https://doi.org/10.1007/978-3-319-69179-4_5

4. Cobârzan, C., et al.: Interactive video search tools: a detailed analysis of the video browser showdown 2015. Multimedia Tools Appl. **76**(4), 5539–5571 (2017)
5. Hu, P., Ramanan, D.: Finding tiny faces. CoRR abs/1612.04402 (2016)
6. Lokoc, J., Bailer, W., Schoeffmann, K., Muenzer, B., Awad, G.: On influential trends in interactive video retrieval: video browser showdown 2015–2017. IEEE Trans. Multimedia **20**(12), 3361–3376 (2018). https://ieeexplore.ieee.org/document/8352047
7. Lokoč, J., Blažek, A., Skopal, T.: Signature-based video browser. In: Gurrin, C., Hopfgartner, F., Hurst, W., Johansen, H., Lee, H., O'Connor, N. (eds.) MMM 2014. LNCS, vol. 8326, pp. 415–418. Springer, Cham (2014). https://doi.org/10.1007/978-3-319-04117-9_49
8. Lokoč, J., Kovalčík, G., Souček, T.: Revisiting SIRET video retrieval tool. In: MultiMedia Modeling - 24th International Conference, MMM 2018, Bangkok, Thailand, Proceedings, Part II, 5–7 February 2018, pp. 419–424 (2018)
9. Lokoč, J., Souček, T., Kovalčík, G.: Using an interactive video retrieval tool for lifelog data. In: Proceedings of the 2018 ACM Workshop on the Lifelog Search Challenge, LSC 2018, pp. 15–19. ACM, New York (2018)
10. Nguyen, P.A., Lu, Y.-J., Zhang, H., Ngo, C.-W.: Enhanced VIREO KIS at VBS 2018. In: Schoeffmann, K., et al. (eds.) MMM 2018. LNCS, vol. 10705, pp. 407–412. Springer, Cham (2018). https://doi.org/10.1007/978-3-319-73600-6_42
11. Primus, M.J., Münzer, B., Leibetseder, A., Schoeffmann, K.: The ITEC collaborative video search system at the video browser showdown 2018. In: Schoeffmann, K., et al. (eds.) MMM 2018. LNCS, vol. 10705, pp. 438–443. Springer, Cham (2018). https://doi.org/10.1007/978-3-319-73600-6_47
12. Rossetto, L., Giangreco, I., Tănase, C., Schuldt, H., Dupont, S., Seddati, O.: Enhanced retrieval and browsing in the IMOTION system. In: Amsaleg, L., Guðmundsson, G.Þ., Gurrin, C., Jónsson, B.Þ., Satoh, S. (eds.) MMM 2017. LNCS, vol. 10133, pp. 469–474. Springer, Cham (2017). https://doi.org/10.1007/978-3-319-51814-5_43
13. Szegedy, C., et al.: Going deeper with convolutions. In: IEEE Conference on Computer Vision and Pattern Recognition, CVPR 2015, Boston, MA, USA, 7–12 June 2015, pp. 1–9 (2015)
14. Zhou, X., et al.: EAST: an efficient and accurate scene text detector. CoRR abs/1704.03155 (2017)
15. Zoph, B., Vasudevan, V., Shlens, J., Le, Q.V.: Learning transferable architectures for scalable image recognition. CoRR abs/1707.07012 (2017)

VERGE in VBS 2019

Stelios Andreadis[1]([⊠]), Anastasia Moumtzidou[1], Damianos Galanopoulos[1],
Foteini Markatopoulou[1], Konstantinos Apostolidis[1], Thanassis Mavropoulos[1],
Ilias Gialampoukidis[1], Stefanos Vrochidis[1], Vasileios Mezaris[1],
Ioannis Kompatsiaris[1], and Ioannis Patras[2]

[1] Information Technologies Institute/Centre for Research and Technology Hellas,
Thessaloniki, Greece
{andreadisst,moumtzid,dgalanop,markatopoulou,kapost,mavrathan,heliasgj,
stefanos,bmezaris,ikom}@iti.gr
[2] School of Electronic Engineering and Computer Science, QMUL, London, UK
i.patras@qmul.ac.uk

Abstract. This paper presents VERGE, an interactive video retrieval
engine that enables browsing and searching into video content. The system implements various retrieval modalities, such as visual or textual
search, concept detection and clustering, as well as a multimodal fusion
and a reranking capability. All results are displayed in a graphical user
interface in an efficient and friendly manner.

1 Introduction

VERGE interactive video search engine integrates a multitude of indexing and
retrieval modules, aiming to provide efficient browsing and search capabilities
inside video collections. During the last decade, VERGE has participated in
several video retrieval related conferences and showcases, with the most recent
being TRECVID [1] and Video Browser Showdown (VBS) [2]. The system is
adapted to support Known Item Search (KIS), Instance Search (INS) and Ad-
Hoc Video Search tasks (AVS). Inspired by other participations in VBS, i.e.
VIREO [3], HTW [4], and SIRET [5], a novel graphical user interface (GUI) was
introduced in 2018, transitioning from a multi- to a single-page website with a
dashboard menu. This year, VERGE incorporates notable improvements regarding the user experience and new approaches to previously ineffective techniques,
e.g. video clustering and fusion. Following the example of SIRET, winner of the
last VBS, an advanced keyword search is also investigated. Section 2 describes
the current version of the search modules and Sect. 3 illustrates the GUI.

2 Video Retrieval System

VERGE serves as a video retrieval system with straightforward browsing in a
friendly environment and diverse search functionalities, which can be combined
either with fusion or reranking the relevant results. So far the following indexing

I. Kompatsiaris et al. (Eds.): MMM 2019, LNCS 11296, pp. 602–608, 2019.
https://doi.org/10.1007/978-3-030-05716-9_53

and retrieval modules have been integrated: (a) Visual Similarity Search; (b) Concept-Based Retrieval; (c) Automatic Query Formulation and Expansion; (d) Clustering; (e) Text-Based Search; and (f) Multimodal Fusion. Utilizing these modules, the user is able to search through a collection of images or videos and the retrieved results are displayed on a GUI. Furthermore, the system allows the user to rerank the top-N results using alternative modalities. The general architecture of the VERGE system is depicted in Fig. 1.

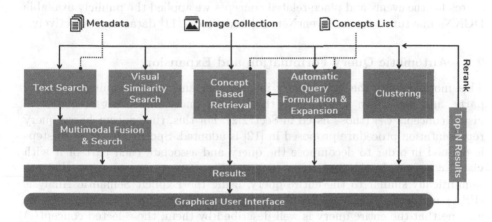

Fig. 1. VERGE system architecture.

2.1 Visual Similarity Search

This module performs content-based retrieval using deep convolutional neural networks (DCNNs). Compared to last year's implementation, which utilized as global keyframe representation the output of the last pooling layer of the GoogleNet trained on 5055 ImageNet concepts, a more complicated feature representation will be evaluated. Specifically, the output of different layers from different networks such as the AlexNet, the GoogleNet, the ResNet, the VGG Net and the CaffeNet will be concatenated into a single feature vector. In the sequel, an IVFADC index database vector will be created for fast indexing and K-Nearest Neighbors will be computed for the query image [6].

2.2 Concept-Based Retrieval

This module indexes each shot that is part of the VBS video collection using a pool of 1000 ImageNet concepts, 345 TRECVID SIN concepts, 500 event-related concepts, and 205 place-related concepts [7]. To obtain scores regarding the 1000 ImageNet concepts, we applied five pre-trained ImageNet deep convolutional neural networks on the shot's keyframes. For each of the 1000 concepts, the average (arithmetic mean) of the output of these networks was used as the final score for the given concept. To obtain scores for the 345 TRECVID SIN concepts, we used the deep learning framework of [8]. This deep architecture learns to annotate video frames not just by looking at each concept separately, but also by explicitly making use of concept relations that exist at two different levels: the (lower) visual representation level, and the (higher) semantic correlations level. Training of the network for the 345 concepts was performed using the 600-hours training portion of the TRECVID-SIN 2013 dataset [9]. Finally, to obtain scores for the event- and place-related concepts we applied the publicly available DCNNs fine-tuned on the EventNet [10] and Places [11] datasets, respectively.

2.3   Automatic Query Formulation and Expansion

This module splits the input query into smaller and more meaningful textual parts, and uses them to translate the original query into a set of high-level visual concepts C_Q (those listed in Sect. 2.2). For this, the concept-based query representation procedure proposed in [12] is adopted. Specifically, a set of steps is defined in order to decompose the query and associate each part of it with visual concepts. In the first step, we search for one or more concepts that are semantically similar to the entire query, using the Explicit Semantic Analysis (ESA) measure. If such concepts are found (according to a threshold θ) we assume that the entire query is well described by them; the selected concept(s) is (are) added in the initially empty set C_Q, and no further action is taken. Otherwise, in a second step we examine if any of the concepts in our concept pool appears in the query by string matching, and if so these concepts are added in C_Q. In the third step the original query is transformed into a set of elementary "subqueries", and for that we search for Noun Phrases in the query. Then in the fourth step, concepts that are semantically similar to any of the "subqueries", are added into the set C_Q. Otherwise, if C_Q is still empty, in a final step the original query and all the "subqueries" are used as input to the zero-example event detection pipeline [13], which attempts to find the concepts that are most closely related to them. The outcome of this procedure is a set of concepts C_Q describing the input query.

2.4   Clustering

Two clustering approaches are applied for the effective visualization of the dataset:

ColorMap Clustering: Video keyframes are clustered by color using three MPEG-7 descriptors related to color, i.e. Color Layout, Color Structure, Scalable Color. These descriptors are extracted for each video frame, and then each frame is mapped to a color of the palette by using either euclidean distance or k-means.

Video Clustering: Videos are clustered by using the visual concepts of their keyframes and their metadata. Specifically, for each video we retrieve the top-N ranked concepts among its keyframes, assuming that these concepts describe accurately the video, since most times a certain topic is presented in their short length. Regarding the video metadata, they are processed by stemming and removing stopwords and punctuation. Thus, each video is represented as a text vector and then Latent Dirichlet Allocation is applied on the vectors in order to identify a predefined number of topics inside the video collection.

2.5 Text-Based Search

This year we evaluate a more sophisticated approach that entails the exploitation of online lexical resources to leverage semantic features. Online databases like WordNet or DBpedia use an elaborate system of interlinked metadata that enables semantically similar words to be interconnected. The process of moving from terms literally occurring in treated text to their semantically corresponding concepts in semantic resources is called conceptualization [14]. Capitalizing on this feature we manage to retrieve words like "client" when the available terms only include "customer". Naturally, not all terms have respective equivalents in these external semantic resources, so only specific concepts can be mapped to the original list of available terms.

2.6 Multimodal Fusion and Search

This module fuses the results of two or more search modules, such as the visual descriptors of Sect. 2.1, the concepts of Sect. 2.2 and the color features of Sect. 2.4. Similar shots are retrieved by performing center-to-center comparisons among video shots by using the selected modules. It is possible to describe the query with more than one features (e.g. a shot, a color and/or some concepts) and in that case one feature, considered as dominant, returns the top-N relevant shots, while the others rerank the initial list by using a non-linear graph-based fusion method [15]. Eventually, on the top-N retrieved shots, reranking is performed, taking into account the adjacent keyframes of the top retrieved shots.

3   VERGE User Interface and Interaction Modes

The VERGE user interface (Fig. 2) is designed in a modern style and aims to be a competitive tool for image or video retrieval. For this year the target is to improve the user experience in terms of responsiveness and intuitiveness.

The GUI[1] can be divided into three main parts: a vertical dashboard-like menu on the left, a results panel that spans to the majority of the screen and a filmstrip on the bottom. From top to bottom, the menu includes a countdown timer that shows the remaining time for submission during the contest, a slider to adjust the image size, a back button to restore results from previous search queries and a switch button to select whether new results will be retrieved or returned results will be reranked by a different approach. The various search

---

[1] http://mklab-services.iti.gr/vbs2018.

options are presented to the user in a compact manner, in the form of sliding boxes. In detail, *Search in Metadata* is a text input field that looks for the typed keywords into the video metadata, e.g. their title or description, (Sect. 2.5), *Search for Concepts* transforms a natural language sentence to suggested concepts (Sect. 2.3), while *Concepts* is the entire list, along with the options of auto-complete search and multiple selection (Sect. 2.2). Moreover, *Events* is a set of predefined queries that combine persons, objects, locations, and activities, *Video Similarity* provides a grouping of videos that are most similar and *Colors* offer a palette in order to retrieve images of a specific shade. The outcome of every search module is displayed on the central and largest panel of the interface either as single shots or group of shots (video) in a grid view, sorted by retrieval scores. Hovering over an image allows users to run the *Visual Similarity Search* (Sect. 2.1) or to submit the shot to the contest. Clicking on the image updates the bottom filmstrip with the complete scene where this frame belongs to, showing the related shots in a chronological order.

Fig. 2. Screenshot of the VERGE web application.

To illustrate the capabilities of the VERGE system, we propose a simple usage scenario. Supposing that we are looking for an image of *a man next to his red car*, we can initiate the retrieval procedure by converting this sentence to concepts, utilizing the corresponding module. The suggested concepts are "Adult Male Human" and "Car", so we can combine these two to get the first results. In order to detect a red car, we are able to rerank the retrieved shots by the color red from the palette. Alternatively, we can search for the word "vehicle" into the videos' metadata and when a shot of a red car appears, we exploit the visual similarity modality to find more related images.

4   Future Work

Future work spans in two directions: on the one hand, we intend to improve the existing search modules as far as it concerns their performance and their responsiveness; on the other hand, we would like to explore novel techniques for video content retrieval, e.g. color sketching.

Acknowledgements. This work was supported by the EU's Horizon 2020 research and innovation programme under grant agreements H2020-779962 V4Desi-gn, H2020-700024 TENSOR, H2020-693092 MOVING and H2020-687786 InVID.

References

1. Awad, G., Butt, A., Fiscus, J., et al.: TRECVID 2017: evaluating ad-hoc and instance video search, events detection, video captioning and hyperlinking. In: Proceedings of TRECVID 2017. NIST, USA (2017)
2. Cobârzan, C., Schoeffmann, K., Bailer, W., et al.: Interactive video search tools: a detailed analysis of the video browser showdown 2015. Multimedia Tools Appl. **76**(4), 5539–5571 (2017)
3. Nguyen, P.A., Lu, Y.-J., Zhang, H., Ngo, C.-W.: Enhanced VIREO KIS at VBS 2018. In: Schoeffmann, K., et al. (eds.) MMM 2018. LNCS, vol. 10705, pp. 407–412. Springer, Cham (2018). https://doi.org/10.1007/978-3-319-73600-6_42
4. Barthel, K.U., Hezel, N., Jung, K.: Fusing keyword search and visual exploration for untagged videos. In: Schoeffmann, K., et al. (eds.) MMM 2018. LNCS, vol. 10705, pp. 413–418. Springer, Cham (2018). https://doi.org/10.1007/978-3-319-73600-6_43
5. Lokoč, J., Kovalčík, G., Souček, T.: Revisiting SIRET video retrieval tool. In: Schoeffmann, K., et al. (eds.) MMM 2018. LNCS, vol. 10705, pp. 419–424. Springer, Cham (2018). https://doi.org/10.1007/978-3-319-73600-6_44
6. Jegou, H., Douze, M., Schmid, C.: Product quantization for nearest neighbor search. IEEE Trans. Patt. Anal. Mach. Intell. **33**(1), 117–128 (2011)
7. Markatopoulou, F., Moumtzidou, A., Galanopoulos, D., et al.: ITI-CERTH participation in TRECVID 2017. In: Proceedings of TRECVID 2017 Workshop, USA (2017)
8. Markatopoulou, F., Mezaris, V., Patras, I.: Implicit and explicit concept relations in deep neural networks for multi-label video/image annotation. IEEE Trans. Circ. Syst. Video Technol. **PP**, 1 (2018)
9. Over, P., et al.: TRECVID 2013 - an overview of the goals, tasks, data, evaluation mechanisms and metrics. In: Proceedings of TRECVID 2013 Workshop, USA (2013)
10. Guangnan, Y., Yitong, L., Hongliang, X., et al.: EventNet: a large scale structured concept library for complex event detection in video. In: Proceedings of ACM Multimedia Conference (ACM MM) (2015)
11. Zhou, B., Lapedriza, A., Xiao, J., et al.: Learning deep features for scene recognition using places database. In: Proceedings of NIPS, pp. 487–495 (2014)
12. Markatopoulou, F., Galanopoulos, D., Mezaris, V., Patras, I.: Query and keyframe representations for ad-hoc video search. In: Proceedings of the 2017 ACM on International Conference on Multimedia Retrieval, pp. 407–411. ACM (2017)

13. Galanopoulos, D., Markatopoulou, F., Mezaris, V., Patras, I.: Concept language models and event-based concept number selection for zero-example event detection. In: Proceedings of the 2017 ACM on International Conference on Multimedia Retrieval, pp. 397–401. ACM (2017)
14. Albitar, S., Fournier, S., Espinasse, B.: The impact of conceptualization on text classification. In: Wang, X.S., Cruz, I., Delis, A., Huang, G. (eds.) WISE 2012. LNCS, vol. 7651, pp. 326–339. Springer, Heidelberg (2012). https://doi.org/10.1007/978-3-642-35063-4_24
15. Gialampoukidis, I., Moumtzidou, A., Liparas, D., Vrochidis, S., Kompatsiaris, I.: A hybrid graph-based and non-linear late fusion approach for multimedia retrieval. In: 2016 14th International Workshop on Content-Based Multimedia Indexing (CBMI), pp. 1–6, June 2016

VIREO @ Video Browser Showdown 2019

Phuong Anh Nguyen[1], Chong-Wah Ngo[1(✉)], Danny Francis[2], and Benoit Huet[2]

[1] Computer Science Department, City University of Hong Kong, Hong Kong, China
panguyen2-c@my.cityu.edu.hk, cscwngo@cityu.edu.hk
[2] Data Science Department, EURECOM, Biot, France
{danny.francis,benoit.huet}@eurecom.fr

Abstract. In this paper, the VIREO team video retrieval tool is described in details. As learned from Video Browser Showdown (VBS) 2018, the visualization of video frames is a critical need to improve the browsing effectiveness. Based on this observation, a hierarchical structure that represents the video frame clusters has been built automatically using k-means and self-organizing-map and used for visualization. Also, the relevance feedback module which relies on real-time support-vector-machine classification becomes unfeasible with the large dataset provided in VBS 2019 and has been replaced by a browsing module with pre-calculated nearest neighbors. The preliminary user study results on IACC.3 dataset show that these modules are able to improve the retrieval accuracy and efficiency in real-time video search system.

Keywords: Video visualization · Video retrieval
Video browser showdown

1 Introduction

The VIREO team has participated in the Video Browser Showdown [1] for two recent years and finished with the best ad-hoc tasks in 2017 [2] and the best visual known-item search tasks in 2018 [3]. The tool of the VIREO team provides two searching methods: color-sketch-based and text-based. Using these two functions, users are able to input queries based on their understanding and their memory. Getting the initial results of queries, users will repeatedly update queries and judge results in a loop until finding correct answers.

In 2018, the VIREO team ranked at 6th position over 9 teams participating in ad-hoc tasks although the concept bank used for text-based retrieval is rich with 14 K concepts. Digging down the problem, we concluded that the tool was lacking of the ability allowing users to explore the dataset with alignments. This is a well-known research topic named image visualization.

From the starting point of Video Browser Showdown, many teams integrated the visualization module to the video retrieval tool and achieved remarkable results. KLU - AAU video browser is the winner in 2012 and the tool relies on the ability of humans to track several video streams by hierarchical or parallel browsing methods [4]. The following version used a 3D thumbnail ring arranged

© Springer Nature Switzerland AG 2019
I. Kompatsiaris et al. (Eds.): MMM 2019, LNCS 11296, pp. 609–615, 2019.
https://doi.org/10.1007/978-3-030-05716-9_54

by color similarity for video browsing [5]. The SIRET team is the winner for two consecutive years in 2014 and 2015. In the version of 2015 [6], the team focused on browsing by using the detected shot boundaries and key-frames displayed in a compact way. The HTW team is the winner in 2016 [7]. The team used a novel browsing approach based on graph hierarchy and visually stored image maps. Visual and semantic features learned from convolutional neural network (CNN) is used to predefine graph structure and perform clustering. Then, the graph is projected to 2D plane, performs discrete optimization and generates hierarchies. These results show that the visualization technique for browsing is a critical module for the video retrieval tool.

Following aforementioned approaches, we propose a simple way to construct the hierarchical visualization of the dataset. Basically, the two main factors determining the effectiveness of browsing using the visualization module are the features and the clustering algorithms used for constructing the hierarchy. In proposed approaches, CNN features and a color histogram are used because their robustness has been proven in image retrieval task. For clustering, k-means and self-organizing-map (SOM) [8] are considered. Setup details and preliminary experiment results are described in the next section.

2   Data Visualization for Browsing

2.1   Feature Extraction

From the video key-frames, we extract two types of features including CNN feature from Deep Residual Net (ResNet) [9] and the color histogram in RGB color space. More precisely, we use ResNet50 which is a 50 layers Residual Network, take the pool 5 layer feature map then perform PCA to reduce the dimension to 128 for clustering. As the color histogram can be built for any kind of color space, the RGB color space is used for simplicity. The pixel values from each channel are discretized into 8 bins and used to form up a 3D color histogram for clustering.

2.2   Clustering and Hierarchy Construction

According to our experiences, the user can observe a limited number of images on the screen at a time. From that, judging all the video key-frames without any alignment is a tedious task for the user. With hierarchical partitioning, the extracted features which contain the color and semantic information are grouped and aligned in an intuitive way for browsing. This hierarchy is built once using all the dataset, while searching and judging, the user can directly navigate to the position of selected shot in the hierarchy to expand the searching area.

A grid with 8 rows and 10 columns is defined on the browsing window, each cell represents an image to the user. Each image is the center of one cluster and it accounts for all the images belonging to that cluster. The user can use left-mouse-click on the images to go down one layer and use right-mouse-click to go up one layer in the hierarchical representation. With this design, users can quickly judge and navigate between clusters to refine browsing results.

To build up the hierarchy, we run self-organizing-map and k-means on the dataset to get 8*10 clusters and recursively do the clustering on the generated clusters with the same parameters (the number of clusters) while the number of images in the new cluster is above 80. The image which is chosen as the representation image is the one closest to the cluster center.

2.3   Preliminary Experiment

For our experiments, the standard IACC.3 video dataset which was introduced in 2016 for video retrieval is used. More precisely, we use the master-shot key-frames provided by TRECVID (TREC Video Retrieval Evaluation series) which contains 335,944 key-frames. By the definition of the master-shot key-frame, key-frames are expected to provide rich information for representing the content of the video shots. Using these images, we treat the problem of video retrieval as image retrieval.

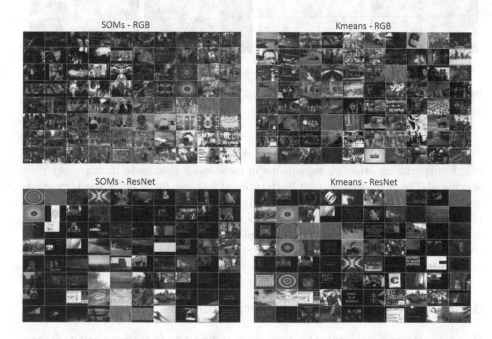

Fig. 1. The visualization of images at the top level of the hierarchy using different clustering algorithms and different types of feature.

Intuitively looking at the clustering results on the tool's interface (in Fig. 1), the clustering result of the SOM is shown in a way that makes the user understand easily with adjacent images a.k.a. clusters look similar. This is the characteristic of SOM that provides a topology preserving mapping from a high dimensional space to a 2D space. The visualization using k-means looks like chaos and creates difficulties for the user in navigation. Besides, comparing between RGB color histogram and ResNet feature for visualization using SOM, RGB color histogram visualization looks more reasonable because the color matches with human vision.

To have a more precise evaluation, a preliminary user study has been held by letting 5 users find some queries using the tool and the searching time has been used to compare and select the best setting of the visualization tool. The selected users are novice users who are trained to use the browsing tool with a ten minutes tutorial and experienced one example before participating in the real user study. In order to provide a better view of the results, two color-favoring-images and two semantic-favoring-images are randomly picked as the queries. Selected queries are shown in Fig. 2.

Query 1   Query 2   Query 3   Query 4

Fig. 2. Selected images for the user study. Two images on the left favor color, two images on the right favor semantic features.

As shown in Table 1, using the same type of features, the visualization using SOM outperforms other visualizations in most cases thanks to its topology preserving ability. It also shows that both types of features including color histogram and ResNet features are useful in visualization for searching. The shortest time to find color-favoring-images belongs to the RGB color histogram, the shortest time to find semantic-favoring-images belongs to the ResNet feature. These results lead us to the decision of using SOM with color histogram and ResNet feature for the visualization tool.

3   Video Retrieval Tool Description

Besides integrating the visualization module into the video retrieval tool, the searching module mostly stays the same as the tool that used in VBS 2018, including:

Color-Sketch Based Query. This is the essential module which brings the VIREO team the best result in 2018 visual known-item-search task. With pre-calculated ranking list for all available queries which is the combination of cells

Table 1. The user study result showing the average searching time of participants who manage to find the correct answer. The number in the parenthesis shows the number of users successfully finding the query image within 3 min (180 s). The infinity symbol (∞) shows that no user manages to find the query image in allocated time.

Query	SOM+RGB	k-means+RGB	SOM+ResNet	k-means+ResNet
No. 1 (color)	**23.8 s (5)**	106.2 s (5)	**45.4 s (5)**	127.75 s (4)
No. 2 (color)	**60.8 s (5)**	∞ (0)	∞ (0)	∞ (0)
No. 3 (semantic)	**98 s (5)**	17.5 s (2)	**18.4 s (5)**	30.6 s (5)
No. 4 (semantic)	**43.33 s (3)**	124.5 s (2)	**12.4 s (5)**	23.4 s (5)

on the uniform grid and the available query colors, the retrieval can be done in real-time. The combination of queries is encouraged to reduce the number of retrieved samples for judging. Two modes of queries are provided to support different attentions of the user: the color distribution of frame-based and shot-based. Because of the robustness and the expand-ability of this approach, the module is kept as the original version.

Text Based Query. In this module, two searching modes are provided: free text search for meta-data and exact text search for concept. The meta-data contains the video name, description, extracted speech and on-screen text. The concept search uses the 14 K concept bank which provides general concepts to fine-grained concepts. However, with the striking development of object detection techniques using CNN, the object detection result of 80 common objects in context (from COCO dataset [10]) is extracted using YOLOv3 [11] and added to the exact text search function.

Filtering. Reducing the number of samples for judging can save a lot of time and favor all the searching modules. Hence, filtering module is helpful in many cases. In the tool, two basic filtering functions are provided: black-borders filter and black and white filter.

Relevance Feedback. Originally, the relevance feedback module has been built based on real-time classification using SVM on the ResNet50 features. The user can pick positive and negative samples then get the classification result for judging. Usually, this module takes 4–5 s to generate new result on IACC.3 dataset. This is unfeasible when the dataset size dramatically increases and not suitable with the coming V3C1 dataset in VBS 2019. Also, collecting positive and negative samples in the judging process is not reasonable to the user. Instead of collecting samples, the user can directly explore the dataset to find similar samples when they look at any positive sample. This process is not time-consuming because the nearest samples for each master-shot key-frame can be calculated in advance. As a result, the relevance feedback module has been replaced by a list of top 1000 nearest neighbors of the picked sample by the user to expand the browsing space.

4   Conclusion

In the latest version, we focus on improving the effectiveness of browsing phase by proposing a simple method to construct the cluster hierarchy of video-frames. This method builds up the hierarchy based on the typical distribution of the dataset and supports the user in understanding the dataset. Besides, the replacement of the relevance feedback module is aiming to help the user expanding their searching space using any positive sample. With current development of the tool, we are looking forward to see how the system works in VBS 2019.

Acknowledgments. The work described in this paper was supported by a grant from the Research Grants Council of the Hong Kong SAR, China (Reference No.: CityU 11250716), and a grant from the PROCORE-France/Hong Kong Joint Research Scheme sponsored by the Research Grants Council of Hong Kong and the Consulate General of France in Hong Kong (Reference No.: F-CityU104/17).

References

1. Cobârzan, C., Schoeffmann, K., Bailer, W., et al.: Interactive video search tools: a detailed analysis of the video browser showdown 2015. Multimedia Tools Appl. **76**, 5539–5571 (2017)
2. Lu, Y.-J., Nguyen, P.A., Zhang, H., Ngo, C.-W.: Concept-based interactive search system. In: Amsaleg, L., Guðmundsson, G.Þ., Gurrin, C., Jónsson, B.Þ., Satoh, S. (eds.) MMM 2017. LNCS, vol. 10133, pp. 463–468. Springer, Cham (2017). https://doi.org/10.1007/978-3-319-51814-5_42
3. Nguyen, P.A., Lu, Y.-J., Zhang, H., Ngo, C.-W.: Enhanced VIREO KIS at VBS 2018. In: Schoeffmann, K., et al. (eds.) MMM 2018. LNCS, vol. 10705, pp. 407–412. Springer, Cham (2018). https://doi.org/10.1007/978-3-319-73600-6_42
4. Del Fabro, M., Münzer, B., Böszörmenyi, L.: AAU video browser with augmented navigation bars. In: Li, S., et al. (eds.) MMM 2013. LNCS, vol. 7733, pp. 544–546. Springer, Heidelberg (2013). https://doi.org/10.1007/978-3-642-35728-2_64
5. Schoeffmann, K., Ahlström, D., Böszörmenyi, L.: Video browsing with a 3D thumbnail ring arranged by color similarity. In: Schoeffmann, K., Merialdo, B., Hauptmann, A.G., Ngo, C.-W., Andreopoulos, Y., Breiteneder, C. (eds.) MMM 2012. LNCS, vol. 7131, pp. 660–661. Springer, Heidelberg (2012). https://doi.org/10.1007/978-3-642-27355-1_70
6. Blažek, A., Lokoč, J., Matzner, F., Skopal, T.: Enhanced signature-based video browser. In: He, X., Luo, S., Tao, D., Xu, C., Yang, J., Hasan, M.A. (eds.) MMM 2015. LNCS, vol. 8936, pp. 243–248. Springer, Cham (2015). https://doi.org/10.1007/978-3-319-14442-9_22
7. Barthel, K.U., Hezel, N., Mackowiak, R.: Navigating a graph of scenes for exploring large video collections. In: Tian, Q., Sebe, N., Qi, G.-J., Huet, B., Hong, R., Liu, X. (eds.) MMM 2016. LNCS, vol. 9517, pp. 418–423. Springer, Cham (2016). https://doi.org/10.1007/978-3-319-27674-8_43

8. Kohonen, T.: The self-organizing map. Proc. IEEE **78**(9), 1464–1480 (1990)

9. He, K., Zhang, X., Ren, S., Sun, J.: Deep residual learning for image recognition. In: CVPR. IEEE Computer Society, pp. 770–778 (2016)

10. Lin, T.-Y., et al.: Microsoft COCO: common objects in context. In: Fleet, D., Pajdla, T., Schiele, B., Tuytelaars, T. (eds.) ECCV 2014. LNCS, vol. 8693, pp. 740–755. Springer, Cham (2014). https://doi.org/10.1007/978-3-319-10602-1_48

11. Redmon, J., Farhadi, A.: YOLOv3: An Incremental Improvement. arXiv:1804.02767 (2018)

Deep Learning-Based Concept Detection in vitrivr

Luca Rossetto[1(✉)], Mahnaz Amiri Parian[1,2], Ralph Gasser[1], Ivan Giangreco[1], Silvan Heller[1], and Heiko Schuldt[1]

[1] Databases and Information Systems Research Group, Department of Mathematics and Computer Science, University of Basel, Basel, Switzerland
{luca.rossetto,mahnaz.amiriparian,ralph.gasser,ivan.giangreco, silvan.heller,heiko.schuldt}@unibas.ch
[2] Numediart Institute, University of Mons, Mons, Belgium

Abstract. This paper presents the most recent additions to the *vitrivr* retrieval stack, which will be put to the test in the context of the 2019 Video Browser Showdown (VBS). The *vitrivr* stack has been extended by approaches for detecting, localizing, or describing concepts and actions in video scenes using various convolutional neural networks. Leveraging those additions, we have added support for searching the video collection based on semantic sketches. Furthermore, *vitrivr* offers new types of labels for text-based retrieval. In the same vein, we have also improved upon *vitrivr*'s pre-existing capabilities for extracting text from video through scene text recognition. Moreover, the user interface has received a major overhaul so as to make it more accessible to novice users, especially for query formulation and result exploration.

1 Introduction

In this paper, we present the latest iteration of the open source, content-based multimedia retrieval stack *vitrivr* [17]. The presented system is a continuation of previous versions, which have been participating in the Video Browser Showdown [3] for several years now, first under the name IMOTION [14,16,18], and since 2018 under its current name – *vitrivr* [13]. In the vein of the mainstreamification of Deep Learning and convolutional neural networks (CNNs), the focus of this year's iteration of the *vitrivr* system lies on augmenting the existing sketch-based retrieval capabilities with semantic concept detection, description, localization, and scene text detection, by making use of various available off-the-shelf tools, pre-trained models, and existing as well as custom training datasets. Moreover, we have made numerous changes to the user interface to improve the user experience particularly for novice users for both query formulation and result exploration.

The remainder of this paper is structured as follows: Sect. 2 provides a brief overview of the overall architecture of the *vitrivr* system stack and its pre-existing capabilities. Section 3 introduces the new functionality which has been added to *vitrivr* for this iteration of the competition. Section 4 concludes.

© Springer Nature Switzerland AG 2019
I. Kompatsiaris et al. (Eds.): MMM 2019, LNCS 11296, pp. 616–621, 2019.
https://doi.org/10.1007/978-3-030-05716-9_55

2   System Overview and Existing Capabilities

vitrivr is a content-based multimedia retrieval stack capable of retrieving from mixed media collections containing images, audio, video, and 3D data. In the context of the VBS competition, only the video retrieval capabilities are relevant. The *vitrivr* stack is comprised of three components: the database system ADAM$_{pro}$ [7], the retrieval engine Cineast [15], and the user interface vitrivr-ng. The user interface is browser-based and can be served either directly by Cineast or via an external web server. More details with respect to the architecture of the entire system can be found in [17].

3   New Functionality

In this section, we highlight the additions made to the *vitrivr* stack. They are primarily based on functionality provided by various neural network architectures. The first group of these additions generates various forms of textual output from a given video scene. These methods include scene text detection and extraction as well as scene labeling and captioning. The second group operates based on concept detection and localization, which is queried via a sketched input. Figure 1 depicts an overview of the different types of features, both new and pre-existing. In addition, the user interface was improved to increase the efficiency in query expression and result browsing in a competitive setting.

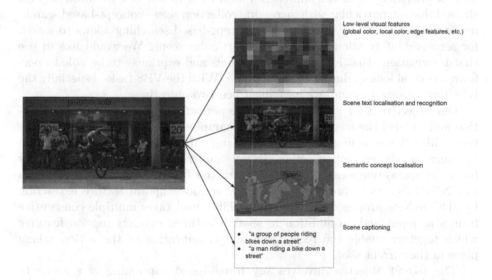

Fig. 1. Overview of the different types of features employed by the *vitrivr* system.

3.1   Scene Text Detection and Recognition

A straightforward way of searching for a particular scene is to use any visible text within that scene as a means for querying. Scene text detection and recognition involves the localization and transcription of textual objects in images. We perform the detection and recognition by leveraging and combining several different neural network-based concept detectors. The new end-to-end scene text detection and recognition module in Cineast is based on a combination of the work presented in [19] and [23] and implemented using the TensorFlow [1] Java API. The module is used during the off-line extraction phase to generate text labels for each keyframe extracted from a video. These labels can then be used on-line, i.e., at retrieval time, during the competition.

The first step during the extraction involves identifying potential text objects in a scene using EAST [23]. EAST leverages a fully connected CNN to generate bounding boxes for areas that contain text. In a second step, we extract the sub-images delimited by those bounding boxes and use a convolutional recurrent neural network (CRNN) – a combination of a CNN and a recurrent neural network, as proposed by [19] – to infer the text in the respective sub-image. We trained the CRNN network using the full MJSynth dataset [8], whereas the pre-trained model provided by the authors was used for EAST.

3.2   Captioning and Labeling

The ex post analysis of the approaches used most at the last iteration of VBS showed that –in particular with increasing collection sizes– concept-based searching is the preferred way of searching. Concept-based searching allows to search for semantic information included in a particular scene. We would like to use that information –that is, the produced labels and captions– to be able to perform a textual lookup during retrieval phase. With the VBS tasks, especially the KIS Textual task in mind, we have identified two objectives:

One objective is for *vitrivr* to be able to perform scene-based action recognition and to label the scenes accordingly. Examples of such action labels involve terms like "horse riding" or "rock climbing" if the scene depicts a person carrying out the respective action. In our implementation, labeling is mainly based on spatio-temporal information extracted from subsequent frames by a 3DCNN [9,20]. More precisely, we employ spatio-temporal feature extraction by 3DConvNets proposed in [20]. This architecture[1] takes multiple consecutive frames as input and, in addition to spatial features, extracts motion features which together enable the recognition and classification of the action taking place in the current shot.

The second objective involves key frame-based captioning of a scene to describe it semantically, that is, describing on a high level what that scene depicts. An example could be a sentence such as "a white cow grazing on a meadow". We use CNN and LSTM networks to achieve this, as proposed by [21].

---

[1] https://github.com/hx173149/C3D-tensorflow

We apply the proposed methods to the representative frame of every shot. The network producing the captions has been trained on [10]. Since this method generates multiple candidate captions, which might describe different aspects of the input image, we store the three most likely captions per segment.

3.3 Semantic Sketches

Inspired by the work presented in [6], we added a new type of sketch-based querying, which uses common semantic concepts rather than colors. We hope that this allows for a more intuitive search, in particular for novice users of the *vitrivr* system. The maps describing the localization of the concepts have been obtained using a DeepLab network [2] trained on three image datasets containing concept-instances from different contexts [4,5,22].

The obtained object maps are quantized into an $n \times n$ grid where the most extensive concept is used as a label for every cell. For every concept, a two-dimensional coordinate point has been pre-computed based on a 2D-embedding [11] of semantic distances [12] between the concepts. To generate a vector from the previously obtained grid, the 2D-coordinates per concept are simply concatenated for every cell in a pre-determined order, resulting in a vector of length $2n^2$. This leads to a compact representation, which still retains some notion of similarity between the different concepts as well as their spatial relation within the scene.

3.4 User Interface Improvements

The extensions of the user interface implemented for the VBS 2019 version of *vitrivr* primarily address the efficiency and speed of both query formulation and results exploration. In particular, the user interface has been improved with novice users in mind to ensure that they are able to use *vitrivr* right away and that the key functionality is accessible in a more intuitive fashion.

While the previous version of the user interface was merely an adaption of a general purpose UI aimed at content-based multimedia retrieval, the UI used in this iteration of the competition is geared more towards the competitive nature of the VBS setting. This is achieved by restructuring several workflows so as to reduce the number of clicks necessary to access the functionality relevant to the competition.

Moreover, we have substantially increased the number of results that are displayed in the interface in order to provide better browsing capabilities. To increase the browsing efficiency, the user interface has been extended by filters for certain visual characteristics (e.g., filter for colored shots or filter for black and white shots) or for excluding previously seen results from a previous query. Especially for the latter, such filter information can also be transmitted to other team members using their own instance of the interface, which enables a high degree of collaboration.

4   Conclusions

In this paper, we have presented recent additions to the *vitrivr* system in order to improve its video retrieval capabilities, especially in a competitive setting. The presented additions have focused on the use of Deep Learning techniques and the improvement of the user interface, in particular towards novice users. The *vitrivr* stack is released as open source software[2] under the MIT license.

References

1. Abadi, M., Barham, P., Chen, J., et al.: Tensorflow: a system for large-scale machine learning. In: Proceedings of the USENIX Symposium on Operating Systems Design and Implementation (OSDI), vol. 16, pp. 265–283. USENIX, Savannah, GA, USA (2016)
2. Chen, L.-C., Zhu, Y., Papandreou, G., Schroff, F., Adam, H.: Encoder-decoder with atrous separable convolution for semantic image segmentation. In: Proceedings of the 15th European Conference on Computer Vision (ECCV), Munich, Germany (2018, page to appear)
3. Cobârzan, C., et al.: Interactive video search tools: a detailed analysis of the video browser showdown 2015. Multimedia Tools and Appl. (MTAP) **76**(4), 5539–5571 (2017)
4. Cordts, M., et al.: The cityscapes dataset for semantic urban scene understanding. In: Proceedings of the IEEE Conference on Computer Vision and Pattern Recognition (CVPR), pp. 3213–3223. IEEE, Las Vegas (2016)
5. Mark Everingham, S.M., Eslami, A., Van Gool, L., Williams, C.K.I., Winn, J., Zisserman, A.: The Pascal visual object classes challenge: a retrospective. Int. J. Comput. Vis. (IJCV) **111**(1), 98–136 (2015)
6. Furuta, R., Inoue, N., Yamasaki, T.: Efficient and interactive spatial-semantic image retrieval. In: Schoeffmann, K., et al. (eds.) MMM 2018. LNCS, vol. 10704, pp. 190–202. Springer, Cham (2018). https://doi.org/10.1007/978-3-319-73603-7_16
7. Giangreco, I., Schuldt, H.: ADAM$_{pro}$: database support for big multimedia retrieval. Datenbank-Spektrum **16**(1), 17–26 (2016)
8. Jaderberg, M., Simonyan, K., Vedaldi, A., Zisserman, A.: Synthetic data and artificial neural networks for natural scene text recognition. arXiv preprint arXiv:1406.2227, pp. 1–10 (2014)
9. Karpathy, A., Toderici, G., Shetty, S., Leung, T., Sukthankar, R., Li, F.-F.: Large-scale video classification with convolutional neural networks. In: Proceedings of the IEEE Conference on Computer Vision and Pattern Recognition (CVPR), pp. 1725–1732. IEEE, Columbus (2014)
10. Lin, T.-Y., et al.: Microsoft COCO: common objects in context. In: Fleet, D., Pajdla, T., Schiele, B., Tuytelaars, T. (eds.) ECCV 2014. LNCS, vol. 8693, pp. 740–755. Springer, Cham (2014). https://doi.org/10.1007/978-3-319-10602-1_48
11. van der Maaten, L., Hinton, G.: Visualizing data using t-SNE. J. Mach. Learn. Res. (JMLR) **9**(Nov), 2579–2605 (2008)
12. Mikolov, T., Chen, K., Corrado, G., Dean, J.: Efficient estimation of word representations in vector space. arXiv preprint arXiv:1301.3781, pp. 1–12 (2013)

---

[2] https://github.com/vitrivr.

13. Rossetto, L., Giangreco, I., Gasser, R., Schuldt, H.: Competitive video retrieval with vitrivr. In: Schoeffmann, K., et al. (eds.) MMM 2018. LNCS, vol. 10705, pp. 403–406. Springer, Cham (2018). https://doi.org/10.1007/978-3-319-73600-6_41
14. Rossetto, L., et al.: IMOTION – searching for video sequences using multi-shot sketch queries. In: Tian, Q., Sebe, N., Qi, G.-J., Huet, B., Hong, R., Liu, X. (eds.) MMM 2016. LNCS, vol. 9517, pp. 377–382. Springer, Cham (2016). https://doi.org/10.1007/978-3-319-27674-8_36
15. Rossetto, L., Giangreco, I., Schuldt, H.: Cineast: a multi-feature sketch-based video retrieval engine. In: Proceedings of the International Symposium on Multimedia (ISM), pp. 18–23. IEEE, Taichung, December 2014
16. Rossetto, L., et al.: IMOTION — a content-based video retrieval engine. In: He, X., Luo, S., Tao, D., Xu, C., Yang, J., Hasan, M.A. (eds.) MMM 2015. LNCS, vol. 8936, pp. 255–260. Springer, Cham (2015). https://doi.org/10.1007/978-3-319-14442-9_24
17. Rossetto, L., Giangreco, I., Tănase, C., Schuldt, H.: vitrivr: a flexible retrieval stack supporting multiple query modesfor searching in multimedia collections. In: Proceedings of the ACM Conference on Multimedia Conference (ACM MM), pp. 1183–1186. ACM, Amsterdam, October 2016
18. Rossetto, L., Giangreco, I., Tănase, C., Schuldt, H., Dupont, S., Seddati, O.: Enhanced retrieval and browsing in the IMOTION system. In: Amsaleg, L., Guðmundsson, G.Þ., Gurrin, C., Jónsson, B.Þ., Satoh, S. (eds.) MMM 2017. LNCS, vol. 10133, pp. 469–474. Springer, Cham (2017). https://doi.org/10.1007/978-3-319-51814-5_43
19. Shi, B., Bai, X., Yao, C.: An end-to-end trainable neural network for image-based sequence recognition and its application to scene text recognition. IEEE Trans. Pattern Anal. Mach. Intell. (TPAMI) 39(11), 2298–2304 (2017)
20. Tran, D., Bourdev, L., Fergus, R., Torresani, L., Paluri, M.: Learning spatiotemporal features with 3D convolutional networks. In: Proceedings of the International Conference on Computer Vision (ICCV), pp. 4489–4497. IEEE, Santiago (2015)
21. Vinyals, O., Toshev, A., Bengio, S., Erhan, D.: Show and tell: lessons learned from the 2015 MSCOCO image captioning challenge. IEEE Trans. Pattern Anal. Mach. Intell. (TPAMI) 39(4), 652–663 (2017)
22. Zhou, B., Zhao, H., Puig, X., Fidler, S., Barriuso, A., Torralba, A.: Scene parsing through ADE20K dataset. In: Proceedings of the IEEE Conference on Computer Vision and Pattern Recognition (CVPR), vol. 1, p. 4. IEEE, Honolulu (2017)
23. Zhou, X., et al.: East: an efficient and accurate scene text detector. In: Proceedings of the IEEE Conference on Computer Vision and Pattern Recognition (CVPR), pp. 2642–2651. IEEE, Honolulu (2017)

MANPU 2019 Workshop Papers

Structure Analysis on Common Plot in Four-Scene Comic Story Dataset

Miki Ueno(✉)

Information and Media Center, Toyohashi University of Technology,
Toyohashi 441-8580, Japan
ueno@imc.tut.ac.jp

Abstract. Comic is the one of the most attractive creative contents and it contains both components of image and words features. Especially, I have been focused in four-scene comics which can represent stories with the simple and clear structure. One of my aims of the researches is to promote collaboration between creators and artificial intelligence. To contribute for the field, I have proposed the original four-scene comics dataset with creative process and meta-data. According to the existing comics, I defined the typical patterns of structure and contents. I provided the character and several information to keep balance of common twenty scenarios based on two types of structure for ten plots. The dataset contains 100 kinds of four-scene comics to keep layer information and several annotations by five artists. Thus, it can be analyzed various expressions in common scenarios. In this research, I show the procedure of creating the dataset. Then, I describe the features of the dataset and results of computational experiment.

Keywords: Story patterns of four-scene comics
Contents creators and artificial intelligence
Creating process · Deep learning · Comic computing

1 Introduction

Creative contents are really attractive [1] because they are composed of lots of sensitive thoughts and complex representation. Comic [2] is one of the most fascinating creative contents, the number of researches becomes so large. In comic computation, several techniques should be combined to take various features. Especially, machine learning are useful to analyze features in comics. On the other hand, creativity in humans is an intellectual activity meaning that it is hard to simulate to whole creative process as computational method. The problem is that the data for machine learning is too small because creative process often contains precious and sensitive data. I have focused on the creating process of both the story [3] and image representation [4]. Thus, I have constructed the original four-scene comic story dataset with creative process and meta-data toward collaboration between "Creators and Artificial Intelligence" [5].

In this research, I show the statistics of original four-scene comics dataset and results of a basic experiment.

© Springer Nature Switzerland AG 2019
I. Kompatsiaris et al. (Eds.): MMM 2019, LNCS 11296, pp. 625–636, 2019.
https://doi.org/10.1007/978-3-030-05716-9_56

1.1   Patterns of Comic Story for Machine Learning

The target of the process of creation is different among researchers. I focused on the process of the creating story. Even if novels and comics, one of the most difficult tasks is to analyze and generate their stories well considering transition of scenes in computational research. Comics are composed of multi-modal components so that it connects several fields, for example, art, philosophy, and engineering. I have been focused on comic, especially four-scene comics because they have a clear and simple structure. I proposed the method to analyze emotion and orders of four-scene comics. On the other hand, there is a limitation with analysis of stories by existing comics. In this research, I show the procedure of creating original datasets and patterns of four-scene comics which are helpful to develop computational research.

1.2   Contribution of the Dataset

To show the contribution of the dataset, the several features are shown for taking tasks as an example.

- Story pattern recognition with different structure: four-scene comics has typical structure to represent interesting stories. The dataset consider two types of structure extracted from several structure patterns.
- Character recognition for different touch: same looks and inner of characters information are shown for five comic artist with different touch. The appearance of characters sometimes change in serial comics for a long-time, animation with several artists, and fan-arts. Human can identify that information compared to characters based on the background knowledge. However, it might be difficult to identify such a information for computational method with only image features. To consider the problem, this dataset has the same characters of the same scenarios with five-touch.

2   Background

In this section, the background of the research is shown against several researches for creative contents. The aims of the field are roughly divided into automatic creation and creation support, analysis and generation.

2.1   Kinds and Features of Creative Contents

Computational researches for creative contents are shown as follows.

Comic. Recognition of objects, automatic layout of scenes, analysis of reviews, estimation of balloons, adjust lines and so on.

Novels. A sentence generation has rapidly developed, however paragraph generation are still difficult. In this field, there has also several researches for creation support.

Animation. Animation creation process requires lots of staffs and component for natural languages, a scene, movie, music and so on. A storyboard has same-sized scenes and natural languages, which is similar to scene comics. On the other hand, there has specific information, the information of camera work and the period of appearance per scene.

Picture Book. The research of interactive picture book has known. Continuous pictures draw story and one page has several small stories sometimes. To analyze the story in picture book, I assume that it is required to separate the area of the same page. Some picture books have an individual page for a text and picture in two facing pages. The others have texts for both sides of pages.

2.2 Existing Dataset of Comic

One of the existing dataset of comic is 109 volumes dataset called MANGA 109 [6]. The dataset contains five volumes of four scene comics, the artist and theme are different. The dataset of eBDtheque [7] contains 100 pages with character words and position of frame. Both of them do not focus on creating way of story information.

2.3 Problem of Existing Dataset: Lack of Process of Creating Story

The different authors seldom draw comic based on the common plot. Therefore, it is difficult to find common story pattern in the dataset at the beginning of research. It is also hard what objects are useful to understand story.

3 Four-Scene Comic Story Patterns

I have proposed the story patterns of four-scene comics. There is the cognitive research [8] on the structure of comics about "peanuts" which is famous in America. The aim of that research is different from my research from the view point of the machine learning. Figure 1 shows seven story patterns.

1. General:

Explanation or starting event in the first scene, events are developing in the second scene, an unexpected event occurs the third scene, and the resulting effect is described in the fourth scene. This pattern is called "Ki-sho-ten-ketsu" in Japanese, which originates in the structure of the four-part organization of Chinese poetry. It is a popular and well-organized structure used for stories such as novels and movies.

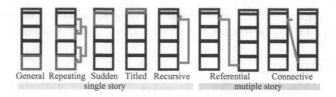

Fig. 1. Seven four-scene comic story pattern * Red line points punch-line and blue line readable order and connection

2. Repeating:
Object transition is continuous for the first and second scene and is similar to that of the third and fourth scene. In most cases, the facial and verbal expressions in the third and fourth scenes are stronger than those in the first and second scenes; e.g. a boy sees the professor in a bad temper and he decides to take a detour between the first and second scenes. Unfortunately, he runs into another professor in a worse temper between the third and fourth scenes.

3. Sudden
Unexpected or special events occur in the first scene. Other scenes are less important than the first scene.

4. Titled
Titles represent the meaning of the entire story.

5. Recursive
It is natural to interpret story even if reading back to the first scene after the fourth scene.

6. Referential
Stories are required to refer a previous story.

7. Connective
Continuous two four-scene comics describes one story. Namely, it seems to be eight-scene comics.

Some comic is used as a component of the news paper and the advertisement. One page usually has two four-scene comics on comic magazines and comic book. In Japan, story four-scene comics is popular. Two types of patterns are considered for story four-scene comics. One is the single story which means that the story is concluded in one four-scene comics. The other is the multiple story which means that it is required to read several four-scene comics in order that the readers understand the story. Mostly, multiple story are composed of several single stories. Story patterns are broadly classified as the structure and contents.

4   Four-Scene Comics Story Dataset

In this research, we focused on two types of the structure story pattern; general and sudden. The content of story pattern is considered as the meta plot which is the abstract text excluding named entity.

4.1   The Concept of Constructing Dataset

The author create characters and location information ten meta plots and plots. Professional comic artist; five different touch: gag, shonen, seinen, shojyo, moe, create 100 comics; twenty kinds of scenarios based on two structure story patterns. In Japan, there are several genres of drawing touches which are according to the magazine including that story. The dataset contains comic images by five comic artists who are introduced by drawing touches they are good at. In different touch, there exists variety of expressions even though the story is same. For example, in gag touch, comic artists tend to use exaggerated expressions with interesting appearance. On the other hand, in moe touch, comic artist tend to use round contour to express something cute.

4.2   The Process of Creation

The process of creation with collaborators is as follows.

I explain the each step to create the original dataset and show the effectiveness for wide-range researches with this dataset to describe the features in each data. Figure 2 shows the whole process with image by shonen-touch comic artist.

1. Define characters and location information[The author]
   - Provide characters information
   - Provide location information
2. Create meta-plot[The author] Meta-plot means the templated plot which are defined referring to popular existing story plots. It has several blanks to be input concrete words. I assume that the punch-line of four-scene comics can be classified into stereotyped story patterns.
3. Create plot based on meta-plot[The author] Plot means the framework of the whole scenario. In this research, I manually input words in order to create plot from the meta-plot. This steps can accept techniques of the cognitive narratology and the natural languages processing based on the database.
4. Create scenario based on plot[The art director and the author] Scenario is composed of concrete character words and actions for each scene. Thinking of characters are represented by words in a specific-shaped speech balloon besides a character. It is useful characteristic of comics to be analyzed an action and a speech-text compared to a character's thinking. Sometimes, the meaning of characters speech-text is far from his/her thinking. This features are important to be analyze emotions and personality of characters.
5. Create rough image based on scenario[Each comic artist] In this step, most of comic artists decide the position characters and character words.
6. Create fair image based on rough image[Each comic artist] In this step, a comic artist draw fair lines and colorize a image with gray-scaled color. Compared between the data in step 5 and 6, we can know which color and the way of painting is appropriate.

1	Character & Location Info.	Author	Hair Length, Eye, Types of Clothes University Laboratory	
2	Meta-Plot	Author	Looks [1] but [2] in actual	*Create two scenarios*
3	Plot	Author	Looks [cute] but have [fair aspect] in actual	*for two structure based on the same scenario*
4	Scenario	Art Director & Author	## Story-2-Structure 2 [1] B returns A his paper with too many stick papers B "I just checked your paper" A "Oh...Thank you... " A thinks (B is so strict) ... ... [4] A thinks (B is so kind), Font by hand "...Usually"	## Story-2-Structure 1 [1] B "A, you looks like pale? Do you have a well sleep?" ... ... [3] A "Well...Will you check my paper?" A gives B his paper [4] Narration "-Tomorrow- B returns A his paper with too many stick papers" A thinks (B is so strict) · *Behavior information for drawing image*

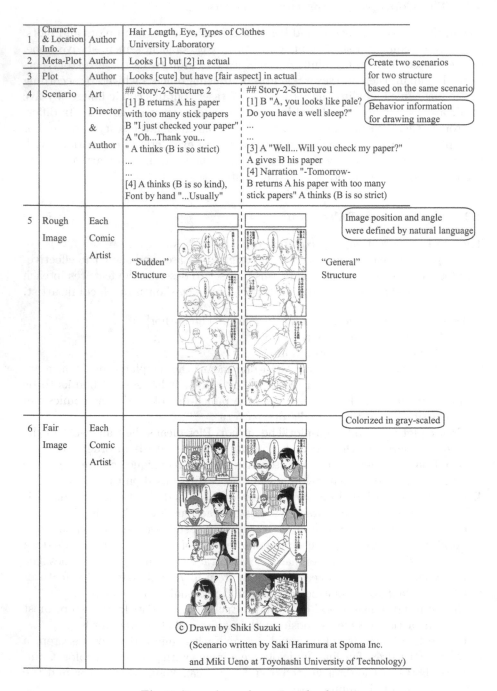

| 5 | Rough Image | Each Comic Artist | "Sudden" Structure | "General" Structure | *Image position and angle were defined by natural language* |
| 6 | Fair Image | Each Comic Artist | | | *Colorized in gray-scaled* |

ⓒ Drawn by Shiki Suzuki

(Scenario written by Saki Harimura at Spoma Inc.
and Miki Ueno at Toyohashi University of Technology)

Fig. 2. Procedure of creating the dataset

Table 1. The first and second story of meta-plot and plot

Story Num.	Meta-plot	Plot
1		A character introduction: Looks [calm] but addicting [something[idol]] in actual
2	Looks [1] but [2] in actual	B character introduction: Looks [cute] but have [fair aspect] in actual

*Meta-plot and plot did not given to the comic artist

Story 1-Structure 1
[1] B "A looks carm." A "Do you think so?"
[2] B thinks (What activities B do on holidays?)
[3] A wears specific clothes for idol concert
[4] A swings cyalume at the favorite idol concert

Story-1-Structure 2
[1] A swings cyalume at the favorite idol concert
[2] Location: Laboratory, A come in the lab. A "Good morning"
[3] B "Good morning, A"
[4] B "A, What activities you do on holidays?"
A "It's a secret" A "You are always so carm"

Story-2-Structure 1
[1] B "A, you looks like pale?Do you have a well sleep?"
A "Umm, no problem"
A think (Yesterday, I had been watching live concert video till midnight...)
[2] B "Please, don't hesitate to ask me"
A thinks (B is so kind)
[3] A "Well...Will you check my paper?" A gives B his paper
[4] Narration "-Tomorrow- B returns A his paper with too many stick papers" A thinks (B is so strict)

Story-2-Structure 2
[1] B returns A his paper with too many stick papers
B "I just checked your paper"
A "Oh...Thank you..." A thinks (B is so strict)
[2] B "A, you looks like pale?
Do you have a well sleep?" A "Umm, no problem"
[3] B "Please, don't hesitate to ask me"
[4] A thinks (B is so kind), Font by hand "...Usually"

Fig. 3. Scenarios of first and second story * Scenarios were given to the comic artist in Japanese

Fig. 4. Two types of structure, above two pages are rough images and the below two pages are fair images in "gag" touch.

* We originally created these image by collaborating with art directors and comic artist.

* Comic can be read right to left in the scene, top to bottom between scenes, and right to left between story in Japan.

* Two four-scene comics per one page. In one page, each right-side comic has the General structure. On the other hand, left-side comic has the Sudden structure. There are four kinds of four-scene comics in the two pages.

Table 2. Parameters of neural network

The number of output units	2
Batch size	20
Linear 1 node size	256
Linear 2 node size	256
The number of epoch	2000
Dropout ratio [10]	0.5
Activation function	ReLU function
Loss function	Softmax cross entropy
Optimizer	Adam:alpha = 1e–6

4.3 Layers Information and Annotate Meta-data

We annotate information to maintain the process of creation.

- Layers information: each frame/facial parts of each character/non-facial parts of each character/each balloon/
- Annotate Meta-data: creators and readers annotate following meta-data
  - Seven types of emotion for each character: six basic emotions [9], neutral
  - Caption to explain the meaning of punch-line

5 Examples and Features of Data

I show location information, character information and the first and second scenario. Table 1 shows meta-plots and plots. Figure 3 shows an example scenario. Figure 4 shows rough images and fair images by the comic artist with gag touch.

Location information. University of laboratory. The protagonists are characters A, B who is bachelor student and master course student respectively.

Character features. Looks information: hair, eyes, height, style of body, clothes information. Inner information: age, grade, personality, and so on.

Common scenarios allow artists to represent variety of expressions. I found several features as follows.

- The perspective of the character is different among artists even in the same scenes.
- Speaker of character words do not necessarily appear in the scene. For example, the speaker is shown as the small face with the balloon of the character words in Fig. 2; the second scene of the right-side story of the right page.

Table 3. CNN layer parameters

	CNN1	CNN2	CNN3	CNN4	CNN5
Filter size	5×5	5×5	5×5	5×5	5×5
Padding size	0	2	1	1	1
Stride	2	1	1	1	1

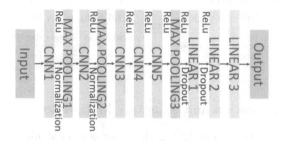

Fig. 5. The architecture of Alex Net

Table 4. Pooling layer parameters

	POOLING1	POOLING2	POOLING3
Filter size	3×3	3×3	3×3
Padding size	0	0	0
Stride	2	2	2

6 Experiment

Computer experiments are carried out for the four-scene comic dataset to show the results to consider features of structure. In the experiment, the input data for Convolutional Neural Network (CNN) is the each scene of four-scene comics with 197×135 pixels. I set the several parameters for AlexNet [11] are same as the our previous paper [12]. Table 2 shows the parameter of the neural network. Tables 3 and 4 shows the CNN layer parameters, the pooling layer parameters respectively. Figure 5 shows the network architectures.

We use following two structures as shown in Sect. 3. I have assumed that there is a big gap between General and Sudden structure. Thus, I focus on these two structure to create the dataset firstly.

General. In the structure of general, the four scene has the punch-line. The fourth scene is the most impressive usually.

Sudden. In the structure of sudden, the first scene has the punch-line so the first scene is impressive. On the other hand, the fourth scene is not so impressive, but sometimes it has also weak punch-line to conclude the story.

Table 5. Classifying two structure in the same order

Num. of order	Acc.
1	0.60
2	0.42
3	0.43
4	0.58

I confirm four kinds of two-class classification. The task of the experiment is to classify which structure by using two same ordered images in the two different structures. e.g. the first scene in the "General" structure is assigned to "Class1" and the first scene in the "Sudden" structure is assigned to "Class2". The number of scenes per each class is 40. The accuracy was calculated by five-fold cross validation. Cross-validation were designed to fix images for each set based on the scenario number to avoid the situation used images from the same scenarios by different comic artists as both for train and the other. For example, images from the first to eighth scenarios are used for train as for first set. The avoided situation is like data-argumentation but not it is truly that because all of images contain different expressions by different comic artists even in the same scenario. Due to the setting, there is a bias in the experiment. Thus, the problem with fixed scenario numbers is more difficult than that with shuffled scenarios. The purpose of the experiment is to show that the images of dataset have specific features for the structure regardless of the number of scenarios and comic artists.

Table 5 shows the result of the experiment. As a result, I indicated that the images of dataset contain specific features in the first scene between two structures regardless of the comic artists. As I mentioned, General structure has the punch-line in the fourth scene. On the other hand, sudden structure has the punch-line in the first scene. Sometimes, it also has small punch-line in the fourth scene. Therefore, the result show the possibility of the gap due to the location of the punch-line. I continue to expand the dataset based on the structure to also analyze existing comics.

7   Conclusion

In this paper, to develop researches for analyzing creating process by both sides of story and image representation, I have shown the procedure of creating original four-scene comics dataset and results of basic experiment to confirm the features of structure.

Followings are future tasks.

- Carry out computational experiments for layer information
- Extend dataset to keep balance
- Collect comments to define applied task

Acknowlegement. I thank to the comic artists and Spoma Inc. to corporate with this research. This work is supported by ACT-I, JST. Grant Number: JPMJPR17U4. A part of this work was supported by JSPS KAKENHI Grant, Grant-in-Aid for Scientific Research(C), 26330282.

References

1. Ueno, M., Fukuda, K., Mori, N.: Can Computers Create Comics and Animations?, Computational and Cognitive Approaches to Narratology, pp. 164–190 (2016)
2. Matsushita, M., et al.: My Book Mark Comic Engineering. Artificial Intelligence, vol. 32 (2017). Advances in Intelligent Systems and Computing, vol. 290, pp. 459–467. Springer (2014)
3. Ueno, M., Isahara, H.: Relationships between features and story description in comics. In: The 30th Annual Conference of the Japanese Society for Artificial Intelligence, 2J5-OS-08b-4in2 (2016)
4. Ueno, M., Mori, N., Matsumoto, K.: 2-scene comic creating system based on the distribution of picture state transition. In: Omatu, S., Bersini, H., Corchado, J.M., Rodríguez, S., Pawlewski, P., Bucciarelli, E. (eds.) Distributed Computing and Artificial Intelligence, 11th International Conference. AISC, vol. 290, pp. 459–467. Springer, Cham (2014). https://doi.org/10.1007/978-3-319-07593-8_53
5. Ueno, M.: Creators and Artificial Intelligence: Four-scene Comics Story Dataset with Creative Process and Metadata towards Collabolation, 4Pin1-16 (2018)
6. Matsui, Y., Ito, K., Aramaki, Y., Yamasaki, T., Aizawa, K.: Sketch-based manga retrieval using manga109 dataset. CoRR, Vol. abs/1510.04389 (2015)
7. Guérin, C., et al.: ebdtheque: a representative database of comics. In: Proceedings of the 12th International Conference on Document Analysis and Recognition (ICDAR) (2013)
8. Cohn, N.: You' re a good structure, Charlie Brown: the distribution of narrative categories in comic strips. Cogn. Sci. **38**(7), 1317–1359 (2014)
9. Ekman, P., Friesen, W.V.: Constants across cultures in the face and emotion. J. Pers. Soc. Psychol. **17**(2), 124 (1971)
10. Hinton, G.E., et al.: Improving neural networks by preventing co-adaptation of feature detectors, arXiv preprint arXiv:1207.0580 (2012)
11. Krizhevsky, A., Sutskever, I., Hinton, G.E.: Imagenet classification with deep convolutional neural networks. In: Advances in Neural Information Processing Systems, pp. 1097–1105 (2012)
12. Ueno, M., Mori, N., Suenaga, T., Isahara, H.: Estimation of structure of four-scene comics by convolutional neural networks. In: Proceedings of the 1st International Workshop on Comics Analysis, Processing and Understanding, MANPU@ICPR 2016, pp. 9:1–9:6 (2016)

Multi-task Model for Comic Book Image Analysis

Nhu-Van Nguyen$^{(\boxtimes)}$, Christophe Rigaud, and Jean-Christophe Burie

Laboratoire L3i, Université de La Rochelle, 17042 La Rochelle CEDEX 1, France
{nhu-van.nguyen,christophe.rigaud,jean-christophe.burie}@univ-lr.fr

Abstract. Comic book image analysis methods often propose multiple algorithms or models for multiple tasks like panels and characters detection, balloons segmentation and text recognition, etc. In this work, we aim to reduce the complexity for comic book image analysis by proposing one model which can learn multiple tasks called Comic MTL. In addition to the detection task and segmentation task, we integrate the relation analysis task for balloons and characters into the Comic MTL model. The experiments with our model are carried out on the eBDtheque dataset which contains the annotations for panels, balloons, characters and also the relations balloon-character. We show that the Comic MTL model can detect the association between balloons and their speakers (comic characters) and handle other tasks like panels, characters detection and balloons segmentation with promising results.

Keywords: Comic book image analysis
Association balloon-character · Multi-task learning · CNN
Deep learning

1 Introduction

Digital comic content is mainly produced to facilitate transport, to reduce cost and to allow reading on screens of devices such as computers, tablets, and mobile phones. To access digital comics in an accurate and user-friendly experience on all mediums, it is necessary to extract and identify comic book elements [4]. Accordingly, the relations between these elements could be investigated further to assist the understanding of the digital form of comic books by a computer. This strategy will help the user to retrieve information very precisely in the image corpus.

Comic book images are composed of different elements such as panel, balloon, text, comic character and their relations (e.g., read before, said by, thought by, addressed to). One research field focuses on analyzing automatically these elements aiming at automatic comics understanding. In early studies, each of them has been first addressed separately and then, in more recent studies, combined all together to get a deeper understanding of the story.

© Springer Nature Switzerland AG 2019
I. Kompatsiaris et al. (Eds.): MMM 2019, LNCS 11296, pp. 637–649, 2019.
https://doi.org/10.1007/978-3-030-05716-9_57

The image analysis community has investigated comics elements extraction for almost ten years, and vary from low-level analysis such as text recognition [3] to high-level analysis such as style recognition [5]. Text detection and recognition in comic book images is one of the most studied elements. The authors from [3,28] proposed several methods based on image processing techniques. In [17], the authors introduced techniques based on deep learning models to recognize text without the segmentation step of characters. Comic characters (protagonists) detection is one of the most challenging tasks because of the comic book creators are entirely free in the drawing of their comic characters, hence their appearance can change a lot from one comic book to another and even within individual comic books. Several methods have been proposed for recognizing comic characters based on deep neural network or hand-crafted feature related techniques [6,15,16,32]. The speech balloon is a key element in comics, which can have various shapes and contours. Current existing methods for extracting balloons are based on conventional techniques in image processing such as contours, region detection, [3,14,18,25]. The method presented in [23] can also associate speech balloons and comic characters. Panel extraction has been studied for a long time [33]. The evolution of screen quality and size of mobile devices such as smartphones and tablets has placed higher demands on accuracy panel extraction recently. Methods in [2,12,13,29] rely on white line cutting, connected component labeling, morphological analysis or region growing. More recently, new methods based on watershed [21], line segmentation using Canny operator and polygon detection [13], region of interest detection [31], and recursive binary splitting [20] have been proposed.

All the existing methods based on deep learning models or conventional techniques treat each comic's element separately. This approach has been used because elements from comic book images are different and hence there is hardly an algorithm that can extract all elements at the same time. For more details about existing methods for comic book analysis, the readers are encouraged to read the survey works in [4,17].

In our work, we investigate a deep learning based approach which processes multiple elements simultaneously. Our approach can help to reduce the process duration of the comic analysis pipeline. Moreover, we propose a new neural network architecture which can detect the relationship between balloons and comic characters. In other words, our model can associate a balloon with its speaker(s).

2   Related Works

2.1   Multi-task Learning

With the success of deep learning approaches, recent works, mostly based on neural network models, have been proposed to extract comic elements [6,8,16,24, 30]. These works include tasks to detect each element separately such as balloon segmentation, panel detection, text recognition or character detection. Hence, the processing pipeline from global images analysis to precise content extraction take much time. In order to reduce the overall processing time for comic book images analysis, we investigate an approach which can handle multiple elements in one deep learning model. Our approach is considered as a multi-task learning (MTL) model among other deep learning models. MTL models aim at learning multiple related tasks jointly to improve the generalization performance of all the tasks [35].

The work in [35] gives a detailed survey for MTL models. We summarize below some popular MTL works based on convolutional neural network (CNN) for the computer vision domain. [36] proposed a deep CNN model which learns jointly different tasks like facial landmark detection, head pose estimation, gender classification, age estimation, facial expression recognition, and facial attribute inference using shared CNN layers. [1] proposed a CNN model to predict attributes in images using individual CNNs for each task and fuses different CNNs in a common layer via a sparse transformation. In [34], the authors proposed a multi-task model to learn the rotate facial task with an auxiliary task as the reconstruction of original images based on generated images. Another popular model is the Mask R-CNN [10] which jointly learns the object detection task and object segmentation task. This model achieves state-of-the-art performances for both segmentation and detection tasks. However, the Mask R-CNN model requires the segmentation masks of the objects.

In order to accomplish the training in our work, we have some elements (classes) that do not have object masks (for example annotations for panels, comic characters and text corresponds to bounding boxes) and elements (classes) that have segmentation masks (balloons). Hence, we extend the Mask R-CNN model to learn both detection and segmentation tasks for panels, comic characters (detection), and balloons (segmentation) using both segmentation masks and bounding boxes.

2.2   Relationship Balloon-Character

The association between balloons and comic characters can create annotations corresponding to story understanding (dialog analysis, situation retrieval). However, whether scanned or digital-born, these relations are not directly encoded in the image but the reader understands them according to other information present in the image. There are few papers in the literature on the topic of relation analysis among comic elements. From our knowledge, only [23] has proposed a method to associate a balloon with its speaker (comic characters). The authors detected firstly panels, balloons and tails of balloons, and comic characters; then they used a geometric graph for each panel where vertices are spatial positions of tail and comic character centroids. Edges are straight-line segments (associations). They formulated an optimization problem by searching for the best pairs (2-tuples) of tail and character corresponding to associations.

In our work, we integrate the association character-balloon into the multitask CNN model. While the method in [23] requires prior knowledge about the positions of panels, balloons and characters, our method does not require any prior information about characters or balloons. Finally, our new model called

Comic-MTL can learn from different kind of annotations (balloon masks, panels and characters bounding boxes, and balloon-character associations) to detect panels and characters, segment balloons, and detect the associations between detected characters and segmented balloons.

3 Proposed Model: Comic-MTL

In this section, we present our proposed Comic-MTL model for comic image analysis which aims at extracting characters, panels, balloons and the associations between characters and balloons. Our model is an extension of the state-of-the-art Mask R-CNN model in instance segmentation [10]. Firstly we modify the loss function for the mask branch in Mask R-CNN to take into account the origin of annotations (masks or bounding boxes), then we add an additional branch which contains a PairPool layer and a binary classifier to detect associations from all possible pairs (a pair contains a balloon and a comic character). The classifier outputs the probabilities of a pair balloon-character to be "has-a-link" and "has-not-a-link". The additional branch requires an extraction step of relevant features for the pairs of balloon-character. We describe our two modifications in the next sub-sections and illustrate them in Fig. 1.

3.1 Multi-task Learning from Bounding Boxes and Object Masks

We consider a detection/segmentation problem where there are classes with bounding box and segmentation mask annotations. In our work, we have to deal with a comic dataset where panels and characters are annotated with bounding boxes and balloons are annotated with masks. While the state-of-the-art model Mask R-CNN [10] can predict both bounding boxes and masks of the objects, it requires the mask annotations for all classes to train the model. In order to learn jointly the detection task and segmentation task from bounding boxes and object masks, we update the model Mask R-CNN where only the object from classes with mask annotations can contribute to the loss in the mask branch.

In the Mask R-CNN model, the multi-task loss on each sampled RoI (region of interest) in the total N sampled RoIs is defined as $L = L_{cls} + L_{box} + L_{mask}$ where L_{cls} and L_{box} are the loss for the detection branch as in Faster R-CNN [22]; L_{mask} is the binary cross-entropy loss in the mask branch of Mask R-CNN [10]. In our model, we simply apply L_{mask} only for RoIs associated with ground-truth classes M which have the mask annotations. For RoIs associated with ground-truth classes $K = N - M$ which have only bounding box annotations, we optimize only the detection branch.

3.2 Relation Analysis for Balloon-Character Pairs

We address the relationship analysis between balloons and comic characters by considering it as a binary classification problem. Each pair of balloon-character

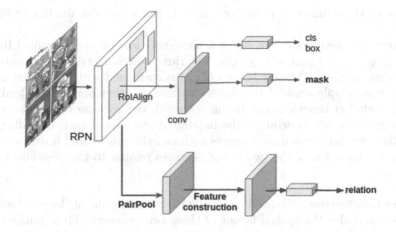

Fig. 1. The Comic MTL framework for comic book image analysis.

needs to be classified as "has a link" or "has not a link". A pair of balloon-character has a link means that the character speaks the text in the balloon. In order to make a binary classifier for the relation analysis, we add a new branch to the model Mask R-CNN.

Mask R-CNN: Similar to Faster R-CNN, in the first stage, Mask R-CNN use the region proposal network (RPN) [22] to get candidate object bounding boxes. Then in the next stage, it uses RoIAlign to extract features of these candidate boxes to feed in parallel into the categorical classifier, bounding-box regressor, and the mask predictor.

Comic MTL: We add an additional branch to the model Mask R-CNN that takes all pair combination of top N anchors candidates from the RPN network as inputs. Then we optimize the branch with the binary cross-entropy loss. The additional classifier output is distinct from the class, box, and mask outputs, requiring a pair combination step and a feature construction step for all pairs. We present these two important steps in the following.

Balloon-Character Pairs Combination - PairPool: Instead of taking into account all combinations of candidate bounding boxes from the RPN stage, we sample all combination between the candidate boxes which have the best overlap (by a threshold α) with the ground-truth balloons and the candidate boxes which have the best overlap with the ground-truth characters. This step can reduce a lot of possible pairs. We keep all positive pairs (the character is the speaker of the balloon in the pair) in the ground-truth and keep the same number of negative pairs randomly. Note that in most cases, the total number of negative pairs is bigger than the total number of positive pairs. Next, we pad the set of pairs with zero or trim the set of pairs to N pairs, where N is configurable. We need to fix the number of pairs because it is the input size for the addtional branch.

In our proposed model, we define a multi-task loss on each sampled RoI as $L = L_{cls} + L_{box} + L_{mask} + L_{rel}$. The first three components were presented in the previous section. The new branch (L_{rel}) is optimized with the binary cross-entropy loss. Simple reuse of the shared features as other branches to feed into this new relation branch is not enough. Indeed, the relation of a balloon and a character does not depend on the individual features of each bounding box but rather depend on multiple features such as individual visual features, visual features of the union of the two boxes, features related to the positions of the two boxes.

Features Construction: We need to encode the visual layout of the pair balloon-character and also the spatial layout of these two elements. Thus, unlike other branches which use a shared feature, we propose to use a combined feature of (1) the visual features of the union of the two bounding boxes, (2) the spatial features.

For the visual features of the union of the two bounding boxes, we reuse the share features as in Mask R-CNN; instead of each individual bounding box, we take into account the box equal to the union of the two bounding boxes in the pair balloon-character. This feature allows preserving the global visual information of a balloon and its speaker.

For the spatial features, let $b = [x_b, y_b, w_b, h_b]$ and $c = [x_c, y_c, w_c, h_c]$ denote two bounding boxes of a pair, where (x, y) are the coordinates of the center of the box, and (w, h) are the width and height of the box, respectively. We encode the spatial features with 5-dimensional vectors which are invariant to translation and scale transformations:

$$[\frac{x_b - x_c}{w_b}, \frac{y_b - y_c}{y_b}, \frac{x_b - x_c}{w_c}, \frac{y_b - y_c}{y_c}, \frac{b \cap c}{b \cup c}] \tag{1}$$

The first four features represent the normalized translation between the two boxes, the fifth feature is the overlap between boxes. In this paper, these features are used directly and are concatenated with the visual features to form the final features. We will investigate further some features embedded methods to map this 5-d feature to a high-dimensional representation.

Network Architecture: To experiment with our approach, we instantiate Mask R-CNN with the default architecture. There are four parts of the architecture: (1) the convolutional backbone architecture used for feature extraction over an entire image, (2) the network head for bounding-box recognition (classification and regression), (3) mask prediction that is applied separately to each RoI and (4) the network head for the relation classifier. We experiment with the backbone architecture using ResNet-50 together with the Feature Pyramid Network (FPN). This backbone with ResNet-50 and FPN is a common choice used in many works [10,22]. For the network heads, we closely follow the architecture of Mask R-CNN and we add the additional relation branch (see Fig. 1).

3.3   Implementation Details

Training: As in Fast R-CNN, a RoI is considered positive if it has IoU (Intersection over Union) with a ground-truth box of at least 0.5 and negative otherwise. We train for 100 epochs with a learning rate of 0.001 which is decreased by 10 at the 80th epoch. We use a weight decay of 0.0001 and a momentum of 0.9. The parameter α is set to 0.6. In a comic page, the number of balloons and characters are 15 and 10 respectively (see Sect. 4) so we set the parameter N to 150 which can cover almost all possible combinations and keeps the computation cost low for the relation branch.

Inference: During the tests, instead of considering the outputs of the RPN network, we take the outputs of the detection branch to construct the pairs of detected balloons and characters. We run the relation prediction branch on these combinations (pairs of balloon-character). This is similar to the approach for the mask branch in Mask R-CNN; although this differs from the parallel computation used in training, it speeds up inference and improves accuracy (due to the use of fewer, more accurate RoIs). Because we only classify on the pairs from detected balloons and characters (we set maximum $N = 150$ pairs for each comic book image), Comic MTL adds marginal runtime to its Mask R-CNN counterpart (5% on typical models).

4   Experiments

We experiment with the Comic MTL model on the public eBDtheque dataset [9]. This is the only dataset to date which has bounding box annotations for comic characters, segmentation masks for panels and balloons, and the association between balloons and its speakers (characters).

This dataset is composed of one hundred comic book images containing 850 panels, 1550 comics characters, 1092 balloons and 4691 text lines in total. More description can be found in the original paper [9]. Because of the limit size of the eBDtheque dataset, we run the cross-validation tests on five different training and testing sets. Each training set contains 90 images and each testing test contains 10 remaining images. The results reported are the average of these five validations.

Balloons Segmentation. In addition to the comparison between Comic MTL and existing works for balloon segmentation presented in [25], we train the state-of-the-art Mask R-CNN model for balloon segmentation and compare it to the Comic MTL model. We used the same configuration, and the same train/test sets without any augmentation for both models Mask R-CNN and Comic MTL. Both models use ImageNet pre-trained weights. In order to compare with existing methods, we use the recall (R), the precision (P), and the F-measure (F1) at pixel-level as metrics, therefore we chose the threshold that maximized the F-measure for Mask R-CNN and Comic MTL models. The result details are given in Table 1.

Table 1. Speech balloon segmentation performance in percent.

Method	Recall	Precision	F-Measure
Arai [3]	18.70	23.14	20.69
Ho [11]	14.78	32.37	20.30
Rigaud [27]	69.81	32.83	44.66
Rigaud [25]	62.92	62.27	63.59
Mask R-CNN [10]	75.31	92.42	82.99
Comic MTL	74.94	92.77	82.91

The neural network models Mask R-CNN and Comic MTL outperform all existing methods with a large margin, 19.4% in the F-measure. The Mask R-CNN model and the Comic MTL model have a similar performance with a slightly lower value for Comic MTL of about 0.08% in the F-measure. However note that the Mask R-CNN can do the balloon segmentation only (because we do not have mask annotations for panels and characters), while balloons segmentation is one of the four tasks that one Comic MTL model can do.

Panels and Characters Detection. We compare our Comic MTL to other existing methods for panels and characters detection. In order to compare with existing methods [3,17,19,26,29], we use the recall (R), the precision (P), and the F-measure (F1) and chose the threshold that maximized the F-measure for the Comic MTL model. We followed PASCAL VOC criteria and used IoU >= 0.5 as threshold for good detections [7]. Result details are given in Table 2.

Table 2. Panels detection performance in percent.

Method	Panels recall	Panels precision	F1
Arai [3]	58.0	75.3	65.6
Rigaud [29]	78.0	73.2	75.5
Rigaud [26]	81.2	86.6	83.8
Ogawa [19]	73.3	76.4	74.8
Comic MTL	76.95	73.19	75.03

Table 2 shows the scores of existing methods (copied from [19]) and the model Comic MTL for panel detection. Comic MTL comes at second place with 8.5% lower compared to [26].

Table 3 shows the scores of existing methods (copied from [19]) and the model Comic MTL for characters detection. For this task, Comic MTL outperforms existing methods with a large improvement, about 17.83% compared to [19]. However, in [19], the authors test a model trained on another dataset than the eBDtheque dataset.

Table 3. Characters detection performance in mAP.

Method	Characters recall	Characters precision	F1
Arai [3]	-	-	-
Rigaud [29]	-	-	-
Rigaud [26]	21.6	40.5	28.2
Ogawa [19]	42.2	58.0	48.8
Comic MTL	62.17	71.79	66.63

Relation Analysis. In this section, we evaluate the relation analysis between balloons and characters. The Comic MTL proposes a number of pairs balloon-character and classifies these pairs into two classes: has-link or not-has-link. A pair is in class "has-link" if the association between the corresponding balloon and character exists in the ground truth. We compare the Comic MTL model to the work in [23].

In the work of [23], panels, balloons, and characters are necessary. The authors use two different settings: (1) panels, balloons, and characters are extracted automatically by some conventional extraction methods; (2) panels, balloons, and characters are available prior.

Table 4. Balloon-character association performance in percent.

Method	Recall	Precision	F1
Setting 1 [23]	-	18.01	-
Setting 2 [23]	-	93.32	-
Comic MTL	28.32	52.88	36.89

Table 4 shows the performance of Comic MTL model compared to [23]. We can see that with the same settings where panels, balloons, and characters are extracted automatically (Setting 1), the model Comic MTL gives better performance. Compared to the performance of [23] when panels, balloons, and characters are available (Setting 2), the Comic MTL is behind. One of the reasons is that the measured error in the Comic MTL model and the Setting 1 of [23] will be a combination of errors from the proposed method and other element extractions (e.g. missed speech balloons, missed comic characters or over-segmentation of panels for [23]). However, we believe that we can investigate further on the features extraction step of the proposed model Comic MTL to improve the results of relation analysis. There is useful information that has not been integrated into the model such as a balloon and a character should be in the same panel to have a link between them, or learning the direction of the balloon tail may help to improve the learning of its association with characters. These features will be included in the next version of our model.

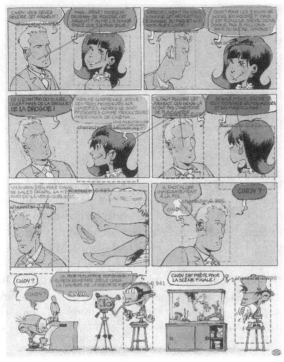

The figure shows the balloon masks, the bounding boxes of characters and the lines that connect a balloon and a character. There are two balloons not detected (at the bottom). There are two characters not detected (second row and last row). There are seven good links detected, and two bad links detected.

Fig. 2. Balloons segmentation, characters detection and their relation analysis by the model Comic MTL.

We visualize some results of the model Comic MTL in Fig. 2, which includes characters detection, balloons segmentation and relation analysis.

5   Conclusion

In this paper, we proposed the Comic MTL model which can handle multiple tasks on one CNN model: characters detection, panels and balloons segmentation, and balloon-character association analysis for comic book images. We compared the Comic MTL model with the model Mask R-CNN and other existing methods on the public eBDtheque dataset. Experiments confirm that the Comic MTL can handle multiple tasks in comic book images analysis (3 compared to 1 of existing models) with promising results compared to the state-of-the-art performance. Further investigation could improve the actual performance of the Comic MTL model, such as detecting the tail and its direction to improve the learning of the association between balloons and characters.

Acknowledgement. This work is supported by the CPER NUMERIC programme funded by the Region Nouvelle Aquitaine, CDA, Charente Maritime French Department, La Rochelle conurbation authority (CDA) and the European Union through the FEDER funding".

References

1. Abdulnabi, A.H., Wang, G., Lu, J., Jia, K.: Multi-task CNN model for attribute prediction. IEEE Trans. Multimedia **17**(11), 1949–1959 (2015)
2. Arai, K., Tolle, H.: Method for automatic e-comic scene frame extraction for reading comic on mobile devices. In: 7th International Conference on Information Technology: New Generations, pp. 370–375. IEEE Computer Society, Washington DC (2010)
3. Arai, K., Tolle, H.: Method for real time text extraction of digital manga comic. Int. J. Image Process. (IJIP) **4**(6), 669–676 (2011)
4. Augereau, O., Iwata, M., Kise, K.: A survey of comics research in computer science. J. Imaging **4** (2018)
5. Chu, W.T., Cheng, W.C.: Manga-specific features and latent style model formanga style analysis. In: 2016 IEEE International Conference on Acoustics, Speech and Signal Processing (ICASSP), pp. 1332–1336, March 2016
6. Chu, W.T., Li, W.W.: Manga FaceNet: face detection in manga based on deep neural network. In: Proceedings of the 2017 ACM on International Conference on Multimedia Retrieval, pp. 412–415. ACM (2017)
7. Everingham, M., Eslami, S.M., Gool, L., Williams, C.K., Winn, J., Zisserman, A.: The pascal visual object classes challenge: a retrospective. Int. J. Comput. Vision **111**(1), 98–136 (2015)
8. Fujino, S., Mori, N., Matsumoto, K.: Recognizing the order of four-scene comics by evolutionary deep learning. In: De La Prieta, F., Omatu, S., Fernández-Caballero, A. (eds.) DCAI 2018. AISC, vol. 800, pp. 136–144. Springer, Cham (2019). https://doi.org/10.1007/978-3-319-94649-8_17
9. Guérin, C., et al.: eBDtheque: a representative database of comics. In: 2013 12th International Conference on Document Analysis and Recognition, pp. 1145–1149, August 2013
10. He, K., Gkioxari, G., Dollár, P., Girshick, R.B.: Mask R-CNN. CoRR abs/1703.06870 (2017)
11. Ho, A.K.N., Burie, J.C., Ogier, J.M.: Panel and speech balloon extraction from comic books. In: 2012 10th IAPR International Workshop on Document Analysis Systems, pp. 424–428, March 2012
12. In, Y., Oie, T., Higuchi, M., Kawasaki, S., Koike, A., Murakami, H.: Fast frame decomposition and sorting by contour tracing for mobile phone comic images. Int. J. Syst. Appl. Eng. Dev. **5**(2), 216–223 (2011)
13. Li, L., Wang, Y., Tang, Z., Gao, L.: Automatic comic page segmentation based on polygon detection. Multimedia Tools Appl. **69**(1), 171–197 (2014)
14. Liu, X., Li, C., Zhu, H., Wong, T.T., Xu, X.: Text-aware balloon extraction from manga. Vis. Computer **32**(4), 501–511 (2016)
15. Matsui, Y., Ito, K., Aramaki, Y., Yamasaki, T., Aizawa, K.: Sketch-based manga retrieval using Manga109 dataset. CoRR abs/1510.04389 (2015)
16. Nguyen, N.V., Rigaud, C., Burie, J.: Comic characters detection using deep learning. In: 2nd International Workshop on coMics Analysis, Processing, and Understanding, MANPU 2017, Kyoto, Japan, 9–15 November 2017, pp. 41–46 (2017)

17. Nguyen, N., Rigaud, C., Burie, J.: Digital comics image indexing based on deep learning. J. Imaging **4**(7), 89 (2018)
18. Obispo, S.L., Kuboi, T.: Element detection in Japanese comic book panels (2014)
19. Ogawa, T., Otsubo, A., Narita, R., Matsui, Y., Yamasaki, T., Aizawa, K.: Object detection for comics using manga109 annotations. CoRR abs/1803.08670 (2018)
20. Pang, X., Cao, Y., Lau, R.W., Chan, A.B.: A robust panel extraction method for manga. In: Proceedings of the 22nd ACM International Conference on Multimedia, MM 2014, pp. 1125–1128. ACM, New York (2014)
21. Ponsard, C., Ramdoyal, R., Dziamski, D.: An OCR-enabled digital comic books viewer. In: Miesenberger, K., Karshmer, A., Penaz, P., Zagler, W. (eds.) ICCHP 2012. LNCS, vol. 7382, pp. 471–478. Springer, Heidelberg (2012). https://doi.org/10.1007/978-3-642-31522-0_71
22. Ren, S., He, K., Girshick, R., Sun, J.: Faster R-CNN: towards real-time object detection with region proposal networks. In: Cortes, C., Lawrence, N.D., Lee, D.D., Sugiyama, M., Garnett, R. (eds.) Advances in Neural Information Processing Systems 28, pp. 91–99. Curran Associates, Inc. (2015)
23. Rigaud, C., et al.: Speech balloon and speaker association for comics and manga understanding. In: 2015 13th International Conference on Document Analysis and Recognition (ICDAR), pp. 351–355, August 2015
24. Rigaud, C., Burie, J., Ogier, J.: Segmentation-free speech text recognition for comic books. In: 2nd International Workshop on coMics Analysis, Processing, and Understanding, Kyoto, Japan, 9–15 November, pp. 29–34 (2017)
25. Rigaud, C., Burie, J.-C., Ogier, J.-M.: Text-independent speech balloon segmentation for comics and manga. In: Lamiroy, B., Dueire Lins, R. (eds.) GREC 2015. LNCS, vol. 9657, pp. 133–147. Springer, Cham (2017). https://doi.org/10.1007/978-3-319-52159-6_10
26. Rigaud, C., Guérin, C., Karatzas, D., Burie, J.C., Ogier, J.M.: Knowledge-driven understanding of images in comic books. Int. J. Doc. Anal. Recogn. (IJDAR) **18**(3), 199–221 (2015)
27. Rigaud, C., Karatzas, D., Van de Weijer, J., Burie, J.C., Ogier, J.M.: An active contour model for speech balloon detection in comics. In: Proceedings of the 12th International Conference on Document Analysis and Recognition (ICDAR), pp. 1240–1244, August 2013
28. Rigaud, C., Karatzas, D., Van de Weijer, J., Burie, J.C., Ogier, J.M.: Automatic text localisation in scanned comic books. In: Proceedings of the 8th International Conference on Computer Vision Theory and Applications (VISAPP) (2013)
29. Rigaud, C., Tsopze, N., Burie, J.-C., Ogier, J.-M.: Robust frame and text extraction from comic books. In: Kwon, Y.-B., Ogier, J.-M. (eds.) GREC 2011. LNCS, vol. 7423, pp. 129–138. Springer, Heidelberg (2013). https://doi.org/10.1007/978-3-642-36824-0_13
30. Singh, S.P., Markovitch, S. (eds.): Proceedings of the Thirty-First AAAI Conference on Artificial Intelligence, 4–9 February 2017, San Francisco, California, USA (2017)
31. Stommel, M., Merhej, L.I., Müller, M.G.: Segmentation-free detection of comic panels. In: Bolc, L., Tadeusiewicz, R., Chmielewski, L.J., Wojciechowski, K. (eds.) ICCVG 2012. LNCS, vol. 7594, pp. 633–640. Springer, Heidelberg (2012). https://doi.org/10.1007/978-3-642-33564-8_76
32. Sun, W., Burie, J.C., Ogier, J.M., Kise, K.: Specific comic character detection using local feature matching. In: 12th International Conference on Document Analysis and Recognition, Washington, DC, USA, pp. 275–279 (2013)

33. Yamada, M., Budiarto, R., Endo, M., Miyazaki, S.: Comic image decomposition for reading comics on cellular phones. IEICE Trans. **87**–**D(6)**, 1370–1376 (2004)
34. Yim, J., Jung, H., Yoo, B., Choi, C., Park, D., Kim, J.: Rotating your face using multi-task deep neural network. In: 2015 IEEE Conference on Computer Vision and Pattern Recognition (CVPR), pp. 676–684, June 2015
35. Zhang, Y., Yang, Q.: A survey on multi-task learning. CoRR abs/1707.08114 (2017). http://arxiv.org/abs/1707.08114
36. Zhang, Z., Luo, P., Loy, C.C., Tang, X.: Facial landmark detection by deep multi-task learning. In: Fleet, D., Pajdla, T., Schiele, B., Tuytelaars, T. (eds.) ECCV 2014. LNCS, vol. 8694, pp. 94–108. Springer, Cham (2014). https://doi.org/10. 1007/978-3-319-10599-4_7

Estimating Comic Content from the Book Cover Information Using Fine-Tuned VGG Model for Comic Search

Byeongseon Park[✉] and Mitsunori Matsushita

Graduate School of Informatics, Kansai University, 2-1-1, Reizanji-cho,
Takatsuki-shi, Osaka 569-1052, Japan
{k281401,t080164}@kansai-u.ac.jp

Abstract. The purpose of this research is to realize retrieval of comic based on content information. Resources of the contents information of existing comics were only the comics itself and review. However, these pieces of information have drawbacks that they can not sufficiently extract information necessary for searching, and that they contain a lot of unnecessary information. In order to solve this problem, we proposed to use the book cover of comics as a resource to grasp the contents of comics. In the proposed method, we estimate the age and cultural background of comics expressed by clothes and belongings written on the cover of comics from the reasoning model which performed fine-tuning from the VGG-16 model. Also, we associated comics with each other based on the obtained semantic vectors and tags. As a result of the experiment, the accuracy of the model was 0.693, and the reproducibility of the tag to the correct data was 0.918. Furthermore, we observed unity in the comics related by the obtained information.

Keywords: Content estimation · Transfer learning · Comic computing

1 Introduction

In Japan, the number of newly published comic book titles is increasing every year, with more than 12,000 titles published in 2017. In such a circumstance, it is difficult for a user to find comics with content that conforms to the interests of the user from such a huge number of comics. To solve this problem, we have developed an interactive comic exploration system [1]. The system supports to grasp the contents of each comic and to select and present them according to a user's interests. The system helps to explore a designed book from the bunch amount of comics, it, however, is difficult to fully extract content information for realizing content-based searches at present. Thus, we propose a method that uses book cover as an information source for easily recognising contents of comics.

The book cover of the comic plays an important role when users purchase a book that has never been read. People often buy a new comic by a first impression got at a glance. This is because the book cover contains advanced information

© Springer Nature Switzerland AG 2019
I. Kompatsiaris et al. (Eds.): MMM 2019, LNCS 11296, pp. 650–661, 2019.
https://doi.org/10.1007/978-3-030-05716-9_58

for the viewer to understand the contents of the comic at a glance. For example, suppose you compare the 3 book covers in Fig. 1 to select the comic book you have never read. Even if you do not know the contents of the comics in Figs. 1a[1] and b[2] you can clearly see that the two comics deal with different era and culture based subjects(hereinafter, this is called Background) by grasping the character's clothing and belongings(e.g., "Robe" and "Sword" in case of Fig. 1a, "Uniform" and "Jacket" in case of Fig. 1b) in the cover. On the other hand, the book cover of Fig. 1c[3] is based on a similar era and culture, although the subject matter is different from Fig. 1b. In this way, the reader interprets the information contained on the book cover, guesses the contents included in the comic, and selects comics that match his/her taste.

We assume that by focusing on such the role of the book cover, we can more easily obtain content information necessary for searching comics that users have never read. In this paper, we propose a method to extract information contained in the book cover of the comic and to correlate each other having a similar worldview. In our method, we acquired information (e.g., clothes, belongings, stage) contained on the book cover by Fine-tuning based on the VGG 16 model [11]. Then, we have topic estimation by LDA [7] is performed from the obtained information, and correlated each comic.

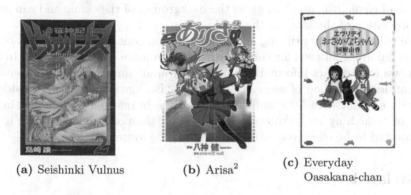

(a) Seishinki Vulnus   (b) Arisa[2]   (c) Everyday
                                                        Oasakana-chan

Fig. 1. Examples of the comic's book cover

2   The Information of the Book Cover

The information that the user can read from the cover of the comic book can be roughly classified as follows.

---

1 © Yuzuru Shimazaki, Kodansha Ltd.
2 © Ken Yagami, Kadokawa Publishing Ltd.
3 © Yuka Kuniki, Takeshobo Ltd.

Style of painting. The external representation technique of author
Story. The Short and implicit scenario
Background. The era and culture that form the basis of the comic

First of all, "Style of painting" refers to information on how the author expresses works using the technique. For example, Fig. 1c shows how to write a deformed person with fewer types of colors used than other comics. Style of painting has an important role to determine the first impression of the comic that users have not read yet. In addition, "Story" refers to information on the short and implicit comic contents expressed on the cover. For example, the characters in Fig. 1b and c can be predicted to have a friendly relationship because they are gently facing each other and lined up on both sides. On the other hand, the character in Fig. 1a is nervous holding a sword and it looks like it is protecting a woman. In this way, the user can use the information contained in the book cover as a material for estimating the story of the comic. Finally, "Background" refers to the historical cultural background as the foundation of the story of the comic. For example, the character in Fig. 1a has a robe and a sword and is similar in appearance to occidental medieval culture. On the other hand, the characters in Fig. 1b and c are dressed in contemporary culture clothes such as uniforms, shirts. Through these elements, even if the user does not know the content of comic, the user can guess the background of the comic and can grasp the foundation of the story of the comic.

We believe that by utilizing all the information contained in the book cover, content information used for comic search can be more easily extracted. In this paper, we first extract information on "Background" among the above elements and consider a method of associating comics. "Background" can be considered to be an element with little individual difference in information amount in the scene of "searching for unknown comics" rather than other elements, so it can be expected to be effectively utilized for searching system for the comic.

3   Related Work

There are direct extraction methods and indirect extraction methods as attempts to extract the information in the comic. Rigaud et al. proposed an expert system that can understand the elements included in the comic [2]. Their expert system realized identification of panel, speech bubbles, characters from images of comics by interact with the low level (image processing) iteratively to progressively understand the content of an image, moving from simple to more complex elements. In addition to Rigaud et al., there are several attempts related to the method for identifying the elements included in the comic [3–5]. These studies are focusing only on the identification of the elements written in the comic, and have not reached the stage of grasping the content of comic. Therefore, information that can be applied to the search from the comic itself (e.g., a summary of the story, structured information based on the story) can not be extracted at present.

As an alternative to such a situation, Park et al. attempted to extract indirect content information such as outline and evaluation of the comic by using the review as a resource of retrievable content information [1]. As a result, the user can search comics suitable for the preference based on the content and evaluation of the comic. However, review often differs greatly in the amount of information included in the review by the author, and it does not necessarily include information directly related to the content of the comic (e.g., explanation of the story or character) in detail.

In this research, we use the book cover of comic as resource for new content information. As mentioned in Sect. 2, the book cover summarizes information that can grasp the outline of the contents of the comic. Furthermore, it is possible to grasp the outline of the story with only one picture, and it is also considered as a long point that noise is less than indirect information like a review. In this paper, we estimate the "Background" which can be expected to effectively utilize in the search among the information contained in the book cover.

4   Proposed Method

In this research, we extracted information included in the book cover based on the hypothesis that "Background of comic expressed on the book cover of a comic has a certain theme (e.g., family, romance, SF)." As shown in Fig. 1, the "Background" included in the book cover is expressed by the clothing of the character, belongings, the stage of the story. By grasping the combination of these elements, I think that it is possible to estimate what theme each comic has.

Furthermore, we estimated the topic from the extracted information. Topic refers to the content of text such as sports, politics, music. Also, the topics included in certain texts are not necessarily single, there are cases where they exist in multiple [8]. Based on the features of such topics, we use it as an approach to estimate topics in the book cover. Then, it is considered that the comics having similar topic distribution patterns have similar "Background."

Also, the cover of certain comics is not necessarily one. In this paper, if there are multiple book covers of a certain comic, information existing on all the cover is set as a set representing one comic and topics are estimated on a comic unit basis. Furthermore, based on a function that can compare the transition of the topics of two comics with different number of book covers, we decided to calculate the similarity between the each comic.

4.1   Information Extraction from the Book Cover

Model Design. There is illustration 2 vec [12] by Saito et al. as an attempt to extract information on illustrations drawn by people, not photographs. Saito et al. proposed a deep convolutional neural networks (CNN) model [6] combining the Network In Network model (NIN) [10] and the VGG model [11] in order to interpret the meaning of the image and to interpret meaning based image search.

The proposed method maps an input illustration into a 4,096-dimensional vector. To build a feature space representing illustrations, they trained the CNN model for predicting binary attributes (also known as "tags") from a single illustration.

Although images mainly targeted by Saito et al. are illustrations freely posted on the web, many of these images are largely different from the features of the book cover (e.g., texts are included, margins are present, color is monotonous) of the comic subject to this paper. Therefore, it is necessary to re-train the model of Saito et al., However, due to the characteristics of CNN, learning using CNN requires a large amount of data. However, unlike the learning data of Saito et al., The cover page of the comic exists only a limited number.

Therefore, in this paper, we perform Fine-tuning using pre-trained network. The fine-tuning is a method of replacing only the discrimination layer of the pre-trained network with that of the target task and the other part using learned parameters as initial values and proceeding with learning by the error back propagation method, and it is widely used as an application method of pre-trained network. Fine-tuning has the advantage that high precision can be obtained even with re-training from less data by using abundant features of Pre-trained network.

In fine-tuning having such characteristics, the performance of the original model itself also greatly affects the accuracy of the final network. For that reason, the 16-layer CNN of Oxford Visual Geometry Group (VGG-16) [11], which was published at ImageNet Large-scale Visual Recognition Challenge (ILSVRC), a competition workshop using ImageNet [9] 1000 class data, is often used. In this paper, we perform fine-tuning from VGG-16 to extract information contained in the book cover of the comic. We replace the discrimination layer of VGG-16 with the discrimination layer for outputting the vector composed of the tags obtained by data collection and re-train from the image of the book cover.

Data Collection. In this paper, we perform Fine-tuning using the VGG-16 model. As the data for training, an image of the book cover of the comic and the tag attached to each image are used. Since there is only book information such as comic title and author name on existing information on the book cover of the comic, information related to "Background" (e.g., clothing of the character, belongings, the stage of the story) written in the image must be newly added. We created tags with the following attributes for 536 book covers of randomly selected 100 comics.

Name. The name of the object
Background Class. The subdivision of the object
Detail Information. The detailed information on the object

The "Name" attribute refers to the name of the object drawn on the book cover. In creating information for expressing "Background", to avoid losing the uniformity of the name of each object, in Name attribute, only the name excluding all named entities (e.g., place name, product name) and modifiers (e.g., color, size, shape) was entered. For example, if there is an object like "Denim Pants", only "Pants" are filled in. The "Background Class" attribute is a subdivision for distinguishing objects having the same name. For example, even if "Castle" is drawn on the book cover, "Castle" has different style depending on country and era (e.g., Neuschwanstein Castle, Osaka Castle). Therefore, in order to distinguish objects even in such a case, we set up four classes as (1) Contemporary, (2) Occidental, (3) Oriental, (4) Future as "Background Class." Finally, the "Detail Information" attribute refers to supplementary information for the object. It is an element for recording information omitted mainly by "Name" attribute. By providing "Detail Information", information omitted by "Name" attribute can arbitrarily be expanded. Examples of tags created based on these rules are "pants:1:denim" for "Denim Pants" and "castle:3:" for "Osaka Castle".

Tags created based on the above rule totaled 560 kinds. Since tags that are too rare as data to be used for training are considered to have a possibility of affecting the accuracy of the model, 100 tags with the highest frequency (frequency of appearance 5 or more) of frequent occurrence on all the covers of the tag were used.

Experiment. After creating the data, we performed Fine-tuning using the VGG-16 model from the obtained data. When training, 20% of the book cover image data was used as validation data. Since the number of data affects accuracy in CNN, it is desirable that the scale of the data used is large. Therefore, we extended the data as (1) Flip upside down, (2) Flip horizontal, (3) Flip 90°, (4) Flip 270°, (5) Used Enhanced Edge Filter, (6) Used More Enhanced Edge Filter, (7) Used Only Edge Filter (total of 7 types) for only train data. Moreover, in order to prevent learning by biased to specific images and tags, the following learning was done after shuffling train data and validation data for each epoch.

The result of learning by the above procedure is shown in Fig. 2. As a result of learning, the accuracy of the model was 0.69309 and the loss score converged at 1.67881. In addition, as a result of comparing the tags that are higher in the certainty factor for each tag of the vector obtained from the learned model and the correct answer data, the degree of reproduction with respect to the correct answer data was 0.91797.

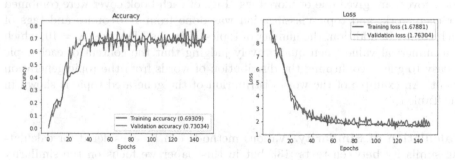

Fig. 2. Result of tag estimation based on VGG-16

4.2   Associating of Comic

Saito et al. made it possible to calculate the similarity in the meaning of illustration by comparing 4,096 dimensional vectors obtained from the CNN model. By using the model proposed in this paper we believe it is also possible to measure the similarity between the book cover of the comic from a 100 dimensional vector expressing "Background." However, compared with the method of Saito et al., The number of dimensions of vectors used in our method is remarkably few. Therefore, when comparing the degree of similarity between vectors, the influence exerted by a specific tag increases, there is a possibility that diversity due to a combination of tags may be lost. Therefore, in this paper, we convert the vector obtained by the model into a tag and perform topic classification based on Latent Dirichlet Allocation (LDA) [7] from the obtained tag.

LDA is a document generation model based on the assumption that words in a document appear not based on independent but on a latent topic. In the LDA, each document is composed of a plurality of topics, and it is an algorithm assuming that words are generated in a form of summing up word distributions of each topic. Therefore, in LDA, a plurality of It is possible to estimate topics. In the estimation of the topic model using the LDA, the probability distribution $P(z_n|d)(n = 1, ..., K)$ of the word w in each topic $z_n(n = 1, ..., K)$ and the topic z_n in each document d, with the set of documents represented by the columns of words w and the number of topics $z_n(n = 1, ..., K)$ as input, Probability distribution $P(w|z_n)(w \in V)$ is estimated. By using LDA, it becomes possible to relate words (tags in this case) that were distinguished by a difference in surface expression.

Since comics are composed of stories from various elements as well as other creations such as novels and movies, "Background" of the comic is not necessarily expressed in one topic. In this paper, we aim to grasp "Background" more easily regardless of tag type by estimating multiple topics included in the cover page of comics using LDA.

In order to perform topic classification by LDA, tags with confidence factor of 0.1 or more were extracted from vectors obtained by the proposed model. The confidence factor threshold value is a numerical value in a state where all the book covers are given one or more tags. Tags of each book cover were combined for each work, and topic classification was done from 100 comics and tags of each comic. In addition, the number of topics K in the LDA uses $K = 10$, which is a numerical value when qualitatively judging that the content of each topic is easy to guess, confirming the distribution of words from the topic generation result. An example of the word distribution of the generated topic is shown in the Table 1.

Calculation of Similarity. Various methods can be considered for calculating similarity between texts [13], but in this paper we focus on the similarity of topic distribution, so we decided to use Bhattacharyya Coefficient [14]. In this method, the total frequency is normalized, and the similarity of the two histograms divided into the same number of bins is calculated by obtaining the

Table 1. Result of topic classification (Top 5 words)

Topic	Words
Topic 0	Jacket:2:, Gun:2:, Combat-clothing:2:, Hair-ornament:2:Iron, Skirt:2:
Topic 1	Hat:1:, Glove:1:, Jacket:1:, Muffler:1:, Coat:1:
Topic 2	Hachimaki:1:, Sword:3:Japanese, Uniform:1:Sailor, Ribbon:1:, Headband:1:
Topic 3	Glasses:1:, Skirt:1:, One-piece-dress:1:, Hat:1:, Uniform:1:
Topic 4	Robe:2:, Dress:2:, T-shirt:1:, Belt:2:Leather, Chalk:2:
Topic 5	Dress:1:, Uniform:1:For-Women, Knee-socks:1:, Coat:1:, Muffler:1:
Topic 6	Dog:1:, Sword:2:, Ribbon:1:, Glasses:1:, Cloak:2:, Swimsuit:1:Bikini
Topic 7	Plush-doll:1:, Tobacco:1:, Uniform:1:, One-piece-dress:1:, School-uniform:1:
Topic 8	Gun:1:, Suit:1:, T-shirt:1:, Guitar:1:Electric, Pants:1:
Topic 9	Shirt:1:, Jacket:1:, Tie:1:, Coat:1:, Hat:1:

product of the frequencies in the corresponding bins. The similarity $s(P,Q)$ of the histograms P and Q divided into the number n bins is Eq. (1).

$$s(P,Q) = \sum_{i=1}^{n} \sqrt{P_i Q_i} \tag{1}$$

P_i and Q_i are the frequencies of the i-th bin of the histograms P and Q, respectively. In this research, topics are estimated on a comic unit basis, and the similarity is calculated by applying Butter Character coefficients to them. In the prototype implemented in this paper, we decided that the value obtained in Expression (1) with the number of bottles as the number of topics ($K = 10$) is similarity, and output comics entered as a query in descending order from this highly similar comic. Based on the above guidelines, in this research, we estimate the topics of the "Background" or the works included in the book cover and express them in the histogram of the topic unit, thereby searching for comics whose topic distribution is similar.

Experiment. Tables 2 and 3 show examples of qualitatively evaluating the results obtained by the created prototype. As samples to be compared at the time of evaluation, (1) similarity when 100 dimension vectors obtained from the model are calculated by Cosine Similarity, (2) average similarity of LDA-based similarity and Vector-based similarity, was used. From the degree of similarity using LDA, while we can expect diversity considering the relationship between tags, the similarity obtained from vectors can be expected to be accurate considering the detailed contents expressed by model inference. Furthermore, the average of the two similarities is used as a flexible similarity considering the viewpoints of both similarities.

The case in Table 2 queries a comic which contains many elements with strong occidental such as dresses, wings, flowers and dragons. Also, in the case

Table 2. The calculation result of similarity based on each method (A)

Query	Type	1st	2nd	3rd	4th	5th
	LDA	Tales of The Abyss[a] 1.000	Vinland Saga[b] 0.994	Kagegari[c] 0.948	FLAGS[d] 0.931	Wizardry[e] 0.877
Dragon Knights[f]	Vector	NEEDLESS[g] 0.456	Tales of The Abyss 0.435	Violinist of Hameln[h] 0.379	Eensy-weensy Monster[i] 0.347	Forest of water[j] 0.304
	LDA + Vector	Tales of The Abyss 0.718	Kagegari 0.591	NEEDLESS 0.569	Vinland Saga 0.561	FLAGS 0.468

[a] ©Sara Yajima, Enterbrain Ltd.
[b] ©Makoto Yukimura, Kodansha Ltd.
[c] ©Takao Saito, Shogakukan Ltd.
[d] ©Satoshi Ueda, Kodansha Ltd.
[e] ©Tamaki Ishigaki, Takarajimasha Ltd.
[f] ©Mineko Okami, Shinshokan Ltd.
[g] ©Kami Imai, Shueisha Ltd.
[h] ©Michiaki Watanabe, Enix Ltd.
[i] ©Masami Tsuda, Hakusensha Ltd.
[j] ©Yugo Kobayashi, Kodansha Ltd.

of Table 3, we use queries that include many elements with strong contemporary nature such as dress and chain saw. There are many Occidental comics in LDA-based similarity, but in case of Vector-based similarity, "Background" is not uniform. As a result of confirming the Vector of each comic, this result was due to the fact that only the local tag is similar to the tag such as the "Dress", "Robe" in the Vector-based similarity. In particular, the comics that were used as the query in Table 2 tend to have low similarity with works that originally have similar backgrounds, since Background of this comic is formed in a complex manner by elements such as flowers and dragons in addition to clothes. On the other hand, in the case of composite type similarity that combines LDA-based

Table 3. The calculation result of similarity based on each method (B)

Query	Type	1st	2nd	3rd	4th	5th
Princess Resurrection[f]	LDA	Ghost Hunt[a] 0.999	Dog Soldier[b] 0.994	Ucchare Goshogawara[c] 0.926	Jyo-Oh[d] 0.822	Musashi no Ken[e] 0.820
	Vector	Jyo-Oh 0.875	Hunter Cats[g] 0.869	Residents of Mister[h] 0.163	Vinland Saga 0.116	Wizardry 0.092
	LDA + Vector	Jyo-Oh 0.843	Hunter Cats 0.773	Ghost Hunt 0.501	Dog Soldier 0.498	Ucchare Goshogawara 0.464

[a] ©Fuyumi Ono, Kadokawa Ltd.
[b] ©Tetsuya Saruwatari, Homesha Ltd.
[c] ©Tsuyoshi Nakaima, Shogakukan Ltd.
[d] ©Ryo Kurashina, Shueisha Ltd.
[e] ©Motoka Murakami, Shogakukan Ltd.
[f] ©Yasunori Mitsunaga, Kodansha Ltd.
[g] ©Aro Hiroshi, Tokumashoten Ltd.
[h] ©Hirokazu Shimada, Gakken Holdings Ltd.

similarity and Vector-based similarity, even in works showing high similarity in LDA-based similarity, similarity decreases greatly due to Vector-based similarity many cases were seen.

5 Discussion

5.1 Information Extraction from the Book Cover

In this paper, by performing Fine-Tuning from the VGG-16 model, it was possible to create a model showing accuracy of 0.69309 and reproducibility of correct answer data of 0.91797. This makes it possible to automatically generate tags required for "Background", and it can be expected to be applied to more comics.

However, it was extremely rare to make a correct estimation when an unknown book cover not being used for learning was given using the current model while holding tags included in train data and validation data. This is because comics are different from photographs, even though they are the same objects, it is thought that the expression method is completely different by the author. In the case of illustration 2 vec of Saito et al. [12], Which also deals with illustrations by people, 1,000,000 images have been used for learning. For future improvement, it is necessary to adjust parameters at learning and increase the population of data so that common points can be found even if there are differences in expressive methods by authors.

5.2   Associating of Comic

In this paper, we associate comics based on inference results obtained from Semantic vector estimation model for Background of the comic. As a method for associating comics, we proposed a method to grasp the distance of comics by calculating the semantic vector of each comic and the similarity between tags. As a result, it is possible to associate comics in which Background is expressed more complexly than in similarity considering only semantic vectors in the method applying LDA. This is considered to be the result that the reason for adopting LDA becomes remarkable. However, the comics in which the background is close by strict similarity of the tags due to the similarity that combines both similarities appears close to the search results. Considering the purpose of this research and the shortness of Vector-based similarity described above, when calculating the average value, by weighting each similarity degree, by adjusting the influence on similarity, We can estimate accurate results. Also, when making a topic estimation of LDA this time, all the evaluations on hyper parameter determination and calculation result of similarity which must be set are qualitative. Since there is a possibility that this will greatly affect the extension of the data of the Semantic vector estimation model in the future, it is necessary to consider a method for quantitatively selecting parameters.

6   Conclusion

The purpose of this research is to realize retrieval of comic based on content information. In this paper, in order to make it possible to realize, we proposed a method to use the book cover as resource to extract content information from comics. In our proposed method, we estimate the age and cultural background of comics expressed by clothes and belongings written on the cover of the comic, and associate comics with each other based on the estimation result. First, in order to extract information related to "Background" from the book cover, Fine-Tuning was performed on 536 images of the book cover of the comic with tags related to Background using the VGG-16 model. As a result, a model in which the degree of reproduction of the tag with respect to the correct data is 0.91797 was created. Also, from the inference results of the background information, we calculated the similarity such similarity based on the semantic vectors and the similarity based on the distribution of topics generated by LDA, and associated the comics. With this method, we were able to confirm multiple cases where it is possible to associate comics with similar backgrounds. On the other hand, there are remaining issues to be solved in the future as there is a lack of necessary data at learning of the semantic vector estimation model, and the need for a quantitative parameter selection method for LDA. In the future, while improving this method, we will examine a method to extract information (Style of painting, Story) contained in the cover other than Background.

Acknowledgments. The authors would like to thank S. Inoue, Y. Baba and Y. Higuchi for assistance with the data collection.

References

1. Park, B., Okamoto, K., Yamashita, R., Matsushita, M.: Designing a comic exploration system using a hierarchical topic classification of reviews. Inf. Eng. Express Int. Instit. Appl. Inform. **3**(2), 45–57 (2017)
2. Rigaud, C., Gurin, C., Karatzas, D., Burie, J.C., Ogier, J.M.: Knowledge-driven understanding of images in comic books. IJDAR **18**(3), 199–221 (2015)
3. Tanaka, T., Shoji, K., Toyama, F., Miyamichi, J.: Layout analysis of tree-structured scene frames in comic images. In: Proceedings of the 20th International Joint Conference on Artificial Intelligence, IJCAI, Hyderabad, pp. 2885–2890 (2007)
4. Arai, K., Tolle H.: Method for automatic E-comic scene frame extraction for reading comic on mobile devices. In: Seventh International Conference on Information Technology, pp. 370–375. IEEE, Las Vegas (2010)
5. Chu, W-T., Li, W-W.: Manga FaceNet: face detection in manga based on deep neural network. In: 17th Proceedings of the 2017 ACM on International Conference on Multimedia Retrieval, ICMR, Bucharest, pp. 412–415 (2017)
6. LeCun, Y., Bottou, L., Bengio, Y., Haffner, P.: Gradient-based learning applied to document recognition. In: Proceedings of the IEEE, pp. 2278–2324. IEEE (1998)
7. Blei, D.M., Andrew, Y., Jordan, M.I.: Latent Dirichlet allocation. J. Mach. Learn. Res. **3**, 993–1022 (2003)
8. Blei, D.M.: Probabilistic topic models. Comun. ACM **55**(4), 77–84 (2012)
9. Deng, J., Dong, W., Socher, R., Li, L.-J., Li, K., Fei-Fei, L.: ImageNet: a large-scale hierarchical image database. In: Proceedings of the 2009 IEEE Conference on Computer Vision and Pattern Recognition, pp. 248–255. IEEE, Miami (2009)
10. Lin, M., Chen, Q., Yan, S.: Network in network. In: International Conference on Learning Representations, San Diego, (2014)
11. Simonyan, K., Zisserman, A.: Very deep convolutional networks for large-scale image recognition. In: International Conference on Learning Representations, San Diego (2015)
12. Saito, M., Matsui, Y.: Illustration2Vec: a semantic vector representation of illustrations. In: SIGGRAPH ASIA 2015 Technical Briefs, No. 5 (2015)
13. Islam, A., Inkpen, D.: Semantic text similarity using corpus-based word similarity and string similarity. ACM Trans. Knowl. Discov. Data **2**(2), 10 (2008)
14. Cha, S.H.: Comprehensive survey on distance/similarity measures between probability density functions. Int. J. Math. Models Methods Appl. Sci. **1**(4), 300–307 (2007)

How Good Is Good Enough? Establishing Quality Thresholds for the Automatic Text Analysis of Retro-Digitized Comics

Rita Hartel[✉] and Alexander Dunst

Paderborn University, Warburger Straße 100, 33098 Paderborn, Germany
rst@upb.de, dunst@mail.upb.de

Abstract. Stylometry in the form of simple statistical text analysis has proven to be a powerful tool for text classification, e.g. in the form of authorship attribution. When analyzing retro-digitized comics, manga and graphic novels, the researcher is confronted with the problem that automated text recognition (ATR) still leads to results that have comparatively high error rates, while the manual transcription of texts remains highly time-consuming. In this paper, we present an approach and measures that specify whether stylometry based on unsupervised ATR will produce reliable results for a given dataset of comics images.

Keywords: Graphic novels · OCR · ATR · Automatic text analysis

1 Introduction

1.1 Motivation

Research on comics has undergone sustained growth over the last two decades in several disciplines and has now become a highly diverse field of inquiry. Although there are wordless and abstract comics, the medium's complex combination of words and images in telling stories has drawn the most sustained interest. Recent advances in image analysis and the explosive growth of the digital humanities (DH) mean that considerable efforts are underway to advance the computational analysis of comics. In previous work, we compared the automatic analysis of comics images with automated text analysis and were confronted with the problem that the quasi-handwritten fonts often used in graphic novels constitute a major challenge for state-of-the-art automatic text recognition (ATR) systems, although approaches for improving the performance of such systems for comics do exist [1]. This challenge led us to the question: "How good is good enough?" In other words: do we need a nearly perfect text recognition in order to perform text analysis, or are there certain tasks (e.g. analyses based on a term-document matrix) that can be performed on automatically recognized texts up to a given quality of recognition. As we show in this paper, text analysis on the basis of an open-source ATR system frequently yields similar results as the analysis of texts transcribed manually in a highly time-consuming annotation process.

© Springer Nature Switzerland AG 2019
I. Kompatsiaris et al. (Eds.): MMM 2019, LNCS 11296, pp. 662–671, 2019.
https://doi.org/10.1007/978-3-030-05716-9_59

1.2   Our Project

Our interdisciplinary project analyzes the different aspects of "hybrid narrative", in our case mainly graphic novels, comics narratives in book length that include fictional and non-fictional stories and are usually aimed at an adult audience. Fully automated analyses of such graphic novels are not yet feasible (beyond recognizing text there are even more difficult challenges, such as the recognition of narrative characters or the point-of-view of a panel). Therefore, our project semi-automatically annotates a corpus of currently around 220 graphic novels, memoirs, and non-fiction, which we call the Graphic Narrative Corpus (GNC) with the help of the M3-Editor developed as part of our project [2].

2   Automatic Text Analysis for Graphic Novels

Stylometry has proven to be a powerful tool for classifying documents, e.g. for authorship attribution. Even in the late nineteenth and early twentieth century, simple stylometric measures such as word-length statistics [3] were used to determine the authorship of parts of the bible or of Shakespeare's plays. Later approaches were based on type-token ratio, i.e., the ratio of 'unique' words relative to text length on the number of *hapax legomena* (i.e., words occurring only once) [4].

Today, approaches to authorship attribution consider different methods. On one side of the spectrum, there are sophisticated methods based on machine learning. On the other hand, there is stylometry in the form of simple statistical text analysis. Machine learning has the disadvantage that it requires comparatively large training sets. Therefore, it might be more applicable to questions such as genre distinction, where the relation between the number of different genres and genre representatives is better than in the case of authorship attribution (more authors than genres, but far less novels per author than per genre). As a consequence, most authorship attribution is based (at least partially) on simple lexical features that are taken to be representative of the individual word usage of an author. These statistical analyses include traditional bag-of-words text representation that researchers use for topic-based text classification (also referred to as term-document matrix) [5]. Therefore, for our analysis, we decided to use 'traditional' stylometric features. Examples of such stylometric features are word-length frequency distribution, sentence length, word or character n-grams, PoS (part of speech) or function words. Specifically, the term-document matrix, i.e., the frequencies of the most common words of a corpus within a document, is used to compute the stylometric distance of several documents and is found to be among the best features for authorship attribution [6, 7].

For many lexical features, text is considered as a bag of words (i.e. an unordered collection containing duplicates) rather than a sequence. Other techniques, including n-grams, consider context [8] but frequently do not perform better than simple word-based features [9]. Furthermore, in this paper we are not interested in semantical analysis, as is the case in part-of-speech-taggers, for instance, but consider words as syntactical units with certain features (e.g. their frequencies).

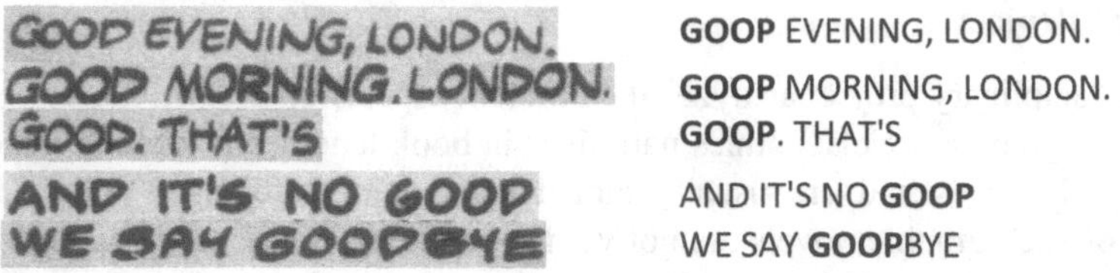

GOOD EVENING, LONDON.
GOOD MORNING. LONDON.
GOOD. THAT'S
AND IT'S NO GOOD
WE SAY GOODBYE
GOOP EVENING, LONDON.
GOOP MORNING, LONDON.
GOOP. THAT'S
AND IT'S NO GOOP
WE SAY GOOPBYE

Fig. 1. Systematic error when recognizing the word GOOD in *V* for Vendetta

Looking at these features, we can see that errors made when automatically recognizing document texts might not constitute a serious problem. This is particularly true if these errors are made systematically: e.g., if a word w is always recognized as the wrong word v throughout the complete text (c.f. Fig. 1). These features may even benefit from systematic errors, if we consider that one author might use the same quasi-handwritten font throughout all of her or his work, whereas different authors will use different fonts (c.f. Fig. 2). That means that the wrong word v might occur only in the texts of author A and not in the texts of other authors.

good GOOD GOOD
GOOD GOOD GOOD
Good good
GOOD GOOD GOOD
good GOOD

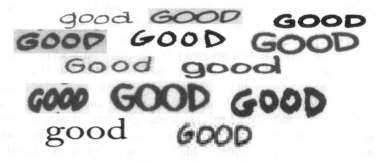

Fig. 2. Different occurrences of word GOOD in our corpus

In this paper, we use a small sample of annotated pages from the GNC to determine if textual analysis based on the output of a given ATR system will produce reliable results.

2.1 Error Rate Measures

When evaluating the performance of systems for tasks like speech recognition, automatic translation, optical character recognition (OCR) or automated text recognition (ATR), two common measures are the character error rate (CER) and the word error rate (WER). For the two texts GT (or 'ground truth', the original text) and R (the recognized text), where R consists of n words, we can define the WER as the "normalized edit distance" of R to GT, i.e., the number of words of R that have to be substituted, deleted or inserted in order to produce the original text GT, divided by the length n (in order to normalize the WER to be independent of text length). Similarly, for the two texts GT and R, where R consists of m symbols, we define the CER as the number of symbols of R that have to be substituted, deleted or inserted in order to produce GT divided by the length m. CER is the more precise measure, i.e., typically, it holds that CER < WER for a document R. As discussed above, many stylometric features do not consider text as a sequence but as a bag of words. If most of the words are recognized correctly but their order was not assigned properly, this might lead to large CERs and WERs although the analysis is not affected, as they result e.g. in a very similar term-document matrix.

For our analysis, we propose a further error measure that we call the *bag error rate (BER)* that does not consider the order of words. Let GT and R be two texts, and let W be a set of words such that for each word $gt \in GT \Rightarrow gt \in W$ and for each word $r \in R \Rightarrow r \in W$. Furthermore, let $freq^D(w) : W \rightarrow \mathbb{N}$ be a function that assigns each word w of W the frequency of w within document D. Then the bag error rate (BER) is defined as:

$$BER := \frac{\sum_{w \in W} |freq^{GT}(w) - freq^R(w)|}{\sum_{w \in W} freq^R(w)}$$

In other words, for each word occurring in either GT or R, we compute the difference in the number of occurrences and calculate them for all words. Then, we normalize this sum by dividing it by the number of words of R. This calculation yields a measure that is robust against changing the order of words and reflects the idea of the term-document matrix. It also follows the idea of other features, for instance, word-length distribution. Note that – although it does not consider the frequencies of words directly – more frequent words influence the BER more strongly than less frequent words. Whenever a word is very frequent but is misrecognized entirely each time, the effect on the BER is stronger than for words that occur less frequently but are mis-recognized completely. The same holds for words that are recognized correctly.

2.2   Quality Measures for Document Distance

In order to decide if text recognition is of sufficient quality for an analysis that uses a term-document matrix, we used the following two evaluations: The analysis based on a term-document matrix considers the distance between documents in an n-dimensional space, where each dimension reflects the occurrences of a frequent word in the corpus. The smaller the distance between them, the more similar are the documents. Thus, a collection of documents should be considered of sufficient quality for analysis if each document is situated close to the corresponding document. The first evaluation – called PERC in this text – computes the distance between all documents that have undergone ATR to each other document. We then calculate what percentage of the other documents is closer to the corresponding original text than the recognized text. The smaller the percentile, the more suitable the recognized document can be considered for automated text analysis. This evaluation considers documents in isolation, that is, without considering their context in the form of all other pages of the same graphic novel.

The second evaluation – called COR in this text – considers the frequency vectors *fo* of the original document and *fr* of the recognized document. It then uses Spearman's Rank Correlation Coefficient to decide if the distances between the original document and all other documents can be correlated to the distances between the recognized document and all other documents. The Spearman correlation between two variables is equal to the Pearson correlation between the rank values of those two variables. In other words, it compares the order of the variable values but ignores real values. The higher the coefficient (i.e., the nearer it is to 1), the more suitable the recognized document can be considered for automated text analysis.

3   Evaluation

The goal of our evaluation is to decide if the bag error rate (BER) is a good measure for selecting a graphic novel for automated text analysis. In order to calculate the BER, we need a ground truth in the form of the original text. Therefore, we also examine what percentage of a graphic novel needs to be manually annotated for the purpose of establishing a ground truth, in order to then compute the text's BER for further determination.

3.1   Method

For our evaluation, we used Tesseract 4 in LSTM mode without additional training to recognize the texts [10]. We ran Tesseract on a complete page of each graphic novel. Note, that running Tesseract on complete pages results in much worse recognition rates compared to running Tesseract on speech bubbles only (we yielded a mean CER of 27%, a mean WER of 44% and a mean BER of 34% for speech bubbles, but only a mean CER of 69%, a mean WER of 82% and a mean BER of 43% for complete pages). We decided to consider complete pages only, as each identification of speech bubbles prior to further analysis would require detection of speech bubbles, either manually with considerable effort, or in an automated fashion (using approaches like [11]), which reaches F1-Scores around 94 but which still introduces an additional source of errors. In a second step, we compared each recognized page to the original text and computed the CER, WER and BER for each pair of pages. Furthermore, we ran a stylometric analysis with the help of the STYLO package within R [12]. The resulting term-document matrix was then analysed with the help of both of our evaluation methods (PERC – percentile of distance and COR – correlation of distances of corresponding documents). Finally, we checked if a correlation between the BER of a page and its PERC and COR value can be found, and what portion of a document has to be evaluated in order to yield a significant correlation between BER of that portion and PERC and COR for the complete graphic novel.

3.2   Corpus

For our evaluation, we used the graphic narrative corpus (GNC) [2], which was designed as a representative corpus as part of our project. As we need a ground truth in order to evaluate the results, and the annotation of a graphic novel is very time-consuming (especially the transcription of the texts), only the part of our corpus that already has been completely annotated could be used. For our evaluation, we analyzed 13 graphic novels (c.f. Table 1), written by different authors and belonging to a number of genres. In total, we analyzed 2,643 pages.

Table 1. Graphic Novels used in our evaluation and their mean error rates

Graphic Novel	CER	WER	BER
A Contract With God	0.64	0.78	0.52
Batman – The Dark Knight Returns	0.74	0.88	0.53
Black Hole	0.55	0.71	0.27
City Of Glass	0.69	0.85	0.4
Fun Home	0.48	0.59	0.22
Gemma Bovery	0.94	0.97	0.73
Cleveland	0.96	0.99	0.74
Jimmy Corrigan	0.66	0.78	0.33
Our Cancer Year	0.76	0.89	0.43
The Complete Maus	0.65	0.88	0.48
The Diary of a Teenage Girl	0.97	0.99	0.91
V for Vendetta	0.68	0.86	0.46
Watchmen	0.63	0.81	0.29

3.3 Results

Our evaluation shows that there is a strong correlation between the bag error rate and our two measures PERC and COR. As shown in Fig. 3, there is also a strong correlation between BER and PERC with a Pearsson's rank coefficient of 0.81 and a p-value of less than $2.2 * 10^{-16}$, as well as a medium strong correlation between BER and COR with a Pearsson's rank coefficient of -0.71 (i.e., the smaller the error, the better the Spearman's correlation of the document's distances) and a p-value of less than $2.2 * 10^{-16}$. If we aggregate the BER, PERC and COR for complete graphic novels, we reach even stronger correlations, with a rank coefficient of 0.89 (and p < 0.000046) for BER/PERC and a rank coefficient of -0.93 (and p < 0.0000029) for BER/COR. These results allow us to state that for our evaluation corpus, the BER of a complete graphic novel functions as a good estimator of the value of ATR for all stylometric analyses that are based on bag of words.

A BER of 0.4–0.5 seems to be a good threshold to yield documents, or graphic novels, with a Spearman's Rank Coefficient of more than 0.6 (or even more than 0.8 in many cases). Therefore, in our successive evaluations, we use the threshold of BER < 0.5 to choose documents for automated text analysis.

As still we need a ground truth, in our second evaluation we compared the fraction of the graphic novel for which we computed the BER with the correlation coefficient of BER to PERC and BER to COR.

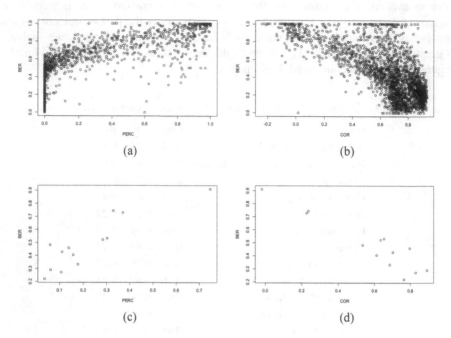

Fig. 3. Correlations for single pages between BER and PERC (a) or COR (b) and correlations for mean values per graphic novel between BER and PERC (c) or COR (d)

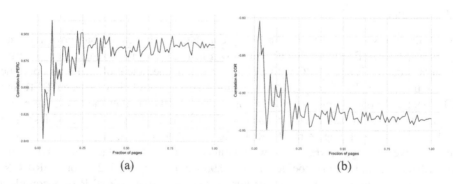

Fig. 4. Progress of correlation coefficient for BER/PERC (a) and BER/COR (b) for growing fraction of pages for each graphic novel used for calculating the BER

Figure 4 shows the results of this second evaluation. Even for small fractions of a graphic novel we can already establish strong correlations between the BER for this fraction and the PERC and COR for the whole graphic novel. When choosing a random sample of around 10% of the pages, we can use the BER as a good estimator. When choosing around 25%, the correlation coefficient remains more or less stable.

We conclude our evaluation with a comparison of automated text analyses and a text analysis on the transcribed texts. We used the term-document matrix and performed a dimension reduction on it with the help of PCA in order to visualize the results. Figure 5(a) and (b) show the visualization of the term-document matrix for Charles Burns' *Black Hole* and Paul Auster, Paul Karasik and David Mazzuchelli's *City of Glass*. As they were written by different authors and belong to different genres (coming of age and crime, respectively), these texts can be expected to possess distinct stylistic qualities. Part (a) shows the visualization of the automated text analysis, whereas part (b) shows the visualization of the analysis of the manually transcribed texts. As we can see in these figures, the two graphic novels can be distinguished quite well and the documents overlap only in a small part at the center of the plot.

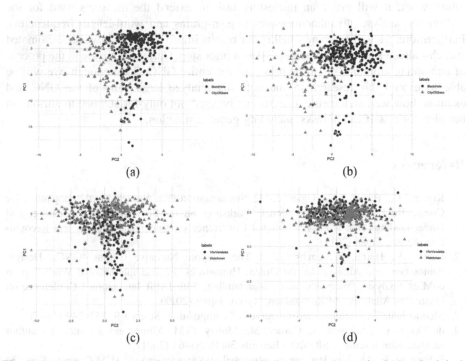

(a)   (b)

(c)   (d)

Fig. 5. Visualization of results for graphic novels with diverse texts (recognized (a) and original (b)) and for graphic novels with similar texts (recognized (c) and original (d))

Figure 5(c) and (d) show the visualization of the term-document matrix of two other graphic novels, *V for Vendetta* and *Watchmen*. Both were written by Alan Moore and, as a consequence, can be expected to possess similar text properties. Part (c) shows the visualization of the automated text analysis, whereas part (d) shows the visualization of the manually transcribed texts. In contrast to the graphic novels that we expected to be distinct stylistically, these two figures are quite similar: in both documents, the two graphic novels overlap. Regions where only one of the two novels can be found are relatively minor in comparison. These examples support the results of our earlier evaluation: when choosing graphic novels that show a BER of less than 0.5, text analysis on the basis of an automated text recognition system yields similar results as the analysis of texts transcribed manually in a highly time-consuming annotation process.

4 Conclusion

In this paper, we evaluated the feasibility of automated text analysis on retro-digitized images of graphic novels, or book-length comics narratives. Within our evaluation, we could show that with the help of the bag error rate (BER) defined in this paper, we were able to establish a good estimator for the reliable stylistic analysis of graphic novels. In future work, it will prove an interesting task to extend the measures used for the stylometric analyses to other measures (e.g. n-grams and word-length frequencies). Furthermore, we will examine whether our results improve further if we use automated speech-balloon segmentation (e.g. [11]) as a prior step. Currently, we are in the process of annotating around 10% of the pages for the entire GNC. Soon enough, we will be able to extend this research to automatically analyze large parts of the GNC and examine how well stylometric analysis can be used not only for authorship attribution but also for classification tasks, including genre distinction.

References

1. Rigaud, C., Burie, J.-C., Ogier, J.-M.: Segmentation-Free Speech Text Recognition for Comic Books. In: 2nd International Workshop on coMics Analysis, Processing, and Understanding, 14th IAPR International Conference on Document Analysis and Recognition, Kyoto, Japan (2017)
2. Dunst, A., Hartel, R., Laubrock, J.: The Graphic Narrative Corpus (GNC): Design, Annotation, and Analysis for the Digital Humanities. In: 2nd International Workshop on coMics Analysis, Processing, and Understanding, 14th IAPR International Conference on Document Analysis and Recognition, Kyoto, Japan (2017)
3. Mendenhall, T.: The characteristic curves of composition. Science **9**, 237–249 (1887)
4. de Vel, O.Y., Anderson, A., Corney, M., Mohay, G.M.: Mining email content for author identification forensics. SIGMOD Records **30**(4), 55–64 (2001)
5. Sebastiani, F.: Machine learning in automated text categorization. ACM Comput. Surv. **34** (1), 1–47 (2002)
6. Burrows, J.: Word patterns and story shapers: the statistical analysis of narrative style. Literary Linguist. Comput. **2**, 61–70 (1987)
7. Argamon, S., Levitan, S.: Measuring the usefulness of function words for authorship attribution. In: Proceedings of the Joint Conference of the Association for Computers and the Humanities and the Association for Literary and Linguistic Computing (2005)
8. Peng, F., Schuurmans, D., Wang, S.: Augmenting Naive Bayes classifiers with statistical language models. Inf. Retrieval J. **7**(3–4), 317–345 (2004)
9. Sanderson, C., Günther, S.: Short text authorship attribution via sequence kernels, Markov Chains and author unmasking: an investigation. In: Proceedings of the 2006 Conference on Empirical Methods in Natural Language Processing, EMNLP 2007, Sydney, Australia (2006)

10. Smith, R.: An overview of the Tesseract OCR Engine. In: 9th International Conference on Document Analysis and Recognition (ICDAR 2007), Curitiba, Paraná, Brazil (2007)
11. Nguyen, N.-V., Rigaud, C., Burie, J.-C.: Digital comics image indexing based on deep learning. J. Imaging **4**(7), 89ff (2018)
12. Eder, M., Kestemont, M., Rybicki, J.: Stylometry with R: a suite of tools. In: Digital Humanities 2013, DH 2013, Lincoln, NE, USA (2013)

Comic Text Detection Using Neural Network Approach

Frédéric Rayar[✉] and Seiichi Uchida

Kyushu University, Fukuoka 819-0395, Japan
{rayar,uchida}@human.ait.kyushu-u.ac.jp

Abstract. Text is a crucial element in comic books; hence text detection is a significant challenge in an endeavour to achieve comic processing. In this work, we study in what extent an off-the-shelf neural network approach for scene text detection can be used to perform comic text detection. Experiment on a public data set shows that such an approach allows to perform as well as methods of the literature, which is promising for building more accurate comic text detector in the future.

Keywords: Comic understanding · Text detection · Neural networks

1 Introduction

Comics are a substantial part of the culture in several countries such as Japan, France, Belgium and USA. Nowadays, they are read all over the world and have become an important medium. Comics also represent an important market worldwide. Let us take the example of Japan: the market in Japan in 2016 was about 4.45 billion USD. It is worth noticing that this market sees an evolution of consumption of its users: in February, 2017 a report [7] from the All Japan Magazine and Book Publisher's and Editor's Association attested that the sales of printed comics saw a 9.3% decrease while those of digital comics saw a 27.5% increase compared to 2015 numbers. Hence, this phenomenon has brought the Document Image Analysis (DIA) research community an opportunity in the last decade to use their techniques to improve comics' analysis, processing and understanding in order to meet the expectation of this new digital era.

Generally speaking, comics are constituted of pictures combined with text and other visual information, in order to narrate a story. However, a comic page can also be considered as a complex layout document: it includes various elements, such as panels, speech balloons, characters, signs, onomatopoeia, background elements, page number, etc.

In this study, we focus on text that can appear in a comic book. Most of the information shared by characters are conveyed by the shape of text appearing in speech balloons. Nevertheless, relevant piece of information are also conveyed by captions and other narrative text (description of a scene or a situation), onomatopoeia (expression of an emotion, an action or a motion), or simply background texts (signs, licence plates, documents, etc). Hence, comic text detection and recognition are important challenges that have to be addressed.

© Springer Nature Switzerland AG 2019
I. Kompatsiaris et al. (Eds.): MMM 2019, LNCS 11296, pp. 672–683, 2019.
https://doi.org/10.1007/978-3-030-05716-9_60

Fig. 1. eBDtheque [3] data set comic page examples.

The presented work deals with text detection in comic pages. In the last decade, only a few methods, based on classic document image analysis techniques, have been proposed to address this challenge. Hence, we aim at evaluating in what extent a cutting-edge algorithm for scene text detection can be used for our purpose. Specifically, we will observe and discuss the results of the EAST (Efficient and Accurate Scene Text Detector) [14] algorithm for Latin script text detection on a public comic data set, namely eBDtheque [3].

This paper is organised as follows: Sect. 2 presents an overview of comic text detection, and introduces the neural-network-based scene text detection algorithm that we aim at evaluating in this work. Section 3 details the experiment that has been conducted in order to evaluate the detection algorithm. Results and discussion are presented in Sect. 4. Finally, Sect. 5 concludes this paper.

2 Related Works

2.1 Comic Text Detection

As mentioned above, comic text detection is a difficult challenge. Indeed, text can appears in speech balloons, out-of-balloons, as onomatopoeia, as signs, etc. Furthermore, the text in comics presents a lot of variations (e.g. font, size, colour, orientation, handwritten, typewritten, etc.). Hence, localisation of such text areas is not trivial. Figure 1 illustrates some of the challenges of detecting text in comic pages: dense picture background, text that appears without balloons, or complex comic layout (no frame). In the last decade, only a few methods have been proposed to detect text areas in comics. They can be categorised in two categories, namely top-down and bottom-up approaches.

In top-down approaches [8,11,13], layout analysis is performed on a given comic page, in order to extract panels and/or speech balloon. Then, from these regions of interest, a connected component extraction and classification is performed to extract text areas. The major limitations of such approaches is that

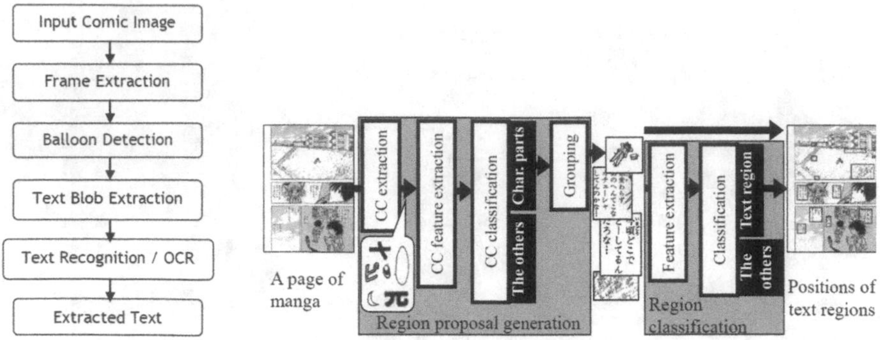

Fig. 2. Workflows of the top-down approach of Arai et al. [11] (left) and the bottom-up approach of Aramaki et al. [1] (right).

they rely on some heuristic rules for the layout analysis; but more importantly, only speech balloon texts can be extracting, discarding other texts. Figure 2 (left) illustrates the workflow of Arai et al. [11].

Bottom-up approaches [1,4,9,10] aim at detecting text areas without any refined page layout analysis, but rather with a text/graphics separation. Connected components are also used to generate potential text region candidates. Then, a classification is performed to output final resulting text areas. In such methods, the connected component analysis is crucial and the classification usually rely on geometrical features (e.g., the area, the perimeter) or heuristic rules. Figure 2 (right) illustrates the workflow of Aramaki et al. [1].

2.2   Scene Text Detection Using Neural Network

Scene text detection is still an active and challenging field of research nowadays. Indeed, one has to deal, among others, with arbitrary sizes, fonts, orientations of text and complex background in natural images. Earlier methods relied on document images analysis techniques where hand crafted features (e.g. colour, edge, texture, shape or frequency features) were used.

Recent advances in neural network approaches, especially convolutional neural networks, have allowed a giant leap towards solving this task. Indeed, such approaches achieve state-of-the-art performances across various benchmark data sets. In the "robust reading competition" held at ICDAR 2017 [2], all the 14 methods proposed to address the scene text localisation challenge used neural-network based approaches.

Recently, EAST (Efficient and Accurate Scene Text Detector) [14] has been proposed to address scene text detection. The authors proposed a single neural network that, given an input image, directly predicts words or text lines of arbitrary orientations. The proposed architecture (See Fig. 3) allows to avoid *"unnecessary intermediate steps (e.g., candidate aggregation and word partitioning)"*. Post-processing steps consist only in thresholding and a non-maximum suppression (NMS) on the predicted geometric shapes. Experiments on bench-mark data sets showed that EAST significantly outperformed state-of-the-art methods in terms of both accuracy and efficiency. One can find more recent methods in the literature, such as FOTS [6] or TextBoxes++ [5].

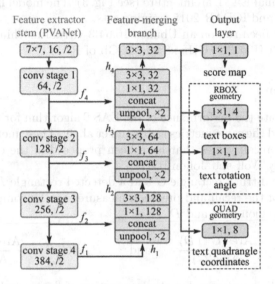

Fig. 3. Original structure of EAST neural network. Illustration from [14].

3   Experiment

3.1   Data Set

The eBDtheque data set [3] contain 100 pages from America, Japan and France comic books. Figure 1 presents three sample of this heterogeneous data set. It is composed of 46 pages that were digitised from 14 albums and 54 web comics. 39 pages are handwritten and 61 computer-generated. 6 pages are in Japanese, 13 in English and 81 in French. 33 pages have out-of-balloon text and 8 have no balloon at all. Only 18 pages contains onomatopoeia.

Annotations about panels, characters, speech balloons and text lines are provided along with the comic pages. More specifically, axis-aligned bounding boxes and transcription of 4667 text lines spread among the 100 comic page are provided.

In this experiment, we have discarded the 6 Japanese comic pages. Indeed, earlier experiments have shown that available pre-trained EAST model did not perform well on Japanese language. Hence, the final data set that we have used in our experiment contain 94 comic pages in Latin scripts, namely English and French.

3.2   Implementation

In order to detect the text areas from the comic pages, we have used the Tensor-flow implementation of the EAST algorithm[1]. For the feature extraction part, this implementation uses a ResNet-50 architecture instead of the PVANet proposed in the original EAST architecture (see Fig. 3). The model has been trained on ICDAR 2013 and ICDAR 2015 training sets.

The code has been run on an Ubuntu 16.04.3 virtual machine, with an Intel Core i7-6850K CPU at 3.60 GHz x8 and 16 Gb of RAM.

3.3   Evaluation

In order to evaluate the performance of the EAST algorithm for detecting comic text, we have used the same metrics as Rigaud et al. [9]. These metrics correspond to precision and recall values that have been proposed in the context of scene text detection, by Wolf and Jolion [12].

Given a ground-truth rectangle G and a detected rectangle D, a straightforward extension of the recall and precision measures can be computed, based on the overlapping region of G and D:

$$R_{AR}(G, D) = \frac{\text{Area}(G \cap D)}{\text{Area}(G)} \quad \text{and} \quad P_{AR}(G, D) = \frac{\text{Area}(G \cap D)}{\text{Area}(D)}$$

The area recall R_{AR} corresponds to the proportion of the ground truth rectangle G that has been correctly detected, while the area precision P_{AR} corresponds to the proportion of the detected rectangle D that is correct with regards to the ground truth. Two rectangles are matched iif. the overlap satisfies quality constraints: $R_{AR}(G, D) > \tau_R$ and $P_{AR}(G, D) > \tau_P$.

Based on these definitions, one can compare two lists $\mathcal{G} = \{G_1, \ldots, G_m\}$ and $\mathcal{D} = \{D_1, \ldots, D_n\}$ of ground-truth and detected rectangles, respectively. In order to take into consideration one-to-one, one-to-many matches (a split ground-truth) and many-to-one matches (merged ground truth), we consider the following recall (R) and precision (P) metrics:

$$R(\mathcal{G}, \mathcal{D}, \tau_R, \tau_P) = \frac{\sum_i \text{Match}_{\mathcal{G}}(G_i, \mathcal{D}, \tau_R, \tau_P)}{|\mathcal{G}|}$$

$$P(\mathcal{G}, \mathcal{D}, \tau_R, \tau_P) = \frac{\sum_j \text{Match}_{\mathcal{D}}(D_j, \mathcal{G}, \tau_R, \tau_P)}{|\mathcal{D}|}$$

with:

$$\text{Match}_{\mathcal{G}}(G_i, \mathcal{D}, \tau_R, \tau_P) = \begin{cases} 0, & \text{if } G_i \text{ matches no rectangle in } \mathcal{D}, \\ 1, & \text{if } G_i \text{ matches one unique rectangle in } \mathcal{D}, \\ f_{sc}, & \text{if } G_i \text{ matches several rectangles in } \mathcal{D}, \end{cases}$$

---

[1] https://github.com/argman/EAST.

and

$$\text{Match}_{\mathcal{D}}(D_j, \mathcal{G}, \tau_R, \tau_P) = \begin{cases} 0, & \text{if } D_j \text{ matches no rectangle in } \mathcal{G}, \\ 1, & \text{if } D_j \text{ matches one unique rectangle in } \mathcal{G}, \\ f_{sc}, & \text{if } D_j \text{ matches several rectangles in } \mathcal{G}, \end{cases}$$

f_{sc} is a parameter controlling the scattering matching punishment. In our experiment, we have set $\tau_R = 0.6$, $\tau_P = 0.4$ and $f_{sc} = 0.8$, according to [9] experiment.

4   Results and Discussion

4.1   Quantitative Results

Table 1 presents the recall and precision obtained on the whole studied data set. The proposed method achieves 62.47% of recall and 78.52% of precision. In term of precision, we perform slightly better than Rigaud et al. [9] (76.15%). However, as one can see, our recall is lower than their score (75.82%). This could be explained by two reasons. First, the ground-truth bounding boxes are axis-aligned, and thus are not always fitted to crooked text (see Fig. 4 (left)). Hence, both recall and precision are affected by this ground truth description. Second, the ground is given at text line level, while the proposed approach detects text areas at word level. The recall is strongly affected by the numerous missing white spaces (see Fig. 4 (right)).

Table 2 gives more details on the recall and precision obtained on 20 comic pages with both Rigaud et al. and the proposed method. Image 14 is a good example of the influence of the text lines ground truth versus detected word: the detection is 100% accurate (precision), but the recall is only 63.48% while 99% of the words have been detected.

Overall, the obtained results are competitive with results of the state of the art, while being promising considering the fact that the model has been pre-trained for scene text detection. Hence, recall and precision could be improved by either parameter tuning, custom training or finetuning.

Table 1. Recall and precision obtained on the 94 comics pages.

Method	Recall (%)	Precision (%)
Rigaud et al. [9]	**75.82**	76.15
Proposed	62.47	**78.52**

4.2   Qualitative Results

We present in this section some qualitative results that highlight advantages and limitations of using EAST algorithm to detect text in comic pages.

Table 2. Comparison of the recall and precision values obtained on 20 comic pages used in [9]. Image 1 and 17 have not been found in the current version of the data set.

Page id	Page name	Rigaud el al. [9]		Proposed	
		Recall (%)	Precision (%)	Recall (%)	Precision (%)
1	?	78.26	64.52	-	-
2	CYB.BUBBLEGOM_T01_005.jpg	84.21	73.61	67.14	85.19
3	CYB.BUBBLEGOM_T01_007.jpg	69.23	40.4	53.58	65.84
4	CYB.COSMOZONE_00.jpg	66.67	61.9	60	18.92
5	CYB.COSMOZONE_010.jpg	84.00	64.71	64.8	38.86
6	CYB.MAGICIENLOOSE_001.jpg	86.11	95	53.33	81.21
7	CYB.MOUETTEMAN_004.jpg	96.43	83.78	78.06	94.05
8	FRED.PHILEMON12.006.jpg	86.11	74.14	45.95	30.93
9	FRED.PHILEMON12.040.jpg	80.95	86.67	60.71	72.89
10	FRED.PHILEMON9.014.jpg	29.23	76	76.62	80.54
11	JOLIVET.BOSTONPOLICEAFFAIREPRADI.003.jpg	100	50.46	75.64	90.97
12	JOLIVET.BOSTONPOLICEAFFAIREPRADI.021.jpg	68.75	91.67	80	62.79
13	LAMISSEB.ETPISTAF_005.jpg	100	82.35	72.86	73.57
14	LAMISSEB.LESNOEILS1_008.jpg	91.3	95.45	63.48	100
15	LAMISSEB.LESNOEILS1_016.jpg	96.55	96.55	82.76	98.85
16	MCCAY.LITTLENEMO_025.jpg	73.33	59.26	62.93	60.45
17	?	65	76.47	-	-
18	ROUDIER.LESTERRESCREUSEES_012.jpg	100	88.24	52.14	95.35
19	TRONDHEIM.LES_TROIS.CHEMINS.003.jpg	79.13	77.24	64.52	63.46
20	WARE.ACME_024.jpg	66.03	89.05	62.84	53.88

Fig. 4. Illustration of the eBDtheque axis-aligned ground-truth text lines and the detected oriented words.

Font Type, Size and Colour. The proposed method allows to detect text independently of the text type, size and colour. Figure 5 illustrates such positive detection. Hence, it could address in a certain extent the large heterogeneity of text that appears in comics (e.g. typewritten vs. handwritten, bold vs. light typeface, etc).

Fig. 5. Different text detected by EAST: text with different font, colour and size, but that appear in the same speech balloon can be detected.

Position and Orientation. The proposed method can detect text that appears out of a classic speech balloon. Figure 6 illustrates such detection. In the top row, an important multi-oriented text, that describes the above picture, is easily detected by the algorithm. In the lower row, an onomatopoeia that appears across several panels (separated by white gutters) is partially detected as several words.

Fig. 6. Text that appear outside of speech balloons, multi-oriented text and onomatopoeia that appear across several panels can be detected by EAST.

Fig. 7. Different comic text detection by the proposed method: background text, onomatopoeia, author signature. In the top-right picture, the "police" and "3949" texts appearing in the licence plate are also correctly detected.

Background Text. As mentioned previously, comic text is not only speech balloon text. Such texts are significant to allow the reader to fully understand the story conveyed by the authors. Figure 7 illustrates difficult texts that have been detected by the proposed method. On top of onomatopoeia, or author signatures, the algorithm can detect text that appears in signs and even in the licence plate of cars (top-right panel of Fig. 7).

False Positive. Apart from non-detected text areas, the algorithm also has some false positive detection. Figure 8 illustrates a few samples of such erroneous detection. As one can see, several vertical stroke shapes seem to be sometimes detected as text (e.g. grass, hairs, etc).

Fig. 8. Samples of false positive text detected by EAST.

Limitations. A few limitations can be observed from our experiment on the eBDtheque data set. The first one is the fact that scattered text is often detected, even for words. Some part of a text lines are also non detected, which may be related to the post process of the method (thresholding and NMS steps). Punctuation marks ('?', '!', '...') and pages numbers are often not detected. Regarding the former, they are not detected whether they appear in speech text or onomatopoeia.

4.3 Computation Times

In the previous studies on comic text detection, not much information was given concerning the computation times of the proposed methods. Rigaud et al. [9] mentions that *"all the dataset was proceeded in less than 5 min on a regular machine with a 2.50 GHz CPU and 8 GB RAM."*

Figure 9 illustrates the distribution of the computation time in milliseconds (ms) of the proposed method on the whole eBDtheque data set. The 100 pages have been processed in 482 ms. One can see that the obtained times are around 1 ms and 7 ms, depending on the dimensions of the comic pages.

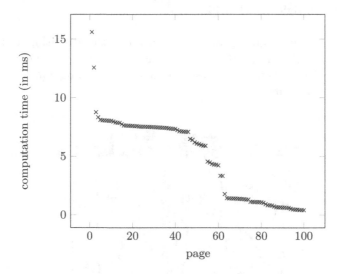

Fig. 9. Distribution of the computation time (in ms) of the proposed text detection method over the 100 comic pages of the whole eBDtheque data set.

5   Conclusion

In this study, we have evaluated a neural-network based approach, namely EAST, to localise text areas in comics pages. The EAST algorithm has originally been proposed and trained for scene text detection, but performs relatively well for comic text detection. The evaluation shows that more than 78.52% of the text lines are detected with 62.47% precision. Furthermore, the method allows to detect oriented text without any layout analysis in a few milliseconds. The extracted text correspond to speech text, but also to onomatopoeia, out-of-balloon speech text and background text.

This first experiment on text detection in comic pages using neural-network approach is a promising step towards automatic processing of text in comics. Future work will address improving the recall and precision of the detection (toward a near-perfect accurate comic text detector), and evaluation of neural networks for text recognition.

Acknowledgements. The authors would like to thank the curators of the eBDtheque data set, along with the authors of the data set's comics, for allowing us to use their works. This research was partially supported by MEXT-Japan (Grant No. 17H06100).

References

1. Aramaki, Y., Matsui, Y., Yamasaki, T., Aizawa, K.: Text detection in manga by combining connected-component-based and region-based classifications, pp. 2901–2905 (2016)
2. Gomez, R., et al.: ICDAR 2017 robust reading challenge on coco-text. In: International Conference on Document Analysis and Recognition, pp. 1435–1443 (2017)
3. Guérin, C., et al.: eBDtheque: a representative database of comics, pp. 1145–1149 (2013)
4. Li, L., Wang, Y., Tang, Z., Lu, X., Gao, L.: Unsupervised speech text localization in comic images, pp. 1190–1194(2013)
5. Liao, M., Shi, B., Bai, X.: Textboxes++: a single-shot oriented scene text detector. CoRR abs/1801.02765 (2018)
6. Liu, X., Liang, D., Yan, S., Chen, D., Qiao, Y., Yan, J.: FOTS: fast oriented text spotting with a unified network. CoRR abs/1801.01671 (2018)
7. All Japan Magazine and Book Publisher's and Editor's Association: Report on printed and digital comics' market. http://www.ajpea.or.jp/book/2-1702/index.html (2017). Accessed 31 Aug 2018
8. Ponsard, C., Ramdoyal, R., Dziamski, D.: An OCR-enabled digital comic books viewer. In: Miesenberger, K., Karshmer, A., Penaz, P., Zagler, W. (eds.) ICCHP 2012. LNCS, vol. 7382, pp. 471–478. Springer, Heidelberg (2012). https://doi.org/10.1007/978-3-642-31522-0_71
9. Rigaud, C., Karatzas, D., Van de Weijer, J., Burie, J.C., Ogier, J.M.: Automatic text localisation in scanned comic books. In: International Conference on Computer Vision Theory and Applications (2013)
10. Su, C., Chang, R., Liu, J.: Recognizing text elements for SVG comic compression and its novel applications, pp. 1329–1333 (2011)
11. Tolle, H., Arai, K.: Method for real time text extraction of digital manga comic. Int. J. Image Process., 669–676 (2011)
12. Wolf, C., Jolion, J.M.: Object count/area graphs for the evaluation of object detection and segmentation algorithms. Int. J. Doc. Anal. Recogn. 8(4), 280–296 (2006)
13. Yamada, M., Budiarto, R., Endo, M., Miyazaki, S.: Comic image decomposition for reading comics on cellular phones. IEICE Trans. Inf. Syst., 1370–1376 (2004). No. 6
14. Zhou, X., et al.: EAST: an efficient and accurate scene text detector. CoRR abs/1704.03155 (2017)

CNN-Based Classification of Illustrator Style in Graphic Novels: Which Features Contribute Most?

Jochen Laubrock[✉] and David Dubray

University of Potsdam, Potsdam, Germany
{laubrock,ddubray}@uni-potsdam.de

Abstract. Can classification of graphic novel illustrators be achieved by convolutional neural network (CNN) features evolved for classifying concepts on photographs? Assuming that basic features at lower network levels generically represent invariants of our environment, they should be reusable. However, features at what level of abstraction are characteristic of illustrator style? We tested transfer learning by classifying roughly 50,000 digitized pages from about 200 comic books of the Graphic Narrative Corpus (GNC, [6]) by illustrator. For comparison, we also classified Manga109 [18] by book. We tested the predictability of visual features by experimentally varying which of the mixed layers of Inception V3 [29] was used to train classifiers. Overall, the top-1 test-set classification accuracy in the artist attribution analysis increased from 92% for mixed-layer 0 to over 97% when adding mixed-layers higher in the hierarchy. Above mixed-layer 5, there were signs of overfitting, suggesting that texture-like mid-level vision features were sufficient. Experiments varying input material show that page layout and coloring scheme are important contributors. Thus, stylistic classification of comics artists is possible re-using pre-trained CNN features, given only a limited amount of additional training material. We propose that CNN features are general enough to provide the foundation of a visual stylometry, potentially useful for comparative art history.

Keywords: Convolutional Neural Network · Classification · Graphic Novels · Stylometry

1 Introduction

What Constitutes Pictorial Style? Pictorial style has been one of the major interests of art history since its beginning, and some of the founding fathers of modern art history were greatly interested in developing a formal theory of style [10,31]. A system enabling a formal and dimensional description of style is extremely useful, because it enables comparative work and allows a scientific

---

Supported by a BMBF eHumanities grant to JL.

I. Kompatsiaris et al. (Eds.): MMM 2019, LNCS 11296, pp. 684–695, 2019.
https://doi.org/10.1007/978-3-030-05716-9_61

judgment and classification of art in terms of agreed-upon categories. Placing artists, artworks and epochs in such a dimensional system enables comparative art-historical and art-critical enquiry into style. Ideally, comparative analysis of the formal organization of pictures will benefit from a set of objective parameters.

Perception-Based Approaches to Style. Artists often play with human perception, and explore its boundaries. Similarly, art historians have been interested in relating art to fundamentals of human sensation and perception. Ernst Gombrich believed that a proper theory of representation had to consider results of scientific research. Perceptual psychology deals with how we perceive and build rich internal representations from a flat retinal image, and how different images differ in memorability and emotional evaluation (e.g. how pleasing is this image?). Art history wants to understand how a flat pictorial image can represent, how representation evolved, and what are the patterns of beauty. Both disciplines are thus naturally interested in the nature of representations, albeit at different levels.

A fundamental insight from psychologist studying perception is that our visual system is hierarchically organized and works in a highly constructive manner: higher levels of visual processing re-construct semantics and depth of real-world scenes from an initial pixel-like coding available at the retinal image. Visual and cognitive processing along the ventral pathway of the brain eventually leads to object representations, but the representations at the initial (lower) stages of cortical processing are rather simple, coding for information such as boundaries, contrast, and color. These simple features are likely to code invariants of our evolutionary environment. The receptive fields of cells at the lower stages are small, so that each neuron only "sees" a small part of the visual scene. Mid-level vision takes their computations as input and combines them to code texture, shape, object parts and proto-objects as well as to separate figure from ground, resolve shadows, etc. Receptive fields get larger the higher up the processing hierarchy we go.

Computational Approaches to Perception. Recent advances in neural modelling using convolutional neural networks (CNNs; [16]) have led to computational models of low- and mid-level vision up to the conceptual level that are a rather good approximation of human vision. Research comparing visual representations in CNN-based models with actual brain recordings has found a striking correspondence [3,32]. CNNs are a class of neural networks specialized in analyzing data with an implicit spatial layout, such as RGB images. CNNs are characterized by local connections, shared weights, pooling, and the use of many layers. Within each convolutional layer, a stack of different filters (feature maps) is trained. Each unit is connected to local patches in the feature maps of the previous layer through a set of learned weights, which describe a filter kernel, and learned by backpropagation [22]. A local weighted sum computed by applying the filter kernel to the image is passed through a non-linearity, often a rectified linear unit (ReLU). All units in a feature map share the same filter kernel; feature maps in a layer differ by using different kernels. The receptive field size of each filter (i.e. the region of the image it responds to) is small at the lower layers, and becomes progressively larger at higher layers. Conversely, the higher the layer, the more complex the features encoded by the filters. Pooling layers typically replacing a local patch by its maximum value are added to further reduce the number of parameters and to provide a more coarse-grained and robust description.

Thus, like the human visual system uses a complex processing hierarchy in learning to categorize objects, CNN-based models learn what combinations of simple and intermediate features are most discriminative for a given object. Lower-level filters often respond well to edges and boundaries and thus resemble simple cells in human visual cortex. Higher-level features, in contrast, can code for complex stimuli like textures or facial parts. Just like the visual system, CNNs compose objects out of simple features by using compositional feature hierarchies. Edges combine into motifs, motifs into parts, and parts into objects. One fundamental insight is that especially the simpler lower-level features represent environmental invariants, so that they are quite generic and can be useful for many different images. For example, a low-level neuron in a CNN as well as simple cells in human early vision (V1, [11]) implement a filter responding to edges of a specific orientation, which may be useful in many contexts. Because lower-level features are quite generic, CNNs pre-trained on large-scale image classification tasks like ImageNet ([5], 14 million images with over 1,000 classes) can often be adapted to specific material by re-training just a few layers. The goal of the present work was to test for transfer to comics drawings.

Computational Approaches to Pictorial Style. The fairly new discipline of the *digital humanities* (DH) has been mostly interested in computational approaches to literature studies, with hallmarks being the so-called "distant reading" of texts [19] and the development of stylometric measures for text, enabling, for example, quantitative style comparison and author identification [12]. Very recently a shift in interest towards visual material can be observed in the DH community. Because CNN models contain examinable representations at several hierarchical levels (objects, proto-objects, textures, colors, orientations, etc), they are likely to provide a highly useful formal description of visual stimuli including comics and visual art. We are convinced that distant reading of art, exploration of the internal representations of deep CNNs trained on artworks, and correlating and mapping them to concepts from art history, will bring new perspectives and possibly even transform the field of art history, in a similar way that distant reading and computational linguistics contributed to the comparative study of literature.

2 Related Work

Machine learning approaches combining visual features with similarity metrics have recently been used with some success to classify artists and styles [24].

Saleh and Elgammal also compared engineered features with CNN features and somewhat surprisingly found that CNN features were not necessarily performing better. However, closer reading of their paper seems to suggest that they used a very late, 'semantic' output feature of a network trained on an unrelated task, thus the contribution of lower-level CNN features is not known.

There have been some successful attempts at classifying the style of artistic paintings using CNN features, which generally performed better than classic, engineered features [4,13]. Benoît Seguin and colleagues have built an image search engine for a large collection of paintings using pre-trained CNN features and paying particular attention to visual links, a category important to art historians [26].

Leon Gatys has described an approach to a general description style using CNN features, and pioneered style transfer, which has become quite popular [8,9]. Style transfer works by transferring style of one image to content of another image. This may be one of the most advanced descriptions of image style to date. A significantly faster approach has recently been presented by Sanakoyeu et al. [25]. Chu and Wu [1] show that learning correlations between deep feature maps improves style representation.

In the domain of comics, there were some approaches using relatively simple summary statistics to describe style. Lev Manovich pioneered this approach in combination with large-scale visualization [17]. Dunst and Hartel describe an approach to stylometry using somewhat more sophisticated engineered features such as a shape descriptor [7], and found some differences between genres.

Saito and Matsui used deep CNN features for computing similarity metrics between a large number of labeled illustrations, for which they were able to compute a semantic vector representation and create an impressive demonstration of 'semantic morphing' [23]. Interestingly, Matsui chose to use classic rather than CNN-based features in the equally impressive sketch-based image-retrieval for Manga109 [18], possibly for performance reasons. Current work from that group, albeit using different material (Kotenseki images), also seems to use deep CNN features [28]. Chu and Li [2] show that CNN features can be used to detect faces in manga.

Rigaud and Burie have a long history of studying comics from a computational perspective. In a recent conference presentation they showed that models based on deep CNN features perform significantly better than other approaches in detecting characters in comics [20]. Such object-level descriptions might well be characteristic of the style of an artist.

We have previously used deep CNN features from VGG-19 [27] in combination with Deep Gaze II [14] predictions of empirical saliency to show that gaze locations of human readers measured using eye-tracking can be well predicted by CNN features [15].

3 CNNs Applied to Graphic Novels

Here we propose a method for a visual stylometry of comics based on CNN features. We test transfer to comics by using a large corpus of graphic narratives.

To illustrate the approach, we use CNN features to classify illustrator, genre, and publisher. We employ an experimental approach to study the effect that some variables such as page layout may have on the classification. In closing we explore how the approach might be used in other domains such as art history.

3.1   Material: GNC

The material we used is the Graphic Narrative Corpus (GNC; [6]). The GNC is a representative collection of graphic novels, i.e., book-length comics that tell continuous stories and are aimed at an adult readership. At the time of analysis, the stratified monitor corpus included 209 graphic narratives amounting to nearly 50,000 digitized pages. A subset of the first chapter of these works is annotated by human annotators with respect to the location and identity of panels, main characters, character relations, captions, speech bubbles, onomatopoeia, and the respective text. Furthermore, eye movement data is collected for these pages to measure readers' attention. Metadata for the GNC includes information on author and illustrator ($N = 161$ at the time of analysis), publisher (78), and genre (24). For comparison, the classifiers were also trained on books of the Manga109 dataset [18].

3.2   CNN Model

In order to test generalization of the features and their transfer to graphic illustrations, we describe material from the GNC using a specific CNN, Inception V3 [29], using pre-trained weights from ImageNet. We chose Inception V3 for stylometry and artist attribution due to its state-of-the art performance, economic parameterization, and relative independence of input sizes. Scanned comic book pages were fed through the CNN to obtain feature maps. For classification, we trained a simple fully-connected neural network with one hidden layer of 1024 units, using average-pooled feature maps from mixed layers as input (see below) and illustrators, genre, or publisher (GNC) or book titles (Manga109) as outputs. The training set contained 90% of pages of each book, 10% of randomly determined pages per comic were held out as a test set to evaluate performance.

4   Experiments

4.1   Design and Procedure

We inspected the predictive value of pre-trained Inception V3 filters for classifying comic illustratorship. Specifically, we used Inception V3 weights from ImageNet classification. Due to our interest in the convolutional part all of the fully connected layers were stripped off. Because we were particularly interested in what type of features are most useful in characterizing illustrator style, we lesioned the CNN at progressively lower layers and compared classification performance to the full model. In order to get a better understanding for what aspects of the material were used in classification, we artificially removed some cues from the material and re-fit the models. First, page layout should become less important if only a randomly cropped part of the page is used. Second, it is possible that a CNN is learning scanning artifacts and page frames for a given book rather than an artist's style. The chance for such artifact-based classification should be much reduced when the boundaries of a page are cropped. Third, to study the contribution of color to style, we compared colored with grayscale versions, using several different methods of thresholding. Finally, we show how an image search engine for our corpus can be implemented using nearest neighbor search in feature space.

Representation. As input to our classifiers we used feature maps obtained by processing the input image with Inception V3 until up to a set of mixed layers. The feature maps were then global average pooled, since we thought that a stylistic signature should be similar in several regions of the image. This results in a fairly compact representation. The mean size of the 49,009 input images was 814 kBytes. The size of the vector we used to represent feature maps ranged from 256 to 2048 entries for single-layer and 10,048 entries for cumulative representations. Table 1 shows the number of filters per layer used, as well as their cumulative sum and the average compression ratios for representations based on single and cumulative layers, assuming single precision and an average image size.

Table 1. Representations and compression ratio.

Layer	N Filters	Cumulative sum	Compression ratio	
			Single	Cumulative
mixed0	256	256	814	814
mixed1	288	544	724	383
mixed2	288	832	724	251
mixed3	768	1600	271	130
mixed4	768	2368	271	88
mixed5	768	3136	271	66
mixed6	768	3904	271	53
mixed7	768	4672	271	45
mixed8	1280	5952	163	35
mixed9	2048	8000	102	26
mixed10	2048	10048	102	21

Lesioning. In the lesioning experiments, we used the output representations of progressively deeper mixed layers of Inception V3 as inputs to the classifier.

Additionally, we computed classifications based on single-layer outputs for mixed layers 0 to 10 vs. outputs up to mixed layer k, $k \in 0, 1, \ldots, 10$.

Binarization, Boundary Removal, Cropping. *Binarization.* To investigate the use of color in classification, color and grayscale images were converted to black-and-white images using two different thresholding methods: Otsu's method [21], and adaptive local thresholding as implemented in scikit-image [30].

Boundary Removal. Boundaries were cropped so as to remove 36% of the image area (20% per side, centered).

Cropping. Classification using the full page ($1024 \times 768\,px$) was compared to classification using various crop sizes: $200 \times 200\,px, 300 \times 300\,px, 400 \times 400\,px$. The centers of the cropped regions were randomly chosen with the constraint that the crop fit into the page.

4.2   Results

Training and Test. Training the neural network classifier on illustrators or book resulted in almost perfect training set performance after some 1000 iterations for both GNC and Manga109, respectively (Fig. 1). The overall accuracy on the test set was over 95% for the GNC and about 93% for the Manga109 data set. The somewhat lower performance on Manga109 might be due to its back-and-white only pages, meaning that features related to coloring scheme could not be used for classification. We further explore the relevance of color below.

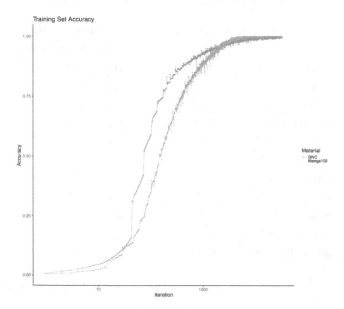

Fig. 1. Example of the evolution of training set accuracy during learning. Note that the x-scale is log10.

Lesioning. Results from the lesioning experiment are presented in Fig. 2. Prediction using lower-level features from bottom layers are not as good as using higher-level features. Interestingly and importantly, very high-level features also don't perform quite as good. This probably indicates that they are too specifically representing concepts useful for ImageNet classification. They also seem to be contributing to overfitting. Overall this result suggests that more generic mid-level features are better suited for classification of artistic style when using pre-trained features.

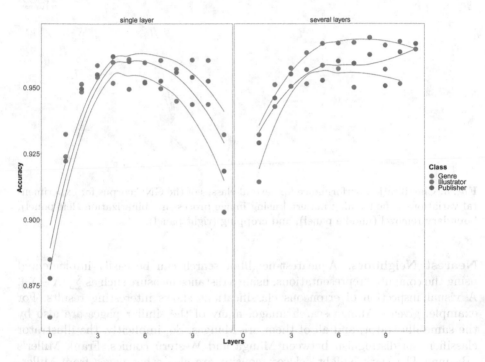

Fig. 2. Classification performance for several classes of the GNC corpus, using either single CNN layers (left panel) or several layers up to a certain layer (right panel). Lines are added by a loess smoother.

Binarization, Boundary Removal, Cropping. Results from the experimental manipulations of the input images using image processing are shown in Fig. 3. Removing color had a much stronger effect on genre than on illustrator classification (left panel). Removing the boundaries did not affect classification much, suggesting that scanning artefacts probably did not play a large role for classification. Destroying the page layout by cropping random elements impaired performance quite strongly, suggesting that page layout is important for all three classifications.

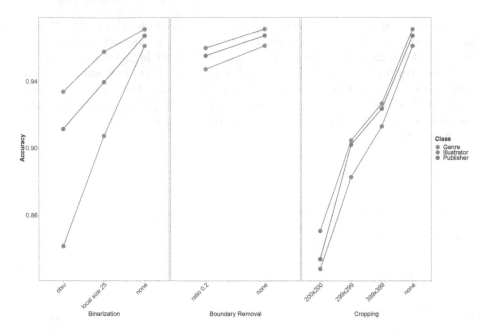

Fig. 3. Classification performance for several classes of the GNC corpus for experimental variation of the training material using image processing: binarization (left panel), boundary removal (middle panel), and cropping (right panel).

Nearest Neighbors. A nearest-neighbor search can be easily implemented using the computed representations, using a distance measure such as $\sum |X - X_i|$. A visual inspection of erroneous classifications shows interesting results. For example, given a Manga search image, many of the similar pages are also by the same illustrator, and all of them are Mangas. So, implicitly, the illustrator classifier can distinguish between Manga and Western comics. Frank Miller's "Batman-The Dark Knight" closest cousins are also other pages from Miller- although there is some confusion with (also action-oriented) Manga. The features even allow to track historical developments within a book. For example, Vincent Mahé's 750 Years in Paris shows the evolution of a house in Paris over several centuries. Generally, using our embedding, pages from similar eras are grouped together.

5   Discussion

We presented a description of illustrator style using a compact representation of CNN features. Overall classification accuracy was very good, thus transfer to illustrations from features obtained by training on photographs generally works well. Mid-level features corresponding to texture and hatching seem to be more important for classification than higher-level features that are closer to object-level descriptions. Visualization of the most discriminative features (not shown) supports this interpretation. Page layout and color do play an important role, whereas scanning artifacts do not contribute much.

The successful transfer suggests that the feature descriptions at the lower and middle levels of CNNs are rather generic, given that they were trained on enough real-world material. After all, an illustration is an abstraction of a visual reality and thus still related to a less abstract photographic depiction. We think that successful transfer implies that CNN features can be successfully employed in several new domains, for example, in describing and computing similarities of artworks in general. While we are pretty confident that they will work well with figurative art, it will be interesting to explore how pre-trained CNN features perform in classifying abstract art.

References

1. Chu, W., Wu, Y.: Image style classification based on learnt deep correlation features. IEEE Trans. Multimedia **20**(9), 2491–2502 (2018). https://doi.org/10.1109/TMM.2018.2801718
2. Chu, W.T., Li, W.W.: Manga FaceNet: face detection in manga based on deep neural network. In: ICMR 2017, pp. 412–415. ACM, New York (2017). https://doi.org/10.1145/3078971.3079031
3. Cichy, R.M., Khosla, A., Pantazis, D., Torralba, A., Oliva, A.: Comparison of deep neural networks to spatio-temporal cortical dynamics of human visual object recognition reveals hierarchical correspondence. Sci. Rep. **6**, 27755 (2016). https://doi.org/10.1038/srep27755
4. Crowley, E.J., Zisserman, A.: In search of art. In: Agapito, L., Bronstein, M.M., Rother, C. (eds.) ECCV 2014. LNCS, vol. 8925, pp. 54–70. Springer, Cham (2015). https://doi.org/10.1007/978-3-319-16178-5_4
5. Deng, J., Dong, W., Socher, R., Li, L.J., Li, K., Fei-Fei, L.: ImageNet: a large-scale hierarchical image database. In: CVPR 2009 (2009)
6. Dunst, A., Hartel, R., Laubrock, J.: The graphic narrative corpus (GNC): design, annotation, and analysis for the digital humanities. In: 2017 14th IAPR International Conference on Document Analysis and Recognition (ICDAR), vol. 03, pp. 15–20, November 2017. https://doi.org/10.1109/ICDAR.2017.286doi.ieeecomputersociety.org/10.1109/ICDAR.2017.286
7. Dunst, A., Hartel, R.: The quantitative analysis of comics: towards a visual stylometry of graphic narrative. In: Dunst, A., Laubrock, J., Wildfeuer, J. (eds.) Empirical Comics Research: Digital, Multimodal, and Cognitive Methods, chap. 12, pp. 239–263. Routledge, New York (2018)
8. Gatys, L.A., Ecker, A.S., Bethge, M.: Image style transfer using convolutional neural networks, pp. 2414–2423, June 2016. https://doi.org/10.1109/CVPR.2016.265
9. Gatys, L.A., Ecker, A.S., Bethge, M.: Texture and art with deep neural networks. Curr. Opin. Neurobiol. **46**, 178–186 (2017). https://doi.org/10.1016/j.conb.2017.08.019
10. Greenberg, C.: American-type painting. Partisan Rev. **22**(2), 179–196 (1955)
11. Hubel, D.H., Wiesel, T.N.: Receptive fields of single neurones in the cat's striate cortex. J. Physiol. **148**, 574–91 (1959)
12. Juola, P.: Authorship attribution. Found. Trends®. Inf. Retrieval 1(3), 233–334 (2008). https://doi.org/10.1561/1500000005

13. Karayev, S., Hertzmann, A., Winnemoeller, H., Agarwala, A., Darrell, T.: Recognizing image style. CoRR abs/1311.3715 (2013). http://arxiv.org/abs/1311.3715
14. Kümmerer, M., Wallis, T.S.A., Gatys, L.A., Bethge, M.: Understanding low- and high-level contributions to fixation prediction. In: The IEEE International Conference on Computer Vision (ICCV), October 2017
15. Laubrock, J., Hohenstein, S., Kümmerer, M.: Attention to comics: Cognitive processing during the reading of graphic literature. In: Dunst, A., Laubrock, J., Wildfeuer, J. (eds.) Empirical Comics Research: Digital, Multimodal, and Cognitive Methods, chap. 12, pp. 239–263. Routledge, New York (2018)
16. LeCun, Y., et al.: Backpropagation applied to handwritten zip code recognition. Neural Comput. 1(4), 541–551 (1989). https://doi.org/10.1162/neco.1989.1.4.541
17. Manovich, L.: How to compare one million images? In: Berry, D.M. (ed.) Understanding Digital Humanities. Palgrave Macmillan, New York (2012)
18. Matsui, Y., et al.: Sketch-based manga retrieval using Manga109 dataset. Multimedia Tools Appl. 76(20), 21811–21838 (2017). https://doi.org/10.1007/s11042-016-4020-z
19. Moretti, F.: Distant Reading. Verso, London/New York (2013)
20. Nguyen, N., Rigaud, C., Burie, J.: Comic characters detection using deep learning. In: 2nd International Workshop on coMics Analysis, Processing, and Understanding, 14th IAPR International Conference on Document Analysis and Recognition, ICDAR 2017, Kyoto, Japan, 9–15 November 2017, pp. 41–46 (2017). https://doi.org/10.1109/ICDAR.2017.290
21. Otsu, N.: A threshold selection method from gray-level histograms. IEEE Trans. Syst. Man. Cybern. 9(1), 62–66 (1979). https://doi.org/10.1109/TSMC.1979.4310076
22. Rumelhart, D.E., Hinton, G.E., Williams, R.J.: Learning representations by back-propagating errors. Nature 323, 533–536 (1986). https://doi.org/10.1038/323533a0
23. Saito, M., Matsui, Y.: Illustration2vec: a semantic vector representation of illustrations. In: SIGGRAPH Asia 2015 Technical Briefs, SA 2015, pp. 5:1–5:4. ACM, New York (2015). https://doi.org/10.1145/2820903.2820907
24. Saleh, B., Elgammal, A.M.: Large-scale classification of fine-art paintings: learning the right metric on the right feature. CoRR abs/1505.00855 (2015). http://arxiv.org/abs/1505.00855
25. Sanakoyeu, A., Kotovenko, D., Lang, S., Ommer, B.: A style-aware content loss for real-time HD style transfer (2018)
26. Seguin, B., Striolo, C., diLenardo, I., Kaplan, F.: Visual link retrieval in a database of paintings. In: Hua, G., Jégou, H. (eds.) ECCV 2016. LNCS, vol. 9913, pp. 753–767. Springer, Cham (2016). https://doi.org/10.1007/978-3-319-46604-0_52
27. Simonyan, K., Zisserman, A.: Very deep convolutional networks for large-scale image recognition. CoRR abs/1409.1556 (2014). http://arxiv.org/abs/1409.1556
28. Sirirattanapol, C., Matsui, Y., Satoh, S., Matsuda, K., Yamamoto, K.: Deep image retrieval applied on kotenseki ancient Japanese literature. In: 2017 IEEE International Symposium on Multimedia (ISM), pp. 495–499, December 2017. https://doi.org/10.1109/ISM.2017.98
29. Szegedy, C., Vanhoucke, V., Ioffe, S., Shlens, J., Wojna, Z.: Rethinking the inception architecture for computer vision. CoRR abs/1512.00567 (2015). http://arxiv.org/abs/1512.00567

30. van der Walt, S., et al.: The scikit-image contributors: scikit-image: image processing in python. PeerJ **2**(e453), 1–18 (2014)
31. Wölfflin, H.: Kunstgeschichtliche Grundbegriffe: Das Problem der Stilentwickelung in der neueren Kunst. Bruckmann, München (1915)
32. Yamins, D.L.K., DiCarlo, J.J.: Using goal-driven deep learning models to understand sensory cortex. Nature Neurosci. **19**(3), 356–365 (2016). https://doi.org/10.1038/nn.4244

Author Index

Printed in the United States
By Bookmasters